The National Hockey League SOURCEBOOK

First Edition
— 1987-88 —

A OFFICIAL PUBLICATION OF THE NHL

AN OWL BOOK

Henry Holt and Company
New York

The National Hockey League SOURCEBOOK

an official publication of the NHL   First Edition, 1987-88

© 1987 by National Hockey League Publishing

All rights reserved. No part of this book may be reproduced in any form or by any means without permission in writing from National Hockey League Publishing.

Senior Editors: Stu Hackel, Gary Meagher
Staff: Steve Charendoff, Dalton Einhorn, Benny Ercolani, Suzanne Greenwald, Shannon Shay.
Contributors: Kenny Albert, Howard Berger, James Duplacey, Jane Freer, Charles Wilkins.
Consulting publisher: Dan Diamond

Typesetting: Q Composition Inc., Toronto
Printing: The Alger Press Limited, Oshawa and Toronto

Library of Congress Catalog Card Number: 87-82762

AN OWL BOOK

Published in the United States of America by Henry Holt and Company Inc., 521 Fifth Avenue, New York, New York 10175

ISBN 0-8050-0782-2

Photo Credits

Special thanks to the Hockey Hall of Fame and Museum, Toronto and to the New York Rangers.

Historical photos: Bruce Bennett, Paul Bereswill, David Bier, Fran Byrne, Melchior Di Giacomo, Jet Photo, Jerry Liebman, Jim Mackey, Rice Studio, Al Ruelle, Robert Shaver, Imperial Oil — Turofsky Collection, Hockey Hall of Fame.

Current photos: Graig Abel, Toronto; A. Biegun, Winnipeg; Bruce Bennett, NY Islanders; Mark Buckner, St. Louis; Gary Fine, Washington; George Kalinsky, NY Rangers; David E. Klutho, St. Louis; Jim Mackey, Detroit; Bob Mummery, Edmonton; Photography Ink, Los Angeles; Andre Pichette, Quebec; Photography, Minnesota; Al Ruelle, Boston; Diane Sobolewski, Hartford; John Tremmel, New Jersey; Brad Watson, Calgary; Bill Wippert, Buffalo.

Front cover photo: Bruce Bennett

The National Hockey League
1155 Metcalfe Street, suite 960, Montreal, Quebec H3B 2W2
650 Fifth Avenue, 33rd floor, New York, New York, 10019
1 Greensboro Drive, suite 200, Toronto, Ontario M9W 1C8   Printed in Canada

Contents

Introduction ... 5

PART ONE: THE 1987-88 NHL

Boston Bruins ... 7
Buffalo Sabres ... 10
Calgary Flames ... 13
Chicago Blackhawks ... 16
Detroit Red Wings ... 19
Edmonton Oilers ... 22
Hartford Whalers ... 25
Los Angeles Kings ... 28
Minnesota North Stars ... 31
Montreal Canadiens ... 34
New Jersey Devils ... 37
New York Islanders ... 40
New York Rangers ... 43
Philadelphia Flyers ... 46
Pittsburgh Penguins ... 49
Quebec Nordiques ... 52
St. Louis Blues ... 55
Toronto Maple Leafs ... 58
Vancouver Canucks ... 61
Washington Capitals ... 64
Winnipeg Jets ... 67

NHL Season Highlights – 1986-87 ... 70
Entry Draft – 1987 prospect profiles ... 81
Transaction Register – trade activity in 1986-87 ... 91
1986-87 Final Statistics ... 93
1986-87 Schedule Results ... 102
Stanley Cup Playoffs – 1987 ... 109

PART TWO: ROOTS & RECORD-SETTERS

Hockey's Early Years ... 111
Franchise History ... 115
NHL Team Records ... 117
NHL Individual Records ... 120
Career Scoring Leaders ... 125
Goaltending Records ... 128
Coaching Records ... 132
Trophies and Awards ... 133
NHL Entry Draft – 1969-86 ... 142
All-Stars – 1987-68 ... 147
Hockey Hall of Fame ... 150

continued

Table of Contents continued

PART THREE: THE STANLEY CUP
Origin of the Trophy	153
Stanley Cup Winners – Final Series details	154
Players on Cup Champions	183
Championship Trophies	191
Champions in Other Leagues	193
Playoff Team Records	195
Playoff Individual Records	197
Overtime	202
Stanley Cup Coaching	204

PART FOUR: PROFESSIONAL HOCKEY INDEX
Section 1: Forwards and Defensemen	205
Section 2: Goaltenders	246
The 1987-88 NHL Schedule	251

INTRODUCTION

THE BOOK YOU ARE READING is the first edition of a new title from National Hockey League Publishing. The NHL Sourcebook brings together images, features and information that hockey fans in Canada and the United States have told us they wanted.

There has never been an intelligent and entertaining hockey information package quite like this one. The NHL Sourcebook brings you the results of special research projects undertaken by members of the League's Communications Department and offers entirely new information about both today's NHL and the earliest days of hockey.

Special features in the Sourcebook include:

Club Profiles (beginning on page 7) outline the strengths and weaknesses of each of the League's 21 teams;

1986-87 Season Highlights (page 70) acknowledge the year's top performances;

Prospect Reports (page 81) provide a "scout's-eye view" on first and second round picks in the June 1987 Entry Draft;

Roots & Record-Setters (page 111) surveys the earliest days of hockey from frozen ponds and clamp-on skates to the first great stars of the Jazz Age;

Stanley Cup Special (page 153) offers much new and detailed information on almost a century of competition for sport's most imposing trophy;

The Professional Hockey Index (page 205) brings together 1986-87 statistics and NHL career totals for more than 1,750 players and goaltenders both in the NHL and in minor pro, college, junior, high school and European hockey. The most complete index of its type in the game.

The NHL Sourcebook reaches beyond statistics and trivia. It attempts to serve all of us who appreciate the game of hockey. The Sourcebook connects Howie Morenz to Wayne Gretzky; the Ottawa Silver Seven to the Philadelphia Flyers; and the 1905 transcontinental trek by a team of Yukon Gold Rush prospectors to the meeting of the Soviet Nationals and NHL All-Stars in Rendez-Vous '87.

Looking to another record-setting year. . . .

– *NHL Publishing*
September 1987

THE NATIONAL HOCKEY LEAGUE

BOARD OF GOVERNORS

Officers
Chairman — William W. Wirtz
Vice-Chairman — Frank A. Griffiths
Secretary — Robert O. Swados

Boston Bruins
(Boston Professional Hockey Association, Inc.)
William D. Hassett, Jr. — Governor
Harry Sinden — Alternate Governor

Buffalo Sabres
(Niagara Frontier Hockey Corporation)
Seymour H. Knox III — Governor
Northrup R. Knox — Alternate Governor
Robert O. Swados — Alternate Governor

Calgary Flames
(Calgary Flames Hockey Club)
Cliff Fletcher — Governor
Norman N. Green — Alternate Governor

Chicago Blackhawks
(Chicago Blackhawk Hockey Team, Inc.)
William W. Wirtz — Governor
Thomas N. Ivan — Alternate Governor
Arthur M. Wirtz, Jr. — Alternate Governor

Detroit Red Wings
(Detroit Red Wings, Inc.)
Michael Ilitch — Governor
James Devellano — Alternate Governor
James Lites — Alternate Governor

Edmonton Oilers
(Pocklington Amalgamated Sports Corp.)
Peter Pocklington — Governor
Glen Sather — Alternate Governor

Hartford Whalers
(Hartford Whalers Hockey Club)
Howard L. Baldwin — Governor
Emile Francis — Alternate Governor
Donald G. Conrad — Alternate Governor

Los Angeles Kings
(Los Angeles Kings, Inc.)
Jerry Buss — Governor
Bruce McNall — Alternate Governor
Ken Doi — Alternate Governor
Rogatien Vachon — Alternate Governor

Minnesota North Stars
(Northstar Hockey Partnership)
George Gund III — Governor
Gordon Gund — Alternate Governor
John F. Karr — Alternate Governor
Lou Nanne — Alternate Governor

Montreal Canadiens
(Le Club de Hockey Canadien Inc.)
Ronald Corey — Governor
Norm Seagram — Alternate Governor
Serge Savard — Alternate Governor

New Jersey Devils
(Meadowlanders, Inc.)
John J. McMullen — Governor
Louis A. Lamoriello — Alternate Governor
John C. Whitehead — Alternate Governor
Robert J. Butera — Alternate Governor

New York Islanders
(Nassau Sports)
John O. Pickett, Jr. — Governor
William Torrey — Alternate Governor
William Skehan — Alternate Governor
John H. Krumpe — Alternate Governor

New York Rangers
(New York Rangers Hockey Club — a division of Madison Square Garden Center, Inc.)
Richard Evans — Governor
Jack Diller — Alternate Governor
Phil Esposito — Alternate Governor
Mel Lowell — Alternate Governor
Ken Munoz — Alternate Governor

Philadelphia Flyers
(Philadelphia Hockey Club, Inc.)
Jay T. Snider — Governor
Edward M. Snider — Alternate Governor
Ronald Rutenberg — Alternate Governor
Keith Allen — Alternate Governor

Pittsburgh Penguins
(Pittsburgh Penguins, Inc.)
J. Paul Martha — Governor
Eddie Johnston — Alternate Governor

Quebec Nordiques
(Le Club de Hockey Les Nordiques (1979) Société en commandite)
Marcel Aubut — Governor
Maurice Filion — Alternate Governor
Gilles Leger — Alternate Governor

St. Louis Blues
(St. Louis Blues Hockey Club, Inc.)
Michael F. Shanahan — Governor
Jack Quinn — Alternate Governor
Ronald Caron — Alternate Governor

Toronto Maple Leafs
(Maple Leafs Gardens Limited)
Harold E. Ballard — Governor
Arthur Gans — Alternate Governor

Vancouver Canucks
(Vancouver Hockey Club, Limited)
Frank A. Griffiths — Governor
Pat Quinn — Alternate Governor
Frank W. Griffiths — Alternate Governor
Arthur R. Griffiths — Alternate Governor

Washington Capitals
(Washington Hockey Limited Partnership)
Abe Pollin — Governor
Richard M. Patrick — Alternate Governor
David Poile — Alternate Governor

Winnipeg Jets
(8 Hockey Ventures, Inc.)
Barry L. Shenkarow — Governor
John B. Ferguson — Alternate Governor
Bill Davis — Alternate Governor

OFFICERS
President — John A. Ziegler, Jr.
Executive Vice-President — Brian F. O'Neill
Vice-President/General Counsel — Gilbert Stein
Vice-President of Finance and Treasurer — Kenneth G. Sawye
Vice-President, Hockey Operations — Jim Gregory
Vice-President, NHL Project Development — Ian Morrison
Vice-President, Broadcasting — Joel Nixon
Vice-President, Marketing/Public Relations — Steve Ryan

BOSTON BRUINS

Bill Ranford and Ray Bourque

1986-87: 39w-34L-7T 85 PTS. Third, Adams Division

1987-88 OUTLOOK: Finally and deservedly, Ray Bourque won the Norris Trophy as the NHL's best defenseman. His consistent blueline excellence and the acquisition of Cam Neely from Vancouver were unfortunately overshadowed by the Bruins fourth consecutive playoff loss to Montreal. This year, however, Boston has bolstered their goaltending by signing free-agent Reggie Lemelin from Calgary. One of the best, Reggie joins Bill Ranford, Roberto Romano and Doug Keans in a fight for top B's netminder and all can do the job. Head coach Terry O'Reilly, who replaced Butch Goring early last season, is a firely presence behind the bench. An excellent two-way player, Neely led Boston with 36 goals. Rick Middleton added 31, Tom McCarthy 30 and Charlie Simmer 29. After that, offense is thin. Keith Crowder and Randy Burridge — a rookie surprise two seasons ago — can score as well as bang, but must both stay healthy. Steve Kasper re-emerged as one of the NHL's top defensive forwards and Ken Linseman is still as feisty as ever. Gord Kluzak, Reed Larson, Allen Pederson, Mats Thelin and Michael Thelven bring defensive depth when all are healthy.

Upcoming Milestones

Ray Bourque — 24 goals to reach 200
Keith Crowder — 13 goals to reach 200
Ken Linseman — 18 goals to reach 200
Rick Middleton — 44 points to reach 1,000
— 15 goals to reach 450
Cam Neely — 13 goals to reach 100

Fan Club

Boston Bruins Fan Club
Janet LePage
144 Rounds St.
New Bedford, MA 02740

Entry Draft Selections 1987

Pick	
3	Glen Wesley
14	Stephane Quintal
56	Todd Lalonde
67	Darwin McPherson
77	Matt Delguidice
98	Ted Donato
119	Matt Glennon
140	Rob Cheevers
161	Chris Winnes
182	Paul Ohman
203	Casey Jones
224	Eric Lemarque
245	Sean Gorman

64th NHL Season

BOSTON BRUINS

Year-by-Year Record 1968-1987

Season	GP	Home W	L	T	Road W	L	T	Overall W	L	T	GF	GA	Pts.	Finished	Playoff Result
1986-87	80	25	11	4	14	23	3	39	34	7	301	276	85	3rd, Adams Div.	Lost Div. Semi-Final
1985-86	80	24	9	7	13	22	5	37	31	12	311	288	86	3rd, Adams Div.	Lost Div. Semi-Final
1984-85	80	21	15	4	15	19	6	36	34	10	303	287	82	4th, Adams Div.	Lost Div. Semi-Final
1983-84	80	25	12	3	24	13	3	49	25	6	336	261	104	1st, Adams Div.	Lost Div. Semi-Final
1982-83	80	28	6	6	22	14	4	50	20	10	327	228	110	1st, Adams Div.	Lost Conf. Championship
1981-82	80	24	12	4	19	15	6	43	27	10	323	285	96	2nd, Adams Div.	Lost Div. Final
1980-81	80	26	10	4	11	20	9	37	30	13	316	272	87	2nd, Adams Div.	Lost Prelim. Round
1979-80	80	27	9	4	19	12	9	46	21	13	310	234	105	2nd, Adams Div.	Lost Quarter-Final
1978-79	80	25	10	5	18	13	9	43	23	14	316	270	100	1st, Adams Div.	Lost Semi-Final
1977-78	80	29	6	5	22	12	6	51	18	11	333	218	113	1st, Adams Div.	Lost Final
1976-77	80	27	7	6	22	16	2	49	23	8	312	240	106	1st, Adams Div.	Lost Final
1975-76	80	27	5	8	21	10	9	48	15	17	313	237	113	1st, Adams Div.	Lost Semi-Final
1974-75	80	29	5	6	11	21	8	40	26	14	345	245	94	2nd, Adams Div.	Lost Prelim. Round
1973-74	78	33	4	2	19	13	7	52	17	9	349	221	113	1st, East Div.	Lost Final
1972-73	78	27	10	2	24	12	3	51	22	5	330	235	107	2nd, East Div.	Lost Quarter-Final
1971-72	78	28	4	7	26	9	4	54	13	11	330	204	119	1st, East Div.	Won Stanley Cup
1970-71	78	33	4	2	24	10	5	57	14	7	399	207	121	1st, East Div.	Lost Quarter-Final
1969-70	76	27	3	8	13	14	11	40	17	19	277	216	99	2nd, East Div.	Won Stanley Cup
1968-69	76	29	3	6	13	15	10	42	18	16	303	221	100	2nd, East Div.	Lost Semi-Final
1967-68	74	22	9	6	15	18	4	37	27	10	259	216	84	3rd, East Div.	Lost Quarter-Final

Playoff History, 1927-87

Versus	Year	Series	Winner	W	L	T	GF	GA
Buffalo	1982	DSF	Boston	3	1		17	11
Buffalo	1983	DF	Boston	4	3		32	23
Chicago	1927	*QF	Boston	1	0	1	10	5
Chicago	1942	QF	Boston	2	1		5	7
Chicago	1970	SF	Boston	4	0		20	10
Chicago	1974	SF	Boston	4	2		28	20
Chicago	1975	PRE	Chicago	1	2		15	12
Chicago	1978	QF	Boston	4	0		19	9
Detroit	1941	F	Boston	3	0		12	6
Detroit	1942	SF	Detroit	0	2		5	9
Detroit	1943	F	Detroit	0	4		5	16
Detroit	1945	SF	Detroit	3	4		22	22
Detroit	1946	SF	Boston	4	1		16	10
Detroit	1953	SF	Boston	4	2		21	21
Detroit	1957	SF	Boston	4	1		15	14
Los Angeles	1976	QF	Boston	4	3		26	14
Los Angeles	1977	QF	Boston	4	2		30	24
Minnesota	1981	PRE	Minnesota	0	3		13	20
Montreal	1929	SF	Boston	3	0		5	2
Montreal	1930	F	Montreal	0	2		3	7
Montreal	1931	SF	Montreal	2	3		13	13
Montreal	1943	SF	Boston	4	0		18	17
Montreal	1946	F	Montreal	1	4		13	19
Montreal	1947	SF	Montreal	1	4		10	16
Montreal	1952	SF	Montreal	3	4		12	18
Montreal	1953	F	Montreal	0	4		9	16
Montreal	1954	SF	Montreal	0	4		4	16
Montreal	1955	SF	Montreal	1	4		9	16
Montreal	1957	F	Montreal	1	4		6	15
Montreal	1958	F	Montreal	2	4		14	16
Montreal	1968	QF	Montreal	0	4		8	15
Montreal	1969	SF	Montreal	2	4		16	15
Montreal	1971	QF	Montreal	3	4		26	28
Montreal	1977	F	Montreal	0	4		6	16
Montreal	1978	F	Montreal	2	4		13	18
Montreal	1979	SF	Montreal	3	4		20	25
Montreal	1984	DSF	Montreal	0	3		2	10
Montreal	1985	DSF	Montreal	2	3		17	19
Montreal	1986	DSF	Montreal	0	3		6	10
Montreal	1987	DSF	Montreal	0	4		11	19
NY Islanders	1980	QF	NY Islanders	1	4		14	19
NY Islanders	1983	SF	NY Islanders	2	4		21	30
NY Rangers	1927	*SF	Boston	1	0	1	3	1
NY Rangers	1928	*SF	NY Rangers	0	1	1	2	5
NY Rangers	1929	F	Boston	2	0		4	1
NY Rangers	1939	SF	Boston	4	3		14	12
NY Rangers	1940	SF	NY Rangers	2	4		9	15
NY Rangers	1958	SF	Boston	4	2		28	16
NY Rangers	1970	QF	Boston	4	2		25	16
NY Rangers	1972	F	Boston	4	2		18	16
NY Rangers	1973	QF	NY Rangers	1	4		11	22
Philadelphia	1974	F	Philadelphia	2	4		13	15
Philadelphia	1976	SF	Philadelphia	1	4		12	19
Philadelphia	1977	SF	Boston	4	0		14	8
Philadelphia	1978	QF	Boston	4	1		15	15
Pittsburgh	1979	QF	Boston	4	0		16	7
Pittsburgh	1980	PRE	Boston	3	2		21	14
Quebec	1982	DF	Quebec	3	4		26	28
Quebec	1983	DSF	Boston	3	1		11	8
St. Louis	1970	F	Boston	4	0		20	7
St. Louis	1972	SF	Boston	4	0		28	8
Toronto	1933	SF	Toronto	2	3		7	9
Toronto	1935	SF	Toronto	1	3		2	7
Toronto	1936	*QF	Toronto	0	2		6	8
Toronto	1938	SF	Toronto	0	3		3	6
Toronto	1939	F	Boston	4	1		12	6
Toronto	1941	SF	Boston	4	3		15	17
Toronto	1948	SF	Toronto	1	4		13	20
Toronto	1949	SF	Toronto	1	4		10	16
Toronto	1951	SF	Toronto	1	4	1	5	17
Toronto	1959	SF	Toronto	3	4		21	20
Toronto	1969	QF	Boston	4	0		24	5
Toronto	1970	QF	Boston	4	1		18	10
Toronto	1974	QF	Boston	4	0		17	9
Ottawa	1927	F	Ottawa	0	2	2	3	7
Maroons	1930	SF	Boston	3	1		11	5
Maroons	1937	QF	Maroons	1	2		6	8

* Total-goals series

BOSTON BRUINS

1986-87 Scoring

Regular Season
*—Rookie

Pos	#	Player	Team	GP	G	A	Pts	+/-	PIM
D	7	Ray Bourque	BOS	78	23	72	95	44	36
F	8	Cam Neely	BOS	75	36	36	72	23	143
F	23	Charlie Simmer	BOS	80	29	40	69	20	59
F	16	Rick Middleton	BOS	76	31	37	68	7	6
F	19	Tom McCarthy	BOS	68	30	29	59	10	31
F	18	Keith Crowder	BOS	58	22	30	52	20	106
F	11	Steve Kasper	BOS	79	20	30	50	4–	51
F	13	Ken Linseman	BOS	64	15	34	49	15	126
F	10	Thomas Gradin	BOS	64	12	31	43	4	18
F	14	Geoff Courtnall	BOS	65	13	23	36	4–	117
D	28	Reed Larson	BOS	66	12	24	36	9	95
F	39	Greg Johnston	BOS	76	12	15	27	7–	79
D	26	Mike Milbury	BOS	68	6	16	22	22	96
F	22	Michael Thelven	BOS	34	5	15	20	2–	18
F	17	Nevin Markwart	BOS	64	10	9	19	6–	225
F	20	Dwight Foster	BOS	47	4	12	16	1	37
D	41	*Allen Pedersen	BOS	79	1	11	12	15–	71
F	38	Kraig Nienhuis	BOS	16	4	2	6	5–	2
F	36	Dave Reid	BOS	12	3	3	6	1–	0
F	42	*Robert Sweeney	BOS	14	2	4	6	5–	21
F	33	Lyndon Byers	BOS	18	2	3	5	1–	53
F	12	Randy Burridge	BOS	23	1	4	5	6–	16
F	29	Jay Miller	BOS	55	1	4	5	1–	208
D	27	Mats Thelin	BOS	59	1	3	4	8–	69
D	38	Wade Campbell	BOS	14	0	3	3	1–	24
G	31	Doug Keans	BOS	36	0	2	2	0	24
F	21	Frank Simonetti	BOS	25	1	0	1	6–	17
F	32	*John Carter	BOS	8	0	1	1	3	0
G	30	*Bill Ranford	BOS	41	0	1	1	0	8
G	35	*Cleon Daskalakis	BOS	2	0	0	0	0	0
D	40	Alain Cote	BOS	3	0	0	0	1–	0
G	1	Roberto Romano	Pit	25	0	0	0	0	0
			Bos	1	0	0	0	0	0
			Total	26	0	0	0	0	0

Playoffs

Pos	#	Player	Team	GP	G	A	Pts	+/-	PIM
F	8	Cam Neely	BOS	4	5	1	6	1–	8
F	16	Rick Middleton	BOS	4	2	2	4	1–	0
F	10	Thomas Gradin	BOS	4	0	4	4	1–	0
D	7	Ray Bourque	BOS	4	1	2	3	1–	0
F	13	Ken Linseman	BOS	4	1	1	2	2–	22
F	19	Tom McCarthy	BOS	4	1	1	2	4–	4
F	11	Steve Kasper	BOS	3	0	2	2	4–	0
D	28	Reed Larson	BOS	4	0	2	2	6–	2
F	12	Randy Burridge	BOS	2	1	0	1	2–	2
F	18	Keith Crowder	BOS	4	0	1	1	1–	4
F	33	Lyndon Byers	BOS	1	0	0	0	1–	0
F	14	Geoff Courtnall	BOS	1	0	0	0	0	0
F	23	Charlie Simmer	BOS	1	0	0	0	1	2
G	31	Doug Keans	BOS	2	0	0	0	0	4
G	30	*Bill Ranford	BOS	2	0	0	0	0	0
F	36	Dave Reid	BOS	2	0	0	0	1–	0
F	20	Dwight Foster	BOS	3	0	0	0	2–	0
F	42	*Robert Sweeney	BOS	3	0	0	0	2–	0
D	38	Wade Campbell	BOS	4	0	0	0	2–	11
F	39	Greg Johnston	BOS	4	0	0	0	4–	0
F	17	Nevin Markwart	BOS	4	0	0	0	3–	9
D	26	Mike Milbury	BOS	4	0	0	0	2–	4
D	41	*Allen Pedersen	BOS	4	0	0	0	5–	4
F	21	Frank Simonetti	BOS	4	0	0	0	1–	6

Club Records

Team
(Figures in brackets for season records are games played; records for fewest points, wins, ties, losses, goals, goals against are for 70 or more games)

Most Points	121	1970-71 (78)
Most Wins	57	1970-71 (78)
Most Ties	21	1954-55 (70)
Most Losses	47	1961-62 (70)
Most Goals	399	1970-71 (78)
Most Goals Against	306	1961-62 (70)
Fewest Points	38	1961-62 (70)
Fewest Wins	14	1962-63 (70)
Fewest Ties	5	1972-73 (78)
Fewest Losses	13	1971-72 (78)
Fewest Goals	147	1955-56 (70)
Fewest Goals Against	172	1952-53 (70)

Individual

Most Seasons	21	John Bucyk
Most Games	1,436	John Bucyk
Most Goals, Career	545	John Bucyk
Most Assists, Career	794	John Bucyk
Most Points, Career	1,339	John Bucyk (545 goals, 794 assists)
Most Pen. Mins., Career	2,095	Terry O'Reilly
Most Shutouts, Career	74	Tiny Thompson
Longest Consecutive Games Streak	418	John Bucyk (Jan. 23/69-Mar. 2/75)
Most Goals, Season	76	Phil Esposito (1970-71)
Most Assists, Season	102	Bobby Orr (1970-71)
Most Points, Season	152	Phil Esposito (1970-71) (76 goals, 76 assists)

Coach

O'REILLY, TERRY
Coach, Boston Bruins. Born in Niagara Falls, Ont., June 7, 1951.

On November 8, 1986, Terry O'Reilly took the Boston Bruins' coaching reins and steered his club to an NHL record 20th consecutive winning season. The 36-year-old former team captain was merely perpetuating a tradition he helped to build. Boston's second pick, 14th overall, in the 1971 Amateur Draft, O'Reilly first joined the Bruins as a player in 1971-72, contributing to the club's last Stanley Cup championship season. From then on, he grew into one of the city's most popular sports figures, playing 14 seasons in Boston through the 1984-85 campaign. As a player, O'Reilly amasssed a 204-402-606 scoring total in 891 games to place eighth among all-time Bruins' scorers.

BUFFALO SABRES

1986-87: 28w-44l-8t 64 pts. Fifth, Adams Division

1987-88 OUTLOOK: After missing the playoffs for the second consecutive season, the Sabres seem to be putting the pieces to their puzzle back together. Ted Sator's appointment as coach led to a second half surge that made up an 18-point gap in December, tying Quebec for fourth in the division on March 8, only to fall back again. A core of young forwards includes top 1987 Entry Draft choice Pierre Turgeon, who Sabre fans are comparing to their first round pick of 1971, Gilbert ("The Franchise") Perreault. John Tucker and Lindy Ruff return from injuries which sidelined them much of last season. Mike Foligno (30 goals, down from 41) is a hustler, while Christian Ruuttu scored 65 points as a rookie. Mammoth forwards Dave Andreychuk (73 points, down from 87) and Adam Creighton (who finally earned a spot on the roster) effectively gain position in front of the net. On defense, perennial all-star Mike Ramsey leads the corps, while Phil Housley (67 points) may have begun to blossom. Much is expected from Swedish rookie Carl Johansson. Youngster Shawn Anderson and ex-Oiler Lee Fogolin round out the blueline crew. Goaltending tandem of Tom Barrasso and Jacques Cloutier can reach excellence. The team responded to Sator after he took over in mid-season and made a run at the last Adams Division playoff spot.

Upcoming Milestones

Scott Arniel — 14 goals to reach 100
Paul Cyr — 16 goals to reach 100
Mike Foligno — 1 goal to reach 250
Lee Fogolin — 11 games to reach 900
Lindy Ruff — 6 goals to reach 100

Fan Club

Buffalo Sabres Booster Club
Jack Brew
23 Cardy Lane
Depew, NY 14043

Entry Draft Selections 1987

Pick
1   Pierre Turgeon
22 Brad Miller
53 Andrew MacVicar
84 John Bradley
85 David Pergola
106 Chris Marshall
127 Paul Flanagan
148 Sean Dooley
153 Tim roberts
169 Grant Tkachuk
190 Ian Herbers
211 David Littman
232 Allan MacIsaac

18th NHL Season

BUFFALO SABRES

Year-by-Year Record 1970-1987

Season	GP	Home W	L	T	Road W	L	T	Overall W	L	T	GF	GA	Pts.	Finished	Playoff Result
1986-87	80	18	18	4	10	26	4	28	44	8	280	308	64	5th, Adams Div.	Out of Playoffs
1985-86	80	23	16	1	14	21	5	37	37	6	296	291	80	5th, Adams Div.	Out of Playoffs
1984-85	80	23	10	7	15	18	7	38	28	14	290	237	90	3rd, Adams Div.	Lost Div. Semi-Final
1983-84	80	25	9	6	23	16	1	48	25	7	315	257	103	2nd, Adams Div.	Lost Div. Semi-Final
1982-83	80	25	7	8	13	22	5	38	29	13	318	285	89	3rd, Adams Div.	Lost Div. Final
1981-82	80	23	8	9	16	18	6	39	26	15	307	273	93	3rd, Adams Div.	Lost Div. Semi-Final
1980-81	80	21	7	12	18	13	9	39	20	21	327	250	99	1st, Adams Div.	Lost Quarter-Final
1979-80	80	27	5	8	20	12	8	47	17	16	318	201	110	1st, Adams Div.	Lost Semi-Final
1978-79	80	19	13	8	17	15	8	36	28	16	280	263	88	2nd, Adams Div.	Lost Prelim. Round
1977-78	80	25	7	8	19	12	9	44	19	17	288	215	105	2nd, Adams Div.	Lost Quarter-Final
1976-77	80	27	8	5	21	16	3	48	24	8	301	220	104	2nd, Adams Div.	Lost Quarter-Final
1975-76	80	28	7	5	18	14	8	46	21	13	339	240	105	2nd, Adams Div.	Lost Quarter-Final
1974-75	80	28	6	6	21	10	9	49	16	15	354	240	113	1st, Adams Div.	Lost Final
1973-74	78	23	10	6	9	24	6	32	34	12	242	250	76	5th, East Div.	Out of Playoffs
1972-73	78	30	6	3	7	21	11	37	27	14	257	219	88	4th, East Div.	Lost Quarter-Final
1971-72	78	11	19	9	5	24	10	16	43	19	203	289	51	6th, East Div.	Out of Playoffs
1970-71	78	16	13	10	8	26	5	24	39	15	217	291	63	5th, East Div.	Out of Playoffs

Playoff History, 1972-87

Versus	Year	Series	Winner	W	L	T	GF	GA
Boston	1982	DSF	Boston	1	3		11	17
Boston	1983	DF	Boston	3	4		23	32
Chicago	1975	QF	Buffalo	4	1		20	10
Chicago	1980	QF	Buffalo	4	0		16	7
Minnesota	1977	PRE	Buffalo	2	0		11	3
Minnesota	1981	QF	Minnesota	1	4		17	23
Montreal	1973	QF	Montreal	2	4		16	21
Montreal	1975	SF	Buffalo	4	2		21	29
Montreal	1983	DSF	Buffalo	3	0		8	2
NY Islanders	1976	QF	NY Islanders	0	4		18	21
NY Islanders	1977	QF	NY Islanders	0	4		10	16
NY Islanders	1980	DSF	NY Islanders	2	4		17	22
NY Rangers	1978	PRE	Buffalo	2	1		11	6
Philadelphia	1975	F	Philadelphia	2	4		12	19
Philadelphia	1978	QF	Philadelphia	1	4		11	16
Pittsburgh	1979	PRE	Pittsburgh	1	2		9	9
Quebec	1984	DSF	Quebec	0	3		5	13
Quebec	1985	DSF	Quebec	2	3		22	22
St. Louis	1976	PRE	Buffalo	2	1		7	8
Vancouver	1980	PRE	Buffalo	3	1		15	7
Vancouver	1981	PRE	Buffalo	3	0		13	7

Club Records

Team

(Figures in brackets for season records are games played; records for fewest points, wins, ties, losses, goals, goals against are for 70 or more games)

Most Points	113	1974-75 (80)
Most Wins	49	1974-75 (80)
Most Ties	21	1980-81 (80)
Most Losses	44	1986-87 (80)
Most Goals	354	1986-87 (80)
Most Goals Against	308	1986-87 (80)
		1974-75 (80)
Fewest Points	51	1971-72 (78)
Fewest Wins	16	1971-72 (78)
Fewest Ties	6	1985-86 (80)
Fewest Losses	16	1974-75 (80)
Fewest Goals	203	1971-72 (78)
Fewest Goals Against	201	1979-80 (80)
Longest Winning Streak		
Over-all	10	Jan. 4-23/84
Home	12	Nov. 12/72-Jan. 7/73
Away	10	Dec. 10/83-Jan. 23/84

continued

Coach

SATOR, THEODORE RICHARD (TED)
Coach, Buffalo Sabres. Born In Utica, N.Y., November 18, 1949.

When he assumed the Buffalo Sabres' coaching duties on December 22, 1986, Ted Sator infused his club with a new winning spirit, leading the team to nine victories in his first 11 games. That kind of positive attitude is one which Sator looks to carry into his first full season behind the Sabres' bench. Of course, the 37-year-old Utica, New York native has been no stranger to winning. After five consecutive championship seasons as a head coach in the Swedish Elite League, Sator joined the Philadelphia Flyers in 1984-85 as an assistant to Mike Keenan and helped that club to the Stanley Cup Finals. In 1985-86, the New York Rangers handed him his first NHL head coaching job, and he responded with playoff victories over both the Flyers and Washington Capitals. A graduate of Bowling Green State University, Sator holds a masters degree in Health and Physical Education.

BUFFALO SABRES

Longest Undefeated Streak
- Over-all .... 14 March 6-April 6/80
- Home .... 21 Oct. 8/72-Jan. 7/73
- Away .... 10 Dec. 10/83-Jan. 23/84 (10 wins)

Longest Losing Streak
- Over-all .... 7 Oct. 25-Nov. 8/70
- Home .... 5 Feb. 15-Mar. 3/85
- Away .... 7 Oct. 14-Nov. 7/70 Feb. 6-27/71

Longest Winless Streak
- Over-all .... 10 Nov. 7-Dec. 1/71 (8 losses, 2 ties)
- Home .... 6 Feb. 27-Mar. 26/72 (3 losses, 3 ties)
- Away .... 23 Oct. 30/71-Feb. 19/72 (15 losses, 8 ties)

Most Shutouts, Season 7 1974-75 (80)
Most Pen. Mins., Season 1,812 1986-87 (80)
Most Goals, Game .... 14 Jan. 21/75 (Wash. 2 at Buf. 14) Mar. 19/81 (Tor. 4 at Buf. 14)

Individual
- Most Seasons .... 17 Gilbert Perreault
- Most Games .... 1,191 Gilbert Perreault
- Most Goals, Career ..... 512 Gilbert Perreault
- Most Assists, Career ..... 814 Gilbert Perreault
- Most Points, Career .... 1,326 Gilbert Perreault
- Most Pen. Mins., Career .. 1,278 Larry Playfair
- Most Shutouts, Career ...... 14 Don Edwards
- Longest Consecutive Games Streak .... 776 Craig Ramsay (Mar. 27/73-Feb. 10/83)
- Most Goals, Season .... 56 Danny Gare (1979-80)
- Most Assists, Season ...... 69 Gilbert Perreault (1975-76)
- Most Points, Season ...... 113 Gilbert Perreault (1975-76) (44 goals, 69 assists)
- Most Pen. Mins., Season .. 258 Larry Playfair (1981-82)
- Most Points, Defenseman Season .... 69 John Van Boxmeer (1980-81) (18 goals, 51 assists)
- Most Points, Center Season .... 113 Gilbert Perreault (1975-76) (44 goals, 69 assists)
- Most Points, Right Wing Season .... 100 René Robert (1974-765) (40 goals, 60 assists)
- Most Points, Left Wing Season .... 95 Richard Martin (1974-75) (52 goals, 43 assists)
- Most Points, Rookie Season .... 74 Richard Martin (1971-72) (44 goals, 30 assists)

1986-87 Scoring
Regular Season   *–Rookie

Pos	#	Player	Team	GP	G	A	Pts	+/–	PIM
F	25	Dave Andreychuk	BUF	77	25	48	73	2	46
D	6	Phil Housley	BUF	78	21	46	67	2–	57
F	21	*Christian Ruuttu	BUF	76	22	43	65	9	62
F	17	Mike Foligno	BUF	75	30	29	59	13	176
F	7	John Tucker	BUF	54	17	34	51	3–	21
F	38	Adam Creighton	BUF	56	18	22	40	4	26
F	15	Doug Smith	BUF	62	16	24	40	20–	106
D	5	Mike Ramsey	BUF	80	8	31	39	1	109
F	27	Wilf Paiement	BUF	56	20	17	37	2	108
F	65	Mark Napier	EDM	62	8	13	21	3	2
			BUF	15	5	5	10	5–	0
			Total	77	13	18	31	2–	2
F	18	Paul Cyr	Buf	73	11	16	27	16–	122
F	39	Clark Gillies	BUF	61	10	17	27	0	81
F	9	Scott Arniel	BUF	63	11	14	25	1–	59
D	28	Tom Kurvers	MTL	1	0	0	0	1	0
			BUF	55	6	17	23	10–	22
			Total	56	6	17	23	9–	22
F	22	Lindy Ruff	BUF	50	6	14	20	12–	74
F	12	*Ken Priestlay	BUF	34	11	6	17	3	8
F	11	Gilbert Perreault	BUF	20	9	7	16	2–	6
D	4	Jim Korn	BUF	52	4	10	14	3–	158
D	37	*Shawn Anderson	BUF	41	2	11	13	0	23
F	26	*Bob Logan	BUF	22	7	3	10	5	0
F	23	Gates Orlando	BUF	27	2	8	10	6–	16
D	31	*Joe Reekie	BUF	56	1	8	9	6	82
F	29	*Jeff Parker	BUF	15	3	3	6	1	7
F	20	*Mike Hartman	BUF	17	3	3	6	2	69
D	33	Lee Fogolin	EDM	35	1	3	4	2–	17
			BUF	9	0	2	2	2–	8
			Total	44	1	5	6	4–	25
F	20	Don Lever	BUF	10	3	2	5	3–	4
D	40	*Uwe Krupp	BUF	26	1	4	5	9–	23
F	16	*Paul Brydges	BUF	15	2	2	4	4	6
D	29	*Mark Ferner	BUF	13	0	3	3	2	9
F	14	Mikael Andersson	BUF	16	0	3	3	2–	0
D	19	Bob Halkidis	BUF	6	1	1	2	3	19
D	26	Phil Russell	BUF	6	0	2	2	0	12
D	24	Bill Hajt	BUF	23	0	2	2	0	4
G	1	Jacques Cloutier	BUF	40	0	2	2	0	10
D	8	Dave Fenyves	BUF	7	1	0	1	3–	0
D	3	Richie Dunn	BUF	2	0	1	1	2	2
D	42	Steve Dykstra	BUF	37	0	1	1	7–	179
G	30	Tom Barrasso	BUF	46	0	1	1	0	22
F	8	*Richard Hajdu	BUF	2	0	0	0	1	0
F	19	*Doug Trapp	BUF	2	0	0	0	0	0
G	35	*Daren Puppa	BUF	3	0	0	0	0	2
D	3	*Jim Hofford	BUF	12	0	0	0	1–	40

Most Shutouts, Season ...... 5 Don Edwards (1977-78) Tom Barrasso (1984-85)
Most Goals, Game .... 5 Dave Andreychuk (Feb. 6/86)
Most Assists, Game .... 5 Gilbert Perreault (Feb. 1/76; Mar. 9/80) Gilbert Perreault (Jan. 4/84)
Most Points, Game .... 7 Gilbert Perreault (Feb. 1/76)

CALGARY FLAMES

Joel Otto

1986-87: 46w-31L-3T 95 PTS. Second, Smythe Division

1987-88 OUTLOOK: After setting a franchise record of 95 points despite numerous key injuries and continuing their mastery over Edmonton in the regular season, the Flames ran into their other divisional nemesis, the Jets and never made it to Rematch 87 with the Oilers. This year, more challenges face Calgary. First is new coach Terry Crisp, who takes over for Bob Johnson and must learn the NHL ropes behind the bench. Second is the loss of Jamie Macoun, a defensive stalwart, who was severly injured in an off-season auto accident. Then there's the gruelling 11-game road trip during the playoff strech drive (February 3 to March 3) while the Olympics play the Saddledone. General manager Cliff Fletcher traded for veteran Flyer Brad McCrimmon to offset Macoun's loss. He joins All-Star Al MacInnis, enigmatic Paul Reinhart and former Calder winner Gary Suter on the blueline. Joe Mullen (47 goals) and Mike Bullard (30 goals) are the Flames' big gunners, while Carey Wilson, Joel Otto and rookie Joe Niewendyk provide depth at center. Goaltender Mike Vernon must carry the bulk of the load since Reggie Lemelin packed his bags for Boston.

Upcoming Milestones

Lanny McDonald – 21 goals to reach 500
                – 36 points to reach 1,000
Doug Risebrough – 60 games to reach 800
                – 15 goals to reach 200
John Tonelli   – 19 games to reach 900
                – 21 goals to reach 250

Entry Draft Selections 1987

Pick	
19	Bryan Deasley
25	Stephane Matteau
40	Kevin Grant
61	Scott Mahoney
70	Tim Harris
103	Tim Corkery
124	Joe Aloi
145	Peter Ciavaglia
166	Theoren Fleury
187	Mark Osiecki
208	William Sedergren
229	Peter Hasselblad
250	Magnus Svensson

16th NHL Season

Year-by-Year Record 1973-1987

Season	GP	Home W L T	Road W L T	Overall W L T	GF	GA	Pts.	Finished	Playoff Result
1986-87	80	25 13 2	21 18 1	46 31 3	318	289	95	2nd, Smythe Div.	Lost Div. Semi-Final
1985-86	80	23 11 6	17 20 3	40 31 9	354	315	89	2nd, Smythe Div.	Lost Final
1984-85	80	23 11 6	18 16 6	41 27 12	363	302	94	3rd, Smythe Div.	Lost Div. Final
1983-84	80	22 11 7	12 21 7	34 32 14	311	314	82	2nd, Smythe Div.	Lost Div. Final
1982-83	80	21 12 7	11 22 7	32 34 14	321	317	78	2nd, Smythe Div.	Lost Div. Final
1980-81	80	20 11 9	9 23 8	39 27 14	329	298	92	3rd, Patrick Div.	Lost Semi-Final
1979-80	80	25 5 10	14 22 4	35 32 13	282	269	83	4th, Patrick Div.	Lost Prelim. Round
1978-79	80	18 15 7	17 17 6	41 31 8	327	280	90	4th, Patrick Div.	Lost Prelim. Round
1977-78	80	25 11 4	16 20 4	34 27 19	274	252	87	3rd, Patrick Div.	Lost Prelim. Round
1976-77	80	20 13 7	14 14 12	34 34 12	264	265	80	3rd, Patrick Div.	Lost Prelim. Round
1975-76	80	22 11 7	12 23 5	35 33 12	262	237	82	3rd, Patrick Div.	Lost Prelim. Round
1974-75	80	19 14 7	16 19 5	34 31 15	243	233	83	4th, Patrick Div.	Out of Playoffs
1973-74	78	24 9 7	10 22 8	30 34 14	214	238	74	4th, West Div.	Lost Quarter-Final
1972-73	78	17 15 7	13 19 7	25 38 15	191	239	65	7th, West Div.	Out of Playoffs

Playoff History, 1973-87

Versus	Year	Series	Winner	W	L	T	GF	GA
Chicago	1981	PRE	Calgary	3	0		15	9
Detroit	1978	PRE	Detroit	0	2		5	8
Edmonton	1983	DF	Edmonton	1	4		13	35
Edmonton	1984	DF	Edmonton	3	4		27	33
Edmonton	1986	DF	Calgary	4	3		25	24
Los Angeles	1976	PRE	Los Angeles	0	2		1	3
Los Angeles	1977	PRE	Los Angeles	1	2		7	11
Minnesota	1981	SF	Minnesota	2	4		18	25
Montreal	1986	F	Montreal	1	4		13	15

Versus	Year	Series	Winner	W	L	T	GF	GA
NY Rangers	1980	PRE	NY Rangers	1	3		8	14
Philadelphia	1974	QF	Philadelphia	0	4		6	17
Philadelphia	1981	QF	Calgary	4	3		22	26
St. Louis	1986	SF	Calgary	4	3		28	22
Vancouver	1982	DSF	Vancouver	0	3		5	8
Vancouver	1983	DSF	Calgary	3	1		17	14
Vancouver	1984	DSF	Calgary	3	1		14	13
Winnipeg	1985	DSF	Winnipeg	1	3		13	15
Winnipeg	1986	DSF	Calgary	3	0		15	8
Winnipeg	1987	DSF	Winnipeg	2	4		15	22

Club Records

Team

(Figures in brackets for season records are games played; records for fewest points, wins, ties, losses, goals, goals against are for 70 or more games)

Most Points	95	1986-87 (80)
Most Wins	46	1986-87 (80)
Most Ties	19	1977-78 (80)
Most Losses	38	1972-73 (78)
Most Goals	363	1984-85 (80)
Most Goals Against	345	1981-82 (80)
Fewest Points	65	1972-73 (78)
Fewest Wins	25	1972-73 (78)
Fewest Ties	3	1986-87 (80)
Fewest Losses	27	1977-78 (80)
		1980-81 (80)
Fewest Goals	191	1972-73 (78)
Fewest Goals Against	233	1974-75 (80)
Longest Winning Streak		
Overall	10	Oct. 14-Nov. 3/78
Home	9	Oct. 17-Nov. 15/78
Away	5	Jan. 26-Feb. 17/87

Longest Undefeated Streak		
Over-all	12	Oct. 11-Nov. 3/78 (10 wins, 2 ties)
Home	18	Mar. 4/78-Nov. 15/78 (12 wins, 6 ties)
Away	7	Mar. 13-Apr. 5/85 (4 wins, 3 ties)
Longest Losing Streak		
Over-all	11	Dec. 14/85-Jan. 7/86
Home	4	Four times
Away	9	Dec. 1/85-Jan. 12/86
Longest Winless Streak		
Over-all	11	Dec. 14/85-Jan. 7/86

Coach

CRISP, TERRY
Coach, Calgary Flames. Born in Parry Sound, Ont., May 28, 1943.

After two seasons as coach and general manager of Calgary's AHL affiliate in Moncton, 44-year-old Terry Crisp earned the Flames' head coaching position on May 22, 1987. A former center with the Boston Bruins, St. Louis Blues, New York Islanders and Philadelphia Flyers, Crisp played 11 seasons in the NHL, compiling a 67-134-201 scoring mark in 537 games and contributing to the Flyers' two Stanley Cup seasons in 1974 and 1975. Following his retirement as a player in 1976, he remained with Philadelphia as an assistant coach during 1977-78 and 1978-79. In 1979-80, he was named head coach of the OHL's Sault Ste. Marie Greyhounds, with whom he captured three regular-season titles and two Coach-of-the-Year awards in six Junior seasons through 1984-85.

CALGARY FLAMES

1986-87 Scoring

Regular Season
*—Rookie

Pos	#	Player	Team	GP	G	A	Pts	+/−	PIM
F	7	Joe Mullen	CGY	79	47	40	87	18	14
D	2	Al MacInnis	CGY	79	20	56	76	20	97
D	23	Paul Reinhart	CGY	76	15	54	69	7	22
F	25	Mike Bullard	PIT	14	2	10	12	1−	17
			CGY	57	28	26	54	10	34
			Total	71	30	36	66	9	51
F	33	Carey Wilson	CGY	80	20	36	56	2−	42
F	27	John Tonelli	CGY	78	20	31	51	2−	72
F	29	Joel Otto	CGY	68	19	31	50	8	185
F	24	Jim Peplinski	CGY	80	18	32	50	13	181
D	20	Gary Suter	CGY	68	9	40	49	10−	70
F	12	Hakan Loob	CGY	68	18	26	44	13−	26
D	34	Jamie Macoun	CGY	79	7	33	40	33	111
F	26	Steve Bozek	CGY	71	17	18	35	3	22
F	14	*Brian Bradley	CGY	40	10	18	28	6	16
F	11	Colin Patterson	CGY	68	13	14	27	7	41
F	9	Lanny McDonald	CGY	58	14	12	26	3−	54
F	19	Tim Hunter	CGY	73	6	15	21	1−	361
F	32	*Gary Roberts	CGY	32	5	9	14	6	85
D	28	*Dale Degray	CGY	27	6	7	13	3−	29
D	5	Neil Sheehy	CGY	54	4	6	10	11	151
F	21	Perry Berezan	CGY	24	5	3	8	4	24
F	22	Nick Fotiu	CGY	42	5	3	8	3−	145
D	32	Kari Eloranta	CGY	13	1	6	7	3	9
F	18	*Joe Nieuwenyk	CGY	9	5	1	6	0	0
F	8	Doug Risebrough	CGY	22	2	3	5	2−	66
D	3	*Kevan Guy	CGY	24	0	4	4	8	19
D	6	Brian Engblom	CGY	32	0	4	4	7−	28
D	4	Paul Baxter	CGY	18	0	2	2	5−	66
G	30	*Mike Vernon	CGY	54	0	2	2	0	14
F	15	*Brett Hull	CGY	5	1	0	1	1−	0
G	36	*Doug Dadswell	CGY	2	0	0	0	0	0
G	31	Rejean Lemelin	CGY	34	0	0	0	0	20

Playoffs

Pos	#	Player	Team	GP	G	A	Pts	+/−	PIM
F	25	Mike Bullard	CGY	6	4	2	6	1	2
F	18	*Joe Nieuwendyk	CGY	6	2	2	4	2−	0
F	15	*Brett Hull	CGY	4	2	1	3	4	0
F	7	Joe Mullen	CGY	6	2	1	3	4−	0
F	12	Hakan Loob	CGY	5	1	2	3	0	0
D	20	Gary Suter	CGY	6	0	3	3	1	10
F	33	Carey Wilson	CGY	6	1	1	2	1−	6
F	21	Perry Berezan	CGY	2	0	2	2	2	7
F	29	Joel Otto	CGY	2	0	2	2	0	6
D	32	Kari Eloranta	CGY	6	0	2	2	5−	0
F	11	Colin Patterson	CGY	6	0	2	2	2−	2
F	26	Steve Bozek	CGY	4	1	0	1	1−	2
D	2	Al MacInnis	CGY	4	1	0	1	1−	0
F	24	Jim Peplinski	CGY	6	1	0	1	2−	24
G	31	Rejean Lemelin	CGY	2	0	1	1	0	0
D	34	Jamie Macoun	CGY	3	0	1	1	2−	8
D	3	*Kevan Guy	CGY	4	0	1	1	0	23
D	23	Paul Reinhart	CGY	4	0	1	1	1−	6
F	8	Doug Risebrough	CGY	4	0	1	1	1−	2
D	4	Paul Baxter	CGY	2	0	0	0	1−	10
F	32	*Gary Roberts	CGY	2	0	0	0	1−	4
F	27	John Tonelli	CGY	3	0	0	0	4	4
F	9	Lanny McDonald	CGY	5	0	0	0	3−	2
G	30	*Mike Vernon	CGY	5	0	0	0	0	0
F	19	Tim Hunter	CGY	6	0	0	0	2−	51
D	5	Neil Sheehy	CGY	6	0	0	0	1	21

Individual

Most Seasons............9	Dan Bouchard	
Most Games...........559	Eric Vail	
Most Goals, Career......229	Kent Nilsson	
Most Assists, Career......336	Guy Chouinard	
Most Points, Career......562	Kent Nilsson (229 goals, 333 assists)	
Most Pen. Mins., Career ..1,267	Willi Plett	
Most Shutouts, Career......20	Dan Bouchard	
Longest Consecutive Games Streak.........257	Brad Marsh (Oct. 11/78- Nov. 10/81)	
Most Goals, Season.......66	Lanny McDonald (1982-83)	
Most Assists, Season......82	Kent Nilsson (1980-81)	
Most Points, Season......131	Kent Nilsson (1980-81) (49 goals, 82 assists)	
Most Pen. Mins., Season ...357	Tim Hunter (1986-87)	
Most Points, Defenseman Season..............76	Paul Reinhart (1982-83) (17 goals, 58 assists) Al MacInnis (1986-87) (20 goals, 56 assists)	
Most Points, Center Season.............131	Kent Nilsson (1980-81) (49 goals, 82 assists)	
Most Points, Right Wing Season.............108	Bob MacMillan (1978-79) (37 goals, 71 assists)	
Most Points, Left Wing Season..............83	Eric Vail (1978-79) (35 goals, 48 assists)	
Most Points, Rookie Season..............72	Carey Wilson (1984-85) (24 goals, 48 assists)	
Most Shutouts, Season......5	Dan Bouchard (1973-74) Phil Myre (1974-75)	
Most Goals, Game.........4	Keith McCreary (Mar. 21/75) Garry Unger (Jan. 11/80) Jim Peplinski (Nov. 17/81) Kent Nilsson (Feb. 27/82) (Dec. 20/84)	
Most Points, Game.........6	Guy Chouinard (Feb. 25/81) Gary Suter (Apr. 4/86)	

CHICAGO BLACKHAWKS

Curt Fraser

1986-87: 29w-37L-14T 72 PTS. Third, Norris Division

1987-88 OUTLOOK: A new face emerges behind the bench at the Stadium in Bob Murdoch, the highly sought-after former assistant coach in Calgary. His Blackhawks have many offensive gunners, but last season sprung big leaks in their own end. General manager Bob Pulford moved to solve at least part of that problem by signing free agent netminder Bob Mason from Washington. Trades have brought defenseman Bob McGill and forwards Rick Vaive, Duane Sutter and Steve Thomas. Magical Denis Savard (90 points) had his least productive season since his rookie year. Troy Murray (28 goals) and Curt Fraser (25 goals), lend a unique blend of scoring and toughness up front. Wayne Presley (32 goals) had an outstanding and unexpected sophomore year and Steve Larmer (28 goals) quietly provided good numbers. All-Star Doug Wilson and Gary Nylund lead a Hawk defense which at times could be solid, but more often non-existent. Bob Murray, Marc Bergevin, Jack O'Callahan and Keith Brown round out the backline. Murdoch will put much of his effort into molding that unit.

Upcoming Milestones

Denis Savard – 43 goals to reach 300
            – 80 points to reach 800
Al Secord – 12 goals to reach 250
Curt Fraser – 18 goals to reach 200
Bob Murray – 18 goals to reach 100
Doug Wilson – 76 games to reach 800
            – 28 points to reach 600

Fan Club

Chicago Blackhawks Standbys
Larry Coffey
5440 W. Agatite Ave.
Chicago, IL 60630

Entry Draft Selections 1987

1987
Pick
8 Jimmy Waite
29 Ryan McGill
50 Cam Russell
60 Mike Dagenais
92 Ulf Sandstrom
113 Mike McCormick
134 Stephen Tepper
155 John Reilly
176 Lance Werness
197 Dale Marquette
218 Bill Lacouture
239 Mike Lappin

62nd NHL Season

CHICAGO BLACKHAWKS

Year-by-Year Record 1968-1987

Season	GP	Home W	Home L	Home T	Road W	Road L	Road T	Overall W	Overall L	Overall T	GF	GA	Pts.	Finished	Playoff Result
1986-87	80	1	13	9	11	24	5	29	37	14	290	310	72	3rd, Norris Div.	Lost Div. Semi-Final
1985-86	80	23	12	5	16	21	3	39	33	8	351	350	86	1st, Norris Div.	Lost Div. Semi-Final
1984-85	80	22	16	2	16	19	5	38	35	7	309	299	83	2nd, Norris Div.	Lost Conf. Championship
1983-84	80	25	13	2	5	29	6	30	42	8	277	311	68	4th, Norris Div.	Lost Div. Semi-Final
1982-83	80	29	8	3	18	15	7	47	23	10	338	268	104	1st, Norris Div.	Lost Conf. Championship
1981-82	80	20	13	7	10	25	5	30	38	12	332	363	72	4th, Norris Div.	Lost Conf. Championship
1980-81	80	21	11	8	10	22	8	31	33	16	304	315	78	2nd, Smythe Div.	Lost Prelim. Round
1979-80	80	21	12	7	13	15	12	34	27	19	241	250	87	1st, Smythe Div.	Lost Quarter-Final
1978-79	80	18	12	10	11	24	5	29	36	15	244	277	73	1st, Smythe Div.	Lost Quarter-Final
1977-78	80	20	9	11	12	20	8	32	29	19	230	220	83	1st, Smythe Div.	Lost Quarter-Final
1976-77	80	19	16	5	7	27	6	26	43	11	240	298	63	3rd, Smythe Div.	Lost Prelim. Round
1975-76	80	17	15	8	15	15	10	32	30	18	254	261	82	1st, Smythe Div.	Lost Quarter-Final
1974-75	80	24	12	4	13	23	4	37	35	8	268	241	82	3rd, Smythe Div.	Lost Quarter-Final
1973-74	78	20	6	13	21	8	10	41	14	23	272	164	105	2nd, West Div.	Lost Semi-Final
1972-73	78	26	9	4	16	18	5	42	27	9	284	225	93	1st, West Div.	Lost Final
1971-72	78	28	3	8	18	14	7	46	17	15	256	166	107	1st, West Div.	Lost Semi-Final
1970-71	78	30	6	3	19	14	6	49	20	9	277	184	107	1st, West Div.	Lost Final
1969-70	76	26	7	5	19	15	4	45	22	9	250	170	99	1st, East Div.	Lost Semi-Final
1968-69	76	20	14	4	14	19	5	34	33	9	280	246	77	6th, East Div.	Out of Playoffs
1967-68	74	20	13	4	12	13	12	32	26	16	212	222	80	4th, East Div.	Lost Semi-Final

Playoff History, 1927-87

Versus	Year	Series	Winner	W	L	T	GF	GA
Boston	1927	*QF	Boston	0	1	1	5	10
Boston	1942	QF	Boston	1	2		7	5
Boston	1970	SF	Boston	0	4		10	20
Boston	1974	SF	Boston	2	4		20	28
Boston	1975	PRE	Chicago	2	1		12	15
Boston	1978	QF	Boston	0	4		9	19
Buffalo	1975	QF	Buffalo	1	4		10	20
Buffalo	1980	QF	Buffalo	0	4		7	16
Calgary	1981	PRE	Calgary	0	3		9	15
Detroit	1934	F	Chicago	3	1		9	7
Detroit	1941	SF	Detroit	0	2		2	5
Detroit	1944	SF	Detroit	4	1		17	8
Detroit	1961	F	Chicago	4	2		19	12
Detroit	1963	SF	Detroit	2	4		19	25
Detroit	1964	SF	Detroit	3	4		18	24
Detroit	1965	SF	Chicago	4	3		23	19
Detroit	1966	SF	Detroit	2	4		10	22
Detroit	1970	QF	Chicago	4	0		16	8
Detroit	1985	DSF	Chicago	3	0		23	8
Detroit	1987	DSF	Detroit	0	4		6	15
Edmonton	1983	SF	Edmonton	0	4		11	25
Edmonton	1985	SF	Edmonton	2	4		25	44
Los Angeles	1974	QF	Chicago	4	1		10	7
Minnesota	1982	DSF	Chicago	3	1		14	14
Minnesota	1983	DF	Chicago	4	1		22	17
Minnesota	1984	DSF	Minnesota	2	3		14	18
Minnesota	1985	DF	Chicago	4	2		32	29
Montreal	1930	*QF	Montreal	0	1	1	2	3
Montreal	1931	F	Montreal	2	3		8	11
Montreal	1934	*QF	Chicago	2	0		4	3
Montreal	1938	QF	Chicago	2	1		11	8
Montreal	1941	QF	Chicago	2	1		8	7
Montreal	1944	F	Montreal	0	4		8	16
Montreal	1946	SF	Montreal	0	4		7	26
Montreal	1953	SF	Montreal	3	4		14	18
Montreal	1959	SF	Montreal	2	4		16	21
Montreal	1960	SF	Montreal	0	4		6	14
Montreal	1961	SF	Chicago	4	2		16	15
Montreal	1962	SF	Chicago	4	2		19	13
Montreal	1965	F	Montreal	3	4		12	18
Montreal	1968	SF	Montreal	1	4		10	22
Montreal	1971	F	Montreal	3	4		18	20
Montreal	1973	F	Montreal	2	4		23	33
Montreal	1976	QF	Montreal	0	4		3	13
NY Islanders	1977	PRE	NY Islanders	0	2		3	7
NY Islanders	1979	QF	NY Islanders	0	4		3	14
NY Rangers	1931	*SF	Chicago	2	0		3	0
NY Rangers	1968	F	Chicago	4	2		18	12
NY Rangers	1971	SF	Chicago	4	3		21	14
NY Rangers	1972	SF	NY Rangers	0	4		9	17
NY Rangers	1973	SF	Chicago	4	1		15	11
Philadelphia	1978	QF	Chicago	4	0		20	8
Pittsburgh	1972	QF	Chicago	4	0		14	8
St. Louis	1973	QF	Chicago	4	1		22	9
St. Louis	1980	PRE	Chicago	3	0		12	4
St. Louis	1982	DF	Chicago	4	2		23	19
St. Louis	1983	DSF	Chicago	3	1		16	10
Toronto	1931	*QF	Chicago	1	0	1	4	3
Toronto	1932	*QF	Toronto	1	1		2	6
Toronto	1938	F	Chicago	3	1		10	8
Toronto	1940	F	Toronto	0	2		3	5
Toronto	1962	F	Toronto	2	4		15	18
Toronto	1967	SF	Toronto	2	4		14	18
Toronto	1986	DSF	Toronto	0	3		9	18
Toronto	1987	DF	Detroit	4	3		20	18
Vancouver	1982	SF	Vancouver	1	4		13	18
Maroons	1934	*SF	Chicago	2	0		6	2
Maroons	1935	*QF	Maroons	0	1	1	0	1
NY Americans	1936	*QF	NY Americans	1	1		5	7
NY Americans	1938	SF	Chicago	2	1		5	5

* Total-goals series

Coach

MURDOCH, ROBERT JOHN (BOB)
Coach, Chicago Blackhawks.
Born in Kirkland Lake, Ont., November 20, 1946.

After eight years in the Calgary Flames' organization, including three as a player and five as an assistant coach, former NHL defenseman Bob Murdoch joined the Chicago Blackhawks as head coach on May 26, 1987. An alumnus of the University of Waterloo in Ontario, Murdoch opened his 12-year NHL playing career with the 1970-71 Stanley Cup champion Montreal Canadiens. After earning another championship ring in 1972-73, he was dealt by Montreal to the Los Angeles Kings, with whom he played until 1978-79, when the Flames acquired his services. At the conclusion of his playing days, Murdoch had registered scoring totals of 60-218-278 in 757 games.

1986-87 Scoring

Regular Season
*—Rookie

Pos	#	Player	Team	GP	G	A	Pts	+/-	PIM
F	18	Denis Savard	CHI	70	40	50	90	15	108
F	28	Steve Larmer	CHI	80	28	56	84	20	22
F	19	Troy Murray	CHI	77	28	43	71	14	59
F	17	Wayne Presley	CHI	80	32	29	61	18-	114
F	20	Al Secord	CHI	77	29	29	58	20-	196
F	16	Ed Olczyk	CHI	79	16	35	51	4-	119
F	8	Curt Fraser	CHI	75	25	25	50	5	182
D	24	Doug Wilson	CHI	69	16	32	48	15	36
D	6	Bob Murray	CHI	79	6	38	44	9-	80
F	14	Bill Watson	CHI	51	13	19	32	19	6
D	22	Gary Nylund	CHI	80	7	20	27	9-	190
D	4	Keith Brown	CHI	73	4	23	27	5	86
F	15	*Mark Lavarre	CHI	58	8	15	23	11	33
F	10	Dave Donnelly	CHI	71	6	12	18	7-	81
F	11	Rich Preston	CHI	73	8	9	17	8-	19
F	29	Steve Ludzik	CHI	52	5	12	17	3-	34
F	27	Darryl Sutter	CHI	44	8	6	14	3-	16
D	2	Marc Bergevin	CHI	66	4	10	14	4	66
D	5	Jack O'Callahan	CHI	48	1	13	14	10	59
F	12	*Mike Stapleton	CHI	39	3	6	9	9-	6
D	3	*Dave Manson	CHI	63	1	8	9	2-	146
F	7	*Everett Sanipass	CHI	7	1	3	4	3	2
G	31	Bob Sauve	CHI	46	0	4	4	0	6
F	26	Rick Paterson	CHI	22	1	2	3	1	6
G	30	Murray Bannerman	CHI	39	0	1	1	0	4
F		*Darin Sceviour	CHI	1	0	0	0	0	0
F	25	*Jim Camazzola	CHI	2	0	0	0	0	0
D	32	*Bruce Cassidy	CHI	2	0	0	0	1-	0
G	40	Warren Skorodenski	CHI	3	0	0	0	0	0

Playoffs

Pos	#	Player	Team	GP	G	A	Pts	+/-	PIM
F	8	Curt Fraser	CHI	2	1	1	2	1-	10
F	16	Ed Olczyk	CHI	4	1	1	2	1	4
D	22	Gary Nylund	CHI	4	0	2	2	1-	11
F	11	Rich Preston	CHI	4	0	2	2	2	4
D	2	Marc Bergevin	CHI	3	1	0	1	1-	2
D	6	Bob Murray	CHI	4	1	0	1	2-	4
F	17	Wayne Presley	CHI	4	1	0	1	2-	9
F	18	Denis Savard	CHI	4	1	0	1	3-	12
D	4	Keith Brown	CHI	4	0	1	1	1-	6
F	14	Bill Watson	CHI	4	0	1	1	1-	0
F	10	Dave Donnelly	CHI	1	0	0	0	0	0
D	5	Jack O'Callahan	CHI	2	0	0	0	0	2
F	27	Darry Sutter	CHI	2	0	0	0	0	0
D	3	*Dave Manson	CHI	3	0	0	0	2-	10
F	32	*Dan Vincelette	CHI	3	0	0	0	4-	0
F	28	Steve Larmer	CHI	4	0	0	0	2-	2
F	29	Steve Ludzik	CHI	4	0	0	0	1-	0
F	19	Troy Murray	CHI	4	0	0	0	3-	5
G	31	Bob Sauve	CHI	4	0	0	0	0	0
F	20	Al Secord	CHI	4	0	0	0	2-	21
F	12	*Mike Stapleton	CHI	4	0	0	0	0	2
D	24	Doug Wilson	CHI	4	0	0	0	2-	0

Club Records

Team
(Figures in brackets for season records are games played; records for fewest points, wins, ties, losses, goals, goals against are for 70 or more games)

Most Points	107	1970-71 (78)
		1971-72 (78)
Most Wins	49	1970-71 (78)
Most Ties	23	1973-74 (78)
Most Losses	51	1953-54 (70)
Most Goals	351	1985-86 (80)
Most Goals Against	363	1981-82 (80)
Fewest Points	31	1953-54 (70)
Fewest Wins	12	1953-54 (70)
Fewest Ties	7	1953-54 (70)
		1957-58 (70)
Fewest Losses	14	1973-74 (78)
Fewest Goals	*133	1953-54 (70)
Fewest Goals Against	164	1973-74 (78)
Longest Winning Streak		
Over-all	8	Dec. 9-26/71
		Jan. 4-21/81
Home	13	Nov. 11-Dec. 20/70
Away	7	Dec. 9-29/64
Longest Undefeated Streak		
Over-all	15	Jan. 14-Feb. 16/67 (12 wins, 3 ties)
Home	18	Oct. 11-Dec. 20/70 (16 wins, 2 ties)
Away	10	Nov. 2-Dec. 16/67 (8 wins, 2 ties)

Individual

Most Seasons	21	Stan Mikita
Most Games	1,394	Stan Mikita
Most Goals, Career	604	Bobby Hull
Most Assists, Career	926	Stan Mikita
Most Points, Career	1,467	Stan Mikita (541 goals, 926 assists)
Most Pen. Mins., Career	1,442	Keith Magnuson
Most Shutouts, Career	74	Tony Esposito
Longest Consecutive Games Streak	509	John Marks (Oct. 27/73-Jan. 2/80)
Most Goals, Season	58	Bobby Hull (1968-69)
Most Assists, Season	87	Denis Savard (1981-82)
Most Points, Season	121	Denis Savard (1982-83) (35 goals, 86 assists)
Most Pen. Mins., Season	303	Al Secord (1981-82)
Most Points, Defenseman Season	85	Doug Wilson (1981-82) (39 goals, 46 assists)
Most Points, Center, Season	121	Denis Savard (1982-83) (35 goals, 86 assists)
Most Points, Right Wing, Season	92	Jim Pappin (1972-73) (41 goals, 51 assists)
Most Points, Left Wing, Season	107	Bobby Hull (1968-9) (58 goals, 49 assists)

DETROIT RED WINGS

Petr Klima

1986-87: 34w-36L-10T 78 PTS. Second, Norris Division

1987-88 OUTLOOK: What happened? The Wings went from 40 points to 78 thanks in part to Adams Trophy winner Jacques Demers. The first-year Red Wing coach was hailed as a miracle worker as the team that finished with the League's worst record in 1986 reached the Campbell Conference final before succumbing to the eventual champion Oilers. Was this fluke or fortune? In Motown they're betting on the latter. Young Steve Yzerman (90 points) emerged as the team leader and Gerard Gallent nearly doubled his goal output (20 to 38). GM Jim Devellano's late-season acquisition of Brent Ashton added another big gun. Petr Klima's offensive talent is tops but must work on his backchecking. The Wings' defense allowed 141 fewer goals than 1985-86, thanks to veteran blueliners and the solid play of goaltenders Greg Stefan and Glen Hanlon. Mike O'Connell, Darren Veitch, Lee Norwood, Dave Lewis, Gilbert Delorme and fan favorite Harold Snepsts – all acquired during the past two seasons – anchored the defense but this crew is getting older. Fans at Joe Louis Arena hope they can hold on until recent draft selections – including 1987 first rounder Yves Racine – are ready to take the reins.

Upcoming Milestones

Harold Snepts – 57 games to reach 900
Mike O'Connell – 6 goals to reach 100
Brent Ashton – 35 goals to reach 200
Mel Bridgman – 8 goals to reach 250
Ric Seiling – 62 games to reach 800

Fan Club

Detroit Red Wing For 'Em Club
Joe Louis Arena
600 Civic Center Drive
Detroit, MI 48226

Entry Draft Selections 1987

Pick	
11	Yves Racine
32	Gordon Kruppke
41	Bob Wilkie
52	Dennis Holland
74	Mark Reimer
95	Radomir Brazda
116	Sean Clifford
137	Mike Gober
158	Kevin Scott
179	Mikko Haapakoski
200	Darin Bannister
221	Craig Quinlan
242	Tomas Jansson

62nd NHL Season

Year-by-Year Record 1968-1987

Season	GP	Home W	L	T	Road W	L	T	Overall W	L	T	GF	GA	Pts.	Finished	Playoff Result
1986-87	80	20	14	6	14	22	4	34	36	10	260	274	78	2nd, Norris Div.	Lost Conf. Championship
1985-86	80	10	26	4	7	31	2	17	57	6	266	415	40	5th, Norris Div.	Out of Playoffs
1984-85	80	19	14	7	8	27	5	27	41	12	313	357	66	3rd, Norris Div.	Lost Div. Semi-Final
1983-84	80	18	20	2	13	22	5	31	42	7	298	323	69	3rd, Norris Div.	Lost Div. Semi-Final
1982-83	80	14	19	7	7	25	8	21	44	15	263	344	57	5th, Norris Div.	Out of Playoffs
1981-82	80	15	19	6	6	28	6	21	47	12	270	351	54	6th, Norris Div.	Out of Playoffs
1980-81	80	16	15	9	3	28	9	19	43	18	252	339	56	5th, Norris Div.	Out of Playoffs
1979-80	80	14	21	5	12	22	6	26	43	11	268	306	63	5th, Norris Div.	Out of Playoffs
1978-79	80	15	17	8	8	24	8	23	41	16	252	295	62	5th, Norris Div.	Out of Playoffs
1977-78	80	22	11	7	10	23	7	32	34	14	252	266	78	2nd, Norris Div.	Lost Quarter-Final
1976-77	80	12	22	6	4	33	3	16	55	9	183	309	41	5th, Norris Div.	Out of Playoffs
1975-76	80	17	15	8	9	29	2	26	44	10	226	300	62	4th, Norris Div.	Out of Playoffs
1974-75	80	17	17	6	6	28	6	23	45	12	259	335	58	4th, Norris Div.	Out of Playoffs
1973-74	78	21	12	6	8	27	4	29	39	10	255	319	68	6th, East Div.	Out of Playoffs
1972-73	78	22	12	5	15	17	7	37	29	12	265	243	86	5th, East Div.	Out of Playoffs
1971-72	78	25	11	3	8	24	7	33	35	10	261	262	76	5th, East Div.	Out of Playoffs
1970-71	78	17	15	7	5	30	4	22	45	11	209	308	55	7th, East Div.	Out of Playoffs
1969-70	76	20	11	7	20	10	8	40	21	15	246	199	95	3rd, East Div.	Lost Quarter-Final
1968-69	76	23	8	7	10	23	5	33	31	12	239	221	78	5th, East Div.	Out of Playoffs
1967-68	74	18	15	4	9	20	8	27	35	12	245	257	66	6th, East Div.	Out of Playoffs

Playoff History, 1927-87

Versus	Year	Series	Winner	W	L	T	GF	GA	Versus	Year	Series	Winner	W	L	T	GF	GA
Boston	1941	F	Boston	0	4		6	12	NY Rangers	1933	*SF	NY Rangers	0	2		3	6
Boston	1942	SF	Detroit	2	0		9	5	NY Rangers	1937	F	Detroit	3	2		9	8
Boston	1943	F	Detroit	4	0		16	5	NY Rangers	1941	QF	Detroit	2	1		6	6
Boston	1945	SF	Detroit	4	3		22	22	NY Rangers	1948	SF	Detroit	4	2		17	12
Boston	1946	SF	Boston	1	4		10	16	NY Rangers	1950	F	Detroit	4	3		22	17
Boston	1953	SF	Boston	2	4		21	21	St. Louis	1984	DSF	St. Louis	1	3		12	13
Boston	1957	SF	Boston	1	4		14	15	Toronto	1929	*QF	Toronto	0	2		2	7
Calgary	1978	PRE	Detroit	2	0		8	5	Toronto	1934	SF	Detroit	3	2		11	12
Chicago	1934	F	Chicago	1	3		7	9	Toronto	1936	F	Detroit	3	1		18	11
Chicago	1941	SF	Detroit	2	0		5	2	Toronto	1939	SF	Toronto	1	2		8	10
Chicago	1944	SF	Chicago	1	4		8	17	Toronto	1940	SF	Toronto	0	2		2	5
Chicago	1961	F	Chicago	2	4		12	19	Toronto	1942	F	Toronto	3	4		19	25
Chicago	1963	SF	Detroit	4	2		25	19	Toronto	1943	SF	Detroit	4	2		20	17
Chicago	1964	SF	Detroit	4	3		24	18	Toronto	1945	F	Toronto	3	4		9	9
Chicago	1965	SF	Chicago	3	4		19	23	Toronto	1947	SF	Toronto	1	4		14	18
Chicago	1966	SF	Detroit	4	2		22	10	Toronto	1948	F	Toronto	0	4		7	18
Chicago	1970	QF	Chicago	0	4		8	16	Toronto	1949	F	Toronto	0	4		5	12
Chicago	1985	DSF	Chicago	0	3		8	23	Toronto	1950	SF	Detroit	4	3		10	11
Chicago	1987	DSF	Detroit	4	0		15	6	Toronto	1952	SF	Detroit	4	0		13	3
Edmonton	1987	CF	Edmonton	1	5		10	16	Toronto	1954	SF	Detroit	4	1		15	8
Montreal	1937	SF	Detroit	3	2		13	8	Toronto	1955	SF	Detroit	4	0		14	6
Montreal	1939	QF	Detroit	2	1		8	5	Toronto	1956	SF	Toronto	1	4		14	10
Montreal	1942	QF	Detroit	2	1		8	8	Toronto	1960	SF	Toronto	2	4		16	20
Montreal	1949	SF	Detroit	4	3		17	14	Toronto	1961	SF	Detroit	4	1		15	8
Montreal	1951	SF	Montreal	2	4		12	13	Toronto	1963	F	Toronto	1	4		10	17
Montreal	1952	F	Detroit	4	0		11	2	Toronto	1964	F	Toronto	3	4		17	22
Montreal	1954	F	Detroit	4	3		14	12	Maroons	1932	*QF	Maroons	0	1	1	1	3
Montreal	1955	F	Detroit	4	3		27	20	Maroons	1933	*QF	Detroit	2	0		5	2
Montreal	1956	F	Montreal	1	4		9	18	Maroons	1936	SF	Detroit	3	0		6	1
Montreal	1958	SF	Montreal	0	4		6	19	NY Americans	1940	QF	Detroit	2	1		9	7
Montreal	1966	F	Montreal	2	4		14	18	* Total-goals series								
Montreal	1978	QF	Montreal	1	4		10	24									

Coach

DEMERS, JACQUES
Coach, Detroit Red Wings. Born in Montreal, Que., August 25, 1944

After a successful three-year stint with the St. Louis Blues, coach Jacques Demers joined the Detroit Red Wings on June 13, 1986, and Joe Louis Arena has never been the same. In addition to bringing an exciting, winning brand of hockey back to the Motor City in 1986-87, Demers led his team to the most improved record in the NHL, a second-place finish in the Norris Division and a trip to the Campbell Conference Finals. For his efforts, the 43-year-old Red Wings' skipper earned the Jack Adams Award as Coach-of-the-Year.

A Montreal native, Demers began coaching in the Quebec Junior League during the late 60's and early 70's. Then, in 1972-73, he jumped to the pro ranks of the newly formed World Hockey Association, in which he piloted the Chicago Cougars and Cincinnati Stingers before joining the WHA's Quebec Nordiques. When Quebec moved into the NHL in 1979-80, Demers remained with the club as coach for one season before taking control of the Nordiques' AHL affiliate in Fredericton. After earning AHL Coach-of-the-Year and Executive-of-the-Year honors in 1982-83, he returned to the NHL as head coach in St. Louis.

1986-87 Scoring

Regular Season
*—Rookie

Pos	#	Player	Team	GP	G	A	Pts	+/-	PIM
F	19	Steve Yzerman	DET	80	31	59	90	1-	43
F	14	Brent Ashton	QUE	46	25	19	44	12-	17
			DET	35	15	16	31	3-	22
			Total	81	40	35	75	15-	39
F	17	Gerard Gallant	DET	80	38	34	72	5-	216
D	5	Darren Veitch	DET	77	13	45	58	14	52
F	85	Petr Klima	DET	77	30	23	53	9-	42
F	11	*Shawn Burr	DET	80	22	25	47	2	107
F	21	Adam Oates	DET	76	15	32	47	0	21
F	15	Mel Bridgman	NJ	51	8	31	39	8-	80
			DET	13	2	2	4	1	19
			Total	64	10	33	43	7-	99
F	22	Dave Barr	STL	2	0	0	0	1	0
			HFD	30	2	4	6	1-	19
			DET	37	13	13	26	7	49
			Total	69	15	17	32	7	68
D	2	Mike O'Connell	DET	77	5	26	31	25-	70
D	23	Lee Norwood	DET	57	6	21	27	23-	163
F	20	Tim Higgins	DET	77	12	14	26	2-	124
F	24	Bob Probert	DET	63	13	11	24	6-	221
F	26	Joey Kocur	DET	77	9	9	18	10-	276
D	27	Harold Snepsts	DET	54	1	13	14	7	129
F	16	Ric Seiling	DET	74	3	8	11	4-	49
F	18	Mark Kumpel	QUE	40	1	8	9	12-	16
			DET	5	0	1	1	2	0
			Total	45	1	9	10	10-	16
D	29	Gilbert Delorme	QUE	19	2	0	2	1-	14
			DET	24	2	3	5	1-	33
			Total	43	4	3	7	2-	47
D	52	Dave Lewis	DET	58	2	5	7	12	66
D	7	Doug Halward	VAN	10	0	3	3	8-	34
			DET	11	0	3	3	4	19
			Total	21	0	6	6	4-	53
D	4	*Rick Zombo	DET	44	1	4	5	6-	59
D	3	*Steve Chiasson	DET	45	1	4	5	7-	73
G	30	Greg Stefan	DET	43	0	4	4	0	24
F	8	*Mark Lamb	DET	22	2	1	3	0	8
F	12	Billy Carroll	DET	31	1	2	3	9-	6
D	4	*Jeff Sharples	DET	3	0	1	1	0	2
G	31	Mark Laforest	DET	5	0	1	1	0	7
F	10	*Joe Murphy	DET	5	0	1	1	0	2
F	15	Chris Cichocki	DET	2	0	0	0	2-	2
F	7	Ed Johnstone	DET	6	0	0	0	1	0
G	34	*Sam St. Laurent	DET	6	0	0	0	0	0
F	28	*Dale Krentz	DET	8	0	0	0	2-	0
G	1	Glen Hanlon	DET	36	0	0	0	0	20

Playoffs

Pos	#	Player	Team	GP	G	A	Pts	+/-	PIM
F	19	Steve Yzerman	DET	16	5	13	18	2-	8
F	17	Gerard Gallant	DET	16	8	6	14	1-	43
F	14	Brent Ashton	DET	16	4	9	13	5	6
F	21	Adam Oates	DET	16	4	7	11	7	6
F	11	*Shawn Burr	DET	16	7	2	9	1	20
F	15	Mel Bridgman	DET	16	5	2	7	6	28
D	5	Darren Veitch	DET	12	3	4	7	3	8
F	24	Bob Probert	DET	16	3	4	7	2	63
D	23	Lee Norwood	DET	16	1	6	7	1-	31
F	26	Joey Kocur	DET	16	2	3	5	1-	71
D	2	Mike O'Connell	DET	16	1	4	5	2	14
D	52	Dave Lewis	DET	14	0	4	4	1	10
F	85	Petr Klima	DET	13	1	2	3	0	4
G	30	Greg Stefan	DET	9	0	2	2	0	0
D	27	Harold Snepsts	DET	11	0	2	2	3	18
D	29	Gilbert Delorme	DET	16	0	2	2	2	14
F	22	Dave Barr	DET	13	1	0	1	3-	14
D	4	*Rick Zombo	DET	7	0	1	1	1-	9
F	20	Tim Higgins	DET	12	0	1	1	4-	16
D	3	*Steve Chiasson	DET	2	0	0	0	0	19
D	4	*Jeff Sharples	DET	2	0	0	0	0	2
F	16	Ric Seiling	DET	7	0	0	0	1	5
G	1	Glen Hanlon	DET	8	0	0	0	0	2
F	18	Mark Kumpel	DET	8	0	0	0	0	4
F	8	*Mark Lamb	DET	11	0	0	0	1-	11

Individual

Most Seasons	*25	Gordie Howe
Most Games	*1,687	Gordie Howe
Most Goals, Career	*786	Gordie Howe
Most Assists, Career	*1,023	Gordie Howe
Most Points, Career	*1,809	Gordie Howe (786 goals, 1,023 assists)
Most Pen. Mins., Career	1,643	Gordie Howe
Most Shutouts, Career	85	Terry Sawchuk
Longest Consecutive Games Streak	548	Alex Delvecchio (Dec. 13/56-Nov. 11/64)
Most Goals, Season	55	John Ogrodnick (1984-85)
Most Assists, Season	74	Marcel Dionne (1974-75)
Most Points, Season	121	Marcel Dionne (1974-75) (47 goals, 74 assists)
Most Pen. Mins., Season	377	Joey Kocur (1985-86)
Most Points, Defenseman Season	74	Reed Larson (1982-83) (22 goals, 52 assists)
Most Points, Center, Season	121	Marcel Dionne (1974-75) (47 goals, 74 assists)
Most Points, Right Wing, Season	103	Gordie Howe (1968-69) (44 goals, 58 assists)
Most Points, Left Wing, Season	105	John Ogrodnick (1984-85) (55 goals, 50 assists)
Most Points, Rookie, Season	87	Steve Yzerman (1983-84) (39 goals, 48 assists)

Club Records

Team

(Figures in brackets for season records are games played; records for fewest points, wins, ties, losses, goals, goals against are for 70 or more games)

Most Points	101	1950-51 (70)
Most Wins	44	1950-51 (70)
		1951-52 (70)
Most Ties	18	1952-53 (70)
		1980-81 (80)
Most Losses	57	1985-86 (80)
Most Goals	313	1984-85 (80)
Most Goals Against	415	1985-86 (80)
Fewest Points	40	1985-86 (80)
Fewest Wins	16	1976-77 (80)
Fewest Ties	4	1966-67 (70)
Fewest Losses	13	1950-51 (70)
Fewest Goals	167	1958-59 (70)
Fewest Goals Against	132	1953-54 (70)

EDMONTON OILERS

Charlie Huddy and Esa Tikkanen

1986-87: 50w-24L-6T 106 PTS. First, Smythe Division

1987-88 OUTLOOK: They may be the Stanley Cup champs, but the Oilers can't ignore the loss of three key role players. Kent Nilsson, hailed as a missing link by Wayne Gretzky after the playoffs, has departed thn NHL for Europe as has Reijo Ruotsalainen who gave the Oilers a second super-skating defenseman. And Randy Gregg, who coach Glen Sather lured from retirement last fall, is gone again, this time to the Canadian Olympic team. But any team with Gretzky, Mark Messier, Glenn Anderson, Jari Kurri, Paul Coffey and Grant Fuhr is still a giant force. His Greatness scored 62 goals last season, Kurri added 54 and linemate Esa Tikkanen came into his own with 34. Messier and Anderson will miss Nillson, but the Oilers checking game, featuring Dave Hunter, Craig MacTavish and Kevin McClelland has never been better. Coffey's decline in production was a source of concern as so much of the Oilers scheme is based on his being the fourth man on the attack. In Kevin Lowe the Oilers have an All-Star defenseman, but he may have health problems. It may be left to Craig Muni, Charlie Huddy and Steve Smith who all came into their own last year to fill the void. Fuhr is one of the NHL's best goaltenders and plays especially well around playoff time.

Upcoming Milestones

Wayne Gretzky – 57 goals to reach 600
– 33 assists to reach 1,000
– 80 points to reach 1,600
Paul Coffey – 40 assists to reach 500
Jari Kurri – 46 goals to reach 400
Mark Messier – 35 goals to reach 300
Craig McTavish – 13 goals to reach 100

Fan Club

Edmonton Oilers Booster Club
P.O. Box 11713
Edmonton, Alberta T5J 3K8

Entry Draft Selections 1987

Pick	
21	Peter Soberlak
42	Brad Werenka
63	Geoff Smith
64	Peter Eriksson
105	Shaun Van Allen
126	Radek Toupal
147	Tomas Srsen
168	Age Ellingsen
189	Gavin Armstrong
210	Mike Tinkham
231	Jeff Pauletti
241	Jesper Duus
252	Igor Viazmikin

9th
NHL
Season

EDMONTON OILERS

Year-by-Year Record 1979-1987

Season	GP	Home W	L	T	Road W	L	T	Overall W	L	T	GF	GA	Pts.	Finished	Playoff Result
1986-87	80	29	6	5	21	18	1	50	24	6	372	284	106	1st, Smythe Div.	Won Stanley Cup
1985-86	80	32	6	2	24	11	5	56	17	7	426	310	119	1st, Smythe Div.	Lost Div. Final
1984-85	80	26	7	7	23	13	4	49	20	11	401	298	109	1st, Smythe Div.	Won Stanley Cup
1983-84	80	31	5	4	26	13	1	57	18	5	446	314	119	1st, Smythe Div.	Won Stanley Cup
1982-83	80	25	9	6	22	12	6	47	21	12	424	315	106	1st, Smythe Div.	Lost Final
1981-82	80	31	5	4	17	12	11	48	17	15	417	295	111	1st, Smythe Div.	Lost Div. Semi-Final
1980-81	80	17	13	10	12	22	6	29	35	16	328	327	74	4th, Smythe Div.	Lost Quarter-Final
1979-80	80	17	14	9	11	25	4	28	39	13	301	322	69	4th, Smythe Div.	Lost Prelim. Round

Playoff History, 1980-87

Versus	Year	Series	Winner	W	L	T	GF	GA
Calgary	1983	DF	Edmonton	4	1		35	13
Calgary	1984	DF	Edmonton	4	3		33	27
Calgary	1986	DF	Calgary	3	4		24	25
Chicago	1983	SF	Edmonton	4	0		25	11
Chicago	1985	SF	Edmonton	4	2		44	25
Detroit	1987	CF	Edmonton	4	1		16	10
Los Angeles	1982	DSF	Los Angeles	2	3		23	27
Los Angeles	1985	DSF	Edmonton	3	0		11	7
Los Angeles	1987	DSF	Edmonton	4	1		32	20
Minnesota	1984	SF	Edmonton	4	0		22	10
Montreal	1981	PRE	Edmonton	3	0		15	6
NY Islanders	1981	QF	NY Islanders	2	4		20	29
NY Islanders	1983	F	NY Islanders	0	4		6	17
NY Islanders	1984	F	Edmonton	4	1		21	12
Philadelphia	1980	PRE	Philadelphia	0	3		6	12
Philadelphia	1985	F	Edmonton	4	1		21	14
Philadelphia	1987	F	Edmonton	4	3		19	17
Vancouver	1986	DSF	Edmonton	3	0		17	5
Winnipeg	1983	DSF	Edmonton	3	0		14	9
Winnipeg	1984	DSF	Edmonton	3	0		18	7
Winnipeg	1985	DF	Edmonton	4	0		22	11
Winnipeg	1987	DF	Edmonton	4	0		17	9

Club Records

Team

(Figures in brackets for season records are games played; records for fewest points, wins, ties, losses, goals, goals against are for 70 or more

Most Points............119	1983-84 (80)	
	1985-86 (80)	
Most Wins..............57	1983-84 (80)	
Most Ties..............16	1980-81 (80)	
Most Losses............39	1979-80 (80)	
Most Goals...........*446	1983-84 (80)	
Most Goals Against......327	1980-81 (80)	
Fewest Points...........69	1979-80 (80)	
Fewest Wins............28	1979-80 (80)	
Fewest Ties.............5	1983-84 (80)	
Fewest Losses..........17	1981-82 (80)	
	1985-86 (80)	
Fewest Goals..........301	1979-80 (80)	
Fewest Goals Against....284	1986-87 (80)	

Longest Winning Streak
Over-all...............8 Several times
Home.................8 Jan. 19/85-
                        Feb. 22/85
Away.................7 Dec. 14/83-
                        Jan. 11/84

Longest Undefeated Streak
Over-all...............15 Oct. 11/84-
                         Nov. 9/84
                         (12 wins, 3 ties)
Home.................12 Oct. 5-
                        Dec. 3/83
                        (10 wins, 2 ties)
Away.................9 Jan. 17-
                       Mar. 2/82
                       (6 wins, 3 ties)

continued

Coach

SATHER, GLEN CAMERON
President, General Manager and Coach, Edmonton Oilers.
Born in High River, Alta., September 2, 1943.

A journeyman left-winger who played for six different teams during his seven-year NHL career, 44-year-old Glen Sather has since become one of the League's most successful coaches ever. Winner of the Jack Adams Award in 1985-86 as the NHL's Coach-of-the-Year, Sather not only has led his club to three Stanley Cup championships in the last four seasons but also has raised his eight-year winning percentage to .635 (364-191-85), the second highest in League history among coaches with 600 or more games.

After closing out his NHL playing career in 1975-76 with an 80-113-193 scoring mark in 660 games, Sather jumped to the Oilers in the World Hockey Association, where he enjoyed his best and last season as a player with totals of 19-34-53 in 81 games. Midway through that 1976-77 campaign, on January 27, 1977, he also assumed the Edmonton coaching duties and led his team to the first of its 11 straight WHA and NHL playoff appearances. Three years later, when the club entered the NHL, Sather took on the added responsibilities of Oilers' President and General Manager, which he currently maintains.

1986-87 Scoring

Regular Season   *—Rookie

Pos	#	Player	Team	GP	G	A	Pts	+/−	PIM
F	99	Wayne Gretzky	EDM	79	62	121	183	70	28
F	17	Jari Kurri	EDM	79	54	54	108	35	41
F	11	Mark Messier	EDM	77	37	70	107	21	73
F	10	Esa Tikkanen	EDM	76	34	44	78	44	120
F	9	Glenn Anderson	EDM	80	35	38	73	27	65
D	7	Paul Coffey	EDM	59	17	50	67	12	49
F	15	Kent Nilsson	MIN	44	13	33	46	2	12
			EDM	17	5	12	17	10	4
			Total	61	18	45	63	12	16
F	26	Mike Krushelnyski	EDM	80	16	35	51	26	67
F	14	Craig MacTavish	EDM	79	20	19	39	9	55
D	4	Kevin Lowe	EDM	77	8	29	37	41	94
F	23	Moe Lemay	VAN	52	9	17	26	2−	128
			EDM	10	1	2	3	2	36
			Total	62	10	19	29	0	164
D	28	Craig Muni	EDM	79	7	22	29	45	85
F	24	Kevin McClelland	EDM	72	12	13	25	4−	238
D	21	Randy Gregg	EDM	52	8	16	24	36	42
D	5	Steve Smith	EDM	62	7	15	22	11	165
D	22	Charlie Huddy	EDM	58	4	15	19	27	35
F	12	Dave Hunter	EDM	77	6	9	15	1	79
D	29	Reijo Ruotsalainen	EDM	16	5	8	13	8	6
F	19	Normand Lacombe	BUF	39	4	7	11	9−	8
			EDM	1	0	0	0	1−	2
			Total	40	4	7	11	10−	10
D	6	*Jeff Beukeboom	EDM	44	3	8	11	7	124
F	33	Marty McSorley	EDM	41	2	4	6	4−	159
F	20	Jaroslav Pouzar	EDM	12	2	3	5	3	6
F	18	Danny Gare	EDM	18	1	3	4	2	6
F	25	Mike Moller	EDM	6	2	1	3	2	0
F	15	*Steve Graves	EDM	12	2	0	2	2−	0
G	31	Grant Fuhr	EDM	44	0	2	2	0	6
G	35	Andy Moog	EDM	46	0	2	2	0	8
F	20	Dave Lumley	EDM	1	0	0	0	0	0
F	8	*Wayne Van Dorp	EDM	3	0	0	0	1−	25

Playoffs

Pos	#	Player	Team	GP	G	A	Pts	+/−	PIM
F	99	Wayne Gretzky	EDM	21	5	29	34	10	6
F	11	Mark Messier	EDM	21	12	16	28	13	16
F	9	Glenn Anderson	EDM	21	14	13	27	13	59
F	17	Jari Kurri	EDM	21	15	10	25	11	20
F	15	Kent Nilsson	EDM	21	6	13	19	11	6
D	7	Paul Coffey	EDM	17	3	8	11	7	30
F	14	Craig MacTavish	EDM	21	1	9	10	1	16
F	10	Esa Tikkanen	EDM	21	7	2	9	1	22
D	21	Randy Gregg	EDM	18	3	6	9	8	17
D	22	Charlie Huddy	EDM	21	1	7	8	12	21
F	33	Marty McSorley	EDM	21	4	3	7	8	65
F	26	Mike Krushelnyski	EDM	21	3	4	7	4	18
D	29	Reijo Ruotsalainen	EDM	21	2	5	7	8	10
F	12	Dave Hunter	EDM	21	3	3	6	4	20
D	4	Kevin Lowe	EDM	21	2	4	6	8	22
F	24	Kevin McClelland	EDM	21	2	3	5	6	43
D	5	Steve Smith	EDM	15	1	3	4	9	45
F	23	Moe Lemay	EDM	9	2	1	3	1	11
F	20	Jaroslav Pouzar	EDM	5	1	1	2	4	2
D	28	Craig Muni	EDM	14	0	2	2	2	17
G	31	Grant Fuhr	EDM	19	0	1	1	0	0
G	35	Andy Moog	EDM	2	0	0	0	0	0
F	16	*Kelly Buchberger	EDM	3	0	0	0	0	5
F	8	*Wayne Van Dorp	EDM	3	0	0	0	0	2

Individual

Most Seasons ....8 Several players
Most Games ....632 Wayne Gretzky
Most Goals, Career......543 Wayne Gretzky
Most Assists, Career......977 Wayne Gretzky
Most Points, Career ....1,520 Wayne Gretzky
(543 goals, 977 assists)
Most Pen. Mins., Career....981 Dave Semenko
Most Shutouts, Career.......4 Andy Moog
Longest Consecutive
Games Streak.........362 Wayne Gretzky
(Nov. 2/79-Feb. 3/84)
Most Goals, Season ......*92 Wayne Gretzky
(1981-82)
Most Assists, Season ....*163 Wayne Gretzky
(1985-86)
Most Points, Season .....*215 Wayne Gretzky
(1985-86)
(52 goals, 163 assists)
Most Pen. Mins., Season ...266 Kevin McClelland
(1985-86)
Most Points, Defenseman,
Season ....138 Paul Coffey
(1985-86)
(48 goals, 90 assists)
Most Points, Center,
Season ....*215 Wayne Gretzky
(1985-86)
(52 goals, 163 assists)
Most Points, Right Wing,
Season ....135 Jari Kurri
(1984-85)
(71 goals, 64 assists)

Most Points, Left Wing,
Season ....102 Glen Anderson
(1985-86)
(54 goals, 48 assists)
Most Points, Rookie,
Season ....75 Jari Kurri
(1980-81)
(32 goals, 43 assists)
Most Shutouts, Season ......1 by 3 goaltenders
Most Goals, Game ....5 Wayne Gretzky
(Feb. 18/81, Dec. 30/81,
Dec. 20/84)
Jari Kurri (Nov. 19/83)
Pat Hughes (Feb. 3/84)
Most Assists, Game ....*7 Wayne Gretzky
(Feb. 15/80; Dec. 11/85;
Feb. 14/86)
Most Points, Game ....8 Wayne Gretzky
(Nov. 19/83)
Paul Coffey
(Mar. 14/86)
Wayne Gretzky
(Jan. 4/84)

* NHL Record.

HARTFORD WHALERS

Kevin Dineen

1986-87: 43w-30L-7T 93 PTS. First, Adams Division

1987-88 OUTLOOK: General manager Emile Francis and coach Jack Evans have assembled a group of players with the potential to challenge for the Stanley Cup. After reaching Game Seven of the Adams Division final against the eventual Cup champion Canadiens two years ago, the Whalers finished in first place last season before being upset by Quebec in last season's playoffs. Hartford is strong from goal on out. Mike Liut is one of the NHL's best netminders, and Steve Weeks has matured into a capable back-up. On defense, the Whalers are solid. Ulf Samuelsson is one of the most physical Europeans ever to play in the NHL. His play last season earned him a spot on Team NHL in Rendez-Vous '87. Samuelsson and his partner, Dana Murzyn, could form one of the League's best defensive tandems for the next decade, while David Babych and Joel Quenneville are outstanding complements. Up front, all that's missing is size. Ron Francis (93 points) and Kevin Dineen (40 goals) are among the NHL's elite forwards, while Sylvain Turgeon must come back from an arm injury suffered during Canada Cup practice. Exceptional scoring balance exists elsewhere with veteran John Anderson (31 goals), Ray Ferraro (27 goals), Dean Evason and Paul Lawless (22 goals each) and Stewart Gavin (20 goals).

Upcoming Milestones

John Anderson – 1 goal to reach 250
Mike Liut – 3 shutouts to reach 20
Doug Jarvis – 38 games to reach 1,000
Kevin Dineen – 2 goals to reach 100
Dave Babych – 8 goals to reach 100

Fan Club

Hartford Whalers Booster Club
P.O. Box 273
Hartford, CT 06141

Entry Draft Selections 1987

Pick
18   Jody Hull
39   Adam Burt
81   Terry Yake
102 Marc Rousseau
123 Jeff St. Cyr
144 Greg Wolf
165 John Moore
186 Joe Day
228 Kevin Sullivan
249 Steve Laurin

9th NHL Season

Year-by-Year Record 1979-1987

Season	GP	Home W	L	T	Road W	L	T	Overall W	L	T	GF	GA	Pts.	Finished	Playoff Result
1986-87	80	26	9	5	17	21	2	43	30	7	287	270	93	1st, Adams Div.	Lost Div. Semi-Final
1985-86	80	21	17	2	19	19	2	40	36	4	332	302	84	4th, Adams Div.	Lost Div. Final
1984-85	80	17	18	5	13	23	4	30	41	9	268	318	69	5th, Adams Div.	Out of Playoffs
1983-84	80	19	16	5	9	26	5	28	42	10	288	320	66	5th, Adams Div.	Out of Playoffs
1982-83	80	13	22	5	6	32	2	19	54	7	261	403	45	5th, Adams Div.	Out of Playoffs
1981-82	80	13	17	10	8	24	8	21	41	18	264	351	60	5th, Adams Div.	Out of Playoffs
1980-81	80	14	17	9	7	24	9	21	41	18	292	372	60	4th, Norris Div.	Out of Playoffs
1979-80	80	22	12	6	5	22	13	27	34	19	303	312	73	4th, Norris Div.	Lost Prelim. Round

Playoff History, 1980-87

Versus	Year	Series	Winner	W	L	T	GF	GA
Montreal	1980	PRE	Montreal	0	3		8	18
Montreal	1986	DF	Montreal	3	4		13	16
Quebec	1986	DSF	Hartford	3	0		16	7
Quebec	1987	DSF	Quebec	2	4		19	27

Club Records

Team

(Figures in brackets for season records are games played; records for fewest points, wins, ties, losses, goals, goals against are for 70 or more games)

Most Points	93	1986-87 (80)
Most Wins	43	1986-87 (80)
Most Ties	19	1979-80 (80)
Most Losses	54	1982-83 (80)
Most Goals	332	1985-86 (80)
Most Goals Against	403	1982-83 (80)
Fewest Points	45	1982-83 (80)
Fewest Wins	19	1982-83 (80)
Fewest Ties	4	1985-86 (80)
Fewest Losses	30	1986-87 (80)
Fewest Goals	261	1982-83 (80)
Fewest Goals Against	270	1986-87 (80)
Longest Winning Streak		
Over-all	7	Mar. 16-29/85
Home	5	Mar. 17-29/85
Away	4	Mar. 7-19/86

Longest Undefeated Streak		
Over-all	10	Jan. 20-Feb. 10/82 (6 wins, 4 ties)
Home	7	Mar. 15-Apr. 15/83 (5 wins, 2 ties)
Away	6	Jan. 23-Feb. 10/82 (3 wins, 3 ties)
Longest Losing Streak		
Over-all	9	Feb. 19/83-Mar. 8/83
Home	6	Feb. 19/83-Mar. 12/83
Away	13	Feb. 10-Mar. 3/85 Dec. 8/82-Feb. 5/83

Coach

EVANS, WILLIAM JOHN (JACK)
Coach, Hartford Whalers. Born in Morriston, South Wales, April 21, 1928.

Since earning the Hartford Whalers' coaching position on July 7, 1983, Jack "Tex" Evans has distinguished himself as the only NHL coach to improve his club in each of the last four seasons. When he took over the Whalers at the outset of 1983-84, Evans inherited a 45-point, last-place club. In the ensuing four years, he steadily lifted his team to its 1986-87 club-high record of 43-30-7 and 93 points, fourth best overall, and its first Adams Division title.

Evans got his first taste of life in the NHL as a rookie defenseman with the New York Rangers in 1948. After nine seasons in the Rangers' organization, he went to the Chicago Blackhawks, contributing to the club's last Stanley Cup season in 1960-61. Finally, he completed his 14-year NHL career in Chicago in 1962-63 with a 19-80-99 scoring record in 752 career games.

When his NHL playing days were over, Evans continued in the minors, acting as player/coach for one season with the AHL's Buffalo Bisons in 1963-64. He then skated nine more seasons in the minors, before moving behind the bench permanently with the Salt Lake City Golden Eagles, whom he led to the CHL title in 1974-75. In 1975-76, Evans returned to the NHL, this time as coach of the California Golden Seals, and during the following two seasons, he piloted the Cleveland Barons. When the Barons merged with the Minnesota North Stars, he returned in 1978-79 to Salt Lake City, where he captured two more CHL titles in five years before joining the Whalers.

HARTFORD WHALERS

1986-87 Scoring

Regular Season
*–Rookie

Pos	#	Player	Team	GP	G	A	Pts	+/−	PIM
F	10	Ron Francis	HFD	75	30	63	93	10	45
F	11	Kevin Dineen	HFD	78	40	39	79	7	110
F	20	John Anderson	HFD	76	31	44	75	11	19
F	26	Ray Ferraro	HFD	80	27	32	59	9−	42
F	12	Dean Evason	HFD	80	22	37	59	5	67
F	28	Paul Lawless	HFD	60	22	32	54	24	14
F	7	Stewart Gavin	HFD	79	20	21	41	10	28
D	44	Dave Babych	HFD	66	8	33	41	18−	44
F	16	Sylvain Turgeon	HFD	41	23	13	36	3−	45
D	5	Ulf Samuelsson	HFD	78	2	31	33	28	162
F	15	Dave Tippett	HFD	80	9	22	31	0	42
D	4	Dana Murzyn	HFD	74	9	19	28	17	95
F	27	Doug Jarvis	HFD	80	9	13	22	0	20
F	23	Paul MacDermid	HFD	72	7	11	18	3	202
D	25	Mike McEwen	HFD	48	8	8	16	9−	32
D	29	Randy Ladouceur	DET	34	3	6	9	4−	70
			HFD	36	2	3	5	6	51
			Total	70	5	9	14	2	121
F	72	Dave Semenko	EDM	5	0	0	0	0	0
			HFD	51	4	8	12	7−	87
			Total	56	4	8	12	7−	87
D	18	Scot Kleinendorst	HFD	66	3	9	12	4	130
D	3	Joel Quenneville	HFD	37	3	7	10	7	24
D	21	Sylvain Cote	HFD	67	2	8	10	11	20
F	24	Pat Hughes	STL	43	1	5	6	6−	26
			HFD	2	0	0	0	1−	2
			Total	45	1	5	6	7−	28
F	8	*Mike Millar	HFD	10	2	2	4	3	0
G	1	Mike Liut	HFD	59	0	2	2	0	4
F	32	Torrie Robertson	HFD	20	1	0	1	6−	98
F	14	Bill Gardner	HFD	8	0	1	1	2−	0
F	22	*Shane Churla	HFD	20	0	1	1	1−	78
F	40	*Greg Britz	HFD	1	0	0	0	0	0
D	33	*Brad Shaw	HFD	2	0	0	0	0	0
F	17	Wayne Babych	HFD	4	0	0	0	5−	4
F	36	*Yves Courteau	HFD	4	0	0	0	6−	0
F	36	Gord Sherven	HFD	7	0	0	0	6−	0
G	31	Steve Weeks	HFD	25	0	0	0	0	0

Playoffs

Pos	#	Player	Team	GP	G	A	Pts	+/−	PIM
F	7	Stewart Gavin	HFD	6	2	4	6	3	10
F	12	Dean Evason	HFD	5	3	2	5	4	35
F	10	Ron Francis	HFD	6	2	2	4	1−	6
D	18	Scot Kleinendorst	HFD	4	1	3	4	1	20
F	11	Kevin Dineen	HFD	6	2	1	3	1−	31
F	23	Paul MacDermid	HFD	6	2	1	3	0	34
D	4	Dana Murzyn	HFD	6	2	1	3	2−	29
F	20	John Anderson	HFD	6	1	2	3	3−	0
F	16	Sylvain Turgeon	HFD	6	1	2	3	2−	4
D	25	Mike McEwen	HFD	1	1	1	2	0	0
D	44	Dave Babych	HFD	6	1	1	2	4−	14
F	26	Ray Ferraro	HFD	6	1	1	2	2−	8
D	21	Sylvain Cote	HFD	2	0	2	2	4	2
F	28	Paul Lawless	HFD	2	0	2	2	1	2
D	29	Randy Ladouceur	HFD	6	0	2	2	1	12
F	15	Dave Tippett	HFD	6	0	2	2	1−	4
D	5	Ulf Samuelsson	HFD	5	0	1	1	2−	41
G	31	Steve Weeks	HFD	1	0	0	0	0	0
F	22	*Shane Churla	HFD	2	0	0	0	0	42
F	24	Pat Hughes	HFD	3	0	0	0	1−	0
F	72	Dave Semenko	HFD	4	0	0	0	1	15
F	27	Doug Jarvis	HFD	6	0	0	0	6−	4
G	1	Mike Liut	HFD	6	0	0	0	0	2
D	3	Joel Quenneville	HFD	6	0	0	0	0	0

Individual

Most Seasons ....7 Ray Neufeld,
Ron Francis,
Paul MacDermid
Most Games ....417 Ron Francis
Most Goals, Career......219 Blaine Stoughton
Most Assists, Career.....335 Ron Francis
Most Points, Career .....489 Ron Francis
(154 goals, 335 assists)
Most Pen. Mins., Career....991 Torrie Robertson
Most Shutouts, Career......7 Mike Liut
Longest Consecutive
Games Streak.........160 Mike Rogers
(Oct. 11/79-Apr. 5/81)
Most Goals, Season ....56 Blaine Stoughton
(1979-80)
Most Assists, Season ......65 Mike Rogers
(1980-81)
Most Points, Season ......105 Mike Rogers
(1979-80)
(44 goals, 61 assists)
(1980-81)
(40 goals, 65 assists)
Torrie Robertson
(1985-86)
Most Pen. Mins., Season ...358 Torrie Robertson
(1985-86)
Most Points, Defenseman
Season ....69 Dave Babych
(1985-86)
(14 goals, 55 assists)

Most Points, Center,
Season ....105 Mike Rogers
(1979-80)
(44 goals, 61 assists)
Mike Rogers
(1980-81)
(40 goals, 65 assists)
Most Points, Right Wing,
Season ....100 Blaine Stoughton
(1979-80)
(56 goals, 44 assists)
Most Points, Left Wing,
Season ....80 Pat Boutette
(1980-81)
(28 goals, 52 assists)
Most Points, Rookie,
Season ....72 Sylvain Turgeon
(1983-84)
(40 goals, 32 assists)
Most Shutouts, Season ......4 Mike Liut
(1986-87)
Most Goals, Game ....5 Jordy Douglas
(Feb. 3/80)
Most Assists, Game ....6 Ron Francis
(Mar. 5/87)
Most Points, Game ....6 Paul Lawless
(Jan. 4/87)
Ron Francis
(Mar. 5/87)

LOS ANGELES KINGS

Bobby Carpenter

1986-87: 31w-41L-8T 70 PTS. Fourth, Smythe Division

1987-88 OUTLOOK: The Kings ushered in a new era last season as superb rookies Luc Robitaille and Jimmy Carson led them into the playoffs for only the second time in five years and took the scoring load off the shoulders of Dave Taylor, Bernie Nicholls and the now-departed Marcel Dionne. Robitaille, a ninth round draft pick, scored 45 goals and won the Calder Trophy while Carson added 37. Playing in the high-scoring Smythe Division, the Kings should have a high supply offense with Robitaille, Carson, Taylor, Nicholls, Bob Carpenter (acquired from the Rangers in the Dionne trade), Jim Fox and Bryan Erickson. The question mark surrounding coach Mike Murphy's club is defense. Only New Jersey allowed more goals last season. Tom Laidlaw, who switched coasts in March along with Carpenter, is a solid veteran, as are Dean Kennedy, Mark Hardy and Jay Wells. Rookie Steve Duchesne had a good rookie year and must continue to improve, while Grant Ledyard has outstanding offensive skills but could still be a defensive liability. Roland Melanson (3.69 last season) and ex-Capital Al Jensen comprise an above average goaltending tandem.

Upcoming Milestones

Dave Williams — 15 goals to reach 200
Bernie Nicholls — 2 goals to reach 200
Dave Taylor — 28 goals to reach 350
— 6 points to reach 800
Morris Lukowich — 1 goal to reach 250
Jimmy Fox — 1 game to reach 500

Fan Club

New Los Angeles Kings Booster Club
P.O. Box 67882
Los Angeles, CA 90067-0082

Entry Draft Selections 1987

Pick	
4	Wayne McBean
27	Mark Fitzpatrick
43	Ross Wilson
90	Mike Vukonich
111	Greg Batters
132	Kyosti Karjalainen
174	Jeff Gawlicki
195	John Preston
216	Rostislav Vlach
237	Mikael Lindholm

21st NHL Season

LOS ANGELES KINGS

Year-by-Year Record 1968-1987

Season	GP	Home W L T	Road W L T	Overall W L T	GF	GA	Pts.	Finished	Playoff Result
1986-87	80	20 17 3	11 24 5	31 41 8	318	341	70	4th, Smythe Div.	Lost Div. Semi-Final
1985-86	80	9 27 4	14 22 4	23 49 8	284	389	54	5th, Smythe Div.	Out of Playoffs
1984-85	80	20 14 6	14 18 8	34 32 14	339	326	82	4th, Smythe Div.	Lost Div. Semi-Final
1983-84	80	13 19 8	10 25 5	23 44 13	309	376	59	5th, Smythe Div.	Out of Playoffs
1982-83	80	20 13 7	7 28 5	27 41 12	308	365	66	5th, Smythe Div.	Out of Playoffs
1981-82	80	19 15 6	5 26 9	24 41 15	314	369	63	4th, Smythe Div.	Lost Div. Final
1980-81	80	22 11 7	21 13 6	43 24 13	337	290	99	2nd, Norris Div.	Lost Prelim. Round
1979-80	80	18 13 9	12 23 5	30 36 14	290	313	74	2nd, Norris Div.	Lost Prelim. Round
1978-79	80	20 13 7	14 21 5	34 34 12	292	286	80	3rd, Norris Div.	Lost Prelim. Round
1977-78	80	18 16 6	13 18 9	31 34 15	243	245	77	3rd, Norris Div.	Lost Prelim. Round
1976-77	80	20 13 7	14 18 8	34 31 15	271	241	83	2nd, Norris Div.	Lost Quarter-Final
1975-76	80	22 13 5	16 20 4	38 33 9	263	265	85	2nd, Norris Div.	Lost Quarter-Final
1974-75	80	22 7 11	20 10 10	42 17 21	269	185	105	2nd, Norris Div.	Lost Prelim. Round
1973-74	78	22 13 4	11 20 8	33 33 12	233	231	78	3rd, West Div.	Lost Quarter-Final
1972-73	78	21 11 7	10 25 4	31 36 11	232	245	73	6th, West Div.	Out of Playoffs
1971-72	78	14 23 2	6 26 7	20 49 9	206	305	49	7th, West Div.	Out of Playoffs
1970-71	78	17 14 8	8 26 5	25 40 13	239	303	63	5th, West Div.	Out of Playoffs
1969-70	76	12 22 4	2 30 6	14 52 10	168	290	38	6th, West Div.	Out of Playoffs
1968-69	76	19 14 5	5 28 5	24 42 10	185	260	58	4th, West Div.	Lost Semi-Final
1967-68	74	20 13 4	11 20 6	31 33 10	200	224	72	2nd, West Div.	Lost Quarter-Final

Playoff History, 1968-87

Versus	Year	Series	Winner	W	L	T	GF	GA
Boston	1976	QF	Boston	3	4		14	26
Boston	1977	QF	Boston	2	4		24	30
Calgary	1976	PRE	Los Angeles	2	0		3	1
Calgary	1977	PRE	Los Angeles	2	1		11	7
Chicago	1974	QF	Chicago	1	4		7	10
Edmonton	1982	DSF	Los Angeles	3	2		27	23
Edmonton	1985	DSF	Edmonton	0	3		7	11
Edmonton	1987	DSF	Edmonton	1	4		20	32
Minnesota	1968	QF	Minnesota	3	4		21	26
NY Islanders	1980	PRE	NY Islanders	1	3		10	21
NY Rangers	1979	PRE	NY Rangers	0	2		2	9
NY Rangers	1981	PRE	NY Rangers	1	3		12	23
St. Louis	1969	SF	St. Louis	0	4		5	16
Toronto	1975	PRE	Toronto	1	2		6	7
Toronto	1978	PRE	Toronto	0	2		3	11
Vancouver	1982	DF	Vancouver	1	4		14	19
Oakland	1969	QF	Los Angeles	4	3		25	23

Club Records

Team

(Figures in brackets for season records are games played; records for fewest points, wins, ties, losses, goals, goals against are for 70 or more games)

Most Points	105	1974-75 (80)
Most Wins	43	1980-81 (80)
Most Ties	21	1974-75 (80)
Most Losses	52	1969-70 (76)
Most Goals	339	1984-85 (80)
Most Goals Against	389	1985-86 (80)
Fewest Points	38	1969-70 (76)
Fewest Wins	14	1969-70 (76)
Fewest Ties	8	1985-86 (80)
Fewest Losses	17	1974-75 (80)
Fewest Goals	168	1969-70 (76)
Fewest Goals Against	185	1974-75 (80)
Longest Winning Streak		
Over-all	8	Oct. 21-Nov. 7/72
Home	7	Four times
Away	8	Dec. 18/74-Jan. 16/75

continued

Coach

MURPHY, MICHAEL JOHN (MIKE)
Coach, Los Angeles Kings. Born in Toronto, Ont., September 12, 1950.

With half a season under his belt behind the Los Angeles Kings' bench, 37-year-old Mike Murphy begins 1987-88 as one of the League's youngest coaches at the helm of one of its youngest and most promising teams. However, Murphy is certainly no stranger to the demands and rigors of life in the big leagues, both on and off the ice. For 12 NHL seasons, he patrolled right wing for the St. Louis Blues, New York Rangers and Kings, amassing a 238-318-556 scoring total in 831 games from 1971-72 through 1982-83. Following his retirement as a player, Murphy remained with Los Angeles as an assistant coach until his appointment as the Kings' head coach on January 9, 1987.

1986-87 Scoring

Regular Season *–Rookie

Pos	#	Player	Team	GP	G	A	Pts	+/−	PIM
F	20	*Luc Robitaille	LA	79	45	39	84	18−	28
F	9	Bernie Nicholls	LA	80	33	48	81	16−	101
F	17	*Jimmy Carson	LA	80	37	42	79	5−	22
F	18	Dave Taylor	LA	67	18	44	62	0	84
F	19	Jim Fox	LA	76	19	42	61	10−	48
F	15	Bryan Erickson	LA	68	20	30	50	12−	26
D	28	*Steve Duchesne	LA	75	13	25	38	8	74
D	4	Grant Ledyard	LA	67	14	23	37	40−	93
D	24	Jay Wells	LA	77	7	29	36	19−	155
F	12	Morris Lukowich	LA	60	14	21	35	0	64
F	22	Dave Williams	LA	76	16	18	34	1−	358
F	10	Sean McKenna	LA	69	14	19	33	11	10
D	5	Mark Hardy	LA	73	3	27	30	16	120
F	21	Bob Carpenter	WSH	22	5	7	12	7−	21
			NYR	28	2	8	10	12−	20
			LA	10	2	3	5	8−	6
			Total	60	9	18	27	27−	47
F	14	Bob Bourne	LA	78	13	9	22	13−	35
F	7	Phil Sykes	LA	58	6	15	21	10	133
D	6	Dean Kennedy	LA	66	6	14	20	9	91
D	3	Tom Laidlaw	NYR	63	1	10	11	18−	65
			LA	11	0	3	3	1	4
			Total	74	1	13	14	17−	69
D	23	Larry Playfair	LA	37	2	7	9	1−	181
D	2	Craig Redmond	LA	16	1	7	8	1−	8
F	8	Paul Guay	LA	35	2	5	7	14−	16
G	31	Roland Melanson	LA	46	0	6	6	0	22
D	25	Dave Langevin	LA	11	0	4	4	3−	7
F	27	Joe Paterson	LA	45	2	1	3	15−	158
F	11	*Lyle Phair	LA	5	2	0	2	1−	2
D	3	*Ken Hammond	LA	10	0	2	2	2	11
D	25	*Peter Dineen	LA	11	0	2	2	9−	8
G	29	Al Jensen	WSH	6	0	0	0	0	0
			LA	5	0	1	1	0	0
			Total	11	0	1	1	0	0
G	35	Darren Eliot	LA	24	0	1	1	0	18
F	26	*Brian Wilks	LA	1	0	0	0	2−	0
F	32	*Craig Duncanson	LA	2	0	0	0	0	24
G	1	Bob Janecyk	LA	7	0	0	0	0−	2

Playoffs

Pos	#	Player	Team	GP	G	A	Pts	+/−	PIM
F	9	Bernie Nicholls	LA	5	2	5	7	1	6
F	19	Jim Fox	LA	5	3	2	5	2−	0
F	22	Dave Williams	LA	5	3	2	5	2	30
F	18	Dave Taylor	LA	5	2	3	5	2−	6
F	20	*Luc Robitaille	LA	5	1	4	5	7−	2
D	28	*Steve Duchesne	LA	5	2	2	4	8−	4
F	14	Bob Bourne	LA	5	2	1	3	2−	0
F	21	Bob Carpenter	LA	5	1	2	3	4−	2
F	17	*Jimmy Carson	LA	5	1	2	3	6−	6
D	5	Mark Hardy	LA	5	1	2	3	3	10
D	24	Jay Wells	LA	5	1	2	3	3−	10
F	15	Bryan Erickson	LA	3	1	1	2	0	0
D	6	Dean Kennedy	LA	5	0	2	2	1	10
F	10	Sean McKenna	LA	5	0	1	1	4−	0
F	7	Phil Sykes	LA	5	0	1	1	2−	8
G	35	Darren Eliot	LA	1	0	0	0	0	0
F	8	Paul Guay	LA	2	0	0	0	1	0
F	27	Joe Paterson	LA	2	0	0	0	2−	0
F	12	Morris Lukowich	LA	3	0	0	0	1	8
D	3	Tom Laidlaw	LA	5	0	0	0	9−	2
D	4	Grant Ledyard	LA	5	0	0	0	2−	10
G	31	Roland Melanson	LA	5	0	0	0	0	4

Individual

Most Seasons 12	Goring, Marcel Dionne
Most Games 921	Marcel Dionne
Most Goals, Career 550	Marcel Dionne
Most Assists, Career 757	Marcel Dionne
Most Points Career..... 1,307	Marcel Dionne
Most Pen. Mins., Career.. 1,287	Jay Wells
Most Shutouts, Career......32	Rogie Vachon
Longest Consecutive Games Streak.........324	Marcel Dionne (Jan. 7/78–Jan. 9/82)
Most Goals, Season 59	Marcel Dionne (1978-79)
Most Assists, Season 84	Marcel Dionne (1979-80)
Most Points, Season......137	Marcel Dionne (1979-80) (53 goals, 84 assists)
Most Pen. Mins., Season ...358	Dave Williams (1986-87)
Most Points, Defenseman Season 76	Larry Murphy (1980-81) (16 goals, 60 assists)
Most Points, Center, Season 137	Marcel Dionne (1979-80) (53 goal, 84 assists)
Most Points, Right Wing, Season 112	Dave Taylor (1980-81) (47 goals, 65 assists)
Most Points, Left Wing, Season 105	Charlie Simmer (1980-81) (56 goals, 49 assists)
Most Points, Rookie, Season 84	Luc Robitaille (1986-87) (45 goals, 39 assists)
Most Shutouts, Season 8	Rogie Vachon (1976-77)
Most Goals, Game 4	Several players
Most Assists, Game 5	Marcel Dionne (Jan. 22/76) Danny Grant (Jan. 14/78) Dave Taylor (Nov. 4/79)
Most Points, Game 6	Butch Goring (Feb. 5/72) Syl Apps (Dec. 21/77) Marcel Dionne (Mar. 14/81)

MINNESOTA NORTH STARS

Neal Broten

1986-87: 30w-40L-10T 70 PTS. Fifth, Norris Division

1987-88 OUTLOOK: Met Center fans got their man when the North Stars named Herb Brooks head coach. The popular St. Paul native will attempt to extract the talent that previous coaches have not. The Stars are loaded with offensive potential led by Dino Ciccarelli (52 goals) one of the League's true snipers. Neal Broten was slowed by a shouler injury last season, but is a main cog in the machine. Brian MacLellan was a find (32 goals). Brian Bellows (26 goals) and Dirk Graham (25 goals) can also light the lamp. Scott Bjugstad disappeared last season after scoring 43 goals in 1985-86. Keith Acton, Dennis Maruk and Brian Lawton provide depth at center. Free-agent Terry Ruskowski brings character and leadership – two urgent qualities. Minnesota performed at a 2-12-3 pace down the stretch last season and didn't make the playoffs. On defense, Craig Hartsburg (61 points) made a big comeback after battling injuries for what seems like an eternity. Gordie Roberts, Ron Wilson, Paul Boutilier and Frantisek Musil. Goalie Don Beaupre has moments of brilliance, perhaps not enough of them. Kari Takko backs him up.

Upcoming Milestones

Dino Ciccarelli – 41 goals to reach 300
Brad Maxwell – 3 goals to reach 100
Dennis Maruk – 1 goal to reach 350
– 40 games to reach 900
Craig Hartsburg – 9 goals to reach 100

Fan Club

Minnesota Star-Gazers
Met Sports Center
7091 Cedar Avenue
Bloomington, MN 55420

Entry Draft Selections 1987

Pick	
6	David Archibald
35	Scott McCrady
48	Kevin Kaminski
73	John Weisbrod
88	Teppo Kivela
109	D'Arcy Norton
130	Timo Kulonen
151	Don Schmidt
172	Jarmo Myllys
193	Larry Olimb
214	Mark Felicio
235	Dave Shields

21st NHL Season

MINNESOTA NORTH STARS

Year-by-Year Record 1968-1987

Season	GP	Home W	L	T	Road W	L	T	Overall W	L	T	GF	GA	Pts.	Finished	Playoff Result
1986-87	80	17	20	3	13	20	7	30	40	10	296	314	70	5th, Norris Div.	Out of Playoffs
1985-86	80	21	15	4	17	18	5	38	33	9	327	305	85	2nd, Norris Div.	Lost Div. Semi-Final
1984-85	80	14	19	7	11	24	5	25	43	12	268	321	62	4th, Norris Div.	Lost Div. Final
1983-84	80	22	14	4	17	17	6	39	31	10	345	344	88	1st, Norris Div.	Lost Conf. Championshi
1982-83	80	23	6	11	17	18	5	40	24	16	321	290	96	2nd, Norris Div.	Lost Div. Final
1981-82	80	21	7	12	16	16	8	37	23	20	346	288	94	1st, Norris Div.	Lost Div. Semi-Final
1980-81	80	23	10	7	12	18	10	35	28	17	291	263	87	3rd, Adams Div.	Lost Final
1979-80	80	25	8	7	11	20	9	36	28	16	311	253	88	3rd, Adams Div.	Lost Semi-Final
1978-79	80	19	15	6	9	25	6	28	40	12	257	289	68	4th, Adams Div.	Out Of Playoffs
1977-78	80	12	24	4	6	29	5	18	53	9	218	325	45	5th, Smythe Div.	Out of Playoffs
1976-77	80	17	14	9	6	25	9	23	39	18	240	310	64	2nd, Smythe Div.	Lost Prelim. Round
1975-76	80	15	22	3	5	31	4	20	53	7	195	303	47	4th, Smythe Div.	Out of Playoffs
1974-75	80	17	20	3	6	30	4	23	50	7	221	341	53	4th, Smythe Div.	Out of Playoffs
1973-74	78	18	15	6	5	23	11	23	38	17	235	275	63	7th, West Div.	Out of Playoffs
1972-73	78	26	8	5	11	22	6	37	30	11	254	230	85	3rd, West Div.	Lost Quarter-Final
1971-72	78	22	11	6	15	18	6	37	29	12	212	191	86	2nd, West Div.	Lost Quarter-Final
1970-71	78	16	15	8	12	19	8	28	34	16	191	223	72	4th, West Div.	Lost Semi-Final
1969-70	76	11	16	11	8	19	11	19	35	22	224	257	60	3rd, West Div.	Lost Quarter-Final
1968-69	76	11	21	6	7	22	9	18	43	15	189	270	51	6th, West Div.	Out of Playoffs
1967-68	74	17	12	8	10	20	7	27	32	15	191	226	69	4th, West Div.	Lost Semi-Final

Playoff History, 1968-87

Versus	Year	Series	Winner	W	L	T	GF	GA
Boston	1981	PRE	Minnesota	3	0		20	13
Buffalo	1977	PRE	Buffalo	0	2		3	11
Buffalo	1981	QF	Minnesota	4	1		23	17
Calgary	1981	SF	Minnesota	4	2		25	18
Chicago	1982	DSF	Chicago	1	3		14	14
Chicago	1983	DF	Chicago	1	4		17	22
Chicago	1984	DSF	Minnesota	3	2		18	14
Chicago	1985	DF	Chicago	2	4		29	32
Edmonton	1984	SF	Edmonton	0	4		10	22
Los Angeles	1968	QF	Minnesota	4	3		26	21
Montreal	1971	SF	Montreal	2	4		19	27
Montreal	1980	QF	Minnesota	4	3		18	21
NY Islanders	1981	F	NY Islanders	1	4		16	26
Philadelphia	1973	QF	Philadelphia	2	4		12	14
Philadelphia	1980	SF	Philadelphia	1	4		14	27
St. Louis	1968	SF	St. Louis	3	4		18	22
St. Louis	1970	QF	St. Louis	2	4		16	20
St. Louis	1971	QF	Minnesota	4	2		16	15
St. Louis	1972	QF	St. Louis	3	4		19	19
St. Louis	1984	DF	Minnesota	4	3		19	17
St. Louis	1985	DSF	Minnesota	3	0		9	5
St. Louis	1986	DSF	St. Louis	2	3		20	18
Toronto	1980	PRE	Minnesota	3	0		17	8
Toronto	1983	DSF	Minnesota	3	1		18	18

Club Records

Team

(Figures in brackets for season records are games played; records for fewest points, wins, ties, losses, goals, goals against are for 70 or more games)

Most Points	96	1982-83 (80)
Most Wins	40	1982-83 (80)
Most Ties	22	1969-70 (76)
Most Losses	53	1975-76 (80)
Most Goals	346	1981-82 (80)
Most Goals Against	344	1983-84 (80)
Fewest Points	45	1977-78 (80)
Fewest Wins	18	1968-69 (76)
		1977-78 (80)
Fewest Ties	7	1974-75 (80)
		1975-76 (80)
Fewest Losses	24	1982-83 (80)
Fewest Goals	189	1968-69 (76)
Fewest Goals Against	191	1971-72 (78)
Longest Winning Streak		
Over-all	7	Mar. 16-28/80
Home	11	Nov. 4-
		Dec. 27/72
Away	5	Dec. 2-16/67
		Feb. 5-
		Mar. 5/83

Coach

BROOKS, HERBERT PAUL (HERB)
Coach, Minnesota North Stars. Born in St. Paul, MN, August 5, 1937.

Upon joining the North Stars on April 27, 1987, Herb Brooks became the first Minnesota native to coach his state's NHL team. the 50-year-old St. Paul native begins his second tour of duty in the NHL, looking to add to another championship to his coaching record.

Hockey fans everywhere, particularly in the United States, will surely never forget the greatest win of Brooks' coaching career – the dramatic, if not shocking, Gold Medal victory for U.S. Olympic Hockey Team at the 1980 Winter Games in Lake Placid. That victory earned him a four-year coaching stint, 1981-82 to 1984-85, with the Rangers in New York, where he earned 100 victories faster than any other coach in that club's storied history.

Prior to the 1980 Olympics, Brooks compiled impressive winning totals as coach of his alma mater, the University of Minnesota Golden Gophers. From 1972 to 1979, he amassed the school's first three NCAA championships (1974, 1976 and 1979) and tallied a .627 winning percentage with a 175-100-20 record.

As an amateur player, Brooks also achieved much success. He played defense for the 1964 and 1968 U.S. Olympic squads, serving as co-captain for the latter, in addition to acting as captain on three of five other U.S. National Teams.

MINNESOTA NORTH STARS

Longest Undefeated Streak
- Over-all 12
- Home 13
- Away 6

Longest Losing Streak
- Over-all 10
- Home 6
- Away 8

Longest Winless Streak
- Over-all 20
- Home 12
- Away 23

Most Shutouts, Season 7
Most Pen. Mins., Season 1,936
Most Goals, Game 15

Individual

Most Seasons 12	Fred Barrett
Most Games 730	Fred Barrett
Most Goals, Career 267	Bill Goldsworthy
Most Assists, Career ... 316	Tim Young
Most Points Career 506	Bill Goldsworthy (267 goals, 239 assists)
Most Pen. Mins., Career .. 1,000	Brad Maxwell
Most Shutouts, Career 26	Cesare Maniago
Longest Consecutive Games Streak 442	Danny Grant (Dec. 4/68-Apr. 7/74
Most Goals, Season 55	Dino Ciccarelli (1981-82)
Most Assists, Season 76	Neal Broten (1985-86)
Most Point, Season 114	Bobby Smith (1981-82) (43 goals, 71 assists)
Most Pen. Mins., Season ... 316	Willi Plett (1983-84)
Most Points, Defenseman Season 77	Craig Hartsburg (1981-82) (17 goals, 60 assists)
Most Points, Center, Season 114	Bobby Smith (1981-82) (43 goals, 71 assists)
Most Points, Right Wing, Season 107	Dino Ciccarelli (1981-82) (55 goals, 52 assists)

Feb. 18-Mar. 15/82 (9 wins, 3 ties)
Oct. 28-Dec. 27/72 (12 wins, 1 tie)
Nov. 21-Jan. 9/80 (10 wins, 3 ties)
Nov. 30-Dec. 16/67 (5 wins, 1 tie)
Nov. 7-27/71 (5 wins, 1 tie)
Nov. 9-Dec. 3/83 (5 wins, 1 tie)

Feb. 1-20/76
Jan. 17-Feb. 4/70
Oct. 19-Nov. 13/75

Jan. 15-Feb. 28/70 (15 losses, 5 ties)
Jan. 17-Feb. 25/70 (8 losses, 4 ties)
Oct. 25/74-Jan. 28/75 (19 losses, 4 ties)
1972-73 (78)

1986-87 (80)
Nov. 11/81 (Wpg. 2 at Minn. 15)

Most Point, Left Wing, Season 85	Steve Payne (1979-80) (42 goals, 43 assists)
Most Points, Rookie, Season 97	Neal Broten (1981-82) (38 goals, 59 assists)
Most Shutouts, Season 6	Cesare Maniago (1967-68)
Most Goals, Game 5	Tim Young (Jan. 15/79)
Most Assists, Game 5	Murray Oliver (Oct. 24/71)
Most Points, Game 7	Bobby Smith (Nov. 11/81)

1986-87 Scoring

Regular Season *—Rookie

Pos	#	Player	Team	GP	G	A	Pts	+/-	PIM
F	20	Dino Ciccarelli	MIN	80	52	51	103	10	88
F	27	Brian MacLellan	MIN	76	32	31	63	12-	69
D	4	Craig Hartsburg	MIN	73	11	50	61	2-	93
F	21	Dirk Graham	MIN	76	25	29	54	2-	142
F	23	Brain Bellows	MIN	65	26	27	53	13-	34
F	7	Neal Brotten	MIN	46	18	35	53	12	33
F	9	Dennis Maruk	MIN	67	16	30	46	5	52
F	12	Keith Acton	MIN	78	16	29	45	15-	56
F	8	Brain Lawton	MIN	66	21	23	44	20	86
D	2	Ron Wilson	MIN	56	12	29	41	9-	36
F	13	Bob Brooke	MIN	15	3	5	8	3-	20
			MIN	65	10	18	28	6-	78
			Total	80	13	23	36	9-	98
D	55	Brad Maxwell	VAN	30	1	7	8	9-	28
			NYR	9	0	4	4	1-	6
			MIN	17	2	7	9	3	31
			Total	56	3	18	21	7-	65
D	26	Paul Boutilier	BOS	52	5	9	14	2-	84
			MIN	10	2	4	6	1	8
			Total	62	7	13	20	1-	92
F	31	*Larry DePalms	MIN	56	9	6	15	7-	219
F	14	Scott Bjugstad	MIN	39	4	9	13	6-	43
D	10	Gordie Roberts	MIN	67	3	10	13	7-	68
D	3	Bob Rouse	MIN	72	2	10	12	6	179
F	24	Willi Plett	MIN	67	6	5	11	1	263
D	6	*Frantisek Musil	MIN	72	2	9	11	0	148
F	16	Mark Pavelich	MIN	12	4	6	10	7	10
F	44	Steve Payne	MIN	48	4	6	10	12-	19
F	15	Raimo Helminen	NYR	21	2	4	6	8-	2
			MIN	6	0	1	1	3-	0
			Total	27	2	5	7	11-	2
D	5	*Jari Gronstrand	MIN	47	1	6	7	4	27
D	36	*Chris Pryor	MIN	50	1	3	4	6-	49
F	16	Marc Habscheid	MIN	15	2	0	2	6-	2
F	37	*Paul Houck	MIN	12	0	2	2	2-	0
D	18	*Emanuel Viveiros	MIN	1	0	1	1	0	0
F	15	*Jim Archibald	MIN	1	0	0	0	1-	2
D	16	Colin Chisholm	MIN	1	0	0	0	0	0
F	11	*Sean Toomey	MIN	1	0	0	0	1-	0
F	32	*Randy Smith	MIN	2	0	0	0	2-	0
G	35	*Mike Sands	MIN	3	0	0	0	0	0
F	28	Mats Hallin	MIN	6	0	0	0	3-	4
F	25	Jack Carlson	MIN	8	0	0	0	0	13
G	1	*Kari Takko	MIN	38	0	0	0	0	14
G	33	Don Beaupre	MIN	47	0	0	0	0	16

MONTREAL CANADIENS

Claude Lemieux

1986-87: 41w-29l-10t 92 pts. Second, Adams Division

1987-88 OUTLOOK: You don't usually think of the Montreal Canadiens as a low-scoring hockey team, but the fabled blue, blanc et rouge finished 19th out of 21 teams in scoring last season. Their 277 goals was the team's lowest output since 1969-70. Fortunately, the Habs had the League's stingiest defense to go along with their anemic offense with many top defensive forwards such as Bob Gainey, Chris Nilan (both of whom were injured for big chunks of the season), Guy Carbonneau, Brian Skrudland, Ryan Walter and Mike McPhee. Still coach Jean Perron would like to see some better numbers. Montreal failed to have a 30 goal scorer last year, the first time that's happened in 20 seasons. Bobby Smith led the team with 28, Mats Naslund slipped from 43 to 2x. Gainey, Nilan and Carbonneau each failed to score at least 20 as they tallied the year before. Claude Lemieux plays a very physical right wing but should improve on his 27 goals. Big things are also expected of Shayne Corson, who also missed games due to injury. An off-season injury to veteran defensive star Larry Robinson will put extra pressure on Rick Green, Chris Chelios, Craig Ludwig, Petr Svoboda and Gaston Gingras. Patrick Roy and Brian Hayward shared the Jennings Trophy last season, but Roy's playoff problems against Quebec thrust Hayward into the number one slot.

Upcoming Milestones

Larry Robinson – 13 goals to reach 200
                 – 25 games to reach 1,100
Bob Gainey   – 67 games to reach 1,100
Mats Naslund   – 35 goals to reach 200
Bobby Smith   – 20 games to reach 700

Fan Club

Fan Club – Club de Hockey Canadien
P.O. Box 18 – Station P.A.T.
Montreal, PQ H1B 5K1

Entry Draft Selections 1987

Pick	
17	Andrew Cassels
33	John Leclair
38	Eric Desjardins
44	Mathieu Schneider
58	Francois Gravel
80	Kris Miller
101	Steve McCool
122	Les Kuntar
143	Rob Kelley
164	Will Geist
185	Eric Tremblay
206	Barry McKinlay
227	Ed Ronan
248	Bryan Herring

71st NHL Season

Playoff History, 1927-87

Versus	Year	Series	Winner	W	L	T	GF	GA
Boston	1929	SF	Boston	0	3		2	5
Boston	1930	F	Montreal	2	0		7	3
Boston	1931	SF	Montreal	3	2		13	13
Boston	1943	SF	Boston	0	4		17	18
Boston	1946	F	Montreal	4	1		19	13
Boston	1947	SF	Montreal	4	1		16	10
Boston	1952	SF	Montreal	4	3		18	12
Boston	1953	F	Montreal	4	0		16	9
Boston	1954	SF	Montreal	4	0		16	4
Boston	1955	SF	Montreal	4	1		16	9
Boston	1957	F	Montreal	4	1		15	6
Boston	1958	F	Montreal	4	2		16	14
Boston	1968	QF	Montreal	4	0		15	8
Boston	1969	SF	Montreal	4	2		15	16
Boston	1971	QF	Montreal	4	3		28	26
Boston	1977	F	Montreal	4	0		16	6
Boston	1978	F	Montreal	4	2		18	13
Boston	1979	SF	Montreal	4	3		25	20
Boston	1984	DSF	Montreal	3	0		10	2
Boston	1985	DSF	Montreal	3	2		19	17
Boston	1986	DSF	Montreal	3	0		10	6
Boston	1987	DSF	Montreal	4	0		19	11
Buffalo	1973	QF	Montreal	4	2		21	16
Buffalo	1975	SF	Buffalo	2	4		29	21
Buffalo	1983	DSF	Buffalo	0	3		2	8
Calgary	1986	F	Montreal	4	1		15	13
Chicago	1930	*QF	Montreal	1	0	1	3	2
Chicago	1931	F	Montreal	3	2		11	8
Chicago	1934	*QF	Chicago	0	2		3	4
Chicago	1938	QF	Chicago	1	2		8	11
Chicago	1941	QF	Chicago	1	2		7	8
Chicago	1944	F	Montreal	4	0		16	8
Chicago	1946	SF	Montreal	4	0		26	7
Chicago	1953	SF	Montreal	4	3		18	14
Chicago	1959	SF	Montreal	4	2		21	16
Chicago	1960	SF	Montreal	4	0		14	6
Chicago	1961	SF	Chicago	2	4		15	16
Chicago	1962	SF	Chicago	2	4		13	19
Chicago	1965	F	Montreal	4	3		18	12
Chicago	1968	SF	Montreal	4	1		22	10
Chicago	1971	F	Montreal	4	3		20	18
Chicago	1973	F	Montreal	4	2		33	23
Chicago	1976	QF	Montreal	4	0		13	3
Detroit	1937	SF	Detroit	2	3		8	13
Detroit	1939	QF	Detroit	1	2		5	8
Detroit	1942	QF	Detroit	1	2		8	8
Detroit	1949	SF	Detroit	3	4		14	17
Detroit	1951	SF	Montreal	4	2		13	12
Detroit	1952	F	Detroit	0	4		2	11
Detroit	1954	F	Detroit	3	4		12	14
Detroit	1955	F	Detroit	3	4		20	27
Detroit	1956	F	Montreal	4	1		18	9
Detroit	1958	SF	Montreal	4	0		19	6
Detroit	1966	F	Montreal	4	2		18	14
Detroit	1978	QF	Montreal	4	1		24	10
Edmonton	1981	PRE	Edmonton	0	3		6	15
Hartford	1980	PRE	Montreal	3	0		18	8
Hartford	1986	DF	Montreal	4	3		16	13
Minnesota	1971	SF	Montreal	4	2		27	19
Minnesota	1980	QF	Minnesota	3	4		21	18
NY Islanders	1976	SF	Montreal	4	1		17	14
NY Islanders	1977	SF	Montreal	4	2		19	13
NY Islanders	1984	SF	NY Islanders	2	4		12	17
NY Rangers	1930	SF	Montreal	2	0		4	1
NY Rangers	1932	SF	NY Rangers	1	3		9	13
NY Rangers	1933	*QF	NY Rangers	0	1	1	5	8
NY Rangers	1935	*QF	Montreal	1	0	1	5	4
NY Rangers	1950	SF	NY Rangers	1	4		7	15
NY Rangers	1956	SF	Montreal	4	1		24	9
NY Rangers	1957	SF	Montreal	4	1		22	12
NY Rangers	1967	SF	Montreal	4	0		14	8
NY Rangers	1969	QF	Montreal	4	0		16	7
NY Rangers	1972	QF	NY Rangers	2	4		14	19
NY Rangers	1974	QF	NY Rangers	2	4		17	21
NY Rangers	1979	F	Montreal	4	1		19	11
NY Rangers	1986	SF	Montreal	4	1		24	24
Philadelphia	1973	SF	Montreal	4	1		19	13
Philadelphia	1976	F	Montreal	4	0		14	9
Philadelphia	1987	F	Philadelphia	2	4		22	22
Quebec	1982	DSF	Quebec	2	3		11	16
Quebec	1984	DF	Montreal	4	2		20	13
Quebec	1985	DF	Quebec	3	4		24	24
Quebec	1987	DF	Montreal	4	3		27	21
St. Louis	1968	F	Montreal	4	0		11	7
St. Louis	1969	F	Montreal	4	0		12	3
St. Louis	1977	QF	Montreal	4	0		19	4
Toronto	1944	SF	Montreal	4	1		23	6
Toronto	1945	SF	Toronto	2	4		21	15
Toronto	1947	F	Toronto	2	4		13	13
Toronto	1951	F	Toronto	1	4		10	13
Toronto	1959	F	Montreal	4	1		18	12
Toronto	1960	F	Montreal	4	0		15	5
Toronto	1963	SF	Toronto	1	4		6	14
Toronto	1964	SF	Toronto	3	4		14	17
Toronto	1965	SF	Montreal	4	2		17	14
Toronto	1966	SF	Montreal	4	0		15	6
Toronto	1967	F	Toronto	2	4		16	17
Toronto	1978	SF	Montreal	4	0		16	6
Toronto	1979	QF	Montreal	4	0		19	10
Vancouver	1975	QF	Montreal	4	1		20	9
Maroons	1927	*QF	Montreal	1	0	1	2	1
Ottawa	1927	*SF	Ottawa	0	1	1	1	5
Maroons	1928	SF	Maroons	0	1	1	2	3

* Total-goals series

Coach

PERRON, JEAN
Coach, Montreal Canadiens. Born in St. Isidore d'Auckland, Que., October 5, 1946

After succeeding Jacques Lemaire as head coach of the Montreal Canadiens on July 29, 1985, Jean Perron masterminded the club's 23rd Stanley Cup title to establish a new professional record for championship seasons. And as a rookie behind the Habs' bench, Perron joined an elite list of 12 other first-year coaches ever to win the coveted trophy.

After completing a successful academic and amateur hockey career at the University of Sherbrooke in 1969, Perron pursued his Master's Degree in Physical Education at Michigan State University, where he also served as assistant coach for the Spartans' hockey team. Following graduation in 1973, he was appointed head coach of the University of Moncton Blue Eagles, whom he led to four regional and two Canadian championships in the ensuing ten years.

In 1983-84, Perron joined Dave King as an assistant coach of the Canadian Olympic Team and helped that club to a fourth-place finish at the 1984 Winter Games in Yugoslavia. Soon after, the Canadiens, impressed by Perron's credentials, brought him to Montreal as an assistant coach for one season before naming him the 20th head coach in their history in 1985-86.

Year-by-Year Record 1968-1987

Season	GP	Home W	L	T	Road W	L	T	Overall W	L	T	GF	GA	Pts.	Finished	Playoff Result
1986-87	80	27	9	4	14	20	6	41	29	10	277	241	92	2nd, Adams Div.	Lost Conf. Championship
1985-86	80	25	11	4	15	22	3	40	33	7	330	280	87	2nd, Adams Div.	**Won Stanley Cup**
1984-85	80	24	10	6	17	17	6	41	27	12	309	262	94	1st, Adams Div.	Lost Div. Final
1983-84	80	19	19	2	16	21	3	35	40	5	286	295	75	4th, Adams Div.	Lost Conf. Championship
1982-83	80	25	6	9	17	18	5	42	24	14	350	286	98	2nd, Adams Div.	Lost Div. Semi-Final
1981-82	80	25	6	9	21	11	8	46	17	17	360	223	109	1st, Adams Div.	Lost Div. Semi-Final
1980-81	80	31	7	2	14	15	11	45	22	13	332	232	103	1st, Norris Div.	Lost Prelim. Round
1979-80	80	30	7	3	17	13	10	47	20	13	328	240	107	1st, Norris Div.	Lost Quarter-Final
1978-79	80	29	6	5	23	11	6	52	17	11	337	204	115	1st, Norris Div.	**Won Stanley Cup**
1977-78	80	32	4	4	27	6	7	59	10	11	359	183	129	1st, Norris Div.	**Won Stanley Cup**
1976-77	80	33	1	6	27	7	6	60	8	12	387	171	132	1st, Norris Div.	**Won Stanley Cup**
1975-76	80	32	3	5	26	8	6	58	11	11	337	174	127	1st, Norris Div.	**Won Stanley Cup**
1974-75	80	27	8	5	20	6	14	47	14	19	374	225	113	1st, Norris Div.	Lost Semi-Final
1973-74	78	24	12	3	21	12	6	45	24	9	293	240	99	2nd, East Div.	Lost Quarter-Final
1972-73	78	29	4	6	23	6	10	52	10	16	329	184	120	1st, East Div.	**Won Stanley Cup**
1971-72	78	29	3	7	17	13	9	46	16	16	307	205	108	3rd, East Div.	Lost Quarter-Final
1970-71	78	29	7	3	13	16	10	42	23	13	291	216	97	3rd, East Div.	**Won Stanley Cup**
1969-70	76	21	9	8	17	13	8	38	22	16	244	201	92	5th, East Div.	Out of Playoffs
1968-69	76	26	7	5	20	12	6	46	19	11	271	202	103	1st, East Div.	**Won Stanley Cup**
1967-68	74	26	5	6	16	17	4	42	22	10	236	167	94	1st, East Div.	Won Stanley Cup

1986-87 Scoring

Regular Season   *–Rookie

Pos	#	Player	Team	GP	G	A	Pts	+/−	PIM
F	26	Mats Naslund	MTL	79	25	55	80	3−	16
F	15	Bobby Smith	MTL	80	28	47	75	6	72
F	32	Claude Lemieux	MTL	76	27	26	53	0	156
D	19	Larry Robinson	MTL	70	13	37	50	24	44
F	11	Ryan Walter	MTL	76	23	23	46	6−	34
F	21	Guy Carbonneau	MTL	79	18	27	45	9	68
D	29	Gaston Gingras	MTL	66	11	34	45	2−	21
D	24	Chris Chelios	MTL	71	11	33	44	5−	124
F	44	Stephane Richer	MTL	57	20	19	39	11	80
F	35	Mike McPhee	MTL	79	18	21	39	7	58
F	36	*Sergio Momesso	MTL	59	14	17	31	0	96
F	39	Brian Skrudland	MTL	79	11	17	28	18	107
F	27	*Shayne Corson	MTL	55	12	11	23	10	144
D	25	Petr Svoboda	MTL	70	5	17	22	14	63
F	20	Kjell Dahlin	MTL	41	12	8	20	3−	0
F	30	Chris Nilan	MTL	44	4	16	20	2	266
F	8	*David Maley	MTL	48	6	12	18	1−	55
F	23	Bob Gainey	MTL	47	8	8	16	0	19
D	17	Craig Ludwig	MTL	75	4	12	16	3	105
D	5	Rick Green	MTL	72	1	9	10	1−	10
D	38	Mike Lalor	MTL	57	0	10	10	5	47
F	31	*John Kordic	MTL	44	5	3	8	7−	151
F	28	*Gilles Thibaudeau	MTL	9	1	3	4	5	0
G	1	Brian Hayward	MTL	37	0	2	2	0	2
G	33	Patrick Roy	MTL	46	0	1	1	0	8
F	12	Serge Boisvert	MTL	1	0	0	0	0	0
D	3	*Scott Sandelin	MTL	1	0	0	0	1	0

Playoffs

Pos	#	Player	Team	GP	G	A	Pts	+/−	PIM
F	26	Mats Naslund	MTL	17	7	15	22	1−	11
D	19	Larry Robinson	MTL	17	3	17	20	4	6
F	11	Ryan Walter	MTL	17	7	12	19	4	10
F	15	Bobby Smith	MTL	17	9	9	18	0	19
D	24	Chris Chelios	MTL	17	4	9	13	1−	38
F	32	Claude Lemieux	MTL	17	4	9	13	7	41
F	27	*Shayne Corson	MTL	17	6	5	11	4	30
F	21	Guy Carbonneau	MTL	17	3	8	11	1	20
F	35	Mike McPhee	MTL	17	7	2	9	2	13
F	20	Kjell Dahlin	MTL	8	2	4	6	5	0
F	39	Brian Skrudland	MTL	14	1	5	6	2	29
F	44	Stephane Richer	MTL	5	3	2	5	3	0
D	17	Craig Ludwig	MTL	17	2	3	5	2	30
D	25	Petr Svoboda	MTL	14	0	5	5	1−	10
F	36	*Sergio Momesso	MTL	11	1	3	4	3	31
F	23	Bob Gainey	MTL	17	1	3	4	7−	6
D	5	Rick Green	MTL	17	0	4	4	13	4
F	30	Chris Nilan	MTL	17	3	0	3	4−	75
D	38	Mike Lalor	MTL	13	2	1	3	1	29
F	31	*John Kordic	MTL	11	2	0	2	1	19
D	29	Gaston Gingras	MTL	5	0	2	2	2−	0
G	33	Patrick Roy	MTL	6	0	0	0	0	0
G	1	Brian Hayward	MTL	13	0	0	0	0	2

Club Records

Team

(Figures in brackets for season records are games played; records for fewest points, wins, ties, losses, goals, goals against are for 70 or more games)

Most Points	*132	1976-77 (80)
Most Wins	*60	1976-77 (80)
Most Ties	23	1962-63 (70)
Most Losses	40	1983-84 (80)
Most Goals	387	1976-77 (80)
Most Goals Against	295	1983-84 (80)
Fewest Points	65	1950-51 (70)
Fewest Wins	25	1950-51 (70)
Fewest Ties	5	1983-84 (80)
Fewest Losses	*8	1976-77 (80)
Fewest Goals	155	1952-53 (70)
Fewest Goals Against	*131	1955-56 (70)

Individual

Most Seasons	20	Henri Richard
Most Games	1,256	Henri Richard
Most Goals Career	544	Maurice Richard
Most Assists, Career	728	Guy Lafleur
Most Points Career	1,246	Guy Lafleur
		(518 goals, 728 assists)
Most Pen. Mins., Career	1,965	Chris Nilan
Most Shutouts, Career	75	George Hainsworth
Longest Consecutive Games Streak	560	Doug Jarvis
		(Oct. 8/75-Apr. 4/82)
Most Goals, Season	60	Steve Shutt
		(1976-77)
		Guy Lafleur
		(1977-78)
Most Assists, Season	82	Peter Mahovlich
		(1974-75)

NEW JERSEY DEVILS

Ken Daneyko

1986-87: 29w-45L-6T 64 PTS. Sixth, Patrick Division

1987-88 OUTLOOK: The Devils have a myriad of young forwards who have improved rapidly over the last few seasons. Their main problem has been in their own end. General manager Max McNab might have begun to solve that problem by signing free-agent netminder Bob Sauve this summer. Alain Chevrier did a good job as the club's number one goaltender the past two years. The combination of Sauve and Chevy (or Craig Billington, or Kirk McLean) could put the Devils in the thick of the Patrick Division playoff race. Up front, captain Kirk Muller (76 points) is among the NHL's hardest workers and best two-way players. Muller, Mark Johnson (25 goals), Greg Adams (20 goals, down from 35 two seasons ago) and first round pick Brendan Shanahan give New Jersey a deep core of talented young centers. Scoring balance also exists on each wing, with Aaron Broten (79 points) and Doug Sulliman (27 goals) manning the left side and Pat Verbeek (35 goals) and John MacLean (31 goals) the right. The Devils yielded a League-high 368 goals last season, as defensemen Bruce Driver, Joe Cirella, Ken Daneyko and Craig Wolanin continue to develop.

Upcoming Milestones
Joe Cirella — 57 games to reach 400
Peter McNab — 46 games to reach 1,000
Kirk Muller — 32 goals to reach 100

Fan Club
New Jersey Devils Fan Club
Ed Nudge
130 First Ave.
Port Reading NJ 07064

Entry Draft Selections 1987
Pick
2   Brendan Shanahan
23 Rickard Persson
65 Brian Sullivan
86 Kevin Dean
107 Ben Hankinson
128 Tom Neziol
149 Jim Dowd
170 John Blessman
191 Peter Fry
212 Alain Charland

14th NHL Season

Year-by-Year Record 1975-1987

Season	GP	Home W	L	T	Road W	L	T	Overall W	L	T	GF	GA	Pts.	Finished	Playoff Result
1986-87	80	20	17	3	9	28	3	29	45	6	293	368	64	6th, Patrick Div.	Out of Playoffs
1985-86	80	17	21	2	11	28	1	28	49	3	300	374	59	6th, Patrick Div.	Out of Playoffs
1984-85	80	13	21	6	7	31	2	22	48	10	264	346	54	5th, Patrick Div.	Out of Playoffs
1983-84	80	10	28	2	7	28	5	17	56	7	231	350	41	5th, Patrick Div.	Out of Playoffs
1982-83	80	11	20	9	6	29	5	17	49	14	230	338	48	5th, Patrick Div.	Out of Playoffs
1981-82	80	14	21	5	4	28	8	18	49	13	241	362	49	5th, Smythe Div.	Out of Playoffs
1980-81	80	15	16	9	7	29	4	22	45	13	258	344	57	5th, Smythe Div.	Out of Playoffs
1979-80	80	12	20	8	7	28	5	19	48	13	234	308	51	6th, Smythe Div.	Out of Playoffs
1978-79	80	8	24	8	7	29	4	15	53	12	210	331	42	4th, Smythe Div.	Out of Playoffs
1977-78	80	17	14	9	2	26	12	19	40	21	257	305	59	2nd, Smythe Div.	Lost Prelim. Round
1976-77	80	12	20	8	8	26	6	20	46	14	226	307	54	5th, Smythe Div.	Out of Playoffs
1975-76	80	8	24	8	4	32	4	12	56	12	190	351	36	5th, Smythe Div.	Out of Playoffs
1974-75	80	12	20	8	3	34	3	15	54	11	184	328	41	5th, Smythe Div.	Out of Playoffs

Playoff History, 1975-87

Versus	Year	Series	Winner	W	L	T	GF	GA
Philadelphia	1978	PRE	Philadelphia	0	2		3	6

Coach

CARPENTER, DOUG
Coach, New Jersey Devils. Born in Cornwall, Ont., July 1, 1942.

45-year-old Doug Carpenter enters his fourth season as head coach of the New Jersey Devils since his appointment on May 31, 1984, looking to build on his club's record-setting campaign of a year ago. Carpenter improved the Devils' on-ice performance for a third straight season last year, taking a 41-point team in 1983-84 to a franchise-high 64 points in 1986-87.

A graduate of Montreal's McGill University in 1962 and Loyola College in 1967, Carpenter spent eight seasons as a minor league defenseman/left-winger in the Eastern and International leagues (1966-74) before joining the head coaching ranks in 1978-79 with the QMJHL's Cornwall Royals. After leading Cornwall to the Memorial Cup in 1979-80, the NHL's Toronto Maple Leafs hired him to pilot their top minor league affiliates, including New Brunswick (AHL) in 1980-81, Cincinnati (CHL) in 1981-82 and St. Catharines (AHL) in 1982-83 and 1983-84.

After completing his rookie season behind the Devils' bench in 1984-85, Carpenter was named head coach of Team Canada at the 1985 World Championships in Czechoslovakia, where he led his squad of Canadian stars to the country's first victory, 3-1, over the Soviet Union in 24 years and a silver medal.

All-time Record vs. Other Clubs
Regular Season

	At Home GP	W	L	T	GF	GA	PTS	On Road GP	W	L	T	GF	GA	PTS	Total GP	W	L	T	GF	GA	PT
Boston	23	2	14	7	60	92	11	23	6	16	1	68	104	13	46	8	30	8	128	196	
Buffalo	23	2	17	4	62	98	8	23	2	19	2	62	116	6	46	4	36	6	124	214	
**Calgary	28	7	18	3	79	110	17	27	2	21	4	64	130	8	55	9	39	7	143	240	
Chicago	29	11	13	5	93	98	27	29	4	21	4	73	127	13	58	15	34	9	166	225	
Detroit	23	12	6	5	87	65	29	23	7	15	1	68	106	15	46	19	21	6	155	171	
Edmonton	16	7	8	1	60	61	15	15	2	11	2	53	86	6	31	9	19	3	113	147	
Hartford	13	5	6	2	45	58	12	13	3	7	3	43	52	9	26	8	13	5	88	110	
Los Angeles	25	9	12	4	83	99	22	26	1	21	4	78	151	6	51	10	33	8	161	250	
Minnesota	28	13	12	3	94	91	29	28	4	19	5	64	121	13	56	17	31	8	158	212	
Montreal	23	4	19	0	55	119	8	23	3	17	3	60	109	9	46	7	36	3	115	228	
NY Islanders	36	9	22	5	109	160	23	35	1	31	3	86	189	5	71	10	53	8	195	349	
NY Rangers	36	11	21	4	118	153	26	35	10	21	4	116	156	24	71	21	42	8	234	309	
Philadelphia	35	11	21	3	122	160	25	35	2	32	1	58	163	5	70	13	53	4	180	323	
Pittsburgh	32	14	12	6	118	120	34	34	11	21	2	116	148	24	66	25	33	8	234	268	
Quebec	13	6	6	1	54	50	13	13	3	8	2	43	66	8	26	9	14	3	97	116	
St. Louis	29	8	14	7	87	89	23	29	5	21	3	87	137	13	58	13	35	10	174	226	
Toronto	23	6	8	9	77	78	21	23	4	17	2	73	109	10	46	10	25	11	150	187	
Vancouver	32	12	14	6	96	111	30	31	6	15	10	98	120	22	63	18	29	16	194	231	
Washington	33	11	16	6	104	109	28	33	4	26	3	82	151	11	66	15	42	9	186	260	
Winnipeg	12	5	5	2	44	45	12	14	2	11	1	32	61	5	26	7	16	3	76	106	
Defunct Clubs	8	4	2	2	25	19	10	8	2	3	3	19	27	7	16	6	5	5	44	46	

Club Records

Team
(Figures in brackets for season records are games played; records for fewest points, wins, ties, losses, goals, goals against are for 70 or more games)

Most Points.............	64	1986-87 (80)
Most Wins..............	29	1986-87 (80)
Most Ties..............	21	1977-78 (80)
Most Losses...........	56	1975-76 (80)
		1983-84 (80)
Most Goals............	300	1985-86 (80)
Most Goals Against......	374	1985-86 (80)
Fewest Points..........	36	1975-76 (80)
Fewest Wins...........	12	1975-76 (80)
Fewest Ties............	3	1985-86 (80)
Fewest Losses.........	40	1977-78 (80)
Fewest Goals..........	184	1974-75 (80)
Fewest Goals Against...	305	1977-78 (80)

Longest Winning Streak
Over-all...............	3	Several times
Home...............	4	Several times
Away...............	3	Dec. 2-9/79

Longest Undefeated Streak
Over-all...............	5	Several times
Home...............	6	Feb. 24-Mar. 19/78 (3 wins, 3 ties)
Away...............	3	Several times

Longest Losing Streak
Over-all...............	14	Dec. 30/75-Jan. 29/76
Home...............	9	Dec. 22/85-Feb. 6/86
Away...............	12	Oct. 19/83-Dec. 1/83

Longest Winless Streak
Over-all...............	27	Feb. 12-Apr. 4/76 (21 losses, 6 ties)
Home...............	14	Feb. 12-Mar. 30/76 (10 losses, 4 ties)
		Feb. 4-Mar. 31/79 (12 losses, 2 ties)
Away...............	32	Nov. 12/77-Mar. 15/78 (22 losses, 10 ties)

Most Shutouts, Season......	2	1983-84 (80)
Most Pen. Mins., Season............	1,735	1986-87 (80)
Most Goals, Game........	9	Apr. 1/79 (St.L. 5 at Col. 9) Feb. 12/82 (Que. 2 at Col. 9) Apr. 6/86 (NYI 7 at N.J. 9)

Individual

Most Seasons...........	8	Mike Kitchen
Most Games...........	474	Mike Kitchen
Most Goals, Career......	153	Wilf Paiement
Most Assists, Career.....	199	Aaron Broten
Most Points, Career.....	336	Wilf Paiement (153 goals, 183 assists)
Most Pen. Mins., Career...	592	Joe Cirella
Most Shutouts, Career...	1	Several players
Longest Consecutive Games Streak.........	266	Aaron Broten (Dec. 6/82-Feb. 15/86)
Most Goals, Season......	41	Wilf Paiement (1976-77)

1986-87 Scoring
Regular Season
*–Rookie

Pos	#	Player	Team	GP	G	A	Pts	+/–	PIM
F	10	Aaron Broten	N.J.	80	26	53	79	5	36
F	9	Kirk Muller	N.J.	79	26	50	76	7–	75
F	15	John MacLean	N.J.	80	31	36	67	23–	120
F	16	Pat Verbeek	N.J.	74	35	24	59	23–	120
F	22	Doug Sulliman	N.J.	78	27	26	53	17–	14
F	12	Mark Johnson	N.J.	68	25	26	51	21–	22
F	24	Greg Adams	N.J.	72	20	27	47	16–	19
F	19	Claude Loiselle	N.J.	75	16	24	40	7–	137
D	23	Bruce Driver	N.J.	74	6	28	34	26–	36
D	2	Joe Cirella	N.J.	65	9	22	31	20–	111
F	26	Andy Brickley	N.J.	51	11	12	23	15–	8
F	7	Peter McNab	N.J.	46	8	12	20	14–	8
D	28	Uli Hiemer	N.J.	40	6	14	20	6–	45
F	20	*Anders Carlsson	N.J.	48	2	18	20	11–	14
F	25	Perry Anderson	N.J.	57	10	9	19	13–	107
D	27	Randy Velischek	N.J.	64	2	16	18	12–	52
F	29	Jan Ludvig	N.J.	47	7	9	16	5–	98
D	3	Ken Daneyko	N.J.	79	2	12	14	13–	183
F	11	*Rich Chernomaz	N.J.	25	6	4	10	11–	8
D	6	Craig Wolanin	N.J.	68	4	6	10	31–	109
D	4	*Gordon Mark	N.J.	36	3	5	8	4–	82
D	21	Steve Richmond	N.J.	44	1	7	8	12–	143
F	33	*Tim Lenardon	N.J.	7	1	1	2	2–	0
D	5	Timo Blomqvist	N.J.	20	0	2	2	3–	29
F	14	*Allan Stewart	N.J.	7	1	0	1	4–	26
F	14	*Douglas Brown	N.J.	4	0	1	1	4–	0
G	34	*Karl Friesen	N.J.	4	0	1	1	0	0
D	33	Murray Brumwell	N.J.	1	0	0	0	1	2
G	32	*Kirk McLean	N.J.	4	0	0	0	0	0
G	35	*Chris Terreri	N.J.	7	0	0	0	0	0
G	31	*Graig Billington	N.J.	22	0	0	0	0	12
G	30	Alain Chevrier	N.J.	58	0	0	0	0	17

Most Assists, Season......	56	Wilf Paiement (1977-78)
Most Points, Season......	87	Wilf Paiement (1977-78) (31 goals, 56 assists)
Most Pen. Mins., Season...	209	Steve Durbano (1975-76)
Most Points, Defenseman Season.............	62	Rob Ramage (1980-81) (20 goals, 42 assists)
Most Points, Center Season.............	77	Greg Adams (1985-86) (35 goals, 42 assists)
Most Points, Right Wing, Season.............	87	Wilf Paiement (1977-78) (31 goals, 56 assists)
Most Points, Left Wing, Season.............	79	Aaron Broten (1986-87) (26 goals, 53 assists)
Most Points, Rookie, Season.............	60	Barry Beck (1977-78) (22 goals, 38 assists)
Most Shutouts, Season......	1	Several players
Most Goals, Game........	4	Bob MacMillan (Jan. 8/82)
Most Assists, Game.......	5	Kirk Muller (Mar. 25/87) Greg Adams (Oct. 10/86)
Most Points, Game.......	6	Kirk Muller (Nov. 29/86) (3 goals, 3 assists)

NEW YORK ISLANDERS

Mike Bossy

1986-87: 35w-33l-12t 82 pts. Third, Patrick Division

1987-88 OUTLOOK: The Islanders have talked about passing the torch to their next generation of players since they surrendered the Cup to Edmonton, but until last year's playoffs, it didn't look like it would happen. Are the Kelly Hrudeys, Pat LaFontaines, Mikko Makelas, Patrick Flatleys, Bob Bassens, Steve Konroyds, Gord Dineens and Ken Leiters for real? Rebounding in the playoffs to eliminate the Capitals and bring the Flyers to a seventh game, these names were as prominent as the Trottiers, Potvins, Morrows, Bossys, Sutters and Smiths, if not more so. Mike Bossy's back problems don't seem any better, however, and the Isles need more scoring from their wingers. LaFontaine's 38 goals tied Bossy for the team lead in goals last season, while Brent Sutter added 27 and Makela 24. Bryan Trottier chipped in with 87 points and continued rugged play. The rest of the Islanders' offense (Rich Kromm, Greg Gilbert, Ari Haanpaa, Alan Kerr, Brad Lauer) remains a question mark. Denis Potvin became the NHL's all-time leading scorer among defensemen, and still has a few years left. Leiter, Randy Boyd, Dineen and Ken Morrow line up alongside Potvin. Hrudey has emerged as the Isles' number one goaltender, pushing aside Hall-of-Fame bound Billy Smith.

Upcoming Milestones

Denis Potvin — 12 games to reach 1,000
— 9 goals to reach 300
Bryan Trottier — 10 goals to reach 450
— 38 assists to reach 800
Mike Bossy — 27 goals to reach 600
— 74 points to reach 1,200
— 15 playoff goals to reach 100
Billy Smith — 9 victories to reach 200
Brent Sutter — 29 goals to reach 200

Fan Club

New York Islander Booster Club
P.O. Box 20
Carle Place, NY 11514

Entry Draft Selections 1987

Pick	
13	Dean Chynoweth
34	Jeff Hackett
55	Dean Ewen
76	George Maneluk
97	Petr Vlk
118	Rob Dimaio
139	Knut Walbye
160	Jeff Saterdalen
181	Shawn Howard
202	John Herlihy
223	Michael Erickson
244	Will Averill

16th NHL Season

WALES CONFERENCE

NEW YORK ISLANDERS

Year-by-Year Record 1972-1987

Season	GP	Home W L T	Road W L T	Overall W L T	GF	GA	Pts.	Finished	Playoff Result
1986-87	80	20 15 5	15 18 7	35 33 12	279	281	82	3rd, Patrick Div.	Lost Div. Semi-Final
1985-86	80	22 11 7	17 18 5	39 29 12	327	284	90	3rd, Patrick Div.	Lost Div. Semi-Final
1984-85	80	26 11 3	14 23 3	40 34 6	345	312	86	3rd, Patrick Div.	Lost Div. Final
1983-84	80	28 11 1	22 15 3	50 26 4	357	269	104	1st, Patrick Div.	Lost Final
1982-83	80	26 11 3	16 15 9	42 26 12	302	226	96	2nd, Patrick Div.	Won Stanley Cup
1981-82	80	33 3 4	21 13 6	54 16 10	385	250	118	1st, Patrick Div.	Won Stanley Cup
1980-81	80	23 6 11	25 12 3	48 18 14	355	260	110	1st, Patrick Div.	Won Stanley Cup
1979-80	80	26 9 5	13 19 8	39 28 13	281	247	91	2nd, Patrick Div.	Won Stanley Cup
1978-79	80	31 3 6	20 12 8	51 15 14	358	214	116	1st, Patrick Div.	Lost Semi-Final
1977-78	80	29 3 8	19 14 7	48 17 15	334	210	111	1st, Patrick Div.	Lost Quarter-Final
1976-77	80	24 11 5	23 10 7	47 21 12	288	193	106	2nd, Patrick Div.	Lost Semi-Final
1975-76	80	24 8 8	18 13 9	42 21 17	297	190	101	2nd, Patrick Div.	Lost Semi-Final
1974-75	80	22 6 12	11 19 10	33 25 22	264	221	88	3rd, Patrick Div.	Lost Semi-Final
1973-74	78	13 17 9	6 24 9	19 41 18	182	247	56	8th, East Div.	Out of Playoffs
1972-73	78	10 25 4	2 35 2	12 60 6	170	347	30	8th, East Div.	Out of Playoffs

Playoff History, 1973-87

Versus	Year	Series	Winner	W	L	T	GF	GA
Boston	1980	QF	NY Islanders	4	1		19	14
Boston	1983	SF	NY Islanders	4	2		30	21
Buffalo	1976	QF	NY Islanders	4	2		21	18
Buffalo	1977	QF	NY Islanders	4	0		16	10
Buffalo	1980	SF	NY Islanders	4	2		22	17
Chicago	1977	PRE	NY Islanders	2	0		7	3
Chicago	1979	QF	NY Islanders	4	0		14	3
Edmonton	1981	QF	NY Islanders	4	2		29	20
Edmonton	1983	F	NY Islanders	4	0		17	6
Edmonton	1984	F	Edmonton	1	4		12	21
Los Angeles	1980	PRE	NY Islanders	1	3		21	10
Minnesota	1981	F	NY Islanders	4	1		26	16
Montreal	1976	SF	Montreal	1	4		14	17
Montreal	1977	SF	Montreal	2	4		13	19
Montreal	1984	SF	NY Islanders	4	2		17	12
NY Rangers	1975	PRE	NY Islanders	2	1		10	13
NY Rangers	1979	SF	NY Rangers	2	4		13	18
NY Rangers	1981	SF	NY Islanders	4	0		22	8
NY Rangers	1982	DF	NY Islanders	4	2		27	20
NY Rangers	1983	DF	NY Islanders	4	2		28	15
NY Rangers	1984	DSF	NY Islanders	3	2		13	14
Philadelphia	1975	SF	Philadelphia	3	4		16	19
Philadelphia	1980	F	NY Islanders	4	2		26	25
Philadelphia	1985	DF	Philadelphia	1	4		11	16
Philadelphia	1987	DF	Philadelphia	3	4		16	23
Pittsburgh	1975	QF	NY Islanders	4	3		21	18
Pittsburgh	1982	DSF	NY Islanders	3	2		22	13
Quebec	1982	SF	NY Islanders	4	0		18	9
Toronto	1978	QF	Toronto	3	4		13	16
Toronto	1981	PRE	NY Islanders	3	0		20	4
Vancouver	1976	PRE	NY Islanders	2	0		8	4
Vancouver	1982	F	NY Islanders	4	0		18	10
Washington	1983	DSF	NY Islanders	3	1		19	11
Washington	1984	DF	NY Islanders	4	1		20	13
Washington	1985	DSF	NY Islanders	3	2		14	12
Washington	1986	DSF	Washington	0	3		4	11
Washington	1987	DSF	NY Islanders	4	3		19	18

Coach

TERRY SIMPSON
Coach, New York Islanders. Born in Brantford, Ont., August 30, 1943.

After completing one of the most impresssive, if not legendary, coaching careers in Minor and Junior hockey history, Terry Simpson assumed the New York Islanders' head coaching position on June 18, 1986. In 1972-73, ironically the Islanders' first year in the NHL, Simpson embarked on a 10-year career with the then-tier II Prince Albert Raiders in Saskatchewan, where he compiled a record of 477-120-10 (.794) and an incredible 10 straight first-place finishes. A 57-3-0 season in 1981-82 was enough to convince anyone that the team should move up a notch, which it did to the WHL.

Although the going was rough at first in the more rugged Junior ranks, Simpson kept his squad on an upward pace and in just three seasons took the Raiders all the way to the 1984-85 Memorial Cup title, symbolic of the Canadian Junior championship.

Now at the highest level of hockey competition, Simpson continues to exhibit his coaching prowess. As an NHL rookie in 1986-87, he steered the Islanders' to their 13th consecutive winning season, maintaining the successful pace which New York fans have come to expect.

1986-87 Scoring

Regular Season
*—Rookie

Pos	#	Player	Team	GP	G	A	Pts	+/−	PIM
F	19	Bryan Trottier	NYI	80	23	64	87	2	50
F	22	Mike Bossy	NYI	63	38	37	75	8−	33
F	16	Pat LaFontaine	NYI	80	38	32	70	10−	70
F	21	Brent Sutter	NYI	69	27	36	63	23	73
F	24	Mikko Makela	NYI	80	24	33	57	3	24
F	26	Patrick Flatley	NYI	63	16	35	51	17	81
D	5	Denis Potvin	NYI	58	12	30	42	6−	70
F	12	Duane Sutter	NYI	80	14	17	31	1	169
D	3	Tomas Jonsson	NYI	47	6	25	31	8−	36
F	35	Rich Kromm	NYI	70	12	17	29	2	20
D	29	*Ken Leiter	NYI	74	9	20	29	1	30
D	8	Randy Boyd	NYI	30	7	17	24	0	37
F	32	*Brad Lauer	NYI	61	7	14	21	0	65
D	33	Steve Konroyd	NYI	72	5	16	21	5−	70
F	10	Alan Kerr	NYI	72	7	10	17	10−	175
F	28	*Bob Bassen	NYI	77	7	10	17	17−	89
D	2	Gord Dineen	NYI	71	4	10	14	8−	110
F	7	Greg Gilbert	NYI	51	6	7	13	12−	26
D	6	Ken Morrow	NYI	64	3	8	11	7	32
F	25	*Ari Haanpaa	NYI	41	6	4	10	8	17
D	34	Brian Curran	NYI	68	0	10	10	3	356
F	20	Dale Henry	NYI	19	3	3	6	2	46
D	4	Gerald Diduck	NYI	30	2	3	5	3−	67
F	36	*Neal Coulter	NYI	9	2	1	3	2−	7
G	31	Billy Smith	NYI	40	0	2	2	0	37
F	11	*Randy Wood	NYI	6	1	0	1	1−	4
F	17	Mark Hamway	NYI	2	0	1	1	1−	0
G	30	Kelly Hrudey	NYI	46	0	1	1	0	37
F	36	*Derek King	NYI	2	0	0	0	0	0

Playoffs

Pos	#	Player	Team	GP	G	A	Pts	+/−	PIM
F	19	Bryan Trottier	NYI	14	8	5	13	6−	12
F	16	Pat LaFontaine	NYI	14	5	7	12	6−	10
F	24	Mikko Makela	NYI	11	2	4	6	4−	8
F	26	Patrick Flatley	NYI	11	3	2	5	2−	6
F	22	Mike Bossy	NYI	6	2	3	5	2−	0
D	3	Tomas Jonsson	NYI	10	1	4	5	2	6
F	10	Alan Kerr	NYI	14	1	4	5	1−	25
D	33	Steve Konroyd	NYI	14	1	4	5	4	10
D	29	*Ken Leiter	NYI	11	0	5	5	2−	6
F	7	Greg Gilbert	NYI	10	2	2	4	3	6
D	5	Denis Potvin	NYI	10	2	2	4	7−	21
D	6	Ken Morrow	NYI	13	1	3	4	6−	2
F	11	*Randy Wood	NYI	13	1	3	4	0	14
F	35	Rich Kromm	NYI	14	1	3	4	0	4
D	2	Gord Dineen	NYI	7	0	4	4	4	4
F	28	*Bob Bassen	NYI	14	1	2	3	2	21
F	32	*Brad Lauer	NYI	6	2	0	2	1	4
F	21	Brent Sutter	NYI	5	1	0	1	4−	4
F	12	Duane Sutter	NYI	14	1	0	1	3−	26
F	36	*Brad Dalgarno	NYI	1	0	1	1	0	0
D	8	Randy Boyd	NYI	4	0	1	1	2−	6
D	4	Gerald Diduck	NYI	14	0	1	1	7−	35
G	31	Billy Smith	NYI	2	0	0	0	0	0
F	25	*Ari Haanpaa	NYI	6	0	0	0	1−	10
D	34	Brian Curran	NYI	8	0	0	0	4−	51
F	20	Dale Henry	NYI	8	0	0	0	5−	2
G	30	Kelly Hrudey	NYI	14	0	0	0	0	0

Club Records

Team
(Figures in brackets for season records are games played; records for fewest points, wins, ties, losses, goals, goals against are for 70 or more games)

Most Points	118	1981-82 (80)
Most Wins	54	1981-82 (80)
Most Ties	22	1974-75 (80)
Most Losses	60	1972-73 (78)
Most Goals	385	1981-82 (80)
Most Goals Against	347	1972-73 (78)
Fewest Points	30	1972-73 (78)
Fewest Wins	12	1972-73 (78)
Fewest Ties	4	1983-84 (80)
Fewest Losses	15	1978-79 (80)
Fewest Goals	170	1972-73 (78)
Fewest Goals Against	190	1975-76 (80)
Longest Winning Streak		
Over-all	*15	Jan. 21/82-Feb. 20/82
Home	14	Jan. 12-26/80 Jan. 2/82-Feb. 25/82
Away	8	Feb. 27/81 Mar. 29/81
Longest Undefeated Streak		
Over-all	15	Jan. 21-Feb. 20/82 (15 wins) Nov. 4-Dec. 2/80 (13 wins, 2 ties)

Individual

Most Seasons	15	Billy Smith
Most Games	988	Denis Potvin
Most Goals, Career	573	Mike Bossy
Most Assists, Career	762	Bryan Trottier
Most Points, Career	1,202	Bryan Trottier (440 goals, 762 assists)
Most Pen. Mins., Career	1,456	Garry Howatt
Most Shutouts, Career	26	Glenn Resch
Longest Consecutive Games Streak	576	Bill Harris (Oct. 7/72-Nov. 30/79)
Most Goals, Season	69	Mike Bossy (1978-79)
Most Assists, Season	87	Bryan Trottier (1978-79)
Most Points, Season	147	Mike Bossy (1981-82) (64 goals, 83 assists)
Most Pen. Mins., Season	356	Brian Curran (1986-87)
Most Points, Defenseman, Season	101	Denis Potvin (1978-79) (31 goals, 70 assists)
Most Points, Center, Season	134	Bryan Trottier (1978-79) (47 goals, 87 assists)
Most Points, Right Wing, Season	147	Mike Bossy (1981-82) (64 goals, 83 assists)

NEW YORK RANGERS

Marcel Dionne and, at rear, Kelly Kisio

1986-87: 34w-38L-8T 76 PTS. Fourth, Patrick Division

1987-88 OUTLOOK: The revolving door policy of general manager Phil Esposito continued through the summer as he traded a first round pick for a coach (Michel Bergeron), acquired Bruce Bell and Brian Mullen in trades, re-signed Barry Beck, and lured ex-first rounder Ulf Dahlen from Sweden. Forwards Tomas Sandstrom and Walt Poddubny each scored 40 goals last season. Marcel Dionne may not post offensive numbers like he did in L.A., but he still is one of the NHL's most creative playmakers. Kelly Kisio (24 goals), Pierre Larouche (63 points), Don Maloney (57 points) and Ron Duguay can also put the puck in the net. Ron Greschner, who can play forward as well as defense, returns for a 14th season as a Ranger, while blueliner James Patrick is emerging into an All-Star. Greschner and Patrick are joined on the backline by compact Curt Giles, Willie Huber, Larry Melnyk, Pat Price, Bell and Beck, who took a year off after irreconcilable differences with ex-coach Ted Sator. The Rangers feature one of the League's top goaltending tandems in John Vanbiesbrouck and Bob Froese.

Upcoming Milestones

Marcel Dionne — 7 goals to reach 700
 — 10 assists to reach 1,000
 — 17 points to reach 1,700
Ron Greschner — 14 goals to reach 200
Pierre Larouche — 8 goals to reach 400
Dan Maloney — 21 goals to reach 200

Fan Club

New York Ranger Fan Club
P.O. Box 1772
New York, NY 10001

Entry Draft Selections 1987

Pick
10 Jayson More
31 Daniel Lacroix
46 Simon Gagne
69 Michael Sullivan
94 Eric O'Borsky
115 Ludek Cajka
136 Clint Thomas
157 Charles Wiegand
178 Eric Burrill
199 David Porter
205 Brett Barnett
220 Lance Marciano

62nd NHL Season

Year-by-Year Record 1968-87

Season	GP	Home W	L	T	Road W	L	T	Overall W	L	T	GF	GA	Pts.	Finished	Playoff Result
1986-87	80	18	18	4	16	20	4	34	38	8	307	323	76	4th, Patrick Div.	Lost Div. Semi-Final
1985-86	80	20	18	2	16	20	4	36	38	6	280	276	78	4th, Patrick Div.	Lost Conf. Championship
1984-85	80	16	18	6	10	26	4	26	44	10	295	345	62	4th, Patrick Div.	Lost Div. Semi-Final
1983-84	80	27	12	1	15	17	8	42	29	9	314	304	93	4th, Patrick Div.	Lost Div. Semi-Final
1982-83	80	24	13	3	11	22	7	35	35	10	306	287	80	4th, Patrick Div.	Lost Div. Final
1981-82	80	19	15	6	20	12	8	39	27	14	316	306	92	2nd, Patrick Div.	Lost Div. Final
1980-81	80	17	13	10	13	23	4	30	36	14	312	317	74	4th, Patrick Div.	Lost Semi-Final
1979-80	80	22	10	8	16	22	2	38	32	10	308	284	86	3rd, Patrick Div.	Lost Quarter-Final
1978-79	80	19	13	8	21	16	3	40	29	11	316	292	91	3rd, Patrick Div.	Lost Final
1977-78	80	18	15	7	12	22	6	30	37	13	279	280	73	4th, Patrick Div.	Lost Prelim. Round
1976-77	80	17	18	5	12	19	9	29	37	14	272	310	72	4th, Patrick Div.	Out of Playoffs
1975-76	80	16	16	8	13	26	1	29	42	9	262	333	67	4th, Patrick Div.	Out of Playoffs
1974-75	80	21	11	8	16	18	6	37	29	14	319	276	88	2nd, Patrick Div.	Lost Prelim. Round
1973-74	78	26	7	6	14	17	8	40	24	14	300	251	94	3rd, East Div.	Lost Semi-Final
1972-73	78	26	8	5	21	15	3	47	23	8	297	208	102	3rd, East Div.	Lost Semi-Final
1971-72	78	26	6	7	22	11	6	48	17	13	317	192	109	2nd, East Div.	Lost Final
1970-71	78	30	2	7	19	16	4	49	18	11	259	177	109	2nd, East Div.	Lost Semi-Final
1969-70	76	22	8	8	16	14	8	38	22	16	246	189	92	4th, East Div.	Lost Quarter-Final
1968-69	76	27	7	4	14	19	5	41	26	9	231	196	91	3rd, East Div.	Lost Quarter-Final
1967-68	74	22	8	7	17	15	5	39	23	12	226	183	90	2nd, East Div.	Lost Quarter-Final

Playoff History, 1927-87

Versus	Year	Series	Winner	W	L	T	GF	GA
Boston	1927	*SF	Boston	0	1	1	1	3
Boston	1928	*SF	NY Rangers	1	0	1	5	2
Boston	1929	F	Boston	0	2		1	4
Boston	1939	SF	Boston	3	4		12	14
Boston	1940	SF	NY Rangers	4	2		15	9
Boston	1958	SF	Boston	2	4		16	28
Boston	1970	QF	Boston	2	4		16	25
Boston	1972	F	Boston	2	4		16	18
Boston	1973	QF	NY Rangers	4	1		22	11
Buffalo	1978	PRE	Buffalo	1	2		6	11
Calgary	1980	PRE	NY Rangers	3	1		8	14
Chicago	1931	*SF	Chicago	0	2		0	3
Chicago	1968	QF	Chicago	2	4		12	18
Chicago	1971	SF	Chicago	3	4		14	21
Chicago	1972	SF	NY Rangers	4	0		17	9
Chicago	1973	SF	Chicago	1	4		11	15
Detroit	1933	*SF	NY Rangers	2	0		6	3
Detroit	1937	F	Detroit	2	3		8	9
Detroit	1941	QF	Detroit	1	2		6	6
Detroit	1948	SF	Detroit	2	4		12	17
Detroit	1950	F	Detroit	3	4		17	22
Los Angeles	1979	PRE	NY Rangers	2	0		9	2
Los Angeles	1981	PRE	NY Rangers	3	1		23	12
Montreal	1930	SF	Montreal	0	2		1	4
Montreal	1932	SF	NY Rangers	3	1		13	9
Montreal	1933	*QF	NY Rangers	1	0	1	8	5
Montreal	1935	*QF	Montreal	0	1	1	4	5
Montreal	1950	SF	NY Rangers	4	1		15	7
Montreal	1956	SF	Montreal	1	4		9	24
Montreal	1957	SF	Montreal	1	4		12	22
Montreal	1967	SF	Montreal	0	4		8	14
Montreal	1969	QF	Montreal	0	4		7	16
Montreal	1972	SF	NY Rangers	4	2		19	14
Montreal	1974	QF	NY Rangers	4	2		21	17
Montreal	1979	F	Montreal	1	4		11	19

Versus	Year	Series	Winner	W	L	T	GF	GA
Montreal	1986	SF	Montreal	1	4		10	15
NY Islanders	1975	PRE	NY Islanders	1	2		13	10
NY Islanders	1979	SF	NY Rangers	4	2		18	13
NY Islanders	1981	SF	NY Islanders	0	4		8	22
NY Islanders	1982	DF	NY Islanders	2	4		20	27
NY Islanders	1983	DF	NY Islanders	2	4		15	28
NY Islanders	1984	DSF	NY Islanders	2	3		14	13
Philadelphia	1974	SF	Philadelphia	3	4		17	22
Philadelphia	1979	QF	NY Rangers	4	1		28	8
Philadelphia	1980	QF	Philadelphia	1	4		7	14
Philadelphia	1982	DSF	NY Rangers	3	1		19	15
Philadelphia	1983	DSF	NY Rangers	3	0		18	9
Philadelphia	1986	DSF	NY Rangers	3	2		18	15
Philadelphia	1987	DSF	Philadelphia	2	4		13	22
St. Louis	1981	QF	NY Rangers	4	2		29	22
Toronto	1929	SF	NY Rangers	2	0		3	1
Toronto	1932	F	Toronto	0	3		10	18
Toronto	1933	F	NY Rangers	3	1		11	5
Toronto	1937	QF	NY Rangers	2	0		5	1
Toronto	1940	F	NY Rangers	4	2		14	11
Toronto	1942	SF	Toronto	2	4		12	13
Toronto	1962	SF	Toronto	2	4		15	22
Toronto	1971	QF	NY Rangers	4	2		16	15
Washington	1986	DF	NY Rangers	4	2		20	25
Pirates	1928	*QF	NY Rangers	1	1		6	4
Maroons	1928	F	NY Rangers	3	2		6	5
NY Americans	1929	*QF	NY Rangers	1	0	1	1	1
Ottawa	1930	*QF	NY Rangers	1	0	1	6	3
Maroons	1931	*QF	NY Rangers	2	0		8	1
Maroons	1934	QF	Maroons	0	1	1	1	2
Maroons	1935	*SF	Maroons	0	1	1	4	5
Maroons	1937	SF	NY Rangers	2	0		5	0
NY Americans	1938	QF	NY Americans	1	2		7	8

* Total-goals series

Coach

BERGERON, JOSEPH ROBERT (MICHEL)
Coach, New York Rangers. Born in Montreal, Que., June 12, 1946.

On June 18, 1987, in one of the most unique transactions in NHL history, the New York Rangers dealt their 1988 first round draft choice to the Quebec Nordiques in exchange for coach Michel Bergeron.

After managing midget teams in his native Montreal, the 41-year-old Bergeron broke into Junior hockey in 1974-75 as coach of the Trois-Rivieres Draveurs in the QMJHL. He piloted the Draveurs for six seasons, leading that club to back-to-back Memorial Cup championships in 1977-78 and 1978-79.

In 1980-81, Bergeron moved into the Nordiques' hierarchy, taking over as coach shortly after the start of the season. He remained in that capacity with the team through 1986-87, compiling a 253-222-79 record in 554 games for a .528 winning percentage and taking two trips to the Wales Conference Final.

1986-87 Scoring

Regular Season
*–Rookie

Pos	#	Player	Team	GP	G	A	Pts	+/−	PIM
F	8	Walt Poddubny	NYR	75	40	47	87	16	49
F	16	Marcel Dionne	L.A.	67	24	50	74	8−	54
			NYR	14	4	6	10	8−	6
			Total	81	28	56	84	16−	60
F	28	Tomas Sandstrom	NYR	64	40	34	74	8	60
F	11	Kelly Kisio	NYR	70	24	40	64	5−	73
F	10	Pierre Larouche	NYR	73	28	35	63	7−	12
F	12	Don Maloney	NYR	72	19	38	57	7	117
D	3	James Patrick	NYR	78	10	45	55	13	62
F	25	Tony McKegney	MIN	11	2	3	5	2	16
			NYR	64	29	17	46	1−	56
			Total	75	31	20	51	1	72
D	4	Ron Greschner	NYR	61	6	34	40	6−	62
F	44	Ron Duguay	PIT	40	5	13	18	8−	30
			NYR	34	9	12	21	8−	9
			Total	74	14	25	39	16−	39
D	27	Willie Huber	NYR	66	8	22	30	13−	68
F	20	Jan Erixon	NYR	68	8	18	26	3	24
D	6	Curt Giles	MIN	11	0	3	3	2	4
			NYR	61	2	17	19	3	50
			Total	72	2	20	22	5	54
F	14	*Jeff Jackson	TOR	55	8	7	15	11−	64
			NYR	9	5	1	6	3−	15
			Total	64	13	8	21	14−	79
D	30	Larry Melnyk	NYR	73	3	12	15	13−	182
D	38	*Terry Carkner	NYR	52	2	13	15	1−	118
F	15	*Chris Jensen	NYR	37	6	7	13	1−	21
F	35	Lucien DeBlois	NYR	40	3	8	11	7−	27
F	21	George McPhee	NYR	21	4	4	8	2−	34
D	47	Pat Price	QUE	47	0	6	6	7−	81
			NYR	13	0	2	2	8−	49
			Total	60	0	8	8	15−	130
F	18	*Stu Kulak	VAN	28	1	1	2	11−	37
			EDM	23	3	1	4	3	41
			NYR	3	0	0	0	1−	0
			Total	54	4	2	6	9−	78
F	9	Dave Gagner	NYR	10	1	4	5	1−	12
D	26	*Jay Caufield	NYR	13	2	1	3	2−	45
F	22	*Mike Donnelly	NYR	5	1	1	2	0	0
G	33	Bob Froese	PHI	3	0	0	0	0	0
			NYR	28	0	2	2	0	56
			Total	31	0	2	2	0	56
F	36	*Gord Walker	NYR	1	1	0	1	2	4
D	29	Don Jackson	NYR	22	1	0	1	1−	91
D	37	*Norm MacIver	NYR	3	0	1	1	5−	0
D	24	Jim Leavins	NYR	4	0	1	1	0	4
G	34	John Vanbiesbrouck	NYR	50	0	1	1	0	18
G	31	*Ron Scott	NYR	1	0	0	0	0	0
F	41	*Mike Siltala	NYR	1	0	0	0	1	0
F	35	*Ron Talakoski	NYR	3	0	0	0	1	21
F	25	*Paul Fenton	NYR	8	0	0	0	5−	2
G	1	Doug Soetaert	NYR	13	0	0	0	0	14

Playoffs

Pos	#	Player	Team	GP	G	A	Pts	+/−	PIM
F	10	Pierre Larouche	NYR	6	3	2	5	4−	4
D	4	Ron Greschner	NYR	6	0	5	5	1−	0
F	12	Don Maloney	NYR	6	2	1	3	3	6
D	3	James Patrick	NYR	6	1	2	3	5−	2
F	28	Tomas Sandstrom	NYR	6	1	2	3	8−	20
F	44	Ron Duguay	NYR	6	2	0	2	21	4
F	16	Marcel Dionne	NYR	6	1	1	2	4−	2
F	14	Jeff Jackson	NYR	6	1	1	2	2−	16
D	27	Willie Huber	NYR	6	0	2	2	6−	6
F	20	Jan Erixon	NYR	6	1	0	1	5−	0
F	21	George McPhee	NYR	6	1	0	1	2−	28
F	11	Kelly Kisio	NYR	4	0	1	1	2−	2
D	47	Pat Price	NYR	6	0	1	1	2−	27
D	38	*Terry Carkner	NYR	1	0	0	0	0	0
F	35	Lucien Deblois	NYR	2	0	0	0	1−	2
D	26	*Jay Caufield	NYR	3	0	0	0	0	12
F	18	Stu Kulak	NYR	3	0	0	0	1−	2
G	33	Bob Froese	NYR	4	0	0	0	0	7
G	34	John Vanbiesbrouck	NYR	4	0	0	0	0	2
D	6	Curt Giles	NYR	5	0	0	0	1	6
F	25	Tony McKegney	NYR	6	0	0	0	3−	12
D	30	*Larry Melnyk	NYR	6	0	0	0	4−	4
F	8	Walt Poddubny	NYR	6	0	0	0	7−	8

Club Records

Team
(Figures in brackets for season records are games played; records for fewest points, wins, ties, losses, goals, goals against are for 70 or more games)

Most Points............109	1970-71 (78)	
	1971-72 (78)	
Most Wins..............49	1970-71 (78)	
Most Ties..............21	1950-51 (70)	
Most Losses............44	1984-85 (80)	
Most Goals............319	1974-75 (80)	
Most Goals Against.....345	1984-85 (80)	
Fewest Points..........47	1965-66 (70)	

Individual

Most Seasons..........17	Harry Howell	
Most Games........1,160	Harry Howell	
Most Goals, Career......406	Rod Gilbert	
Most Assists, Career....615	Rod Gilbert	
Most Points, Career...1,021	Rod Gilbert	
	(406 goals, 615 assists)	
Most Pen. Mins., Career..1,147	Harry Howell	
Most Shutouts, Career....49	Ed Giacomin	
Longest Consecutive		
Games Streak........560	Andy Hebenton	
	(Oct. 7/55-Mar. 24/63)	
Most Goals, Season......50	Vic Hadfield	
	(1971-72)	

PHILADELPHIA FLYERS

Dave Poulin

1986-87: 46w-26l-8t 100 pts. First, Patrick Division

1987-88 OUTLOOK: The Flyers lost in the Stanley Cup finals for the second time in three years last spring, but in both cases their top gunner, 50-plus goal scorer Tim Kerr was out of the lineup and team leader Dave Poulin was in but crippled. Can they go all the way this year? One key is in goal where rookie netminder Ron Hextall emerged as one of the NHL's best – and most aggressive – goaltenders. A healthy Kerr (who still has shoulder problems), Brian Propp (31 goals), Peter Zezel (38 goals) and Poulin (70 points) must remain productive. Rick Tocchet (21 goals) is emerging as a star rugged forward. His chronic back problems might hinder Mark Howe (+57), an exceptional leader on defense. Doug Crossman and Brad Marsh are among Howe's efficient partners. The Spectrum crowds are among the most inspirational in the League and visitors will have to learn to solve the Flyers home ice mastery. The intellect of coach Mike Keenan permeates the entire roster to create a sound, methodical approach.

Upcoming Milestones

Mark Howe	– 3 goals to reach 150
	– 32 assists to reach 400
Tim Kerr	– 22 goals to reach 300
Doug Crossman	– 25 games to reach 500
Brian Propp	– 3 goals to reach 300

Fan Club

Philadelphia Flyers Fan Club
Jack Schott
Spectrum, Pattison Place
Philadelphia, PA 19148

Entry Draft Selections 1987

Pick	
20	Darren Rumble
30	Jeff Harding
62	Martin Hostak
83	Tomaz Eriksson
104	Bill Gall
125	Tony Link
146	Mark Strapon
167	Darryl Ingham
188	Bruce McDonald
209	Steve Morrow
230	Darius Rusnak
251	Dale Roehl

21st NHL Season

PHILADELPHIA FLYERS 47

Year-by-Year Record 1968-1987

Season	GP	Home W	L	T	Road W	L	T	Overall W	L	T	GF	GA	Pts.	Finished	Playoff Result
1986-87	80	29	9	2	17	17	6	46	26	8	310	245	100	1st, Patrick Div.	Lost Final
1985-86	80	33	6	1	20	17	3	53	23	4	335	241	110	1st, Patrick Div.	Lost Div. Semi-Final
1984-85	80	32	4	4	21	16	3	53	20	7	348	241	113	1st, Patrick Div.	Lost Final
1983-84	80	25	10	5	19	16	5	44	26	10	350	290	98	3rd, Patrick Div.	Lost Div. Semi-Final
1982-83	80	29	8	3	20	15	5	49	23	8	326	240	106	1st, Patrick Div.	Lost Div. Semi-Final
1981-82	80	25	10	5	13	21	6	38	31	11	325	313	87	3rd, Patrick Div.	Lost Div. Semi-Final
1980-81	80	23	9	8	18	15	7	41	24	15	313	249	97	2nd, Patrick Div.	Lost Quarter-Final
1979-80	80	27	5	8	21	7	12	48	12	20	327	254	116	1st, Patrick Div.	Lost Final
1978-79	80	26	10	4	14	15	11	40	25	15	281	248	95	2nd, Patrick Div.	Lost Quarter-Final
1977-78	80	29	6	5	16	14	10	45	20	15	296	200	105	2nd, Patrick Div.	Lost Semi-Final
1976-77	80	33	6	1	15	10	15	48	16	16	323	213	112	1st, Patrick Div.	Lost Semi-Final
1975-76	80	36	2	2	15	11	14	51	13	16	348	209	118	1st, Patrick Div.	Lost Final
1974-75	**80**	**32**	**6**	**2**	**19**	**12**	**9**	**51**	**18**	**11**	**293**	**181**	**113**	**1st, Patrick Div.**	**Won Stanley Cup**
1973-74	**78**	**28**	**6**	**5**	**22**	**10**	**7**	**50**	**16**	**12**	**273**	**164**	**112**	**1st, West Div.**	**Won Stanley Cup**
1972-73	78	27	8	4	10	22	7	37	30	11	296	256	85	2nd, West Div.	Lost Semi-Final
1971-72	78	19	13	7	7	25	7	26	38	14	200	236	66	5th, West Div.	Out of Playoffs
1970-71	78	20	10	9	8	23	8	28	33	17	207	225	73	3rd, West Div.	Lost Quarter-Final
1969-70	76	11	14	13	6	21	11	17	35	24	197	225	58	5th, West Div.	Out of Playoffs
1968-69	76	14	16	8	6	19	13	20	35	21	174	225	61	3rd, West Div.	Lost Quarter-Final
1967-68	74	17	13	7	14	19	4	31	32	11	173	179	73	1st, West Div.	Lost Quarter-Final

Playoff History, 1968-87

Versus	Year	Series	Winner	W	L	T	GF	GA
Boston	1974	F	Philadelphia	4	2		15	13
Boston	1976	SF	Philadelphia	4	1		19	12
Boston	1977	SF	Boston	0	4		8	14
Boston	1978	QF	Boston	1	4		15	21
Buffalo	1975	F	Philadelphia	4	2		19	12
Buffalo	1978	QF	Philadelphia	4	1		16	11
Calgary	1974	QF	Philadelphia	4	0		17	8
Calgary	1981	QF	Calgary	3	4		22	26
Chicago	1971	QF	Chicago	0	4		8	20
Edmonton	1980	PRE	Philadelphia	3	0		12	6
Edmonton	1985	F	Edmonton	1	4		14	21
Edmonton	1987	F	Edmonton	3	4		17	19
Minnesota	1973	QF	Philadelphia	4	2		14	12
Minnesota	1980	SF	Philadelphia	4	1		27	14
Montreal	1973	SF	Montreal	1	4		13	19
Montreal	1976	F	Montreal	0	4		9	14
Montreal	1987	CF	Philadelphia	4	2		22	22
New Jersey	1978	PRE	Philadelphia	2	0		6	3
NY Islanders	1975	SF	Philadelphia	4	3		19	16
NY Islanders	1980	F	NY Islanders	2	4		25	26
NY Islanders	1985	DF	Philadelphia	4	1		16	11
NY Islanders	1987	DF	Philadelphia	4	3		23	16
NY Rangers	1974	SF	Philadelphia	4	3		22	17
NY Rangers	1979	QF	NY Rangers	1	4		28	8
NY Rangers	1980	QF	Philadelphia	4	1		14	7
NY Rangers	1982	DSF	NY Rangers	1	3		15	19
NY Rangers	1983	DSF	NY Rangers	0	3		9	18
NY Rangers	1986	DSF	NY Rangers	2	3		15	18
NY Rangers	1987	DSF	Philadelphia	4	2		22	13
Quebec	1981	PRE	Philadelphia	3	2		22	17
Quebec	1985	SF	Philadelphia	4	2		17	12
St. Louis	1968	QF	St. Louis	3	4		17	17
St. Louis	1969	QF	St. Louis	0	4		3	17
Toronto	1975	QF	Philadelphia	4	0		15	6
Toronto	1976	QF	Philadelphia	4	3		33	23
Toronto	1977	QF	Philadelphia	4	2		19	18
Vancouver	1979	PRE	Philadelphia	2	1		15	9
Washington	1984	DSF	Washington	0	3		5	15

Coach

KEENAN, MICHAEL (MIKE)
Coach, Philadelphia Flyers. Born in Toronto, Ont., October 21, 1949.

Since his appointment as head coach of the Philadelphia Flyers on May 24, 1984, Mike Keenan has not only taken his team to the Stanley Cup Finals twice in three seasons but also distinguished himself as the first coach in NHL history to post 40 or more wins in each of his first three seasons. Moreover, he has achieved 150 wins faster than any coach in League history. Entering the 1987-88 campaign, his three-year record stands at 152-69-19 in 240 games for a .673 winning percentage, the best among all active coaches.

A former team captain of the St. Lawrence University Saints, Keenan began coaching at the Junior B level, winning back-to-back championships in the Metro Toronto League. After leading the OHL's Peterborough Petes to the 1979-80 Memorial Cup Finals, he joined the AHL's Rochester Americans, carrying that team to the 1982-83 Calder Cup title. The following season, 1983-84, immediately preceding his tenure with the Flyers, Keenan posted yet another championship, this time taking the CIAU Canadian college title with the University of Toronto Blues.

1986-87 Scoring

Regular Season *–Rookie

Pos	#	Player	Team	GP	G	A	Pts	+/–	PIM
F	12	Tim Kerr	PHI	75	58	37	95	38	57
F	25	Peter Zezel	PHI	71	33	39	72	21	71
F	20	Dave Poulin	PHI	75	25	45	70	47	53
F	26	Brian Propp	PHI	53	31	36	67	39	45
D	2	Mark Howe	PHI	69	15	43	58	57	37
F	9	Per-Erik Eklund	PHI	72	14	41	55	2–	2
F	32	Murray Craven	PHI	77	19	30	49	1	38
F	22	Rick Tocchet	PHI	69	21	26	47	16	288
D	3	Doug Crossman	PHI	78	9	31	40	18	29
D	10	Brad McCrimmon	PHI	71	10	29	39	45	52
F	19	*Scott Mellanby	PHI	71	11	21	32	8	94
F	24	Derrick Smith	PHI	71	11	21	32	4–	34
F	23	Ilkka Sinisalo	PHI	42	10	21	31	14	8
F	14	Ron Sutter	PHI	39	10	17	27	10	69
F	18	Lindsay Carson	PHI	71	11	15	26	2–	141
D	15	J.J. Daigneault	PHI	77	6	16	22	12	56
D	28	*Kjell Samuelsson	NYR	30	2	6	8	2–	50
			PHI	46	1	6	7	9–	86
			Total	76	3	12	15	11–	136
D	8	Brad Marsh	PHI	77	2	9	11	9	124
F	21	Dave Brown	PHI	62	7	3	10	7–	274
G	27	*Ron Hextall	PHI	66	0	6	6	0	104
F	11	*Glen Seabrooke	PHI	10	1	4	5	2	2
D	17	Ed Hospodar	PHI	45	2	2	4	8–	136
F	7	*Brian Dobbin	PHI	12	2	1	3	2	14
D	29	*Darryl Stanley	PHI	33	1	2	3	6	76
D	41	*John Stevens	PHI	6	0	2	2	0	14
F	28	Al Hill	PHI	7	0	2	2	1	4
F	42	Don Nachbaur	PHI	23	0	2	2	1	87
F	37	*Mark Freer	PHI	1	0	1	1	1	0
D	6	*Jeff Chychrun	PHI	1	0	0	0	0	4
F	34	Jere Gillis	PHI	1	0	0	0	0	0
D	40	*Greg Smyth	PHI	1	0	0	0	2–	0
F	36	Ray Allison	PHI	2	0	0	0	2–	0
D	36	Kevin McCarthy	PHI	2	0	0	0	1–	0
D	5	*Steve Smith	PHI	2	0	0	0	0	6
D	44	*Mike Stothers	PHI	2	0	0	0	0	4
F	37	Tim Tookey	PHI	2	0	0	0	0	0
F	34	*Craig Berube	PHI	7	0	0	0	2	57
D	5	*Kerry Huffman	PHI	9	0	0	0	5	2
G	33	Glenn Resch	PHI	7	0	0	0	0	0

Playoffs

Pos	#	Player	Team	GP	G	A	Pts	+/–	PIM
F	26	Brian Propp	PHI	26	12	16	28	11	10
F	9	Per-Erik Eklund	PHI	26	7	20	27	11	2
F	22	Rick Tocchet	PHI	26	11	10	21	7	72
D	3	Doug Crossman	PHI	26	4	14	18	0	31
F	12	Tim Kerr	PHI	12	8	5	13	3	2
F	25	Peter Zezel	PHI	25	3	10	13	6	10
D	2	Mark Howe	PHI	26	2	10	12	14	4
F	24	Derrick Smith	PHI	26	6	4	10	3	26
F	19	*Scott Mellanby	PHI	24	5	5	10	7	46
F	18	Lindsay Carson	PHI	24	3	5	8	3	22
D	10	Brad McCrimmon	PHI	26	3	5	8	9	30
F	14	Ron Sutter	PHI	16	1	7	8	3–	12
D	8	Brad Marsh	PHI	26	3	4	7	2	16
F	23	Ilkka Sinisalo	PHI	18	5	1	6	6–	4
F	20	Dave Poulin	PHI	15	3	3	6	1	14
F	32	Murray Craven	PHI	12	3	1	4	4–	9
F	37	Tim Tookey	PHI	10	1	3	4	1	2
D	28	*Kjell Samuelsson	PHI	26	0	4	4	4	25
F	28	Al Hill	PHI	9	2	1	3	2	0
F	21	Dave Brown	PHI	26	1	2	3	1	59
F	42	Don Nachbaur	PHI	7	1	1	2	2	15
D	15	J.J. Daigneault	PHI	9	1	0	1	1–	0
G	27	*Ron Hextall	PHI	26	0	1	1	0	43
G	33	Glenn Resch	PHI	2	0	0	0	0	0
D	40	*Greg Smyth	PHI	1	0	0	0	0	2
D	44	*Mike Stothers	PHI	2	0	0	0	1	7
F	34	*Craig Berube	PHI	5	0	0	0	0	17
D	17	Ed Hospodar	PHI	5	0	0	0	0	2
D	29	Darryl Stanley	PHI	13	0	0	0	3–	9

Club Records

Team
(Figures in brackets for season records are games played; records for fewest points, wins, ties, losses, goals, goals against are for 70 or more games)

Most Points............	118	1975-76 (80)
Most Wins..............	53	1984-85 (80)
		1985-86 (80)
Most Ties..............	*24	1969-70 (76)
Most Losses............	38	1971-72 (78)
Most Goals.............	350	1983-84 (80)
Most Goals Against.....	313	1981-82 (78)
Fewest Points..........	58	1969-70 (76)
Fewest Wins............	17	1969-70 (76)
Fewest Ties............	4	1985-86 (80)
Fewest Losses..........	12	1979-80 (80)
Fewest Goals...........	173	1967-68 (74)
Fewest Goals Against...	164	1973-74 (78)

Longest Winning Streak
Over-all...............	13	Oct. 19-Nov. 17/85
Home..................	*20	Jan. 4-Apr. 3/76
Away..................	8	Dec. 22/82-Jan. 16/83

Individual

Most Seasons...........	15	Bobby Clarke
Most Games.............	1,144	Bobby Clarke
Most Goals, Career.....	420	Bill Barber
Most Assists, Career...	852	Bobby Clarke
Most Points, Career....	1,210	Bobby Clarke (358 goals, 852 assists)
Most Pen Mins., Career.	1,600	Paul Holmgren
Most Shoutouts, Career.	50	Bernie Parent

Longest Consecutive
Game Streak...........	287	Rick MacLeish (Oct. 6/72-Feb. 5/76)
Most Goals, Season....	61	Reggie Leach (1975-76)
Most Assists, Season..	89	Bobby Clarke (1974-75; 1975-76)
Most Points, Season...	119	Bobby Clarke (1975-76) (30 goals, 89 assists)
Most Pen. Mins., Season	*472	Dave Schultz (1974-75)
Most Points, Defenseman, Season..............	82	Mark Howe (1985-86) (24 goals, 58 assists)

* NHL Record.

PITTSBURGH PENGUINS

Willy Lindstrom

1986-87: 30w-38l-12t 72 pts. Fifth, Patrick Division

1987-88 OUTLOOK: Mario Lemieux is the best athlete to have hit Pittsburgh since Terry Bradshaw and could be approaching Wayne Gretzky as the NHL's best player. Lemieux almost singlehandedly led the Penguins to victories in their first eight games last season. Although the club missed the playoffs for the fifth consecutive season, the addition of coach Pierre Creamer – who has been a consistent winner in junior hockey – and spunky veteran Wilf Paiement could lead Pittsburgh to a post-season position. One of Creamer's top chores will be to motivate Mario to play with top intensity each game. Dan Quinn (80 points) is one of the NHL's best power-play specialists, while Craig Simpson (26 goals) proved why he was the second player selected in the 1985 Entry Draft – especially when Lemieux was injured. Randy Cunneyworth (26 goals) has developed into a solid left winger. But the right wingers were far less productive. The Penguins' defense has improved rapidly over the past few seasons as Doug Bodger, Moe Mantha, Ville Siren and Jim Johnson have become solid NHL defensemen. They're joined on the backline by veterans Rod Buskas and Randy Hillier. Veteran goaltenders Gilles Meloche and Pat Riggin combine 25 years of NHL experience.

Upcoming Milestones

Mario Lemieux – 5 goals to reach 150
Kevin LaVallee – 9 goals to reach 100
Willy Lindstrom – 18 games to reach 600
Terry Ruskowski – 20 games to reach 600

Fan Club

Pittsburgh Penguins Fan Club
Jack Bauman
P.O. Box 903
Pittsburgh, PA 15230

Entry Draft Selections 1987

Pick	
5	Chris Joseph
26	Richard Tabaracci
47	Jamie Leach
68	Risto Kurkinen
89	Jeff Waver
110	Shawn McEachern
131	Jim Bodden
152	Jiri Kucera
173	Jack MacDougall
194	Daryn McBride
215	Mark Carlson
236	Ake Lilljebjorn

21st NHL Season

WALES CONFERENCE

Year-by-Year Record 1968-1987

Season	GP	Home W	L	T	Road W	L	T	Overall W	L	T	GF	GA	Pts.	Finished	Playoff Result
1986-87	80	19	15	6	11	23	6	30	38	12	297	290	72	5th, Patrick Div.	Out of Playoffs
1985-86	80	20	15	5	14	23	3	34	38	8	313	305	76	5th, Patrick Div.	Out of Playoffs
1984-85	80	17	20	3	7	31	2	24	51	5	276	385	53	6th, Patrick Div.	Out of Playoffs
1983-84	80	7	29	4	9	29	2	16	58	6	254	390	38	6th, Patrick Div.	Out of Playoffs
1982-83	80	14	22	4	4	31	5	18	53	9	257	394	45	6th, Patrick Div.	Out of Playoffs
1981-82	80	21	11	8	10	25	5	31	36	13	310	337	75	4th, Patrick Div.	Lost Div. Semi-Final
1980-81	80	21	16	3	9	21	10	30	37	13	302	345	73	3rd, Norris Div.	Lost Prelim. Round
1979-80	80	20	13	7	10	24	6	30	37	13	251	303	73	3rd, Norris Div.	Lost Prelim. Round
1978-79	80	23	12	5	13	19	8	36	31	13	281	279	85	2nd, Norris Div.	Lost Quarter-Final
1977-78	80	16	15	9	9	22	9	25	37	18	254	321	68	4th, Norris Div.	Out of Playoffs
1976-77	80	22	12	6	12	21	7	34	33	13	240	252	81	3rd, Norris Div.	Lost Prelim. Round
1975-76	80	23	11	6	12	22	6	35	33	12	339	303	82	3rd, Norris Div.	Lost Prelim. Round
1974-75	80	25	5	10	12	23	5	37	28	15	326	289	89	3rd, Norris Div.	Lost Quarter-Final
1973-74	78	15	18	6	13	23	3	28	41	9	242	273	65	5th, West Div.	Out of Playoffs
1972-73	78	24	11	4	8	26	5	32	37	9	257	265	73	5th, West Div.	Out of Playoffs
1971-72	78	18	15	6	8	23	8	26	38	14	220	258	66	4th, West Div.	Lost Quarter-Final
1970-71	78	18	12	9	3	25	11	21	37	20	221	240	62	6th, West Div.	Out of Playoffs
1969-70	76	17	13	8	9	25	4	26	38	12	182	238	64	2nd, West Div.	Lost Semi-Final
1968-69	76	12	20	6	8	25	5	20	45	11	189	252	51	5th, West Div.	Out of Playoffs
1967-68	74	15	12	10	12	22	3	27	34	13	195	216	67	5th, West Div.	Out of Playoffs

Playoff History, 1968-87

Versus	Year	Series	Winner	W	L	T	GF	GA
Boston	1979	QF	Boston	0	4		7	16
Boston	1980	PRE	Boston	2	3		14	21
Buffalo	1979	PRE	Pittsburgh	2	1		9	9
Chicago	1972	QF	Chicago	0	4		8	14
NY Islanders	1975	QF	NY Islanders	3	4		18	21
NY Islanders	1982	DSF	NY Islanders	2	3		13	22
St. Louis	1970	SF	St. Louis	2	4		10	19
St. Louis	1975	PRE	Pittsburgh	2	0		9	6
St. Louis	1981	PRE	St. Louis	2	3		21	20
Toronto	1976	PRE	Toronto	1	2		3	8
Toronto	1977	PRE	Toronto	1	2		10	13
Oakland	1970	QF	Pittsburgh	4	0		13	6

Coach

CREAMER, PIERRE
Coach, Pittsburgh Penguins. Born in Chomedy, Que., July 6, 1944.

After an outstanding coaching career in Junior and minor league hockey, Pierre Creamer was selected head coach of the Pittsburgh Penguins on June 4, 1987. In 1980-81, Creamer earned his first coaching position with the Montreal (later Verdun) Junior Canadiens and, within three seasons, carried his team to the QMJHL championship and the Memorial Cup Finals. During his four-year tenure with the Junior Canadiens through 1983-84, he amasssed an impressive record of 165-105-6 for a .609 winning percentage. In 1984-85, Creamer moved into the professional ranks with the Sherbrooke Canadiens, leading that club to the AHL championship in his first year. He remained with Sherbrooke for two more seasons, reaching the Calder Cup Finals again in 1986-87 on the strength of a 50-30-0 (.625) regular-season finish.

Club Records

Team

(Figures in brackets for season records are games played; records for fewest points, wins, ties, losses, goals, goals against are for 70 or more games)

Most Points	89	1974-75 (80)
Most Wins	37	1974-75 (80)
Most Ties	20	1970-71 (78)
Most Losses	58	1983-84 (80)
Most Goals	339	1975-76 (80)
Most Goals Against	394	1982-83 (80)
Fewest Points	38	1983-84 (80)
Fewest Wins	16	1983-84 (80)
Fewest Ties	6	1983-84 (80)
Fewest Losses	28	1974-75 (80)
Fewest Goals	182	1969-70 (76)
Fewest Goals Against	216	1967-68 (74)

Longest Winning Streak

Over-all	7	Oct. 9-Oct. 22/86
Home	9	Feb. 26-Apr. 5/75
Away	4	Oct. 14-Nov. 2/84

Longest Undefeated Streak

Over-all	11	Feb. 7-28/76 (7 wins, 4 ties)
Home	20	Nov. 30/74-Feb. 22/75 (12 wins, 8 ties)
Away	7	Mar. 13-27/79 (5 wins, 2 ties)

Longest Losing Streak

Over-all	11	Jan. 22/83-Feb. 10/83
Home	7	Oct. 8-29/83
Away	18	Dec. 23/82-Mar. 4/83

Longest Winless Streak

Over-all	18	Jan. 2/83-Feb. 10/83 (17 losses, 1 tie) Oct. 8-Nov. 19/83 (9 losses, 2 ties)
Home	11	Oct. 25/70-Jan. 14/71 (11 losses, 7 ties) Dec. 23/82-Mar. 4/83 (18 losses)
Away	18	

Most Shutouts, Season	6	1967-68 (74) 1976-77 (80) 1981-82 (80)
Most Pen. Mins., Season	2,210	
Most Goals, Game	12	Mar. 15/75 (Wash. 1 at Pit. 12)

Individual

Most Seasons	11	Rick Kehoe
Most Games	753	Jean Pronovost
Most Goals, Career	316	Jean Pronovost
Most Assists, Career	349	Syl Apps
Most Points, Career	636	Rick Kehoe (312 goals, 324 assists)
Most Pen. Mins., Career	871	Bryan Watson
Most Shutouts, Career	11	Les Binkley
Longest Consecutive Games Streak	320	Ron Schock (Oct. 24/73-Apr. 3/77)

1986-87 Scoring

Regular Season   *-Rookie

Pos	#	Player	Team	GP	G	A	Pts	+/-	PIM
F	66	Mario Lemieux	PIT	63	54	53	107	13	57
F	10	Dan Quinn	CGY	16	3	6	9	6-	14
			PIT	64	28	43	71	14	40
			Total	80	31	49	80	8	54
F	15	Randy Cunneyworth	PIT	79	26	27	53	14	142
F	18	Craig Simpson	PIT	72	26	25	51	11	57
F	8	Terry Ruskowski	PIT	70	14	37	51	8	145
D	3	Doug Bodger	PIT	76	11	38	49	6	52
D	20	Moe Mantha	PIT	62	9	31	40	6-	44
F	9	John Chabot	PIT	72	14	22	36	7-	8
F	12	Bob Errey	PIT	72	16	18	34	5-	46
D	6	Jim Johnson	PIT	80	5	25	30	6	116
F	28	Dan Frawley	PIT	78	14	14	28	10-	218
F	16	Kevin LaVallee	PIT	33	8	20	28	2-	4
F	32	Dave Hannan	PIT	58	10	15	25	2-	56
F	19	Willy Lindstrom	PIT	60	10	13	23	9	6
D	5	Ville Siren	PIT	69	5	17	22	8	50
F	35	Warren Young	PIT	50	8	13	21	5-	103
D	7	Rod Buskas	PIT	68	3	15	18	2	123
F	14	Chris Kontos	PIT	31	8	9	17	6-	6
F	24	Troy Loney	PIT	23	8	7	15	0	22
D	23	Randy Hillier	PIT	55	4	8	12	12	97
D	4	Dwight Schofield	PIT	25	1	6	7	4	59
D	25	Norm Schmidt	PIT	20	1	5	6	8-	4
F	29	*Phil Bourque	PIT	22	2	3	5	2-	32
F	22	Jim McGeough	PIT	11	1	4	5	5-	8
F	33	*Mitch Wilson	PIT	17	2	1	3	3-	83
F	11	*Lee Giffin	PIT	8	1	1	2	2	0
F	26	Mike Blaisdell	PIT	10	1	1	2	2	2
D	22	Neil Belland	PIT	3	0	1	1	0	0
F	11	*Dwight Mathiasen	PIT	6	0	1	1	1-	0
D	2	*Chris Dahlquist	PIT	19	0	1	1	2-	20
G	1	Pat Riggin	BOS	10	0	0	0	0	0
			PIT	17	0	1	1	0	2
			Total	27	0	1	1	0	2
G	27	Gilles Meloche	PIT	43	0	1	1	0	20
D	34	Todd Charlesworth	PIT	1	0	0	0	0	0
F	11	Alain Lemieux	PIT	1	0	0	0	1-	0
G	1	*Steve Guenette	PIT	2	0	0	0	0	0
D	33	*Mike Rowe	PIT	2	0	0	0	2-	0
F	31	Carl Mokosak	PIT	3	0	0	0	4-	4

Most Goals, Season	55	Rick Kehoe (1980-81)
Most Assists, Season	93	Mario Lemieux (1985-86)
Most Points, Season	141	Mario Lemieux (1985-86)
Most Pen. Mins., Season	407	Paul Baxter (1981-82)
Most Points, Defenseman Season	83	Randy Carlyle (1980-81) (16 goals, 67 assists)
Most Points, Center, Season	141	Mario Lemieux (1985-86) (48 goals, 93 assists)
Most Points, Right Wing, Season	104	Jean Pronovost (1975-76) (52 goals, 52 assists)
Most Points, Left Wing, Season	82	Lowell MacDonald (1973-74) (43 goals, 39 assists)

QUEBEC NORDIQUES

Peter Stastny

1986-87: 31w-39L-10T 72 PTS. Fourth, Adams Division

1987-88 OUTLOOK: It's a new day in Quebec, as the Nordiques performed a face-lift both on their bench and behind it. "Le Petit Tigre" is now part of the Big Apple as popular coach Michel Bergeron has departed for the Rangers. In his place is former NHL winger Andre Savard, who piloted the Nords' Fredericton farm club the past two seasons. Savard will rebuild without sparkplug Dale Hunter and goaltender Clint Malarchuk, who were shipped to the Caps for two forwards Alan Haworth (who emerged as a scorer in Washington) and Gaetan Duchesne (who became a reliable defensive forward). The Nords still have top marksmen Michel Goulet (49 goals) and the Stastny brothers Peter and Anton. But sniper John Ogrodnick, obtained from Detroit last season, requested a trade before training camp. Paul Gillis and Richard Zemlack will try to fill Hunter's skates, but the rest of the forwards are iffy. Mario Gosselin replaced Malarchuk as Quebec's starting goaltender with a strong second half last season, while rookie Mario Brunetta will likely back-up. With Risto Siltanen returning to Europe, Quebec does not have an offensive threat among its defensemen. Jeff Brown, Robert Picard, David Shaw, Normand Rochefort and Randy Moller combined for 26 goals. Rochefort, however, has become one of the NHL's best defensive defensemen.

Upcoming Milestones

John Ogrodnick – 30 goals to reach 300
Peter Stastny – 25 goals to reach 300
– 10 points to reach 800
Anton Stastny – 32 goals to reach 250
Greg Malone – 3 goals to reach 200
Michel Goulet – 34 goals to reach 400
– 70 points to reach 800

Entry Draft Selections 1987

Pick	
9	Bryan Fogarty
15	Joe Sakic
51	Jim Sprott
72	Kip Miller
93	Rob Mendel
114	Garth Snow
135	Tim Hanus
156	Jake Enebak
177	Jaroslav Sevcik
183	Ladislav Tresl
198	Darren Nauss
219	Mike Williams

WALES CONFERENCE

9th NHL Season

QUEBEC NORDIQUES

Year-by-Year Record 1979-1987

Season	GP	Home W	L	T	Road W	L	T	Overall W	L	T	GF	GA	Pts.	Finished	Playoff Result
1986-87	80	20	13	7	11	26	3	31	39	10	267	276	72	4th, Adams Div.	Lost Div. Final
1985-86	80	23	13	4	20	18	2	43	31	6	330	289	92	1st, Adams Div.	Lost Div. Semi-Final
1984-85	80	24	12	4	17	18	5	41	30	9	323	275	91	2nd, Adams Div.	Lost Conf. Championship
1983-84	80	24	11	5	18	17	5	42	28	10	360	278	94	3rd, Adams Div.	Lost Div. Final
1982-83	80	23	10	7	11	24	5	34	34	12	343	336	80	4th, Adams Div.	Lost Div. Semi-Final
1981-82	80	24	13	3	9	18	13	33	31	16	356	345	82	4th, Adams Div.	Lost Conf. Championship
1980-81	80	18	11	11	12	21	7	30	32	18	314	318	78	4th, Adams Div.	Lost Prelim. Round
1979-80	80	17	16	7	8	28	4	25	44	11	248	313	61	5th, Adams Div.	Out of Playoffs

Playoff History, 1980-87

Versus	Year	Series	Winner	W	L	T	GF	GA	Versus	Year	Series	Winner	W	L	T	GF	GA
Boston	1982	DF	Quebec	4	3		28	26	Montreal	1982	DSF	Quebec	3	2		16	11
Boston	1983	DSF	Boston	1	3		8	11	Montreal	1984	DF	Montreal	2	4		13	20
Buffalo	1984	DF	Quebec	3	0		13	5	Montreal	1985	DF	Quebec	4	3		24	24
Buffalo	1985	DSF	Quebec	3	2		22	22	Montreal	1987	DF	Montreal	3	4		21	27
Hartford	1986	DSF	Hartford	0	3		7	16	NY Islanders	1982	SF	NY Islanders	0	4		9	18
Hartford	1987	DSF	Quebec	4	2		27	19	Philadelphia	1981	PRE	Philadelphia	2	3		17	22
									Philadelphia	1985	SF	Philadelphia	2	4		12	17

Club Records

Team
(Figures in brackets for season records are games played; records for fewest points, wins, ties, losses, goals, goals against are for 70 or more games)

Most Points............94	1983-84 (80)	
Most Wins.............43	1985-86 (80)	
Most Ties.............18	1980-81 (80)	
Most Losses...........44	1979-80 (80)	
Most Goals............360	1983-84 (80)	
Most Goals Against.....345	1981-82 (80)	
Fewest Points..........61	1979-80 (80)	
Fewest Wins...........25	1979-80 (80)	
Fewest Ties............6	1985-86 (80)	
Fewest Losses.........28	1983-84 (80)	
Fewest Goals..........248	1979-80 (80)	
Fewest Goals Against..275	1984-85 (80)	
Longest Winning Streak		
Over-all..............7	Nov. 24-Dec. 10/83	
Home................10	Nov. 26/83-Jan. 10/84	
Away.................4	Feb. 17-22/81	
Longest Undefeated Streak		
Over-all.............11	Mar. 10-31/81 (7 wins, 4 ties)	
Home................14	Nov. 19/83-Jan. 21/84 (11 wins, 3 ties)	
Away.................8	Feb. 17/81-Mar. 22/81 (6 wins, 2 ties)	
Longest Losing Streak		
Over-all..............7	Feb. 9-23/80	
Home.................4	Mar. 12-30/80	
Away.................9	Feb. 2-Mar. 19/80	
Longest Winless Streak		
Over-all.............13	Oct. 12-Nov. 11/80 (9 losses, 4 ties)	
Home.................8	Dec. 23/80-Jan. 28/81 (4 losses, 4 ties)	
Away................13	Jan. 11-Mar. 19/80 (12 losses, 1 tie)	

Individual

Most Seasons............8	Several players	
Most Games............366	Michel Goulet	
Most Goals, Career......515	Michel Goulet	
Most Assists, Career....462	Peter Stastny	
Most Points, Career.....790	Peter Stastny (275 goals, 515 assists)	
Most Pen. Mins., Career..1,545	Dale Hunter	
Most Shutouts, Career.....5	Clint Malarchuk	
Longest Consecutive Games Streak........312	Dale Hunter (Oct. 9/80-Mar. 13/84)	
Most Goals, Season......57	Michel Goulet (1982-83)	
Most Assists, Season....93	Peter Stastny (1980-81, 1981-82)	
Most Points, Season....139	Peter Stastny (1981-82) (46 goals, 93 assists)	
Most Pen. Mins., Season...272	Dale Hunter (1981-82)	
Most Points,Defenseman Season.............46	Mario Marois (1983-84) (13 goals, 36 assists)	
Most Points, Center, Season.............139	Peter Stastny (1981-82) (46 goals, 93 assists)	
Most Points, Right Wing, Season............97	Réal Cloutier (1981-82) (37 goals, 60 assists)	
Most Points, Left Wing, Season...........121	Michel Goulet (1983-84) (56 goals, 65 assists)	
Most Points, Rookie, Season...........109	Peter Stastny (1980-81) (39 goals, 70 assists)	
Most Shutouts, Season.....4	Clint Malarchuk (1985-86)	
Most Goals, Game........4	Michel Goulet (Dec. 14/85; Mar. 17/86)	

1986-87 Scoring

Regular Season   *–Rookie

Pos	#	Player	Team	GP	G	A	Pts	+/-	PIM
F	16	Michel Goulet	QUE	75	49	47	96	12-	61
F	26	Peter Stastny	QUE	64	24	53	77	21-	43
F	25	John Ogrodnick	DET	39	12	28	40	2-	6
			QUE	32	11	16	27	6-	4
			Total	71	23	44	67	8-	10
F	20	Anton Stastny	QUE	77	27	35	62	3	8
F	23	Paul Gillis	QUE	76	13	26	39	5-	267
F	32	Dale Hunter	QUE	46	10	29	39	4	135
D	12	Risto Siltanen	QUE	66	10	29	39	2-	32
F	19	Alain Cote	QUE	80	12	24	36	4-	38
F	11	Mike Eagles	QUE	73	13	19	32	15-	55
D	22	*Jeff Brown	QUE	44	7	22	29	11	16
F	15	*Jason Lafreniere	QUE	56	13	15	28	3-	8
D	24	Robert Picard	QUE	78	8	20	28	17-	71
F	9	Doug Shedden	DET	33	6	12	18	3	6
			QUE	16	0	2	2	5-	8
			Total	49	6	14	20	2-	14
D	4	David Shaw	QUE	75	0	19	19	35-	69
F	17	Basil McRae	DET	36	2	2	4	3-	193
			QUE	33	9	5	14	1	149
			Total	69	11	7	18	2-	342
F	10	Bill Derlago	WPG	30	3	6	9	3-	12
			QUE	18	3	5	8	4-	6
			Total	48	6	11	17	7-	18
D	5	Normand Rochefort	QUE	70	6	9	15	2	46
F	7	Lane Lambert	NYR	18	2	2	4	2	33
			QUE	15	5	5	10	1-	18
			Total	33	7	7	14	1	51
F	18	Mike Hough	QUE	56	6	8	14	8-	79
D	21	Randy Moller	QUE	71	5	9	14	11-	144
F	44	*Ken Quinney	QUE	25	2	7	9	2	16
D	29	*Steven Finn	QUE	36	2	5	7	8-	40
F	14	Jean F. Sauve	QUE	14	2	3	5	4-	4
F	10	*Max Middendorf	QUE	6	1	4	5	2-	4
G	33	Mario Gosselin	QUE	30	0	3	3	0	20
F	37	*Richard Zemlak	QUE	20	0	2	2	0	47
D	34	Gord Donnelly	QUE	38	0	2	2	3-	143
G	30	Clint Malarchuk	QUE	54	0	2	2	0	37
F	14	*Trevor Stienberg	QUE	6	1	0	1	0	12
F	25	Greg Malone	QUE	6	0	1	1	0	0
F	29	*Yves Heroux	QUE	1	0	0	0	0	0
D	6	*Scott Shaunessy	QUE	3	0	0	0	1-	7
G	1	Richard Sevigny	QUE	4	0	0	0	0	14
D	2	*Daniel Poudrier	QUE	6	0	0	0	2-	0

Playoffs

Pos	#	Player	Team	GP	G	A	Pts	+/-	PIM
F	26	Peter Stastny	QUE	13	6	9	15	3	12
F	16	Michel Goulet	QUE	13	9	5	14	2-	35
F	25	John Ogrodnick	QUE	13	9	4	13	0	6
D	24	Robert Picard	QUE	13	2	10	12	3	10
F	20	Anton Stastny	QUE	13	3	8	11	0	6
D	12	Risto Siltanen	QUE	13	1	9	10	4-	8
F	32	Dale Hunter	QUE	13	1	7	8	5-	56
D	22	*Jeff Brown	QUE	13	3	3	6	3-	2
F	23	Paul Gillis	QUE	13	2	4	6	3	65
F	7	Lane Lambert	QUE	13	2	4	6	2	30
F	15	*Jason Lafreniere	QUE	12	1	5	6	1-	2
F	19	Alain Cote	QUE	13	2	3	5	0	2
D	21	Randy Moller	QUE	13	1	4	5	5	23
F	17	Basil McRae	QUE	13	3	1	4	1-	99
D	5	Normand Rochefort	QUE	13	2	1	3	3-	26
F	18	*Mike Hough	QUE	9	0	3	3	1-	26
D	29	*Steven Finn	QUE	13	0	2	2	1	29
F	11	Mike Eagles	QUE	4	1	0	1	1-	10
F	25	Greg Malone	QUE	1	0	0	0	0	0
G	30	Clint Malarchuk	QUE	3	0	0	0	0	0
G	33	Mario Gosselin	QUE	11	0	0	0	0	2
D	34	Gord Donnelly	QUE	13	0	0	0	2-	53

Coach

SAVARD, ANDRÉ
Coach, Quebec Nordiques. Born in Temiscaming, Que., September 2, 1953.

After four seasons in the Quebec organization, including the last two as head coach of the AHL's Fredericton Express, André Savard earned the Nordiques' top coaching position on June 19, 1987. 34-year-old Savard enters the 1987-88 campaign as the youngest of all active NHL coaches.

Chosen sixth overall from the QMJHL's Quebec Remparts by Boston in the 1973 Amateur Draft, Savard played his first three NHL seasons at center for the Bruins from 1973-74 to 1975-76, before signing as a free agent with the Buffalo Sabres for 1976-77. After concluding his seven-year stint with Buffalo in 1982-83, Savard was acquired by Quebec, where he played out the remaining two years of his career. In 12 NHL seasons, Savard compiled a scoring totals of 211-271-482 in 790 career games.

ST. LOUIS BLUES

Goaltender Greg Millen

1986-87: 32w-33l-15t 79 pts. First, Norris Division

1987-88 OUTLOOK: Residents of the Show Me State quickly forgot about the painful departure of coach Jacques Demers as another Jacques – Martin – led the Blues to a first place Norris Division finish on the final night of the regular season. Doug Gilmour continued his torrid pace of the 1986 playoffs and finished with 105 points. Bernie Federko (72 points), Mark Hunter (36 goals) and Greg Paslawski (29 goals) also pitched in offensively, while St. Louis added veterans Tony McKegney (35 goals) and Perry Turnbull during the off-season. In addition, Hobey Baker Award winner Tony Hrkac should provide some scoring punch. Rookie defenseman Rob Nordmark brings formidable credentials from Sweden. He will join Brian Benning (49 points), Rob Ramage and Charles Bourgeois on a stubborn Blues backline. St. Louis has two front-line goaltenders in Greg Millen (3.53) and Rick Wamsley (3.54).

Upcoming Milestones

Bernie Federko – 83 points to reach 1,000
Brian Sutter – 12 goals to reach 300
Ron Flockhart – 10 goals to reach 150
Doug Gilmour – 37 goals to reach 150

Fan Club

St. Louis Blueliners
P.O. Box 805
St. Louis, MO 63188

Entry Draft Selections 1987

Pick	
12	Keith Osborne
54	Kevin Miehm
59	Robert Nordmark
75	Darin Smith
82	Andy Rymsha
117	Rob Robinson
138	Tobb Crabtree
159	Guy Hebert
180	Robert Dumas
201	David Marvin
207	Andy Cesarski
222	Dan Rolfe
243	Ray Savard

21st NHL Season

Year-by-Year Record 1968-1987

Season	GP	Home W	L	T	Road W	L	T	Overall W	L	T	GF	GA	Pts.	Finished	Playoff Result
1986-87	80	21	12	7	11	21	8	32	33	15	281	293	79	1st, Norris Div.	Lost Div. Semi-Final
1985-86	80	23	11	6	14	23	3	37	34	9	302	291	85	3rd, Norris Div.	Lost Conf. Championship
1984-85	80	21	12	7	16	19	5	37	31	12	299	288	86	1st, Norris Div.	Lost Div. Semi-Final
1983-84	80	23	14	3	9	27	4	32	41	7	293	316	71	2nd, Norris Div.	Lost Div. Final
1982-83	80	16	16	8	9	24	7	25	40	15	285	316	65	4th, Norris Div.	Lost Div. Semi-Final
1981-82	80	22	14	4	10	26	4	32	40	8	315	349	72	3rd Norris Div.	Lost Div. Final
1980-81	80	29	7	4	16	11	13	45	18	17	352	281	107	1st, Smythe Div.	Lost Quarter-Final
1979-80	80	20	13	7	14	21	5	34	34	12	266	278	80	2nd, Smythe Div.	Lost Prelim. Round
1978-79	80	14	20	6	4	30	6	18	50	12	249	348	48	3rd, Smythe Div.	Out of Playoffs
1977-78	80	12	20	8	8	27	5	20	47	13	195	304	53	4th, Smythe Div.	Out of Playoffs
1976-77	80	22	13	5	10	26	4	32	39	9	239	276	73	1st, Smythe Div.	Lost Quarter-Final
1975-76	80	20	12	8	9	25	6	29	37	14	249	290	72	3rd, Smythe Div.	Lost Prelim. Round
1974-75	80	23	13	4	12	18	10	35	31	14	269	267	84	2nd, Smythe Div.	Lost Prelim. Round
1973-74	78	16	16	7	10	24	5	26	40	12	206	248	64	6th, West Div.	Out of Playoffs
1972-73	78	21	11	7	11	23	5	32	34	12	233	251	76	4th, West Div.	Lost Quarter-Final
1971-72	78	17	17	5	11	22	6	28	39	11	208	247	67	3rd, West Div.	Lost Semi-Final
1970-71	78	23	7	9	11	18	10	34	25	19	223	208	87	2nd, West Div.	Lost Quarter-Final
1969-70	76	24	9	5	13	18	7	37	27	12	224	179	86	1st, West Div.	Lost Final
1968-69	76	21	8	9	16	17	5	37	25	14	204	157	88	1st, West Div.	Lost Final
1967-68	74	18	12	7	9	19	9	27	31	16	177	191	70	3rd, West Div.	Lost Final

Playoff History, 1968-87

Versus	Year	Series	Winner	W	L	T	GF	GA
Boston	1970	F	Boston	0	4		7	20
Boston	1972	SF	Boston	0	4		8	28
Buffalo	1978	PRE	Buffalo	1	2		8	7
Calgary	1986	SF	Calgary	3	4		22	28
Chicago	1973	QF	Chicago	1	4		9	22
Chicago	1980	PRE	Chicago	0	3		4	12
Chicago	1982	DF	Chicago	2	4		19	23
Chicago	1983	DSF	Chicago	1	3		10	16
Detroit	1984	DSF	St. Louis	3	1		13	12
Los Angeles	1969	SF	St. Louis	4	0		16	5
Minnesota	1968	SF	St. Louis	4	3		22	18
Minnesota	1970	QF	St. Louis	4	2		20	16
Minnesota	1971	QF	Minnesota	2	4		15	16
Minnesota	1972	QF	St. Louis	4	3		19	19
Minnesota	1984	DF	Minnesota	3	4		17	19
Minnesota	1985	DSF	Minnesota	0	3		5	9
Minnesota	1986	DSF	St. Louis	3	2		18	20
Montreal	1968	F	Montreal	0	4		7	11
Montreal	1969	F	Montreal	0	4		3	12
Montreal	1977	QF	Montreal	0	4		4	19
NY Rangers	1981	QF	NY Rangers	2	4		22	29
Philadelphia	1968	QF	St. Louis	4	3		17	17
Philadelphia	1969	QF	St. Louis	4	0		17	3
Pittsburgh	1970	SF	St. Louis	4	2		19	10
Pittsburgh	1975	PRE	Pittsburgh	0	2		6	9
Pittsburgh	1981	PRE	St. Louis	3	2		20	21
Toronto	1986	DF	St. Louis	4	3		24	22
Toronto	1987	DSF	Toronto	2	4		11	15
Winnipeg	1982	DSF	St. Louis	3	1		20	13

Club Records

Team
(Figures in brackets for season records are games played; records for fewest points, wins, ties, losses, goals, goals against are for 70 or more games)

Most Points............107 1980-81 (80)
Most Wins.............45 1980-81 (80)
Most Ties 19 1970-71 (78)
Most Losses 50 1978-79 (80)
Most Goals...........352 1980-81 (80)
Most Goals Against......349 1981-82 (80)
Fewest Points 48 1978-79 (80)
Fewest Wins 18 1978-79 (80)
Fewest Ties............ 7 1983-84 (80)
Fewest Losses..........18 1980-81 (80)
Fewest Goals...........177 1967-68 (74)
Fewest Goals Against 157 1968-69 (76)
Longest Winning Streak
 Over-all .... 5 Feb. 12-19/69
     Jan. 6-16/72
 Home .... 7 Nov. 28-
     Dec. 29/81
 Away................ 4 Dec. 16/73-
     Jan. 8/74
Longest Undefeated Streak
 Over-all ....12 Nov. 10-
     Dec. 8/68
     (5 wins, 7 ties)
 Home ....11 Feb. 12-
     Mar. 19/69
     (5 wins, 6 ties)
     Feb. 7-
     Mar. 29/75
     (9 wins, 2 ties)
 Away .... 6 Feb. 1-17/81
     (3 wins, 3 ties)

Coach

MARTIN, JACQUES
Coach, St. Louis Blues. Born in Rockland, Ont., October 1, 1952

When he came to the St. Louis Blues on June 26, 1986, Jacques Martin looked to build on his highly successful coaching career. And build on it he did, rallying the Blues to their sixth division title and 17th playoff appearance in their 20-year team history.

The 35-year-old St. Louis skipper began coaching in 1979-80 with the Rockland Nationals Junior B squad, before moving on to the OHL's Peterborough Petes in 1983-84. After leading the Petes to a divisional championship in 1984-85, Martin was named coach of the Guelph Platers, winning the 1985-86 OHL title, the Memorial Cup and the OHL Coach of the Year award. In three OHL seasons, Martin amassed a 126-76-10 record and a .618 winning percentage.

ST. LOUIS BLUES

1986-87 Scoring

Regular Season
*–Rookie

Pos	#	Player	Team	GP	G	A	Pts	+/-	PIM
F	94	Doug Gilmour	STL	80	42	63	105	2-	58
F	24	Bernie Federko	STL	64	20	52	72	25-	32
F	20	Mark Hunter	STL	74	36	33	69	19-	167
F	28	Greg Paslawski	STL	76	29	35	64	1	27
D	2	Brian Benning	STL	78	13	36	49	2	110
F	17	Gino Cavallini	STL	80	18	26	44	4	54
F	22	Rick Meagher	STL	80	18	21	39	9-	52
D	5	Rob Ramage	STL	59	11	28	39	12-	108
F	12	Ron Flockhart	STL	60	16	19	35	9-	12
F	14	Doug Wickenheiser	STL	80	13	15	28	22-	37
D	27	Ric Nattress	STL	73	6	22	28	34-	24
F	7	*Cliff Ronning	STL	42	11	14	25	1-	6
F	15	Mark Reeds	STL	68	9	16	25	20-	16
D	6	Tim Bothwell	HFD	4	1	0	1	5-	0
			STL	72	5	16	21	14-	46
			Total	76	6	16	22	19-	46
F	16	*Jocelyn Lemieux	STL	53	10	8	18	1	94
F	25	*Herb Raglan	STL	62	6	10	16	6	159
D	10	Bruce Bell	STL	45	3	13	16	3	18
F	32	Doug Evans	STL	53	3	13	16	2	91
D	4	Charles Bourgeois	STL	66	2	12	14	16	164
D	35	Jim Pavese	STL	69	2	9	11	21-	0
F	11	Brian Sutter	STL	14	3	3	6	5-	18
D	26	*Micheal Dark	STL	13	2	0	2	0	2
F	21	*Todd Ewen	STL	23	2	0	2	1-	84
G	29	Greg Millen	STL	42	0	2	2	0	12
D	34	*Mike Posavad	STL	2	0	0	0	1	0
D	23	Larry Trader	STL	26	5	0	0	0	5
G	30	Rick Wamsley	STL	41	0	0	0	0	10

Playoffs

Pos	#	Player	Team	GP	G	A	Pts	+/-	PIM
F	24	Bernie Federko	STL	6	3	3	620xm		18
F	17	Gino Cavallini	STL	6	3	1	4	0	2
F	9	Doug Gilmour	STL	6	2	2	4	1	16
D	5	Rob Ramage	STL	6	2	2	4	0	21
D	2	*Brian Benning	STL	6	0	4	4	0	9
F	20	Mark Hunter	STL	5	0	3	3	1-	10
D	10	Bruce Bell	STL	4	1	1	2	1-	7
F	28	Greg Paslawski	STL	6	1	1	2	1-	4
F	7	*Cliff Ronning	STL	4	0	1	1	1-	0
F	16	*Jocelyn Lemieux	STL	5	0	1	1	1-	6
F	15	Mark Reeds	STL	6	0	1	1	0	2
D	35	Jim Pavese	STL	2	0	0	0	1-	2
G	30	Rick Wamsley	STL	2	0	0	0	0	0
F	18	*Tony Hrkac	STL	3	0	0	0	0	0
F	21	*Todd Ewen	STL	4	0	0	0	0	23
G	29	Greg Millen	STL	4	0	0	0	0	0
F	25	*Herb Raglan	STL	4	0	0	0	3-	0
F	32	*Doug Evans	STL	5	0	0	0	2-	10
D	6	Tim Bothwell	STL	6	0	0	0	5-	6
D	4	Charles Bourgeois	STL	6	0	0	0	3-	27
F	22	Rick Meagher	STL	6	0	0	0	4-	11
D	27	Ric Nattress	STL	6	0	0	0	3-	2
F	14	Doug Wickenheiser	STL	6	0	0	0	3-	2

Longest Losing Streak
Over-all .... 7 Nov. 12-26/67
Home .... 5 Nov. 19-Dec. 6/77
Away............. 10 Jan. 20/82-Mar. 8/82

Longest Winless Streak
Over-all .... 12 Jan. 17-Feb. 15/78 (10 losses, 2 ties)
Home .... 7 Dec. 28/82-Jan. 25/83 (6 losses, 1 tie)
Away............. 17 Jan. 23-Apr. 7/74 (14 losses, 3 ties)

Most Shutouts, Season 13 1968-69 (76)
Most Pen. Mins.,
 Season............. 1,657 1980-81 (80)
Most Goals, Game .... 10 Feb. 2/82 (Wpg. 6 at St. L. 10) Dec. 1/84 (Det. 5 at St. L. 10)

Individual

Most Seasons .... 11 Bob Plager, Bernie Federko, Brian Sutter
Most Games .... 718 Bernie Federko
Most Goals, Career .... 310 Bernie Federko
Most Assists, Career .... 607 Bernie Federko
Most Points, Career ..... 917 Bernie Federko
Most Pen. Mins., Career .. 1,639 Brian Sutter
Most Shutouts, Career .... 16 Glenn Hall
Longest Consecutive
 Games Streak .... 662 Garry Unger (Feb. 7/71-Apr. 8/79)

Most Goals, Season .... 54 Wayne Babych (1980-81)
Most Assists, Season ..... 73 Bernie Federko (1980-81)
Most Points, Season ..... 107 Bernie Federko (1983-84, 1984-85) (41 goals, 66 assists)
Most Pen. Mins., Season ... 306 Bob Gassoff (1975-76)
Most Points, Defenseman
 Season .... 66 Rob Ramage (1985-86) (10 goals, 56 assists)
Most Points, Center,
 Season .... 107 Bernie Federko (1983-84) (41 goals, 66 assists)
Most Points, Right Wing,
 Season .... 96 Wayne Babych (1980-81) (54 goals, 42 assists)
Most Points, Left Wing,
 Season .... 85 Chuck Lefley (1975-76) (43 goals, 42 assists)
Most Points, Rookie,
 Season .... 73 Jorgen Pettersson (1980-81) (37 goals, 36 assists)
Most Shutouts, Season ..... 8 Glenn Hall (1968-69)
Most Goals, Game .... 6 Red Berenson (Nov. 7/68)
Most Assists, Game ...... 4 Several players
Most Points, Game .... 7 Red Berenson (Nov. 7/68) Garry Unger (Mar. 13/71)

TORONTO MAPLE LEAFS

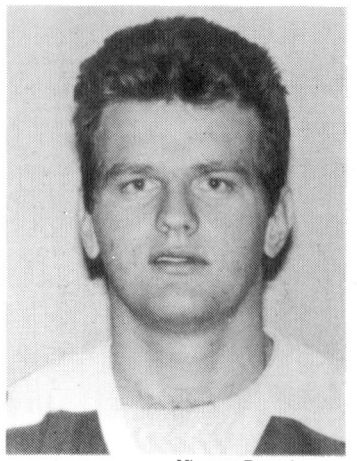

Vincent Damphousse   *Wendel Clark*

1986-87: 32w-42l-6t 70 pts. Fourth, Norris Division

1987-88 OUTLOOK: Toronto's hopes are based on a continuing trend towards eliminating defensive blunders. Showing much improved discipline last season under rookie coach John Brophy, the Maple Leafs reduced their goals-against by 67 from 1985-86. Continued progress will depend on upgrading their power play, which was 20th in the NHL and badly requires a proficient set-up man. Off-season deals brought three big forwards to Toronto as Ed Olczyk, Al Secord and Dave Semenko will attempt to make the Leafs more formidable in the corners. The undisputed team leader is third-year pro Wendel Clark who tops the club in goals (37 last year) and spirit. Returning forwards include Russ Courtnall (73 points), fine rookie Vince Damphousse (21 goals) and Mark Osborne (22 goals). The Leafs are hopeful that skilled center Tom Fergus can shake the mysterious virus that sidelined him for the second half of last season. Veteran Borje Salming returns for a 15th season on defense and is still reliable. Al Iafrate, Todd Gill, Chris Kotsopoulos and Rick Lanz may be joined by mammoth first-round draft pick Luke Richardson (6-foot-4, 208 pounds). Goalie Ken Wregget has been exceptional in the playoffs in each of the past two years.

Upcoming Milestones

Rick Vaive — 38 goals to reach 350
Borje Salming — 30 games to reach 1,000
Wendel Clark — 29 goals to reach 100
Peter Ihnacak — 10 goals to reach 100
Greg Terrion — 3 games to reach 500

Entry Draft Selections 1987

Pick	
7	Luke Richardson
28	Daniel Marois
49	John McIntyre
71	Joe Sacco
91	Mike Eastwood
112	Damian Rhodes
133	Trevor Jobe
154	Chris Jensen
175	Brian Blad
196	Ron Bernacci
217	Ken Alexander
238	Alex Weinrich

71st NHL Season

TORONTO MAPLE LEAFS

Year-by-Year Record 1968-1987

Season	GP	Home W	L	T	Road W	L	T	Overall W	L	T	GF	GA	Pts.	Finished	Playoff Result
1986-87	80	22	14	4	10	28	2	32	42	6	286	319	70	4th, Norris Div.	Lost Div. Final
1985-86	80	16	21	3	9	27	4	25	48	7	311	386	57	4th, Norris Div.	Lost Div. Final
1984-85	80	10	28	2	10	24	6	20	52	8	253	358	48	5th, Norris Div.	Out of Playoffs
1983-84	80	17	16	7	9	29	2	26	45	9	303	287	61	5th, Norris Div.	Out of Playoffs
1982-83	80	20	15	5	8	25	7	28	40	12	293	330	68	3rd, Norris Div.	Lost Div. Semi-Final
1981-82	80	12	20	8	8	24	8	20	44	16	298	380	56	5th, Norris Div.	Out of Playoffs
1980-81	80	14	21	5	14	16	10	28	37	15	322	367	71	5th, Adams Div.	Lost Prelim. Round
1979-80	80	17	19	4	18	21	1	35	40	5	304	327	75	4th, Adams Div.	Lost Prelim. Round
1978-79	80	20	12	8	14	21	5	34	33	13	267	252	81	3rd, Adams Div.	Lost Quarter-Final
1977-78	80	21	13	6	20	16	4	41	29	10	271	237	92	3rd, Adams Div.	Lost Semi-Final
1976-77	80	18	13	9	15	19	6	33	32	15	301	285	81	3rd, Adams Div.	Lost Quarter-Final
1975-76	80	23	12	5	11	19	10	34	31	15	294	276	83	3rd, Adams Div.	Lost Quarter-Final
1974-75	80	19	12	9	12	21	7	31	33	16	280	309	78	3rd, Adams Div.	Lost Quarter-Final
1973-74	78	21	11	7	14	16	9	35	27	16	274	230	86	4th, East Div.	Lost Quarter-Final
1972-73	78	20	12	7	7	29	3	27	41	10	247	279	64	6th, East Div.	Out of Playoffs
1971-72	78	21	11	7	12	20	7	33	31	14	209	208	80	4th, East Div.	Lost Quarter-Final
1970-71	78	24	9	6	13	24	2	37	33	8	248	211	82	4th, East Div.	Lost Quarter-Final
1969-70	76	18	13	7	11	21	6	29	34	13	222	242	71	6th, East Div.	Out of Playoffs
1968-69	76	20	8	10	15	18	5	35	26	15	234	217	85	4th, East Div.	Lost Quarter-Final
1967-68	74	24	9	4	9	22	6	33	31	10	209	176	76	5th, East Div.	Out of Playoffs

Playoff History, 1927-87

Versus	Year	Series	Winner	W	L	T	GF	GA
Boston	1933	SF	Toronto	3	2		9	7
Boston	1935	SF	Toronto	3	1		7	2
Boston	1936	*QF	Toronto	2	0		8	6
Boston	1938	SF	Toronto	3	0		6	3
Boston	1939	F	Boston	1	4		6	12
Boston	1941	SF	Boston	3	4		17	15
Boston	1948	SF	Toronto	4	1		20	13
Boston	1949	SF	Toronto	4	1		16	10
Boston	1951	SF	Toronto	4	1	1	17	5
Boston	1959	SF	Toronto	4	3		20	21
Boston	1969	QF	Boston	0	4		5	24
Boston	1970	QF	Boston	1	4		10	18
Boston	1974	QF	Boston	0	4		9	17
Calgary	1979	PRE	Toronto	2	0		9	5
Chicago	1931	*QF	Chicago	0	1	1	3	4
Chicago	1932	*QF	Toronto	1	1		6	2
Chicago	1938	F	Chicago	1	3		8	10
Chicago	1940	QF	Toronto	2	0		5	3
Chicago	1962	F	Toronto	4	2		18	15
Chicago	1967	SF	Toronto	4	2		18	14
Chicago	1986	DSF	Toronto	3	0		18	8
Detroit	1929	*QF	Toronto	2	0		7	2
Detroit	1934	SF	Detroit	2	3		12	11
Detroit	1936	F	Detroit	1	3		11	18
Detroit	1939	SF	Toronto	2	1		10	8
Detroit	1940	SF	Toronto	2	0		5	2
Detroit	1942	F	Toronto	4	3		25	19
Detroit	1943	SF	Detroit	2	4		17	10
Detroit	1945	F	Toronto	4	3		9	9
Detroit	1947	SF	Toronto	4	1		18	14
Detroit	1948	F	Toronto	4	0		18	7
Detroit	1949	F	Toronto	4	0		12	5
Detroit	1950	SF	Detroit	3	4		11	10
Detroit	1952	SF	Detroit	0	4		3	13
Detroit	1954	SF	Detroit	1	4		8	15
Detroit	1955	SF	Detroit	0	4		6	14
Detroit	1956	SF	Detroit	1	4		10	14
Detroit	1960	SF	Toronto	4	2		20	16
Detroit	1961	SF	Detroit	1	4		8	15
Detroit	1963	F	Toronto	4	1		17	10
Detroit	1964	F	Toronto	4	3		22	17
Detroit	1987	DF	Detroit	3	4		18	20
Los Angeles	1975	PRE	Toronto	2	1		7	6
Los Angeles	1978	PRE	Toronto	2	0		11	3
Minnesota	1980	PRE	Minnesota	0	3		8	17
Minnesota	1983	DSF	Minnesota	1	3		18	18
Montreal	1944	SF	Montreal	1	4		6	23
Montreal	1945	SF	Toronto	4	2		15	21
Montreal	1947	F	Toronto	4	2		13	13
Montreal	1951	F	Toronto	4	1		13	10
Montreal	1959	F	Montreal	1	4		12	18
Montreal	1960	F	Montreal	0	4		5	15
Montreal	1963	SF	Toronto	4	1		14	6
Montreal	1964	SF	Toronto	4	3		17	14
Montreal	1965	SF	Montreal	2	4		14	17
Montreal	1966	SF	Montreal	0	4		6	15
Montreal	1967	F	Toronto	4	2		17	16
Montreal	1978	SF	Montreal	0	4		6	16
Montreal	1979	QF	Montreal	0	4		10	19
NY Islanders	1978	QF	Toronto	4	3		17	8
NY Islanders	1981	PRE	NY Islanders	0	3		4	20
NY Rangers	1929	SF	NY Rangers	0	2		1	3
NY Rangers	1932	F	Toronto	3	0		18	10
NY Rangers	1933	F	NY Rangers	1	3		5	11
NY Rangers	1937	QF	NY Rangers	0	2		1	5
NY Rangers	1940	F	NY Rangers	2	4		11	14
NY Rangers	1942	SF	Toronto	4	2		13	12
NY Rangers	1962	SF	Toronto	4	2		22	15
NY Rangers	1971	QF	NY Rangers	2	4		15	16
Philadelphia	1975	QF	Philadelphia	0	4		8	15
Philadelphia	1976	QF	Philadelphia	3	4		23	33
Philadelphia	1975	QF	Philadelphia	2	4		18	19
Pittsburgh	1976	PRE	Toronto	2	1		8	3
Pittsburgh	1977	PRE	Toronto	2	1		13	10
St. Louis	1986	DSF	St. Louis	3	4		22	24
St. Louis	1987	DSF	Toronto	4	2		15	11

* Total-goals series

1986-87 Scoring

Regular Season *–Rookie

Pos	#	Player	Team	GP	G	A	Pts	+/−	PIM
F	9	Russ Courtnall	TOR	79	29	44	73	20−	90
F	22	Rick Vaive	TOR	73	32	34	66	12	61
F	32	Steve Thomas	TOR	78	35	27	62	3−	114
F	17	Wendel Clark	TOR	80	37	23	60	23−	271
F	11	Gary Leeman	TOR	80	21	31	52	26−	66
F	19	Tom Fergus	TOR	57	21	28	49	1	57
F	12	Mark Osborne	NYR	58	17	15	32	15−	101
			TOR	16	5	10	15	1−	12
			TOTAL	74	22	25	47	16−	113
F	10	*Vincent Damphouse	TOR	80	21	25	46	6−	26
F	18	Peter Ihnacak	TOR	58	12	27	39	5	16
D	23	Todd Gill	TOR	61	4	27	31	3−	92
D	33	Al Iafrate	TOR	80	9	21	30	18−	55
D	4	Rick Lanz	VAN	17	1	6	7	13−	10
			TOR	44	2	19	21	4	32
			TOTAL	61	3	25	28	9−	42
F	8	Mike Allison	TOR	71	7	16	23	1	66
D	21	Borje Salming	TOR	56	4	16	20	17	42
F	14	Miroslav Frycer	TOR	29	7	8	15	15−	28
F	7	Greg Terrion	TOR	67	7	8	15	5−	6
F	29	Brad Smith	TOR	47	5	7	12	15	172
D	26	Chris Kotsopoulos	TOR	43	2	10	12	8	75
F	27	*Miroslav Ihnacak	TOR	34	6	5	11	3	12
F	16	Ken Yaremchuk	TOR	20	3	8	11	0	16
F	24	Dan Daoust	TOR	33	4	3	7	0	35
D	25	Bill Root	TOR	34	3	3	6	9−	37
D	15	Bob McGill	TOR	56	1	4	5	2−	103
G	31	Ken Wregget	TOR	56	0	4	4	0	20
F	3	Daryl Evans	TOR	2	1	0	1	2−	0
D	2	*Ted Fauss	TOR	15	0	1	1	4	11
D	20	Terry Johnson	TOR	48	0	1	1	5−	104
G	1	Tim Bernhardt	TOR	1	0	0	0	0	0
F	28	*Derek Laxdal	TOR	2	0	0	0	1−	7
F	28	*Val James	TOR	4	0	0	0	0	14
D	2	Jerome Dupont	TOR	13	0	0	0	5−	23
F	28	*Kevin Maguire	TOR	17	0	0	0	6	74
G	30	Allan Bester	TOR	36	0	0	0	0	8

Playoffs

Pos	#	Player	Team	GP	G	A	Pts	+/−	PIM
F	17	Wendel Clark	TOR	13	6	5	11	6	38
F	8	Mike Allison	TOR	13	3	5	8	0	15
F	24	Dan Daoust	TOR	13	5	2	7	2−	42
F	9	Russ Courtnall	TOR	13	3	4	7	1	11
F	22	Rick Vaive	TOR	13	4	2	6	1−	23
F	18	Peter Ihnacak	TOR	13	2	4	6	3	9
F	10	*Vincent Damphousse	TOR	12	1	5	6	3−	8
F	32	Steve Thomas	TOR	13	2	3	5	4−	13
D	23	Todd Gill	TOR	13	2	2	4	2	42
F	12	Mark Osborne	TOR	9	1	3	4	1	6
D	33	Al Iafrate	TOR	13	1	3	4	1−	11
D	4	Rick Lanz	TOR	13	1	3	4	2	27
D	21	Borje Salming	TOR	13	0	3	3	1−	14
F	29	Brad Smith	Tor	11	1	1	2	2−	24
F	7	Greg Terrion	TOR	13	0	2	2	1−	14
D	25	Bill Root	TOR	13	1	0	1	0	12
F	19	Tom Fergus	TOR	2	0	1	1	1	2
F	11	Gary Leeman	TOR	5	0	1	1	1	14
G	31	Den Wregget	TOR	13	0	1	1	0	4
G	30	Allan Bester	TOR	1	0	0	0	0	0
F	3	Daryl Evans	TOR	1	0	0	0	0	0
F	27	*Miroslav Ihnacak	TOR	1	0	0	0	0	0
F	28	*Kevin Maguire	TOR	1	0	0	0	0	0
F	16	Wes Jarvis	TOR	2	0	0	0	0	2
D	20	Terry Johnson	TOR	2	0	0	0	2−	0
D	15	BobMcGill	TOR	4	0	0	0	1−	0
F	16	Ken Yaremchuk	TOR	6	0	0	0	0	0
D	26	Chris Kotsopoulos	TOR	7	0	0	0	0	14

Individual

Most Seasons	20	George Armstrong
Most Games	1,187	George Armstrong
Most Goals, Career	389	Darryl Sittler
Most Assists, Career	527	Darryl Sittler
Most Points, Career	916	Darryl Sittler (389 goals, 527 assists)
Most Pen. Mins., Career	1,670	Dave Williams
Most Shutouts, Career	62	Turk Broda
Longest Consecutive Games Streak	486	Tim Horton (Feb. 11/61-Feb. 4/68)
Most Goals, Season	54	Rick Vaive (1981-82)

Club Records

Team

(Figures in brackets for season records are games played; records for fewest points, wins, ties, losses, goals, goals against are for 70 or more games)

Most Points	95	1950-51 (70)
Most Wins	41	1950-51 (70)
		1977-78 (80)
Most Ties	22	1954-55 (70)
Most Losses	52	1984-85 (80)
Most Goals	322	1980-81 (80)
Most Goals Against	387	1983-84 (80)
Fewest Points	48	1984-85 (80)
Fewest Wins	20	1981-82, 1984-85 (80)
Fewest Ties	5	1979-80 (80)
Fewest Losses	16	1950-51 (70)
Fewest Goals	146	1954-55 (70)
Fewest Goals Against	*131	1953-54 (70)

* NHL Record

Coach

BROPHY, JOHN
Coach, Toronto Maple Leafs. Born in Antigonish. N.S., January 20, 1933.

Named to the Toronto Maple Leafs' head coaching post on July 3, 1986, the 54-year-old Brophy rallied the Leafs to their best regular-season finish (70 points) since 1980-81 and their highest win total (32) since 1979-80.

Although he never made it to the NHL as a player, Brophy did compile one of the longest playing careers in minor league history, lasting 21 seasons from the mid-50's to mid-70's. Immediately following his retirement, he applied his wealth of hockey knowledge to the technical side of the game as an assistant coach, first with the Hampton club in the Southern League and then with the Cincinnati Stingers and Birmingham Bulls in the World Hockey Association.

In 1978-79, Brophy took on the head coaching responsibilities at Birmingham and won Coach-of-the-Year honors. Among his disciples that season were several future NHL stars, including Michel Goulet, Rick Vaive and Craig Hartsburg. Although the city's WHA team folded, Brophy stayed in Birmingham to pilot the Calgary Flames' CHL affiliate for the 1979-80 and 1980-81 seasons. In 1981-82, the Montreal Canadiens lured him back to his native Nova Scotia, where he coached the AHL's Voyageurs through 1983-84.

In 1984-85, Brophy joined the Toronto organization as an assistant coach before moving on in 1985-86 as head coach of the Leaf's AHL affiliate St. Catharines Saints.

VANCOUVER CANUCKS

Patrik Sundstrom

1986-87: 29w-43L-8T 66 PTS. Fifth, Smythe Division

1987-88 OUTLOOK: After missing the playoffs last spring, the Canucks' new management team of general manager Pat Quinn and coach Bob McCammon will attempt to expand Vancouver's nucleus of talent and make the club competitive in the tough Smythe Division. The Canucks have scoring punch up front with Tony Tanti (41 goals), Petri Skriko (33 goals), Barry Pederson (76 points) and Patrik Sundstrom (71 points). Add Jim Sandlak, Stan Smyl, Rich Sutter and Raimo Summanen and the Canucks could turn on many a red light. However, Vancouver lacks depth on defense. Doug Lidster is still a youngster, but has developed into a fine defenseman. Michel Petit, Garth Butcher, Jim Benning and Dave Richter are still question marks. Richard Brodeur will be in his 16th season of professional hockey, yet can still handle himself in the nets. The back-up job will be fought over by Frank Caprice and Troy Gamble.

Upcoming Milestones

Tony Tanti – 27 goals to reach 200
Stan Smyl – 10 goals to reach 250
Barry Pederson – 13 goals to reach 200
Petri Skriko – 8 goals to reach 100

Fan Club

Vancouver Canucks Booster Club
Tracy Graham
225 West 17th. St. North
Vancouver, B.C. V7M 1V7

Entry Draft Selections 1987

Pick	
24	Rob Murphy
45	Steve Veilleux
66	Doug Torrel
87	Sean Fabian
108	Gary Valk
129	Todd Fanning
150	Viktor Tumineu
171	Craig Daly
192	John Fletcher
213	Roger Hansson
233	Neil Eisenhut
234	Matt Evo

CAMPBELL CONFERENCE

18th NHL Season

Year-by-Year Record 1971-1987

Season	GP	Home W	L	T	Road W	L	T	W	L	T	GF	GA	Overall Pts.	Finished	Playoff Result
1986-87	80	17	19	4	12	24	4	29	43	8	282	314	66	5th, Smythe Div.	Out of Playoffs
1985-86	80	17	18	5	6	26	8	23	44	13	282	333	59	4th, Smythe Div.	Lost Div. Semi-Final
1984-85	80	15	21	4	10	25	5	25	46	9	284	401	59	5th, Smythe Div.	Out of Playoffs
1983-84	80	20	16	4	12	23	5	32	39	9	306	328	73	3rd, Smythe Div.	Lost Div. Semi-Final
1982-83	80	20	12	8	10	23	7	30	35	15	303	309	75	3rd, Smythe Div.	Lost Div. Semi-Final
1981-82	80	20	8	12	10	25	5	30	33	17	290	286	77	2nd, Smythe Div.	Lost Stanley Cup Final
1980-81	80	17	12	11	11	20	9	28	32	20	289	301	76	3rd, Smythe Div.	Lost Prelim. Round
1979-80	80	14	17	9	13	20	7	27	37	16	256	281	70	3rd, Smythe Div.	Lost Prelim. Round
1978-79	80	15	18	7	10	24	6	25	42	13	217	291	63	2nd, Smythe Div.	Lost Prelim. Round
1977-78	80	13	15	12	7	28	5	20	43	17	239	320	57	3rd, Smythe Div.	Out of Playoffs
1976-77	80	13	21	6	12	21	7	25	42	13	235	294	63	4th, Smythe Div.	Out of Playoffs
1975-76	80	22	11	7	11	21	8	33	32	15	271	272	81	2nd, Smythe Div.	Lost Prelim. Round
1974-75	80	23	12	5	15	20	5	38	32	10	271	254	86	1st, Smythe Div.	Lost Quarter-Final
1973-74	78	14	18	7	10	25	4	24	43	11	224	296	59	7th, East Div.	Out of Playoffs
1972-73	78	17	18	4	5	29	5	22	47	9	233	339	53	7th, East Div.	Out of Playoffs
1971-72	78	14	20	5	6	30	3	20	50	8	203	297	48	7th, East Div.	Out of Playoffs
1970-71	78	17	18	4	7	28	4	24	46	8	229	296	56	6th, East Div.	Out of Playoffs

Playoff History, 1971-87

Versus	Year	Series	Winner	W	L	T	GF	GA
Buffalo	1980	PRE	Buffalo	1	3		7	15
Buffalo	1981	PRE	Buffalo	0	3		7	13
Calgary	1982	DSF	Vancouver	3	0		8	5
Calgary	1983	DSF	Calgary	1	3		14	17
Calgary	1984	DSF	Calgary	1	3		13	14
Chicago	1982	SF	Vancouver	4	1		18	13
Edmonton	1986	DSF	Edmonton	0	3		5	17
Los Angeles	1982	DF	Vancouver	4	1		19	14
Montreal	1975	QF	Montreal	1	4		9	20
NY Islanders	1976	PRE	NY Islanders	0	2		4	8
NY Islanders	1982	F	NY Islanders	0	4		10	18
Philadelphia	1979	PRE	Philadelphia	1	2		9	15

Club Records

Team

(Figures in brackets for season records are games played; records for fewest points, wins, ties, losses, goals, goals against are for 70 or more games)

Most Points	86	1974-75 (80)
Most Wins	38	1974-75 (80)
Most Ties	20	1980-81 (80)
Most Losses	50	1971-72 (78)
Most Goals	306	1983-84 (80)
Most Goals Against	401	1984-85 (80)
Fewest Points	48	1971-72 (78)
Fewest Wins	20	1971-72 (78)
Fewest Ties	8	1970-71 (78)
		1971-72 (78)

continued

Coach

MCCAMMON, BOB
Coach, Vancouver Canucks. Born in Kenora, Ont., April 14, 1941.

On June 22, 1987, the Vancouver Canucks named Bob McCammon as the club's new head coach for the 1987-88 season. McCammon joins Vancouver with impressive coaching credentials.

After retiring from his 11-year minor league playing career with the Port Huron Flags in 1972-73, McCammon remained with the IHL club as coach through 1976-77. The following season, he joined the Philadelphia Flyers' organization as coach of the Maine Mariners, their top farm club in the AHL, leading them to the AHL's Calder Cup championship and earning Coach-of-the-Year honors.

In 1978-79, the Flyers named McCammon to their head coaching position and then guided the NHL team to a 22-17-11 record in 50 games before returning to Maine in mid-season. In each of the next three years, he piloted the Mariners to 40 or more wins and again won AHL Coach-of-the-Year honors in 1980-81.

Late in the 1981-82 season, McCammon worked his way back to the Flyers as head coach and was promoted to general manager/head coach in 1983-84. In 218 NHL games with Philadelphia, he compiled a record of 119-68-31 for a .617 winning percentage.

In 1985-86, McCammon was named to an assistant coaching position with the Edmonton Oilers and last year became that club's Head of Player Development.

VANCOUVER CANUCKS

Fewest Losses..........32	1974-75 (80) 1975-76 (80) 1980-81 (80)
Fewest Goals..........203	1971-72 (78)
Fewest Goals Against.....254	1974-75 (80)
Longest Winning Streak	
Over-all...............5	Mar. 2-12/83
Home................8	Feb. 27/83- Mar. 21/83
Away.................3	Eight times
Longest Undefeated Streak	
Over-all..............10	Mar. 5-25/77 (5 wins, 5 ties)
Home................12	Oct. 29- Dec. 17/74 (11 wins, 1 tie)
Away.................5	Three times
Longest Losing Streak	
Over-all...............9	Three times
Home.................6	Dec. 18/70- Jan. 20/71 Nov. 3-18/78
Away................12	Nov. 28/81- Feb. 6/82
Longest Winless Streak	
Over-all..............13	Nov. 9- Dec. 7/73 (10 losses, 3 ties) Dec. 18/70- Feb. 6/71 (10 losses, 1 tie)
Home................11	
Away................20	Jan. 2/86- Apr. 2/86 (14 losses, 6 ties)
Most Shutouts, Season......8	1974-75 (80)
Most Pen. Mins., Season............1,917	1986-87 (80)
Most Goals, Game........11	Mar. 28/71 (Cal. 5 at Van. 11) Nov. 25/86 (Van. 11 at L.A. 5)

1986-87 Scoring

Regular Season
*–Rookie

Pos	#	Player	Team	GP	G	A	Pts	+/−	PIM
F	9	Tony Tanti	VAN	77	41	38	79	5	84
F	7	Barry Pederson	VAN	79	24	52	76	13−	50
F	26	Petri Skriko	VAN	76	33	41	74	4−	44
F	17	Patrick Sundstrom	VAN	72	29	42	71	9	40
D	3	Doug Lidster	VAN	80	12	51	63	35−	40
F	12	Stan Smyl	VAN	66	20	23	43	20−	84
F	15	Rich Sutter	VAN	74	20	22	42	17	113
F	20	Steve Tambellini	VAN	72	16	20	36	22−	14
F	19	*Jim Sandlak	VAN	78	15	21	36	4−	66
F	14	Raimo Summanen	EDM	48	10	7	17	1−	15
			VAN	10	4	4	8	1−	0
			TOTAL	58	14	11	25	2−	15
D	24	Michel Petit	VAN	69	12	13	25	5−	131
F	16	Dan Hodgson	VAN	43	9	13	22	9−	25
F	10	Brent Peterson	VAN	69	7	15	22	14−	77
D	5	Garth Butcher	VAN	70	5	15	20	12−	207
F	22	Dave Lowry	VAN	70	8	10	18	23−	176
D	6	Dave Richter	VAN	78	2	15	17	2−	172
F	25	*David Bruce	VAN	50	9	7	16	2−	109
D	4	Jim Benning	TOR	5	0	0	0	0	4
			VAN	54	2	11	13	9	40
			TOTAL	59	2	11	13	9	44
F	18	Marc Crawford	VAN	21	0	3	3	8−	67
F	27	*John LeBlanc	VAN	2	1	0	1	1	0
F	21	Craig Coxe	VAN	15	1	0	1	3−	31
G	1	*Wendell Young	VAN	8	0	1	1	0	0
D	2	Craig Levie	VAN	9	0	1	1	3	13
D	32	*Robin Bartel	VAN	40	0	1	1	2	14
G	31	*Troy Gamble	VAN	1	0	0	0	0	0
D	2	*Jim Agnew	VAN	4	0	0	0	0	0
F	8	Taylor Hall	VAN	4	0	0	0	2−	0
D	29	Glen Cochrane	VAN	14	0	0	0	0	52
G	30	Frank Caprice	VAN	25	0	0	0	0	9
G	35	Richard Brodeur	VAN	53	0	0	0	0	2

Individual

Most Seasons...........10	Dennis Kearns Harold Snepsts
Most Games..........683	Harold Snepsts
Most Goals, Career......240	Stan Smyl
Most Assists, Career.....353	Thomas Gradin
Most Points, Career.....581	Stan Smyl (240 goals, 341 assists)
Most Pen. Mins., Career..1,352	Harold Snepsts
Most Shutouts, Career......11	Gary Smith
Longest Consecutive Games Streak........437	Don Lever (Oct. 7/72-Jan. 14/78)
Most Goals, Season.......45	Tony Tanti (1983-84)
Most Assists, Deason.....62	André Boudrias (1974-75)
Most Points, Season......91	Patrik Sundstrom (1983-84) (38 goals, 53 assists)
Most Pen. Mins., Season...343	Dave Williams (1980-81)
Most Points, Defenseman, Season..............63	Doug Lidster (1986-87) (12 goals, 51 assists)
Most Points, Center, Season..............91	Patrik Sundstrom (1983-84) (38 goals, 53 assists)
Most Points, Right Wing, Season..............88	Stan Smyl (1982-83) (38 goals, 50 assists)
Most Points, Left Wing, Season..............81	Darcy Rota (1982-83) (42 goals, 398 assists)
Most Points, Rookie, Season..............60	Ivan Hlinka (1981-82) (23 goals, 37 assists)
Most Shutouts, Season......6	Gary Smith (1974-75)
Most Goals, Game.........4	Several players
Most Assists, Game........6	Patrik Sundstrom (Feb. 29/84)
Most Points, Game.........7	Patrik Sundstrom (Feb. 29/84)

* NHL Record.

WASHINGTON CAPITALS

Scott Stevens and Bob Gould

1986-87: 38w-32L-10T 86 PTS. Second, Patrick Division

1987-88 OUTLOOK: After another disappointing playoff which culminated with a four overtime periods loss to the Islanders in the seventh game of the first round, the Capitals shook up the club a bit by obtaining feisty Dale Hunter from Quebec. The Caps also received goaltender Clint Malarchuk, while parting with forwards Alan Haworth and Gaetan Duchesne. A healthy Hunter should provide the spark the Caps need to complement their balanced scoring and excellent defensive play. Mike Gartner (41 goals) and Mike Ridley (31 goals) are Washington's top offensive guns, while Dave Christian (23 goals), Bob Gould (23 goals) and Craig Laughlin (22 goals) are also adequate around the net. The return of Bengt Gustafsson, who spent a year in Europe, makes the Caps forwards probably the most diligent two-way crew in the League. Defenseman Larry Murphy (81 points) led the club in scoring last season and also improved defensively. He's joined on the backline by Scott Stevens (61 points), team leader Rod Langway, Kevin Hatcher and Garry Galley returning the team to the defensive posture that made them an NHL power. Although Pete Peeters (3.21) has had his problems, along with Malarchuk the Caps have retained their steady goaltending tandem.

Upcoming Milestones

Dave Christian — 2 goals to reach 200
Rod Langway — 44 games to reach 700
Mike Gartner — 27 goals to reach 350
Gaetan Duchesne — 13 goals to reach 100

Fan Club

Washington Capitals Fan Club, Ltd.
P.O. Box 306
Lanham, MD 20706

Entry Draft Selections 1987

Pick
36 Jeff Ballantyne
57 Steve Maltais
78 Tyler Larter
99 Pat Beauchesne
120 Rich Defreitas
141 Devon Oleniuk
162 Thomas Sjogren
204 Chris Clarke
225 Milos Vanik
240 Dan Brettschneider
246 Ryan Kummu

14th NHL Season

WASHINGTON CAPITALS

Year-by-Year Record 1974-1987

Season	GP	Home W-L-T	Road W-L-T	Overall W-L-T	GF	GA	Pts.	Finished	Playoff Result
1986-87	80	22 15 3	16 17 7	38 32 10	285	278	86	2nd, Patrick Div.	Lost Div. Semi-Final
1985-86	80	30 8 2	20 15 5	50 23 7	315	272	107	2nd, Patrick Div.	Lost Div. Final
1984-85	80	27 11 2	19 14 7	46 25 9	322	240	101	2nd, Patrick Div.	Lost Div. Semi-Final
1983-84	80	26 11 3	22 16 2	48 27 5	308	226	101	2nd, Patrick Div.	Lost Div. Final
1982-83	80	22 12 6	17 13 10	39 25 16	306	283	94	3rd, Patrick Div.	Lost Div. Semi-Final
1981-82	80	16 16 8	10 25 5	26 41 13	319	338	65	5th, Patrick Div.	Out of Playoffs
1980-81	80	16 17 7	10 19 11	26 36 18	286	317	70	5th, Patrick Div.	Out of Playoffs
1979-80	80	20 14 6	7 26 7	27 40 13	261	293	67	5th, Patrick Div.	Out of Playoffs
1978-79	80	15 19 6	9 22 9	24 41 15	273	338	63	4th, Norris Div.	Out of Playoffs
1977-78	80	10 23 7	7 26 7	17 49 14	195	321	48	5th, Norris Div.	Out of Playoffs
1976-77	80	17 15 8	7 27 6	24 42 14	221	307	62	4th, Norris Div.	Out of Playoffs
1975-76	80	6 26 8	5 33 2	11 59 10	224	394	32	5th, Norris Div.	Out of Playoffs
1974-75	80	7 28 5	1 39 0	8 67 5	181	446	21	5th, Norris Div.	Out of Playoffs

Playoff History, 1975-87

Versus	Year	Series	Winner	W	L	T	GF	GA
NY Islanders	1983	DSF	NY Islanders	1	3		11	19
NY Islanders	1984	DF	NY Islanders	1	4		13	20
NY Islanders	1985	DSF	NY Islanders	2	3		12	14
NY Islanders	1986	DSF	Washington	4	2		11	4
NY Islanders	1987	DSF	NY Islanders	3	4		18	19
NY Rangers	1986	DF	NY Rangers	2	4		25	20
Philadelphia	1984	DSF	Washington	3	0		15	5

Club Records

Team

(Figures in brackets for season records are games played; records for fewest points, wins, ties, losses, goals, goals against are for 70 or more games)

Most Points	107	1985-86 (80)
Most Wins	50	1985-86 (80)
Most Ties	18	1980-81 (80)
Most Losses	*67	1974-75 (80)
Most Goals	322	1984-85 (80)
Most Goals Against	*446	1974-75 (80)
Fewest Points	*21	1974-75 (80)
Fewest Wins	*8	1974-75 (80)
Fewest Ties	5	1974-75 (80)
		1983-84 (80)
Fewest Losses	23	1985-86 (80)
Fewest Goals	181	1974-75 (80)
Fewest Goals Against	226	1983-84 (80)

Longest Winning Streak
Over-all ....10 Jan. 27-Feb. 18/84
Home ....7 Jan. 17-Feb. 11/84
Away ....6 Feb. 26-Apr. 1/84

Longest Undefeated Streak
Over-all ....14 Nov. 12-Dec. 23/82 (9 wins, 5 ties) Jan. 17-Feb. 18/84 (13 wins, 1 tie)
Home ....12 Nov. 7/82-Dec. 14/82 (9 wins, 3 ties)
Away ....10 Nov. 24/82-Jan. 8/83

Longest Losing Streak
Over-all ....*17 Feb. 18-Mar. 26/75
Home ....*11 Feb. 18-Mar. 30/75
Away ....*37 Oct. 9/74-Mar. 26/75

Longest Winless Streak
Over-all ....25 Nov. 29/75-Jan. 21/76 (22 losses, 3 ties)
Home ....14 Dec. 3/75-Jan. 21/76 (11 losses, 3 ties)
Away ....*37 Oct. 9/74-Mar. 26/75 (37 losses)

continued

Coach

MURRAY, BRYAN CLARENCE
Coach, Washington Capitals. Born in Shawville, Que., December 5, 1942.

In less than six full seasons behind the Washington Capitals' bench, Bryan Murray has achieved more success than any other coach in the team's 13-year history. After a partial season with the club in 1981-82, Murray led the Caps in 1982-83 to two franchise firsts – a winning season and a playoff berth. Since that time, Washington has become one of the NHL top teams, finishing with over 100 points in three of the last four years, and Murray has become one of the League's top coaches, having earned the Jack Adams Award in 1983-84 as Coach-of-the-Year.

A graduate of McGill University, Murray became the school's athletic director and hockey coach from 1972-73 to 1975-76, after which he returned to coach in his hometown of Shawville, Quebec. In 1979-80, he took over the last-place Regina Pats and carried the team to the WHL championship. His one-year success in Regina translated into a professional coaching job in 1980-81 with the Capitals' AHL farm team, the Hershey Bears, whom he guided to their best season in over 40 years. That first-year effort netted him the Hockey News Minor League Coach-of-the-Year honors. Although he began the 1981-82 campaign in Hershey, Murray was promoted to Washington on November 11, 1981.

1986-87 Scoring

Regular Season
*—Rookie

Pos	#	Player	Team	GP	G	A	Pts	+/−	PIM
D	8	Larry Murphy	WSH	80	23	58	81	25	39
F	11	Mike Gartner	WSH	78	41	32	73	1	61
F	17	Mike Ridley	NYR	38	16	20	36	10−	20
			WSH	40	15	19	34	1−	20
			Total	78	31	39	70	11−	40
D	3	Scott Stevens	WSH	77	10	51	61	13	283
F	18	Craig Laughlin	WSH	80	22	30	52	3−	67
F	14	Gaetan Duchesne	WSH	74	17	35	52	18	53
F	27	Dave Christian	WSH	76	23	27	50	5−	8
F	23	Bob Gould	WSH	78	23	27	50	18	74
F	22	Greg Adams	WSH	67	14	30	44	9	184
F	20	*Michal Pivonka	WSH	73	18	25	43	19−	41
F	10	Kelly Miller	NYR	38	6	14	20	5−	22
			WSH	39	10	12	22	10	26
			Total	77	16	26	42	5	48
F	15	Alan Haworth	WSH	50	25	16	41	3	43
D	12	Garry Galley	L.A.	30	5	11	16	9−	57
			WSH	18	1	10	11	3	10
			Total	48	6	21	27	6−	67
D	5	Rod Langway	WSH	78	2	25	27	11	53
D	4	Kevin Hatcher	WSH	78	8	16	24	29−	144
F	32	Lou Franceschetti	WSH	75	12	9	21	9−	127
F	9	Dave Jensen	WSH	46	8	8	16	10−	12
D	17	John Blum	WSH	66	2	8	10	1	133
D	19	Greg Smith	WSH	45	0	9	9	6−	31
D	6	John Barrett	WSH	55	2	2	4	16−	43
G	1	Pete Peeters	WSH	37	0	4	4	0	16
F	12	Gary Sampson	WSH	25	1	2	3	9−	4
F	24	*Jeff Greenlaw	WSH	22	0	3	3	2	44
F	26	*Yvon Corriveau	WSH	17	1	1	2	4−	24
F	29	*Ed Kastelic	WSH	23	1	1	2	3−	83
D	30	*Paul Cavallini	WSH	6	0	2	2	4−	8
F	21	Stephen Leach	WSH	15	1	0	1	4−	6
D	38	*Yves Beaudoin	WSH	6	0	0	0	4−	5
F	25	Grant Martin	WSH	9	0	0	0	1−	4
F	37	*Jim Thomson	WSH	10	0	0	0	2−	35
F	25	Bob Crawford	NYR	3	0	0	0	1−	2
			WSH	12	0	0	0	0	0
			Total	15	0	0	0	1−	2
G	31	*Bob Mason	WSH	45	0	0	0	0	0

Playoffs

Pos	#	Player	Team	GP	G	A	Pts	+/−	PIM
F	11	Mike Gartner	WSH	7	4	3	7	0	14
D	3	Scott Stevens	WSH	7	0	5	5	4	19
F	10	Kelly Miller	WSH	7	2	2	4	2	0
D	8	Larry Murphy	WSH	7	2	2	4	3	6
F	22	Greg Adams	WSH	7	1	3	4	0	38
F	27	Dave Christian	WSH	7	1	3	4	1	6
F	14	Gaetan Duchesne	WSH	7	3	0	3	3	14
F	17	Mike Ridley	WSH	7	2	1	3	5−	6
F	15	Alan Haworth	WSH	6	0	3	3	2	7
F	23	Bob Gould	WSH	7	0	3	3	3	8
F	20	*Michal Pivonka	WSH	7	1	1	2	2	2
F	25	Grant Martin	WSH	1	1	0	1	1	2
F	29	*Ed Kastelic	WSH	5	1	0	1	1	13
D	4	Kevin Hatcher	WSH	7	1	0	1	2−	20
D	17	John Blum	WSH	6	0	1	1	2−	4
D	5	Rod Langway	WSH	7	0	1	1	0	2
F	18	Craig Laughlin	WSH	1	0	0	0	0	0
D	12	Gary Galley	WSH	2	0	0	0	0	0
G	1	Pete Peeters	WSH	3	0	0	0	0	2
G	31	*Bob Mason	WSH	4	0	0	0	0	0
F	32	Lou Franceschetti	WSH	7	0	0	0	4−	23
F	9	Dave Jensen	WSH	7	0	0	0	2−	2
D	19	Greg Smith	WSH	7	0	0	0	1	11

Individual

Most Seasons	8	Mike Gartner
Most Games	622	Mike Gartner,
Most Goals, Career	323	Mike Gartner
Most Assists, Career	330	Mike Gartner
Most Points, Career	653	Mike Gartner (282 goals, 298 assists)
Most Pen. Mins., Career	1,067	Scott Stevens
Most Shutouts, Career	7	Al Jensen
Longest Consecutive Games Streak	422	Bob Carpenter
Most Goals, Season	60	Dennis Maruk (1981-82)
Most Assists, Season	76	Dennis Maruk (1981-82)
Most Points, Season	136	Dennis Maruk (1981-82) (60 goals, 76 assists)
Most Pen. Mins., Season	285	Scott Stevens (1986-87)
Most Points, Defenseman, Season	81	Larry Murphy (1986-87) (23 goals, 53 assists) Scott Stevens (1984-85) (21 goals, 44 assists)
Most Points, Center, Season	136	Dennis Maruk (1981-82) (60 goals, 76 assists)
Most Points, Right Wing, Season	102	Mike Gartner (1984-85) (50 goals, 52 assists)
Most Points, Left Wing, Season	87	Ryan Walter (1981-82) (38 goals, 49 assists)
Most Points, Rookie, Season	67	Bobby Carpenter (1981-82) (32 goals, 35 assists) Chris Valentine (1981-82) (30 goals, 37 assists)
Most Shutouts, Season	4	Al Jensen, Pat Riggin (1983-84)
Most Goals, Game	5	Bengt Gustafsson (Jan. 8/84)
Most Assists, Game	4	Several players
Most Points, Game	6	Several players

* NHL Record.

WINNIPEG JETS

Dale Hawerchuk

1986-87: 40w-32L-8T 88 PTS. Third, Smythe Division

1987-88 OUTLOOK: An 88 point season and a solid performance against Calgary in the opening playoff round put the Jets back on their flight path last season. Dan Maloney vied for top coaching honors as he led the Jets back from their disastrous 1985-86 campaign which saw them dip to 59 points from 96 in 1984-85. Still they must get past Edmonton. The guy who leads the way is captain Dale Hawerchuk, who could be a Hart Trophy winner in any but the Gretzky era. Yet he may have to make some adjustments: One linemate, Brian Mullen, has been dealt to the Rangers and his other, Paul MacLean, is the subject of trade rumors. MacLean is a tough, big scorer who, along with Thomas Steen, Gilles Hamel and Doug Smail, provide the balance of Winnipeg's punch. More scoring is needed. Defensively, things look bright. Last year, two rookie goaltenders – Eldon "Pokey" Reddick and Daniel Berthiaume – teamed for the 4th best goals-against-average in the NHL. Randy Carlyle (16 goals), Tim Watters, Dave Ellett, Fredrik Olausson, Mario Marois and Jim Kyte are the stalwarts on defense. If they can generate more offense without sacrificing on defense, the Jets could challenge the Oilers for Smythe Division honors this season.

Upcoming Milestones

Dale Hawerchuk – 32 goals to reach 300
                – 37 assists to reach 400
Randy Carlyle – 25 assists to reach 400
Gilles Hamel – 31 goals to reach 150
Brian Mullen – 26 goals to reach 150

Fan Club

Winnipeg Jets Booster Club, Inc.
Lesley Cass
19 Emerald Grove Dr.
Winnipeg, Manitoba R3J 1H3

Entry Draft Selections 1987

Pick	
16	Bryan Marchment
37	Patrik Eriksson
79	Don McLennan
96	Ken Gernander
100	Darrin Amundson
121	Joe Harwell
142	Todd Hartje
163	Markku Kyllonen
184	Jim Fernholz
226	Roger Rougelot
247	Hans Goran Elo

9th NHL Season

Year-by-Year Record 1979-1987

Season	GP	Home W	L	T	Road W	L	T	Overall W	L	T	GF	GA	Pts.	Finished	Playoff Result
1986-87	80	25	12	3	15	20	5	40	32	8	279	271	8	3rd, Smythe Div.	Lost Div. Final
1985-86	80	18	19	3	8	28	4	26	47	7	295	372	59	3rd, Smythe Div.	Lost Div. Semi-Final
1984-85	80	21	13	6	22	14	4	43	27	10	358	332	96	2nd, Smythe Div.	Lost Div. Final
1983-84	80	17	15	8	14	23	3	31	38	11	340	374	73	4th, Smythe Div.	Lost Div. Semi-Final
1982-83	80	22	16	2	11	23	6	33	39	8	311	333	74	4th, Smythe Div.	Lost Div. Semi-Final
1981-82	80	18	13	9	15	20	5	33	33	14	319	332	80	2nd, Norris Div.	Lost Div. Semi-Final
1980-81	80	7	25	8	2	32	6	9	57	14	246	400	32	6th, Smythe Div.	Out of Playoffs
1979-80	80	13	19	8	7	30	3	20	49	11	214	314	51	5th, Smythe Div.	Out of Playoffs

Playoff History, 1980-87

Versus	Year	Series	Winner	W	L	T	GF	GA
Calgary	1985	DSF	Winnipeg	3	1		15	13
Calgary	1986	DSF	Calgary	0	3		8	15
Calgary	1987	DSF	Winnipeg	4	2		22	15
Edmonton	1983	DSF	Edmonton	0	3		9	14
Edmonton	1984	DSF	Edmonton	0	3		7	18
Edmonton	1985	DF	Edmonton	0	4		11	22
Edmonton	1987	DF	Edmonton	0	4		9	17
St. Louis	1982	DSF	St. Louis	1	3		13	20

Club Records

Team
(Figures in brackets for season records are games played; records for fewest points, wins, ties, losses, goals, goals against are for 70 or more games)

Most Points	96	1984-85 (80)
Most Wins	43	1984-85 (80)
Most Ties	14	1980-81 (80)
		1981-82 (80)
Most Losses	57	1980-81 (80)
Most Goals	358	1984-85 (80)
Most Goals Against	400	1980-81 (80)
Fewest Points	32	1980-81 (80)
Fewest Wins	9	1980-81 (80)
Fewest Ties	8	1982-83 (80)
Fewest Losses	27	1984-85 (80)
Fewest Goals	214	1979-80 (80)
Fewest Goals Against	271	1986-87 (80)

Longest Winning Streak
 Over-all 9   Mar. 8-27/85
 Home 6   Feb. 28-Mar. 24/82
                          Dec. 2-22/84
 Away 8   Feb. 25-Apr. 6/85

Longest Undefeated Streak
 Over-all .... 13 Mar. 8-Apr. 7/85
                          (10 wins, 3 ties)
 Home .... 11 Dec. 23/83
                          Feb. 5/84
                          (6 wins, 5 ties)
 Away 9   Feb. 25-Apr. 7/85 (8 wins, 1 tie)

Longest Losing Streak
 Over-all .... 10 Nov. 30-
                          Dec. 20/80
 Home 4   Four times
 Away 9   Dec. 26/79-
                          Jan. 20/80

Longest Winless Streak
 Over-all .... *30 Oct. 19-
                          Dec. 20/80
                          (23 losses, 7 ties)
 Home .... 14 Oct. 19-
                          Dec. 14/80
                          (9 losses, 5 ties)
 Away .... 18 Oct. 10-
                          Dec. 20/80
                          (16 losses, 2 ties)

Most Shutouts, Season 3 1981-82 (80)
Most Pen. Mins.,
 Season 1,784 1985-86 (80)
Most Goals, Game .... 12 Feb. 25/85
                              (Wpg. 12 at NYR. 5)

Coach

MALONEY, DAN
Coach, Winnipeg Jets. Born in Barrie, Ont., September 24, 1950.

On June 20, 1986, Dan Maloney began his tenure as coach of the Jets, bringing to Winnipeg the same determination that made him so successful as a player for 11 NHL seasons and as a coach with the Toronto Maple Leafs for two. That style certainly worked well in 1986-87, as his new club skated to its second best all-time finish in the regular-season, 40-32-8 and sixth overall, and to the Smythe Division Final in the playoffs.

Chicago's first choice, 14th overall, in the 1970 Amateur Draft, Maloney began his playing career with the Blackhawks in 1970-71. After spending the 1971-72 season with Dallas in the CHL, he returned to the NHL for good, playing left wing for Chicago, Los Angeles, Detroit and Toronto while compiling a 192-259-451 scoring total in 737 career games.

Following his retirement in 1981-82, Maloney stayed on with Toronto as an assistant coach for one season, and when the Maple Leafs' head coaching position opened up in 1984-85, he stepped right in. By the end of his second season behind the Toronto bench, Maloney had molded the Leafs into a contender as the team battled its way to a seventh game in the Norris Division Final.

1986-87 Scoring

Regular Season
*—Rookie

Pos	#	Player	Team	GP	G	A	Pts	+/−	PIM
F	10	Dale Hawerchuk	WPG	80	47	53	100	3	52
F	15	Paul MacLean	WPG	72	32	42	74	12	75
F	19	Brian Mullen	WPG	69	19	32	51	2−	20
F	25	Thomas Steen	WPG	75	17	33	50	7	59
F	11	Gilles Hamel	WPG	79	27	21	48	3	24
D	2	Dave Ellett	WPG	78	13	31	44	19	53
D	22	Mario Marois	WPG	79	4	40	44	1−	106
F	9	Doug Smail	WPG	78	25	18	43	18	36
D	8	Randy Carlyle	WPG	71	16	26	42	6−	93
F	16	Laurie Boschman	WPG	80	17	24	41	17−	152
F	28	Ray Neufeld	WPG	80	18	18	36	13−	105
D	4	Fredrick Olausson	WPG	72	7	29	36	3−	26
F	20	Andrew McBain	WPG	71	11	21	32	6	106
D	7	Tim Watters	WPG	63	3	13	16	5	119
F	24	Ron Wilson	WPG	80	3	13	16	10	13
D	6	Jim Kyte	WPG	72	5	5	10	4	162
D	29	*Brad Berry	WPG	52	2	8	10	6	60
F	13	*Hannu Jarvenpaa	WPG	20	1	8	9	4−	8
F	17	Jim Nill	WPG	36	3	4	7	1	52
F	27	Perry Turnbull	WPG	26	1	5	6	2−	44
F	18	Steve Rooney	MTL	2	0	0	0	0	22
			WPG	30	2	3	5	4−	57
			Total	32	2	3	5	4−	79
F	36	*Iain Duncan	WPG	6	1	2	3	1	0
F	38	*Brad Jones	WPG	4	1	0	1	2	0
F	21	*Tom Martin	WPG	11	1	0	1	1	49
F	14	*Craig Endean	WPG	2	0	1	1	1	0
F	40	*Joel Baillargeon	WPG	11	0	1	1	3−	15
F	39	*Randy Gilhen	WPG	2	0	0	0	2−	0
F	32	Peter Taglianetti	WPG	3	0	0	0	4−	12
F	12	*Peter Douris	WPG	6	0	0	0	1−	0
G	37	Steve Penney	WPG	7	0	0	0	0	7
G	30	*Daniel Berthiaume	WPG	31	0	0	0	0	2
G	33	*Eldon Reddick	WPG	48	0	0	0	0	8

Playoffs

Pos	#	Player	Team	GP	G	A	Pts	+/−	PIM
F	10	Dale Hawerchuck	WPG	10	5	8	13	4−	4
D	2	Dave Ellett	WPG	10	0	8	8	1−	2
F	15	Paul MacLean	WPG	10	5	2	7	2−	16
F	25	Thomas Steen	WPG	10	3	4	7	1−	8
F	19	Brian Mullen	WPG	9	4	2	6	2−	0
D	8	Randy Carlyle	WPG	10	1	5	6	4−	18
F	16	Laurie Boschman	WPG	10	2	3	5	2−	32
D	4	*Frederick Olausson	WPG	10	2	3	5	0	4
F	9	Doug Smail	WPG	10	4	0	4	2	10
D	22	Mario Marois	WPG	10	1	3	4	2	23
D	6	Jim Kyte	WPG	10	0	4	4	3	36
F	24	Ron Wilson	WPG	10	1	2	3	1−	0
F	11	Gilles Hamel	WPG	8	2	0	2	3−	2
F	28	Ray Neufeld	WPG	8	1	1	2	0	30
F	36	*Iain Duncan	WPG	7	0	2	2	3	6
F	20	Andrew McBain	WPG	9	0	2	2	3	10
D	29	*Brad Berry	WPG	7	0	1	1	2	14
F	27	Perry Turnbull	WPG	1	0	0	0	2−	10
F	17	Jim Nill	WPG	3	0	0	0	6−	7
G	33	*Eldon Reddick	WPG	3	0	0	0	0	0
G	30	*Daniel Berthiaume	WPG	8	0	0	0	0	0
F	18	Steve Rooney	WPG	8	0	0	0	2	34
D	7	Tim Watters	WPG	10	0	0	0	4−	21

Individual

Most Seasons .... 7 Ron Wilson
Most Games .... 479 Dale Hawerchuk
Most Goals, Career .... 268 Dale Hawerchuk
Most Assists, Career ...... 363 Dale Hawerchuk
Most Points, Career ...... 631 Dale Hawerchuk
(221 goals, 310 assists)
Most Pen. Mins., Career ... 598 Jimmy Mann
Most Shutouts, Career ...... 3 Markus Mattsson
Longest Consecutive
Games Streak .... 212 Dave Christian
(Mar. 2/80-Jan. 1/83)
Most Goals, Season .... 53 Dale Hawerchuk
(1984-85)
Most Assists, Season ...... 77 Dale Hawerchuk
(1984-85)
Most Points, Season ...... 130 Dale Hawerchuk
(1984-85)
(53 goals, 77 assists)
Most Pen. Mins., Season ... 287 Jimmy Mann
(1979-80)
Most Points, Defenseman
Season .... 74 David Babych
(1982-83)
(13 goals, 61 assists)
Most Points, Center,
Season .... 130 Dale Hawerchuk
(1984-85)
(53 goals, 77 assists)
Most Points, Right Wing,
Season .... 101 Paul Maclean
(1984-85)
(41 goals, 60 assists)

Most Points, Left Wing,
Season .... 92 Morris Lukowich
(1981-82)
(43 goals, 49 assists)
Most Points, Rookie,
Season .... 103 Dale Hawerchuk
(1981-82)
(45 goals, 58 assists)
Most Shutouts, Season ...... 2 Markus Mattsson
(1979-80)
Doug Soetaert
(1981-82)
Dan Bouchard
(1985-86)
Most Goals, Game .... 5 Willy Lindstrom
(Mar. 2/82)
Most Assists, Game .... 5 Dale Hawerchuk
(Mar. 6/84)
Most Points, Game .... 6 Willy Lindstrom
(Mar. 2/82)
Dale Hawerchuk
(Dec. 14/83)
Thomas Steen
(Oct. 24/84)

* NHL Record.

1986-87 NHL Season Highlights

October 9, 1986
The Calgary Flames and Boston Bruins inaugurated the **National Hockey League's** 70th year of competition in Game One, the 22,602nd regular-season contest in League history. Bruins' right-winger Rick Middleton scored the season's first goal, raising the all-time NHL scoring tally to 139,327.

Los Angeles Kings' center **Marcel Dionne**, the NHL's second all-time leading scorer behind Hall-of-Famer Gordie Howe (1,850 points), notched his 1600th career point in his 1,164th career game, a 4-3 loss to the St. Louis Blues. The 35-year-old Dionne assisted Luc Robitaille's first-period goal.

October 11, 1986
Edmonton Oilers' right-winger **Jari Kurri** successfully converted the first of 25 penalty shots awarded during the 1986-87 campaign. Kurri's goal helped the Oilers defeat the defending Stanley Cup champion Montreal Canadiens 5-4.

Left-winger **Wendel Clark** posted the first four-goal game of his career and the first by 11 players during the 1986-87 campaign, lifting the Toronto Maple Leafs to a 5-5 tie with the Buffalo Sabres.

October 13, 1986
Washington Capitals' right-winger **Mike Gartner** tallied his 300th career assist to extend his all-time club record. Also the Capitals' leader in career games, goals and points, Gartner posted the milestone assist in the second period before adding an overtime goal to defeat the New York Rangers 7-6.

October 16, 1986
Denis Potvin of the New York Islanders registered his 684th career assist to shatter Brad Park's career record (683) for a defenseman. Potvin, who ranks first among NHL defensemen in career goals and points as well, assisted Bryan Trottier's first-period goal to help New York down the Washington Capitals 7-4.

October 18, 1986
The **Montreal Canadiens** defeated the Winnipeg Jets 5-3 to earn their 5001st NHL point in club history. The win raised Montreal's 70-year League totals to 2174-1290-653 in 4117 games.

October 22, 1986
The **Pittsburgh Penguins** defeated the Buffalo Sabres 5-4 in overtime to win their seventh straight game from the start of the season. The streak, longest in club history, fell one short of an NHL record – eight in a row from season's start – shared by the 1934-35 Toronto Maple Leafs and 1975-76 Sabres.

October 24, 1986
Center **Gilbert Perreault** of the Buffalo Sabres scored his 508th career goal to surpass Hall-of-Famer Jean Beliveau (507) for 11th place on the all-time scoring list. However, Edmonton Oilers' center Wayne Gretzky would soon move past Perreault, dropping the Sabres' captain back a notch into 12th place.

Edmonton Oilers' center **Wayne Gretzky** posted his 874th career assist to move past Hall-of-Famer Phil Esposito (873) into fourth place on the all-time NHL list. Edmonton downed the Boston Bruins 6-2.

SEASON HIGHLIGHTS, 1986-87

October 26, 1986
Leading his team to an 8-4 win over the Winnipeg Jets, Chicago Blackhawks' center **Denis Savard** notched his 641st career point with two goals and one assist to move past Dennis Hull (640) into third place on the club's all-time scoring list. Only Hall-of-Famers Stan Mikita (1,467) and Bobby Hull (1,153) have scored more points in a Blackhawks' uniform.

October 29, 1986
New Jersey Devils' center **Kirk Muller** scored six points, including three goals and three assists, to establish a new club single-game scoring record. Muller, who led the Devils over the Pittsburgh Penguins 8-6, eclipsed the previous mark of five points he had shared with five other players.

October 31, 1986
Edmonton Oilers' center **Wayne Gretzky** recorded two goals and one assist in a 6-2 win over the Vancouver Canucks to move past Hall-of-Famer Johnny Bucyk (1,369) into fifth place on the NHL's all-time point-scoring list.

November 1, 1986
Center **Bernie Federko** notched his 293rd career goal to become the St. Louis Blues' all-time leading scorer. Federko, who posted the record-breaker at 1:14 of the second period in St. Louis' 3-3 tie with the Pittsburgh Penguins, surpassed the previous club mark held by Garry Unger (292).

November 2, 1986
Coaching his final game of 1986-87, **Scotty Bowman** steered the Buffalo Sabres to a 7-1 win over the Bruins in Boston. The game marked Bowman's 739th career victory, ranking him first among all-time NHL coaches. Bowman left the Sabres' bench with a lifetime coaching total of 739-327-210 in 1276 games.

November 11, 1986
In his 15th game of the season, Minnesota North Stars' right-winger **Dino Ciccarelli** scored twice to set a modern NHL record (post-1926) for the quickest 20 goals from the start of a season. Hall-of-Fame forward Joe Malone set the all-time mark for the fastest 20 goals with the Montreal Canadiens in 1917-18, when he netted 20 in the first eight games of the season.

November 13, 1986
Calgary Flames' coach **Bob Johnson** posted his 157th career victory, 4-3 over the Hartford Whalers, to become the winningest coach in club history. Johnson surpassed the record set by Fred Creighton (156) from 1974 to 1979.

November 15, 1986
Boston Bruins' right-winger **Rick Middleton** cracked the 900-point barrier with an third-period assist to help tie the New Jersey Devils 5-5. Middleton became the 27th player in NHL history to amass at least 900 points in a career.

Buffalo Sabres' captain **Gilbert Perreault** posted his last NHL point with one assist in a 4-2 loss to the Montreal Canadiens. The tally, which topped off a career scoring record of 512-814-1326, lifted Perreault past Hall-of-Famer John Bucyk (813) into eighth place on the NHL's all-time assist list.

Center **Ron Francis** played his 358th career game, a 6-2 win over the Edmonton Oilers, as a Hartford Whaler to surpass right-winger Blaine Stoughton's club record (357) in games played.

November 16, 1986
NY Islanders' right-winger **Mike Bossy** scored his 10th goal of the season and the 545th of his career to pass Hall-of-Famer Maurice "Rocket" Richard (544) for sixth place on the all-time NHL scoring list.

Petri Skriko

November 18, 1986
Left-winger **Petri Skriko** set a Vancouver Canucks' record by scoring two short-handed goals during the same penalty. After Canucks' captain Stan Smyl drew a two-minute minor for highsticking at 13:05 of the second period, Skriko scored at 13:21 and 14:32 to establish the new club mark.

November 20, 1986
The NHL's active leader in career wins, 35-year-old goalie **Billy Smith** of the New York Islanders registered his 271st career win, 6-4 over the Toronto Maple Leafs, to move past Hall-of-Famer Bernie Parent (270) into 12th place on the NHL's all-time victory list.

November 21, 1986
New York Rangers' General Manager **Phil Esposito** made his NHL coaching debut with an 8-5 win over the Vancouver Canucks. Esposito, who took over the bench duties from Ted Sator, rallied his club from a 4-1 deficit to earn his first career victory as coach.

November 22, 1986
In his 575th career game, 26-year-old center **Wayne Gretzky** scored the 500th goal mark of his career, his third of the game, to boost the Edmonton Oilers over the Vancouver Canucks 5-2. The youngest of 13 players ever to score 500 goals, Gretzky achieved the feat in fewer games than any player in NHL history, eclipsing the mark previously held by Mike Bossy (689).

November 22, 1986
17-year veteran **Gilbert Perreault** skated in the 1,191st and final game of his career, a 3-1 loss to the Nordiques in Quebec City. The 36-year-old center closed out his playing days 22nd in all-time games played, four ahead of former Toronto Maple Leafs' captain George Armstrong (1,187).

SEASON HIGHLIGHTS, 1986-87 73

November 25, 1986
The **Vancouver Canucks** tied a club record by scoring 11 goals in one game as they defeated the Los Angeles Kings 11-5, matching their record first set on March 28, 1971.

December 4, 1986
Toronto Maple Leafs' right-winger **Rick Vaive** recorded the first successful penalty shot against the Los Angeles Kings. Vaive, the 11th player awarded a penalty shot against the Kings in their 20-year history, converted the attempt at 7:48 of the second period against goaltender Darren Eliot.

December 5, 1986
Posting two assists in the Edmonton Oilers' 4-2 win over the Pittsburgh Penguins, **Wayne Gretzky** joined Gordie Howe (1,850), Marcel Dionne (1,600+), Phil Esposito (1,590) and Stan Mikita (1,467) in the NHL's elite 1,400-point club.

December 11, 1986
35-year-old **Larry Robinson** helped the Montreal Canadiens to a 6-2 win over the New York Rangers with his 600th career assist, adding to his fourth-ranked total among all-time defensemen. At the close of the season, Robinson (626) trailed Denis Potvin (710), Brad Park (683) and Bobby Orr (645) on the all-time list among defensemen.

December 12, 1986
Wayne Gretzky recorded his 900th career assist as the Edmonton Oilers downed the Winnipeg Jets 6-1. Only three other players in NHL history – Gordie Howe, Marcel Dionne and Stan Mikita – have amassed as many as 900 in a career.

December 14, 1986
Captain **Stan Smyl** registered his fifth career hat-trick to lead the Vancouver Canucks over the Chicago Blackhawks 7-3 and become the club's' all-time leading point-scorer. The three-goal performance gave Smyl 354th career points to pass Thomas Gradin (353) for the overall club leadership.

December 19, 1986
Right-winger **Mike Gartner** scored his seventh goal of the season to become the first player in Washington Capitals' history ever to amass 600 points in a career. The game, a 6-4 win for New Jersey, raised the **Devils** to 16-14-2, their best record in franchise history ever after 32 games.

December 20, 1986
Edmonton Oilers' center **Wayne Gretzky** concluded the longest point-scoring streak of the season at 19 games with a five-point effort to help tie the Los Angeles Kings 8-8. Gretzky posted a total of 22 goals and 26 assists during the 19-game span.

December 23, 1986
Ted Sator took over the Buffalo Sabres' coaching duties, leading his new club to a 2-1 win over the Philadelphia Flyers. The Sabres, whose previous record had been 7-22-4 and 18 points out of fourth place, rallied around their new bench boss with wins in nine out of Sator's first 11 games.

Right-winger **Mike Bossy** scored at 3:25 of overtime to boost the New York Islanders over the Pittsburgh Penguins 4-3. The goal, his 22nd of the season and 557th of his career, lifted Bossy past Hall-of-Famer Johnny Bucyk (556) into fifth place on the all-time list.

December 26, 1986
"Ironman" center **Doug Jarvis** of the Hartford Whalers played his 915th straight game to establish a new NHL record. Jarvis, who started the streak with the Montreal Canadiens on October 8, 1975, shattered the mark set by Garry Unger (914).

December 27, 1986
Minneapolis-native **Reed Larson** became the first American-born player in NHL history ever to score 600 points in a career. The 30-year-old Boston Bruins' defenseman tallied one assist in the game, a 2-1 overtime loss to the Los Angeles Kings, to set the new mark.

December 27, 1986
Center **Marcel Dionne** of the Los Angeles Kings skated in his 1,200th career game, ranking him 21st all-time. Dionne played his first 299 games with the Detroit Red Wings before joining the Kings in 1975-76.

Paul Lawless

January 4, 1987
Left-winger **Paul Lawless** of the Hartford Whalers broke a club record with six points in one game. Lawless, who recorded two goals and four assists to lead Hartford over the Toronto Maple Leafs 8-3, surpassed the old mark of five points shared by seven other Whalers.

January 5, 1987
The **Washington Capitals** celebrated their 1,000th NHL game with a 6-4 win over the St. Louis Blues. The victory raised the Capitals' all-time record to 360-495-145 as they hit the 40-game mark of their 13th season. Washington had originally entered the League with the New Jersey Devils – nee the Kansas City Scouts – as an expansion franchise in 1974-75.

Montreal Canadiens' captain **Bob Gainey** skated in the 1,000th game of his NHL career. The 14-year veteran left-winger joined Henri Richard (1256), Jean Beliveau (1125) and current teammate Larry Robinson as the only 1,000-game performers in the club's 70-year NHL history.

The **Detroit Red Wings** tied the Boston Bruins 4-4 to earn their 40th point of the season and equal their total point production during the 1985-86 campaign. The Red Wings would go on to post a League-high 38-point improvement over last season.

SEASON HIGHLIGHTS, 1986-87

January 6, 1987
The **New Jersey Devils** hit the 1,000-game mark in franchise history, posting a 4-0 loss to the Philadelphia Flyers. In 1974-75, the Devils had entered the NHL as the expansion Kansas City Scouts, but after two seasons headed for Denver, where they were renamed the Colorado Rockies. In 1982-83, the team relocated again, becoming the New Jersey Devils.

January 11, 1987
Edmonton's **Wayne Gretzky** registered his 100th point of the season, an assist in the Oilers' 5-3 win over the Calgary Flames, to tie Marcel Dionne's NHL record of eight 100-or-more point seasons. Gretzky has scored a minimum of 137 points in each of his first eight years in the League.

January 12, 1987
Left-winger **Charlie Simmer** registered the 13,000th goal in Boston Bruins' history in this 4-1 win over the New York Rangers. Simmer's milestone goal, a power-play tally at 14:56 of the second period, was scored over 62 years after the Bruins' Fred Harris posted the club's first goal ever at 3:30 of the second period in a 2-1 win over the Montreal Maroons on December 1, 1924.

January 15, 1987
Three Boston Bruins – defensemen **Ray Bourque** and **Reed Larson** and right-winger **Rick Middleton** – reached major career milestones in this 6-4 win against the Hartford Whalers. Bourque tallied his 400th career assist, while Larson scored twice to become the first American-born player and the sixth defenseman in League history to score 200 career goals. Middleton became the 35th NHL player ever to post 500 assists.

January 21, 1987
Defenseman **Mark Howe** of the Philadelphia Flyers cracked the 1,000-point mark of his professional career. Howe, who scored 504 points with the Houston Aeros and New England Whalers in the now-defunct World Hockey Association, posted his 496th NHL point and 1,000th overall as a pro in this 5-5 tie with the Chicago Blackhawks.

January 22, 1987
Goaltender **Alain Chevrier** turned aside 29 shots to defeat the Calgary Flames 7-5 and establish a new club record with 17 wins. The 25-year-old netminder eclipsed the old mark of 16 victories set by Glenn "Chico" Resch in 1981-82 as a member of the Colorado Rockies. Amidst one of the worst snowstorms in the New Jersey region, the Devils and Flames played before the smallest crowd in NHL history – 334 – despite a paid attendance of 11,249.

January 23, 1987
Winnipeg Jets' left-winger **Gilles Hamel** tied a club record by scoring goals in seven consecutive games. The streak, which began January 13, included eight goals and nine points. Current Jets' right-winger Paul MacLean first set the team mark in 1984-85.

Edmonton's **Wayne Gretzky** posted his 927th career assist, his 71st of the season, passing Stan Mikita (926) for the third highest total in NHL history as the Oilers downed the New York Rangers 7-4.

January 27, 1987
Pittsburgh Penguins' goaltender **Gilles Meloche** registered his 259th career victory, 7-5 over Washington, to move past Hall-of-Famer Ken Dryden (258) into 14th place on the all-time NHL win list.

January 30, 1987
The **Washington Capitals** tied the New York Islanders 3-3 with two late goals from right-winger Mike Gartner to extend their overtime undefeated streak to 35 games. Washington's streak, which began March 18, 1984, ranks second in NHL history behind the 37-game overtime unbeaten string set by the Boston Bruins between December 30, 1934, and November 15, 1938.

January 31, 1987
Bob Pulford of the Chicago Blackhawks coached his 743rd career game, a 4-4 tie with the St. Louis Blues, to move past Red Kelly (742) into 10th place all-time. Pulford, also the NHL's active leader in games coached, began his career behind the bench with Los Angeles in 1972-73 and joined the Blackhawks in 1977-78.

February 1, 1987
Edmonton Oilers' center **Wayne Gretzky** registered his 1,468th career point, an assist, to pass Stan Mikita (1,467) for fourth place on the NHL's all-time point-scoring list. The Chicago Blackhawks defeated the Oilers 6-4.

February 4, 1987
Winnipeg Jets' center **Dale Hawerchuk** distinguished himself as the second youngest player in NHL history to score 600 points. Hawerchuk, at 23 years and 10 months old, scored twice against Flyers' rookie goaltender Ron Hextall to defeat Philadelphia 5-3. Edmonton center Wayne Gretzky set the record as the youngest when he scored 600 points at the age of 22 years, four days old.

Wayne Gretzky of Edmonton extended his streak of 50-goal seasons to eight, scoring at 9:49 of the third period to help the Oilers beat the Minnesota North Stars 6-5. Only Mike Bossy (9) has recorded more 50-goal seasons in a career.

February 8, 1987
13-year veteran right-winger **Wilf Paiement** notched his 800th career point, an assist, to lead the Buffalo Sabres over the Chicago Blackhawks 7-4. The assist, his third point of the night, tied him with former NHLer Ken Hodge (800) for 43rd place in all-time scoring.

February 11, 1987
Philadelphia Flyers' captain **Dave Poulin** scored with 1:15 remaining in regulation time to power Team NHL over the Soviet Union 4-3 at Rendez-Vous 87 in Quebec City. Jari Kurri and Glenn Anderson of the Edmonton Oilers and Kevin Dineen of the Hartford Whalers also scored for the NHL.

February 13, 1987
Valeri Kamensky and **Vladimir Krutov** scored two goals apiece to boost the Soviets to a 5-3 victory over Team NHL and deadlock the Rendez-Vous 87 series at 1-1. Edmonton Oilers' center Wayne Gretzky, named the series' most outstanding player, tallied three assists in a losing effort.

SEASON HIGHLIGHTS, 1986-87

February 15, 1987
Washington Capitals' right-winger **Mike Gartner** skated in his 600th career game to extend his all-time club record in that category. Gartner played his first game as a Capital on October 7, 1979.

February 18, 1987
Los Angeles Kings' left-winger **Luc Robitaille** set a new club record with his 34th goal of the season, eclipsing the rookie mark set by Steve Bozek (33) in 1981-82, to help defeat the Washington Capitals 7-4.

February 25, 1987
Montreal Canadiens' defenseman **Larry Robinson** moved into a tie with Ken Hodge for 43rd place among all-time NHL scorers when he scored the 800th point of his career. Robinson recorded the milestone tally in a 3-3 tie with the Chicago Blackhawks.

New Jersey's **Aaron Broten** posted his 184th career assist to shatter Wilf Paiement's all-time club record (183) as the Devils defeated Edmonton 4-2.

In a 3-3 tie with the Montreal Canadiens, Chicago's **Doug Wilson** registered his 401st career assist to pass Pierre Pilote (400) as the Blackhawks' all-time leader in assists by a defenseman.

February 26, 1987
Right-winger **Tony Tanti** became the first player in Vancouver Canucks' history to score 30-or-more goals in four straight seasons. Tanti, who had posted 45, 39 and 39 goals in his previous three campaigns, scored his 30th goal of the year as the Detroit Red Wings defeated Vancouver 5-4.

March 3, 1987
Philadelphia Flyers' defenseman **Mark Howe** notched his 500th NHL point, a third-period goal versus netminder Tom Barrasso, to help defeat the Buffalo Sabres 4-2. The milestone tally left the 31-year-old Howe with career scoring totals of 142-358-500 in 562 NHL games.

March 5, 1987
Hartford Whalers' center **Ron Francis** shattered a club record with six assists in one game en route to a 10-2 victory over the Boston Bruins. Francis also equalled the team's single-game mark of six points set earlier in the season by left-winger Paul Lawless.

March 7, 1987
Right-winger **Dino Ciccarelli**, the only player ever to score 50 goals in a season for the Minnesota North Stars, reached the 50-goal mark for the second time in his career. Ciccarelli, who notched 55 goals in his first full season with the North Stars in 1981-82, scored twice against goalie Gilles Meloche in this 7-3 loss to the Pittsburgh Penguins. Ciccarelli also became the second player of the season to score 50 goals, joining Edmonton's Wayne Gretzky.

March 9, 1987
En route to a 3-2 overtime victory against the Toronto Maple Leafs, St. Louis Blues' center **Bernie Federko** registered three assists to reach the 900-point plateau of his career. Federko, who currently holds club records for games, goals, assists and points, became only the 28th player in NHL history ever to score as many as 900 points in a career.

March 10, 1987
With the trading deadline minutes away, the Los Angeles Kings dealt center **Marcel Dionne**, the NHL's second all-time leading scorer, and minor league left-winger Jeff Crossman to the New York Rangers in exchange for center Bob Carpenter and defenseman Tom Laidlaw. The deal capped off the final two days of trading which had 14 players transferred among 11 teams.

March 11, 1987
Wayne Gretzky tallied a goal and three assists in the Edmonton Oilers' 6-3 victory over Detroit to reach the 1,500-point mark in his career. Only Gordie Howe (1,850), Marcel Dionne (1,600+) and Phil Esposito (1,590) have scored more career points.

Tim Kerr   Glenn Resch

March 15, 1987
38-year-old goalie **Glenn "Chico" Resch**, the oldest active player in the NHL, posted his 231st career win to move past Hall-of-Famer Gerry Cheevers (230) into 20th place on the NHL's all-time win list. Resch kicked out 37 shots to lead the Philadelphia Flyers over the New York Rangers 5-2.

March 17, 1987
Right-wingers **Tim Kerr** of the Philadelphia Flyers and **Jari Kurri** of the Edmonton Oilers joined Wayne Gretzky as the League's only three players to score 50-or-more goals in each of the last four seasons. Kerr, whose streak set a new club record, scored twice to lead Philadelphia over the New York Rangers 4-1, while Kurri helped the Oilers defeat the New Jersey Devils 7-4.

March 18, 1987
Hartford Whalers' goalie **Mike Liut** broke his own team record with his 28th win of the season, defeating the New York Rangers 5-3. Liut had set the club mark in 1985-86, when he posted 27 victories in the Whalers' first winning season since joining the National Hockey League in 1979-80.

En route to a 5-4 win over St. Louis, Pittsburgh Penguins' center **Mario Lemieux** topped the 100-point mark on the season with a goal and two assists and joined Wayne Gretzky, Mike Rogers and Peter Stastny as the fourth player ever to score 100-or-more points in each of his first three NHL seasons.

SEASON HIGHLIGHTS, 1986-87

March 19, 1987
Edmonton's **Wayne Gretzky** scored his 542nd career goal to move past Stan Mikita (541) into seventh place among all-time NHL scorers.

March 20, 1987
Vancouver Canucks' left-winger **Tony Tanti** scored his 68th career power-play goal to shatter captain Stan Smyl's all-time team record in that category. Tanti, who notched the game-winning goal in overtime as the Canucks downed the Winnipeg Jets 6-5, also surpassed the 300-point plateau to move into eighth place on the club's all-time scoring list.

Pat Verbeek

March 21, 1987
New Jersey Devils' left-winger **Pat Verbeek** became the fifth player in club history ever to score 30 goals in a season. Verbeek, who scored twice in the game, notched his 30th of the season at 3:12 into overtime to lift New Jersey past the St. Louis Blues 7-6. Verbeek joined Wilf Paiement, Paul Gardner, Lanny McDonald and Greg Adams on the Devils' 30-goal list.
  St. Louis Blues' center **Bernie Federko** posted his 600th career assist, becoming the first player in club history ever to achieve the milestone.

March 22, 1987
The **Hartford Whalers** beat the Los Angeles Kings 6-3 to set a new club record for points in a season with 85. The Whalers had set the previous club mark (84) in 1985-86, their first winning year since joining the NHL in 1979-80.

March 25, 1987

Los Angeles Kings' left-winger **Luc Robitaille** notched his 77th point of the season to shatter the club's rookie scoring record set by Larry Murphy (76) in 1980-81.

The **New Jersey Devils** defeated the New York Rangers 8-2 to earn a franchise record 60 points in one season. Also in the game, Devils' center **Kirk Muller** tallied five assists to tie the club's single-game assist mark set by center Greg Adams on October 10, 1985.

March 28, 1987

The **Calgary Flames** set a new team record by winning their 46th game of the season, 4-3 over the Los Angeles Kings.

March 29, 1987

Doug Lidster of the Vancouver Canucks scored his 61st point to establish a new club record for points in a season by a defenseman. The 26-year-old blueliner surpassed the former mark set by Dennis Kearns (5-55-60) in 1976-77.

April 1, 1987

Minnesota North Stars' right-winger **Dino Ciccarelli** tallied his final point of the season, a third-period assist, to tie Bill Goldsworthy with 506 career points for a share of the club's all-time scoring title. In 470 games, Ciccarelli has compiled a 259-247-506 career mark, while Goldsworthy posted totals of 267-239-506 in 670 games with the club.

April 2, 1987

Center **Doug Gilmour** tallied two assists to become the second player in St. Louis Blues' history to score 100 points in a season. Gilmour, who led the Blues to a 5-3 victory over the Buffalo Sabres, joined teammate Bernie Federko on the club's 100-point list. Federko has accomplished the feat four times in his 11-year career.

The **Edmonton Oilers** captured the Presidents' Trophy – awarded to the club posting the NHL's best overall record – for the second straight season after tying the Calgary Flames 4-4. The Oilers later concluded the season with a 50-24-6 mark for 106 points, tops in the League.

April 4, 1987

Denis Potvin of the New York Islanders became the first defenseman and 21st player overall in NHL history to score 1,000 points in a career. The 14-year veteran scored at 19:43 of the third period against Buffalo Sabres' goaltender Jacques Cloutier to reach the milestone and lift the Islanders to a 6-6 tie.

April 5, 1987

Los Angeles Kings' left-winger **Luc Robitaille** registered his 45th goal of the season, tying Winnipeg Jets' center Dale Hawerchuk as the second highest goal-scoring rookie in NHL history. Robitaille and Hawerchuk trail New York Islanders' right-winger Mike Bossy, who set the all-time rookie record with 53 goals in 1977-78.

New York Islanders' center **Bryan Trottier** tallied four assists in a 9-5 victory over the Philadelphia Flyers, becoming the 14th player in NHL history to surpass the 1,200-point mark in a career.

Calgary's **Al MacInnis** registered his 76th point of the season, an assist on the Flames' lone goal, breaking Paul Reinhart's club record (75 in 1982-83) for points by a defenseman in a season.

14-year-veteran right-winger **Lanny McDonald** of the Calgary Flames skated in his 1,000th career game, a 3-1 loss to the Winnipeg Jets. McDonald, who made his NHL debut with the Toronto Maple Leafs in 1973-74, became the 59th player in history to appear in as many games.

1987 Entry Draft
Round #1 — Choices 1-21

1. Buffalo
TURGEON, PIERRE
Center, shoots left
6.01, 200 lbs.
Born: August 29, 1969 in Rouyn, Que.

YEAR	TEAM	LEAGUE	GP	G	A	PTS	PIM
1986-87	Granby	QMJHL	58	69	85	154	8
1985-86	Granby	QMJHL	69	47	67	114	31

Moves with exceptional strength, speed and acceleration....packs a highly potent scoring punch....employs a wide variety of scoring techniques....positions himself to maximize his scoring chances....has a knack for scoring the big goals....shoots at the proper moments....possesses strong wristshots and slapshots....passes very effectively ....finds the open man....stickhandles excellently....uses his body to protect the puck....can handle the puck with his skates....excels on the power-play....takes advantage of the open ice....can take a check....stands up in tough situations....plays a finesse checking game....takes face-offs well....works hard for the team....possesses an excellent hockey sense.

2. New Jersey
SHANAHAN, BRENDAN
Center, shoots right
6.03, 200 lbs.
Born: January 23, 1969, in Mimico, Ont.

YEAR	TEAM	LEAGUE	GP	G	A	PTS	PIM
1986-87	London	OHL	56	39	53	92	128
1985-86	London	OHL	59	28	34	62	70

Skates powerfully....can score with either finesse or strength....sets up the play well....works hard for his points ....executes well....shoots accurately ....has a sound slapshot and quick wristshot....sees the play developing.... passes equally well to both sides....controls the puck skillfully....uses his body effectively to hide the puck....plays a strong two-way game....helps out his defensemen....can play right wing....takes face-offs....loves to hit....bulls his way through traffic....plays hurt....stands up for his teammates....can be easily motivated....plays a highly intelligent game....leads by example.

3. Boston
WESLEY, GLEN
Defense, shoots left
6.01, 192 lbs.
Born: October 2, 1968, in Red Deer, Alta.

YEAR	TEAM	LEAGUE	GP	G	A	PTS	PIM
1986-87	Portland	WHL	63	16	46	62	72
1985-86	Portland	WHL	69	16	75	91	96

Skates with good power, quickness and acceleration.... moves backwards well ....possesses excellent scoring talent....shoots quick and accurate slapshots and wristshots....passes very skillfully to either side....anticipates his teammates' moves....finds the open man....controls and carries the puck excellently....can rush with the puck from end to end....has outstanding defensive skills....plays the point on the power-play effectively....recovers quickly.... checks well in the open ice....possesses mental toughness ....plays with poise and confidence.

4. Los Angeles
McBEAN, WAYNE
Defense, shoots left
6.02, 185 lbs.
Born: February 21, 1969, in Calgary, Alta.

YEAR	TEAM	LEAGUE	GP	G	A	PTS	PIM
1986-87	Medicine Hat	WHL	71	12	41	53	163
1985-86	Medicine Hat	WHL	67	1	14	15	73

Skates excellently in all directions....accelerates quickly.... pivots deftly....scores well for a defenseman....gets his shots on net....has excellent wristshots and slapshots.... possesses outstanding stickhandling and passing abilities ....finds the open man....carries the puck out of his own end very well....likes to rush with the puck....recovers quickly.... pokechecks skillfully....takes his man out well along the boards and in the corners.... uses his size advantageously ....plays a physical game and won't back away ....learns quickly....possesses a strong desire to win.

5. Pittsburgh
JOSEPH, CHRIS
Defense, shoots right
6.01, 194 lbs.
Born: September 10, 1969, in Burnaby, B.C.

YEAR	TEAM	LEAGUE	GP	G	A	PTS	PIM
1986-87	Seattle	WHL	67	13	45	58	155
1985-86	Seattle	WHL	72	4	8	12	50

Skates with excellent strength, agility, mobility and balance ....pivots well....possesses excellent scoring talent.... releases hard, accurate wristshots and slapshots....shoots the puck low from the point....passes at the appropriate times....controls the puck well....can stickhandle out of his own zone....rushes well....has good playmaking qualities ....reads the play well ....solid at both ends....clears the front of the net....checks with authority....ties his man up effectively....pinches in well....blocks shots skillfully....gets involved....won't be intimidated....has excellent desire and strong leadership qualities....wants to excel....plays confidently.

6. Minnesota
ARCHIBALD, DAVID
Center, shoots left
6.01, 192 lbs.
Born: April 14, 1969, in Chilliwack, B.C.

YEAR	TEAM	LEAGUE	GP	G	A	PTS	PIM
1986-87	Portland	WHL	65	50	57	107	40
1985-86	Portland	WHL	70	29	35	64	56

Skates with exceptional balance and agility....moves deceivingly fast.... changes pace skillfully....plays an excellent offensive game....scores in a variety of ways.... utilizes great shot selection....owns a hard, accurate wristshot....passes excellently....uses his wingers well....moves the puck at the right times....finds the openings with and without the puck.... stickhandles and controls the puck well ....possesses outstanding playmaking talent....works equally well one-on-one or in traffic....anticipates the play ....performs strongly in the neutral zone....plays an excellent two-way game, including power-play and penalty-killing situations....takes a hit to make the play....checks well at both ends of the ice....hides the puck effectively....prefers the finesse game....combines strong desire and attitude with excellent creativity.

7. Toronto
RICHARDSON, LUKE
Defense, shoots left
6.04, 208 lbs.
Born: March 26, 1969, in Ottawa, Ont.

YEAR	TEAM	LEAGUE	GP	G	A	PTS	PIM
1986-87	Peterborough	OHL	59	13	32	45	70
1985-86	Peterborough	OHL	63	6	18	24	57

Has outstanding skating talents....skates backwards quickly and with solid lateral mobility....accelerates well in all directions....possesses a heavy and accurate slapshot....passes with precision....plays a defensive style, strong in front of the net and in the corners....seldom gets caught out of position but recovers quickly....hits cleanly and effectively, particularly in the open ice....is a coach's player....possesses a great attitude....leads both on and off the ice.

8. Chicago
WAITE, JIMMY
Goaltender, catches left
6.00, 163 lbs.
Born: April 15, 1969, in Sherbrooke, Que.

YEAR	TEAM	LEAGUE	GP	MINS	GA	SO	AVG
1986-87	Chicoutimi	QMJHL	50	2569	209	2	4.88
1985-86	Canonniers	Midget	29	1643	143	0	5.22

Uses his body well to block shots....recovers quickly....comes out to challenge the shooter....possesses excellent reflexes....knows his position relative to the net at all times ....skates well in the crease....has an outstanding glove hand....blocks well....uses his stick effectively to stop the puck behind the net....covers up well....directs the rebounds to the corners or to teammates....cuts down the angles skillfully....reads the play as it develops....comes up with the key saves....can single-handedly win a game or keep his team close....exudes a tremendous amount of confidence and determination....displays plenty of endurance....listens and learns....plays equally well at home or on the road.

9. Quebec
FOGARTY, BRYAN
Defense, shoots left
6.01, 189 lbs.
Born: June 11, 1969, in Brantford, Ont.

YEAR	TEAM	LEAGUE	GP	G	A	PTS	PIM
1986-87	Kingston	OHL	56	20	50	70	46
1985-86	Kingston	OHL	47	2	19	21	14

Skates smoothly with solid balance and mobility....accelerates well....has excellent offensive capabilities....shoots accurately....waits for the right moment....passes and receives the puck effectively on either side....sees and hits the open man....controls and moves the puck skillfully....anticipates the play....can rush with the puck....plays effectively on the power-play and in all short-handed situations ....plays with poise and confidence....ties up his opponents in the corners....stickchecks well....has good size and strength....will not be intimidated....wants to win....works very hard....can make the big play....plays a polished and unselfish game.

10. N.Y. Rangers
MORE, JAYSON
Defense, shoots right
6.01, 191 lbs.
Born: January 12, 1969, in Souris, Man.

YEAR	TEAM	LEAGUE	GP	G	A	PTS	PIM
1986-87	New Westminster	WHL	64	8	29	37	217
1985-86	Lethbridge	WHL	61	7	18	25	155

Moves with good balance and agility....skates well backwards....shoots low and accurately....possesses hard wristshots and slapshots....passes off and leads his man well....controls the puck and rushes effectively....plays the point on the power-play....kills penalties....makes solid contact with the body....pins his opponents skillfully....likes to hit....clears the front of the net....uses his strength advantageously....plays a highly tough and physical game....leads by example....wants to excel.

11. Detroit
RACINE, YVES
Defense, shoots left
6.00, 183 lbs.
Born: February 7, 1969, in Matane, Que.

YEAR	TEAM	LEAGUE	GP	G	A	PTS	PIM
1986-87	Longueuil	QMJHL	70	7	43	50	50
1985-86	Ste. Foy	Midget	42	4	38	42	66

Skates with outstanding mobility and balance....accelerates well....uses wide choice of shots....times the play and positions himself to maximize scoring opportunities....shoots with power and accuracy....can make either the soft lead or the firm, crisp pass....always keeps his options open....stickhandles well....can control the puck with his skates....stands up to make the play at the blueline....reads the play and pinches in....plays both power-play and penalty-killing situations....helps his goaltender....checks effectively in the corners and along the boards....protects the puck....blocks shots.... plays a physical yet clean game....wants to excel in all phases of the game ....works hard....listens and learns.

12. St. Louis
OSBORNE, KEITH
Right wing, shoots right
6.01, 181 lbs.
Born: April 2, 1969, in Toronto, Ont.

YEAR	TEAM	LEAGUE	GP	G	A	PTS	PIM
1986-87	North Bay	OHL	61	34	55	89	31
1985-86	Toronto	Midget	42	28	63	111	36

Accelerates quickly....moves to the net well....scores in a variety of ways....will take punishment in front of the net....shoots accurately....has a solid wristshot....passes both softly and crisply....receives the puck well....handles the puck skillfully in traffic....will go into the corners for the puck....will take a hit to make the play....forechecks and backchecks....plays in both power-play and penalty-killing situations....has the potential to become a very strong, imposing player....works hard and unselfishly....plays with a lot of determination.

13. N.Y. Islanders
CHYNOWETH, DEAN
Defense, shoots right
6.01, 185 lbs.
Born: October 30, 1968, in Calgary, Alta.

YEAR	TEAM	LEAGUE	GP	G	A	PTS	PIM
1986-87	Medicine Hat	WHL	67	3	18	21	285
1985-86	Medicine Hat	WHL	69	3	12	15	208

Maintains good balance on his skates....plays a predominantly defensive style ....shoots the puck well from the point ....passes adeptly to his wingers.... finds and hits the open man....makes the sure play....plays a solid positional game ....takes his opponents out along the boards and in the corners....stickhandles skillfully....uses his body masterfully when checking ....likes to hit....plays a tough, aggressive style....always plays up to his potential....shows great desire and attitude....wants to improve.

14. Boston
QUINTAL, STEPHANE
Defense, shoots right
6.03, 214 lbs.
Born: October 22, 1968, in Boucherville, Que.

YEAR	TEAM	LEAGUE	GP	G	A	PTS	PIM
1986-87	Granby	QMJHL	67	13	41	54	178
1985-86	Granby	QMJHL	67	2	17	19	144

Possesses excellent speed, balance and agility....pivots and moves laterally well....employs a wide variety of shots ....maximizes his scoring chances....shoots accurately and powerfully....knows when to release the puck....passes very well to either side....leads his man accurately....has soft hands....uses partner effectively....stickhandles well....kills penalties....plays the power-play....rushes with the puck....ties his man up without tying himself up....protects the goalie ....moves the screen from the path of the puck....clears the puck well....uses his body effectively....sacrifices himself for the team....blocks shots....works hard....is mentally tough....aware of the overall play around him.

15. Quebec
SAKIC, JOE
Center, shoots left
5.11, 181 lbs.
Born: July 7, 1969, in Burnaby, B.C.

YEAR	TEAM	LEAGUE	GP	G	A	PTS	PIM
1986-87	Swift Current	WHL	72	60	73	133	31
1985-86	Burnaby	Midget	60	83	73	156	96

Skates with good speed and acceleration....possesses an excellent scoring talent....scores in a variety of creative ways....releases his shots very quickly and accurately....has an outstanding wristshot and a solid slapshot....backhands the puck well....passes very well off the forehand and backhand ....can pick out the open man....controls the puck effectively in traffic....has great playmaking qualities ....plays skillfully without the puck....checks proficiently, forcing his man off the play....kills penalties....plays a tenacious game....has excellent stamina and endurance....will not be intimidated....possesses extraordinary hockey sense ....sees and anticipates.

16. Winnipeg
MARCHMENT, BRYAN
Defense, shoots left
6.01, 195 lbs.
Born: May 1, 1969, in West Hill, Ont.

YEAR	TEAM	LEAGUE	GP	G	A	PTS	PIM
1986-87	Belleville	OHL	52	6	38	44	238
1985-86	Belleville	OHL	57	5	14	19	225

Possesses good strength on his skates....accelerates well ....scores well for a defenseman....concentrates on his defensive work....shoots hard....can make a good pass to either side....plays positionally sound defense....bodychecks masterfully....hits anywhere on the ice....punishes opponents with physical play....uses outstanding size and strength to his advantage....plays very aggressively....does everything to win....works relentlessly for the team.

17. Montreal
CASSELS, ANDREW
Center, shoots left
6.00, 167 lbs.
Born: July 23, 1969, in Bramalea, Ont.

YEAR	TEAM	LEAGUE	GP	G	A	PTS	PIM
1986-87	Ottawa	OHL	66	26	66	92	28
1985-86	Bramalea	Jr. B	33	18	25	43	26

Skates with good balance, agility, speed and acceleration.... uses his intelligence to create a variety of scoring chances ....releases wristshots quickly and accurately....passes excellently, with quick hands and a soft touch....leads his man well....moves the puck at the proper times....breaks into the clear once the pass is made....anticipates the play effectively.... takes face-offs skillfully....kills penalties....checks both ways....remains unaffected by physical play....cannot be intimidated....wants to excel... listens and learns.... possesses excellent hockey sense.

18. Hartford
HULL, JODY
Center/Right wing, shoots right
6.02, 198 lbs.
Born: February 2, 1969, in Cambridge, Ont.

YEAR	TEAM	LEAGUE	GP	G	A	PTS	PIM
1986-87	Peterborough	OHL	49	18	34	52	22
1985-86	Peterborough	OHL	61	20	22	42	29

Balances and accelerates well....skates with exceptional strength....works hard for his points....has a good feel for the net....shoots well....passes and receives the puck crisply and accurately....stickhandles well through traffic....controls the puck effectively in the corners and along the boards.... plays a tough and aggressive game, particularly in the corners and in front of the net....dishes out solid checks.... uses his size favorably.... works hard for the team....has excellent versatility, playing all three forward positions.

19. Calgary
DEASLEY, BRYAN
Left wing, shoots left
6.03, 205 lbs.
Born: November 26, 1968, in Toronto, Ont.

YEAR	TEAM	LEAGUE	GP	G	A	PTS	PIM
1986-87	U. of Michigan	CCHA	38	13	11	24	74
1985-86	St. Mike's	H.S.	30	17	20	37	88

Moves very well on the straight-away....possesses strong balance....works hard for his goals....owns a heavy slapshot and an accurate wristshot....passes effectively to all areas of the ice....plays the left side skillfully at both ends of the ice....checks well along the boards and in the corners ....uses size and strength advantageously....thrives under tough, competitive circumstances....plays very aggressively when needed....shows strong desire and attitude.

20. Philadelphia
RUMBLE, DARREN
Defense, shoots left
6.01, 187 lbs.
Born: January 23, 1969, in Barrie, Ont.

YEAR	TEAM	LEAGUE	GP	G	A	PTS	PIM
196-87	Kitchener	OHL	64	11	32	43	44
1985-86	Barrie	Jr. B	46	14	32	46	91

Possesses an excellent skating ability....accelerates fast.... knows what to do in the offensive zone....releases his shots quickly and accurately....anticipates well....passes outstandingly....moves the puck very fast....controls the puck and sets up the play with great effectiveness....takes the play to the outside....contains his check along the boards.... plays a finesse game....rides his man out of the play....will not be intimidated....has great natural ability....plays consistently well at home and on the road....owns a highly polished repertoire of skills.

21. Edmonton
SOBERLAK, PETER
Left wing, shoots left
6.02, 185 lbs.
Born: May 12, 1969, in Kamloops, B.C.

YEAR	TEAM	LEAGUE	GP	G	A	PTS	PIM
1986-87	Swift Current	WHL	68	33	42	75	45
1985-86	Kamloops	WHL	55	10	11	21	46

Skates powerfully....accelerates quickly....moves with deceptive speed....has good hands....plays very intelligently around the net....wrists and slaps the puck accurately.... finds the open man....passes crisply....handles the puck effectively along the boards and in the corners....moves well through traffic....adjusts well from center to left wing.... maintains solid positioning in checking situations....uses his body advantageously....plays a tough, aggressive style when required....possesses a good team attitude and a strong hockey sense.

Round #2 — Choices 22-42

22. Buffalo
MILLER, BRAD
Defense, shoots left
6.04, 202 lbs.
Born: July 23, 1969, in Edmonton, Alta.

YEAR	TEAM	LEAGUE	GP	G	A	PTS	PIM
1986-87	Regina	WHL	67	10	38	48	154
1985-86	Regina	WHL	71	2	14	16	99

Skates deceptively fast....is strong on his skates....shows good scoring touch for a defenseman....has good hands.... shoots low, hard and accurate wristshots and slapshots from the point....passes accurately....leads his man well.... controls the puck....can carry the puck out of his own end ....plays the power-play....uses long reach to check....positions himself well on incoming players....uses his body size and strength efficiently....loves to play a hard-hitting, aggressive style....displays an excellent attitude and desire ....will play hurt.

23. New Jersey
PERSSON, LARS RICKARD
Defense, shoots left
6.01, 196 lbs.
Born: August 24 1969, in Ostersund, Sweden

YEAR	TEAM	LEAGUE	GP	G	A	PTS	PIM
1986-87	Ostersund	Sweden	31	10	11	21	2
1985-86	Ostersund	Sweden	24	4	7	11	N/A

Skates strongly both forwards and backwards....has a strong sense of balance....passes effectively to both sides ....controls the puck well....stickhandles skillfully....plays a well developed defensive game....takes the man out in front of the net and along the boards....works hard all the time.... plays hard for the team....possesses an excellent attitude.

24. Vancouver
MURPHY, ROB
Center, shoots left
6.03, 195 lbs.
Born: April 7, 1969, in Hull, Que.

YEAR	TEAM	LEAGUE	GP	G	A	PTS	PIM
1986-87	Laval	QMJHL	70	35	54	89	86
1985-86	Outaouais	Midget	41	17	33	50	47

Can deceive opponents with his speed....skates with agility and balance....can score several ways....has good hands and a nice touch around the net....slaps and wrists the puck hard and accurately....moves and passes the puck excellently....gets into the clear after making the pass.... can stickhandle in traffic....plays positionally sound game ....utilizes his wingers effectively....forechecks and backchecks....uses his body favorably....works hard...will not be intimidated....plays hard for the team....shows lots of desire ....possesses exceptional creativity.

1987 ENTRY DRAFT

25. Calgary
MATTEAU, STEPHANE
Left wing, shoots left
6.04, 183 lbs.
Born: September 2, 1969, in Rouyn, Que.

YEAR	TEAM	LEAGUE	GP	G	A	PTS	PIM
1986-87	Hull	QMJHL	69	27	48	75	113
1985-86	Hull	QMJHL	60	6	8	14	19

Starts and stops well....skates with good balance and mobility for a big man....can score in a variety of ways....handles himself well in close to the net....uses excellent size and reach to complete plays around the net....stickhandles, passes and receives the puck well....anticipates the play.... backchecks solidly....uses his body favorably ....will not be intimidated.... good desire and attitude.... learns quickly.

26. Pittsburgh
TABARACCI, RICHARD
Goaltender, catches left
5.10, 186 lbs.
Born: January 2, 1969, in Toronto, Ont.

YEAR	TEAM	LEAGUE	GP	MINS	GA	SO	AVG
1986-87	Cornwall	OHL	59	3347	290	1	5.20
1985-86	Markham	Tier II	40	2176	188	1	5.18

Cuts down the angles with outstanding precision....likes to position himself initially far out of the net....can make the save on his feet....possesses good quickness....concentrates well....uses the blocker effectively....clears his own rebounds....never freezes the puck unnecessarily....displays excellent stamina....plays an aggressive style.... handles the puck adeptly....manages well with a heavy work load....usually rebounds from bad performances with very strong ones.

27. Los Angeles
FITZPATRICK, MARK
Goaltender, catches left
6.01, 190 lbs.
Born: November 13, 1968, in Kitmat, B.C.

YEAR	TEAM	LEAGUE	GP	MINS	GA	SO	AVG
1986-87	Medicine Hat	WHL	50	2844	159	4	3.55
1985-86	Medicine Hat	WHL	41	2074	99	1	2.86

Stands his ground....moves quickly for a big man....concentrates well.... always stays close to the crease....reads and anticipates the play excellently....blocks and catches effectively....positions his glove close to the ice....allows few rebounds....uses his size and strength to his advantage, particularly in cutting the angle from incoming shooters.... plays a stand-up style....shoots the puck adeptly....performs exceptionally well under pressure.

28. Toronto
MAROIS, DANIEL
Right wing, shoots right
6.01, 180 lbs.
Born: October 3, 1968, in Montreal, Que.

YEAR	TEAM	LEAGUE	GP	G	A	PTS	PIM
1986-87	Verdun	QMJHL	40	22	26	48	143
1985-86	Verdun	QMJHL	58	42	35	77	110

Cuts to the net with quick acceleration....plays very cleverly in the offensive zone....uses a wide selection of shots.... passes the puck at the right moments....takes a check to complete the play....can handle the puck in his skates.... uses the body well....plays a physical but clean style....has good size....will not be intimidated....shows lots of desire and a good team spirit....plays the power-play....possesses solid skills in all facets of the game.

29. Chicago
McGILL, RYAN
Defense, shoots right
6.02, 197 lbs.
Born: February 28, 1969, in Sherwood Park, Alta.

YEAR	TEAM	LEAGUE	GP	G	A	PTS	PIM
1986-87	Swift Current	WHL	72	12	36	48	226
1985-86	Lethbridge	WHL	64	5	10	15	171

Moves with good speed and acceleration....skates well backwards....pivots effectively to either side....shoots a low, hard and accurate shot....passes on forehand and backhand....finds and hits the open man....controls and rushes with the puck....plays the point on the power-play....checks well all over the ice....likes to hit....uses his excellent size and strength to his advantage....loves the tough, aggressive game....plays with confidence and poise.

30. Philadelphia
HARDING, JEFF
Right wing, shoots right
6.04, 207 lbs.
Born: April 6, 1969.

YEAR	TEAM	LEAGUE	GP	G	A	PTS	PIM
1986-87	St. Michael's	Jr. B	22	22	8	30	97
1985-86	Henry Carr	H.S.	23	14	10	24	30

Skates with deceptive speed and mobility for a big man.... takes advantage of his scoring abilities....possesses very hard and accurate snapshots and wristshots....releases the puck quickly....passes and receives the puck sharply and crisply....plays excellently in front of his opponent's net ....checks efficiently along the boards and in the corners ....plays a physical and often punishing game....never backs down.

31. N.Y. Rangers
LACROIX, DANIEL
Left wing, shoots left
6.02, 185 lbs.
Born: March 11, 1969, in Montreal, Que.

YEAR	TEAM	LEAGUE	GP	G	A	PTS	PIM
1986-87	Granby	QMJHL	54	9	16	25	311
1985-86	Hull	Midget	37	10	13	23	46

Balances well on his skates....releases hard slapshots and wristshots.... leads his man well with crisp and accurate passes....plays his position well....controls the left side effectively....forechecks and backchecks skillfully and tenaciously....uses the body favorably in the corners and along the boards....angles his man well....sticks with his man.... always gets involved....plays a physical and aggressive game....hits at every opportunity ....possesses excellent size and strength....sacrifices himself to complete the play....commands the respect of his teammates....leads by example.

32. Detroit
KRUPPKE, GORD
Defense, shoots right
6.01 202 lbs.
Born: April 2, 1969, in Slave Lake, Alta.

YEAR	TEAM	LEAGUE	GP	G	A	PTS	PIM
1986-87	Prince Albert	WHL	49	2	10	12	129
1985-86	Prince Albert	WHL	62	1	8	9	81

Possesses strength and balance on his feet....skates well backwards....shoots hard, accurate slapshots....leads his man well....plays a sound positional game....likes the stay-at-home style of defense....maintains good positioning when checking....uses his body effectively along the boards and in the corners....has good overall size and strength.... plays physically....clears traffic in front of the net....plays an aggressive and intimidating style.... works hard at all times....learns quickly....possesses mental and physical toughness.

33. Montreal
LeCLAIR, JOHN
Center, shoots left
6.01, 185 lbs.
Born: July 5, 1969, in St. Albans, VT.

YEAR	TEAM	LEAGUE	GP	G	A	PTS	PIM
1986-87	Bellows Free Acad. H.S.		23	44	40	84	25
1985-86	Bellows Free Acad. H.S.		22	41	28	69	145

Accelerates well....skates with good balance and a long stride....has an excellent scoring touch....displays exceptional creativity in the offensive zone....shoots accurately ....passes and leads well to both sides....stickhandles skillfully....knows how to set up the play....uses his body favorably, particularly in hiding the puck....plays a finesse game but can be tough and aggressive....has excellent desire, attitude and hockey sense.

34. N.Y. Islanders
HACKETT, JEFF
Goaltender, catches left
6.01, 175 lbs.
Born: June 1, 1968, in London, Ont.

YEAR	TEAM	LEAGUE	GP	MINS	GA	SO	AVG
1986-87	Oshawa	OHL	31	1672	85	2	3.05
1985-86	London	Jr. B	19	1150	66	0	3.43

Uses the butterfly with great effectiveness....blocks shots excellently with body and leg pads....recovers and controls quickly....has outstanding concentration....follows the puck well through traffic....moves with agility ....catches the puck whenever possible....positions himself well for the second shot....likes to challenge the shooters....stands his ground in close shooting situations....handles the puck skillfully.

35. Minnesota
McCRADY, SCOTT
Defense, shoots right
6.01, 195 lbs.
Born: October 30, 1968, in Calgary, Alta.

YEAR	TEAM	LEAGUE	GP	G	A	PTS	PIM
1986-87	Medicine Hat	WHL	70	10	66	76	157
1985-86	Medicine Hat	WHL	65	8	25	33	144

Turns well both ways....skates with good balance and agility ....moves well backwards....plays an offensive game....can either set up the play or score on his own....shoots well from the point....has excellent passing skills....finds and leads the open man....stickhandles and carries the puck skillfully out of his own end....recovers quickly....uses his body effectively along the boards and in the corners.... completes his checks....plays an aggressive game.... utilizes exceptional creativity in making his plays.

36. Washington
BALLANTYNE, JEFF
Defense, shoots left
6.02, 193 lbs.
Born: January 7, 1969, in Elmira, Ont.

YEAR	TEAM	LEAGUE	GP	G	A	PTS	PIM
1986-87	Ottawa	OHL	65	2	13	15	75
1984-85	Owen Sound	Jr. A	44	2	18	20	128

Skates with agility and strength....moves well backwards.... focuses primarily on his defensive role....passes the puck quickly....leads his man well....puckhandles skillfully.... takes the sure play....shows exceptional poise and confidence....reads and anticipates the play effectively....plays his man well....maintains solid positioning when checking ....angles attacking players away from the net....uses his body effectively along the boards and in the corners.... clears the front of the net with authority....will not be intimidated....works extremely hard....displays great attitude.... plays a steady defensive game.

37. Winnipeg
ERICKSON, PATRIK
Center/Right wing, shoots left
5.11, 169 lbs.
Born: March 13, 1969

YEAR	TEAM	LEAGUE	GP	G	A	PTS	PIM
1986-87	Brynas	Sweden	25	10	5	15	8
1985-86	Brynas	Sweden	30	20	16	36	14

Skates exceptionally well....releases a good, quick, accurate shot....handles the puck excellently....reads the play well and resonds accordingly....anticipates and thinks ahead ....has excellent hockey sense....possesses great technical skills....plays creatively.

38. Montreal
DESJARDINS, ERIC
Defense, shoots right
6.01, 185 lbs.
Born: June 14, 1969, in Rouyn, Que.

YEAR	TEAM	LEAGUE	GP	G	A	PTS	PIM
1986-87	Granby	QMJHL	66	14	24	38	75
1985-86	Laval	QMJHL	42	6	30	36	54

Skates well with balance and acceleration....moves right and left equally well....pivots and crosses over deftly.... shoots accurately from the point ....possesses a variety of powerful shots....passes crisply and accurately....keeps his options open....performs adeptly in both power-play and penalty-killing situations....plays a sound positional checking game.... stickchecks deftly....ties up his man in front of the net and in the corners....angles well....plays a sound, clean game....possesses physical and mental toughness....sticks to the game plan....blocks shots.... wants to excel....plays unselfishly....listens and learns.... works hard.

39. Hartford
BURT, ADAM
Defense, shoots left
6.02, 192 lbs.
Born: January 15, 1969, in Detroit, Mich.

YEAR	TEAM	LEAGUE	GP	G	A	PTS	PIM
1986-87	North Bay	OHL	57	4	27	31	138
1985-86	North Bay	OHL	49	0	11	11	81

Moves with good speed, balance and strength....concentrates mainly on defensive aspects of the game....shoots powerfully....passes well to either side....handles the puck deftly....moves skillfully out of his own zone.... clears traffic away from the net....plays a strong game along the boards and in the corners....hits and takes a hit very well....uses his body to his advantage....challenges opponents.... performs with strong competitive spirit and work ethic.... wants to improve with every outing....possesses a sound hockey sense.

40. Calgary
GRANT, KEVIN
Defense, shoots right
6.04, 210 lbs.
Born: January 9, 1969, in Halifax, N.S.

YEAR	TEAM	LEAGUE	GP	G	A	PTS	PIM
1986-87	Kitchener	OHL	52	5	18	23	125
1985-86	Kitchener	OHL	63	2	15	17	204

Skates well....shoots adeptly from the point....moves into scoring position quickly....checks solidly....clears out well in front of the net....hits at every opportunity....possesses excellent size and strength....gets involved in the action.... plays a tough game home or away....knows what to do in all situations....plays relentlessly.

41. Detroit
WILKIE, BOB
Defense, shoots right
6.02, 200 lbs.
Born: February 11, 1969, in Calgary, Alta.

YEAR	TEAM	LEAGUE	GP	G	A	PTS	PIM
1986-87	Swift Current	WHL	65	12	38	50	50
1985-86	Calgary	WHL	63	8	19	27	56

Skates with a long, smooth stride....pivots well....moves backwards deftly.....possesses an exceptional scoring talent for a defenseman....shoots accurately....passes and stickhandles excellently....finds the open man....likes to rush with the puck....plays an offensive style....recovers well.... has good size and strength.

42. Edmonton
WERENKA, BRAD
Defense, shoots left
6.02, 205 lbs.
Born: February 12, 1969, in Two Hills, Alta.

YEAR	TEAM	LEAGUE	GP	G	A	PTS	PIM
1986-87	Northern Michigan	WCHA	30	4	4	8	35
1985-86	Fort Saskatchewan	Tier II	29	12	23	35	24

Skates with strong balance and acceleration....possesses accurate wristshots and slapshots....keeps his passing options open at all times....uses his partner effectively ....passes firmly and crisply....moves the puck up the ice quickly....knows how to tie his man up....clears traffic in front of the net....reads the attack and adjusts appropriately ....angles and pinches in on his opponents excellently at both ends of the ice....protects the puck with his body.... takes his man out along the boards and in the corners.... plays a physically clean game....blocks shots....has an outstanding hockey sense.

Rounds 3-12 — Choices 43-252

Transferred draft choice notation:
Example: L.A.-Phi. represents a draft choice transferred from Los Angeles to Philadelphia.

ROUND # 3

#	Player	Team	School/Club
43	WILSON, Ross	Buf.-L.A.	Peterborough
44	SCHNEIDER, Mathieu	N.J.-Mtl.	Cornwall
45	VEILLEUX, Steve	Van.	Trois Rivieres
46	GAGNE, Simon	Min.-NYR	Laval
47	LEACH, Jamie	Pit.	Hamilton
48	KAMINSKI, Kevin	L.A.-Min.	Saskatoon
49	McINTYRE, John	Tor.	Guelph
50	RUSSELL, Cam	Chi.	Hull
51	SPROTT, Jim	Que.	London
52	HOLLAND, Dennis	NYR-Det.	Portland
53	MacVICAR, Andrew	Det.-N.J.-Buf.	Peterborough
54	MIEHM, Kevin	St.L.	Oshawa
55	EWEN, Dean	NYI	Spokane
56	LALONDE, Todd	Bos.	Sudbury
57	MALTAIS, Steve	Wsh.	Cornwall
58	GRAVEL, Francois	Wpg.-Mtl.	Shawinigan
59	NORDMARK, Robert	Mtl.-St.L.	Lulea, Sweden
60	DAGENAIS, Mike	Hfd.-Chi.	Peterborough
61	MAHONEY, Scott	Cgy.	Oshawa
62	HOSTAK, Martin	Phi.	Sparta Praha, Czech.
63	SMITH, Geoff	Edm.	St. Albert Tier II

ROUND # 6

#	Player	Team	School/Club
106	MARSHALL, Chris	Buf.	B.C. HS
107	HANKINSON, Ben	N.J.	Edina HS
108	VALK, Gary	Van.	Sherwood Park HS
109	NORTON, D'arcy	Min.	Kamloops
110	McEACHERN, Shawn	Pit.	Matignon HS
111	BATTERS, Greg	L.A.	Victoria
112	RHODES, Damian	Tor.	Richfield HS
113	McCORMICK, Mike	Chi.	Richmond, Tier II
114	SNOW, Garth	Que.	Mt. St. Charles HS
115	CAJKA, Ludek	NYR	Dukla Jihlava, Czech
116	CLIFFORD, Sean	Det.	Ohio State
117	ROBINSON, Rob	St.L.	Miami Univ.
118	DIMAIO, Rob	NYI	Medicine Hat
119	GLENNON, Matt	Bos.	Archbishop Wms. HS
120	DEFREITAS, Rich	Wsh.	St. Mark's HS
121	HARWELL, Joe	Wpg.	Hill Murray HS
122	KUNTAR, Les	Mtl.	Nichols HS
123	ST. CYR, Jeff	Hfd.	Michigan Tech
124	ALOI, Joe	Cgy.	Hull
125	LINK, Tony	Phi.	Dimond Alaska HS
126	TOUPAL, Radek	Edm.	Motor Budejovice, Czech.

ROUND # 4

#	Player	Team	School/Club
64	ERIKSSON, Peter	Buf.-Edm.	HV 71, Sweden
65	SULLIVAN, Brian	N.J.	Springfield Jrs.
66	TORREL, Doug	Van.	Hibbing HS
67	McPHERSON, Darwin	Min.-Bos.	New Westminster
68	KURKINEN, Risto	Pit.	Jypht, Finland
69	SULLIVAN, Michael	L.A.-NYR	Boston Univ.
70	HARRIS, Tim	Tor.-Cgy.	Pickering Jr. B
71	SACCO, Joe	Chi.-Tor.	Medford HS
72	MILLER, Kip	Que.	Michigan State
73	WEISBROD, John	NYR-Min.	Choate HS
74	REIMER, Mark	Det.	Saskatoon
75	SMITH, Darin	St.L.	North Bay
76	MANELUK, George	NYI	Brandon
77	DELGUIDICE, Matt	Bos.	St. Anselm College
78	LARTER, Tyler	Wsh.	Sault Ste. Marie
79	McLENNAN, Don	Wpg.	U. of Denver
80	MILLER, Kris	Mtl.	Greenway HS
81	YAKE, Terry	Hfd.	Brandon
82	RYMSHA, Andy	Cgy.-St.L.	Western Michigan
83	ERIKSSON, Tomaz	Phi.	Djurgardens, Sweden
84	BRADLEY, John	Edm.-Buf.	New Hampton HS

ROUND # 7

#	Player	Team	School/Club
127	FLANAGAN, Paul	Buf.	New Hampton HS
128	NEZIOL, Tom	N.J.	Miami Univ.
129	FANNING, Todd	Van.	Ohio State
130	KULDMEN, Timo	Min.	Kalpa, Finland
131	BODDEN, Jim	Pit.	Chatham Jr. B
132	KARJALAINEN, Kyosti	L.A.	Brynas, Sweden
133	JOBE, Trevor	Tor.	Moose Jaw
134	TEPPER, Stephen	Chi.	Westboro HS
135	HANUS, Tim	Que.	Minnetonka HS
136	THOMAS, Clint	NYR	Bartlett Alaska HS
137	BOBER, Mike	Det.	Laval
138	CRABTREE, Todd	St.L.	Governor Dummer
139	WALBYE, Knut	NYI	Furuset, Norway
140	CHEEVERS, Rob	Bos.	Boston College
141	OLENIUK, Devon	Wsh.	Kamloops
142	HARTJE, Todd	Wpg.	Harvard Univ.
143	KELLEY, Rob	Mtl.	Matignon HS
144	WOLF, Greg	Hfd.	Buffalo Regal Midget
145	CIAVAGLIA, Peter	Cgy.	Nichols HS
146	STRAPON, Mark	Phi.	Hayward HS
147	SRSEN, Tomas	Edm.	Zetor Brno, Czech.

ROUND # 5

#	Player	Team	School/Club
85	PERGOLA, David	Buf.	Belmont Hill HS
86	DEAN, Kevin	N.J.	Culver Military
87	FABIAN, Sean	Van.	Hill Murray HS
88	KIVELA, Teppo	Min.	Jokerit, Finland
89	WAVER, Jeff	Pit.	Hamilton
90	VUKONICH, Mike	L.A.	Duluth Denfeld HS
91	EASTWOOD, Mike	Tor.	Pembroke
92	SANDSTROM, Ulf	Chi.	Mo Do, Sweden
93	MENDEL, Rob	Que.	U. of Wisconsin
94	O'BORSKY, Eric	NYR	Yale Univ.
95	BRAZDA, Radomir	Det.	Pardubice, Czech.
96	GERENDER, Ken	St.L.-Wpg.	Greenway HS
97	VLK, Petr	NYI	Dukla Jihlava, Czech.
98	DONATO, Ted	Bos.	Catholic Memorial HS
99	BEAUCHESNE, Pat	Wsh.	Moose Jaw
100	AMUNDSON, Darrin	Wpg.	Duluth East HS
101	McCOOL, Steve	Mtl.	Hill HS
102	ROUSSEAU, Marc	Hfd.	U. of Denver
103	CORKERY, Tim	Cgy.	Ferris State College
104	GALL, Bill	Phi.	New Hampton HS
105	VAN ALLEN, Shaun	Edm.	Saskatoon

ROUND # 8

#	Player	Team	School/Club
148	DOOLEY, Sean	Buf.	Groton HS
149	DOWD, Jim	N.J.	Brick HS
150	TUMINEU, Viktor	Van.	Sparta Moscow, U.S.S.R.
151	SCHMIDT, Don	Min.	Kamloops
152	KUCERA, Jiri	Pit.	Dukla Jihlava, Czech
153	ROBERTS, Tim	L.A.-Buf.	Deerfield Academy
154	JENSEN, Chris	Tor.	Northwood HS
155	REILLY, John	Chi.	Phillips Andover HS
156	ENEBAK, Jake	Que.	Northfield HS
157	WIEGAND, Charles	NYR	Essex Junction HS
158	SCOTT, Kevin	Det.	Vernon Tier II
159	HEBERT, Guy	St.L.	Hamilton College
160	SATERDALEN, Jeff	NYI	Jefferson HS
161	WINNES, Chris	Bos.	Northwood HS
162	SJOGREN, Thomas	Wsh.	Vastra Frolunda, Sweden
163	KYLLONEN, Markku	Wpg.	Finland
164	GEIST, Will	Mtl.	St. Paul Academy
165	MOORE, John	Hfd.	Yale Univ.
166	FLEURY, Theoren	Cgy.	Moose Jaw
167	INGHAM, Darryl	Phi.	U. of Manitoba
168	ELLINGSEN, Age	Edm.	Storhamer, Norway

1987 ENTRY DRAFT

ROUND # 9
169	TKACHUK, Grant	Buf.	Saskatoon
170	BLESSMAN, John	N.J.	Toronto
171	DALY, Craig	Van.	New Hampton Prep
172	MYLLYS, Jarmo	Min.	Lukko, Finland
173	MacDOUGALL, Jack	Pit.	New Prep HS
174	GAWLICKI, Jeff	L.A.	N. Michigan
175	BLAD, Brian	Tor.	Belleville
176	WERNESS, Lance	Chi.	Burnsville HS
177	SEVCIK, Jaroslav	Que.	Zetor Brno, Czech.
178	BURRILL, Eric	NYR	Tartan HS
179	HAAPAKOSKI, Mikko	Det.	Karpat, Finland
180	DUMAS, Robert	St.L.	Seattle
181	HOWARD, Shawn	NYI	Penticton Tier II
182	OHMAN, Paul	Bos.	St. John HS
183	TRESL, Ladislav	Wsh.-Que.	Zetor Brno, Czech.
184	FERNOLZ, Jim	Wpg.	White Bear Lake HS
185	TREMBLAY, Eric	Mtl.	Drummondville
186	DAY, Joe	Hfd.	St. Lawrence Univ.
187	OSIECKI, Mark	Cgy.	Madison Jr.
188	McDONALD, Bruce	Phi.	Loomis-Chaffee HS
189	ARMSTRONG, Gavin	Edm.	RPI

ROUND # 10
190	HERBERS, Ian	Buf.	Swift Current
191	FRY, Peter	N.J.	Victoria
192	FLETCHER, John	Van.	Clarkson College
193	OLIMB, Larry	Min.	Warroad HS
194	McBRIDE, Daryn	Pit.	U. of Denver
195	PRESTON, John	L.A.	Boston Univ.
196	BERNACCI, Ron	Tor.	Hamilton
197	MARQUETTE, Dale	Chi.	Brandon
198	NAUSS, Darren	Que.	N. Battleford Tier II
199	PORTER, David	NYR	N. Michigan
200	BANNISTER, Darin	Det.	U. Illinois-Chicago
201	MARVIN, David	St.L.	Warroad HS
202	HERLIHY, John	NYI	Babson College
203	JONES, Casey	Bos.	Cornell Univ.
204	CLARKE, Chris	Wsh.	Pembroke
205	BARNETT, Brett	Wpg.-NYR	Wexford Jr.B
206	McKINLAY, Barry	Mtl.	U. Illinois-Chicago
207	CESARSKI, Andy	Hfd.-St.L.	Culver Military
208	SEDERGREN, William	Cgy.	Springfield Jrs.
209	MORROW, Steve	Phi.	Westminster HS
210	TINKHAM, Mike	Edm.	Newburyport HS

ROUND # 11
211	LITTMAN, David	Buf.	Boston College
212	CHARLAND, Alain	N.J.	Drummondville
213	HANSSON, Roger	Van.	Rogle, Sweden
214	FELICIO, Mark	Min.	Northwood HS
215	CARLSON, Mark	Pit.	Philadelphia Jrs.
216	VLACH, Rostislav	L.A.	Gottwaldov, Czech.
217	ALEXANDER, Ken	Tor.	Hamilton
218	LACOUTURE, Bill	Chi.	Natick HS
219	WILLIAMS, Mike	Que.	Ferris State College
220	MARCIANO, Lance	NYR	Choate HS
221	QUINLAN, Craig	Det.	Hill Murrary HS
222	ROLFE, Dan	St.L.	Brockville
223	ERICKSON, Michael	NYI	St John's Hill HS
224	LEMARQUE, Eric	Bos.	N. Michigan Univ.
225	VANIK, Milos	Wsh.	EHC Freiburg, Germany
226	ROUGELOT, Roger	Wpg.	Madison Jrs.
227	RONAN, Ed	Mtl.	Andover Academy
228	SULLIVAN, Kevin	Hfd.	Princeton Univ.
229	HASSELBLAD, Peter	Cgy.	Orebro, Sweden
230	RUSNAK, Darius	Phi.	Bratislava, Czech.
231	PAULETTI, Jeff	Edm.	U. of Minnesota

ROUND # 12
232	MacISAAC, Allan	Buf.	Guelph
233	EISENHUT, Neil	N.J.-Van.	Langley
234	EVO, Matt	Van.	Country Day HS
235	SHIELDS, Dave	Min.	U. of Denver
236	LILLJEBJORN, Ake	Pit.	Brynas, Sweden
237	LINDHOLM, Mikael	L.A.	Brynas, Sweden
238	WEINRICH, Alex	Tor.	North Yarmouth Acad.
239	LAPPIN, Mike	Chi.	Northwood HS
240	BRETTSCHNEIDER, Dan	Que.-Wsh.	Burnsville HS
241	DUUS, Jesper	NYR-Edm.	Rodoure SK, Denmark
242	JANSSON, Tomas	Det.	IK Talje, Sweden
243	SAVARD, Ray	St.L.	Regina
244	AVERILL, Will	NYI	Belmont Hill HS
245	GORMAN, Sean	Bos.	Matignon HS
246	KUMMU, Ryan	Wsh.	RPI
247	GORAN ELO, Hans	Wpg.	Djurgardens, Sweden
248	HERRING, Bryan	Mtl.	Dubuque Jrs.
249	LAURIN, Steve	Hfd.	Dartmouth College
250	SVENSSON, Magnus	Cgy.	Leksand, Sweden
251	ROEHL, Dale	Phi.	Minnetonka HS
252	VIAZMIKIN, Igor	Edm.	USSR

1986-87 Transaction Register

June 1986

- **21st** - **Scott Arniel** to Buffalo from Winnipeg for **Gilles Hamel**.
- **25th** - **Alfie Turcotte** to Edmonton from Montreal for future considerations.
- **30th** - **Tim Higgins** to Detroit from New Jersey for **Claude Loiselle**

July

- **3rd** - **Murray Eaves** to Edmonton from Winnipeg for future considerations.
- **29th** - **Kelly Kisio, Jim Leavins, Lane Lambert** and Detroit's 5th round pick in 1988 to NY Rangers from Detroit for **Glen Hanlon** and NY Rangers' 3rd round pick **(Dennis Holland)** in 1987 and 3rd round pick in 1988.

August

- **7th** - **Lee Norwood** to Detroit from St. Louis for **Larry Trader**.
- **15th** - **Brian Hayward** to Montreal from Winnipeg for **Steve Penney** and **Jan Ingman**.
- **18th** - **Steve Richmond** to New Jersey from Detroit for **Sam St. Laurent**.
- - **Walt Poddubny** to NY Rangers from Toronto for **Mike Allison**.

September

- **6th** - **Paul Boutilier** to Boston from NY Islanders as compensation for signing free agent **Brian Curran**.
- - **Jerome Dupont, Ken Yaremchuk** and Chicago's 4th round pick in 1987, **Joe Sacco**, to Toronto from Chicago as compensation for signing free agent **Gary Nylund**.
- **8th** - **Brian MacLellan** to Minnesota from NY Rangers for Minnesota's 3rd pick **(Simon Gagne)** in 1987.
- **17th** - NHL Supplemental Draft:

Boston	**Chris Olsen** (U. of Denver)
Buffalo	**Jeff Capello** (U. of Vermont)
	John Cullen (Boston U.)
Calgary	**Steve MacSwain** (U. of Minnesota)
Chicago	**Dave Randall** (Northern Michigan)
Detroit	**Rob Doyle** (Colorado College)
Edmonton	**Peter Heinze** (U. of Lowell)
Hartford	**Joe Tracy** (Ohio State)
Los Angeles	**Robert Kudelski** (Yale)
	Grant Paranika (North Dakota)
Minnesota	**Brian McKee** (Bowling Green)
Montreal	**Randy Exelby** (Lake Superior)
New Jersey	**Glen Engevik** (Northern Arizona)
	Tim Barakett (Harvard)
NY Islanders	**Gary Kruzich** (Bowling Green)
NY Rangers	**Gary Emmons** (Michigan)
Pittsburgh	**Jeff Lamb** (U. of Denver)
	Randy Taylor (Harvard)
Quebec	**Mike Natyshak** (Bowling Green)
St. Louis	**Marty Raus** (Northeastern U.)
Toronto	**Art Fitzgerald** (Trinity College)
Vancouver	**David Gourlie** (U. of Denver)
Washington	**Steve Cousins** (U. of Alberta)
Winnipeg	**Chris Levasseur** (U. of Alaska-Anchorage)

October

- **2nd** - **Don Jackson, Mike Golden** and **Miloslav Horava** to NY Rangers from Edmonton for **Reijo Ruotsalainen, Ville Kentala, Clark Donatelli** and **Jim Wiemer**.
- - **Craig Muni** to Buffalo from Edmonton for cash.
- **3rd** - **Brad Maxwell** to Vancouver from Toronto for Vancouver's 5th round pick in 1988.
- - **Terry Johnson** to Toronto from Calgary for **Jim Korn**.
- - **Jim Korn** to Buffalo from Calgary for **Brian Engblom**.
- - **Craig Muni** to Pittsburgh from Buffalo for future considerations.
- **6th** - **Craig Muni** to Edmonton from Pittsburgh for completion of **Gilles Meloche** deal, of September 11, 1985.
- - NHL Waiver Draft:

Buffalo	**Clark Gillies** (NY Islanders)
	Wilf Paiement (NY Rangers)
Hartford	**Gord Sherven** (Edmonton)
Los Angeles	**Bob Bourne** (NY Islanders)
	Mal Davis (Buffalo)
St. Louis	**Pat Hughes** (Buffalo)
Washington	**John Blum** (Boston)

- **7th** - **Yves Courteau** to Hartford from Calgary for **Mark Paterson**.
- - **Ric Seiling** to Detroit from Buffalo for future considerations.
- **8th** - **Dwight Schofield** to Pittsburgh from Washington for cash.
- - **Warren Young** to Pittsburgh from Detroit for cash.
- **15th** - **Shawn Evans** to Edmonton from St. Louis for **Todd Ewen**.
- **21st** - **Dave Barr** to Hartford from St. Louis for **Tim Bothwell**.
- **24th** - **Mark Pavelich** to Minnesota from NY Rangers for Minnesota's 3rd or 4th round pick in 1988.
- **30th** - **Dom Campedelli** to Philadelphia from Montreal for **Andre Villeneuve**.

November

- **12th** - **Dan Quinn** to Pittsburgh from Calgary for **Mike Bullard**.
- **13th** - **Curt Giles, Tony McKegney** and Minnesota's 2nd round pick in 1988 to NY Rangers from Minnesota for **Bob Brooke** and NY Rangers' rights to Minnesota's 4th round pick in 1988 (previously acquired by NY Rangers in **Mark Pavelich** trade).
- **18th** - **Tom Kurvers** to Buffalo from Montreal for Buffalo's 2nd round pick in 1988.
- **21st** - **Doug Halward** to Detroit from Vancouver for Detroit's 6th round pick in 1988.

December

- **2nd** - **Jim Benning** and **Dan Hodgson** to Vancouver from Toronto for **Rick Lanz**.
- **11th** - **Stu Kulak** to Edmonton from Vancouver for cash.
- - **Dave Semenko** to Hartford from Edmonton for Hartford's 3rd round pick in 1988.
- **18th** - **Bob Froese** to NY Rangers from Philadelphia for **Kjell Samuelsson** and NY Rangers' 2nd round pick in 1989.

TRADES & TRANSACTIONS

January, 1987

1st - **Bob Carpenter** and Washington's 2nd round pick in 1989 to NY Rangers from Washington for **Mike Ridley, Kelly Miller** and **Bob Crawford**.

5th - **Bill Derlago** to Quebec from Winnipeg for Quebec's 4th round pick in 1989.

12th - **Dave Barr** to Detroit from Hartford for **Randy Ladouceur**.

17th - **John Ogrodnick, Doug Shedden** and **Basil McRae** to Quebec from Detroit for **Brent Ashton, Gilbert Delorme** and **Mark Kumpel**.

21st - **Ron Duguay** to NY Rangers from Pittsburgh for **Chris Kontos**.

February

14th - **Garry Galley** to Washington from Los Angeles for **Al Jensen**.

24th - **Brad Maxwell** to Minnesota from NY Rangers for future considerations.

March

2nd- **Kent Nilsson** to Edmonton from Minnesota for future considerations.

5th - **Mark Osborne** to Toronto from NY Rangers for **Jeff Jackson** and Toronto's 3rd round pick in 1989.

- **Lane Lambert** to Quebec from NY Rangers for **Pat Price**.

6th - **Lee Fogolin** and **Mark Napier** to Buffalo from Edmonton for **Normand Lacombe, Wayne Van Dorp** and future considerations.

9th - **Mel Bridgman** to Detroit from New Jersey for **Chris Cichocki** and Detroit's 3rd round pick (**Andrew MacVicar**) in 1987.

- **Dom Campedelli** to Edmonton from Philadelphia for **Jeff Brubaker**.

10th - **Paul Boutilier** to Minnesota from Boston for Minnesota's 4th round pick (**Darwin MacPherson**) in 1987.

- **Raimo Helminen** to Minnesota from NY Rangers for future considerations.

- **Pat Hughes** to Hartford from St. Louis for cash.

- **Raimo Summanen** to Vancouver from Edmonton for **Moe Lemay**.

- **Stu Kulak** to NY Rangers from Edmonton for completion of **Reijo Ruotsalainen** trade October 2, 1986.

- **Marcel Dionne, Jeff Crossman** and Los Angeles' 3rd round pick in 1989 to NY Rangers for **Bob Carpenter** and **Tom Laidlaw**.

May

14th - **Alfie Turcotte** to Montreal from Edmonton for cash.

22nd- **Jan Ludvig** to Buffalo from New Jersey for **Jim Korn**.

- **Mark Paterson** to Chicago from Calgary for cash.

28th - **Tony McKegney** and **Rob Whistle** to St. Louis from NY Rangers for **Bruce Bell** and St. Louis' 3rd and 4th round picks in 1988.

29th - **Warren Young** to Detroit from Pittsburgh for cash.

June

1st - **John Blum** to Boston from Washington for Boston's 7th round pick in 1988.

- Rights to **Shane Doyle** to New Jersey from Vancouver for New Jersey's 12th round pick (**Neil Eisenhut**) in 1987.

5th - **Perry Turnbull** to St. Louis from Winnipeg for St. Louis' 5th round pick (**Ken Gernander**) in 1987.

8th - **Brian Mullen** and Winnipeg's 10th round pick (**Brett Barnett**) in 1987 to NY Rangers from Winnipeg for NY Rangers' 5th round pick in 1988 and 3rd round pick in 1989.

13th - **Gaetan Duchesne, Alan Haworth** and Washington's 1st round pick (**Joe Sakic**) in 1987 to Quebec from Washington for **Clint Malarchuk** and **Dale Hunter**.

- **Mark LaForest** to Philadelphia from Detroit for Philadelphia's 2nd round choice (**Bob Wilkie**) in 1987.

- **Ric Nattress** to Calgary from St. Louis for Calgary's 4th round pick (**Andy Rymsha**) in 1987 and 5th round pick in 1988.

- **David Maley** to New Jersey from Monteal for New Jersey's 3rd round pick (**Mathieu Schneider**) in 1987.

- **Tom Kurvers** to New Jersey from Buffalo for rights to Detroit's 3rd round pick (**Andrew MacVicar**) in 1987 (previously acquired by New Jersey in **Mel Bridgman** trade).

- NHL Supplemental Draft:

Boston	**Mike Jeffrey** (Northern Michigan U.)
Buffalo	**Dave Snuggerud** (U. of Minnesota)
	Mike DeCarle (Lake Superior)
Calgary	**Peter Lappin** (St. Lawrence U.)
Detroit	**Mike LaMoine** (U. of North Dakota)
Hartford	**Ken Lovesin** (U. of Saskatchewan)
Los Angeles	**Chris Panek** (Plattsburgh State U.)
Minnesota	**Shawn Chambers** (U. of Alaska-Fairbanks)
	Rick Boh (Colorado College)
Montreal	**Wayne Gagne** (Western Michigan)
New Jersey	**John Walker** (N. Alberta Institute of Technology)
	Jeff Madill (Ohio State)
NY Islanders	**Howie Vandermast** (Potsdam State)
NY Rangers	**Joe Lockwood** (U. of Michigan)
Philadelphia	**David Whyte** (Boston College)
Pittsburgh	**Dan Shea** (Boston College)
	John Leonard (Bowdoin College)
Quebec	**Mike Hitner** (U. of Alaska-Anchorage)
Vancouver	**Steve Johnson** (U. of North Dakota)
Washington	**Mark Anderson** (Ohio State)
Winnipeg	**Rob Fowler** (Merrimack College)

18th - Coach **Michel Bergeron** to NY Rangers from Quebec for NY Rangers' 1st round pick in 1988.

July

21st - **Jeff Brubaker** to NY Rangers from Philadelphia for cash.

August

26th - **Brad McCrimmon** to Calgary from Philadelphia for a choice of Calgary's 1st round selection in 1988 and 3rd round selection in 1989 Entry Drafts or Calgary's 3rd round selection in 1988 and 1st round selection in 1989 Entry Drafts.

27th - **Darren Jensen** and **Daryl Stanley** to Vancouver from Philadelphia for **Wendell Young**.

September

4th - **Bob McGill, Steve Thomas** and **Rick Vaive** to Chicago from Toronto for **Ed Olczyk** and **Al Secord**.

5th - **Duane Sutter** to Chicago from NY Islanders for future considerations.

Wayne Gretzky was hockey's dominant player in 1986-87. He was selected top player of the tournament at Rendez-Vous '87, the two-game series between the NHL All-Stars and Soviet Nationals played in Quebec in February. In the NHL, he captained the Oilers to a Stanley Cup win while capturing the Ross and Hart Trophies as League scoring leader and MVP.

Final Statistics 1986-87

Standings
Abbreviations: GA – goals against; **GF** – goals for; **GP** – games played; **L** – losses; **PTS** – points; **T** – ties; **W** – wins; **%** – percentage of games won.

CLARENCE CAMPBELL CONFERENCE
Norris Division

	GP	W	L	T	GF	GA	PTS	%
St. Louis	80	32	33	15	281	293	79	.494
Detroit	80	34	36	10	260	274	78	.488
Chicago	80	29	37	14	290	310	72	.450
Toronto	80	32	42	6	286	319	70	.438
Minnesota	80	30	40	10	296	314	70	.438

Smythe Division

	GP	W	L	T	GF	GA	PTS	%
Edmonton	80	50	24	6	372	284	106	.663
Calgary	80	46	31	3	318	289	95	.594
Winnipeg	80	40	32	8	279	271	88	.550
Los Angeles	80	31	41	8	318	341	70	.438
Vancouver	80	29	43	8	282	314	66	.413

PRINCE OF WALES CONFERENCE
Adams Division

	GP	W	L	T	GF	GA	PTS	%
Hartford	80	43	30	7	287	270	93	.581
Montreal	80	41	29	10	277	241	92	.575
Boston	80	39	34	7	301	276	85	.531
Quebec	80	31	39	10	267	276	72	.450
Buffalo	80	28	44	8	280	308	64	.400

Patrick Division

	GP	W	L	T	GF	GA	PTS	%
Philadelphia	80	46	26	8	310	245	100	.625
Washington	80	38	32	10	285	278	86	.538
NY Islanders	80	35	33	12	279	281	82	.513
NY Rangers	80	34	38	8	307	323	76	.475
Pittsburgh	80	30	38	12	297	290	72	.450
New Jersey	80	29	45	6	293	368	64	.400

Individual Leaders
Abbreviations: * – rookie eligible for Calder Trophy; **A** – assists; **G** – goals; **GP** – games played; **GT** – game-tying goals; **GW** – game-winning goals; **PIM** – penalties in minutes; **PP** – power play goals; **PTS** – points; **S** – shots on goal; **SH** – short-handed goals; **%** – percentage of shots resulting in goals; **+/−** – difference between Goals For (**GF**) scored when a player is on the ice with his team at even strength or short-handed and Goals Against (**GA**) scored when the same player is on the ice with his team at even strength or on a power play.

Individual Scoring Leaders for Art Ross Trophy

Player	Team	GP	G	A	PTS	+/−	PIM	PP	SH	GW	GT	S	%
Wayne Gretzky	Edmonton	79	62	121	183	70	28	13	7	4	0	288	21.5
Jari Kurri	Edmonton	79	54	54	108	35	41	12	5	10	0	211	25.6
Mario Lemieux	Pittsburgh	63	54	53	107	13	57	19	0	4	2	267	20.2
Mark Messier	Edmonton	77	37	70	107	21	73	7	4	5	0	208	17.8
Doug Gilmour	St. Louis	80	42	63	105	2−	58	17	1	2	1	207	20.3
Dino Ciccarelli	Minnesota	80	52	51	103	10	88	22	0	5	3	255	20.4
D. Hawerchuk	Winnipeg	80	47	53	100	3	52	10	0	4	2	267	17.6
Michel Goulet	Quebec	75	49	47	96	12−	61	17	0	6	2	276	17.8
Tim Kerr	Philadelphia	75	58	37	95	38	57	26	0	10	0	261	22.2
Ray Bourque	Boston	78	23	72	95	44	36	6	1	3	2	334	6.9
Ron Francis	Hartford	75	30	63	93	10	45	7	0	7	0	189	15.9
Denis Savard	Chicago	70	40	50	90	15	108	7	0	7	1	237	16.9
Steve Yzerman	Detroit	80	31	59	90	1−	43	9	1	2	1	217	14.3

FINAL STATISTICS, 1986-87

INDIVIDUAL LEADERS

Goal Scoring
Player	Team	GP	G
Wayne Gretzky	Edm.	79	62
Tim Kerr	Phi.	75	58
Mario Lemieux	Pit.	63	54
Jari Kurri	Edm.	79	54
Dino Ciccarelli	Min.	80	52
Michel Goulet	Que.	75	49

Assists
Player	Team	GP	A
Wayne Gretzky	Edm.	79	121
Ray Bourque	Bos.	78	72
Mark Messier	Edm.	77	70
Bryan Trottier	NYI	80	64
Ron Francis	Hfd.	75	63
Doug Gilmour	St. L.	80	63

Power Play Goals
Player	Team	GP	PP
Tim Kerr	Phi.	75	26
Dino Ciccarelli	Min.	80	22
Pat LaFontaine	NYI	80	19
Mario Lemieux	Pit.	63	19
*Jimmy Carson	L.A.	80	18
*Luc Robitaille	L.A.	79	18

Short-Hand Goals
Player	Team	GP	SH
Wayne Gretzky	Edm.	79	7
Russ Courtnall	Tor.	79	6
Mike Gartner	Wsh.	78	6
Petri Skriko	Van.	76	6
Dirk Graham	Min.	76	5
Jari Kurri	Edm.	79	5
Brian Propp	Phi.	53	5

Game-Winning Goals
Player	Team	GP	GW
Joe Mullen	Cgy.	79	12
Tim Kerr	Phi.	75	10
Mike Gartner	Wsh.	78	10
Jari Kurri	Edm.	79	10
Brent Sutter	NYI	69	8

Game-Tying Goals
Player	Team	GP	GT
Dino Ciccarelli	Min.	80	3

15 players with two each

Shots
Player	Team	GP	S
Ray Bourque	Bos.	78	334
Mike Gartner	Wsh.	78	317
Wayne Gretzky	Edm.	79	288
Russ Courtnall	Tor.	79	282

First Goals
Player	Team	GP	FG
Tim Kerr	Phi.	75	10
Doug Gilmour	St. L.	80	9
Michel Goulet	Que.	75	9
Wayne Presley	Chi.	80	8

At right: Dino Ciccarelli; opposite; Clint Malarchuk stops Rick Middleton.

INDIVIDUAL ROOKIE SCORING LEADERS

Rookie Leaders

Rookie	Team	GP	G	A	PTS	+/-	PIM	PP	SH	GW	GT	S	%
Luc Robitaille	Los Angeles	79	45	39	84	18-	28	18	0	3	1	199	22.6
Jimmy Carson	Los Angeles	80	37	42	79	5-	22	18	0	2	0	215	17.2
Christian Ruuttu	Buffalo	76	22	43	65	9	62	3	1	1	1	167	13.2
Brian Benning	St. Louis	78	13	36	49	2	110	7	0	2	0	144	9.0
Shawn Burr	Detroit	80	22	25	47	2	107	1	2	1	0	153	14.4
V. Damphousse	Toronto	80	21	25	46	6-	26	4	0	1	0	142	14.8
Michal Pivonka	Washington	73	18	25	43	19-	41	4	0	2	0	117	15.4
Steve Duchesne	Los Angeles	75	13	25	38	8	74	5	0	2	1	113	11.5
Jim Sandlak	Vancouver	78	15	21	36	4-	66	2	0	3	0	114	13.2
Fredrick Olausson	Winnipeg	72	7	29	36	3-	26	1	0	2	0	119	5.9

Goaltending Statistics

All goals against a team in any game are charged to the goaltender of that game for purposes of awarding the Bill Jennings Trophy.

Won-Lost-Tied record is based upon which goaltender was playing when the winning or tying goal was scored.

Empty-net goals are not counted in personal averages but are included in the team total and the shot(s) is included in the goaltender's shots against (**SA**) total.

GPI - games played in; **MINS** - minutes played; **AVG** - 60 minute average; **ENG** - empty-net goals against; **SO** - shutouts; **GA** - goals against; **SA** - shots against; **S%** - save percentage; *rookie eligible for Calder Trophy.

Goaltender	GPI	MINS	AVG	W	L	T	EN	SO	GA	SA	S%
MONTREAL											
Brian Hayward	37	2178	2.81	19	13	4	2	1	102	959	.893
Patrick Roy	46	2686	2.93	22	16	6	6	1	131	1210	.891
Totals	80	4864	2.97	41	29	10		2	241	2169	.889
PHILADELPHIA											
Bob Froese	3	180	2.67	3	0	0	0	0	8	88	.909
Glenn Resch	17	867	2.91	6	5	2	1	0	42	436	.903
*Ron Hextall	66	3799	3.00	37	21	6	4	1	190	1933	.902
Totals	80	4846	3.03	46	26	8		1	245	2457	.900
HARTFORD											
Mike Liut	59	3476	3.23	31	22	5	3	4	187	1625	.885
Steve Weeks	25	1367	3.42	12	8	2	2	1	78	615	.873
Totals	80	4843	3.35	43	30	7		5	270	2240	.879
WINNIPEG											
*Daniel Berthiaume	31	1758	3.17	18	7	3	1	1	93	810	.885
*Eldon Reddick	48	2762	3.24	21	21	4	2	0	149	1256	.881
Steve Penney	7	327	4.59	1	4	1	1	0	25	134	.812
Totals	80	4847	3.35	40	32	8		2	271	2200	.877

(Berthiaume and Reddick shared shutout January 9)

Goaltender	GPI	MINS	AVG	W	L	T	EN	SO	GA	SA	S%
DETROIT											
*Sam St. Laurent	6	342	2.81	1	2	2	0	0	16	135	.881
Glen Hanlon	36	1963	3.18	11	16	5	3	0	104	975	.893
Mark Laforest	5	219	3.29	2	1	0	0	0	12	111	.892
Greg Stefan	43	2351	3.45	20	17	3	4	1	135	1082	.875
Totals	80	4875	3.37	34	36	10		2	274	2303	.881
QUEBEC											
Mario Gosselin	30	1625	3.18	13	11	1	3	0	86	758	.886
Clint Malarchuk	54	3092	3.40	18	26	9	1	1	175	1512	.884
Richard Sevigny	4	144	4.58	0	2	0	0	0	11	56	.804
Totals	80	4861	3.41	31	39	10		1	276	2326	.881

GOALTENDING STATISTICS continued

Goaltender	GPI	MINS	AVG	W	L	T	EN	SO	GA	SA	S%
BOSTON											
*Bill Ranford	41	2234	3.33	16	20	2	1	3	124	1137	.891
Doug Keans	36	1942	3.34	18	8	4	1	0	108	909	.881
Pat Riggin	10	513	3.39	3	5	1	0	0	29	236	.877
*Cleon Daskalakis	2	97	4.43	2	0	0	0	0	7	51	.863
Roberto Romano	1	60	6.00	0	1	0	0	0	6	34	.824
Totals	**80**	**4846**	**3.42**	**39**	**34**	**7**		**3**	**276**	**2367**	**.883**
WASHINGTON											
Pete Peeters	37	2002	3.21	17	11	4	3	0	107	930	.885
*Bob Mason	45	2536	3.24	20	18	5	3	0	137	1247	.890
Al Jensen	6	328	4.94	1	3	1	1	0	27	184	.852
Totals	**80**	**4866**	**3.43**	**38**	**32**	**10**		**0**	**278**	**2361**	**.882**
NY ISLANDERS											
Kelly Hrudey	46	2634	3.30	21	15	7	1	0	145	1219	.881
Billy Smith	40	2252	3.52	14	18	5	3	1	132	1007	.869
Totals	**80**	**4886**	**3.45**	**35**	**33**	**12**		**1**	**281**	**2226**	**.874**
EDMONTON											
Grant Fuhr	44	2388	3.44	22	13	3	1	0	137	1149	.881
Andy Moog	46	2461	3.51	28	11	3	2	0	144	1218	.882
Totals	**80**	**4849**	**3.51**	**50**	**24**	**6**		**0**	**284**	**2367**	**.880**
PITTSBURGH											
Pat Riggin	17	988	3.34	8	6	3	0	0	55	465	.882
Gilles Meloche	43	2343	3.43	13	19	7	3	0	134	1123	.880
Roberto Romano	25	1438	3.63	9	11	2	1	0	87	713	.878
*Steve Guenette	2	113	4.25	0	2	0	2	0	8	54	.846
Totals	**80**	**4882**	**3.56**	**30**	**38**	**12**		**1**	**290**	**2355**	**.877**

(Meloche and Romano shared shutout January 23)

ST. LOUIS											
Greg Millen	42	2482	3.53	15	18	9	3	0	146	1152	.873
Rick Wamsley	41	2410	3.54	17	15	6	2	0	142	1212	.883
Totals	**80**	**4892**	**3.59**	**32**	**33**	**15**		**0**	**293**	**2364**	**.876**

Mike Vernon

CALGARY											
Rejean Lemelin	34	1735	3.25	16	9	1	4	2	94	825	.886
*Mike Vernon	54	2957	3.61	30	21	1	2	1	178	1528	.883
*Doug Dadswell	2	125	4.80	0	1	1	1	0	10	73	.861
Totals	**80**	**4817**	**3.60**	**46**	**31**	**3**		**3**	**289**	**2426**	**.881**
BUFFALO											
Tom Barrasso	46	2501	3.65	17	23	2	4	2	152	1202	.873
Jacques Cloutier	40	2167	3.79	11	19	5	1	0	137	1035	.868
*Daren Puppa	3	185	4.22	0	2	1	1	0	13	80	.835
Totals	**80**	**4853**	**3.81**	**28**	**44**	**8**		**2**	**308**	**2317**	**.867**

FINAL STATISTICS, 1986-87

Goaltender	GPI	MINS	AVG	W	L	T	EN	SO	GA	SA	S%
CHICAGO											
Warren Skorodenski	3	155	2.71	1	0	1	0	0	7	90	.922
Bob Sauve	46	2660	3.59	19	19	5	0	1	159	1497	.894
Murray Bannerman	39	2059	4.14	9	18	8	2	0	142	1122	.873
Totals	**80**	**4874**	**3.82**	**29**	**37**	**14**		**1**	**310**	**2709**	**.886**
MINNESOTA											
*Kari Takko	38	2075	3.44	13	18	4	4	0	119	1061	.887
Don Beaupre	47	2622	3.98	17	20	6	4	1	174	1439	.879
*Mike Sands	3	163	4.42	0	2	0	1	0	12	104	.883
Totals	**80**	**4860**	**3.88**	**30**	**40**	**10**		**1**	**314**	**2604**	**.879**
VANCOUVER											
Richard Brodeur	53	2972	3.59	20	25	5	3	1	178	1391	.872
Frank Caprice	25	1390	3.84	8	11	2	2	0	89	643	.861
*Troy Gamble	1	60	4.00	0	1	0	1	0	4	23	.818
*Wendell Young	8	420	5.00	1	6	1	2	0	35	224	.842
Totals	**80**	**4842**	**3.89**	**29**	**43**	**8**		**1**	**314**	**2281**	**.862**
TORONTO											
Allan Bester	36	1808	3.65	10	14	3	3	2	110	991	.889
Ken Wregget	56	3026	3.97	22	28	3	3	0	200	1598	.875
Tim Bernhardt	1	20	9.00	0	0	0	0	0	3	7	.571
Totals	**80**	**4854**	**3.94**	**32**	**42**	**6**		**2**	**319**	**2596**	**.877**
NY RANGERS											
John Vanbiesbrouck	50	2656	3.64	18	20	5	6	0	161	1369	.882
Bob Froese	28	1474	3.74	14	11	0	1	0	92	784	.883
*Ron Scott	1	65	4.62	0	0	1	0	0	5	35	.857
Doug Soetaert	13	675	5.16	2	7	2	1	0	58	368	.842
Totals	**80**	**4870**	**3.99**	**34**	**38**	**8**		**0**	**324**	**2556**	**.873**
LOS ANGELES											
Roland Melanson	46	2734	3.69	18	21	6	3	1	168	1420	.881
Darren Eliot	24	1404	4.40	8	13	2	5	1	103	692	.850
Bob Janecyk	7	420	4.86	4	3	0	0	0	34	222	.847
Al Jensen	5	300	5.40	1	4	0	1	0	27	154	.824
Totals	**80**	**4858**	**4.21**	**31**	**41**	**8**		**2**	**341**	**2488**	**.863**
NEW JERSEY											
*Kirk Mclean	4	160	3.75	1	1	0	1	0	10	73	.861
Alain Chevrier	58	3153	4.32	24	26	2	3	0	227	1793	.873
*Chris Terreri	7	286	4.41	0	3	1	1	0	21	173	.878
*Craig Billington	22	1114	4.79	4	13	2	0	0	89	569	.844
*Karl Friesen	4	130	7.38	0	2	1	0	0	16	80	.800
Totals	**80**	**4843**	**4.56**	**29**	**45**	**6**		**0**	**368**	**2688**	**.863**

Tom Barrasso

Mike Liut

GOALTENDING LEADERS

Goals Against Average Minimum 25 games

Goaltender	Team	GPI	MINS	GA	AVG
Brian Hayward	Montreal	37	2178	102	2.81
Patrick Roy	Montreal	46	2686	131	2.93
*Ron Hextall	Philadelphia	66	3799	190	3.00
*Daniel Berthiaume	Winnipeg	31	1758	93	3.17
Glen Hanlon	Detroit	36	1963	104	3.18
Mario Gosselin	Quebec	30	1625	86	3.18

Wins

Goaltender	Team	GPI	MINS	W	L	T
*Ron Hextall	Philadelphia	66	3799	37	21	6
Mike Liut	Hartford	59	3476	31	22	5
*Mike Vernon	Calgary	54	2957	30	21	1
Andy Moog	Edmonton	46	2461	28	11	3
Alain Chevrier	New Jersey	58	3153	24	26	2

Save Percentage

Goaltender	Team	GPI	MINS	GA	SA	S%	W	L	T
*Ron Hextall	Philadelphia	66	3799	190	1933	.902	37	21	6
Bob Sauve	Chicago	46	2660	159	1497	.894	19	19	5
Glen Hanlon	Detroit	36	1963	104	975	.893	11	16	5
Brian Hayward	Montreal	37	2178	102	959	,893	19	13	4
*Bill Ranford	Boston	41	2234	124	1137	.891	16	20	2
Patrick Roy	Montreal	46	2686	131	1210	.891	22	16	6

Shutouts

Goaltender	Team	GPI	MINS	SO	W	L	T
Mike Liut	Hartford	59	3476	4	31	22	5
*Bill Ranford	Boston	41	2234	3	16	20	2
Tom Barrasso	Buffalo	46	2501	2	17	23	2
Rejean Lemelin	Calgary	34	1735	2	16	9	1
Allan Bester	Toronto	36	1808	2	10	14	3

Team Statistics

TEAMS' HOME-ROAD RECORD

Norris Division

Home

	GP	W	L	T	GF	GA	PTS	%
STL	40	21	12	7	153	135	49	.613
DET	40	20	14	6	137	116	46	.575
CHI	40	18	13	9	168	152	45	.563
TOR	40	22	14	4	167	139	48	.600
MIN	40	17	20	3	150	143	37	.463
TOT	200	98	73	29	775	685	225	.563

Road

	GP	W	L	T	GF	GA	PTS	%
STL	40	11	21	8	128	158	30	.375
DET	40	14	22	4	123	158	32	.400
CHI	40	11	24	5	122	158	27	.338
TOR	40	10	28	2	119	180	22	.275
MIN	40	13	20	7	146	171	33	.413
TOT	200	59	115	26	638	825	144	.360

Smythe Division

Home

	GP	W	L	T	GF	GA	PTS	%
EDM	40	29	6	5	199	124	63	.788
CGY	40	25	13	2	162	128	52	.650
WPG	40	25	12	3	150	116	53	.663
LA	40	20	17	3	164	156	43	.538
VAN	40	17	19	4	157	159	38	.475
TOT	200	116	67	17	832	683	249	.623

Road

	GP	W	L	T	GF	GA	PTS	%
EDM	40	21	18	1	173	160	43	.538
CGY	40	21	18	1	156	161	43	.538
WPG	40	15	20	5	129	155	35	.438
LA	40	11	24	5	154	185	27	.338
VAN	40	12	24	4	125	155	28	.350
TOT	200	80	104	16	737	816	176	.440

Adams Division

Home

	GP	W	L	T	GF	GA	PTS	%
HFD	40	26	9	5	150	112	57	.713
MTL	40	27	9	4	164	113	58	.725
BOS	40	25	11	4	174	132	54	.675
QUE	40	20	13	7	145	132	47	.588
BUF	40	18	18	4	153	144	40	.500
TOT	200	116	60	24	786	633	256	.640

Road

	GP	W	L	T	GF	GA	PTS	%
HFD	40	17	21	2	137	158	36	.450
MTL	40	14	20	6	113	128	34	.425
BOS	40	14	23	3	127	144	31	.388
QUE	40	11	26	3	122	144	25	.313
BUF	40	10	26	4	127	164	24	.300
TOT	200	66	116	18	626	738	150	.375

Patrick Division

Home

	GP	W	L	T	GF	GA	PTS	%
PHI	40	29	9	2	168	111	60	.750
WSH	40	22	15	3	144	125	47	.588
NYI	40	20	15	5	148	139	45	.563
NYR	40	18	18	4	152	156	40	.500
PIT	40	19	15	6	164	145	44	.550
NJ	40	20	17	3	155	164	43	.538
TOT	240	128	89	23	931	840	279	.581

Road

	GP	W	L	T	GF	GA	PTS	%
PHI	40	17	17	6	142	134	40	.500
WSH	40	16	17	7	141	153	39	.488
NYI	40	15	18	7	131	142	37	.463
NYR	40	16	20	4	155	167	36	.450
PIT	40	11	23	6	133	145	28	.350
NJ	40	9	28	3	138	204	21	.263
TOT	240	84	123	33	840	945	201	.419

TEAMS' DIVISIONAL RECORD

Norris Division

Against Own Division

	GP	W	L	T	GF	GA	PTS	%
STL	32	17	8	7	123	107	41	.641
DET	32	16	12	4	103	96	36	.563
CHI	32	10	15	7	114	122	27	.422
TOR	32	13	17	2	96	109	28	.438
MIN	32	12	16	4	125	127	28	.438
TOT	160	68	68	24	561	561	160	.500

Against Other Divisions

	GP	W	L	T	GF	GA	PTS	%
STL	48	15	25	8	158	186	38	.396
DET	48	18	24	6	157	178	42	.438
CHI	48	19	22	7	176	188	45	.469
TOR	48	19	25	4	190	210	42	.438
MIN	48	18	24	6	171	187	42	.438
TOT	240	89	120	31	852	949	209	.435

Smythe Division

Against Own Division

	GP	W	L	T	GF	GA	PTS	%
EDM	32	17	11	4	154	124	38	.594
CGY	32	17	14	1	118	125	35	.547
WPG	32	19	13	0	125	109	38	.594
LA	32	10	19	3	120	151	23	.359
VAN	32	12	18	2	121	129	26	.406
TOT	160	75	75	10	638	638	160	.500

Against Other Divisions

	GP	W	L	T	GF	GA	PTS	%
EDM	48	33	13	2	218	160	68	.708
CGY	48	29	17	2	200	164	60	.625
WPG	48	21	19	8	154	162	50	.521
LA	48	21	22	5	198	190	47	.490
VAN	48	17	25	6	161	185	40	.417
TOT	240	121	96	23	931	861	265	.552

Adams Division

Against Own Division

	GP	W	L	T	GF	GA	PTS	%
HFD	32	17	12	3	104	103	37	.578
MTL	32	18	10	4	104	87	40	.625
BOS	32	13	17	2	115	118	28	.438
QUE	32	12	17	3	98	103	27	.422
BUF	32	12	16	4	100	110	28	.438
TOT	160	72	72	16	521	521	160	.500

Against Other Divisions

	GP	W	L	T	GF	GA	PTS	%
HFD	48	26	18	4	183	167	56	.583
MTL	48	23	19	6	173	154	52	.542
BOS	48	26	17	5	186	158	57	.594
QUE	48	19	22	7	169	173	45	.469
BUF	48	16	28	4	180	198	36	.375
TOT	240	110	104	26	891	850	246	.513

Patrick Division

Against Own Division

	GP	W	L	T	GF	GA	PTS	%
PHI	35	20	11	4	139	102	44	.629
WSH	35	16	16	3	115	128	35	.500
NYI	35	18	12	5	141	114	41	.586
NYR	35	17	15	3	128	129	37	.529
PIT	35	10	19	6	128	140	26	.371
NJ	35	13	21	1	133	171	27	.386
TOT	210	94	94	22	784	784	210	.500

Against Other Divisions

	GP	W	L	T	GF	GA	PTS	%
PHI	45	26	15	4	171	143	56	.622
WSH	45	22	16	7	170	150	51	.567
NYI	45	17	21	7	138	167	41	.456
NYR	45	17	23	5	179	194	39	.433
PIT	45	20	19	6	169	150	46	.511
NJ	45	16	24	5	160	197	37	.411
TOT	270	118	118	34	987	1001	270	.500

PENALTIES AND POWER-PLAYS

TEAMS' POWER-PLAY RECORDS

Abbreviations: ADV – total advantages; **PPGF** – power-play goals for; **%** – arrived by dividing number of power-play goals by total advantages.

Home

	Team	ADV	PPGF	%
1	MIN	178	47	26.4
2	VAN	180	47	26.1
3	NYI	169	44	26.0
4	STL	169	42	24.9
5	CGY	174	42	24.1
6	LA	198	47	23.7
7	BOS	166	39	23.5
8	MTL	166	38	22.9
9	QUE	174	39	22.4
10	WSH	190	41	21.6
11	PIT	202	43	21.3
12	N.J	193	41	21.2
13	BUF	201	40	20.4
14	HFD	189	38	20.1
15	EDM	163	32	19.6
16	NYR	205	40	19.5
17	CHI	180	35	19.4
18	TOR	177	33	18.6
19	DET	177	32	18.1
20	PHI	180	32	17.8
21	WPG	153	25	16.3
	TOTAL	3784	818	21.6

Road

Team	ADV	PPGF	%
CGY	144	38	26.4
LA	191	50	26.2
EDM	155	38	24.5
STL	155	37	23.9
NYI	168	40	23.8
DET	159	37	23.3
NJ	189	41	21.7
HFD	163	35	21.5
NYR	170	35	20.6
PHI	175	36	20.6
QUE	180	37	20.6
MIN	177	36	20.3
VAN	173	35	20.2
MTL	155	29	18.7
WPG	147	27	18.4
PIT	176	31	17.6
BUF	163	27	16.6
BOS	168	26	15.5
TOR	126	19	15.1
WSH	165	24	14.5
CHI	144	20	13.9
	3443	698	20.3

Overall

Team	ADV	PPGF	%
CGY	318	80	25.2
NYI	337	84	24.9
LA	389	97	24.9
STL	324	79	24.4
MIN	355	83	23.4
VAN	353	82	23.2
EDM	318	70	22.0
QUE	354	76	21.5
NJ	382	82	21.5
MTL	321	67	20.9
HFD	352	73	20.7
DET	336	69	20.5
NYR	375	75	20.0
PIT	378	74	19.6
BOS	334	65	19.5
PHI	355	68	19.2
BUF	364	68	18.7
WSH	355	65	18.3
WPG	300	52	17.3
TOR	303	52	17.2
CHI	324	55	17.0
	7227	1516	21.0

SHORT HAND GOALS FOR

Home

	Team	SHGF
1	EDM	14
2	PHI	11
3	TOR	7
4	VAN	7
5	BOS	6
6	HFD	6
7	LA	6
8	NYI	6
9	QUE	6
10	WPG	5
11	DET	4
12	MIN	4
13	NJ	4
14	PIT	4
15	STL	4
16	CGY	3
17	MTL	3
18	NYR	3
19	WSH	3
20	BUF	1
21	CHI	1
	TOTAL	108

Road

Team	SHGF
EDM	14
PHI	11
TOR	10
NYR	9
BOS	7
WSH	6
DET	5
HFD	5
MIN	5
NJ	5
BUF	4
CGY	4
CHI	4
LA	3
MTL	3
PIT	3
VAN	3
WPG	3
NYI	2
QUE	2
STL	2
	110

Overall

Team	SHGF
EDM	28
PHI	22
TOR	17
BOS	13
NYR	12
HFD	11
VAN	10
DET	9
LA	9
MIN	9
NJ	9
WSH	9
NYI	8
QUE	8
WPG	8
CGY	7
PIT	7
MTL	6
STL	6
BUF	5
CHI	5
	218

SHORT HAND GOALS AGAINST

Home

	Team	SHGA
1	BOS	1
2	MTL	2
3	DET	3
4	PHI	3
5	WPG	3
6	NJ	4
7	NYI	4
8	CGY	5
9	CHI	5
10	EDM	5
11	HFD	5
12	STL	5
13	WSH	5
14	BUF	6
15	PIT	6
16	QUE	6
17	LA	7
18	VAN	7
19	TOR	8
20	NYR	9
21	MIN	11
	TOTAL	110

Road

Team	SHGA
PHI	2
TOR	2
BUF	3
EDM	3
PIT	3
BOS	4
CHI	4
DET	4
MTL	4
VAN	4
HFD	5
NYI	5
NJ	6
NYR	6
QUE	6
STL	6
WPG	6
MIN	7
CGY	9
LA	9
WSH	10
	108

Overall

Team	SHGA
BOS	5
PHI	5
MTL	6
DET	7
EDM	8
BUF	9
CHI	9
NYI	9
PIT	9
WPG	9
HFD	10
NJ	10
TOR	10
STL	11
VAN	11
QUE	12
CGY	14
NYR	15
WSH	15
LA	16
MIN	18
	218

TEAM PENALTIES

Abbreviations: GP - games played; **PEN** - total penalty minutes, including bench penalties; **BMI** - total bench minor minutes; **AVG** - average penalty minutes/calculated by dividing total penalty minutes by games played.

Team	GP	PEN	BMI	AVG	Team	GP	PEN	BMI	AVG
HFD	80	1496	12	18.7	BUF	80	1810	24	22.6
WPG	80	1537	10	19.2	TOR	80	1827	14	22.8
STL	80	1572	6	19.7	NYI	80	1857	26	23.2
CHI	80	1692	16	21.2	BOS	80	1870	30	23.4
PIT	80	1693	16	21.2	VAN	80	1917	20	24.0
EDM	80	1721	26	21.5	MIN	80	1936	20	24.2
NYR	80	1718	16	21.5	CGY	80	2036	18	25.5
WSH	80	1720	18	21.5	LA	80	2038	18	25.5
NJ	80	1735	22	21.7	PHI	80	2082	14	26.0
QUE	80	1741	12	21.8	DET	80	2209	12	27.6
MTL	80	1802	32	22.5	TOTAL	840	38009	382	45.2

TEAMS' PENALTY KILLING RECORDS

Abbreviations: TSH – times short-handed; **PPGA** – power-play goals against; **%** – arrived by dividing – times short minus power-play goals against — by times short.

Home

	Team	TSH	PPGA	%
1	WSH	150	20	86.7
2	STL	143	19	86.7
3	WPG	148	24	83.8
4	QUE	146	24	83.6
5	HFD	159	27	83.0
6	TOR	160	28	82.5
7	NYR	182	32	82.4
8	PHI	206	37	82.0
9	MTL	150	27	82.0
10	DET	165	30	81.8
11	BOS	157	29	81.5
12	NYI	170	35	79.4
13	CGY	187	40	78.6
14	MIN	176	39	77.8
15	EDM	162	36	77.8
16	BUF	169	38	77.5
17	LA	181	44	75.7
18	NJ	171	44	74.3
19	PIT	150	40	73.3
20	CHI	161	44	72.7
21	VAN	150	41	72.7
	TOTAL	3443	698	79.7

Road

Team	TSH	PPGA	%
MTL	154	24	84.4
WPG	176	29	83.5
QUE	165	28	83.0
PHI	196	34	82.7
EDM	210	38	81.9
BOS	168	31	81.5
PIT	168	32	81.0
CGY	181	35	80.7
NYR	197	39	80.2
CHI	180	37	79.4
VAN	169	36	78.7
WSH	176	38	78.4
DET	192	43	77.6
NYI	211	48	77.3
STL	160	39	75.6
HFD	177	44	75.1
BUF	186	48	74.2
TOR	163	43	73.6
MIN	200	53	73.5
NJ	190	51	73.2
LA	165	48	70.9
	3784	818	78.4

Overall

Team	TSH	PPGA	%
WPG	324	53	83.6
QUE	311	52	83.3
MTL	304	51	83.2
PHI	402	71	82.3
WSH	326	58	82.2
BOS	325	60	81.5
NYR	379	71	81.3
STL	303	58	80.9
EDM	372	74	80.1
CGY	368	75	79.6
DET	357	73	79.6
HFD	336	71	78.9
NYI	381	83	78.2
TOR	323	71	78.0
PIT	318	72	77.4
CHI	341	81	76.2
VAN	319	77	75.9
BUF	355	86	75.8
MIN	376	92	75.5
NJ	361	95	73.7
LA	346	92	73.4
	7227	1516	79.0

Overtime Results

	1986-87				1985-86				1984-85				1983-84			
Team	GP	W	L	T	GP	W	L	T	GP	W	L	T	GP	W	L	T
Boston	12	2	3	7	17	2	3	12	18	4	4	10	7	1	0	6
Buffalo	13	1	4	8	9	1	2	6	17	0	3	14	13	5	1	7
Calgary	4	1	0	3	12	1	2	9	14	1	1	12	18	4	0	14
Chicago	15	1	0	14	12	3	1	8	12	2	3	7	9	0	1	8
Detroit	17	2	5	10	13	2	5	6	14	0	2	12	11	3	1	7
Edmonton	14	5	3	6	14	5	2	7	12	0	1	11	9	4	0	5
Hartford	9	2	0	7	7	1	2	4	17	4	4	9	15	2	3	10
Los Angeles	12	2	2	8	14	3	3	8	19	3	2	14	17	1	3	13
Minnesota	14	2	2	10	15	4	2	9	15	1	2	12	18	5	3	10
Montreal	16	2	4	10	14	1	6	7	18	3	3	12	7	1	1	5
New Jersey	13	3	4	6	10	4	3	3	12	0	2	10	15	1	7	7
NY Islanders	20	5	3	12	17	4	1	12	15	1	8	6	10	3	3	4
NY Rangers	19	5	6	8	13	0	7	6	17	2	5	10	17	5	3	9
Philadelphia	10	1	1	8	9	4	1	4	9	1	1	7	14	3	1	10
Pittsburgh	21	5	4	12	14	3	3	8	8	3	0	5	12	1	5	6
Quebec	14	0	4	10	11	4	1	6	14	3	2	9	15	0	5	10
St. Louis	21	4	2	15	17	5	3	9	15	2	1	12	11	3	1	7
Toronto	13	3	4	6	17	4	6	7	15	5	2	8	13	1	3	9
Vancouver	10	2	0	8	16	1	2	13	17	7	1	9	16	3	4	9
Washington	17	5	2	10	11	4	0	7	12	3	0	9	9	1	3	5
Winnipeg	11	2	1	8	8	0	1	7	14	3	1	10	24	7	6	11
Totals	148	55		93	135	56		79	152	48		104	140	54		86

1986-87
Home Team Wins: 31
Visiting Team Wins: 24

1986-87 Schedule Results

Game #	Visitor		Home	
Thur. Oct. 9				
1	Calgary	5	Boston	3
2	Buffalo	2	Winnipeg	3
3	Montreal	4	Toronto	7
4	Detroit	1	Quebec	6
5	NY Islanders	2	Chicago	3
6	New Jersey	5	NY Rangers	3
7	Edmonton	1	Philadelphia	2
8	Washington	4	Pittsburgh	5
9	St. Louis	4	Los Angeles	3
Sat. Oct. 11				
10	Boston	4	New Jersey	5
11	Calgary	5	Hartford	6
12	Buffalo	5	Toronto	5
13	Edmonton	5	Montreal	4
14	Minnesota	4	Quebec	4
15	NY Islanders	4	Los Angeles	5
16	NY Rangers	5	Pittsburgh	6
17	Philadelphia	6	Washington	1
18	Chicago	3	Detroit	4
19	St. Louis	3	Vancouver	4
Sun. Oct. 12				
20	Hartford	2	Boston	7
21	Calgary	4	Buffalo	2
22	Pittsburgh	4	Chicago	1
23	Edmonton	3	Winnipeg	5
Mon. Oct. 13				
24	Minnesota	4	Montreal	6
25	Quebec	7	Vancouver	1
26	Washington	7	NY Rangers	6
Tues. Oct. 14				
27	Boston	2	Winnipeg	1
28	Los Angeles	3	Pittsburgh	4
29	St. Louis	2	Toronto	1
Wed. Oct. 15				
30	Montreal	0	Buffalo	0
31	Quebec	2	Edmonton	5
32	NY Rangers	5	Chicago	5
33	Vancouver	2	New Jersey	3
34	Los Angeles	4	Detroit	3
Thur. Oct. 16				
35	Boston	5	Minnesota	3
36	Winnipeg	4	Hartford	4
37	Quebec	4	Calgary	2
38	Washington	4	NY Islanders	7
39	Vancouver	2	Philadelphia	6
Fri. Oct. 17				
40	Pittsburgh	7	Buffalo	3
41	Toronto	3	New Jersey	2
42	Detroit	3	Edmonton	4
Sat. Oct. 18				
43	Boston	4	Los Angeles	1
44	Philadelphia	6	Hartford	3
45	Buffalo	4	Washington	2
46	Winnipeg	3	Montreal	5
47	Quebec	3	St. Louis	4
48	NY Rangers	4	NY Islanders	2
49	New Jersey	4	Pittsburgh	8
50	Chicago	2	Toronto	3
51	Detroit	5	Calgary	3
52	Vancouver	1	Minnesota	3
Sun. Oct. 19				
53	NY Islanders	2	NY Rangers	2
54	Winnipeg	1	Philadelphia	3
55	Minnesota	8	Chicago	5
56	Edmonton	6	Los Angeles	7
Mon. Oct. 20				
57	Washington	5	Montreal	4
Tues. Oct. 21				
58	Washington	4	Quebec	4
59	New Jersey	3	NY Islanders	6
60	Chicago	2	Edmonton	9
Wed. Oct. 22				
61	Boston	1	Vancouver	3
62	Buffalo	4	Pittsburgh	5
63	Montreal	4	Detroit	3
64	Quebec	7	Toronto	1
65	Los Angeles	4	NY Rangers	5
66	Minnesota	4	St. Louis	3
67	Edmonton	3	Calgary	6

Game #	Visitor		Home	
Thur. Oct. 23				
68	Los Angeles	3	New Jersey	5
69	Pittsburgh	3	Philadelphia	5
Fri. Oct. 24				
70	Boston	2	Edmonton	6
71	Hartford	5	Buffalo	4
72	Minnesota	2	Washington	8
73	St. Louis	1	Detroit	1
74	Chicago	2	Vancouver	2
75	Calgary	2	Winnipeg	5
Sat. Oct. 25				
76	Buffalo	2	Hartford	3
77	NY Rangers	3	Montreal	3
78	Toronto	3	Quebec	4
79	Los Angeles	3	NY Islanders	4
80	New Jersey	1	Washington	2
81	Philadelphia	2	Pittsburgh	4
82	Detroit	3	St. Louis	1
Sun. Oct. 26				
83	Boston	6	Calgary	0
84	Toronto	3	NY Rangers	3
85	Minnesota	1	Philadelphia	4
86	Chicago	8	Winnipeg	4
87	Vancouver	2	Edmonton	3
Mon. Oct. 27				
88	Los Angeles	5	Montreal	6
Tues. Oct. 28				
89	Pittsburgh	2	Hartford	5
90	Los Angeles	2	Quebec	6
91	Philadelphia	1	NY Islanders	2
92	Washington	5	Vancouver	2
93	Chicago	1	Toronto	2
94	Calgary	4	Minnesota	7
Wed. Oct. 29				
95	Buffalo	2	Montreal	5
96	NY Rangers	2	St. Louis	7
97	New Jersey	8	Pittsburgh	5
98	Washington	3	Edmonton	6
99	Chicago	2	Detroit	5
100	Calgary	2	Winnipeg	6
Thur. Oct. 30				
101	Montreal	3	Boston	3
102	Hartford	2	Toronto	6
103	Quebec	3	Philadelphia	6
104	NY Islanders	6	New Jersey	7
105	Detroit	3	Minnesota	1
Fri. Oct. 31				
106	Edmonton	6	Vancouver	2
Sat. Nov. 1				
107	Boston	3	Philadelphia	4
108	Quebec	2	Hartford	2
109	Buffalo	3	New Jersey	1
110	Winnipeg	4	NY Islanders	7
111	Pittsburgh	3	St. Louis	3
112	Washington	1	Calgary	4
113	Detroit	0	Toronto	2
114	Chicago	6	Minnesota	5
Sun. Nov. 2				
115	Buffalo	7	Boston	1
116	Hartford	3	Quebec	3
117	Montreal	5	NY Rangers	4
118	Winnipeg	5	St. Louis	7
119	Chicago	3	St. Louis	7
120	Los Angeles	5	Edmonton	5
Mon. Nov. 3				
121	Los Angeles	2	Calgary	4
Tues. Nov. 4				
122	Winnipeg	6	Quebec	3
123	Washington	3	NY Islanders	7
124	New Jersey	1	Philadelphia	7
125	Vancouver	2	Pittsburgh	2
Wed. Nov. 5				
126	Boston	3	Buffalo	8
127	NY Islanders	3	Hartford	5
128	NY Rangers	4	Detroit	5
129	Vancouver	2	Washington	5
130	St. Louis	2	Toronto	6
131	Minnesota	2	Chicago	4
132	Calgary	3	Edmonton	1

Game #	Visitor		Home	
Thur. Nov. 6				
133	Montreal	6	Los Angeles	4
134	Philadelphia	5	New Jersey	5
135	Toronto	1	Minnesota	4
Fri. Nov. 7				
136	Vancouver	7	Buffalo	6
137	St. Louis	0	Winnipeg	2
138	Edmonton	4	Calgary	6
Sat. Nov. 8				
139	Boston	5	Quebec	1
140	Hartford	3	Los Angeles	4
141	Montreal	3	Edmonton	4
142	Detroit	1	NY Islanders	2
143	*NY Rangers	3	Philadelphia	2
144	Pittsburgh	4	Minnesota	2
145	Chicago	2	Washington	3
146	Vancouver	5	Toronto	3
Sun. Nov. 9				
147	NY Islanders	4	Buffalo	3
148	Montreal	0	Calgary	3
149	NY Rangers	5	Quebec	6
150	New Jersey	1	Winnipeg	8
151	Pittsburgh	1	Detroit	2
152	St. Louis	4	Chicago	4
Tues. Nov. 11				
153	Edmonton	3	NY Islanders	2
154	Washington	2	Minnesota	2
155	Winnipeg	3	Los Angeles	4
156	Vancouver	3	Calgary	5
Wed. Nov 12				
157	Boston	1	Pittsburgh	2
158	Hartford	4	Vancouver	2
159	Buffalo	1	NY Rangers	2
160	Quebec	3	Montreal	4
161	Detroit	3	New Jersey	5
162	Washington	2	Chicago	2
163	Toronto	3	St. Louis	4
Thur. Nov. 13				
164	Edmonton	3	Boston	4
165	Hartford	3	Calgary	3
166	Detroit	5	Philadelphia	7
167	Winnipeg	6	Los Angeles	5
Fri. Nov. 14				
168	Quebec	4	Washington	3
169	Philadelphia	1	NY Rangers	2
170	Pittsburgh	4	New Jersey	5
171	Winnipeg	4	Vancouver	2
Sat. Nov. 15				
172	New Jersey	5	Boston	5
173	Edmonton	2	Hartford	6
174	Buffalo	2	Montreal	3
175	Quebec	5	Pittsburgh	5
176	NY Islanders	7	Minnesota	3
177	Detroit	0	Toronto	6
178	Chicago	3	St. Louis	2
179	Calgary	1	Los Angeles	4
Sun. Nov. 16				
180	NY Islanders	1	Winnipeg	3
181	Edmonton	9	NY Rangers	6
182	Washington	2	Philadelphia	7
183	Toronto	7	Chicago	3
Mon. Nov. 17				
184	Boston	2	Montreal	3
185	NY Rangers	2	New Jersey	3
Tues. Nov. 18				
186	NY Islanders	4	Quebec	3
187	Pittsburgh	1	Winnipeg	3
188	Los Angeles	6	Washington	5
189	St. Louis	3	Minnesota	3
190	Calgary	0	Vancouver	5
Wed. Nov. 19				
191	Boston	4	Buffalo	5
192	Montreal	4	Hartford	1
193	NY Rangers	5	Edmonton	3
194	New Jersey	4	Detroit	3
195	Philadelphia	2	Toronto	3
196	Los Angeles	4	Chicago	4
197	Minnesota	5	St. Louis	7

SCHEDULE RESULTS, 1986-87

Denotes Afternoon Game

Game #	Visitor		Home	
Thur. Nov. 20				
198	Montreal	3	Boston	1
199	Toronto	4	NY Islanders	6
200	Chicago	1	Philadelphia	5
201	Pittsburgh	5	Calgary	2
Fri. Nov. 21				
202	St. Louis	0	Hartford	4
203	Quebec	6	Buffalo	1
204	NY Rangers	8	Vancouver	5
205	Washington	3	Detroit	3
206	Los Angeles	4	Winnipeg	1
Sat. Nov. 22				
207	St. Louis	5	Boston	6
208	Hartford	6	NY Islanders	3
209	Buffalo	1	Quebec	3
210	Detroit	4	Montreal	3
211	NY Rangers	5	Calgary	8
212	New Jersey	2	Minnesota	6
213	Toronto	1	Philadelphia	6
214	Pittsburgh	5	Washington	4
215	Vancouver	2	Edmonton	5
Sun. Nov. 23				
216	New Jersey	3	Chicago	5
217	Los Angeles	2	Winnipeg	3
Mon. Nov. 24				
218	Boston	3	Toronto	2
219	Edmonton	5	Calgary	6
Tues. Nov. 25				
220	Montreal	1	Quebec	2
221	Pittsburgh	1	NY Islanders	5
222	Los Angeles	5	Vancouver	11

Game #	Visitor		Home	
Wed. Nov. 26				
223	Boston	2	Washington	2
224	Buffalo	0	Hartford	3
225	Montreal	2	Philadelphia	4
226	Quebec	2	NY Rangers	4
227	NY Islanders	3	Pittsburgh	2
228	New Jersey	5	St. Louis	1
229	Toronto	3	Detroit	1
230	Chicago	2	Minnesota	5
231	Winnipeg	3	Edmonton	5
232	Vancouver	5	Los Angeles	3
Thur. Nov 27				
233	Winnipeg	4	Calgary	3
Fri. Nov. 28				
234	Boston	3	Buffalo	4
235	Philadelphia	4	Washington	2
236	Toronto	3	Minnesota	6
237	St. Louis	2	Detroit	1
238	Chicago	6	Edmonton	5
Sat. Nov. 29				
239	Buffalo	2	Boston	6
240	Hartford	7	Montreal	5
241	Washington	3	Quebec	4
242	Philadelphia	6	NY Islanders	5
243	NY Rangers	5	Pittsburgh	5
244	New Jersey	6	Los Angeles	9
245	Minnesota	7	Toronto	2
246	Detroit	4	St. Louis	2
247	Chicago	4	Calgary	5
248	Winnipeg	6	Vancouver	3
Sun. Nov. 30				
249	Pittsburgh	2	NY Rangers	2
Mon. Dec. 1				
250	Hartford	1	Quebec	4
251	Washington	2	Montreal	1

Game #	Visitor		Home	
Tues. Dec. 2				
252	Minnesota	5	Buffalo	4
253	NY Islanders	3	Calgary	3
254	NY Rangers	5	New Jersey	8
255	St. Louis	1	Philadelphia	7
256	Detroit	4	Los Angeles	5
257	Chicago	4	Vancouver	2
Wed. Dec. 3				
258	Quebec	1	Hartford	2
259	St. Louis	3	Montreal	4
260	NY Islanders	1	Edmonton	7
261	Washington	3	Winnipeg	3
Thur. Dec. 4				
262	Quebec	2	Boston	3
263	Hartford	2	Philadelphia	1
264	Minnesota	3	New Jersey	3
265	Toronto	3	Los Angeles	3
266	Chicago	1	Calgary	4
Fri. Dec. 5				
267	St. Louis	6	Buffalo	5
268	Montreal	3	Detroit	3
269	NY Islanders	4	Vancouver	3
270	NY Rangers	5	Winnipeg	3
271	Edmonton	4	Pittsburgh	2
Sat. Dec. 6				
272	*Philadelphia	0	Boston	5
273	Detroit	4	Hartford	1
274	Buffalo	3	New Jersey	4
275	Montreal	1	Washington	3
276	Calgary	3	Quebec	2
277	Minnesota	2	Pittsburgh	5
278	Chicago	2	Los Angeles	7
Sun. Dec. 7				
279	NY Islanders	1	Boston	3
280	Edmonton	2	Philadelphia	5
281	Toronto	3	St. Louis	5
282	Vancouver	3	Winnipeg	1
Mon. Dec. 8				
283	Calgary	3	Montreal	5

Washington goaltender Bob Mason and Boston's Keith Crowder.

1986-87 NHL Schedule Results continued

Game #	Visitor		Home	
Tues. Dec. 9				
284	Buffalo	5	Detroit	5
285	St. Louis	4	Quebec	1
286	Los Angeles	7	NY Islanders	2
287	New Jersey	2	Washington	4
288	Vancouver	3	Philadelphia	6
289	Edmonton	3	Minnesota	2
Wed. Dec. 10				
290	St. Louis	2	Hartford	6
291	Buffalo	3	Chicago	6
292	Los Angeles	4	NY Rangers	5
293	Calgary	6	Pittsburgh	4
294	Washington	2	Toronto	8
295	Edmonton	7	Winnipeg	4
Thur. Dec. 11				
296	Vancouver	2	Boston	4
297	NY Rangers	2	Montreal	6
298	NY Islanders	8	New Jersey	4
299	Calgary	3	Philadelphia	5
300	Minnesota	6	Detroit	6
Fri. Dec. 12				
301	Toronto	3	Pittsburgh	8
302	Winnipeg	1	Edmonton	6
Sat. Dec. 13				
303	Boston	4	Montreal	2
304	Vancouver	2	Hartford	2
305	Buffalo	0	Quebec	7
306	New Jersey	2	NY Islanders	4
307	Philadelphia	4	Minnesota	5
308	Pittsburgh	2	Toronto	3
309	Chicago	4	St. Louis	4
310	Calgary	6	Los Angeles	3
Sun. Dec. 14				
311	Boston	6	Quebec	2
312	Hartford	3	Buffalo	4
313	Montreal	2	New Jersey	4
314	*NY Rangers	3	Washington	1
315	Vancouver	7	Chicago	3
316	Philadelphia	4	Winnipeg	1
317	Edmonton	4	Los Angeles	2
Mon. Dec. 15				
318	Minnesota	4	NY Rangers	3
Tues. Dec. 16				
319	Montreal	4	St. Louis	2
320	Minnesota	2	NY Islanders	4
321	Detroit	3	Calgary	8
Wed. Dec. 17				
322	Buffalo	3	Hartford	4
323	Quebec	3	Edmonton	5
324	Washington	1	NY Rangers	6
325	Toronto	2	New Jersey	3
326	Pittsburgh	0	Los Angeles	3
327	Detroit	5	Vancouver	4
328	Winnipeg	1	Chicago	5
Thur. Dec. 18				
329	Hartford	6	Boston	5
330	Quebec	2	Calgary	6
331	NY Islanders	4	Philadelphia	9
332	Minnesota	6	Toronto	5
333	Winnipeg	3	St. Louis	3
Fri. Dec. 19				
334	Montreal	2	Buffalo	3
335	Washington	4	New Jersey	6
336	Vancouver	2	Edmonton	3
Sat. Dec. 20				
337	Chicago	6	Boston	2
338	Hartford	2	Detroit	2
339	Buffalo	4	Toronto	5
340	New Jersey	2	Montreal	5
341	Quebec	4	Minnesota	1
342	NY Rangers	2	NY Islanders	5
343	Philadelphia	6	Pittsburgh	4
344	St. Louis	3	Washington	5
345	Calgary	5	Vancouver	3
346	Los Angeles	8	Edmonton	8
Sun. Dec. 21				
347	Hartford	4	NY Rangers	3
348	Quebec	4	Winnipeg	4
349	St. Louis	6	Philadelphia	7
350	Detroit	4	Chicago	7
Mon. Dec. 22				
351	Pittsburgh	4	Montreal	4
352	Los Angeles	5	Calgary	3
Tues. Dec. 23				
353	Boston	0	Hartford	2
354	Philadelphia	1	Buffalo	2
355	Pittsburgh	3	NY Islanders	4
356	New Jersey	5	NY Rangers	8
357	Toronto	4	Minnesota	3
358	Chicago	1	Detroit	3
359	Winnipeg	2	Edmonton	1
360	Los Angeles	4	Vancouver	6
Fri. Dec. 26				
361	Montreal	1	Hartford	1
362	Pittsburgh	3	Buffalo	3
363	NY Islanders	1	Washington	3
364	NY Rangers	7	New Jersey	4
365	Toronto	2	Detroit	4
366	St. Louis	6	Chicago	8
367	Winnipeg	2	Minnesota	4
Sat. Dec. 27				
368	Boston	1	Los Angeles	2
369	Hartford	2	Montreal	6
370	New Jersey	2	Quebec	2
371	NY Islanders	3	Pittsburgh	3
372	NY Rangers	2	St. Louis	3
373	Philadelphia	2	Vancouver	4
374	Detroit	5	Toronto	5
Sun. Dec. 28				
375	Calgary	4	Buffalo	1
376	Philadelphia	4	Edmonton	6
377	Washington	5	Chicago	7
378	Minnesota	4	Winnipeg	5
Tues. Dec. 30				
379	Boston	3	St. Louis	4
380	Hartford	3	Washington	1
381	Montreal	3	Quebec	6
382	Chicago	5	NY Islanders	3
383	NY Rangers	5	Pittsburgh	3
384	Calgary	4	New Jersey	3
385	Philadelphia	1	Los Angeles	4
386	Edmonton	7	Vancouver	3

Keith Acton

SCHEDULE RESULTS, 1986-87

*Denotes Afternoon Game

Game	# Visitor		Home	
Wed. Dec. 31				
387	Hartford	2	Minnesota	5
388	Chicago	2	Buffalo	5
389	Quebec	1	Montreal	4
390	NY Islanders	3	NY Rangers	4
391	Winnipeg	1	Toronto	6
392	Calgary	4	Detroit	6
Thur. Jan. 1				
393	*Pittsburgh	3	Washington	4
Fri. Jan 2				
394	Boston	7	New Jersey	2
395	Winnipeg	6	Buffalo	3
396	Minnesota	1	Detroit	2
397	Los Angeles	3	Vancouver	3
Sat. Jan. 3				
398	Boston	5	NY Islanders	4
399	*Chicago	3	Hartford	2
400	Montreal	3	Pittsburgh	6
401	NY Rangers	5	Quebec	2
402	New Jersey	2	Toronto	7
403	Philadelphia	4	Washington	1
404	Detroit	3	Minnesota	2
405	Calgary	2	St Louis	7
406	Edmonton	8	Los Angeles	1
Sun. Jan. 4				
407	Toronto	3	Hartford	8
408	Quebec	2	Buffalo	7
409	Calgary	4	Chicago	1
410	Vancouver	2	Winnipeg	4
Mon. Jan. 5				
411	Montreal	2	Boston	1
412	Minnesota	3	NY Rangers	3
413	Washington	6	St Louis	4
Tues. Jan. 6				
414	Vancouver	2	Quebec	3
415	Minnesota	3	NY Islanders	5
416	New Jersey	0	Philadelphia	4
417	Toronto	3	Detroit	1
Wed. Jan. 7				
418	Hartford	3	St Louis	6
419	Buffalo	4	Winnipeg	2
420	Vancouver	3	Montreal	2
421	Philadelphia	6	NY Rangers	3
422	Washington	3	Pittsburgh	5
423	Toronto	4	Chicago	6
424	Los Angeles	6	Edmonton	1
Thur. Jan. 8				
425	Detroit	3	Boston	4
426	Buffalo	4	Minnesota	5
427	Quebec	4	New Jersey	4
428	Los Angeles	4	Calgary	5
Fri. Jan. 9				
429	Hartford	0	Winnipeg	3
430	NY Islanders	3	NY Rangers	1
431	Pittsburgh	2	Wahsington	3
432	St Louis	1	Edmonton	5
Sat. Jan. 10				
433	*Philadelphia	5	Boston	3
434	Hartford	3	Minnesota	4
435	Buffalo	8	Los Angeles	5
436	Quebec	2	Montreal	5
437	Toronto	2	NY Islanders	3
438	*Vancouver	2	New Jersey	2
439	Winnipeg	5	Detroit	2
440	St Louis	2	Calgary	5
Sun. Jan. 11				
441	Vancouver	3	NY Rangers	8
442	Washington	2	Philadelphia	2
443	Detroit	3	Chicago	5
444	Calgary	3	Edmonton	5
Mon. Jan. 12				
445	NY Rangers	1	Boston	4
446	Hartford	5	New Jersey	7
447	Toronto	1	Montreal	4
448	St Louis	4	Minnesota	2
Tues. Jan. 13				
449	Pittsburgh	3	NY Islanders	3
450	Winnipeg	3	Washington	2
451	Edmonton	5	Detroit	2

Game	# Visitor		Home	
Wed. Jan. 14				
452	Boston	1	Hartford	3
453	Montreal	3	Buffalo	3
454	NY Rangers	8	Calgary	5
455	NY Jersey	3	Chicago	1
456	Winnipeg	4	Pittsburgh	3
457	Minnesota	3	Toronto	2
458	Vancouver	0	Los Angeles	4
Thur. Jan. 15				
459	Hartford	4	Boston	6
460	Montreal	3	Philadelphia	6
461	Edmonton	4	Quebec	1
462	Washington	3	NY Islanders	2
463	Toronto	3	Detroit	1
Fri. Jan. 16				
464	Winnipeg	5	New Jersey	4
465	Los Angeles	5	St. Louis	3
466	Calgary	5	Vancouver	9
Sat. Jan. 17				
467	*Pittsburgh	2	Boston	4
468	Washington	6	Hartford	1
469	Buffalo	2	Montreal	4
470	Quebec	2	Detroit	3
471	Philadelphia	4	NY Islanders	2
472	Edmonton	7	Toronto	4
473	Chicago	2	Minnesota	3
474	Los Angeles	4	St Louis	4
475	Vancouver	4	Calgary	3
Sun. Jan. 18				
476	Edmonton	5	Buffalo	6
477	Quebec	5	Chicago	3
478	NY Islanders	3	Philadelphia	1
479	Washington	6	New Jersey	1
480	Detroit	1	Pittsburgh	0
481	Minnesota	3	Winnipeg	5
Mon. Jan. 19				
482	Hartford	5	Montreal	4
483	NY Rangers	2	Hartford	2
484	Vancouver	4	Winnipeg	5
Tues. Jan. 20				
485	Boston	5	Quebec	3
486	Buffalo	0	Minnesota	5
487	Calgary	3	NY Islanders	1
488	New Jersey	3	Washingtom	6
Wed. Jan. 21				
489	Montreal	1	Hartford	3
490	NY Islanders	5	Detroit	8
491	NY Rangers	3	Vancouver	5
492	*Philadelphia	5	Chicago	5
493	Pittsburgh	5	Los Angeles	10
494	St. Louis	2	Toronto	4
495	Edmonton	5	Winnipeg	3
Thur. Jan. 22				
496	Montreal	3	Boston	7
497	Calgary	5	New Jersey	7
Fri. Jan. 23				
498	Quebec	2	Hartford	3
499	Washington	3	Buffalo	2
500	NY Rangers	3	Edmonton	7
501	Chicago	3	Philadelphia	4
502	Pittsburgh	6	Vancouver	0
503	Toronto	5	Winnipeg	7
504	St. Louis	3	Detroit	4
505	Minnesota	6	Los Angeles	3
Sat. Jan. 24				
506	*Calgary	3	Boston	5
507	Hartford	3	Toronto	5
508	Buffalo	5	Washington	3
509	Chicago	1	Montreal	3
510	NY Islanders	2	Quebec	1
511	Philadelphia	4	New Jersey	5
512	Pittsburgh	2	Edmonton	4
513	Detroit	3	St. Louis	5
Mon. Jan. 26				
514	Buffalo	2	Boston	6
515	Montreal	3	Chicago	2
516	New Jersey	3	NY Rangers	6
517	Calgary	6	Toronto	5

Game	# Visitor		Home	
Tues. Jan. 27				
518	Hartford	2	Quebec	4
519	Montreal	1	St. Louis	2
520	Winnipeg	2	NY Islanders	2
521	Washington	5	Pittsburgh	7
522	Edmonton	4	Vancouver	4
Wed. Jan. 28				
523	Philadelphia	7	Buffalo	4
524	Winnipeg	2	NY Rangers	1
525	New Jersey	2	Los Angeles	6
526	Washington	2	Detroit	1
527	Toronto	0	Chicago	5
528	Vancouver	3	Edmonton	7
Thur. Jan. 29				
529	Hartford	6	Boston	3
530	Pittsburgh	3	Philadelphia	5
531	Toronto	2	St. Louis	4
532	Minnesota	3	Calgary	3
Fri. Jan. 30				
533	Quebec	1	Buffalo	5
534	NY Islanders	3	Washington	5
535	New Jersey	4	Vancouver	3
536	Minnesota	2	Edmonton	2
Sat. Jan. 31				
537	*Winnipeg	3	Boston	6
538	Hartford	2	NY Islanders	4
539	Los Angeles	3	Montreal	5
540	*NY Rangers	3	Philadelphia	1
541	New Jersey	3	Calgary	5
542	Detroit	4	Toronto	3
543	Chicago	4	St. Louis	4
Sun. Feb. 1				
544	Boston	3	NY Rangers	5
545	Hartford	8	Pittsburgh	6
546	Detroit	1	Buffalo	5
547	Los Angeles	2	Quebec	3
548	*Winnipeg	4	Washington	6
549	Edmonton	4	Chicago	3
550	Minnesota	4	Vancouver	3
Mon. Feb. 2				
551	Philadelphia	4	Toronto	8
Tues. Feb. 3				
552	Montreal	1	Quebec	3
553	*Edmonton	4	St. Louis	2
554	Vancouver	4	Calgary	2
Wed. Feb. 4				
555	Buffalo	3	Hartford	1
556	Quebec	3	Montreal	4
557	NY Islanders	1	Vancouver	4
558	Washington	2	NY Rangers	3
559	Philadelphia	3	Winnipeg	5
560	Los Angeles	4	Toronto	3
561	Detroit	4	Chicago	5
562	Edmonton	6	Minnesota	5
Thur. Feb. 5				
563	Pittsburgh	5	Boston	6
564	St. Louis	2	Calgary	1
Fri. Feb. 6				
565	Hartford	5	Washington	2
566	NY Islanders	3	Edmonton	2
567	Minnesota	4	Detroit	2
568	St. Louis	2	Vancouver	2
569	Los Angeles	1	Winnipeg	6
Sat. Feb. 7				
570	*Toronto	5	Boston	8
571	Montreal	1	Hartford	3
572	*Buffalo	2	Quebec	5
573	NY Islanders	1	Calgary	3
574	NY Rangers	3	Washington	4
575	*Philadelphia	2	New Jersey	3
576	Chicago	1	Pittsburgh	2
577	Detroit	5	Minnesota	3
Sun. Feb. 8				
578	*Quebec	2	Boston	1
579	Chicago	2	Buffalo	7
580	Toronto	5	NY Rangers	4
581	Pittsburgh	2	New Jersey	1
582	St. Louis	4	Edmonton	6
583	Los Angeles	1	Winnipeg	3
584	Calgary	3	Vancouver	2

SCHEDULE RESULTS, 1986-87

1986-87 NHL Schedule Results continued

Game #	Visitor		Home	
Feb. 9-13				
	NHL All-Stars	3	USSR	2
	USSR	5	NHL All-Stars	3
Sat. Feb. 14				
585	Boston	4	Toronto	5
586	Hartford	2	Los Angeles	5
587	Buffalo	5	NY Islanders	1
588	Winnipeg	2	Montreal	5
589	*New Jersey	1	Detroit	5
590	Philadelphia	4	St. Louis	2
591	Vancouver	3	Pittsburgh	3
592	Calgary	3	Minnesota	2
Sun. Feb. 15				
593	*Quebec	4	Chicago	6
594	Pittsburgh	1	NY Rangers	4
595	Washington	5	Edmonton	3
596	St. Louis	2	Minnesota	3
Mon. Feb. 16				
597	Boston	3	Montreal	7
598	*Calgary	5	Philadelphia	0
599	*Toronto	1	Los Angeles	1
Tues. Feb. 17				
600	Hartford	5	Chicago	4
601	Winnipeg	3	Quebec	3
602	Philadelphia	3	NY Islanders	2
603	Detroit	2	NY Rangers	6
604	Calgary	3	Pittsburgh	1
605	Vancouver	4	St. Louis	3
Wed. Feb. 18				
606	Boston	3	Buffalo	4
607	Hartford	6	New Jersey	3
608	NY Islanders	1	Montreal	1
609	Washington	4	Los Angeles	7
610	Toronto	2	Edmonton	9
611	Winnipeg	2	Detroit	5
612	Vancouver	3	Minnesota	7
Thur. Feb. 19				
613	NY Rangers	2	Chicago	5
614	Pittsburgh	4	Philadelphia	4
615	Minnesota	3	St. Louis	6
Fri. Feb. 20				
616	Boston	2	Winnipeg	6
617	Buffalo	6	NY Rangers	6
618	Quebec	3	Detroit	6
619	Washington	6	Vancouver	3
620	Toronto	2	Calgary	7
Sat. Feb. 21				
621	Boston	1	Minnesota	0
622	Chicago	6	Hartford	3
623	Montreal	5	NY Islanders	6
624	Quebec	3	St. Louis	4
625	New Jersey	6	Pittsburgh	5
626	Philadelphia	4	Los Angeles	2
Sun. Feb. 22				
627	Hartford	3	Buffalo	5
628	NY Islanders	7	New Jersey	0
629	Pittsburgh	4	NY Rangers	2
630	Washington	5	Calgary	2
631	Toronto	2	Vancouver	3
632	Detroit	2	Chicago	2
633	*Edmonton	2	Winnipeg	5
Mon. Feb. 23				
634	Minnesota	4	Montreal	3
Tues. Feb. 24				
635	NY Rangers	6	Buffalo	3
636	Minnesota	4	Quebec	5
637	NY Islanders	2	St. Louis	3
638	Edmonton	2	Pittsburgh	5
639	Detroit	2	Washington	8
640	Winnipeg	3	Los Angeles	8
641	Vancouver	0	Calgary	2
Wed. Feb. 25				
642	Boston	4	Hartford	6
643	Montreal	3	Chicago	3
644	NY Rangers	4	Toronto	2
645	Edmonton	2	New Jersey	4
Thur. Feb. 26				
646	Quebec	2	Boston	6
647	St. Louis	3	Buffalo	6
648	Pittsburgh	4	NY Islanders	5
649	Philadelphia	3	Calgary	4
650	Vancouver	5	Detroit	5
651	Winnipeg	6	Los Angeles	3

Game #	Visitor		Home	
Fri. Feb. 27				
652	Edmonton	2	Washington	5
Sat. Feb. 28				
653	*Buffalo	1	Boston	5
654	Quebec	1	Hartford	2
655	*New Jersey	2	Montreal	3
656	St. Louis	3	NY Islanders	3
657	*NY Rangers	1	Detroit	4
658	Chicago	2	Pittsburgh	1
659	Vancouver	6	Toronto	8
660	*Los Angeles	3	Minnesota	6
661	Winnipeg	3	Calgary	5
Sun. Mar. 1				
662	*New Jersey	5	Hartford	5
663	Vancouver	4	Buffalo	2
664	*NY Rangers	3	Washington	7
665	Philadelphia	4	Minnesota	5
666	St. Louis	5	Pittsburgh	5
667	Los Angeles	1	Chicago	6
668	Calgary	3	Winnipeg	6
Mon. Mar. 2				
669	Detroit	4	Boston	3
Tues. Mar. 3				
670	Boston	4	NY Islanders	4
671	Detroit	3	Hartford	5
672	Buffalo	2	Philadelphia	4
673	Montreal	4	Calgary	2
674	Pittsburgh	8	Quebec	1
675	New Jersey	2	Washington	3
676	St. Louis	4	Toronto	1
677	Minnesota	4	Los Angeles	4
Wed. Mar. 4				
678	NY Islanders	5	NY Rangers	7
679	Winnipeg	2	Chicago	3
680	Edmonton	8	Vancouver	5
Thur. Mar. 5				
681	Boston	2	Hartford	10
682	New Jersey	4	Buffalo	6
683	Washington	2	Philadelphia	4
684	Pittsburgh	2	Toronto	7
685	Minnesota	3	Detroit	9
686	Winnipeg	1	St. Louis	1
687	Los Angeles	2	Calgary	7
Fri. Mar. 6				
688	Montreal	1	Vancouver	4
689	Los Angeles	3	Edmonton	9
Sat. Mar. 7				
690	*Washington	2	Boston	3
691	Philadelphia	3	Hartford	5
692	Buffalo	5	Quebec	3
693	Montreal	3	Edmonton	5
694	NY Islanders	2	Toronto	7
695	Chicago	4	New Jersey	3
696	Pittsburgh	7	Minnesota	3
697	Detroit	3	St. Louis	5
Sun. Mar. 8				
698	Quebec	1	Buffalo	5
699	NY Islanders	6	Chicago	5
700	Calgary	7	NY Rangers	4
701	*New Jersey	3	Philadelphia	7
702	Pittsburgh	5	Winnipeg	3
703	*Vancouver	2	Los Angeles	5
Mon. Mar. 9				
704	Montreal	5	Minnesota	4
705	Toronto	2	St. Louis	3
Tues. Mar. 10				
706	Harford	4	Quebec	6
707	NY Islanders	6	Pittsburgh	3
708	Calgary	3	Washington	3
709	Detroit	4	Vancouver	7
Wed. Mar. 11				
710	Boston	2	NY Rangers	3
711	Calgary	6	Hartford	1
712	Buffalo	3	Los Angeles	2
713	Montreal	1	Winnipeg	2
714	Philadelphia	5	New Jersey	4
715	Toronto	4	Minnesota	2
716	Detroit	3	Edmonton	6
717	St. Louis	2	Chicago	2
Thur. Mar. 12				
718	St. Louis	4	Boston	6
719	Quebec	3	Pittsburgh	6
720	NY Rangers	6	Philadelphia	1

Game #	Visitor		Home	
Fri. Mar. 13				
721	Hartford	3	Winnipeg	0
722	Buffalo	4	Vancouver	6
723	NY Islanders	1	New Jersey	4
724	Toronto	2	Washington	10
Sat. Mar. 14				
725	*Chicago	4	Boston	4
726	Buffalo	3	Edmonton	5
727	Philadelphia	3	Montreal	3
728	Quebec	6	Los Angeles	3
729	New Jersey	6	NY Islanders	7
730	NY Rangers	3	Pittsburgh	2
731	Washington	3	St. Louis	3
732	Calgary	4	Toronto	6
733	*Detroit	4	Minnesota	5
Sun. Mar. 15				
734	Hartford	1	Edmonton	4
735	Philadelphia	5	NY Rangers	2
736	*Detroit	1	Winnipeg	1
737	*Minnesota	4	Chicago	2
Mon. Mar. 16				
738	NY Islanders	0	Montreal	3
Tues. Mar. 17				
739	Boston	1	Detroit	3
740	Buffalo	2	Calgary	6
741	Quebec	2	Vancouver	5
742	NY Rangers	3	Philadelphia	4
743	New Jersey	4	Edmonton	7
744	Los Angeles	5	Washington	4
745	Chicago	3	Minnesota	3
Wed. Mar. 18				
746	Hartford	5	NY Rangers	3
747	New Jersey	3	Winnipeg	4
748	St. Louis	4	Pittsburgh	5
749	Chicago	6	Toronto	5
Thurs. Mar. 19				
750	Minnesota	2	Boston	6
751	NY Islanders	3	Detroit	2
752	Los Angeles	5	Philadelphia	2
753	Edmonton	4	Calgary	5
Fri. Mar. 20				
754	Montreal	3	Buffalo	2
755	Toronto	4	Quebec	5
756	Pittsburgh	3	Washington	4
757	Winnipeg	5	Vancouver	6
758	Calgary	6	Edmonton	3
Sat. Mar. 21				
759	*Los Angeles	6	Boston	8
760	Minnesota	1	Hartford	5
761	Toronto	4	Montreal	9
762	Philadelphia	2	Quebec	2
763	NY Rangers	3	NY Islanders	4
764	New Jersey	7	St. Louis	6
765	Chicago	0	Detroit	3
Sun. Mar. 22				
766	*Boston	3	Washington	3
767	*Los Angeles	3	Hartford	6
768	Detroit	2	Buffalo	3
769	Chicago	3	NY Rangers	5
770	Pittsburgh	1	Philadelphia	3
771	*Vancouver	5	Winnipeg	6
Mon. Mar. 23				
772	Edmonton	7	New Jersey	4
773	St. Louis	8	Minnesota	5
Tues. Mar. 24				
774	Toronto	6	Buffalo	5
775	Montreal	4	Quebec	5
776	Washington	3	NY Islanders	1
777	Philadelphia	3	Pittsburgh	2
Wed. Mar. 25				
778	Edmonton	6	Hartford	5
779	New Jersey	8	NY Rangers	2
780	Minnesota	6	Toronto	2
781	Los Angeles	2	Detroit	1
782	St. Louis	4	Chicago	4
783	Calgary	1	Winnipeg	10
Thurs. Mar. 26				
784	Edmonton	1	Boston	4
785	Los Angeles	5	Buffalo	5
786	Quebec	2	Philadelphia	5
787	Vancouver	5	NY Islanders	4
788	Winnipeg	1	Calgary	5

SCHEDULE RESULTS, 1986-87

Game	#Visitor		Home	
Fri. Mar. 27				
789	NY Islanders	2	Washington	2
790	St Louis	4	NY Rangers	6
791	Minnesota	2	New Jersey	5
Sat. Mar. 28				
792	*Vancouver	1	Boston	2
793	Pittsburgh	4	Hartford	5
794	Buffalo	3	Montreal	6
795	Chicago	4	Quebec	5
796	*Detroit	5	Philadelphia	1
797	Edmonton	2	Toronto	4
798	Calgary	4	Los Angeles	3
Sun. Mar. 29				
799	Boston	8	Chicago	6
800	*Vancouver	4	Hartford	7
801	Edmonton	3	Buffalo	2
802	Montreal	4	Pittsburgh	1
803	*St. Louis	4	New Jersey	1
804	*Minnesota	2	Washington	4
805	Toronto	6	Winnipeg	2
Mon. Mar. 30				
806	NY Rangers	6	Minnesota	5
807	Calgary	4	Los Angeles	5

Game	#Visitor		Home	
Tues. Mar. 31				
808	Boston	4	Quebec	3
809	NY Islanders	4	St. Louis	3
810	Pittsburgh	3	New Jersey	5
811	Toronto	2	Washington	4
812	Winnipeg	4	Edmonton	5
Wed. Apr. 1				
813	Hartford	2	Montreal	3
814	Washington	5	NY Rangers	1
815	Philadelphia	2	Detroit	1
816	Minnesota	4	Chicago	4
817	Vancouver	8	Los Angeles	3
Thurs. Apr. 2				
818	Buffalo	3	St. Louis	5
819	Quebec	4	NY Islanders	1
820	New Jersey	2	Pittsburgh	6
821	Calgary	4	Edmonton	4
Fri. Apr. 3				
822	Winnipeg	4	Vancouver	6

Game	#Visitor		Home	
Sat. Apr. 4				
823	Boston	1	Montreal	3
824	NY Rangers	3	Hartford	5
825	Buffalo	6	NY Islanders	6
826	New Jersey	4	Quebec	8
827	Philadelphia	2	Washington	3
828	Detroit	3	Pittsburgh	4
829	Chicago	1	Toronto	3
830	Minnesota	1	St Louis	4
831	Edmonton	7	Los Angeles	3
Sun. Apr. 5				
832	Quebec	6	Boston	4
833	Hartford	0	Buffalo	6
834	Montreal	8	NY Rangers	2
835	NY Islanders	9	Philadelphia	5
836	Washington	6	New Jersey	5
837	Toronto	2	Chicago	5
838	St Louis	3	Detroit	2
839	*Winnipeg	3	Calgary	1
840	Los Angeles	2	Vancouver	5

* Denotes Afternoon Game

NHL Attendance

Season	Regular Season Games	Regular Season Attendance	Playoffs Games	Playoffs Attendance	Total Attendance
1960-61	210	2,317,142	17	242,000	2,559,142
1961-62	210	2,435,424	18	277,000	2,712,424
1962-63	210	2,590,574	16	220,906	2,811,480
1963-64	210	2,732,642	21	309,149	3,041,791
1964-65	210	2,822,635	20	303,859	3,126,494
1965-66	210	2,941,164	16	249,000	3,190,184
1966-67	210	3,084,759	16	248,336	3,333,095
1967-68[1]	444	4,938,043	40	495,089	5,433,132
1968-69	456	5,550,613	33	431,739	5,982,352
1969-70	456	5,992,065	34	461,694	6,453,759
1970-71[2]	546	7,257,677	43	707,633	7,965,310
1971-72	546	7,609,368	36	582,666	8,192,034
1972-73[3]	624	8,575,651	38	624,637	9,200,288
1973-74	624	8,640,978	38	600,442	9,241,420
1974-75[4]	720	9,521,536	51	784,181	10,305,717
1975-76	720	9,103,761	48	726,279	9,830,040
1976-77	720	8,563,890	44	646,279	9,210,169
1977-78	720	8,526,564	45	686,634	9,213,198
1978-79	680	7,758,053	45	694,521	8,452,574
1979-80[5]	840	10,533,623	63	976,699	11,510,322
1980-81	840	10,726,198	68	966,390	11,692,588
1981-82	840	10,710,894	71	1,058,948	11,769,842
1982-83	840	11,020,610	66	1,088,222	12,028,832
1983-84	840	11,359,386	70	1,107,400	12,466,786
1984-85	840	11,633,730	70	1,107,500	12,741,230
1985-86	840	11,621,000	72	1,152,503	12,773,503
1986-87	840	11,855,880	87	1,383,967	13,239,847

[1] First expansion: Los Angeles, Pittsburgh, California, Philadelphia, St. Louis and Minnesota
[2] Second expansion: Buffalo and Vancouver
[3] Third expansion: Atlanta and New York Islanders
[4] Fourth expansion: Kansas City (Colorado) and Washington
[5] Fifth expansion: Edmonton, Hartford, Quebec and Winnipeg

Conn Smythe Trophy-winning rookie goaltender Ron Hextall and the Flyers took Edmonton to seven games before goals by Jari Kurri and Glenn Anderson gave the Oilers a 3-1 home-ice victory and the Stanley Cup.

1987 Stanley Cup Playoffs

Results

WALES CONFERENCE

DIVISION SEMI-FINALS
(Best of seven series)

Series 'A'
Wed. Apr. 8	Quebec 2	at	Hartford 3*
Thur. Apr. 9	Quebec 4	at	Hartford 5
Sat. Apr. 11	Hartford 1	at	Quebec 5
Sun. Apr. 12	Hartford 1	at	Quebec 4
Tues. Apr. 14	Quebec 7	at	Hartford 5
Thur. Apr. 16	Hartford 4	at	Quebec 5**

* Paul MacDermid scored at 2:20 of overtime
* Peter Stastny scored at 6:05 of overtime
Quebec won series 4-2

Series 'B'
Wed. Apr. 8	Boston 2	at	Montreal 6
Thur. Apr. 9	Boston 3	at	Montreal 4*
Sat. Apr. 11	Montreal 5	at	Boston 4
Sun. Apr. 12	Montreal 4	at	Boston 2

* Mats Naslund scored at 2:38 of overtime
Montreal won series 4-0

Series 'C'
Wed. Apr. 8	NY Rangers 3	at	Philadelphia 0
Thur. Apr. 9	NY Rangers 3	at	Philadelphia 8
Sat. Apr. 11	Philadelphia 3	at	NY Rangers 0
Sun. Apr. 12	Philadelphia 3	at	NY Rangers 6
Tues. Apr. 14	NY Rangers 1	at	Philadelphia 3
Thur. Apr. 16	Philadelphia 5	at	NY Rangers 0

Philadelphia won series 4-2

Series 'D'
Wed. Apr. 8	NY Islanders 3	at	Washington 4
Thur. Apr. 9	NY Islanders 3	at	Washington 1
Sat. Apr. 11	Washington 2	at	NY Islanders 0
Sun. Apr. 12	Washington 4	at	NY Islanders 1
Tues. Apr. 14	NY Islanders 4	at	Washington 2
Thur. Apr. 16	Washington 4	at	NY Islanders 5
Sat. Apr. 18	NY Islanders 3	at	Washington 2*

* Pat LaFontaine scored at 68:47 of overtime
NY Islanders won series 4-3

CAMPBELL CONFERENCE

Series 'E'
Wed. Apr. 8	Toronto 1	at	St. Louis 3
Thur. Apr. 9	Toronto 3	at	St. Louis 2*
Sat. Apr. 11	St. Louis 5	at	Toronto 3
Sun. Apr. 12	St. Louis 1	at	Toronto 2
Tues. Apr. 14	Toronto 2	at	St. Louis 1
Thur. Apr. 16	St. Louis 0	at	Toronto 4

* Rick Lanz scored at 10:17 of overtime
Toronto won series 4-2

Series 'F'
Wed. Apr. 8	Chicago 1	at	Detroit 3
Thur. Apr. 9	Chicago 1	at	Detroit 5
Sat. Apr. 11	Detroit 4	at	Chicago 3*
Sun. Apr. 12	Detroit 3	at	Chicago 1

* Shawn Burr scored at 4:51 of overtime
Detroit won series 4-0

Series 'G'
Wed. Apr. 8	Los Angeles 5	at	Edmonton 2
Thur. Apr. 9	Los Angeles 3	at	Edmonton 13
Sat. Apr. 11	Edmonton 6	at	Los Angeles 5
Sun. Apr. 12	Edmonton 6	at	Los Angeles 3
Tues. Apr. 14	Los Angeles 4	at	Edmonton 5

Edmonton won series 4-1

Series 'H'
Wed. Apr. 8	Winnipeg 4	at	Calgary 2
Thur. Apr. 9	Winnipeg 3	at	Calgary 2
Sat. Apr. 11	Calgary 3	at	Winnipeg 2*
Sun. Apr. 12	Calgary 3	at	Winnipeg 4
Tues. Apr. 14	Winnipeg 3	at	Calgary 4
Thur. Apr. 16	Calgary 1	at	Winnipeg 6

* Mike Bullard scored at 3:53 of overtime
Winnipeg won series 4-2

DIVISION FINALS
(Best-of-seven series)

Series 'I'
Mon. Apr. 20	Quebec 7	at	Montreal 5
Wed. Apr. 22	Quebec 2	at	Montreal 1
Fri. Apr. 24	Montreal 7	at	Quebec 2
Sun. Apr. 26	Montreal 3	at	Quebec 2*
Tues. Apr. 28	Quebec 2	at	Montreal 3
Thur. Apr. 30	Montreal 2	at	Quebec 3
Sat. May 2	Quebec 3	at	Montreal 5

Mats Naslund scored at 5:30 of overtime
Montreal won series 4-3

Series 'J'
Mon. Apr. 20	NY Islanders 2	at	Philadelphia 4
Wed. Apr. 22	NY Islanders 2	at	Philadelphia 1
Fri. Apr. 24	Philadelphia 4	at	NY Islanders 1
Sun. Apr. 26	Philadelphia 6	at	NY Islanders 4
Tues. Apr. 28	NY Islanders 2	at	Philadelphia 1
Thur. Apr. 30	Philadelphia 2	at	NY Islanders 4
Sat. May 2	NY Islanders 1	at	Philadelphia 5

Philadelphia won series 4-3

Series 'K'
Tues. Apr. 21	Toronto 4	at	Detroit 2
Thur. Apr. 23	Toronto 7	at	Detroit 2
Sat. Apr. 25	Detroit 4	at	Toronto 2
Mon. Apr. 27	Detroit 2	at	Toronto 3*
Wed. Apr. 29	Toronto 0	at	Detroit 3
Fri. May 1	Detroit 4	at	Toronto 2
Sun. May 3	Toronto 0	at	Detroit 3

Mike Allison scored at 9:31 of overtime
Detroit won series 4-3

Series 'L'
Tues. Apr. 21	Winnipeg 2	at	Edmonton 3*
Thur. Apr. 23	Winnipeg 3	at	Edmonton 5
Sat. Apr. 25	Edmonton 5	at	Winnipeg 2
Mon. Apr. 27	Edmonton 4	at	Winnipeg 2

Glenn Anderson scored at 0:36 of overtime
Edmonton won series 4-0

CONFERENCE CHAMPIONSHIPS
(Best-of-seven series)

Series 'M'
Mon. May 4	Montreal 3	at	Philadelphia 4*
Wed. May 6	Montreal 5	at	Philadelphia 2
Fri. May 8	Philadelphia 4	at	Montreal 3
Sun. May 10	Philadelphia 6	at	Montreal 3
Tues. May 12	Montreal 5	at	Philadelphia 2
Thur. May 14	Philadelphia 4	at	Montreal 3

Ilkka Sinisalo scored at 9:11 of overtime
Philadelphia won series 4-2

Series 'N'
Tues. May 5	Detroit 3	at	Edmonton 1
Thur. May 7	Detroit 1	at	Edmonton 4
Sat. May 9	Edmonton 2	at	Detroit 1
Mon. May 11	Edmonton 3	at	Detroit 2
Wed. May 13	Detroit 3	at	Edmonton 6

Edmonton won series 4-1

STANLEY CUP CHAMPIONSHIP
(Best-of-seven series)

Series 'O'
Sun. May 17	Philadelphia 2	at	Edmonton 4
Wed. May 20	Philadelphia 2	at	Edmonton 3*
Fri. May 22	Edmonton 3	at	Philadelphia 5
Sun. May 24	Edmonton 4	at	Philadelphia 1
Tues. May 26	Philadelphia 4	at	Edmonton 3
Thur. May 28	Edmonton 2	at	Philadelphia 3
Sun. May 31	Philadelphia 1	at	Edmonton 3

Jari Kurri scored at 6:50 of overtime
Edmonton won series 4-3

Team Playoff Records

	GP	W	L	GF	GA	%
Edmonton	21	16	5	87	57	.762
Philadelphia	26	15	11	85	73	.577
Montreal	17	10	7	67	54	.588
Detroit	16	9	7	45	40	.563
Quebec	13	7	6	48	45	.538
Toronto	13	7	6	33	32	.538
NY Islanders	14	7	7	35	42	.500
Winnipeg	10	4	6	31	32	.400
Washington	7	3	4	19	19	.429
Hartford	6	2	4	19	27	.333
Calgary	6	2	4	15	22	.333
NY Rangers	6	2	4	13	22	.333
St. Louis	6	2	4	12	15	.333
Los Angeles	5	1	4	20	32	.200
Boston	4	0	4	11	19	.000
Chicago	4	0	4	6	15	.000

Playoff Scoring Leaders

Player	GP	G	A	Pts	+/-
Wayne Gretzky	21	5	29	34	10
Mark Messier	21	12	16	28	18
Brian Propp	26	12	16	28	11
Glenn Anderson	21	14	13	27	13
Per-Erik Eklund	26	7	20	27	11
Jari Kurri	21	15	10	25	11
Mats Naslund	17	7	15	22	1 —
Rick Tocchet	26	11	10	21	7
Larry Robinson	17	43	17	20	4
Ryan Walter	17	7	12	19	4
Kent Nilsson	21	6	13	19	11
Bobby Smith	17	9	9	18	0
Steve Yzerman	16	5	13	18	2 —
Doug Crossman	26	4	14	18	0
Peter Stastny	13	6	9	15	3
Michel Goulet	13	9	5	14	2 —
Gerard Gallant	16	8	6	14	1 —

PART TWO: **ROOTS & RECORD-SETTERS**

Hockey's Early Years

AT ONE TIME or another, most North American hockey fans have read or heard that ice hockey was first played at Kingston, Ontario, during the early 1870s, on the frozen waters of the St. Lawrence River. "The winters seemed long and dreary to the young men of Canada," wrote the late sports journalist Bill Roche. "Happily, someone thought of using the abundant ice surfaces for a new game to be played on skates. The general pattern of the game was possibly England's field hockey."

Unknown to Mr. Roche and to the majority of North Americans, a version of hockey was being played in northern Europe at least as early as the 16th century. One of the few pieces of evidence of this is a painting, 'The Hunters', by the Flemish artist Peter Breugel, whose career spanned the middle decades of the 1500s. In the background of the painting, on a frozen river or canal, there are a number of tiny figures carrying what could only be described as hockey sticks. Their various poses indicate that they are skating. (Primitive wooden and metal skates, perhaps like those used by the fabled Hans Brinker, are known to have existed in Holland as early as the Middle Ages.) Because of the scale of the painting, it is impossible to see a puck, though the presence of the sticks is strong evidence that an object of some sort is being shoved around on the ice.

It might be argued that the game being played in the painting was not hockey as we know it. In the same vein, nor was hockey played in the 19th century hockey as we know it. One of the first Canadian games on record was a crowded fracas played in Montreal in the mid-1870s by 30 McGill University students, all of whom were on the ice at once. Some wore skates, some street shoes. The game was played with a ball.

By the time the first league was formed in 1885 in Kingston, the game had evolved, but was still being played under relatively primitive conditions. There were no goal nets, for instance – only small mounds of snow to indicate the width of the goal. There were no waist-high boards or bluelines, and the condition of the ice was often atrocious. In a game played in Rat Portage (now Kenora, Ontario) during the 1880s, the puck was reported to have vanished into a wide crack in the ice, from which it could not be recovered.

The players of the day wore no specialized equipment other than their skates, which were not entirely satisfactory pieces of gear. The skate blades, like those worn in Europe, were not riveted onto boots but were clamped onto street shoes in much the way that the inexpensive roller skates of the future would be attached to children's shoes. Often, when hit by a puck or stick, the trigger-type fasteners on a skate would spring open, and the skate would go flying across the ice, leaving its owner hobbling in pursuit.

Until well into the 1890s, players, including goaltenders, wore no pads. They didn't have to; no one had yet figured out how to raise the puck, and errant sticks were not yet considered a sufficient threat to the shins. Then some bright innovator discovered the "backhand lift" shot, and within weeks goaltenders were showing up at rinks in borrowed cricket pads. Defensemen soon wore shinguards made of cane, while forwards wore a light leather pad on their lower legs. Early goaltenders were not allowed to kneel or sprawl on the ice, but had to remain standing.

By the mid 1890s, four-foot wooden poles bearing red flags were being hammered into the ice to serve as goal posts, and in 1900 crossbars and nets were introduced. It is easy to imagine that upright goaltenders, poorly padded, would allow vast numbers of goals. But the remarkable goaltenders of the 1890s – Herb Collins of Montreal, Fred Chittick of Ottawa and Gordon Lewis of Victoria among them – permitted an average of only three goals a game... better than most goalies of the modern era.

It is sharp evidence of hockey's popularity that, by 1893, leagues had been established across Canada, rules had been laid down, and the Governor General of the country, Lord Stanley, had donated the Stanley Cup, to be held by the top team in the Dominion, whether professional or amateur. For the first 23 years of the Cup's existence, any team in Canada (and from 1916 to 1926, any team anywhere), could challenge for it at any time during the hockey season. There were some unlikely claimants to the trophy. In 1905, the Ottawa Silver Seven, who held the Cup, were challenged by an irrepressible team of prospectors from Dawson City. It is a tale verging on myth how the Yukon team journeyed 4,000 miles – by dogsled to Skagway, Alaska, by boat to Vancouver and train to Ottawa, where they were trashed 9-2 and 23-2 in successive games. Later that year, the Silver Seven were challenged by a team from Rat Portage, which they defeated with equal ease.

In 1919, the Stanley Cup final between the Montreal Canadiens and the Seattle Metropolitans was terminated after five games by the great flu epidemic that swept the continent that year, claiming thousands of lives. "Bad" Joe Hall, a Montreal star of the era, retired early from the fifth game and died two days later in a Seattle hospital.

In all, teams from 17 leagues challenged for the Cup. After the founding of the NHL in 1917, the strongest challenges came from the Pacific Coast Hockey Association, the Western Canada Hockey League and the Western Hockey League, many of whose players were professionals. In 1917, the Seattle Metropolitans of the Pacific Coast Association became the first American team to win the Cup. By 1926, however, all three western leagues had folded, and many of their best players – Eddie Shore, Bill and Bun Cook, Dick Irvin, Newsy Lalonde, Jack Adams, Fred "Cyclone" Taylor, Alf Skinner, and others – had joined the burgeoning NHL. That year, the Stanley Cup became the NHL's exclusive property.

As furious as the early game must have appeared to its fans, it would likely seem unmercifully slow to observers today. For one thing, players spent the entire game on the ice (some did so right up into the 1930s). For a contemporary player to play even 60 percent of a game – say, 35 minutes – is considered a Herculean accomplishment, even with regular rests on the bench. Anyone who has ever played even 15 minutes of spirited, non-stop hockey will understand, from the severe stress on the legs and lungs, that early players must have spent a fair portion of any game dawdling behind the play, attempting desperately to catch their wind. Moreover, the ice was crowded by nine-man teams, then seven-man teams, until 1911, when the six-man rule was introduced. As a further retardant, the early blades had flat blades, unlike today's "rockered" blades which add immeasurably to a skater's maneuverability. What's more, the ice was often snowy or soft, or badly chipped. When the Ottawa Silver Seven travelled to Rat Portage for the first Stanley Cup series between the teams in 1903, the home-town fans, not content to let the already faulty ice of their rink bring their renowned opponents into check, stole to the rink the night before the first game and sprinkled salt on the ice.

Perhaps the greatest contributor to the slow pace of early hockey was that it was an "onside" game, meaning that no forward passes were permitted and that the puck could only be advanced by the puck carrier. Those familiar with the game of rugger, which is also an onside game, will know that such games progress not by rapid acceleration of the sort that can be achieved by a forward pass but by the sheer cunning or brute force with which the lead man in the attack can move across the playing surface. Since, in hockey, the puck carrier's options were not great in number, checkers could easily gang up on him. In a tight spot, often the best he could do was drop the puck to a teammate, give it up to the opposition, or struggle on at the risk of being racked by a bodycheck.

The fact that many of hockey's best players were small and fast compensated somewhat for the game's inherent slowness. It was not until well into the 1930s and '40s that larger players began to outnumber the smaller ones. One of the finest forward lines of the 1920s – Aurel Joliet, Howie Morenz and Bill Boucher of the Montreal Canadiens – averaged only 145 lbs. in weight.

Within a year of the founding of the NHL, league governors introduced a new rule permitting forward passing, at least in the neutral zone between bluelines. It would be 1929 before the forward pass would be allowed in all zones of the rink, but, nonetheless, the game sped up immeasurably with the 1918 ruling. Not surprisingly, the game also made great gains in popularity. By 1926, the original four-team NHL (Montreal Wanderers, Montreal Canadiens, Ottawa Senators and Toronto Arenas) had increased to 10 teams, including six in the United States.

At left: Aurel Joliat; below: the 1917 Seattle Metropolitans, the first U.S. team to win the Stanley Cup.

But pro hockey's popularity did not increase entirely on the merits of the game. By the mid-1920s, it had a host of ambassadors and heroes, including the greatest player of the day, Howie Morenz of the Montreal Canadiens. "He would challenge the opposing defenses by dazzling dash and deception," sports journalist Andy O'Brien once wrote. "You didn't have to know anything about hockey to be lifted from your seat by Morenz – just as you didn't have to know anything about baseball to be thrilled by a towering home run by Babe Ruth." Morenz was, in fact, sometimes referred to as the Babe Ruth of hockey.

When he died in 1937 of complications from a severe hockey injury, 14,000 silent fans crowded the Montreal Forum for his funeral. Another 200,000 are said to have jammed the streets to watch his cortege roll past on the way to Mount Royal cemetery.

It was only a year after Morenz joined the Canadiens in 1924 that the NHL crossed the American border for the first time to Boston. There, a new star rose in the person of Eddie Shore, the "Edmonton Express". Shore is said to have played his position on defense in a style similar to that of a future Boston star, Bobby Orr, making frequent lightning rushes on the opposition goal. He was also renowned for his toughness and endurance.

Eddie Shore

If one man could be named as the game's greatest early ambassador, however, it would not be a player at all, but a shrill-voiced broadcaster named Foster Hewitt, who, in 1923, began broadcasting NHL games from Toronto's Mutual Street Arena. Over the years, Hewitt's broadcasts would reach millions of listeners in Canada and the United States, and he would achieve a legendary acclaim normally accorded only to the games finest players.

In 1925, the New York Americans and Pittsburgh Pirates, a team that lasted only five seasons, joined the NHL. The following year, the league made its biggest expansion prior to 1967, as three more American teams materialized: the Chicago Black Hawks, the New York Rangers and the Detroit Cougars, a predecessor of the modern-day Red Wings.

The NHL continued to evolve – and, indeed, still evolves yearly to meet the changing demands of hockey and its fans – but by 1926 it had established itself as the first major sports league of truly international proportion, a status it enjoys to this day.

NHL Franchise History

Location	Club Name	NHL Seasons	Franchise Activity	Divisional Alignment
Atlanta	Flames	1973-80	transferred to Calgary	West 1973-79 Patrick 1980
Boston	Bruins	1925 to date		American 1927-38 East 1968-74 Adams 1975 to date
Brooklyn	Americans	1942	formerly NY Americans	Canadian
Buffalo	Sabres	1971 to date		East 1971-74 Adams 1975 to date
California	Seals	1968	renamed Oakland mid-season	West
	Golden Seals	1971 to 1976	transferred to Cleveland	West 1971 Adams 1975-76
Calgary	Flames	1981 to date	transferred from Atlanta	Smythe
Chicago	Black Hawks	1927 to date		American 1927-38 East 1968-70 West 1971-74 Smythe 1975-81 Norris 1982 to date
Cleveland	Barons	1977, 1978	transferred from Oakland merged with Minnesota	Adams
Colorado	Rockies	1977-82	transferred from Kansas City transferred to New Jersey	Smythe
Detroit	Cougars	1927-30	renamed Falcons 1931	American 1927-38
	Falcons	1931-33	renamed Red Wings 1934	East 1968-74
	Red Wings	1934 to date		Norris 1975 to date
Edmonton	Oilers	1980 to date	former WHA franchise	Smythe
Hamilton	Tigers	1921-25	sold to NY Americans	
Hartford	Whalers	1980 to date	former WHA franchise	Norris 1980, 1981 Adams 1982 to date
Kansas City	Scouts	1975, 1976	transferred to Colorado	Smythe
Long Island	NY Islanders	1973 to date		East 1973, 1974 Patrick 1975 to date
Los Angeles	Kings	1968 to date		West 1968-74 Norris 1975-81 Smythe 1982 to date
Minnesota	North Stars	1968 to date	merged with Cleveland	West 1968-74 Smythe 1975-78 Adams 1979-82 Norris 1982 to date
Montreal	Canadiens	1918 to date		Canadian 1927-38 East 1968-74 Norris 1975-81 Adams 1982 to date
	Wanderers	1918		
	Maroons	1925-38		Canadian 1927-38
New Jersey	Devils	1983 to date	transferred from Colorado	Patrick
New York	Americans	1926-41	shifted to Brooklyn 1942	Canadian 1927-41
	Rangers	1927 to date		American 1927-38 East 1968-74 Patrick 1975 to date
Oakland	Seals	1968-70	name changed from California mid-season (Renamed California Golden Seals 1971	West 1968-70
Ottawa	Senators	1918-31 1933, 1934	did not play in 1932 transferred to St. Louis	Canadian 1927-31 Canadian 1933, 1934
Philadelphia	Quakers	1931		American
	Flyers	1968 to date		East 1968-74 Patrick 1975 to date
Pittsburgh	Pirates	1926-30	transferred to Philadelphia	American 1927-30
	Penguins	1968 to date		West 1968-74 Norris 1975-81 Patrick 1982 to date

1912 Cup-champion Quebec Bulldogs

1987 Quebec Nordiques

Location	Club Name	NHL Seasons	Franchise Activity	Divisional Alignment
Quebec	Bulldogs	1920	transferred to Hamilton	
	Nordiques	1980 to date	former WHA franchise	Adams
St. Louis	Eagles	1935	transferred from Ottawa	Canadian 1935
	Blues	1968 to date		West 1967-74
				Smythe 1975-81
				Norris 1982 to date
Toronto	Arenas	1918, 1919	renamed St. Patricks	
	St. Patricks	1920-26	renamed Maple Leafs	
	Maple Leafs	1927 to date		Canadian 1927-38
				Norris 1982 to date
Vancouver	Canucks	1971 to date		East 1971-74
				Smythe 1975 to date
Washington	Capitals	1975 to date		Patrick
Winnipeg	Jets	1980 to date	former WHA franchise	Smythe 1980, 1981
				Norris 1982
				Smythe 1983 to date

Note: All references to years in this table refer to the NHL season ending in the stated calendar year. "1918" refers to the 1917-18 NHL season. "1918, 1919" refers to the 1917-18 and 1918-19 NHL seasons.

NHL Record Book
TEAM RECORDS

BEST WINNING PERCENTAGE, ONE SEASON:
.875 — **Boston Bruins,** 1929-30. 38w-5L-1T. 77PTS in 44GP
.830 — Montreal Canadiens, 1943-44. 38w-5L-7T. 83PTS in 50GP
.825 — Montreal Canadiens, 1976-77. 60w-8L-12T. 132PTS in 80GP
.806 — Montreal Canadiens, 1977-78. 59w-10L-11T. 129PTS in 80GP
.800 — Montreal Canadiens, 1944-45. 38w-8L-4T. 80PTS in 50GP

MOST POINTS, ONE SEASON:
132 — Montreal Canadiens, 1976-77. 60w-8L-12T. 80GP
129 — Montreal Canadiens, 1977-78. 59w-10L-11T. 80GP
127 — Montreal Canadiens, 1975-76. 58w-11L-11T. 80GP

FEWEST POINTS, ONE SEASON:
8 — Quebec Bulldogs, 1919-20. 4w-20L-0T. 24GP
10 — Toronto Arenas, 1918-19. 5w-13L-0T. 18GP
12 — Hamilton Tigers, 1920-21. 6w-18L-0T. 24GP
— Hamilton Tigers, 1922-23. 6w-18L-0T. 24GP
— Boston Bruins, 1924-25. 6w-24L-0T. 30GP
— Philadelphia Quakers, 1930-31. 4w-36L-4T. 44GP

FEWEST POINTS, ONE SEASON (MINIMUM 70-GAME SCHEDULE):
21 — Washington Capitals, 8w-67L-5T. 80GP
30 — New York Islanders, 1972-73. 12w-60L-6T. 78GP
31 — Chicago Black Hawks, 1953-54. 12w-51L-7T. 70GP

MOST WINS, ONE SEASON:
60 — Montreal Canadiens, 1976-77. 80GP
59 — Montreal Canadiens, 1977-78. 80GP
58 — Montreal Canadiens, 1975-76. 80GP

MOST LOSSES, ONE SEASON:
67 — Washington Capitals, 1974-75. 80GP
60 — New York Islanders, 1972-73. 78GP
59 — Washington Capitals, 1975-76. 80GP

FEWEST LOSSES, ONE SEASON:
5 — Ottawa Senators, 1919-20. 24GP
—Boston Bruins, 1929-30. 44GP
—Montreal Canadiens, 1943-44. 50GP

FEWEST LOSSES, ONE SEASON (MINIMUM 70-GAME SCHEDULE):
8 — Montreal Canadiens, 1976-77. 80GP
10 — Montreal Canadiens, 1972-73. 78GP
— Montreal Canadiens, 1977-78. 80GP
11 — Montreal Canadiens, 1975-76. 80GP

MOST TIES, ONE SEASON:
24 — Philadelphia Flyers, 1969-70. 76GP
23 — Montreal Canadiens, 1962-63. 70GP
— Chicago Black Hawks, 1973-74. 78GP
22 — Toronto Maple Leafs, 1954-55. 70GP
— New York Islanders, 1974-75. 80GP
— Minnesota North Stars, 1969-70. 76GP

LONGEST UNDEFEATED STREAK (ONE SEASON):
35 Games — Philadelphia Flyers, Oct. 14, 1979 - Jan. 6, 1980. 25w-10T.
28 Games — Montreal Canadiens, Dec. 18, 1977 - Feb. 23, 1978. 23w-5T.
23 Games — Boston Bruins, Dec. 22, 1940 - Feb. 23, 1941. 15w-8T.
— Philadelphia Flyers, Jan. 29, 1976 - Mar. 18, 1976. 17w-6T.

LONGEST UNDEFEATED STREAK FROM START OF SEASON:
15 Games — Edmonton Oilers, 1984-85. 12w-3T
14 Games — Montreal Canadiens, 1943-44. 11w-3T
13 Games — Montreal Canadiens, 1972-73. 9w-4T
12 Games — Atlanta Flames, 1979-80. 10w-2T
10 Games — Buffalo Sabres, 1972-73. 6w-4T
— Montreal Canadiens, 1981-82. 6w-4T
— Detroit Red Wings, 1962-63. 8w-2T

LONGEST LOSING STREAK (ONE SEASON):
17 Games — **Washington Capitals,** Feb. 18, 1975 - Mar. 26, 1975.
15 Games — Philadelphia Quakers, Nov. 29, 1930 - Jan. 8, 1931.

LONGEST WINLESS STREAK (ONE SEASON):
30 Games — **Winnipeg Jets,** Oct. 19, 1980 - Dec. 28, 1980. 23L-7T.
27 Games — Kansas City Scouts, Feb. 12, 1976 - April 4, 1976. 21L-6T.
25 Games — Washington Capitals, Nov. 29, 1975 - Jan. 21, 1976. 22L-3T.

LONGEST WINLESS STREAK FROM START OF SEASON:
15 Games — **New York Rangers,** 1943-44. 14L-1T
12 Games — Pittsburgh Pirates, 1927-28. 9L-3T
11 Games — Minnesota North Stars, 1973-74. 5L-6T
10 Games — Detroit Red Wings, 1975-76. 7L-3T

MOST CONSECUTIVE GAMES SHUT OUT:
8 — **Chicago Black Hawks,** 1928-29.

MOST SHUTOUTS, ONE SEASON:
22 — **Montreal Canadiens,** 1928-29. All by George Hainsworth. 44GP
16 — New York Americans, 1928-29. Roy Worters had 13; Flat Walsh 3. 44GP
15 — Ottawa Senators, 1925-26. All by Alex Connell. 36GP
— Ottawa Senators, 1927-28. All by Alex Connell. 44GP
— Boston Bruins, 1927-28. All by Hal Winkler. 44GP
— Chicago Black Hawks, 1969-70. All by Tony Esposito. 76GP

MOST GOALS, ONE SEASON:
446 — **Edmonton Oilers,** 1983-84. 80GP
426 — Edmonton Oilers, 1985-86. 80GP
424 — Edmonton Oilers, 1982-83. 80GP
417 — Edmonton Oilers, 1981-82. 80GP
401 — Edmonton Oilers, 1984-85. 80GP

HIGHEST GOALS-PER-GAME AVERAGE, ONE SEASON:
5.58 — **Edmonton Oilers,** 1983-84. 446G in 80GP.
5.38 — Montreal Canadiens, 1919-20. 129G in 24GP.
5.33 — Edmonton Oilers, 1985-86. 426G in 80GP.
5.30 — Edmonton Oilers, 1982-83. 424G in 80GP.
5.23 — Montreal Canadiens, 1917-18. 115G in 22GP.

FEWEST GOALS, ONE SEASON:
33 — **Chicago Black Hawks,** 1928-29. 44GP
45 — Montreal Maroons, 1924-25. 30GP
46 — Pittsburgh Pirates, 1928-29. 44GP

FEWEST GOALS, ONE SEASON (MINIMUM 70-GAME SCHEDULE):
133 — **Chicago Black Hawks,** 1953-54. 70GP
147 — Toronto Maple Leafs, 1954-55. 70GP
— Boston Bruins, 1955-56. 70GP
150 — New York Rangers, 1954-55. 70GP

MOST GOALS AGAINST, ONE SEASON:
446 — **Washington Capitals,** 1974-75. 80GP
415 — Detroit Red Wings, 1985-86. 80GP
403 — Hartford Whalers, 1982-83. 80GP
401 — Vancouver Canucks, 1984-85. 80GP
400 — Winnipeg Jets, 1980-81. 80GP

FEWEST GOALS AGAINST, ONE SEASON:
42 — **Ottawa Senators,** 1925-26. 36GP
43 — Montreal Canadiens, 1928-29. 44GP
48 — Montreal Canadiens, 1923-24. 24GP
— Montreal Canadiens, 1927-28. 44GP

FEWEST GOALS AGAINST, ONE SEASON (MINIMUM 70-GAME SCHEDULE):
131 — **Toronto Maple Leafs,** 1953-54. 70GP
— **Montreal Canadiens,** 1955-56. 70GP
132 — Detroit Red Wings, 1953-54. 70GP
133 — Detroit Red Wings, 1951-52 70GP

MOST POWER-PLAY GOALS, ONE SEASON:
99 — **Pittsburgh Penguins,** 1981-82. 80GP
— **Quebec Nordiques,** 1985-86. 80GP
97 — Los Angeles Kings, 1986-87. 80GP
95 — Boston Bruins, 1985-86. 80GP

NHL TEAM RECORDS

MOST SHORTHAND GOALS, ONE SEASON:
36 — **Edmonton Oilers**, 1983-84. 80GP
28 — Edmonton Oilers, 1986-87. 80GP
27 — Edmonton Oilers, 1985-86. 80GP
25 — Boston Bruins, 1970-71. 78GP
— Edmonton Oilers, 1984-85. 80GP

MOST ASSISTS, ONE SEASON:
737 — **Edmonton Oilers**, 1985-86. 80GP
736 — Edmonton Oilers, 1983-84. 80GP
723 — Edmonton Oilers, 1982-83. 80GP
706 — Edmonton Oilers, 1981-82. 80GP
697 — Boston Bruins, 1970-71. 78GP
690 — Edmonton Oilers, 1984-85. 80GP

FEWEST ASSISTS, ONE SEASON:
45 — **New York Rangers**, 1926-27. 44GP

FEWEST ASSISTS, ONE SEASON (MINIMUM 70-GAME SCHEDULE):
206 — **Chicago Black Hawks**, 1953-54. 70GP

1984 Edmonton Oilers

MOST SCORING POINTS, ONE SEASON:
1,182 — **Edmonton Oilers**, 1983-84. 80GP
1,163 — Edmonton Oilers, 1985-86. 80GP
1,129 — Edmonton Oilers, 1982-83. 80GP
1,123 — Edmonton Oilers, 1981-82. 80GP
1,096 — Boston Bruins, 1970-71. 78GP

MOST 50-OR-MORE-GOAL SCORERS, ONE SEASON:
3 — **Edmonton Oilers**, 1983-84. Wayne Gretzky, 87; Glenn Anderson, 54; Jari Kurri, 52 80GP.
— **Edmonton Oilers**, 1985-86. Jari Kurri, 68; Glenn Anderson, 54; Wayne Gretzky, 52. 80GP.

MOST 40-OR-MORE-GOAL SCORERS, ONE SEASON:
4 — **Edmonton Oilers**, 1982-83. Wayne Gretzky, 71; Glenn Anderson, 48; Mark Messier, 48; Jari Kurri, 45. 80GP
— **Edmonton Oilers**, 1983-84. Wayne Gretzky, 87; Glenn Anderson, 54; Jari Kurri, 52; Paul Coffey, 40. 80GP
— **Edmonton Oilers**, 1984-85. Wayne Gretzky, 73; Jari Kurri, 71; Mike Krushelnyski, 43; Glenn Anderson, 42. 80GP
— **Edmonton Oilers**, 1985-86. Jari Kurri, 68; Glenn Anderson, 54; Wayne Gretzky, 52; Paul Coffey, 48. 80GP

MOST 30-OR-MORE GOAL SCORERS, ONE SEASON:
6 — **Buffalo Sabres**, 1974-75. Rick Martin, 52; René Robert, 40; Gilbert Perreault, 39; Don Luce, 33; Rick Dudley, Danny Gare, 31 each. 80GP
— **New York Islanders**, 1977-78, Mike Bossy, 53; Bryan Trottier, 46; Clark Gillies, 35; Denis Potvin, Bob Nystrom, Bob Bourne, 30 each. 80GP
— **Winnipeg Jets**, 1984-85. Dale Hawerchuk, 53; Paul MacLean, 41; Thomas Steen, 30; Laurie Boschman, 32; Brian Mullen, 32; Doug Smail, 31. 80GP

MOST 20-OR-MORE GOAL SCORERS, ONE SEASON:
11 — **Boston Bruins**, 1977-78; Peter McNab, 41; Terry O'Reilly, 29; Bobby Schmautz, Stan Jonathan, 27 each; Jean Ratelle, Rick Middleton, 25 each; Wayne Cashman, 24; Gregg Sheppard, 23; Brad Park, 22; Don Marcotte, Bob Miller, 20 each. 80GP

MOST 100 OR-MORE-POINT SCORERS, ONE SEASON:
4 — **Boston Bruins**, 1970-71, Phil Esposito, 76G-76A-152PTS; Bobby Orr, 37G-102A-139PTS; John Bucyk, 51G-65A-116PTS; Ken Hodge, 43G-62A-105PTS. 78GP
— **Edmonton Oilers**, 1982-83, Wayne Gretzky, 71G-125A-196PTS; Mark Messier, 48G-58A-106PTS; Glenn Anderson, 48G-58A-104PTS; Jari Kurri, 45G-59A-104PTS. 80GP.
— **Edmonton Oilers**, 1983-84, Wayne Gretzky, 87G-118A-205PTS; Paul Coffey, 40G-86A-126PTS; Jari Kurri, 52G-61A-113PTS; Mark Messier, 37G-64A-101PTS. 80GP.
— **Edmonton Oilers**, 1985-86, Wayne Gretzky, 52G-163A-215PTS; Paul Coffey, 48G-90A-138PTS; Jari Kurri, 68G-63A-131PTS; Glenn Anderson, 54G-48A-102PTS. 80GP

MOST PENALTY MINUTES, ONE SEASON:
2,621 — **Philadelphia Flyers**, 1980-81. 80GP
2,493 — Philadelphia Flyers, 1981-82. 80GP
2,393 — Detroit Red Wings, 1985-86. 80GP
2,297 — Calgary Flames, 1985-86. 80GP

INDIVIDUAL RECORDS

Career

MOST SEASONS:
26 — **Gordie Howe,** Detroit Red Wings, 1946-47 – 1970-71; Hartford Whalers, 1979-80.
23 — Alex Delvecchio, Detroit Red Wings, 1951-52 – 1973-74.
— John Bucyk, Detroit, Boston, 1955-56 – 1977-78.

MOST GAMES:
1,767 — **Gordie Howe,** Detroit Red Wings, 1946-47 – 1970-71; Hartford Whalers, 1979-80.
1,549 — Alex Delvecchio, Detroit Red Wings, 1950-51 – 1973-74.
1,540 — John Bucyk, Detroit, Boston, 1955-56 – 1977-78.

MOST GOALS:
801 — **Gordie Howe,** Detroit Red Wings, Hartford Whalers, in 26 seasons, 1,767GP.
717 — Phil Esposito, Chicago Black Hawks, Boston Bruins, New York Rangers, in 18 seasons, 1,282GP.
693 — Marcel Dionne, Detroit Red Wings, Los Angeles Kings, New York Rangers, in 16 seasons, 1,244GP.
610 — Bobby Hull, Chicago Black Hawks, Winnipeg Jets, Hartford Whalers, in 16 seasons, 1,063GP.

MOST ASSISTS:
1,049 — **Gordie Howe,** Detroit Red Wings, Hartford Whalers in 26 seasons, 1,767GP.
990 — Marcel Dionne, Detroit, Los Angeles, NY Rangers in 16 seasons, 1,244GP.
977 — Wayne Gretzky, Edmonton Oilers, in 8 seasons, 632GP.

MOST POINTS:
1,850 — **Gordie Howe,** Detroit Red Wings, Hartford Whalers, in 26 seasons, 1,767GP (801G-1049A).
1,683 — Marcel Dionne, Detroit, Los Angeles, NY Rangers, in 16 seasons, 1,244GP (693G-990A).
1,590 — Phil Esposito, Chicago, Boston, NY Rangers in 18 seasons, 1,282GP (717G-873A).

MOST GOALS BY A CENTER, CAREER
717 — **Phil Esposito,** Chicago, Boston, NY Rangers, in 18 seasons.

MOST ASSISTS BY A CENTER, CAREER;
990 — **Marcel Dionne,** Detroit, Los Angeles, NY Rangers, in 16 seasons.

MOST POINTS BY A CENTER, CAREER:
1,683 — **Marcel Dionne,** Detroit, Los Angeles, NY Rangers, in 16 seasons.

MOST GOALS BY A LEFT WING, CAREER:
610 — **Bobby Hull,** Chicago, Winnipeg, Hartford, in 16 seasons.

MOST ASSISTS BY A LEFT WING, CAREER:
813 — **John Bucyk,** Detroit, Boston, in 23 seasons.

MOST POINTS BY A LEFT WING, CAREER:
1,369 — **John Bucyk,** Detroit, Boston, in 23 seasons.

MOST GOALS BY A RIGHT WING, CAREER:
801 — **Gordie Howe,** Detroit, Hartford, in 26 seasons.

MOST ASSISTS BY A RIGHT WING, CAREER:
1,049 — **Gordie Howe,** Detroit, Hartford, in 26 seasons.

MOST POINTS BY A RIGHT WING, CAREER:
1,850 — **Gordie Howe,** Detroit, Hartford, in 26 seasons.

MOST GOALS BY A DEFENSEMAN, CAREER:
291 — **Denis Potvin,** NY Islanders, in 14 seasons.

MOST ASSISTS BY A DEFENSEMAN, CAREER:
710 — **Denis Potvin,** NY Islanders, in 14 seasons.

MOST POINTS BY A DEFENSEMAN, CAREER:
1,001 — **Denis Potvin,** NY Islanders, in 14 seasons.

MOST GAMES, INCLUDING PLAYOFFS:
1,924 — **Gordie Howe,** Detroit Red Wings, Hartford Whalers, 1,767 regular-season and 157 playoff games.
1,670 — Alex Delvecchio, Detroit Red Wings, 1,549 regular-season and 121 playoff games.
1,664 — John Bucyk, Detroit, Boston, 1,540 regular-season and 124 playoff games.

Bobby Hull

MOST GOALS, INCLUDING PLAYOFFS:
869 — **Gordie Howe,** Detroit Red Wings, Hartford Whalers, 801 regular-season goals and 68 playoff goals.
778 — **Phil Esposito,** Chicago, Boston, NY Rangers, 717 regular-season and 61 playoff goals.
714 — **Marcel Dionne,** Detroit Red Wings, Los Angeles Kings, NY Rangers, 693 regular-season and 21 playoff goals.
672 — **Bobby Hull,** Chicago, Winnipeg, Hartford, 610 regular-season and 62 playoff goals.

MOST ASSISTS, INCLUDING PLAYOFFS:
1,141 — **Gordie Howe,** Detroit Red Wings, Hartford Whalers, 1,049 regular-season and 92 playoff assists.
1,117 — **Wayne Gretzky,** Edmonton Oilers, 977 regular-season and 140 playoff assists.
1,017 — **Stan Mikita,** Chicago, 926 regular-season and 91 playoff assists.

MOST POINTS, INCLUDING PLAYOFFS:
2,010 — **Gordie Howe,** Detroit Red Wings, Hartford Whalers, 1,850 regular-season and 160 playoff points.
1,729 — **Wayne Gretzky,** Edmonton Oilers, 1,520 regular-season and 209 playoff points.
1,728 — **Marcel Dionne,** Detroit, Los Angeles, 1,683 regular-season and 45 playoff points.

MOST CONSECUTIVE GAMES:
962 — **Doug Jarvis,** Montreal, Washington, Hartford, from Oct. 8, 1975 – Apr. 5, 1987.
914 — **Garry Unger,** Toronto, Detroit, St. Louis, Atlanta from Feb. 24, 1968, – Dec. 21, 1979.
776 — **Craig Ramsay,** Buffalo Sabres, from March 27, 1973, – Feb. 10, 1983.

MOST GAMES APPEARED IN BY A GOALTENDER, CAREER:
971 — **Terry Sawchuk,** Detroit, Boston, Toronto, Los Angeles, NY Rangers from 1949-50 - 1969-70.
906 — **Glenn Hall,** Detroit, Chicago, St. Louis from 1952-53 through 1970-71.
886 — **Tony Esposito,** Montreal, Chicago from 1968-69 - 1983-84.

MOST CONSECUTIVE COMPLETE GAMES BY A GOALTENDER:
502 — **Glenn Hall,** Detroit, Chicago. Played 502 games from beginning of 1955-56 season - first 12 games of 1962-63. In his 503rd straight game, Nov. 7, 1962, at Chicago, Hall was removed from the game against Boston with a back injury in the first period.

MOST SHUTOUTS BY A GOALTENDER, CAREER:
103 — **Terry Sawchuk,** Detroit, Boston, Toronto, Los Angeles, NY Rangers in 20 seasons.
94 — **George Hainsworth,** Montreal Canadiens, Toronto in 10 seasons.
84 — **Glenn Hall,** Detroit, Chicago, St. Louis in 16 seasons.

MOST GAMES SCORING THREE-OR-MORE GOALS:
41 — **Wayne Gretzky,** Edmonton, in 8 seasons, 29 three-goal games, 9 four-goal games, 3 five-goal games.

MOST 20-OR-MORE GOAL SEASONS:
22 — **Gordie Howe,** Detroit Red Wings, Hartford Whalers in 26 seasons.

MOST CONSECUTIVE 20-OR-MORE GOAL SEASONS:
22 — **Gordie Howe,** Detroit Red Wings, 1949-50 – 1970-71.

MOST 30-OR-MORE GOAL SEASONS:
14 — **Gordie Howe,** Detroit Red Wings, in 25 seasons.

MOST CONSECUTIVE 30-OR-MORE GOAL SEASONS:
13 — **Bobby Hull,** Chicago Black Hawks, 1959-60 – 1971-72.
— **Phil Esposito,** Boston, NY Rangers, 1967-68 – 1979-80.

MOST 40-OR-MORE GOAL SEASONS:
10 — **Marcel Dionne,** Detroit, Los Angeles, NY Rangers, in 15 seasons.

MOST CONSECUTIVE 40-OR-MORE GOAL SEASONS:
9 — **Mike Bossy,** New York Islanders, 1977-78 – 1985-86.

MOST 50-OR-MORE GOAL SEASONS:
9 — **Mike Bossy,** NY Islanders, in 10 seasons.

MOST CONSECUTIVE 50-OR-MORE GOAL SEASONS:
9 — **Mike Bossy,** NY Islanders, 1977-78 – 1985-86.

MOST 100-OR-MORE POINT SEASONS:
8 — **Marcel Dionne,** Detroit, 1974-75; Los Angeles, 1976-77; 1978-79 – 1982-83; 1984-85.
— **Wayne Gretzky,** Edmonton, 1979-80 – 1986-87.

MOST CONSECUTIVE 100-OR-MORE POINT SEASONS:
8 — **Wayne Gretzky,** Edmonton Oilers, 1979-80 – 1986-87.

Single Season

MOST GOALS, ONE SEASON:
92 — **Wayne Gretzky,** Edmonton Oilers, 1981-82. 80 game schedule.
87 — Wayne Gretzky, Edmonton Oilers, 1983-84. 80 game schedule.
76 — Phil Esposito, Boston Bruins, 1970-71. 78 game schedule.

MOST ASSISTS, ONE SEASON:
163 — **Wayne Gretzky,** Edmonton Oilers, 1985-86. 80 game schedule.
135 — Wayne Gretzky, Edmonton Oilers, 1984-85. 80 game schedule.
125 — Wayne Gretzky, Edmonton Oilers, 1982-83. 80 game schedule.

MOST POINTS, ONE SEASON:
215 — **Wayne Gretzky,** Edmonton Oilers, 1985-86. 80 game schedule.
212 — Wayne Gretzky, Edmonton Oilers, 1981-82. 80 game schedule.
208 — Wayne Gretzky, Edmonton Oilers, 1984-85. 80 game schedule.

MOST GOALS, ONE SEASON, BY A DEFENSEMAN:
48 — **Paul Coffey,** Edmonton Oilers, 1985-86. 80 game schedule.

MOST GOALS, ONE SEASON, BY A CENTER:
92 — **Wayne Gretzky,** Edmonton Oilers, 1981-82. 80 game schedule.

MOST GOALS, ONE SEASON, BY A RIGHT WINGER:
71 — **Jari Kurri,** Edmonton Oilers, 1984-85. 80 game schedule.

MOST GOALS, ONE SEASON, BY A LEFT WINGER:
60 — **Steve Shutt,** Montreal Canadiens, 1976-77. 80 game schedule.

MOST GOALS, ONE SEASON, BY A ROOKIE:
53 — **Mike Bossy,** NY Islanders, 1977-78. 80 game schedule.

MOST ASSISTS, ONE SEASON, BY A DEFENSEMAN:
102 — **Bobby Orr,** Boston Bruins, 1970-71. 78 game schedule.

MOST ASSISTS, ONE SEASON, BY A CENTER:
163 — **Wayne Gretzky,** Edmonton Oilers, 1985-86. 80 game schedule.

MOST ASSISTS, ONE SEASON, BY A RIGHT WINGER:
83 — **Mike Bossy,** New York Islanders, 1981-82. 80 game schedule.

MOST ASSISTS, ONE SEASON, BY A LEFT WINGER:
67 — **Mats Naslund,** Montreal Canadiens, 1985-86. 80 game schedule.

MOST ASSISTS, ONE SEASON, BY A ROOKIE:
70 — **Peter Stastny,** Quebec Nordiques, 1980-81. 80 game schedule.

MOST ASSISTS, ONE SEASON, BY A ROOKIE DEFENSEMAN:
60 — **Larry Murphy,** Los Angeles Kings, 1980-81. 80 game schedule.

MOST POINTS, ONE SEASON, BY A DEFENSEMAN:
139 — **Bobby Orr,** Boston Bruins, 1970-71. 78 game schedule.

MOST POINTS, ONE SEASON, BY A CENTER:
215 — **Wayne Gretzky,** Edmonton Oilers, 1985-86. 80 game schedule.

MOST POINTS, ONE SEASON, BY A RIGHT WINGER:
147 — **Mike Bossy,** New York Islanders, 1981-82. 80 game schedule.

MOST POINTS, ONE SEASON, BY A LEFT WINGER:
121 — **Michel Goulet,** Quebec Nordiques, 1983-84. 80 game schedule.

MOST POINTS, ONE SEASON, BY A ROOKIE:
109 — **Peter Stastny,** Quebec Nordiques, 1980-81. 80 game schedule.

MOST POWER-PLAY GOALS, ONE SEASON:
34 — **Tim Kerr,** Philadelphia Flyers, 1985-86. 80 game schedule.

MOST SHORTHAND GOALS, ONE SEASON:
12 — **Wayne Gretzky,** Edmonton Oilers, 1983-84. 80 game schedule.

MOST SHOTS ON GOAL, ONE SEASON:
550 — **Phil Esposito, Boston Bruins,** 1970-71. 78 game schedule.

MOST SHUTOUTS, ONE SEASON:
22 — **George Hainsworth,** Montreal Canadiens, 1928-29. 22GP.

Phil Esposi

NHL INDIVIDUAL RECORDS

LONGEST UNDEFEATED STREAK BY A GOALTENDER:
32 Games — **Gerry Cheevers,** Boston Bruins, 1971-72. 24w-8t.

MOST GAMES, ONE SEASON, BY A GOALTENDER:
73 — **Bernie Parent,** Philadelphia, 1973-74.

MOST WINS, ONE SEASON, BY A GOALTENDER:
47 — **Bernie Parent,** Philadelphia, 1973-74.

LONGEST WINNING STREAK, ONE SEASON, BY A GOALTENDER:
17 — **Gilles Gilbert,** Boston Bruins, 1975-76.

Single Game

Gilles Gilbert

MOST GOALS, ONE GAME:
7 — **Joe Malone,** Quebec Bulldogs, Jan. 31, 1920, at Quebec City. Quebec 10, Toronto St. Pats 6.
6 — Newsy Lalonde, Montreal Canadiens, Jan. 10, 1920, at Montreal. Canadiens 14, Toronto St. Pats 7.
— Joe Malone, Quebec Bulldogs, March 10, 1920, at Quebec City. Quebec 10, Ottawa Senators 4.
— Corb Denneny, Toronto St. Patricks, Jan. 26, 1921, at Toronto. Toronto 10, Hamilton Tigers 3.
— Cy Denneny, Ottawa Senators, March 7, 1921, at Ottawa. Ottawa 12, Hamilton Tigers 5.
— Syd Howe, Detroit Red Wings, Feb. 3, 1944, at Detroit. Detroit 12, New York Rangers 2.
— Red Berenson, St. Louis Blues, Nov. 7, 1968, at Philadelphia. St. Louis 8, Philadelphia 0
— Darryl Sittler, Toronto Maple Leafs, Feb. 7, 1976, at Toronto. Toronto 11, Boston 4.

MOST ASSISTS, ONE GAME:
7 — **Billy Taylor,** Detroit Red Wings, March 16, 1947, at Chicago. Detroit 10, Chicago 6.
— **Wayne Gretzky,** Edmonton Oilers, Feb. 15, 1980, at Edmonton. Edmonton 8, Washington 2.
— **Wayne Gretzky,** Edmonton Oilers, Dec. 11, 1985, at Chicago. Edmonton 12, Chicago 9.
— **Wayne Gretzky,** Edmonton Oilers, Feb. 14, 1986, at Edmonton. Edmonton 8, Quebec 2.

MOST POINTS, ONE GAME:
10 — **Darryl Sittler,** Toronto Maple Leafs, Feb. 7, 1976, at Toronto, 6g-4a. Toronto 11, Boston 4.

MOST GOALS, ONE GAME, BY A DEFENSEMAN:
5 — **Ian Turnbull,** Toronto Maple Leafs, Feb. 2, 1977, at Toronto. Toronto 9, Detroit 1.

MOST GOALS BY ONE PLAYER IN HIS FIRST NHL GAME:
3 — **Alex Smart,** Montreal Canadiens, Jan. 14, 1943, at Montreal. Canadiens 5, Chicago 1.
— **Real Cloutier,** Quebec Nordiques, Oct. 10, 1979, at Quebec. Atlanta 5, Quebec 3.

MOST GOALS, ONE GAME, BY A PLAYER IN HIS FIRST NHL SEASON:
5 — **Howie Meeker,** Toronto Maple Leafs, Jan. 8, 1944, at Toronto. Toronto 10, Chicago 4.
— **Don Murdoch,** New York Rangers, Oct. 12, 1976, at Minnesota. NY Rangers 10, Minnesota 4.

MOST ASSISTS, ONE GAME, BY A DEFENSEMAN:
6 — **Babe Pratt,** Toronto Maple Leafs, Jan. 8, 1944, at Toronto. Toronto 12, Boston 3.
— **Pat Stapleton,** Chicago Black Hawks, March 30, 1969, at Chicago. Chicago 9, Detroit 5.
— **Bobby Orr,** Boston Bruins, Jan. 1, 1973, at Vancouver, Boston 8, Vancouver 2.
— **Ron Stackhouse,** Pittsburgh Penguins, March 8, 1975, at Pittsburgh. Pittsburgh 8, Philadelphia 2.
— **Paul Coffey,** Edmonton Oilers, Mar. 14, 1986, at Edmonton. Edmonton 12, Detroit 3.
— **Gary Suter,** Calgary Flames, Apr. 4, 1986, at Calgary. Calgary 9, Edmonton 3.

MOST ASSISTS BY ONE PLAYER IN HIS FIRST NHL GAME:
4 — **Earl (Dutch) Reibel,** Detroit Red Wings, Oct. 8, 1953, at Detroit. Detroit 4, New York Rangers 1.
— **Roland Eriksson,** Minnesota North Stars, Oct. 6, 1976, at New York. Rangers 6, Minnesota 5.

MOST ASSISTS, ONE GAME, BY A PLAYER IN HIS FIRST NHL SEASON:
7 — **Wayne Gretzky,** Edmonton Oilers, Feb. 15, 1980, at Edmonton. Edmonton 8, Washington 2.

MOST POINTS, ONE GAME, BY A DEFENSEMAN:
8 — **Tom Bladon,** Philadelphia Flyers, Dec. 11, 1977, at Philadelphia. 4g-4a. Philadelphia 11, Cleveland 1.
— **Paul Coffey,** Edmonton Oilers, Mar. 14, 1986, at Edmonton. 2g-6a. Edmonton 12, Detroit 3.

MOST POINTS BY ONE PLAYER IN HIS FIRST NHL GAME:
5 — **Al Hill,** Philadelphia Flyers, Feb. 14, 1977, at Philadelphia. 2g-3a. Philadelphia 6, St. Louis 4.

MOST POINTS, ONE GAME, BY A PLAYER IN HIS FIRST NHL SEASON:
8 — **Peter Stastny,** Quebec Nordiques, Feb. 22, 1981, at Washington. 4g-4a. Quebec 11, Washington 7.
— **Anton Stastny,** Quebec Nordiques, Feb. 22, 1981, at Washington. 3g-5a. Quebec 11, Washington 7.

MOST GOALS, ONE PERIOD:
 4 — **Harvey (Busher) Jackson,** Toronto Maple Leafs, Nov. 20, 1934, at St. Louis, third period. Toronto 5, St. Louis Eagles 2.
 — **Max Bentley,** Chicago Black Hawks, Jan. 28, 1943, at Chicago, third period. Chicago 10, New York Rangers 1.
 — **Clint Smith,** Chicago Black Hawks, March 4, 1945, at Chicago, third period. Chicago 6, Montreal Canadiens 4.
 — **Red Berenson,** St. Louis Blues, Nov. 7, 1968, at Philadelphia, second period. St. Louis 8, Philadelphia Flyers 0.
 — **Wayne Gretzky,** Edmonton Oilers, Feb. 18, 1981, at Edmonton, third period. Edmonton 9, St. Louis 2.
 — **Grant Mulvey,** Chicago Black Hawks, Feb. 3, 1982, at Chicago, first period. Chicago 9, St. Louis 5.
 — **Bryan Trottier,** New York Islanders, Feb 13, 1982, at New York, second period. Islanders 8 Philadelphia 2.
 — **Al Secord,** Chicago Black Hawks, Jan. 7, 1987 at Chicago, second period. Chicago 6, Toronto Maple Leafs 4.

MOST ASSISTS, ONE PERIOD:
 5 — **Dale Hawerchuk,** Winnipeg Jets, Mar. 6, 1984, at Los Angeles, second period. Winnipeg 7, Los Angeles 3.

MOST POINTS, ONE PERIOD:
 6 — **Bryan Trottier,** New York Islanders, Dec. 23, 1978, at New York, second period. 3G, 3A. New York Rangers 4 at New York Islanders 9.

FASTEST GOAL FROM START OF GAME:
 5 Seconds — **Bryan Trottier,** New York Islanders, Mar. 22, 1984, at Boston. NY Islanders 3, Boston 3
 — **Doug Smail,** Winnipeg Jets, Dec. 20, 1981, at Winnipeg. Winnipeg 5, St. Louis 4.

FASTEST GOAL FROM START OF A PERIOD:
 4 Seconds — **Claude Provost,** Montreal Canadiens, Nov. 9, 1957, at Montreal, second period. Montreal 4, Boston 2.
 — **Denis Savard,** Chicago Blackhawks, Jan. 12, 1986, at Chicago, third period. Chicago 4, Hartford 2.

FASTEST TWO GOALS:
 4 Seconds — **Nels Stewart,** Montreal Maroons, Jan. 3, 1931, at Montreal at 8:24 and 8:28, third period. Montreal 5, Boston 3.

FASTEST THREE GOALS:
 21 Seconds — **Bill Mosienko,** Chicago Black Hawks, March 23, 1952, at New York, against goaltender Lorne Anderson. Mosienko scored at 6:09, 6:20 and 6:30, third period, all with both teams as full strength. Chicago 7, NY Rangers 6.

FASTEST THREE ASSISTS:
 21 Seconds — **Gus Bodnar,** Chicago Black Hawks, March 23, 1952, at New York, Bodnar assisted on Bill Mosienko's three goals at 6:09, 6:20, 6:30 of third Period. Chicago 7, NY Rangers 6.

Gus Bodnar

All-Time Goal-Scoring Leaders
* active player
(figures in parentheses indicate ranking of top 10 by goals per game)

Player		Seasons	Games	Goals	Goals per game
1. Gordie Howe	Detroit	25	1,687	786	.466
	Hartford	1	80	15	.188
	Total	26	1,767	801	.453
2. Phil Esposito	Chicago	4	235	74	.315
	Boston	8 1/4	625	459	.734
	NY Rangers	5 3/4	422	184	.436
	Total	18	1,282	717	.572 (8)
* 3. Marcel Dionne	Detroit	4	309	139	.450
	Los Angeles	11 3/4	921	550	.597
	New York	1/4	14	4	.286
	Total	15	1,244	693	.557
4. Bobby Hull	Chicago	15	1,036	604	.583
	Winnipeg	2/3	18	4	.222
	Hartford	1/3	9	2	.222
	Total	16	1,063	610	.574 (7)
* 5. Mike Bossy	NY Islanders	10	752	573	.762 (2)
6. John Bucyk	Detroit	2	104	11	.106
	Boston	21	1,436	545	.380
	Total	23	1,540	556	.361
7. Maurice Richard	Montreal	18	978	544	.556
* 8. Wayne Gretzky	Edmonton	8	632	543	.859 (1)
9. Stan Mikita	Chicago	22	1,394	541	.388
10. Frank Mahovlich	Toronto	11 2/3	720	296	.411
	Detroit	2 2/3	198	108	.545
	Montreal	3 2/3	263	129	.490
	Total	18	1,181	533	.451
11. Guy Lafleur, Montreal		14	961	518	.539
12. Gilbert Perreault, Buffalo		17	1,191	512	.430
13. Jean Beliveau, Montreal		18	1,125	507	.451
14. Jean Ratelle, NY Rangers, Boston		21	1,281	491	.383
15. Norm Ullman, Detroit, Toronto		20	1,410	490	.348
16. Darryl Sittler, Toronto, Philadelphia, Detroit		15	1096	484	.442
* 17. Lanny McDonald, Toronto, Colorado, Calgary		14	1000	479	.479
18. Alex Delvecchio, Detroit		23	1,549	456	.294
* 19. Bryan Trottier, NY Islanders		12	914	440	.481
* 20. Rick Middleton, NY Rangers, Boston		13	946	435	.460
21. Yvan Cournoyer, Montreal		16	968	428	.442
22. Steve Shutt, Montreal, Los Angeles		13	930	424	.456
23. Bill Barber, Philadelphia		12	903	420	.465
24. Garry Unger, Toronto, Detroit, St. Louis, Atlanta, Los Angeles, Edmonton		16	1105	413	.374
25. Rod Gilbert, NY Rangers		18	1,065	406	.381
26. Dave Keon, Toronto, Hartford		18	1,296	396	.305
27. Bernie Geoffrion, Montreal, NY Rangers		16	883	393	.445
* 28. Pierre Larouche, Pittsburgh, Montreal, Hartford, NY Rangers		13	802	392	.489
29. Jean Pronovost, Pittsburgh, Atlanta, Washington		13	998	391	.392
30. Dean Prentice, NY Rangers, Boston, Detroit, Pittsburgh, Minnesota		22	1378	391	.284
31. Richard Martin, Buffalo, Los Angeles		11	685	384	.561 (9)
32. Reggie Leach, Boston, California, Philadelphia, Detroit		13	934	381	.408
33. Ted Lindsay, Detroit, Chicago		17	1,068	379	.355
34. Butch Goring, Los Angeles, NY Islanders, Boston		16	1,107	375	.339
35. Rick Kehoe, Toronto, Pittsburgh		14	906	371	.409
* 36. Michel Goulet, Quebec		8	607	366	.603 (5)
37. Jacques Lemaire, Montreal		12	853	366	.429
* 38. Peter McNab, Buffalo, Boston, Vancouver, New Jersey		14	954	363	.381
39. Rick MacLeish, Philadelphia, Hartford, Pittsburgh, Detroit		14	863	361	.418
40. Ivan Boldirev, Boston, California, Atlanta, Vancouver, Detroit		15	1052	361	.343
41. Bobby Clarke, Philadelphia		15	1,144	358	.313
42. Henri Richard, Montreal		20	1,256	358	.285
* 43. Jari Kurri, Edmonton		7	520	354	.681 (3)
44. Danny Gare, Buffalo, Detroit Edmonton		13	827	354	.428
45. Wilf Paiement, Kansas City, Colorado, Toronto, Quebec, NY Rangers, Buffalo		13	923	354	.384
* 46. Dennis Maruk, California, Cleveland, Washington, Minnesota		12	860	349	.406

125

All-Time Assist Leaders

* active player
(figures in parentheses indicates ranking of top 10 in order of assists per game)

	Player	Team	Seasons	Games	Assists	Assists per game
	1. Gordie Howe	Detroit	25	1,687	1,023	.606
		Hartford	1	80	26	.325
		Total	26	1,767	1,049	.594
*	2. Marcel Dionne	Detroit	4	309	227	.735
		Los Angeles	11³/₄	921	757	.822
		New York	¹/₄	14	6	.429
		Total	15	1,244	990	.796 (7)
*	3. Wayne Gretzky	Edmonton	8	632	977	1.546 (1)
	4. Stan Mikita	Chicago	22	1,394	926	.664
	5. Phil Esposito	Chicago	4	235	100	.426
		Boston	8¹/₄	625	553	.885
		NY Rangers	5³/₄	422	220	.521
		Total	18	1,282	873	.681
	6. Bobby Clarke	Philadelphia	15	1,144	852	.745
	7. Alex Delvecchio	Detroit	23	1,549	825	.533
	8. Gilbert Perreault	Buffalo	17	1,191	814	.683
	9. John Bucyk	Detroit	2	104	19	.183
		Boston	21	1,436	794	.553
		Total	23	1,540	813	.528
	10. Jean Ratelle	NY Rangers	15¹/₄	862	481	.558
		Boston	5³/₄	419	295	.704
		Total	21	1,281	776	.605
	11. Norm Ullman, Detroit, Toronto		20	1,410	739	.524
*	12. Bryan Trottier, NY Islanders		12	914	762	.834 (6)
	13. Guy Lafleur, Montreal		14	961	728	.757
	14. Jean Beliveau, Montreal		20	1,125	712	.633
*	15. Denis Potvin, NY Islanders		14	988	710	.719
	16. Henri Richard, Montreal		20	1,256	688	.548
	17. Brad Park, NY Rangers, Boston, Detroit		17	1,113	683	.614
	18. Bobby Orr, Boston, Chicago		12	657	645	.982 (2)
	19. Darryl Sittler, Toronto, Philadelphia, Detroit		15	1,096	637	.581
*	20. Larry Robinson, Montreal		14	1,075	626	.582
	21. Andy Bathgate, NY Rangers, Toronto, Detroit, Pittsburgh		17	1,069	624	.584
	22. Rod Gilbert, NY Rangers		18	1,065	615	.577
	23. Dave Keon, Toronto, Hartford		18	1,296	590	.455
*	24. Bernie Federko, St. Louis		11	782	607	.776 (8)
*	25. Borje Salming, Toronto		14	970	579	.597
	26. Frank Mahovlich, Toronto, Detroit, Montreal		18	1,181	570	.483
	27. Bobby Hull, Chicago, Winnipeg, Hartford		16	1,063	560	.527
	28. Mike Bossy, NY Islanders		10	752	553	.735
	29. Tom Lysiak, Atlanta, Chicago		13	919	551	.596
	30. Red Kelly, Detroit, Toronto		20	1,316	542	.412
*	31. Rick Middleton, NY Rangers, Boston		13	946	521	.551
	32. Denis Maruk, California, Cleveland, Washington, Minnesota		12	860	517	.601
	33. Wayne Cashman, Boston		17	1,027	516	.502
*	34. Peter Stastny, Quebec		7	527	515	.977 (3)
	35. Butch Goring, Los Angeles, NY Islanders, Boston		16	1,107	513	.463
	36. Ivan Boldirev, Boston, California, Chicago, Atlanta, Vancouver, Detroit		15	1,052	505	.480
*	37. Lanny McDonald, Toronto, Colorado, Calgary		14	1000	486	.486
	38. Peter Mahovlich, Montreal, Pittsburgh		16	884	486	.549
	39. Pit Martin, Detroit, Boston, Chicago, Vancouver		17	1,101	485	.441
*	40. Bobby Smith, Minnesota, Montreal		9	680	473	.696
*	41. Dave Taylor, Los Angeles		10	684	473	.692
	42. Ken Hodge, Chicago, Boston, NY Rangers		14	881	472	.536
	43. Ted Lindsay, Detroit, Chicago		17	1,068	472	.442
	44. Jacques Lemaire, Montreal		12	853	469	.550
	45. Dean Prentice, NY Rangers, Boston, Detroit, Pittsburgh, Minnesota		22	1,378	469	.340
	46. Phil Goyette, Montreal, NY Rangers, St. Louis, Buffalo		16	941	467	.496
	47. Bill Barber, Philadelphia		12	903	463	.513
*	48. Denis Savard, Chicago		7	538	463	.861 (5)
	49. Doug Mohns, Boston, Chicago, Minnesota, Atlanta, Washington		22	1,390	462	.332
*	50. Paul Coffey, Edmonton		7	532	460	.865 (4)

All-Time Point Leaders

* active player
(figures in parentheses indicate ranking of top 10 by points per game)

Player		Seasons	Games	Goals	Assists	Points	Points per game
1. Gordie Howe	Detroit	25	1,687	786	1,023	1,809	1.072
	Hartford	1	80	15	26	41	.513
	Total	26	1,767	801	1,049	**1,850**	1.047
* 2. Marcel Dionne	Detroit	4	309	139	227	366	1.184
	LA	11³/₄	921	550	757	1,307	1.419
	New York	¹/₄	14	4	6	10	.714
	Total	15	1,244	693	990	**1,683**	1.353 (6)
3. Phil Esposito	Chicago	4	235	74	100	174	.740
	Boston	8¹/₄	625	459	553	1,012	1.619
	NYR	5³/₄	422	184	220	404	.957
	Total	18	1,282	717	873	**1,590**	1.240
* 4. Wayne Gretzky	Edmonton	8	632	543	977	**1,520**	2.405 (1)
5. Stan Mikita	Chicago	22	1,394	541	926	**1,467**	1.052
6. John Bucyk	Detroit	2	104	11	19	30	.288
	Boston	21	1,436	545	794	1,339	.932
	Total	23	1,540	556	813	**1,369**	.889
7. Gilbert Perreault	Buffalo	17	1,191	512	814	**1,326**	1.113
8. Alex Delvecchio	Detroit	24	1,549	456	825	**1,281**	.827
9. Jean Ratelle	NYR	15¹/₄	862	336	481	817	.948
	Boston	5³/₄	419	155	295	450	1.074
	Total	21	1,281	491	776	**1,267**	.989
10. Guy Lafleur	Montreal	14	961	518	728	**1,246**	1.296 (10)
11. Norm Ullman, Detroit, Toronto		20	1,410	490	739	**1,229**	.872
12. Jean Beliveau, Montreal		20	1,125	507	712	**1,219**	1.084
13. Bobby Clarke, Philadelphia		15	1,144	358	852	**1,210**	1.057
* 14. Bryan Trottier, NY Islanders		12	914	440	762	**1,202**	1.315 (9)
15. Bobby Hull, Chicago, Winnipeg, Hartford		16	1,063	610	560	**1,170**	1.100
* 16. Mike Bossy, NY Islanders		10	752	573	553	**1,126**	1.497 (3)
17. Darryl Sittler, Toronto, Philadelphia		15	1,096	484	637	**1,121**	1.023
18. Frank Mahovlich, Toronto, Detroit, Montreal		18	1,181	533	570	**1,103**	.934
19. Henri Richard, Montreal		20	1,256	358	688	**1,046**	.833
20. Rod Gilbert, NY Rangers		18	1,065	406	615	**1,021**	.959
* 21. Denis Potvin, NY Islanders		14	988	291	710	**1001**	1.013
22. Dave Keon, Toronto, Hartford		18	1,296	396	590	**986**	.761
23. Andy Bathgate, NY Rangers, Toronto, Detroit, Pittsburgh		17	1,069	349	624	**973**	.910
* 24. Lanny McDonald, Toronto, Colorado, Calgary		14	1000	479	486	**965**	.965
25. Maurice Richard, Montreal		18	978	544	421	**965**	.987
* 26. Rick Middleton, NY Rangers, Boston		13	946	435	521	**956**	1.011
* 27. Bernie Federko, St. Louis		11	782	310	607	**917**	1.173
28. Bobby Orr, Boston, Chicago		12	657	270	645	**915**	1.393 (5)
29. Brad Park, NY Rangers, Boston, Detroit		17	1,113	213	683	**896**	.805
30. Butch Goring, Los Angeles, NY Islanders, Boston		16	1,107	375	513	**888**	.802
31. Bill Barber, Philadelphia		12	903	420	463	**883**	.978
* 32. Denis Maruk, California, Cleveland, Washington, Minnesota		12	860	349	517	**866**	1.007
33. Ivan Boldirev, Boston, California, Chicago, Atlanta, Vancouver, Detroit		15	1,052	361	505	**866**	.823
34. Yvan Cournoyer, Montreal		16	968	428	435	**863**	.892
35. Dean Prentice, NY Rangers, Boston, Detroit, Pittsburgh, Minnesota		22	1,318	391	469	**860**	.624
36. Ted Lindsay, Detroit, Chicago		17	1,068	379	472	**851**	.797
37. Jacques Lemaire, Montreal		12	853	366	469	**835**	.979
38. Red Kelly, Detroit, Toronto		20	1,316	281	542	**823**	.625
39. Bernie Geoffrion, Montreal, NY Rangers		16	883	393	429	**822**	.931
40. Steve Shutt, Montreal, Los Angeles		13	930	424	393	**817**	.878
* 41. Peter McNab, Buffalo, Boston, Vancouver, New Jersey		14	954	363	450	**813**	.852
* 42. Larry Robinson, Montreal		14	1,075	187	626	**813**	.756
* 43. Pierre Larouche, Pittsburgh, Montreal, Hartford, NY Rangers		13	802	392	418	**810**	1.010
* 44. Wilf Paiement, Kansas City, Colorado, Toronto, Quebec, NY Rangers		13	923	354	452	**806**	.873
45. Garry Unger, Toronto, Detroit, St. Louis, Atlanta, Los Angeles, Edmonton		16	1,105	413	391	**804**	.728
46. Ken Hodge, Chicago, Boston, NY Rangers		14	881	328	472	**800**	.908
* 47. Dave Taylor, Los Angeles		10	684	321	473	**794**	1.161
48. Wayne Cashman, Boston		17	1,027	277	516	**793**	.772

127

Goaltending Records

All-Time Shutout Leaders

Goaltender	Team	Seasons	Games	Shutouts
Terry Sawchuk	Detroit	14	734	85
(1949-1970)	Boston	2	102	11
	Toronto	3	91	4
	Los Angeles	1	36	2
	NY Rangers	1	8	1
	Total	21	971	**103**
George Hainsworth	Montreal	7½	317	75
(1926-1937)	Toronto	3½	145	19
	Total	11	464	**94**
Glenn Hall	Detroit	4	148	17
(1952-1971)	Chicago	10	618	51
	St. Louis	4	140	16
	Total	18	906	**84**
Jacques Plante	Montreal	11	556	58
(1952-1973)	NY Rangers	2	98	5
	St. Louis	2	69	10
	Toronto	2½	106	7
	Boston	½	8	2
	Total	18	837	**82**
Tiny Thompson	Boston	10⅓	467	74
(1928-1940)	Detroit	1⅔	85	7
	Total	12	552	**81**
Alex Connell	Ottawa	8	292	63
(1925-1937)	Detroit	1	48	6
	NY Americans	1	1	0
	Mtl. Maroons	2	75	11
	Total	12	416	**80**
Tony Esposito	Montreal	1	13	2
(1968-1984)	Chicago	15	873	74
	Total	16	886	**76**
Lorne Chabot	NY Rangers	2	80	21
(1926-1937)	Toronto	5	215	33
	Montreal	1	47	8
	Chicago	1	48	8
	Mtl. Maroons	1	16	2
	NY Americans	1	6	1
	Total	11	412	**73**
Harry Lumley	Detroit	7	324	26
(1943-1960)	Chicago	2	134	5
	Toronto	4	267	34
	Boston	3	78	6
	Total	16	803	**71**
Roy Worters	Pittsburgh Pirates	3	123	22
(1925-1937)	NY Americans	9	364	44
	*Montreal		1	0
	Total	12	488	**66**
Turk Broda	Toronto	12	628	**62**
(1936-1952)				
Clint Benedict	Ottawa	7	158	19
(1917-1926)	Mtl. Maroons	6	202	39
	Total	13	360	**58**
John Roach	Toronto	7	223	13
(1921-1935)	NY Rangers	4	89	30
	Detroit	3	180	15
	Total	14	492	**58**
Bernie Parent	Boston	2	57	1
(1965-1979)	Philadelphia	9½	486	50
	Toronto	1½	65	4
	Total	13	608	**55**
Ed Giacomin	NY Rangers	10	539	49
(1965-1978)	Detroit	3	71	5
	Total	13	610	**54**
David Kerr	Mtl. Maroons	3	102	11
(1930-1941)	NY Americans	1	1	0
	NY Rangers	7	324	40
	Total	11	427	**51**

*Played 1 game for Canadiens in 1929-30.

GOALTENDING RECORDS

Frank Brimsek

Goaltender	Team	Seasons	Games	Shutouts
Rogie Vachon	Montreal	5½	206	13
(1966-1982)	Los Angeles	6⅔	389	32
	Detroit	2	109	4
	Boston	2	91	2
	Total	**16**	**795**	**51**
Ken Dryden	Montreal	8	397	**46**
(1970-1979)				
Gump Worsley	NY Rangers	10	582	24
(1952-1974)	Montreal	6½	171	16
	Minnesota	4½	107	3
	Total	**21**	**860**	**43**
Chuck Gardiner	Chicago	7	316	**42**
(1927-1934)				
Frank Brimsek	Boston	9	445	35
(1938-1950)	Chicago	1	70	5
	Total	**10**	**515**	**40**
Johnny Bower	NY Rangers	3	77	5
(1953-1970)	Toronto	12	475	32
	Total	**15**	**552**	**37**
Bill Durnan	Montreal	7	383	**34**
(1943-1950)				
Eddie Johnston	Boston	11	444	27
(1962-1978)	Toronto	1	26	1
	St. Louis	3⅔	118	4
	Chicago	⅓	4	0
	Total	**16**	**502**	**32**
Roger Crozier	Detroit	7	313	20
(1963-1977)	Buffalo	6	202	10
	Washington	1	3	0
	Total	**14**	**518**	**30**
Cesare Maniago	Toronto	⅓	7	0
(1960-1978)	Montreal	⅓	14	0
	NY Rangers	2	34	2
	Minnesota	9	420	26
	Vancouver	2	93	2
	Total	**14**	**568**	**30**

Goaltending Records continued

All-Time Win Leaders
(Minimum 200 Wins)

Wins	Goaltender	GP	MINS	%
435	Terry Sawchuk	971	57,114	.551
434	Jacques Plante	837	49,533	.615
423	Tony Esposito	886	52,585	.566
407	Glenn Hall	906	53,464	.544
355	Rogie Vachon	795	46,298	.542
335	Gump Worsley	862	50,232	.489
332	Harry Lumley	804	48,097	.505
302	Turk Broda	629	38,167	.560
289	Ed Giacomin	610	35,693	.570
286	Dan Bouchard	655	37,919	.543
284	Tiny Thompson	553	34,174	.581
281	*Billy Smith	625	35,594	.579
270	Bernie Parent	608	35,136	.562
262	*Gilles Meloche	761	44,007	.445
258	Ken Dryden	397	23,352	.758
252	Frank Brimsek	514	31,210	.568
251	Johnny Bower	549	32,016	.551

Active Goaltending Leaders
(Ranked by winning percentage; minimum 250 games played)

Goaltender	Seasons	GP	W	L	T	Winning %
Grant Fuhr	6	255	148	56	33	.645
Pete Peeters	9	371	202	116	37	.594
Rick Wamsley	7	254	134	82	30	.587
Billy Smith	16	625	281	191	95	.526
Bob Sauve	11	371	168	133	54	.526
Pat Riggin	8	328	146	112	48	.518
Reggie Lemelin	9	324	144	90	46	.515
Mike Liut	8	476	214	185	62	.515
Don Beaupre	7	272	116	102	42	.504
Glenn Resch	14	571	231	224	82	.476
Doug Soetaert	12	284	110	103	44	.465
Murray Bannerman	8	289	116	125	33	.458
Gilles Meloche	17	761	262	342	126	.427
Richard Brodeur	8	368	124	168	60	.418
Greg Millen	9	442	150	217	67	.415
Glen Hanlon	10	327	113	147	40	.407

Active Shutout Leaders

Goaltender	Seasons	Games	Shutouts
Glenn Resch	14	571	26
Billy Smith	16	625	20
Gilles Meloche	17	761	20
Mike Liut	8	476	17
Pete Peeters	9	371	13
Bob Froese	5	172	12
Tom Barrasso	4	202	11
Pat Riggin	8	328	11
Greg Millen	9	442	9
Al Jensen	7	179	8
Bob Sauve	11	371	8

Tony Esposito

Terry Sawchuk

Goals Against Average Leaders

Season	Goaltender and Club	GP	GA	AVG.
1986-87	Brian Hayward, Montreal	37	102	2.81
	Patrick Roy, Montreal	46	131	2.93
1985-86	Bob Froese, Philadelphia	51	116	2.55
	Darren Jensen, Philadelphia	29	88	3.68
1984-85	Tom Barrasso, Buffalo	54	144	2.66
	Bob Sauve, Buffalo	27	84	3.22
1983-84	Pat Riggin, Washington	41	102	2.66
	Al Jensen, Washington	43	117	
1982-83	Roland Melanson, NY Islanders	44	109	2.66
	Billy Smith, NY Islanders	41	112	2.87
1981-82	Denis Herron, Montreal	27	68	2.64
	Rick Wamsley, Montreal	38	101	2.75
1980-81	Richard Sevigny, Montreal	33	71	2.40
	Michel Larocque, Montreal	28	82	3.03
	Denis Herron, Montreal	25	67	3.50
1979-80	Bob Sauvé, Buffalo	32	74	2.36
	Don Edwards, Buffalo	49	125	2.57
1978-79	Ken Dryden, Montreal	47	108	2.30
	Michel Larocque, Montreal	34	94	2.84
1977-78	Ken Dryden, Montreal	52	105	2.05
	Michel Larocque, Montreal	30	77	2.67
1976-77	Michel Larocque, Montreal	26	53	2.09
	Ken Dryden, Montreal	56	117	2.14
1975-76	Ken Dryden, Montreal	62	121	2.03
1974-75	Bernie Parent, Philadelphia	68	137	2.03
1973-74	Bernie Parent, Philadelphia	73	136	1.89
	Tony Esposito, Chicago	70	141	2.04
1972-73	Ken Dryden, Montreal	54	119	2.26
1971-72	Tony Esposito, Chicago	48	82	1.76
	Gary Smith, Chicago	28	62	2.41
1970-71	Ed Giacomin, NY Rangers	45	95	2.15
	Gilles Villemure, NY Rangers	34	78	2.29
1969-70	Tony Esposito, Chicago	63	136	2.17
1968-69	Jacques Plante, St. Louis	37	70	1.96
	Glenn Hall, St. Louis	41	85	2.17
1967-68	Lorne Worsley, Montreal	40	73	1.98
	Rogatien Vachon, Montreal	39	92	2.48
1966-67	Glenn Hall, Chicago	32	66	2.38
	Denis DeJordy, Chicago	44	104	2.46
1965-66	Lorne Worsley, Montreal	51	114	2.36
	Charlie Hodge, Montreal	26	56	2.58
1964-65	Johnny Bower, Toronto	34	81	2.38
	Terry Sawchuk, Toronto	36	92	2.56
1963-64	Charlie Hodge, Montreal	62	140	2.26
1962-63	Glenn Hall, Chicago	66	166	2.51
1961-62	Jacques Plante, Montreal	70	166	2.37
1960-61	Johnny Bower, Toronto	58	145	2.50
1959-60	Jacques Plante, Montreal	69	175	2.54
1958-59	Jacques Plante, Montreal	67	144	2.18
1957-58	Jacques Plante, Montreal	57	119	2.11
1956-57	Jacques Plante, Montreal	61	123	2.02
1955-56	Jacques Plante, Montreal	64	119	1.86
1954-55	Terry Sawchuk, Detroit	68	132	1.94
1953-54	Harry Lumley, Toronto	69	128	1.85
1952-53	Terry Sawchuk, Detroit	63	120	1.90
1951-52	Terry Sawchuk, Detroit	70	133	1.90
1950-51	Al Rollins, Toronto	40	70	1.75
1949-50	Bill Durnan, Montreal	64	141	2.20
1948-49	Bill Durnan, Montreal	60	126	2.10
1947-48	Turk Broda, Toronto	60	143	2.38
1946-47	Bill Durnan, Montreal	60	138	2.30
1945-46	Bill Durnan, Montreal	40	104	2.60
1944-45	Bill Durnan, Montreal	50	121	2.42
1943-44	Bill Durnan, Montreal	50	109	2.18
1942-43	Johnny Mowers, Detroit	50	124	2.48
1941-42	Frank Brimsek, Boston	47	115	2.44
1940-41	Turk Broda, Toronto	48	99	2.06
1939-40	Dave Kerr, NY Rangers	48	77	1.60
1938-39	Frank Brimsek, Boston	44	70	1.59
1937-38	Tiny Thompson, Boston	48	89	1.85
1936-37	Normie Smith, Detroit	48	102	2.13
1935-36	Tiny Thompson, Boston	48	83	1.73
1934-35	Lorne Chabot, Chicago	48	88	1.83
1933-34	Chuck Gardiner, Chicago	48	83	1.73
1932-33	Tiny Thompson, Boston	48	88	1.83
1931-32	Chuck Gardiner, Chicago	48	101	2.10
1930-31	Roy Worters, NY Americans	44	74	1.68
1929-30	Tiny Thompson, Boston	44	98	2.23
1928-29	George Hainsworth, Montreal	44	43	0.98
1927-28	George Hainsworth, Montreal	44	48	1.09
1926-27	George Hainsworth, Montreal	44	67	1.52

* Goaltender(s) with lowest goals-against average awarded Vezina Trophy up to and including 1980-81 season. Beginning with 1982-83 season, William Jennings Trophy awarded.

Billy Smith

Coaching Records

(Minimum 600 regular-season games. Ranked by number of games coached.)

Coach	Team	Seasons	Games	Wins	Losses	Ties	%*
Dick Irvin	Chicago	1930-31; 55-56	114	43	56	15	.443
	Toronto	1931-40	427	216	152	59	.575
	Montreal	1940-55	896	431	313	152	.566
	Total		**1,437**	**690**	**521**	**226**	**.559**
Scott Bowman	St. Louis	1967-71	238	110	83	45	.557
	Montreal	1971-79	634	419	110	105	.744
	Buffalo	1979-87	404	210	134	60	.594
	Total		**1,276**	**739**	**327**	**210**	**.661**
Al Arbour	St. Louis	1970-73	107	42	40	25	.509
	NY Islanders	1973-86	1,039	552	317	169	.612
	Total		**1,146**	**594**	**357**	**194**	**.603**
Billy Reay	Toronto	1957-59	90	26	50	14	.367
	Chicago	1963-77	1,012	516	335	161	.589
	Total		**1,102**	**542**	**385**	**175**	**.571**
Jack Adams	Detroit	1927-44	**964**	**413**	**390**	**161**	**.512**
Sid Abel	Chicago	1952-54	140	39	79	22	.357
	Detroit	1957-68; 69-70	810	340	338	132	.501
	St. Louis	1971-72	10	3	6	1	.350
	Kansas City	1975-76	3	0	3	0	.000
	Total		**963**	**382**	**426**	**155**	**.477**
Punch Imlach	Toronto	1958-69; 79-81	840	391	311	138	.548
	Buffalo	1970-72	119	32	62	25	.374
	Total		**959**	**423**	**373**	**163**	**.526**
Toe Blake	Montreal	1955-68	**914**	**500**	**255**	**159**	**.634**
Emile Francis	NY Rangers	1965-75	654	347	209	98	.606
	St. Louis	1976-77, 81-83	124	46	64	14	.427
	Total		**778**	**393**	**273**	**112**	**.577**
Bob Pulford	Los Angeles	1972-77	396	178	150	68	.535
	Chicago	1977-79; 1981-82; 84-87	375	158	155	62	.504
	Total		**771**	**336**	**305**	**130**	**.520**
Milt Schmidt	Boston	1954-61; 62-66	726	245	360	121	.421
	Washington	1974-76	43	5	33	5	.174
	Total		**769**	**250**	**393**	**126**	**.407**
Red Kelly	Los Angeles	1967-69	150	55	75	20	.433
	Pittsburgh	1969-73	274	90	132	52	.423
	Toronto	1973-77	318	133	123	62	.516
	Total		**742**	**278**	**330**	**134**	**465**
Fred Shero	Philadelphia	1971-78	554	308	151	95	.642
	NY Rangers	1978-81	180	82	74	24	.522
	Total		**734**	**390**	**225**	**119**	**.612**
Art Ross	Boston	1924-45	**728**	**361**	**277**	**90**	**.558**
Bob Berry	Los Angeles	1978-81	240	107	94	39	.527
	Montreal	1981-84	223	116	71	36	.601
	Pittsburgh	1984-87	240	88	127	25	.419
	Total		**703**	**311**	**292**	**100**	**.514**
Glen Sather	Edmonton	1979-87	**640**	**364**	**191**	**85**	**.635**
Tommy Ivan	Detroit	1947-54	470	262	118	90	.653
	Chicago	1956-58	140	40	78	22	.364
	Total		**610**	**302**	**196**	**112**	**.587**
Lester Patrick	NY Rangers	1926-39	**604**	**281**	**216**	**107**	**.554**

* % arrived at by dividing possible points into actual points.

ёё # Individual Awards

ART ROSS TROPHY

An annual award "to the player who leads the league in scoring points at the end of the regular season." Overall winner receives $3,000 and the overall runner-up $1,000.

History: Arthur Howie Ross, former manager-coach of Boston Bruins, presented the trophy to the National Hockey League in 1947. If two players finish the schedule with the same number of points, the trophy is awarded in the following manner: 1. Player with most goals. 2. Player with fewer games played. 3. Player scoring first goal of the season.

1986-87 Winner: Wayne Gretzky, Edmonton
Runners-up: Jari Kurri, Edmonton
Mario Lemieux, Pittsburgh
Mark Messier, Edmonton

HART MEMORIAL TROPHY

An annual award "to the player adjudged to be the most valuable to his team". Winner selected in poll by Professional Hockey Writers' Association in the 21 NHL cities at the end of the regular schedule. The winner receives $1,500 and the runner-up $750.

History: The Hart Memorial Trophy was presented by the National Hockey League in 1960 after the original Hart Trophy was retired to the Hockey Hall of Fame. The original Hart Trophy was donated to the NHL in 1923 by Dr. David A. Hart, father of Cecil Hart, former manager-coach of the Montreal Canadiens.

1986-87 Winner: Wayne Gretzky, Edmonton
Runners-up: Ray Bourque, Boston
Mike Liut, Hartford

CALDER MEMORIAL TROPHY

An annual award "to the player selected as the most proficient in his first year of competition in the National Hockey League". Winner selected in poll by Professional Hockey Writers' Association at the end of the regular schedule. The winner receives $3,000 and the runner-up $1,500.

History: From 1936-37 until his death in 1943, Frank Calder, NHL President, bought a trophy each year to be given permanently to the outstanding rookie. After Calder's death, the NHL presented the Calder Memorial Trophy in his memory and the trophy is to be kept in perpetuity. To be eligible for the award, a player cannot have played more than 25 games in any single preceding season nor in six or more games in each of any two preceding seasons in any major professional league.

1986-87 Winner: Luc Robitaille, Los Angeles
Runners-up: Ron Hextall, Philadelphia
Jimmy Carson, Los Angeles

JAMES NORRIS MEMORIAL TROPHY

An annual award "to the defense player who demonstrates throughout the season the greatest all-round ability in the position." Winner selected in poll by Professional Hockey Writers' Association at the end of the regular schedule. The winner receives $3,000 and the runner-up $1,500.

History: The James Norris Memorial Trophy was presented in 1953 by the four children of the late James Norris in memory of the former owner-president of the Detroit Red Wings.

1986-87 Winner: Ray Bourque, Boston
   Runners-up: Mark Howe, Philadelphia
         Larry Murphy, Washington

LADY BYNG MEMORIAL TROPHY

An annual award "to the player adjudged to have exhibited the best type of sportsmanship and gentlemanly conduct combined with a high standard of playing ability." Winner selected in poll by Professional Hockey Writers' Association at the end of the regular schedule. The winner receives $3,000 and the runner-up $1,500.

History: Lady Byng, wife of Canada's Governor-General at the time, presented the Lady Byng Trophy in 1925. After Frank Boucher of New York Rangers won the award seven times in eight seasons, he was given the trophy to keep and Lady Byng donated another trophy in 1936. After Lady Byng's death in 1949, the National Hockey League presented a new trophy, changing the name to Lady Byng Memorial Trophy.

1986-87 Winner: Joe Mullen, Calgary
   Runners-up: Wayne Gretzky, Edmonton
         Rick Middleton, Boston

VEZINA TROPHY

An annual award "to the goalkeeper adjudged to be the best at his position" as voted by the general managers of each of the 21 clubs. Over-all winner receives $3,000, runner-up $1,500.

History: Leo Dandurand, Louis Letourneau and Joe Cattarinich, former owners of the Montreal Canadiens, presented the trophy to the National Hockey League in 1926-27 in memory of Georges Vezina, outstanding goalkeeper of the Canadiens who collapsed during an NHL game November 28, 1925, and died of tuberculosis a few months later. Until the 1981-82 season, the goalkeeper(s) of the team allowing the fewest number of goals during the regular-season were awarded the Vezina Trophy.

1986-87 Winner: Ron Hextall, Philadelphia
   Runners-up: Mike Liut, Hartford
         Grant Fuhr, Edmonton

FRANK J. SELKE TROPHY

An annual award "to the forward who best excels in the defensive aspects of the game." Winner selected in poll by Professional Hockey Writers' Association at the end of the regular schedule. The winner receives $3,000 and the runner-up $1,500.

History: Presented to the National Hockey League in 1977 by the Board of Governors of the NHL in honour of Frank J. Selke, one of the great architects of NHL championship teams.

1986-87 Winner: Dave Poulin, Philadelphia
Runners-up: Guy Carbonneau, Montreal
Bob Gould, Washington

CONN SMYTHE TROPHY

An annual award "to the most valuable player for his team in the playoffs." Winner selected by the Professional Hockey Writers' Association at the conclusion of the final game in the Stanley Cup Finals. The winner receives $3,000.

History: Presented by Maple Leaf Gardens Limited in 1964 to honor Conn Smythe, the former coach, manager, president and owner-governor of the Toronto Maple Leafs.

1986-87 Winner: Ron Hextall, Philadelphia

JACK ADAMS AWARD

An annual award presented by the National Hockey League Broadcasters' Association to "the NHL coach adjudged to have contributed the most to his team's success." Winner selected by poll among members of the NHL Broadcasters' Association at the end of the regular season. The winner receives $1,000 from the NHLBA.

History: The award was presented by the NHL Broadcasters' Association in 1974 to commemorate the late Jack Adams, coach and general manager of Detroit Red Wings, whose lifetime dedication to hockey serves as an inspiration to all who aspire to further the game.

1986-87 Winner: Jacques Demers, Detroit
Runners-up: Jack Evans, Hartford
Dan Maloney, Winnipeg

WILLIAM M. JENNINGS TROPHY

An annual award "to the goalkeeper(s) having played a minimum of 25 games for the team with the fewest goals scored against it." Winners selected on regular-season play. Overall winner receives $3,000, runner-up $1,500. Leader at end of first half of season and leader in second half each receive $250.

History: The Jennings Trophy was presented in 1981-82 by the National Hockey League's Board of Governors to honor the late William M. Jennings, longtime governor and president of the New York Rangers and one of the great builders of hockey in the United States.

1986-87 Winners: Brian Hayward and Patrick Roy, Montreal
Runners-up: Ron Hextall, Philadelphia
Mike Liut and Steve Weeks, Hartford

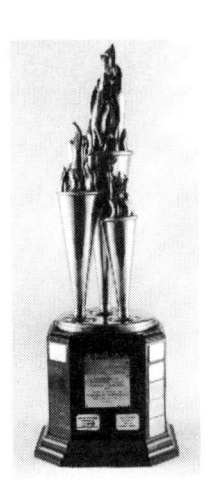

BILL MASTERTON MEMORIAL TROPHY

An annual award under the trusteeship of the Professional Hockey Writers' Association to "the National Hockey League player who best exemplifies the qualities of perseverance, sportsmanship and dedication to hockey." Winner selected by poll among the 21 chapters of the PHWA at the end of the regular season. A $1,500 grant from the PHWA is awarded annually to the Bill Masterton Scholarship Fund, based in Bloomington, MN, in the name of the Masterton Trophy winner.

History: The trophy was presented by the NHL Writers' Association in 1968 to commemorate the late William Masterton, a player of the Minnesota North Stars, who exhibited to a high degree the qualities of perseverance, sportsmanship and dedication to hockey, and who died January 15, 1968.

1986-87 Winner: Doug Jarvis, Hartford

LESTER PATRICK TROPHY

An annual award "for outstanding service to hockey in the United States." Eligible recipients are players, officials, coaches, executives and referees. Winner selected by an award committee consisting of the President of the NHL, an NHL Governor, a hockey writer for a U.S. national news service, a nationally syndicated sports columnist, an ex-player in the Hockey Hall of Fame and a sports representative of a U.S. national radio-TV network. Each except the League president is rotated annually. The winner receives a miniature of the trophy.

History: Presented by the New York Rangers in 1966 to honor the late Lester Patrick, longtime general manager and coach of the New York Rangers, whose teams finished out of the playoffs only once in his first 16 years with the club.

1986-87 Winners: Hobey Baker and Frank Mathers

TROPHIES & AWARDS

LESTER B. PEARSON AWARD
An annual award presented to the NHL's outstanding player as selected by the members of the National Hockey League Players' Association.

History: The award was presented in 1970-71 by the NHLPA in honor of the late Lester B. Pearson, former Prime Minister of Canada.

1986-87 Winner: Wayne Gretzky, Edmonton

EMERY EDGE AWARD
An annual award "to the player who appears in a minimum of 60 games and leads the National Hockey League in plus-minus statistics". Overall winner receives $2,000. Each team leader receives $500, to be donated in his name to the charity of his choice.

History: The award was presented to the NHL in 1982-83 by Emery Worldwide, of Wilton, Connecticut, to recognize the League leader in plus-minus statistics. Plus-minus statistics are calculated by giving a player a "plus" when on-ice for an even-strength or shorthand goal scored by his team. He receives a "minus" when on-ice for an even-strength or shorthand goal scored by the opposing team.

1986-87 Winner: Wayne Gretzky, Edmonton
Runner-up: Mark Howe, Philadelphia

DODGE PERFORMER OF THE YEAR AWARD
An annual award presented by Dodge to the National Hockey League's most outstanding performer in the regular-season. The winner receives the Dodge vehicle of his choice.

History: The award was first presented in 1984-85 to recognize the NHL's top player. Dodge also sponsors the Performer of the Week and Performer of the Month awards, donating $500 and $1,000, respectively, to youth hockey organizations across North America in the recipients' honor.

1986-87 Winner: Wayne Gretzky, Edmonton

L.B. Pearson Award   *Emery Edge Award*

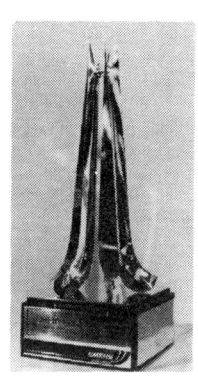

Team Award

PRESIDENTS' TROPHY
An annual award to the club finishing the regular-season with the best overall record. The winner receives $200,000, to be split evenly between the team and its players. Based on 20 players in each game during the regular-season, a player who appears in all 80 games receives $5,000. Players appearing in less than 80 games receive pro-rated amounts.

History: Presented to the National Hockey League in 1985-86 by the NHL Board of Governors to recognize the team compiling the top regular-season record.

1986-87 Winner: Edmonton Oilers
Runners-up: Philadelphia Flyers
           Calgary Flames

NATIONAL HOCKEY LEAGUE INDIVIDUAL AWARD WINNERS

ART ROSS TROPHY WINNERS

1987	Wayne Gretzky	Edmonton
1986	Wayne Gretzky	Edmonton
1985	Wayne Gretzky	Edmonton
1984	Wayne Gretzky	Edmonton
1983	Wayne Gretzky	Edmonton
1982	Wayne Gretzky	Edmonton
1981	Wayne Gretzky	Edmonton
1980	Marcel Dionne	Los Angeles
1979	Bryan Trottier	NY Islanders
1978	Guy Lafleur	Montreal
1977	Guy Lafleur	Montreal
1976	Guy Lafleur	Montreal
1975	Bobby Orr	Boston
1974	Phil Esposito	Boston
1973	Phil Esposito	Boston
1972	Phil Esposito	Boston
1971	Phil Esposito	Boston
1970	Bobby Orr	Boston
1969	Phil Esposito	Boston
1968	Stan Mikita	Chicago
1967	Stan Mikita	Chicago
1966	Bobby Hull	Chicago
1965	Stan Mikita	Chicago
1964	Stan Mikita	Chicago
1963	Gordie Howe	Detroit
1962	Bobby Hull	Chicago
1961	Bernie Geoffrion	Montreal
1960	Bobby Hull	Chicago
1959	Dickie Moore	Montreal
1958	Dickie Moore	Montreal
1957	Gordie Howe	Detroit
1956	Jean Béliveau	Montreal
1955	Bernie Geoffrion	Montreal
1954	Gordie Howe	Detroit
1953	Gordie Howe	Detroit
1952	Gordie Howe	Detroit
1951	Gordie Howe	Detroit
1950	Ted Lindsay	Detroit
1949	Roy Conacher	Chicago
1948	Elmer Lach	Montreal
1947*	Max Bentley	Chicago
1946	Max Bentley	Chicago
1945	Elmer Lach	Montreal
1944	Herbie Cain	Boston
1943	Doug Bentley	Chicago
1942	Bryan Hextall	NY Rangers
1941	Bill Cowley	Boston
1940	Milt Schmidt	Boston
1939	Toe Blake	Montreal
1938	Gordie Drillon	Toronto
1937	Dave Schriner	NY Americans
1936	Dave Schriner	NY Americans
1935	Charlie Conacher	Toronto
1934	Charlie Conacher	Toronto
1933	Bill Cook	NY Rangers
1932	Harvey Jackson	Toronto
1931	Howie Morenz	Montreal
1930	Cooney Weiland	Boston
1929	Ace Bailey	Toronto
1928	Howie Morenz	Montreal
1927	Bill Cook	NY Rangers
1926	Nels Stewart	Mtl. Maroons
1925	Babe Dye	Toronto
1924	Cy Denneny	Ottawa
1923	Babe Dye	Toronto
1922	Punch Broadbent	Ottawa
1921	Newsy Lalonde	Montreal
1920	Joe Malone	Quebec
1919	Newsy Lalonde	Montreal
1918	Joe Malone	Montreal

* Scoring leaders prior to inception of Art Ross Trophy in 1947-48

HART TROPHY WINNERS

1987	Wayne Gretzky	Edmonton
1986	Wayne Gretzky	Edmonton
1985	Wayne Gretzky	Edmonton
1984	Wayne Gretzky	Edmonton
1983	Wayne Gretzky	Edmonton
1982	Wayne Gretzky	Edmonton
1981	Wayne Gretzky	Edmonton
1980	Wayne Gretzky	Edmonton
1979	Bryan Trottier	NY Islanders
1978	Guy Lafleur	Montreal
1977	Guy Lafleur	Montreal
1976	Bobby Clarke	Philadelphia
1975	Bobby Clarke	Philadelphia
1974	Phil Esposito	Boston
1973	Bobby Clarke	Philadelphia
1972	Bobby Orr	Boston
1971	Bobby Orr	Boston
1970	Bobby Orr	Boston
1969	Phil Esposito	Boston
1968	Stan Mikita	Chicago
1967	Stan Mikita	Chicago
1966	Bobby Hull	Chicago
1965	Bobby Hull	Chicago
1964	Jean Béliveau	Montreal
1963	Gordie Howe	Detroit
1962	Jacques Plante	Montreal
1961	Bernie Geoffrion	Montreal
1960	Gordie Howe	Detroit
1959	Andy Bathgate	NY Rangers
1958	Gordie Howe	Detroit
1957	Gordie Howe	Detroit
1956	Jean Béliveau	Montreal
1955	Ted Kennedy	Toronto
1954	Al Rollins	Chicago
1953	Gordie Howe	Detroit
1952	Gordie Howe	Detroit
1951	Milt Schmidt	Boston
1950	Charlie Rayner	NY Rangers
1949	Sid Abel	Detroit
1948	Buddy O'Connor	NY Rangers
1947	Maurice Richard	Montreal
1946	Max Bentley	Chicago
1945	Elmer Lach	Montreal
1944	Babe Pratt	Toronto
1943	Bill Cowley	Boston
1942	Tom Anderson	NY Americans
1941	Bill Cowley	Boston
1940	Ebbie Goodfellow	Detroit
1939	Toe Blake	Montreal
1938	Eddie Shore	Boston
1937	Babe Siebert	Montreal
1936	Eddie Shore	Boston
1935	Eddie Shore	Boston
1934	Aurel Joliat	Montreal
1933	Eddie Shore	Boston
1932	Howie Morenz	Montreal
1931	Howie Morenz	Montreal
1930	Nels Stewart	Mtl. Maroons
1929	Roy Worters	NY Americans
1928	Howie Morenz	Montreal
1927	Herb Gardiner	Montreal
1926	Nels Stewart	Mtl. Maroons
1925	Billy Burch	Hamilton
1924	Frank Nighbor	Ottawa

TROPHIES & AWARDS

CALDER MEMORIAL TROPHY WINNERS

1987	Luc Robitaille	Los Angeles
1986	Gary Suter	Calgary
1985	Mario Lemieux	Pittsburgh
1984	Tom Barrasso	Buffalo
1983	Steve Larmer	Chicago
1982	Dale Hawerchuk	Winnipeg
1981	Peter Stastny	Quebec
1980	Raymond Bourque	Boston
1979	Bobby Smith	Minnesota
1978	Mike Bossy	NY Islanders
1977	Willi Plett	Atlanta
1976	Bryan Trottier	NY Islanders
1975	Eric Vail	Atlanta
1974	Denis Potvin	NY Islanders
1973	Steve Vickers	NY Rangers
1972	Ken Dryden	Montreal
1971	Gilbert Perreault	Buffalo
1970	Tony Esposito	Chicago
1969	Danny Grant	Minnesota
1968	Derek Sanderson	Boston
1967	Bobby Orr	Boston
1966	Brit Selby	Toronto
1965	Roger Crozier	Detroit
1964	Jacques Laperrière	Montreal
1963	Kent Douglas	Toronto
1962	Bobby Rousseau	Montreal
1961	Dave Keon	Toronto
1960	Bill Hay	Chicago
1959	Ralph Backstrom	Montreal
1958	Frank Mahovlich	Toronto
1957	Larry Regan	Boston
1956	Glenn Hall	Detroit
1955	Ed Litzenberger	Chicago
1954	Camille Henry	NY Rangers
1953	Lorne Worsley	NY Rangers
1952	Bernie Geoffrion	Montreal
1951	Terry Sawchuk	Detroit
1950	Jack Gelineau	Boston
1949	Pentti Lund	NY Rangers
1948	Jim McFadden	Detroit
1947	Howie Meeker	Toronto
1946	Edgar Laprade	NY Rangers
1945	Frank McCool	Toronto
1944	Gus Bodnar	Toronto
1943	Gaye Stewart	Toronto
1942	Grant Warwick	NY Rangers
1941	Johnny Quilty	Montreal
1940	Kilby MacDonald	NY Rangers
1939	Frank Brimsek	Boston
1938	Cully Dahlstrom	Chicago
1937	Syl Apps	Toronto
1936	Mike Karakas	Chicago
1935	Dave Schriner	NY Americans
1934	Russ Blinko	Mtl. Maroons
1933	Carl Voss	Detroit

LESTER B. PEARSON AWARD WINNERS

1987	Wayne Gretzky	Edmonton
1986	Mario Lemieux	Pittsburgh
1985	Wayne Gretzky	Edmonton
1984	Wayne Gretzky	Edmonton
1983	Wayne Gretzky	Edmonton
1982	Wayne Gretzky	Edmonton
1981	Mike Liut	St. Louis
1980	Marcel Dionne	Los Angeles
1979	Marcel Dionne	Los Angeles
1978	Guy Lafleur	Montreal
1977	Guy Lafleur	Montreal
1976	Guy Lafleur	Montreal
1975	Bobby Orr	Boston
1974	Bobby Clarke	Philadelphia
1973	Phil Esposito	Boston
1972	Jean Ratelle	NY Rangers
1971	Phil Esposito	Boston

JAMES NORRIS TROPHY WINNERS

1987	Ray Bourque	Boston
1986	Paul Coffey	Edmonton
1985	Paul Coffey	Edmonton
1984	Rod Langway	Washington
1983	Rod Langway	Washington
1982	Doug Wilson	Chicago
1981	Randy Carlyle	Pittsburgh
1980	Larry Robinson	Montreal
1979	Denis Potvin	NY Islanders
1978	Denis Potvin	NY Islanders
1977	Larry Robinson	Montreal
1976	Denis Potvin	NY Islanders
1975	Bobby Orr	Boston
1974	Bobby Orr	Boston
1973	Bobby Orr	Boston
1972	Bobby Orr	Boston
1971	Bobby Orr	Boston
1970	Bobby Orr	Boston
1969	Bobby Orr	Boston
1968	Bobby Orr	Boston
1967	Harry Howell	NY Rangers
1966	Jacques Laperrière	Montreal
1965	Pierre Pilote	Chicago
1964	Pierre Pilote	Chicago
1963	Pierre Pilote	Chicago
1962	Doug Harvey	NY Rangers
1961	Doug Harvey	Montreal
1960	Doug Harvey	Montreal
1959	Tom Johnson	Montreal
1958	Doug Harvey	Montreal
1957	Doug Harvey	Montreal
1956	Doug Harvey	Montreal
1955	Doug Harvey	Montreal
1954	Red Kelly	Detroit

Doug Harvey

NHL Award Winners continued

LADY BYNG TROPHY WINNERS

1987	Joe Mullen	Calgary
1986	Mike Bossy	NY Islanders
1985	Jari Kurri	Edmonton
1984	Mike Bossy	NY Islanders
1983	Mike Bossy	NY Islanders
1982	Rick Middleton	Boston
1981	Rick Kehoe	Pittsburgh
1980	Wayne Gretzky	Edmonton
1979	Bob MacMillan	Atlanta
1978	Butch Goring	Los Angeles
1977	Marcel Dionne	Los Angeles
1976	Jean Ratelle	NY Rangers-Boston
1975	Marcel Dionne	Detroit
1974	John Bucyk	Boston
1973	Gilbert Perreault	Buffalo
1972	Jean Ratelle	NY Rangers
1971	John Bucyk	Boston
1970	Phil Goyette	St. Louis
1969	Alex Delvecchio	Detroit
1968	Stan Mikita	Chicago
1967	Stan Mikita	Chicago
1966	Alex Delvecchio	Detroit
1965	Bobby Hull	Chicago
1964	Ken Wharram	Chicago
1963	Dave Keon	Toronto
1962	Dave Keon	Toronto
1961	Red Kelly	Toronto
1960	Don McKenney	Boston
1959	Alex Delvecchio	Detroit
1958	Camille Henry	NY Rangers
1957	Andy Hebenton	NY Rangers
1956	Earl Reibel	Detroit
1955	Sid Smith	Toronto
1954	Red Kelly	Detroit
1953	Red Kelly	Detroit
1952	Sid Smith	Toronto
1951	Red Kelly	Detroit
1950	Edgar Laprade	NY Rangers
1949	Bill Quackenbush	Detroit
1948	Buddy O'Connor	NY Rangers
1947	Bobby Bauer	Boston
1946	Toe Blake	Montreal
1945	Bill Mosienko	Chicago
1944	Clint Smith	Chicago
1943	Max Bentley	Chicago
1942	Syl Apps	Toronto
1941	Bobby Bauer	Boston
1940	Bobby Bauer	Boston
1939	Clint Smith	NY Rangers
1938	Gordie Drillon	Toronto
1937	Marty Barry	Detroit
1936	Doc Romnes	Chicago
1935	Frank Boucher	NY Rangers
1934	Frank Boucher	NY Rangers
1933	Frank Boucher	NY Rangers
1932	Joe Primeau	Toronto
1931	Frank Boucher	NY Rangers
1930	Frank Boucher	NY Rangers
1929	Frank Boucher	NY Rangers
1928	Frank Boucher	NY Rangers
1927	Billy Burch	NY Americans
1926	Frank Nighbor	Ottawa
1925	Frank Nighbor	Ottawa

EMERY EDGE AWARD WINNERS

1987	Wayne Gretzky	Edmonton
1986	Mark Howe	Philadelphia
1985	Wayne Gretzky	Edmonton
1984	Wayne Gretzky	Edmonton
1983	Charlie Huddy	Edmonton

VEZINA TROPHY WINNERS

1987	Ron Hextall	Philadelphia
1986	John Vanbiesbrouck	NY Rangers
1985	Pelle Lindbergh	Philadelphia
1984	Tom Barrasso	Buffalo
1983	Pete Peeters	Boston
1982	Bill Smith	NY Islanders
1981	Richard Sevigny	Montreal
	Denis Herron	
	Michel Larocque	
1980	Bob Sauvé	Buffalo
	Don Edwards	
1979	Ken Dryden	Montreal
	Michel Larocque	
1978	Ken Dryden	Montreal
	Michel Larocque	
1977	Ken Dryden	Montreal
	Michel Larocque	
1976	Ken Dryden	Montreal
1975	Bernie Parent	Philadelphia
1974	Bernie Parent	Philadelphia
	Tony Esposito	Chicago
1973	Ken Dryden	Montreal
1972	Tony Esposito	Chicago
	Gary Smith	
1971	Ed Giacomin	NY Rangers
	Gilles Villemure	
1970	Tony Esposito	Chicago
1969	Jacques Plante	St. Louis
	Glenn Hall	
1968	Lorne Worsley	Montreal
	Rogie Vachon	
1967	Glenn Hall	Chicago
	Denis Dejordy	
1966	Lorne Worsley	Montreal
	Charlie Hodge	
1965	Terry Sawchuk	Toronto
	Johnny Bower	
1964	Charlie Hodge	Montreal
1963	Glenn Hall	Chicago
1962	Jacques Plante	Montreal
1961	Johnny Bower	Toronto
1960	Jacques Plante	Montreal
1959	Jacques Plante	Montreal
1958	Jacques Plante	Montreal
1957	Jacques Plante	Montreal
1956	Jacques Plante	Montreal
1955	Terry Sawchuk	Detroit
1954	Harry Lumley	Toronto
1953	Terry Sawchuk	Detroit
1952	Terry Sawchuk	Detroit
1951	Al Rollins	Toronto
1950	Bill Durnan	Montreal
1949	Bill Durnan	Montreal
1948	Turk Broda	Toronto
1947	Bill Durnan	Montreal
1946	Bill Durnan	Montreal
1945	Bill Durnan	Montreal
1944	Bill Durnan	Montreal
1943	Johnny Mowers	Detroit
1942	Frank Brimsek	Boston
1941	Turk Broda	Toronto
1940	Dave Kerr	NY Rangers
1939	Frank Brimsek	Boston
1938	Tiny Thompson	Boston
1937	Normie Smith	Detroit
1936	Tiny Thompson	Boston
1935	Lorne Chabot	Chicago
1934	Charlie Gardiner	Chicago
1933	Tiny Thompson	Boston
1932	Charlie Gardiner	Chicago
1931	Roy Worters	NY Americans
1930	Tiny Thompson	Boston
1929	George Hainsworth	Montreal
1928	George Hainsworth	Montreal
1927	George Hainsworth	Montreal

TROPHIES & AWARDS

FRANK J. SELKE TROPHY WINNERS
1987	Dave Poulin	Philadelphia
1986	Troy Murray	Chicago
1985	Craig Ramsay	Buffalo
1984	Doug Jarvis	Washington
1983	Bobby Clarke	Philadelphia
1982	Steve Kasper	Boston
1981	Bob Gainey	Montreal
1980	Bob Gainey	Montreal
1979	Bob Gainey	Montreal
1978	Bob Gainey	Montreal

CONN SMYTHE TROPHY WINNERS
1987	Ron Hextall	Philadelphia
1986	Patrick Roy	Montreal
1985	Wayne Gretzky	Edmonton
1984	Mark Messier	Edmonton
1983	Bill Smith	NY Islanders
1982	Mike Bossy	NY Islanders
1981	Butch Goring	NY Islanders
1980	Bryan Trottier	NY Islanders
1979	Bob Gainey	Montreal
1978	Larry Robinson	Montreal
1977	Guy Lafleur	Montreal
1976	Reggie Leach	Philadelphia
1975	Bernie Parent	Philadelphia
1974	Bernie Parent	Philadelphia
1973	Yvan Cournoyer	Montreal
1972	Bobby Orr	Boston
1971	Ken Dryden	Montreal
1970	Bobby Orr	Boston
1969	Serge Savard	Montreal
1968	Glenn Hall	St. Louis
1967	Dave Keon	Toronto
1966	Roger Crozier	Detroit
1965	Jean Béliveau	Montreal

JACK ADAMS AWARD WINNERS
Year	Coach	Team
1987	Jack Demers	Detroit
1986	Glen Sather	Edmonton
1985	Mike Keenan	Philadelphia
1984	Bryan Murray	Washington
1983	Orval Tessier	Chicago
1982	Tom Watt	Winnipeg
1981	Gordon (Red) Berenson	St. Louis
1980	Pat Quinn	Philadelphia
1979	Al Arbour	NY Islanders
1978	Bobby Kromm	Detroit
1977	Scott Bowman	Montreal
1976	Don Cherry	Boston
1975	Bob Pulford	Los Angeles
1974	Fred Shero	Philadelphia

WILLIAM M. JENNINGS TROPHY WINNERS
1987	Patrick Roy, Brian Hayward	Montreal
1986	Bob Froese, Darren Jensen	Philadelphia
1985	Tom Barrasso, Bob Sauve	Buffalo
1984	Al Jensen, Pat Riggin	Washington
1983	Roland Melanson, Bill Smith	NY Islanders
1982	Rick Wamsley, Denis Herron	Montreal

DODGE PERFORMER OF THE YEAR AWARD WINNERS
1987	Wayne Gretzky	Edmonton
1986	Wayne Gretzky	Edmonton
1985	Wayne Gretzky	Edmonton

PRESIDENTS' TROPHY WINNERS
1986-87	Edmonton Oilers
1985-86	Edmonton Oilers

BILL MASTERTON TROPHY WINNERS
1987	Doug Jarvis	Hartford
1986	Charlie Simmer	Boston
1985	Anders Hedberg	NY Rangers
1984	Brad Park	Detroit
1983	Lanny McDonald	Calgary
1982	Glenn Resch	Colorado
1981	Blake Dunlop	St. Louis
1980	Al MacAdam	Minnesota
1979	Serge Savard	Montreal
1978	Butch Goring	Los Angeles
1977	Ed Westfall	NY Islanders
1976	Rod Gilbert	NY Rangers
1975	Don Luce	Buffalo
1974	Henri Richard	Montreal
1973	Lowell MacDonald	Pittsburgh
1972	Bobby Clarke	Philadelphia
1971	Jean Ratelle	NY Rangers
1970	Pit Martin	Chicago
1969	Ted Hampson	Oakland
1968	Claude Provost	Montreal

LESTER PATRICK TROPHY WINNERS
1987	*Hobey Bakey
	Frank Mathers
1986	John MacInnes
	Jack Riley
1985	Jack Butterfield
	Arthur M. Wirtz
1984	John A. Ziegler Jr.
	*Arthur Howie Ross
1983	Bill Torrey
1982	Emile P. Francis
1981	Charles M. Schulz
1980	Bobby Clarke
	Edward M. Snider
	Frederick A. Shero
	1980 U.S. Olympic Hockey Team
1979	Bobby Orr
1978	Philip A. Esposito
	Tom Fitzgerald
	William T. Tutt
	William W. Wirtz
1977	John P. Bucyk
	Murray A. Armstrong
	John Mariucci
1976	Stanley Mikita
	George A. Leader
	Bruce A. Norris
1975	Donald M. Clark
	William L. Chadwick
	Thomas N. Ivan
1974	Alex Delvecchio
	Murray Murdoch
	*Weston W. Adams, Sr.
	*Charles L. Crovat
1973	Walter L. Bush, Jr.
1972	Clarence S. Campbell
	John Kelly
	Ralph "Cooney" Weiland
	*James D. Norris
1971	William M. Jennings
	*John B. Sollenberger
	*Terrance G. Sawchuk
1970	Edward W. Shore
	*James C. V. Hendy
1969	Robert M. Hull
	*Edward J. Jeremiah
1968	Thomas F. Lockhart
	*Walter A. Brown
	*Gen. John R. Kilpatrick
1967	Gordon Howe
	*Charles F. Adams
	*James Norris, Sr.
1966	J.J. "Jack" Adams

* awarded posthumously

NHL Entry Draft

Pierre Turgeon, 1st pick 1987

First Selections

Year	Player	Pos	Drafted By
1969	Rejean Houle	LW	Montreal
1970	Gilbert Perreault	C	Buffalo
1971	Guy Lafleur	RW	Montreal
1972	Billy Harris	RW	NY Islanders
1973	Denis Potvin	D	NY Islanders
1974	Greg Joly	D	Washington
1975	Mel Bridgman	C	Philadelphia
1976	Rick Green	D	Washington
1977	Dale McCourt	C	Detroit
1978	Bobby Smith	C	Minnesota
1979	Bob Ramage	D	Colorado
1980	Doug Wickenheiser	C	Montreal
1981	Dale Hawerchuk	C	Winnipeg
1982	Gord Kluzak	D	Boston
1983	Brian Lawton	C	Minnesota
1984	Mario Lemieux	C	Pittsburgh
1985	Wendel Clark	LW/D	Toronto
1986	Joe Murphy	C	Detroit
1987	Pierre Turgeon	C	Buffalo

Draft Summary

Following is a summary of the number of players drafted from the Ontario Hockey League (OHL), Western Hockey League (WHL), Quebec Major Junior Hockey League (Que.), United States Colleges (USC), United States High Schools (USH), European Leagues (Eur.) and other Leagues throughout North America since 1969:

	OHL	WHL	Que.	USC	USH	Eur.	Other
1969	36	20	11	7	0	1	9
1970	51	22	13	16	0	0	13
1971	41	28	13	22	0	0	13
1972	46	44	30	21	0	0	11
1973	56	49	24	25	0	0	14
1974	69	66	40	41	0	6	24
1975	45	54	28	59	0	6	25
1976	47	33	18	26	0	8	3
1977	42	44	40	49	0	5	5
1978	59	48	22	71	0	15	19
1979	48	37	19	15	0	7	2
1980	73	41	24	42	7	13	10
1981	59	36	28	21	17	32	18
1982	60	55	17	20	47	35	18
1983	57	41	24	14	35	34	37
1984	55	38	16	22	44	40	35
1985	59	43	15	20	48	30	37
1986	66	32	22	22	40	28	42
1987	32	36	17	40	69	38	20
Total	1001	767	421	553	307	298	355

Mario Lemieux, 1st pick 1984

Draft Choices, 1986-69

1986
FIRST ROUND

Selection	Claimed By	Amateur Club
1. MURPHY, Joe	Det.	Michigan State
2. CARSON, Jimmy	L.A.	Verdun Juniors
3. BRADY, Neil	N.J.	Medicine Hat Tigers
4. ZALAPSKI, Zarley	Pit.	Team Canada
5. ANDERSON, Shawn	Buf.	Team Canada
6. DAMPHOUSSE, Vincent	Tor.	Laval Olympiques
7. WOODLEY, Dan	Van.	Portland Winterhawks
8. ELYNUIK, Pat	Wpg.	Prince Albert Raiders
9. LEETCH, Brian	NYR	Avon Old Farms HS
10. LEMIEUX, Jocelyn	St.L.	Laval Olympiques
11. YOUNG, Scott	Hfd.	Bos. University
12. BABE, Warren	Min.	Lethbridge Broncos
13. JANNEY, Craig	Bos.	Bos. College
14. SANIPASS, Everett	Chi.	Verdun Juniors
15. PEDERSON, Mark	Mtl.	Medicine Hat Tigers
16. PELAWA, George	Cgy.	Bemidji HS
17. FITZGERALD, Tom	NYI	Austin Prep
18. McRAE, Ken	Que.	Sudbury Wolves
19. GREENLAW, Jeff	Wsh.	Team Canada
20. HUFFMAN, Kerry	Phi.	Guelph Platers
21. ISSEL, Kim	Edm.	Prince Albert Raiders

1985
FIRST ROUND

Selection	Claimed By	Amateur Club
1. CLARK, Wendel	Tor.	Saskatoon Blades
2. SIMPSON, Craig	Pit.	Michigan State
3. WOLANIN, Craig	N.J.	Kitchener Rangers
4. SANDLAK, Jim	Van.	London Knights
5. MURZYN, Dana	Hfd.	Cgy. Wranglers
6. DALGARNO, Brad	NYI	Hamilton Steelhawks
7. DAHLEN, Ulf	NYR	Ostersund (Sweden)
8. FEDYK, Brent	Det.	Regina Pats
9. DUNCANSON, Craig	L.A.	Sudbury Wolves
10. GRATTON, Dan	L.A.	Oshawa Generals
11. MANSON, David	Chi.	Prince Albert Raiders
12. CHARBONNEAU, Jose	Mtl.	Drummondville
13. KING, Derek	NYI	Sault Greyhounds
14. JOHANSSON, Carl	Buf.	V. Frolunda (Sweden)
15. LATTA, Dave	Que.	Kitchener Rangers
16. CHORSKE, Tom	Mtl.	Minneapolis HS
17. BIOTTI, Chris	Cgy.	Belmont Hill HS
18. STEWART, Ryan	Wpg.	Kamloops Blazers
19. CORRIVEAU, Yvon	Wsh.	Tor. Marlboros
20. METCALFE, Scott	Edm.	Kingston Canadians
21. SEABROOKE, Glen	Phi.	Peterborough Petes

1984
FIRST ROUND

Selection	Claimed By	Amateur Club
1. LEMIEUX, Mario	Pit.	Laval Voisins
2. MULLER, Kirk	N.J.	Team Canada-Guelph
3. OLCZYK, Ed	Chi.	Team USA
4. IAFRATE, Al	Tor.	Team USA-Belleville
5. SVOBODA, Petr	Mtl.	Czechoslovakia Jr.
6. REDMOND, Craig	L.A.	Team Canada
7. BURR, Shawn	Det.	Kitchener Rangers
8. CORSON, Shayne	Mtl.	Brantford Alexanders
9. BODGER, Doug	Pit.	Kamloops Jr. Oilers
10. DAIGNEAULT, J.J.	Van.	Canada-Longueuil
11. COTE, Sylvain	Hfd.	Que. Remparts
12. ROBERTS, Gary	Cgy.	Ottawa 67's
13. QUINN, David	Min.	Kent High School
14. CARKNER, Terry	NYR	Peterborough Petes
15. STIENBURG, Trevor	Que.	Guelph Platers
16. BELANGER, Roger	Pit.	Kingston Canadians
17. HATCHER, Kevin	Wsh.	North Bay Centennials
18. ANDERSSON, Bo Mikael	Buf.	V. Frolunda (Sweden)
19. PASIN, Dave	Bos.	Prince Albert Raiders
20. MACPHERSON, Duncan	NYI	Saskatoon Blades
21. ODELEIN, Selmar	Edm.	Regina Pats

1983
FIRST ROUND

Selection	Claimed By	Amateur Club
1. LAWTON, Brian	Min.	Mount St. Charles HS
2. TURGEON, Sylvain	Hfd.	Hull Olympiques
3. LAFONTAINE, Pat	NYI	Verdun Juniors
4. YZERMAN, Steve	Det.	Peterborough Petes
5. BARRASSO, Tom	Buf.	Acton-Boxboro HS
6. MacLEAN, John	N.J.	Oshawa Generals
7. COURTNALL, Russ	Tor.	Victoria Cougars
8. McBAIN, Andrew	Wpg.	North Bay Centennials
9. NEELY, Cam	Van.	Portland Winter Hawks
10. LACOMBE, Normand	Buf.	New Hampshire
11. CREIGHTON, Adam	Buf.	Ottawa 67's
12. GAGNER, Dave	NYR	Brantford Alexanders
13. QUINN, Dan	Cgy.	Belleville Bulls
14. DOLLAS, Bobby	Wpg.	Laval Voisins
15. ERREY, Bob	Pit.	Peterborough Petes
16. DIDUCK, Gerald	NYI	Lethbridge Broncos
17. TURCOTTE, Alfie	Mtl.	Portland Winter Hawks
18. CASSIDY, Bruce	Chi.	Ottawa 67's
19. BEUKEBOOM, Jeff	Edm.	Sault Greyhounds
20. JENSEN, David	Hfd.	Lawrence Academy
21. MARKWART, Nevin	Bos.	Regina Pats

Ed Olczyk, 3rd pick 1984

1982
FIRST ROUND

Selection	Claimed By	Amateur Club
1. KLUZAK, Gord	Bos.	Nanaimo Islanders
2. BELLOWS, Brian	Min.	Kitchener Rangers
3. NYLUND, Gary	Tor.	Portland Winter Hawks
4. SUTTER, Ron	Phi.	Lethbridge Broncos
5. STEVENS, Scott	Wsh.	Kitchener Rangers
6. HOUSLEY, Phil	Buf.	S. St. Paul High School
7. YAREMCHUK, Ken	Chi.	Portland Winter Hawks
8. TROTTIER, Rocky	N.J.	Nanaimo Islanders
9. CYR, Paul	Buf.	Victoria Cougars
10. SUTTER, Rich	Pit.	Lethbridge Broncos
11. PETIT, Michel	Van.	Sherbrooke Castors
12. KYTE, Jim	Wpg.	Cornwall Royals
13. SHAW, David	Que.	Kitchener Rangers
14. LAWLESS, Paul	Hfd.	Windsor Spitfires
15. KONTOS, Chris	NYR	Tor. Marlboros
16. ANDREYCHUK, Dave	Buf.	Oshawa Generals
17. CRAVEN, Murray	Det.	Medicine Hat Tigers
18. DANEYKO, Ken	N.J.	Seattle Breakers
19. HEROUX, Alain	Mtl.	Chicoutimi Sagueneens
20. PLAYFAIR, Jim	Edm.	Portland Winter Hawks
21. FLATLEY, Pat	NYI	University of Wisconsin

1981
FIRST ROUND

Selection	Claimed By	Amateur Club
1. HAWERCHUK, Dale	Wpg.	Cornwall Royals
2. SMITH, Doug	L.A.	Ottawa 67's
3. CARPENTER, Bobby	Wsh.	St. John's High School
4. FRANCIS, Ron	Hfd.	Sault Greyhounds
5. CIRELLA, Joe	Col.	Oshawa Generals
6. BENNING, Jim	Tor.	Portland Winter Hawks
7. HUNTER, Mark	Mtl.	Brantford Alexanders
8. FUHR, Grant	Edm.	Victoria Cougars
9. PATRICK, James	NYR	U. of North Dakota
10. BUTCHER, Garth	Van.	Regina Pats
11. MOLLER, Randy	Que.	Lethbridge Broncos
12. TANTI, Tony	Chi.	Oshawa Generals
13. MEIGHAN, Ron	Min.	Niagara Falls Flyers
14. LEVEILLE, Normand	Bos.	Chicoutimi Sagueneens
15. MacINNIS, Allan	Cgy.	Kitchener Rangers
16. SMITH, Steve	Phi.	Sault Greyhounds
17. DUDACEK, Jiri	Buf.	Kladno (Czech.)
18. DELORME, Gilbert	Mtl.	Chicoutimi Sagueneens
19. INGMAN, Jan	Mtl.	Sweden
20. RUFF, Marty	St.L.	Lethbridge Broncos
21. BOUTILIER, Paul	NYI	Sherbrooke Castors

Gord Kluzak, 1st pick 1982

1980
FIRST ROUND

Selection	Claimed By	Amateur Club
1. WICKENHEISER, Doug	Mtl.	Regina Pats
2. BABYCH, Dave	Wpg.	Portland Winter Hawks
3. SAVARD, Denis	Chi.	Mtl. Juniors
4. MURPHY, Larry	L.A.	Peterborough Petes
5. VEITCH, Darren	Wsh.	Regina Pats
6. COFFEY, Paul	Edm.	Kitchener Rangers
7. LANZ, Rick	Van.	Oshawa Generals
8. ARTHUR, Fred	Hfd.	Cornwall Royals
9. BULLARD, Mike	Pit.	Brantford Alexanders
10. FOX, Jimmy	L.A.	Ottawa 67's
11. BLAISDELL, Mike	Det.	Regina Pats
12. WILSON, Rik	St.L.	Kingston Canadians
13. CYR, Denis	Cgy.	Mtl. Juniors
14. MALONE, Jim	NYR	Tor. Marlboros
15. DUPONT, Jerome	Chi.	Tor. Marlboros
16. PALMER, Brad	Min.	Victoria Cougars
17. SUTTER, Brent	NYI	Red Deer Rustlers
18. PEDERSON, Barry	Bos.	Victoria Cougars
19. GAGNE, Paul	Col.	Windsor Spitfires
20. PATRICK, Steve	Buf.	Brandon Wheat Kings
21. STOTHERS, Mike	Phi.	Kingston Canadians

1979
FIRST ROUND

Selection	Claimed By	Amateur Club
1. RAMAGE, Rob	Col.	London Knights
2. TURNBULL, Perry	St.L.	Portland Winter Hawks
3. FOLIGNO, Mike	Det.	Sudbury Wolves
4. GARTNER, Mike	Wsh.	Niagara Falls Flyers
5. VAIVE, Rick	Van.	Sherbrooke Castors
6. HARTSBURG, Craig	Min.	Sault Greyhounds
7. BROWN, Keith	Chi.	Portland Winter Hawks
8. BOURQUE, Raymond	Bos.	Verdun Black Hawks
9. BOSCHMAN, Laurie	Tor.	Brandon Wheat Kings
10. McCARTHY, Tom	Min.	Oshawa Generals
11. RAMSEY, Mike	Buf.	University of Min.
12. REINHART, Paul	Atlanta	Kitchener Rangers
13. SULLIMAN, Doug	NYR	Kitchener Rangers
14. PROPP, Brian	Phi.	Brandon Wheat Kings
15. McCRIMMON, Brad	Bos.	Brandon Wheat Kings
16. WELLS, Jay	L.A.	Kingston Canadians
17. SUTTER, Duane	NYI	Lethbridge Broncos
18. ALLISON, Ray	Hfd.	Brandon Wheat Kings
19. MANN, Jimmy	Wpg.	Sherbrooke Beavers
20. GOULET, Michel	Que.	Que. Remparts
21. LOWE, Kevin	Edm.	Que. Remparts

ENTRY DRAFT – 1969-86   **145**

1978
FIRST ROUND

Selection	Claimed By	Amateur Club
1. SMITH, Bobby	Min.	Ottawa 67's
2. WALTER, Ryan	Wsh.	Seattle Breakers
3. BABYCH, Wayne	St.L.	Portland Winter Hawks
4. DERLAGO, Bill	Van.	Brandon Wheat Kings
5. GILLIS, Mike	Col.	Kingston Canadians
6. WILSON, Behn	Phi.	Kingston Canadians
7. LINSEMAN, Ken	Phi.	Kingston Canadians
8. GEOFFRION, Danny	Mtl.	Cornwall Royals
9. HUBER, Willie	Det.	Hamilton Fincups
10. HIGGINS, Tim	Chi.	Ottawa 67's
11. MARSH, Brad	Atl.	London Knights
12. PETERSON, Brent	Det.	Portland Winter Hawks
13. PLAYFAIR, Larry	Buf.	Portland Winter Hawks
14. LUCAS, Danny	Phi.	Sault Greyhounds
15. TAMBELLINI, Steve	NYI	Lethbridge Broncos
16. SECORD, Al	Bos.	Hamilton Fincups
17. HUNTER, Dave	Mtl.	Sudbury Wolves
18. COULIS, Tim	Wsh.	Hamilton Fincups

1975
FIRST ROUND

Selection	Claimed By	Amateur Club
1. BRIDGMAN, Mel	Phi.	Victoria Cougars
2. DEAN, Barry	K.C.	Medicine Hat Tigers
3. KLASSEN, Ralph	Cal.	Saskatoon Blades
4. MAXWELL, Brian	Min.	Medicine Hat Tigers
5. LAPOINTE, Rick	Det.	Victoria Cougars
6. ASHBY, Don	Tor.	Cgy. Centennials
7. VAYDIK, Greg	Chi.	Medicine Hat Tigers
8. MULHERN, Richard	Atl.	Sherbrooke Beavers
9. SADLER, Robin	Mtl.	Edm. Oil Kings
10. BLIGHT, Rick	Van.	Brandon Wheat Kings
11. PRICE, Pat	NYI	Saskatoon Blades
12. DILLON, Wayne	NYR	Tor. Marlboros
13. LAXTON, Gord	Pit.	New Westminster
14. HALWARD, Doug	Bos.	Peterborough Petes
15. MONDOU, Pierre	Mtl.	Montreal Juniors
16. YOUNG, Tim	L.A.	Ottawa 67's
17. SAUVE, Bob	Buf.	Laval Nationales
18. FORSYTH, Alex	Wsh.	Kingston Canadians

1977
FIRST ROUND

Selection	Claimed By	Amateur Club
1. McCOURT, Dale	Det.	St. Catharines Fincups
2. BECK, Barry	Col.	New Westminster
3. PICARD, Robert	Wsh.	Mtl. Jrs.
4. GILLIS, Jere	Van.	Sherbrooke Castors
5. CROMBEEN, Mike	Cle.	Kingston Canadians
6. WILSON, Doug	Chi.	Ottawa 67's
7. MAXWELL, Brad	Min.	New Westminster
8. DEBLOIS, Lucien	NYR	Sorel Black Hawks
9. CAMPBELL, Scott	St.L.	London Knights
10. NAPIER, Mark	Mtl.	Tor. Marlboros
11. ANDERSON, John	Tor.	Tor. Marlboros
12. JOHANSON, Trevor	Tor.	Tor. Marlboros
13. DUGUAY, Ron	NYR	Sudbury Wolves
14. SEILING, Ric	Buf.	St. Catharines Fincups
15. BOSSY, Mike	NYI	Laval Nationales
16. FOSTER, Dwight	Bos.	Kitchener Rangers
17. McCARTHY, Kevin	Phi.	Wpg. Monarchs
18. DUPONT, Norm	Mtl.	Montreal Jrs.

1974
FIRST ROUND

Selection	Claimed By	Amateur Club
1. JOLY, Greg	Wsh.	Regina Pats
2. PAIEMENT, Wilfred	K.C.	St. Catharines Hawks
3. HAMPTON, Rick	Cal.	St. Catharines Hawks
4. GILLIES, Clark	NYI	Regina Pats
5. CONNOR, Cam	Mtl.	Flin Flon Bombers
6. HICKS, Doug	Min.	Flin Flon Bombers
7. RISEBROUGH, Doug	Mtl.	Kitchener Rangers
8. LAROUCHE, Pierre	Pit.	Sorel Black Hawks
9. LOCHEAD, Bill	Det.	Oshawa Generals
10. CHARTRAW, Rick	Mtl.	Kitchener Rangers
11. FOGOLIN, Lee	Buf.	Oshawa Generals
12. TREMBLAY, Mario	Mtl.	Montreal Juniors
13. VALIQUETTE, Jack	Mtl.	Sault Greyhounds
14. MALONEY, Dave	NYR	Kitchener Rangers
15. McTAVISH, Gord	Mtl.	Sudbury Wolves
16. MULVEY, Grant	Chi.	Cgy. Centennials
17. CHIPPERFIELD, Ron	Cal.	Brandon Wheat Kings
18. LARWAY, Don	Bos.	Swift Current Broncos

1976
FIRST ROUND

Selection	Claimed By	Amateur Club
1. GREEN, Rick	Wsh.	London Knights
2. CHAPMAN, Blair	Pit.	Saskatoon Blades
3. SHARPLEY, Glen	Min.	Hull Festivals
4. WILLIAMS, Fred	Det.	Saskatoon Blades
5. JOHANSSON, Bjorn	Cal.	Sweden
6. MURDOCH, Don	NYR	Medicine Hat Tigers
7. FEDERKO, Bernie	St.L.	Saskatoon Blades
8. SHAND, Dave	Atl.	Peterborough Petes
9. CLOUTIER, Real	Chi.	Que. Remparts
10. PHILLIPOFF, Harold	Atl.	New Westminster
11. GARDNER, Paul	K.C.	Oshawa Generals
12. LEE, Peter	Mtl.	Ottawa 67's
13. SCHUTT, Rod	Mtl.	Sudbury Wolves
14. McKENDRY, Alex	NYI	Sudbury Wolves
15. CARROLL, Greg	Wsh.	Medicine Hat Tigers
16. PACHAL, Clayton	Bos.	New Westminster
17. SUZOR, Mark	Phi.	Kingston Canadians
18. BAKER, Bruce	Mtl.	Ottawa 67's

1973
FIRST ROUND

Selection	Claimed By	Amateur Club
1. POTVIN, Denis	NYI	Ottawa 67's
2. LYSIAK, Tom	Atl.	Medicine Hat Tigers
3. VERVERGAERT, Dennis	Van.	London Knights
4. McDONALD, Lanny	Tor.	Medicine Hat Tigers
5. DAVIDSON, John	St.L.	Cgy. Centennials
6. SAVARD, Andre	Bos.	Que. Remparts
7. STOUGHTON, Blaine	Pit.	Flin Flon Bombers
8. GAINEY, Bob	Mtl.	Peterborough Petes
9. DAILEY, Bob	Van.	Tor. Marlboros
10. NEELEY, Bob	Tor.	Peterborough Petes
11. RICHARDSON, Terry	Det.	New Westminster
12. TITANIC, Morris	Buf.	Sudbury Wolves
13. ROTA, Darcy	Chi.	Edm. Oil Kings
14. MIDDLETON, Rick	NYR	Oshawa Generals
15. TURNBULL, Ian	Tor.	Ottawa 67's
16. MERCREDI, Vic	Atl.	New Westminster

1972
FIRST ROUND

Selection	Claimed By	Amateur Club
1. HARRIS, Billy	NYI	Tor. Marlboros
2. RICHARD, Jacques	Atl.	Que. Remparts
3. LEVER, Don	Van.	Niagara Falls Flyers
4. SHUTT, Steve	Mtl.	Tor. Marlboros
5. SCHOENFELD, Jim	Buf.	Niagara Falls Flyers
6. LAROCQUE, Michel	Mtl.	Ottawa 67's
7. BARBER, Bill	Phi.	Kitchener Rangers
8. GARDNER, Dave	Mtl.	Tor. Marlboros
9. MERRICK, Wayne	St.L.	Ottawa 67's
10. BLANCHARD, Albert	NYR	Kitchener Rangers
11. FERGUSON, George	Tor.	Tor. Marlboros
12. BYERS, Jerry	Min.	Kitchener Rangers
13. RUSSELL, Phil	Chi.	Edm. Oil Kings
14. VAN BOXMEER, John	Mtl.	Guelph Juniors
15. MacMILLAN, Bobby	NYR	St. Catharines Hawks
16. BLOOM, Mike	Bos.	St. Catharines Hawks

Jacques Richard, 2nd pick 1972

1971
FIRST ROUND

Selection	Claimed By	Amateur Club
1. LAFLEUR, Guy	Mtl.	Que. Remparts
2. DIONNE, Marcel	Det.	St. Catharines Hawks
3. GUEVREMONT, Jocelyn	Van.	Mtl. Junior Canadiens
4. CARR, Gene	St.L.	Flin Flon Bombers
5. MARTIN, Rick	Buf.	Mtl. Junior Canadiens
6. JONES, Ron	Bos.	Edm. Oil Kings
7. ARNASON, Chuck	Mtl.	Flinflon Bombers
8. WRIGHT, Larry	Phi.	Regina Pats
9. PLANTE, Pierre	Phi.	Drummondville Rangers
10. VICKERS, Steve	NYR	Tor. Marlboros
11. WILSON, Murray	Mtl.	Ottawa 67's
12. SPRING, Dan	Chi.	Edm. Oil Kings
13. DURBANO, Steve	NYR	Tor. Marlboros
14. O'REILLY, Terry	Bos.	Oshawa Generals

1970
FIRST ROUND

Selection	Claimed By	Amateur Club
1. PERREAULT, Gilbert	Buf.	Mtl. Junior Canadiens
2. TALLON, Dale	Van.	Tor. Marlboros
3. LEACH, Reg	Bos.	Flin Flon Bombers
4. MacLEISH, Rick	Bos.	Peterborough Petes
5. MARTINIUK, Ray	Mtl.	Flin Flon Bombers
6. LEFLEY, Chuck	Mtl.	Canadian Nationals
7. POLIS, Greg	Pit.	Estevan Bruins
8. SITTLER, Darryl	Tor.	London Knights
9. PLUMB, Ron	Bos.	Peterborough Petes
10. ODDLEIFSON, Chris	Oak.	Wpg. Jets
11. GRATTON, Norm	NYR	Mtl. Junior Canadiens
12. LAJEUNESSE, Serge	Det.	Mtl. Junior Canadiens
13. STEWART, Bob	Bos.	Oshawa Generals
14. MALONEY, Dan	Chi.	London Knights

Marcel Dionne, 2nd pick 1971

1969
FIRST ROUND

Selection	Claimed By	Amateur Club
1. HOULE, Rejean	Mtl.	Mon. Junior Canadiens
2. TARDIF, Marc	Mtl.	Mon. Junior Canadiens
3. TANNAHILL, Don	Bos.	Niagara Falls Flyers
4. SPRING, Frank	Bos.	Edm. Oil Kings
5. REDMOND, Dick	Min.	St. Catharines Hawks
6. CURRIER, Bob	Phi.	Cornwall Royals
7. FEATHERSTONE, Tony	Oak.	Peterborough Petes
8. DUPONT, André	NYR	Mtl. Junior Canadiens
9. MOSER, Ernie	Tor.	Estevan Bruins
10. RUTHERFORD, Jim	Det.	Hamilton Red Wings
11. BOLDIREV, Ivan	Bos.	Oshawa Generals
12. JARRY, Pierre	NYR	Ottawa 67's
13. BORDELEAU, J.-P.	Chi.	Mtl. Junior Canadiens
14. O'BRIEN, Dennis	Min.	St. Catharines Hawks

J.-P. Bordeleau, 13th pick 1969

All-Star Teams
1987-68

Voting for the NHL All-Star Team is conducted among the representatives of the Professional Hockey Writers' Association at the end of the season. Following is a list of the First and Second All-Star Teams since 1967-68.

1986-87

First Team		Second Team	
Hextall, Ron, Phi.	G	Liut, Mike, Hfd.	
Bourque, Raymond, Bos.	D	Murphy, Larry, Wsh.	
Howe, Mark, Phi.	D	MacInnis, Al, Cgy.	
Gretzky, Wayne, Edm.	C	Lemieux, Mario, Pit.	
Kurri, Jari, Edm.	RW	Kerr, Tim, Phi.	
Goulet, Michel, Que.	LW	Robitaille, Luc, L.A.	

1985-86

Vanbiesbrouck, J., NYR	G	Froese, Bob Phi.	
Coffey, Paul, Edm.	D	Robinson, Larry, Mtl.	
Howe, Mark, Phi.	D	Bourque, Raymond, Bos.	
Gretzky, Wayne, Edm.	C	Lemieux, Mario, Pit.	
Bossy, Mike, NYI	RW	Kurri, Jari, Edm.	
Goulet, Michel, Que.	LW	Naslund, Mats, Mtl.	

1984-85

First Team		Second Team	
Lindbergh, Pelle, Phi.	G	Barrasso, Tom Buf.	
Coffey, Paul, Edm.	D	Langway, Rod, Wsh.	
Bourque, Raymond, Bos.	D	Wilson, Doug, Chi.	
Gretzky, Wayne, Edm.	C	Hawerchuk, Dale, Wpg.	
Kurri, Jari, Edm.	RW	Bossy, Mike, NYI	
Ogrodnick, John, Det.	LW	Tonelli, John, NYI	

1983-84

Barrasso, Tom, Buf.	G	Riggin, Pat Wsh.	
Langway, Rod, Wsh.	D	Coffey, Paul, Edm.	
Bourque, Raymond, Bos.	D	Potvin, Denis, NYI	
Gretzky, Wayne, Edm.	C	Trottier, Bryan, NYI	
Bossy, Mike, NYI	RW	Kurri, Jari, Edm.	
Goulet, Michel, Que.	LW	Messier, Mark, Edm.	

Tom Barrasso

ALL-STAR TEAMS

Pete Peeters

1982-83

First Team
Peeters, Pete, Bos. — G
Howe, Mark, Phi. — D
Langway, Rod, Wsh. — D
Gretzky, Wayne, Edm. — C
Bossy, Mike, NYI — RW
Messier, Mark, Edm. — LW

Second Team
Melanson, Roland, NYI — G
Bourque, Raymond, Bos. — D
Coffey, Paul, Edm. — D
Savard, Denis, Chi. — C
McDonald, Lanny, Cgy. — RW
Goulet, Michel, Que. — LW

1981-82

First Team
Smith, Bill, NYI — G
Wilson, Doug, Chi. — D
Bourque, Raymond, Bos. — D
Gretzky, Wayne, Edm. — C
Bossy, Mike, NYI — RW
Messier, Mark, Edm. — LW

Second Team
Fuhr, Grant, Edm. — G
Coffey, Paul, Edm. — D
Engblom, Brian, Mtl. — D
Trottier, Bryan, NYI — C
Middleton, Rick, Bos. — RW
Tonelli, John, NYI — LW

1980-81

First Team
Liut, Mike, St.L. — G
Potvin, Denis, NYI — D
Carlyle, Randy, Pit. — D
Gretzky, Wayne, Edm. — C
Bossy, Mike, NYI — RW
Simmer, Charlie, L.A. — LW

Second Team
Lessard, Mario, L.A. — G
Robinson, Larry, Mtl. — D
Bourque, Raymond, Bos. — D
Dionne, Marcel, L.A. — C
Taylor, Dave, L.A. — RW
Barber, Bill, Phi. — LW

1979-80

First Team
Esposito, Tony, Chi. — G
Robinson, Larry, Mtl. — D
Bourque, Raymond, Bos. — D
Dionne, Marcel, L.A. — C
Lafleur, Guy, Mtl. — RW
Simmer, Charlie, L.A. — LW

Second Team
Edwards, Don, Buf. — G
Salming, Borje, Tor. — D
Schoenfeld, Jim, Buf. — D
Gretzky, Wayne, Edm. — C
Gare, Danny, Buf. — RW
Shutt, Steve, Mtl. — LW

1978-79

First Team
Dryden, Ken, Mtl. — G
Potvin, Denis, NYI — D
Robinson, Larry, Mtl. — D
Trottier, Bryan, NYI — C
Lafleur, Guy, Mtl. — RW
Gillies, Clark, NYI — LW

Second Team
Resch, Glenn, NYI — G
Salming, Borje, Tor. — D
Savard, Serge, Mtl. — D
Dionne, Marcel, L.A. — C
Bossy, Mike, NYI — RW
Barber, Bill, Phi. — LW

1977-78

First Team
Dryden, Ken, Mtl. — G
Potvin, Denis, NYI — D
Park, Brad, Bos. — D
Trottier, Bryan, NYI — C
Lafleur, Guy, Mtl. — RW
Gillies, Clark, NYI — LW

Second Team
Edwards, Don, Buf. — G
Robinson, Larry, Mtl. — D
Salming, Borje, Tor. — D
Sittler, Darryl, Tor. — C
Bossy, Mike, NYI — RW
Shutt, Steve, Mtl. — LW

1976-77

First Team
Dryden, Ken, Mtl. — G
Robinson, Larry, Mtl. — D
Salming, Borje, Tor. — D
Dionne, Marcel, L.A. — C
Lafleur, Guy, Mtl. — RW
Shutt, Steve, Mtl. — LW

Second Team
Vachon, Rogatien, L.A. — G
Potvin, Denis, NYI — D
Lapointe, Guy, Mtl. — D
Perreault, Gilbert, Buf. — C
McDonald, Lanny, Tor. — RW
Martin, Richard, Buf. — LW

1975-76

First Team
Dryden, Ken, Mtl. — G
Potvin, Denis, NYI — D
Park, Brad, Bos. — D
Clarke, Bobby, Phi. — C
Lafleur, Guy, Mtl. — RW
Barber, Bill, Phi. — LW

Second Team
Resch, Glenn, NYI — G
Salming, Borje, Tor. — D
Lapointe, Guy, Mtl. — D
Perreault, Gilbert, Buf. — C
Leach, Reggie, Phi. — RW
Martin, Richard, Buf. — LW

ALL-STAR TEAMS

1974-75

First Team
Parent, Bernie, Phi.	G
Orr, Bobby, Bos.	D
Potvin, Denis, NYI	D
Clarke, Bobby, Phi.	C
Lafleur, Guy, Mtl.	RW
Martin, Richard, Buf.	LW

Second Team
Vachon, Rogie, L.A.	G
Lapointe, Guy, Mtl.	D
Salming, Borje, Tor.	D
Esposito, Phil, Bos.	C
Robert, René, Buf.	RW
Vickers, Steve, NYR	LW

1973-74

First Team
Parent, Bernie, Phi.	G
Orr, Bobby, Bos.	D
Park, Brad, NYR	D
Esposito, Phil, Bos.	C
Hodge, Ken, Bos.	RW
Martin, Richard, Buf.	LW

Second Team
Esposito, Tony, Chi.	G
White, Bill, Chi.	D
Ashbee, Barry, Phi.	D
Clarke, Bobby, Phi.	C
Redmond, Mickey, Det.	RW
Cashman, Wayne, Bos.	LW

1972-73

First Team
Dryden, Ken, Mtl.	G
Orr, Bobby, Bos.	D
Lapointe, Guy, Mtl.	D
Esposito, Phil, Bos.	C
Redmond, Mickey, Det.	RW
Mahovlich, Frank, Mtl.	LW

Second Team
Esposito, Tony, Chi.	G
Park, Brad, NYR	D
White, Bill, Chi.	D
Clarke, Bobby, Phi.	C
Cournoyer, Yvan, Mtl.	RW
Hull, Dennis, Chi.	LW

1971-72

First Team
Esposito, Tony, Chi.	G
Orr, Bobby, Bos.	D
Park, Brad, NYR	D
Esposito, Phil, Bos.	C
Gilbert, Rod, NYR	RW
Hull, Bobby, Chi.	LW

Second Team
Dryden, Ken, Mtl.	G
White, Bill, Chi.	D
Stapleton, Pat, Chi.	D
Ratelle, Jean, NYR	C
Cournoyer, Yvan, Mtl.	RW
Hadfield, Vic, NYR	LW

1970-71

First Team
Giacomin, Ed, NYR	G
Orr, Bobby, Bos.	D
Tremblay, J.C., Mtl.	D
Esposito, Phil, Bos.	C
Hodge, Ken, Bos.	RW
Bucyk, John, Bos.	LW

Second Team
Plante, Jacques, Tor.	G
Park, Brad, NYR	D
Stapleton, Pat, Chi.	D
Keon, Dave, Tor.	C
Cournoyer, Yvan, Mtl.	RW
Hull, Bobby, Chi.	LW

1969-70

First Team
Esposito, Tony, Chi.	G
Orr, Bobby, Bos.	D
Park, Brad, NYR	D
Esposito, Phil, Bos.	C
Howe, Gordie, Det.	RW
Hull, Bobby, Chi.	LW

Second Team
Giacomin, Ed, NYR	G
Brewer, Carl, Det.	D
Laperrière, Jacques, Mtl	D
Mikita, Stan, Chi.	C
McKenzie, John, Bos.	RW
Mahovlich, Frank, Det.	LW

1968-69

First Team
Hall, Glenn, St.L.	G
Orr, Bobby, Bos.	D
Horton, Tim, Tor.	D
Esposito, Phil, Bos.	C
Howe, Gordie, Det.	RW
Hull, Bobby, Chi.	LW

Second Team
Giacomin, Ed, NYR	G
Green, Ted, Bos.	D
Harris, Ted, Mtl.	D
Béliveau, Jean, Mtl.	C
Cournoyer, Yvan, Mtl.	RW
Mahovlich, Frank, Det.	LW

1967-68

First Team
Worsley, Lorne, Mtl.	G
Orr, Bobby, Bos.	D
Horton, Tim, Tor.	D
Mikita, Stan, Chi.	C
Howe, Gordie, Det.	RW
Hull, Bobby, Chi.	LW

Second Team
Giacomin, Ed, NYR	G
Tremblay, J.C., Mtl.	D
Neilson, Jim, NYR	D
Esposito, Phil, Bos.	C
Gilbert, Rod, NYR	RW
Bucyk, John, Bos.	LW

Bobby Orr earned nine all-star selections including eight consecutive First All-Star Team berths from 1968 to 1975.

Hockey Hall of Fame

Location: Toronto's Exhibition Park, on the shore of Lake Ontario, adjacent to Ontario Place and Exhibition Stadium. The Hockey Hall of Fame building is in the middle of Exhibition Place, directly north of the stadium.
Telephone: (416) 595-1345.
Eligibility Requirements: Any person who is, or has been distinguished in hockey as a player, executive or on-ice official, shall be eligible for election. Player and On-ice Official candidates will normally have completed their active participating careers three years prior to election, but in exceptional cases this period may be shortened by the Hockey Hall of Fame Board of Directors. Candidates for election as executives and on-ice officials shall be nominated only by the Board of Directors and upon election shall be known as Builders or On-Ice Officials. Candidates for election as players shall be chosen on the basis of "playing ability, integrity, character and their contribution to their team and the game of hockey in general."
Honor Roll: There are 261 Honored Members of the Hockey Hall of Fame. Of the total, 182 are listed as players, 69 as Builders and ten as On-Ice Officials. Ian (Scotty) Morrison is President and M. H. (Lefty) Reid is Curator of the Hall.
(Year of election to the Hall is indicated in brackets after the Members' names).

PLAYERS
Abel, Sidney Gerald (1969)
*Adams, John James "Jack" (1959)
Apps, Charles Joseph Sylvanus "Syl" (1961)
Armstrong, George Edward (1975)
Bailey, Irvine Wallace "Ace" (1975)
*Bain, Donald H. "Dan" (1945)
*Baker, Hobart "Hobey" (1945)
*Barry, Martin J. "Marty" (1965)
Bathgate, Andrew James "Andy" (1978)
Beliveau, Jean Arthur (1972)
*Benedict, Clinton S. (1965)
*Bentley, Douglas Wagner (1964)
*Bentley, Maxwell H. L. (1966)
Blake, Hector "Toe" (1966)
Boivin, Leo Joseph (1986)
*Boon, Richard R. "Dickie" (1952)
Bouchard, Emile Joseph "Butch" (1966)
*Boucher, Frank (1958)
*Boucher, George "Buck" (1960)
Bower, John William (1976)
*Bowie, Russell (1945)
Brimsek, Francis Charles (1966)
*Broadbent, Harry L. "Punch" (1962)
*Broda, Walter Edward "Turk" (1967)
Bucyk, John Paul (1981)
*Burch, Billy (1974)
*Cameron, Harold Hugh "Harry" (1962)
Cheevers, Gerald Michael "Gerry" (1985)
*Clancy, Francis Michael "King" (1958)
*Clapper, Aubrey "Dit" (1945)
Clarke, Robert "Bobby" (1987)
*Cleghorn, Sprague (1958)
Colville, Neil MacNeil (1967)
*Conacher, Charles W. (1961)
*Connell, Alex (1958)
*Cook, William Osser (1952)
Coulter, Arthur Edmund (1974)
Cournoyer, Yvan Serge (1982)
Cowley, William Mailes (1968)
*Crawford, Samuel Russell "Rusty" (1962)
*Darragh, John Proctor "Jack" (1962)
*Davidson, Allan M. "Scotty" (1950)
Day, Clarence Henry "Hap" (1961)
Delvecchio, Alex (1977)
*Denneny, Cyril "Cy" (1959)
*Drillon, Gordon Arthur (1975)
*Drinkwater, Charles Graham (1950)
Dryden, Kenneth Wayne (1983)
*Dunderdale, Thomas (1974)
*Durnan, William Ronald (1964)
*Dutton, Mervyn A. "Red" (1958)
*Dye, Cecil Henry "Babe" (1970)
Esposito, Philip Anthony (1984)
*Farrell, Arthur F. (1965)
*Foyston, Frank (1958)
*Frederickson, Frank (1958)

Cy Denneny

HALL OF FAME

Gadsby, William Alexander (1970)
*Gardiner, Charles Robert "Chuck" (1945)
*Gardiner, Herbert Martin "Herb" (1958)
*Gardner, James Henry "Jimmy" (1962)
Geoffrion, Jos. A. Bernard "Boom Boom" (1972)
*Gerard, Eddie (1945)
Giacomin, Edward "Eddie" (1987)
Gilbert, Rodrigue Gabriel "Rod" (1982)
*Gilmour, Hamilton Livingstone "Billy" (1962)
*Goheen, Frank Xavier "Moose" (1952)
*Goodfellow, Ebenezer R. "Ebbie" (1963)
*Grant, Michael "Mike" (1950)
*Green, Wilfred "Shorty" (1962)
*Griffis, Silas Seth "Si" (1950)
*Hainsworth, George (1961)
Hall, Glenn Henry (1975)
*Hall, Joseph Henry (1961)
Harvey, Douglas Norman (1973)
*Hay, George (1958)
*Hern, William Milton "Riley" (1962)
*Hextall, Bryan Aldwyn (1969)
*Holmes, Harry "Hap" (1972)
*Hooper, Charles Thomas "Tom" (1962)
Horner, George Reginald "Red" (1965)
*Horton, Miles Gilbert "Tim" (1977)
Howe, Gordon (1972)
*Howe, Sydney Harris (1965)
Howell, Henry Vernon "Harry" (1979)
Hull, Robert Marvin (1983)
*Hutton, John Bower "Bouse" (1962)
*Hyland, Harry M. (1962)
*Irvin, James Dickenson "Dick" (1958)
*Jackson, Harvey "Busher" (1971)
*Johnson, Ernest "Moose" (1952)
*Johnson, Ivan "Ching" (1958)
Johnson, Thomas Christian (1970)
*Joliat, Aurel (1947)
*Keats, Gordon "Duke" (1958)
Kelly, Leonard Patrick "Red" (1969)
Kennedy, Theodore Samuel "Teeder" (1966)
Keon, David Michael (1986)
Lach, Elmer James (1966)
*Lalonde, Edouard Charles "Newsy" (1950)
Laperriere, Jacques (1987)
*Laviolette, Jean Baptiste "Jack" (1962)
*Lehman, Hugh (1958)
Lemaire, Jacques Gerard (1984)
LeSueur, Percy (1961)
Lindsay, Robert Blake Theodore "Ted" (1966)
Lumley, Harry (1980)
*MacKay, Duncan "Mickey" (1952)
Mahovlich, Frank William (1981)
*Malone, Joseph "Joe" (1950)
*Mantha, Sylvio (1960)
*Marshall, John "Jack" (1965)
*Maxwell, Fred G. "Steamer" (1962)
*McGee, Frank (1945)
*McGimsie, William George "Billy" (1962)
*McNamara, George (1958)
Mikita, Stanley (1983)
Moore, Richard Winston (1974)
*Moran, Patrick Joseph "Paddy" (1958)
*Morenz, Howie (1945)
*Mosienko, William "Billy" (1965)
*Nighbor, Frank (1945)
*Noble, Edward Reginald "Reg" (1962)
*Oliver, Harry (1967)
Olmstead, Murray Bert "Bert" (1985)
Orr, Robert Gordon (1979)
Parent, Bernard Marcel (1984)
*Patrick, Joseph Lynn (1980)
*Patrick, Lester (1945)
*Phillips, Tommy (1945)
Pilote, Joseph Albert Pierre Paul (1975)
*Pitre, Didier "Pit" (1962)
*Plante, Joseph Jacques Omer (1978)
Pratt, Walter "Babe" (1966)

Charlie Gardiner

Primeau, A. Joseph (1963)
Pronovost, Joseph René Marcel (1978)
*Pulford, Harvey (1945)
Quackenbush, Hubert George "Bill" (1976)
*Rankin, Frank (1961)
Ratelle, Joseph Gilbert Yvan Jean "Jean" (1985)
Rayner, Claude Earl "Chuck" (1973)
Reardon, Kenneth Joseph (1966)
Richard, Joseph Henri (1979)
*Richard, Joseph Henri Maurice "Rocket" (1961)
*Richardson, George Taylor (1950)
*Roberts, Gordon (1971)
*Ross, Arthur Howie (1945)
*Russel, Blair (1965)
*Russell, Ernest (1965)
*Ruttan, J.D. "Jack" (1962)
Savard, Serge A. (1986)
*Sawchuk, Terrance Gordon "Terry" (1971)
*Scanlan, Fred (1965)
Schmidt, Milton Conrad "Milt" (1961)
Schriner, David "Sweeney" (1962)
Seibert, Earl Walter (1963)
*Seibert, Oliver Levi (1961)
*Shore, Edward W. "Eddie" (1945)
*Siebert, Albert C. "Babe" (1964)
*Simpson, Harold Edward "Bullet Joe" (1962)
*Smith, Alfred E. (1962)
*Smith, Reginald "Hooley" (1972)
*Smith, Thomas James (1973)
Stanley, Allan Herbert (1981)
*Stanley, Russell "Barney" (1962)
*Stewart, John Sherratt "Black Jack" (1964)
*Stewart, Nelson "Nels" (1962)
*Stuart, Bruce (1961)
*Stuart, Hod (1945)
*Taylor, Frederic "Cyclone" (O.B.E.) (1945)
*Thompson, Cecil R. "Tiny" (1959)
*Trihey, Col. Harry J. (1950)
Ullman, Norman Victor Alexander "Norm" (1982)
*Vezina, Georges (1945)
*Walker, John Phillip "Jack" (1960)
*Walsh, Martin "Marty" (1962)
*Watson, Harry E. (1962)
*Weiland, Ralph "Cooney" (1971)
*Westwick, Harry (1962)
*Whitcroft, Fred (1962)
*Wilson, Gordon Allan "Phat" (1962)
Worsley, Lorne John "Gump" (1980)
*Worters, Roy (1969)

BUILDERS
*Adams, Charles Francis (1960)
*Adams, Weston W. (1972)
*Ahearn, Thomas Franklin "Frank" (1962)
*Ahearne, John Francis "Bunny" (1977)
*Allan, Sir Montague (C.V.O.) (1945)
Ballard, Harold Edwin (1977)
*Bickell, John Paris (1978)
*Brown, George V. (1961)
*Brown, Walter A. (1962)
Buckland, Frank (1975)
Butterfield, Jack Arlington (1980)
*Calder, Frank (1945)
*Campbell, Angus D. (1964)
*Campbell, Clarence Sutherland (1966)
*Cattarinich, Joseph (1977)
*Dandurand, Joseph Viateur "Leo" (1963)
Dilio, Francis Paul (1964)
*Dudley, George S. (1958)
*Dunn, James A. (1968)
Francis, Emile (1982)
*Gibson, Dr. John L. "Jack" (1976)
*Gorman, Thomas Patrick "Tommy" (1963)
Hanley, William (1986)
*Hay, Charles (1974)
Hendy, James C. (1968)
*Hewitt, Foster (1965)
*Hewitt, William Abraham (1945)
*Hume, Fred J. (1962)
Imlach, George "Punch" (1984)
Ivan, Thomas N. (1974)
*Jennings, William M. (1975)
Juckes, Gordon W. (1979)
*Kilpatrick, Gen. John Reed (1960)
*Leader, George Alfred (1969)
LeBel, Robert (1970)
*Lockhart, Thomas F. (1965)
*Loicq, Paul (1961)
*Mariucci, John (1985)
*McLaughlin, Major Frederic (1963)
*Milford, John "Jake" (1984)
Molson, Hon. Hartland de Montarville (1973)
*Nelson, Francis (1945)
*Norris, Bruce A. (1969)
*Norris, Sr., James (1958)
*Norris, James Dougan (1962)
*Northey, William M. (1945)
*O'Brien, John Ambrose (1962)
*Patrick, Frank (1958)
*Pickard, Allan W. (1958)
Pilous, Rudy (1985)
Pollock, Samuel Patterson Smyth (1978)
*Raymond, Sen. Donat (1958)
*Robertson, John Ross (1945)
*Robinson, Claude C. (1945)
*Ross, Philip D. (1976)
*Selke, Frank J. (1960)
Sinden, Harry James (1983)
*Smith, Frank D. (1962)
*Smythe, Conn (1958)
*Stanley of Preston, Lord (G.C.B.) (1945)
*Sutherland, Cap. James T. (1945)
Tarasov, Anatoli V. (1974)
*Turner, Lloyd (1958)
Tutt, William Thayer (1978)
Voss, Carl Potter (1974)
*Waghorn, Fred C. (1961)
*Wirtz, Arthur Michael (1971)
Wirtz, William W. "Bill" (1976)
Ziegler, John A. Jr. (1987)

ON-ICE OFFICIALS
Ashley, John George (1981)
Chadwick, William L. (1964)
*Elliott, Chaucer (1961)
*Hewitson, Robert W. (1963)
*Ion, Fred J. "Mickey" (1961)
Pavelich, Matt (1987)
*Rodden, Michael J. "Mike" (1962)
*Smeaton, J. Cooper (1961)
Storey, Roy Alvin "Red" (1967)
Udvari, Frank Joseph (1973)

*Deceased

United States Hockey Hall of Fame

PLAYERS
*Abel, Clarence "Taffy"
*Baker, Hobart "Hobey"
Bartholome, Earl
Bessone, Peter
Blake, Robert
Brimsek, Frank
*Chaisson, Ray
Chase, John P.
Christian, William "Bill"
Cleary, Robert
Cleary, William
*Conroy, Anthony
Dahlstrom, Carl "Cully"
DesJardins, Victor
Dill, Robert
Everett, Doug
Garrison, John B.
Garrity, Jack
*Goheen, Frank "Moose"
Harding, Austin "Austie"
Iglehart, Stewart
Johnson, Virgil
Karakas, Mike
Kirrane, Jack
Lane, Myles J.
*Linder, Joseph
*LoPresti, Sam L.
*Mariucci, John
Mayasich, John
McCartan, Jack
Moe, William
Moseley, Fred
*Murray, Hugh "Muzz" Sr.
*Nelson, Hubert "Hub"
Olson, Eddie
*Owen, Jr., George
*Palmer, Winthrop
Purpur, Clifford "Fido"
Riley, William
*Romnes, Elwin "Doc"
Rondeau, Richard
Williams, Thomas
*Winters, Frank "Coddy"
Yackel, Ken

COACHES
*Almquist, Oscar
*Gordon, Malcolm K.
Heyliger, Victor
*Jeremiah, Edward J.
*Kelley, John "Snooks"
Riley, Jack
*Thompson, Clifford, R.
*Stewart, William
*Winsor, Alfred "Ralph"

ADMINISTRATORS
*Brown, George V.
*Brown, Walter A.
Bush, Walter
Clark, Donald
*Gibson, J.C. "Doc"
*Jennings, William M.
*Kahler, Nick
*Lockhart, Thomas F.
Marvin, Cal
Ridder, Robert
Trumble, Harold
Tutt, William Thayer
Wirtz, William W. "Bill"
*Wright, Lyle Z.

REFEREE
Chadwick, William

*Deceased

Origin of the Stanley Cup

The 1893 Montreal AAA *Lord Stanley*

On March 18, 1892, at a dinner of the Ottawa Amateur Athletic Association, Lord Kilcoursie, a player with the Ottawa Rebels from Government House, read the following message on behalf of Lord Stanley of Preston, the Governor-General of Canada:

> "I have for some time been thinking that it would be a good thing if there were a challenge cup which should be held year to year by the champion hockey team in the Dominion (of Canada)."
>
> "There does not appear to be any such outward sign of a championship at present, and considering the general interest which matches now elicit, and the importance of having the game played fairly and under rules generally recognized, I am willing to give a cup which shall be held from year to year by the winning team."

Later that year, Lord Stanley purchased a silver bowl for the sum of 10 pounds or approximately $50. Ironically, he would never witness a Stanley Cup game, having returned to his native England before the end of the 1893 season.

Prior to his departure from Canada, Lord Stanley appointed two Ottawa gentlemen – Sherriff John Sweetland and Philip D. Ross – to act as trustees of the Cup and laid down the following preliminary conditions to govern the annual Cup competition:

1. The winners to return the Cup in good order when required by the trustees in order that it may be handed over to any other team which may win it.
2. Each winning team to have the club name and year engraved on a silver ring fitted on the Cup.
3. The Cup to remain a challenge competition and not the property of any one team, even if won more than once.
4. The trustees to maintain absolute authority in all situations or disputes over the winner of the Cup.
5. A substitute trustee to be named in the event that one of the existing trustees drops out.

Lord Stanley also directed that as winners of the Amateur Hockey Association (AHA) of Canada in 1893, the Montreal Amateur Athletic Association (AAA) would become the first Stanley Cup Champions.

Although Lord Stanley could not have envisioned the significance of his trophy would eventually carry, the Stanley Cup has endured for nearly a century. It has become the world's oldest trophy still actively competed for and one of only two, including tennis' Davis Cup (1894), which dates to the nineteenth century.

Stanley Cup Winners

1987 – EDMONTON OILERS

The Oilers won the first two games of the series on home ice and split the next two in Philadelphia. It appeared that they were about to capture the Cup at home in game five, but the Flyers played brilliantly, winning the contest by a goal. In game six, J.J. Daigneault's shot from the point lifted the Flyers to a comeback victory, and the NHL Finals were pushed to a seventh game for the first time since 1971.

With the Cup on the line, the Oilers set a torrid pace in game seven and, despite a first-period goal by Philadelphia, controlled play and took the lead in the second period on a goal by Jari Kurri. The Flyers put up a strong defensive effort, but, with just three minutes left in the game, Edmonton's Glenn Anderson put the Oilers up 3-1, and they went on to capture the Cup for the third time in their eight years in the NHL.

Philadelphia goaltender Ron Hextall was awarded the Conn Smythe Trophy for his outstanding, play throughout the series.

1986-87 — Edmonton Oilers — Glenn Anderson, Jeff Beukeboom, Kelly Buchberger, Paul Coffey, Grant Fuhr, Randy Gregg, Wayne Gretzky, Charlie Huddy, Dave Hunter, Mike Krushelnyski, Jari Kurri, Moe Lemay, Kevin Lowe, Craig MacTavish, Kevin McClelland, Marty McSorley, Mark Messier, Andy Moog, Craig Muni, Kent Nilsson, Jaroslav Pouzar, Reijo Ruotsalainen, Steve Smith, Esa Tikkanen, Peter Pocklington (Owner), Glen Sather (General Manager/Coach), John Muckler (Co-Coach), Ted Green (Ass't. Coach), Ron Low (Ass't. Coach), Bruce MacGregor (Ass't. General Manager), Barry Fraser (Director of Player Personnel), Peter Millar (Athletic Therapist), Barrie Stafford (Trainer), Lyle Kulchisky (Ass't Trainer).
Scores: May 17 at Edmonton — Edmonton 4, Philadelphia 3; May 20 at Edmonton — Edmonton 3, Philadelphia 2; May 22 at Philadelphia — Philadelphia 5, Edmonton 3; May 24 at Philadelphia — Edmonton 4, Philadelphia 1; May 26 at Edmonton — Philadelphia 4, Edmonton 3; May 28 at Philadelphia — Philadelphia 3, Edmonton 2; May 31 at Edmonton — Edmonton 3, Philadelphia 1.

1986 – MONTREAL CANADIENS

The Montreal Canadiens set a new record for professional sports championships, winning their 23rd Stanley Cup title. Montreal had been tied with the New York Yankees, who have amassed 22 World Series titles in their history.

The series marked the first All-Canadian Finals since Montreal and Toronto faced each other in the 1967 Finals.

Patrick Roy of the Canadiens and Mike Vernon of the Flames became the second pair of rookie goaltenders to oppose each other in Final play. Detroit's Harry Lumley and Toronto's Frank McCool were the first when they met in 1945.

Brian Skrudland scored nine seconds into overtime in game two to set a new record for the fastest overtime goal in playoff history, eclipsing the old mark of 11 seconds set by J.P. Parise of the NY Islanders on April 11, 1975.

Montreal's Jean Perron became the 13th rookie coach to win the Stanley Cup, and 20-year-old goaltender Patrick Roy became the youngest player to earn the Conn Smythe Trophy in the 22-year history of the award. Roy posted a record-tying 15 playoff wins (15-5) and a 1.92 average in 20 post-season games.

1985-86 — Montreal Canadiens — Bob Gainey, Doug Soetaert, Patrick Roy, Rick Green, David Maley, Ryan Walter, Serge Boisvert, Mario Tremblay, Bobby Smith, Craig Ludwig, Tom Kurvers, Kjell Dahlin, Larry Robinson, Guy Carbonneau, Chris Chelios, Petr Svoboda, Mats Naslund, Lucien DeBlois, Steve Rooney, Gaston Gingras, Mike Lalor, Chris Nilan, John Kordic, Claude Lemieux, Mike McPhee, Brian Skrudland, Stephane Richer, Ronald Corey (President), Serge Savard (General Manager), Jean Perron (Coach), Jacques Laperriere (Ass't. Coach), Jean Beliveau (Vice President), Francois-Xavier Seigneur (Vice President), Fred Steer (Vice President), Jacques Lemaire (Ass't. General Manager), Andre Boudrias (Ass't. General Manager), Claude Ruel, Yves Belanger (Athletic Therapist), Gaetan Lefebvre (Ass't. Athletic Therapist), Eddy Palchek (Trainer), Sylvain Toupin (Ass't. Trainer).
Scores: May 16 at Calgary — Calgary 5, Montreal 3; May 18 at Calgary — Montreal 3, Calgary 2; May 20 at Montreal — Montreal 5, Calgary 3; May 22 at Montreal — Montreal 1, Calgary 0; May 24 at Calgary — Montreal 4, Calgary 3.

CUP FINALS – 1985, 1984							155

1985 – EDMONTON OILERS

The irrepressible Edmonton Oilers surprised few people in winning their second consecutive Stanley Cup. Conn Smythe Trophy winner Wayne Gretzky set new records for assists (30) and points (47) in one playoff year with a 17-30-47 mark in 18 games, eclipsing his own records set in 1983, when he posted totals of 12-26-38 in 16 games. Gretzky also tied the record shared by Montreal's Jean Beliveau (1956) and Mike Bossy (1982) for most goals in the Stanley Cup Finals with seven in five games.

Jari Kurri scored 19 goals in 18 games to tie the record for goals in one playoff year. Former Philadelphia Flyer Reggie Leach first set the mark in 1976 with 19 goals in 16 post-season games. Kurri also broke teammate Mark Messier's record for most hat-tricks in a playoff year with four, including a four-goal game.

Paul Coffey, who registered a 12-25-37 mark in 18 games, shattered the one-year playoff records for goals, assists and points by a defenseman. Coffey broke Boston Bruin Bobby Orr's records for goals (9 in 1970) and assists (19 in 1972) and New York Islander Denis Potvin's record for points (25 in 1981).

Grant Fuhr tied New York Islanders' goaltender Billy Smith for most wins, 15, in a playoff year. Fuhr posted a 15-3 record in 18 games.

For the first time in the Finals, two penalty shots were awarded in the same series. Philadelphia's Ron Sutter and Dave Poulin attempted the two penalty shots, and both were stopped by the Oilers' Grant Fuhr.

1984-85 — Edmonton Oilers — Glenn Anderson, Bill Carrol, Paul Coffey, Lee Fogolin, Grant Fuhr, Randy Gregg, Wayne Gretzky, Charlie Huddy, Pat Hughes, Dave Hunter, Don Jackson, Mike Krushelnyski, Jari Kurri, Willy Lindstrom, Kevin Lowe, Dave Lumley, Kevin McClelland, Larry Melnyk, Mark Messier, Andy Moog, Mark Napier, Jaroslav Pouzar, Dave Semenko, Esa Tikkanen, Peter Pocklington (Owner), Glen Sather (General Manager/Coach), John Muckler (Ass't. Coach), Ted Green (Ass't. Coach), Bruce MacGregor (Ass't. General Manager), Barry Fraser (Director of Player Personnel/Chief Scout), Peter Millar (Athletic Therapist), Barrie Stafford, Lyle Kulchisky (Trainers)
Scores: May 21 at Philadelphia — Philadelphia 4, Edmonton 1; May 23 at Philadelphia — Edmonton 3, Philadelphia 1; May 25 at Edmonton — Edmonton 4, Philadelphia 3; May 28 at Edmonton — Edmonton 5, Philadelphia 3; May 30 at Edmonton — Edmonton 8, Philadelphia 3.

1984 – EDMONTON OILERS

The Edmonton Oilers, who joined the NHL in 1979-80 with the Hartford Whalers, Quebec Nordiques and Winnipeg Jets, became the first of the four former World Hockey Association clubs to win the Stanley Cup.

In his first championship game, Oilers' goalie Grant Fuhr posted a shutout to hand the defending champion New York Islanders their first loss in 10 Final series games.

Four different Oilers – Kevin McClelland, Glenn Anderson, Mark Messier and Ken Linseman – scored game winning goals.

Messier won the Conn Smyth Trophy with an 8-18-26 mark in 19 games.

1983-84 — Edmonton Oilers — Glenn Anderson, Paul Coffey, Pat Conacher, Lee Fogolin, Grant Fuhr, Randy Gregg, Wayne Gretzky, Charlie Huddy, Pat Hughes, Dave Hunter, Don Jackson, Jari Kurri, Willy Lindstrom, Ken Linseman, Kevin Lowe, Dave Lumley, Kevin McClelland, Mark Messier, Andy Moog, Jaroslav Pouzar, Dave Semenko, Peter Pocklington (Owner), Glen Sather (General Manager/Coach), John Muckler (Ass't. Coach), Ted Green (Ass't. Coach), Bruce MacGregor (Ass't. General Manager), Barry Fraser (Director of Player Personnel/Chief Scout), Peter Millar (Athletic Therapist), Barrie Stafford (Trainer)
Scores: May 10 at New York — Edmonton 1, NY Islanders 0; May 12 at New York — NY Islanders 6, Edmonton 1; May 15 at Edmonton — Edmonton 7, NY Islanders 2; May 17 at Edmonton — Edmonton 7, NY Islanders 2; May 19 at Edmonton — Edmonton 5, NY Islanders 2.

1983 – NEW YORK ISLANDERS

The New York Islanders won their fourth straight Stanley Cup to become only the second NHL franchise in history to gain four championships in a row. The Montreal Canadiens own the record with five consecutive Cups from 1956 to 1960 and four more between 1976 and 1979.

Goaltender Billy Smith won the Conn Smythe Trophy after limiting the Edmonton Oilers to six goals in four games and shutting out the Campbell Conference champions in seven of 12 periods of play.

In his first appearance in the Finals, Wayne Gretzky tallied four assists.

1982-83 — New York Islanders — Mike Bossy, Bob Bourne, Paul Boutilier, Bill Carroll, Greg Gilbert, Clark Gillies, Butch Goring, Mats Hallin, Tomas Jonsson, Anders Kallur, Gord Lane, Dave Langevin, Mike McEwen, Roland Melanson, Wayne Merrick, Ken Morrow, Bob Nystrom, Stefan Persson, Denis Potvin, Bill Smith, Brent Sutter, Duane Sutter, John Tonelli, Bryan Trottier, Al Arbour (coach), Lorne Henning (ass't coach), Bill Torrey (general manager), Ron Waske, Jim Pickard (trainers)
Scores: May 10 at Edmonton — NY Islanders 2, Edmonton 0; May 12 at Edmonton — NY Islanders 6, Edmonton 3; May 14 at New York — NY Islanders 5, Edmonton 1; May 17 at New York — NY Islanders 4, Edmonton 2

1982 – NEW YORK ISLANDERS

With a sweep of the Vancouver Canucks, the Islanders distinguished themselves as the first American-based team in history to win three consecutive Stanley Cups

The Canucks, meanwhile, became the first Vancouver team since the 1924 Maroons of the WCHL to appear in the Finals.

Mike Bossy won the Conn Smythe Trophy with seven goals in the four-game series, tying the record for most goals in a Final set by Jean Beliveau in 1956.

Bryan Trottier tallied 32 playoff assists in 19 games to set a new record, while goalie Billy Smith achieved a 15-4-0 mark to equal his own record for playoff wins.

1981-82 — New York Islanders — Mike Bossy, Bob Bourne, Bill Carroll, Butch Goring, Greg Gilbert, Clark Gillies, Tomas Jonsson, Anders Kallur, Gord Lane, Dave Langevin, Hector Marini, Mike McEwen, Roland Melanson, Wayne Merrick, Ken Morrow, Bob Nystrom, Stefan Persson, Denis Potvin, Bill Smith, Brent Sutter, Duane Sutter, John Tonelli, Bryan Trottier, Al Arbour (coach), Lorne Henning (ass't coach), Bill Torrey (general manager), Ron Waske, Jim Pickard (trainers)
Scores: May 8 at New York — NY Islanders 6, Vancouver 5; May 11 at New York — NY Islanders 6, Vancouver 4; May 13 at Vancouver — NY Islanders 3, Vancouver 0; May 16 at Vancouver — NY Islanders 3, Vancouver 1

1981 – NEW YORK ISLANDERS

The New York Islanders captured a second consecutive Stanley Cup with a five-game series triumph over the Minnesota North Stars. For Minnesota, it marked the club's first trip to the Finals since joining the NHL in 1967-68.

New York's Mike Bossy shattered playoff records for points (17-18-35) and power-play goals (9) in his 18 post-season outings.

Dino Ciccarelli of Minnesota broke Don Maloney's rookie scoring record with 21 playoff points and Steve Christoff's rookie mark for playoff goals with 14.

1980-81 — New York Islanders — Denis Potvin, Mike McEwen, Ken Morrow, Gord Lane, Bob Lorimer, Stefan Persson, Dave Langevin, Mike Bossy, Bryan Trottier, Butch Goring, Wayne Merrick, Clark Gillies, John Tonelli, Bob Nystrom, Bill Carroll, Bob Bourne, Hector Marini, Anders Kallur, Duane Sutter, Garry Howatt, Lorne Henning, Bill Smith, Roland Melanson, Al Arbour (coach), Bill Torrey (general manager), Ron Waske, Jim Pickard (trainers).
Scores: May 12 at New York — NY Islanders 6, Minnesota 3; May 14 at New York — NY Islanders 6, Minnesota 3; May 17 at Minnesota — NY Islanders 7, Minnesota 5; May 19 at Minnesota— Minnesota 4, NY Islanders 2; May 21 at New York — NY Islanders 5, Minnesota 1.

CUP FINALS — 1980-78

1980 — NEW YORK ISLANDERS

In their eighth NHL season, the New York Islanders became the second expansion team to win the Stanley Cup. Two players, goalie Billy Smith and right-winger Bob Nystrom, had been with the team since its inception in 1972-73.

In game one, Denis Potvin recorded the first power-play goal scored in overtime in Stanley Cup history. The Flyers' Jimmy Watson went off at 2:08, and Potvin scored one minute and fifty nine seconds later to end the game and give the Islanders their first win in the Finals.

Nystrom also scored an overtime goal, the Cup-winner in game six, to raise his career total to four. Maurice "Rocket" Richard, who scored six overtime goals in the playoffs, owns the record.

Two other Islanders set playoff records in the finale. Smith posted his 15th win of the playoffs to establish a new mark, and Conn Smythe Trophy recipient Bryan Trottier registered two assists to finish the playoffs with a record 29 points.

1979-80 — New York Islanders — Gord Lane, Jean Potvin, Bob Lorimer, Denis Potvin, Stefan Persson, Ken Morrow, Dave Langevin, Duane Sutter, Garry Howatt, Clark Gillies, Lorne Henning, Wayne Merrick, Bob Bourne, Steve Tambellini, Bryan Trottier, Mike Bossy, Bob Nystrom, John Tonelli, Anders Kallur, Butch Goring, Alex McKendry, Glenn Resch, Billy Smith, Al Arbour (coach), Bill Torrey (general manager), Ron Waske, Jim Pickard (trainers).
Scores: May 13 at Philadelphia — NY Islanders 4, Philadelphia 3; May 15 at Philadelphia — Philadelphia 8, NY Islanders 3; May 17 at Long Island — NY Islanders 6, Philadelphia 2; May 19 at Long Island — NY Islanders 5, Philadelphia 2; May 22 at Philadelphia — Philadelphia 6, NY Islanders 3; May 24 at Long Island — NY Islanders 5, Philadelphia 4.

1979 — MONTREAL CANADIENS

The Montreal Canadiens captured their fourth straight Stanley Cup to record the second longest streak of championships in NHL history. Only the Canadiens' five-year stronghold on the Cup from 1956 to 1960 lasted longer.

Montreal's game five series-winning effort also marked the first time since 1968 that the Canadiens had won the Cup on home ice.

At the conclusion of the series, Jacques Lemaire, Yvan Cournoyer and Ken Dryden retired from the NHL. The trio left the game with a combined total of 24 Cups among them.

Scotty Bowman, who had amassed his fifth Cup in seven seasons behind the Canadiens' bench, also made his farewell appearance with the team as he joined the Buffalo Sabres the following season.

1978-79 — Montreal Canadiens — Ken Dryden, Larry Robinson, Serge Savard, Guy Lapointe, Brian Engblom, Gilles Lupien, Rick Chartraw, Guy Lafleur, Steve Shutt, Jacques Lemaire, Yvan Cournoyer, Rejean Houle, Pierre Mondou, Bob Gainey, Doug Jarvis, Yvon Lambert, Doug Risebrough, Pierre Larouche, Mario Tremblay, Cam Connor, Pat Hughes, Rod Langway, Mark Napier, Michel Larocque, Richard Sevigny, Scotty Bowman (coach), Irving Grundman (managing director), Eddy Palchak, Pierre Meilleur (trainers).
Scores: May 13 at Montreal — NY Rangers 4, Montreal 1; May 15 at Montreal — Montreal 6, NY Rangers 2; May 17 at New York — Montreal 4, NY Rangers 1; May 19 at New York — Montreal 4, NY Rangers 3; May 21 at Montreal — Montreal 4, NY Rangers 1.

1978 — MONTREAL CANADIENS

Conn Smythe Trophy winner Larry Robinson led all playoff performers with 17 assists and tied teammate Guy Lafleur (10-11-21) for the overall playoff scoring lead with 21 points. Robinson was one of three Canadiens, including Doug Jarvis and Steve Shutt, to appear in all 95 games during the course of the season.

Ken Dryden sparkled in goal once again with a 12-3-0 record and a 1.89 average in Montreal's 15 post-season contests.

1977-78 — Montreal Canadiens — Ken Dryden, Larry Robinson, Serge Savard, Guy Lapointe, Bill Nyrop, Pierre Bouchard, Brian Engblom, Gilles Lupien, Rick Chartraw, Guy Lafleur, Steve Shutt, Jacques Lemaire, Yvan Cournoyer, Rejean Houle, Pierre Mondou, Bob Gainey, Doug Jarvis, Yvon Lambert, Doug Risebrough, Pierre Larouche, Mario Tremblay, Michel Larocque, Scotty Bowman (coach), Sam Pollock (general manager), Eddy Palchak, Pierre Meilleur (trainers).
Scores: May 13 at Montreal — Montreal 4, Boston 1; May 16 at Montreal — Montreal 3, Boston 2; May 18 at Boston — Boston 4, Montreal 0; May 21 at Boston — Boston 4, Montreal 3; May 23 at Montreal — Montreal 4, Boston 1; May 25 at Boston — Montreal 4, Boston 1.

1977 – MONTREAL CANADIENS

Winning their second consecutive Stanley Cup, the Canadiens extended their undefeated streak against Boston in the Finals to six straight series.

In Game Two, Ken Dryden posted his fourth shutout of the playoffs to tie a record shared by six goaltenders.

Jacques Lemaire, who scored three of Montreal's game-winning goals, including the Cup-winner in overtime, joined Maurice Richard (3) and Don Raleigh (2) in recording more than one career overtime goal in a Stanley Cup championship series. Lemaire first scored in overtime against the St. Louis Blues in the 1968 Finals.

Guy Lafleur won the Conn Smythe Trophy with a 9-17-26 mark in 14 playoff games.

1976-77 — Montreal Canadiens — Ken Dryden, Guy Lapointe, Larry Robinson, Serge Savard, Jimmy Roberts, Rick Chartraw, Bill Nyrop, Pierre Bouchard, Brian Engblom, Yvan Cournoyer, Guy Lafleur, Jacques Lemaire, Steve Shutt, Pete Mahovlich, Murray Wilson, Doug Jarvis, Yvon Lambert, Bob Gainey, Doug Risebrough, Mario Tremblay, Rejean Houle, Pierre Mondou, Mike Polich, Michel Larocque, Scotty Bowman (coach), Sam Pollock (general manager), Eddy Palchak, Pierre Meilleur (trainers).
Scores: May 7 at Montreal — Montreal 7, Boston 3; May 10 at Montreal — Montreal 3, Boston 0; May 12 at Boston — Montreal 4, Boston 2; May 14 at Boston — Montreal 2, Boston 1.

1976 – MONTREAL CANADIENS

The Montreal Canadiens returned to the Stanley Cup Finals against the Flyers after a two-year absence.

Guy Lafleur scored his first two goals in Final play and both proved to be game-winners.

Philadelphia's Reggie Leach scored four times in the series to finish the playoffs with the all-time record of 19 post-season goals. Leach became the third player on a Stanley Cup loser to earn the Conn Smythe Trophy.

1975-76 — Montreal Canadiens — Ken Dryden, Serge Savard, Guy Lapointe, Larry Robinson, Bill Nyrop, Pierre Bouchard, Jim Roberts, Guy Lafleur, Steve Shutt, Pete Mahovlich, Yvan Cournoyer, Jacques Lemaire, Yvon Lambert, Bob Gainey, Doug Jarvis, Doug Risebrough, Murray Wilson, Mario Tremblay, Rick Chartraw, Michel Larocque, Scotty Bowman (coach), Sam Pollock (general manager), Eddy Palchak, Pierre Meilleur (trainers).
Scores: May 9 at Montreal — Montreal 4, Philadelphia 3; May 11 at Montreal — Montreal 2, Philadelphia 1; May 13 at Philadelphia — Montreal 3, Philadelphia 2; May 16 at Philadelphia — Montreal 5, Philadelphia 3.

1975 – PHILADELPHIA FLYERS

For the first time, two former expansion teams met in the Finals, with the Flyers becoming the first to defend the Stanley Cup successfully.

Bernie Parent's netminding highlighted the series as he allowed only 12 goals in six games and recorded his second consecutive Cup-winning shutout. Parent became the first player to win back-to-back Conn Smythe Trophies and joined Boston's Bobby Orr in winning the award twice.

1974-75 — Philadelphia Flyers — Bernie Parent, Wayne Stephenson, Ed Van Impe, Tom Bladon, André Dupont, Joe Watson, Jim Watson, Ted Harris, Larry Goodenough, Rick MacLeish, Bobby Clarke, Bill Barber, Reggie Leach, Gary Dornhoefer, Ross Lonsberry, Bob Kelly, Terry Crisp, Don Saleski, Dave Schultz, Orest Kindrachuk, Bill Clement, Fred Shero (coach), Keith Allen (general manager), Frank Lewis, Jim McKenzie (trainers).
Scores: May 15 at Philadelphia — Philadelphia 4, Buffalo 1; May 18 at Philadelphia — Philadelphia 2, Buffalo 1; May 20 at Buffalo — Buffalo 5, Philadelphia 4; May 22 at Buffalo — Buffalo 4, Philadelphia 2; May 25 at Philadelphia — Philadelphia 5, Buffalo 1; May 27 at Buffalo — Philadelphia 2, Buffalo 0.

Bernie Parent

1974 – PHILADELPHIA FLYERS

Owning a 17-0-2 record in their previous 19 home games against Philadelphia, Boston was a heavy favorite coming into this series with home-ice advantage.

Flyers' captain Bobby Clarke ended his team's drought at the Garden in game two with a great individual effort, in recording two goals, the second in sudden-death, and one assist to overcome an early 2-0 deficit.

Goaltender Bernie Parent limited the Bruins to three goals in his three remaining wins, including a sixth-game shutout as the Flyers became the first expansion team to win the Stanley Cup, after only seven years in the NHL.

Parent earned the Conn Smythe Trophy with a 2.02 average in 17 playoff games.

1973-74 — Philadelphia Flyers — Bernie Parent, Ed Van Impe, Tom Bladon, André Dupont, Joe Watson, Jim Watson, Barry Ashbee, Bill Barber, Dave Schultz, Don Saleski, Gary Dornhoefer, Terry Crisp, Bobby Clarke, Simon Nolet, Ross Lonsberry, Rick MacLeish, Bill Flett, Orest Kindrachuk, Bill Clement, Bob Kelly, Bruce Cowick, Al MacAdam, Bobby Taylor, Fred Shero (coach), Keith Allen (general manager), Frank Lewis, Jim McKenzie (trainers).
Scores: May 7 at Boston — Boston 3, Philadelphia 2; May 9 at Boston — Philadelphia 3, Boston 2; May 12 at Philadelphia — Philadelphia 4, Boston 1; May 14 at Philadelphia — Philadelphia 4, Boston 2; May 16 at Boston — Boston 5, Philadelphia 1; May 19 at Philadelphia — Philadelphia 1, Boston 0.

1973 – MONTREAL CANADIENS

The Canadiens and Blackhawks met in a rematch of their Final series two years earlier. Chicago's Tony Esposito and Montreal's Ken Dryden, former teammates in the noted 1972 Summit Series against the Soviet Union, now faced each other at opposite ends of the ice.

Yvan Cournoyer, who recorded game-winning goals in the second and sixth contests, finished the playoffs with a new record of 15 goals en route to winning the Conn Smythe Trophy. Cournoyer (6-6-12) and Jacques Lemaire (3-9-12) both tied Gordie Howe's record for points in a Final series, while Lemaire set a new record for assists in the Finals with nine.

Henri Richard became the first player to play for 11 Stanley Cup champions and tied the overall record held by Toe Blake, who played on three Cup winners and coached eight before retiring in 1968.

After coaching the St. Louis Blues to three successive Finals from 1968 to 1970, Montreal's Scotty Bowman earned his first Stanley Cup ring.

1972-73 — **Montreal Canadiens** — Ken Dryden, Guy Lapointe, Serge Savard, Larry Robinson, Jacques Laperriere, Bob Murdoch, Pierre Bouchard, Jim Roberts, Yvan Cournoyer, Frank Mahovlich, Jacques Lemaire, Pete Mahovlich, Marc Tardif, Henri Richard, Rejean Houle, Guy Lafleur, Chuck Lefley, Claude Larose, Murray Wilson, Steve Shutt, Michel Plasse, Scotty Bowman (coach), Sam Pollock (general manager), Ed Palchak, Bob Williams (trainers).
Scores: April 29 at Montreal — Montreal 8, Chicago 3; May 1 at Montreal — Montreal 4, Chicago 1; May 3 at Chicago — Chicago 7, Montreal 4; May 6 at Chicago — Montreal 4, Chicago 0; May 8 at Montreal — Chicago 8, Montreal 7; May 10 at Chicago — Montreal 6, Chicago 4.

1972 – BOSTON BRUINS

After 43 years, the New York Rangers finally got a chance to avenge their 1929 loss to the Boston Bruins in the Stanley Cup Finals. However, history would repeat itself, as the Bruins again defeated the Rangers in this six-game confrontation.

Bobby Orr, who scored his second Cup-winning goal in three years, became the first two-time winner of the Conn Smythe Trophy. With a 4-4-8 mark in the Finals, Orr raised his playoff totals to 5-19-24, breaking Jean Beliveau's assist mark set in 1971.

1971-72 — **Boston Bruins** — Gerry Cheevers, Ed Johnston, Bobby Orr, Ted Green, Carol Vadnais, Dallas Smith, Don Awrey, Phil Esposito, Ken Hodge, John Bucyk, Mike Walton, Wayne Cashman, Garnet Bailey, Derek Sanderson, Fred Stanfield, Ed Westfall, John McKenzie, Don Marcotte, Garry Peters, Chris Hayes, Tom Johnson (coach), Milt Schmidt (general manager), Dan Canney, John Forristall (trainers).
Scores: April 30 at Boston — Boston 6, New York Rangers 5; May 2 at Boston — Boston 2, New York 1; May 4 at New York — New York 5, Boston 2; May 7 at New York — Boston 3, New York 2; May 9 at Boston — New York 3, Boston 2; May 11 at New York — Boston 3, New York 0.

Ed Westfall

CUP FINALS – 1971, 1970   **161**

1971 – MONTREAL CANADIENS

After missing the playoffs for the first time in 22 years in 1970, the Canadiens rebounded in 1971 to win their 16th Stanley Cup.

Brothers Frank and Peter Mahovlich were reunited in mid-season, and the two responded with a total of nine goals in the seven-game Final. Frank achieved the unusual distinction of being awarded a penalty shot in game six, but failed to score. He did, however, set a new playoff record with 14 goals and tied Phil Esposito's record 27-point performance of 1970.

After Chicago went ahead 2-0 in game seven, Henri Richard scored the tying and winning goals.

The hero of the playoffs turned out to be 23-year-old rookie goaltender Ken Dryden, who appeared in all 20 post-season games after only six starts during the regular season. Dryden's performance, which included a 12-8 record and 3.00 average, earned him the Conn Smythe Trophy.

While the series heralded the beginning of Dryden's career in the Montreal nets, it marked the conclusion of Jean Beliveau's playing days. Beliveau, who finished the playoffs with six goals and a record 16 assists, left the sport as the all-time leader in playoff assists (97) and points (176) and temporarily shared first place with Henri Richard in Stanley Cups won as a player, with 10.

1970-71 — Montreal Canadiens — Ken Dryden, Rogatien Vachon, Jacques Laperriere, Jean-Claude Tremblay, Guy Lapointe, Terry Harper, Pierre Bouchard, Jean Beliveau, Marc Tardif, Yvan Cournoyer, Rejean Houle, Claude Larose, Henri Richard, Phil Roberto, Pete Mahovlich, Leon Rochefort, John Ferguson, Bobby Sheehan, Jacques Lemaire, Frank Mahovlich, Bob Murdoch, Chuck Lefley, Al MacNeil (coach), Sam Pollock (general manager), Yvon Belanger, Ed Palchak (trainers).
Scores: May 4 at Chicago — Chicago 2, Montreal 1; May 6 at Chicago — Chicago 5, Montreal 3; May 9 at Montreal — Montreal 4, Chicago 2; May 11 at Montreal — Montreal 5, Chicago 2; May 13 at Chicago — Chicago 2, Montreal 0; May 16 at Montreal — Montreal 4, Chicago 3; May 18 at Chicago — Montreal 3, Chicago 2.

1970 – BOSTON BRUINS

For the third straight year, the St. Louis Blues qualified for the Finals but this year faced new rivals in the Boston Bruins, led by the first 100-point defenseman in hockey history, Bobby Orr.

After winning the first three games by margins of five, four and three goals, the Bruins were pushed into overtime in the fourth game. But Conn Smythe Trophy winner Orr ended the affair at the 40 second mark with his first goal of the series. Orr literally flew through the air on the play, which has become one of the most memorable images of Stanley Cup competition.

The series victory gave the Bruins their first Stanley Cup in 29 years, closing the club's longest period without a championship.

Phil Esposito established new playoff records for goals with 13 – breaking the record set by Jean Beliveau in 1956 – and for points with 27, eclipsing the mark set by Stan Mikita in 1962.

1969-70 — Boston Bruins — Gerry Cheevers, Ed Johnston, Bobby Orr, Rick Smith, Dallas Smith, Bill Speer, Gary Doak, Don Awrey, Phil Esposito, Ken Hodge, John Bucyk, Wayne Carleton, Wayne Cashman, Derek Sanderson, Fred Stanfield, Ed Westfall, John McKenzie, Jim Lorentz, Don Marcotte, Bill Lesuk, Dan Schock, Harry Sinden (coach), Milt Schmidt (general manager), Dan Canney, John Forristall (trainers).
Scores: May 3 at St. Louis — Boston 6, St. Louis 1; May 5 at St. Louis — Boston 6, St. Louis 2; May 7 at Boston — Boston 4, St. Louis 1; May 10 at Boston — Boston 4, St. Louis 3.

1969 – MONTREAL CANADIENS

Following in his predecessor's footsteps, Claude Ruel won the Stanley Cup in his first season behind the Canadiens' bench and became the 11th rookie coach in NHL history to go the distance with his team.

Ruel's squad had an easier time with St. Louis in this rematch of the previous year's Final, winning the series without the aid of overtime heroics.

Goaltender Rogie Vachon limited St. Louis to three goals in four games and registered his first playoff shutout in game three.

Serge Savard tallied a goal and an assist and became the first defenseman to win the Conn Smythe Trophy.

1968-69 — Montreal Canadiens — Lorne Worsley, Rogatien Vachon, Jacques Laperriere, Jean-Claude Tremblay, Ted Harris, Serge Savard, Terry Harper, Larry Hillman, Jean Beliveau, Ralph Backstrom, Dick Duff, Yvan Cournoyer, Claude Provost, Bobby Rousseau, Henri Richard, John Ferguson, Christian Bordeleau, Mickey Redmond, Jacques Lemaire, Lucien Grenier, Tony Esposito, Claude Ruel (coach), Sam Pollock (general manager), Larry Aubut, Eddy Palchak (trainers).
Scores: April 27 at Montreal — Montreal 3, St. Louis 1; April 29 at Montreal — Montreal 3, St. Louis 1; May 1 at St. Louis — Montreal 4, St. Louis 0; May 4 at St. Louis — Montreal 2, St. Louis 1.

1968 – MONTREAL CANADIENS

Before the start of the 1967-68 season, the NHL doubled in size with the addition of six expansion teams which formed a new Western division. In the playoffs, Montreal won the East and St. Louis won the West to earn a chance at the Stanley Cup.

The Blues' line-up included several aging superstars, among them the goaltending tandem of two-time Vezina Trophy winners Glenn Hall and Gump Worsley, two-time Art Ross Trophy winner Dickie Moore and seven-time Norris Trophy recipient Doug Harvey. The four were no strangers to playoff action with 50 years of post-season experience among them.

Although the Canadiens won in straight games, the series was a tightly contested affair with all four games decided by one goal and two determined in overtime.

Rookie defenseman Serge Savard, who would gather seven Stanley Cup rings in his career, scored his first two career playoff goals short-handed in games two and three to tie a Final series record.

Toe Blake retired after capturing his eighth Stanley Cup in 13 years as coach of the Canadiens and set a record as the first person to win a total of 11 Cups in a career. Blake also played on championship teams with the Montreal Maroons in 1926 and Canadiens in 1944 and 1946.

Glenn Hall became the second player from a losing team to earn the Conn Smythe Trophy, joining fellow goaltender Roger Crozier who won the award in 1966.

1967-68 — Montreal Canadiens — Lorne Worsley, Rogatien Vachon, Jacques Laperriere, Jean-Claude Tremblay, Ted Harris, Serge Savard, Terry Harper, Carol Vadnais, Jean Beliveau, Gilles Tremblay, Ralph Backstrom, Dick Duff, Claude Larose, Yvan Cournoyer, Claude Provost, Bobby Rousseau, Henri Richard, John Ferguson, Danny Grant, Jacques Lemaire, Mickey Redmond, Toe Blake (coach), Sam Pollock (general manager), Larry Aubut, Eddy Palchak (trainers).
Scores: May 5 at St. Louis — Montreal 3, St. Louis 2; May 7 at St. Louis — Montreal 1, St. Louis 0; May 9 at Montreal — Montreal 4, St. Louis 3; May 11 at Montreal — Montreal 3, St. Louis 2.

1967 – TORONTO MAPLE LEAFS

With an average age of over 31 years, the Toronto Maple Leafs iced the oldest line-up ever to win a Stanley Cup. Goaltender Johnny Bower (42) and defenseman Allan Stanley (41) were the senior citizens of the squad, which included seven players over 35 and 12 members over 30.

27-year-old "youngster" Dave Keon, who scored a goal and assist in the series, captured the Conn Smythe Trophy on the basis of an outstanding defensive performance.

1966-67 — Toronto Maple Leafs — Johnny Bower, Terry Sawchuk, Larry Hillman, Marcel Pronovost, Tim Horton, Bob Baun, Aut Erickson, Allan Stanley, Red Kelly, Ron Ellis, George Armstrong, Pete Stemkowski, Dave Keon, Mike Walton, Jim Pappin, Bob Pulford, Brian Conacher, Eddie Shack, Frank Mahovlich, Milan Marcetta, Larry Jeffrey, Bruce Gamble, Punch Imlach (manager-coach), Bob Haggart (trainer).
Scores: April 20 at Montreal — Toronto 2, Montreal 6; April 22 at Montreal — Toronto 3, Montreal 0; April 25 at Toronto — Toronto 3, Montreal 2; April 27 at Toronto — Toronto 2, Montreal 6; April 29 at Montreal — Toronto 4, Montreal 1; May 2 at Toronto — Toronto 3, Montreal 1.

John Ferguson

1966 – MONTREAL CANADIENS

The Canadiens repeated as champions to give coach Toe Blake his seventh title in 11 years behind the Montreal bench.

Henri Richard, a member of each of those seven Stanley Cup teams, scored the game-winner in overtime in game six, marking the ninth time in history that a series-winning goal had been scored in overtime.

Despite his team's loss in the Finals, goaltender Roger Crozier received the Conn Smythe Trophy by posting a 2.17 average and one shutout in 12 playoff games.

1965-66 — Montreal Canadiens — Lorne Worsley, Charlie Hodge, Jean-Claude Tremblay, Ted Harris, Jean-Guy Talbot, Terry Harper, Jacques Laperriere, Noel Price, Jean Beliveau, Ralph Backstrom, Dick Duff, Gilles Tremblay, Claude Larose, Yvan Cournoyer, Claude Provost, Bobby Rousseau, Henri Richard, Dave Balon, John Ferguson, Leon Rochefort, Jim Roberts, Toe Blake (coach), Sam Pollock (general manager), Larry Aubut, Andy Galley (trainers).
Scores: April 24 at Montreal — Detroit 3, Montreal 2; April 26 at Montreal — Detroit 5, Montreal 2; April 28 at Detroit — Montreal 4, Detroit 2; May 1 at Detroit — Montreal 2, Detroit 1; May 3 at Montreal — Montreal 5, Detroit 1; May 5 at Detroit — Montreal 3, Detroit 2.

1965 – MONTREAL CANADIENS

Repeating the feat accomplished in 1955, the home teams won every game in the Finals.

Lorne "Gump" Worsley, appearing in his first Stanley Cup after 12 seasons in the NHL, recorded two shutouts in four starts, including one in game seven. Sharing the goaltending duties, Charlie Hodge also posted a shutout in his three outings.

Jean Beliveau captured the inaugural Conn Smythe Trophy as the most valuable player to his team in the playoffs after recording eight goals and eight assists in 13 games.

1964-65 — Montreal Canadiens — Lorne Worsley, Charlie Hodge, Jean-Claude Tremblay, Ted Harris, Jean-Guy Talbot, Terry Harper, Jacques Laperriere, Jean Gauthier, Noel Picard, Jean Beliveau, Ralph Backstrom, Dick Duff, Claude Larose, Yvan Cournoyer, Claude Provost, Bobby Rousseau, Henri Richard, Dave Balon, John Ferguson, Red Berenson, Jim Roberts, Toe Blake (coach), Sam Pollock (general manager), Larry Aubut, Andy Galley (trainers).
Scores: April 17 at Montreal — Montreal 3, Chicago 2; April 20 at Montreal — Montreal 2, Chicago 0; April 22 at Chicago — Montreal 1, Chicago 3; April 25 at Chicago — Montreal 1, Chicago 5; April 27 at Montreal — Montreal 6, Chicago 0; April 29 at Chicago — Montreal 1, Chicago 2; May 1 at Montreal — Montreal 4, Chicago 0.

Bob Baun

1964 – TORONTO MAPLE LEAFS

Toronto captured the Cup for a third consecutive season, tying their club record set in 1947-49. Only one NHL team – the Montreal Canadiens (1956-60) – had ever won more championships in a row.

In each of the first three games, the winning goal was scored within the final minute of play. After Toronto took game one on Bob Pulford's goal with two seconds remaining in regulation time, Detroit skated to consecutive last-minute victories, with Larry Jeffrey netting the game-winner at 7:52 of overtime in game two and Alex Delvecchio potting the tie-breaker with 17 seconds to play in game three.

With the score tied 3-3 late in game six, Maple Leafs' defenseman Bobby Baun took a Gordie Howe slapshot on his skate and dropped to the ice with an apparently sprained ankle. After freezing and taping the injury, he returned for overtime and scored the winning goal at 2:43 of the extra period. On crutches for the next two days, he would later suit up for the series finale and never miss a shift as Toronto won the Cup. the following day, X rays confirmed what Baun had known all along, that the ankle was in fact broken. The Leafs' blueliner spent two more months on crutches.

Toronto's Red Kelly closed out his playing days in the finale, raising his record total to 142 career playoff games.

1963-64 — Toronto Maple Leafs — Johnny Bower, Carl Brewer, Tim Horton, Bob Baun, Allan Stanley, Larry Hillman, Al Arbour, Red Kelly, Gerry Ehman, Andy Bathgate, George Armstrong, Ron Stewart, Dave Keon, Billy Harris, Don McKenney, Jim Pappin, Bob Pulford, Eddie Shack, Frank Mahovlich, Eddie Litzenberger, Punch Imlach (manager-coach), Bob Haggert (trainer).
Scores: April 11 at Toronto — Toronto 3, Detroit 2; April 14 at Toronto — Toronto 3, Detroit 4; April 16 at Detroit — Toronto 3, Detroit 4; April 18 at Detroit — Toronto 4, Detroit 2; April 21 at Toronto — Toronto 1, Detroit 2; April 23 at Detroit — Toronto 4, Detroit 3; April 25 at Toronto — Toronto 4, Detroit 0.

CUP FINALS – 1963-60

1963 – TORONTO MAPLE LEAFS

Five different Maple Leafs – Bob Nevin, Dick Duff, Ron Stewart, Red Kelly and Dave Keon – recorded multiple-goal performances in Toronto's four victories, and 38-year-old goaltender Johnny Bower limited Detroit to 10 goals in five games.

Keon scored twice in game five with a Toronto player in the penalty box, establishing a new playoff record for short-handed goals in one game.

1962-63 — Toronto Maple Leafs — Johnny Bower, Don Simmons, Carl Brewer, Tim Horton, Kent Douglas, Allan Stanley, Bob Baun, Larry Hillman, Red Kelly, Dick Duff, George Armstrong, Bob Nevin, Ron Stewart, Dave Keon, Billy Harris, Bob Pulford, Eddie Shack, Ed Litzenberger, Frank Mahovlich, John MacMillan, Punch Imlach (manager-coach), Bob Haggert (trainer).
Scores: April 9 at Toronto — Toronto 4, Detroit 2; April 11 at Toronto — Toronto 4, Detroit 2; April 14 at Detroit — Toronto 2, Detroit 3; April 16 at Detroit — Toronto 4, Detroit 2; April 18 at Toronto — Toronto 3, Detroit 1.

1962 – TORONTO MAPLE LEAFS

The Maple Leafs regained the Stanley Cup after 11 years, putting an end to the club's longest period without a championship in its 45-year NHL history.

In his Stanley Cup debut, 22-year-old Dave Keon scored a goal and added an assist in game one.

Stan Mikita tallied two assists in game five to set new playoff records for assists (15) and points (21), breaking Gordie Howe's mark of 20 points set in the 1955 playoffs.

1961-62 — Toronto Maple Leafs — Johnny Bower, Don Simmons, Carl Brewer, Tim Horton, Bob Baun, Allan Stanley, Al Arbour, Larry Hillman, Red Kelly, Dick Duff, George Armstrong, Frank Mahovlich, Bob Nevin, Ron Stewart, Bill Harris, Bert Olmstead, Bob Pulford, Eddie Shack, Dave Keon, Ed Litzenberger, John MacMillan, Punch Imlach (manager-coach), Bob Haggert (trainer).
Scores: April 10 at Toronto — Toronto 4, Chicago 1; April 12 at Toronto — Toronto 3, Chicago 2; April 15 at Chicago — Toronto 0, Chicago 3; April 17 at Chicago — Toronto 1, Chicago 4; April 19 at Toronto — Toronto 8, Chicago 4; April 22 at Chicago — Toronto 2, Chicago 1.

1961 – CHICAGO BLACKHAWKS

In their fifth appearance in the Finals, the Chicago Blackhawks captured their first Stanley Cup since 1938 and their third championship overall since joining the NHL in 1926-27.

Two of the greatest athletes in Chicago sports history, Bobby Hull and Stan Mikita, made their premier Stanley Cup appearances, and both figured prominently in the outcome. "The Golden Jet" sparkled in game one with his first two Cup goals, including the game-winner, while Mikita scored the winner in game five.

1960-61 — Chicago Black Hawks — Glenn Hall, Al Arbour, Pierre Pilote, Elmer Vasko, Jack Evans, Dollard St. Laurent, Reg Fleming, Tod Sloan, Ron Murphy, Eddie Litzenberger, Bill Hay, Bobby Hull, Ab McDonald, Eric Nesterenko, Ken Wharram, Earl Balfour, Stan Mikita, Murray Balfour, Chico Maki, Tommy Ivan (manager), Rudy Pilous (coach), Nick Garen (trainer).
Scores: April 6 at Chicago — Chicago 3, Detroit 2; April 8 at Detroit — Detroit 3, Chicago 1; April 10 at Chicago — Chicago 3, Detroit 1; April 12 at Detroit — Detroit 2, Chicago 1; April 14 at Chicago — Chicago 6, Detroit 3; April 16 at Detroit — Chicago 5, Detroit 1.

1960 – MONTREAL CANADIENS

The Canadiens retained the Stanley Cup for an unprecedented fifth straight season. No team has since matched the record-setting achievement.

Jacques Plante, who introduced the goal mask to the hockey world on November 1, 1959, in New York, was stellar in his self-designed face guard. His performance, in fact, played a large part in the acceptance of the mask by goaltenders world-wide.

For Maurice Richard, this series was a fine finale to a great career. In game three, he scored his 82nd and final playoff goal, extending his all-time record in that category.

1959-60 — Montreal Canadiens — Jacques Plante, Charlie Hodge, Doug Harvey, Tom Johnson, Bob Turner, Jean-Guy Talbot, Albert Langlois, Ralph Backstrom, Jean Beliveau, Marcel Bonin, Bernie Geoffrion, Phil Goyette, Bill Hicke, Don Marshall, Ab McDonald, Dickie Moore, André Pronovost, Claude Provost, Henri Richard, Maurice Richard, Frank Selke (manager), Toe Blake (coach), Hector Dubois, Larry Aubut (trainers).
Scores: April 7 at Montreal — Canadiens 4, Toronto 2; April 9 at Montreal — Canadiens 2, Toronto 1; April 12 at Toronto — Canadiens 5, Toronto 2; April 14 at Toronto — Canadiens 4, Toronto 0.

1959 – MONTREAL CANADIENS

The Canadiens skated to a fourth consecutive Cup championship, breaking the record of three they had shared with Toronto (1947-49).

1958-59 — **Montreal Canadiens** — Jacques Plante, Charlie Hodge, Doug Harvey, Tom Johnson, Bob Turner, Jean-Guy Talbot, Albert Langlois, Bernie Geoffrion, Ralph Backstrom, Bill Hicke, Maurice Richard, Dickie Moore, Claude Provost, Ab McDonald, Henri Richard, Marcel Bonin, Phil Goyette, Don Marshall, André Pronovost, Jean Béliveau, Frank Selke (manager), Toe Blake (coach), Hector Dubois, Larry Aubut (trainers).
Scores: April 9 at Montreal — Canadiens 5, Toronto 3; April 11 at Montreal — Canadiens 3, Toronto 1; April 14 at Toronto — Toronto 3, Canadiens 2; April 16 at Toronto — Canadiens 3, Toronto 2; April 18 at Montreal — Canadiens 5, Toronto 3.

1958 – MONTREAL CANADIENS

The Canadiens' third straight Stanley Cup title equalled the NHL record set by the Toronto Maple in 1947-49.

Maurice Richard, the top overall playoff goal-scorer with 11, notched his third career overtime goal in final play and sixth in playoffs in game five to extend his own record in each category. Neither record has been broken.

1957-58 — **Montreal Canadiens** — Jacques Plante, Gerry McNeil, Doug Harvey, Tom Johnson, Bob Turner, Dollard St-Laurent, Jean-Guy Talbot, Albert Langlois, Jean Béliveau, Bernie Geoffrion, Maurice Richard, Dickie Moore, Claude Provost, Floyd Curry, Bert Olmstead, Henri Richard, Marcel Bonin, Phil Goyette, Don Marshall, André Pronovost, Connie Broden, Frank Selke (manager), Toe Blake (coach), Hector Dubois, Larry Aubut (trainers).
Scores: April 8 at Montreal — Canadiens 2, Boston 1; April 10 at Montreal — Boston 5, Canadiens 2; April 13 at Boston — Canadiens 3, Boston 0; April 15 at Boston — Boston 3, Canadiens 1; April 17 at Montreal — Canadiens 3, Boston 2; April 20 at Boston — Canadiens 5, Boston 3.

1957 – MONTREAL CANADIENS

Maurice "Rocket" Richard scored four times in game one to equal Ted Lindsay's modern Stanley Cup record for goals in a game.

Jacques Plante held the Bruins to six goals in five games.

1956-57 — **Montreal Canadiens** — Jacques Plante, Gerry McNeil, Doug Harvey, Tom Johnson, Bob Turner, Dollard St. Laurent, Jean-Guy Talbot, Jean Béliveau, Bernie Geoffrion, Floyd Curry, Dickie Moore, Maurice Richard, Claude Provost, Bert Olmstead, Henri Richard, Phil Goyette, Don Marshall, André Pronovost, Connie Broden, Frank Selke (manager), Toe Blake (coach), Hector Dubois, Larry Aubut (trainers).
Scores: April 6, at Montreal — Canadiens 5, Boston 1; April 9, at Montreal — Canadiens 1, Boston 0; April 11, at Boston — Canadiens 4, Boston 2; April 14, at Boston — Boston 2, Canadiens 0; April 16, at Montreal — Canadiens 5, Boston 1.

1956 – MONTREAL CANADIENS

Two rookies played integral roles for the Montreal Canadiens on this first of five consecutive Stanley Cup championship teams. Former star Toe Blake took over for Dick Irvin behind the Canadiens' bench as coach, while rookie center Henri Richard joined his famous brother Maurice on the ice.

In game one, Blake coached his first winning game as a Finalist, and young Richard notched his first Stanley Cup goal.

Jean Beliveau scored seven times in the series, including at least one goal in each game, to set a record for goals in the Finals and tie Maurice Richard's overall playoff record of 12 goals set in 1944.

1955-56 — **Montreal Canadiens** — Jacques Plante, Doug Harvey, Emile Bouchard, Bob Turner, Tom Johnson, Jean-Guy Talbot, Dollard St. Laurent, Jean Béliveau, Bernie Geoffrion, Bert Olmstead, Floyd Curry, Jackie Leclair, Maurice Richard, Dickie Moore, Henri Richard, Ken Mosdell, Don Marshall, Claude Provost, Frank Selke (manager), Toe Blake (coach), Hector Dubois (trainer).
Scores: March 31, at Montreal — Canadiens 6, Detroit 4; April 3, at Montreal — Canadiens 5, Detroit 1; April 5, at Detroit — Detroit 3, Canadiens 1; April 8, at Detroit — Canadiens 3, Detroit 0; April 10, at Montreal — Canadiens 3, Detroit 1.

Maurice Richard

1955 – DETROIT RED WINGS

On March 13, Maurice Richard had been suspended for the remainder of the regular season and playoffs by NHL President Clarence Campbell because of a fight, and the high-scoring right-winger's absence was sorely felt by the Canadiens.

In game two, Detroit's Ted Lindsay scored four times to set a modern record for goals in a championship game, and the Red Wings won their 15th consecutive contest to establish another NHL record.

Lindsay then tallied an assist, his last of the series, in game four, to tie Elmer Lach's record of 12 playoff assists.

Gordie Howe set a Final-series scoring record (5-7-12) and an overall playoff scoring record (9-11-20) in 11 games.

For the first time in a best-of-seven Final, the home teams won all seven games.

1954-55 — Detroit Red Wings — Terry Sawchuk, Red Kelly, Bob Goldham, Marcel Pronovost, Ben Woit, Jim Hay, Larry Hillman, Ted Lindsay, Tony Leswick, Gordie Howe, Alex Delvecchio, Marty Pavelich, Glen Skov, Earl Reibel, John Wilson, Bill Dineen, Vic Stasiuk, Marcel Bonin, Jack Adams (manager), Jimmy Skinner (coach), Carl Mattson (trainer).
Scores: April 3, at Detroit — Detroit 4, Canadiens 2; April 5, at Detroit — Detroit 7, Canadiens 1; April 7 at Montreal — Canadiens 4, Detroit 2; April 9, at Montreal — Canadiens 5, Detroit 3; April 10, at Detroit — Detroit 5, Canadiens 1; April 12, at Montreal — Canadiens 6, Detroit 3; April 14, at Detroit — Detroit 3, Canadiens 1.

Ted Lindsay kisses the Cup after Tony Leswick's deflected flip shot counted as the overtime winner in game seven.

1954 – DETROIT RED WINGS

Tony Leswick's Cup-winning tally was the second overtime goal ever scored in the seventh game of a Final series. Leswick, who notched the winner at 4:29 of the first extra period, matched the feat first accomplished by former Red Wing Pete Babando in 1950.

Marguerite Norris, President of the Detroit club, was presented with the Stanley Cup by NHL President Clarence Campbell at the conclusion of the series. Mrs. Norris became the only woman in history to have her name engraved into the Stanley Cup.

1953-54 — Detroit Red Wings — Terry Sawchuk, Red Kelly, Bob Goldham, Ben Woit, Marcel Pronovost, Al Arbour, Keith Allen, Ted Lindsay, Tony Leswick, Gordie Howe, Marty Pavelich, Alex Delvecchio, Metro Prystai, Glen Skov, John Wilson, Bill Dineen, Jim Peters, Earl Reibel, Vic Stasiuk, Jack Adams (manager), Tommy Ivan (coach), Carl Mattson (trainer).
Scores: April 4, at Detroit — Detroit 3, Canadiens 1; April 6, at Detroit — Canadiens 3, Detroit 1; April 8, at Montreal — Detroit 5, Canadiens 2; April 10, at Montreal — Detroit 2, Canadiens 0; April 11, at Detroit — Canadiens 1, Detroit 0; April 13, at Montreal — Canadiens 4, Detroit 1; April 16, at Detroit — Detroit 2, Canadiens 1.

CUP FINALS – 1953-51 **169**

1953 – MONTREAL CANADIENS

After goaltender Jacques Plante recorded a loss in the second game of the series, Canadiens' coach Dick Irvin sent Gerry McNeil into the nets. The move resulted in two shutouts in three games, and Montreal regained the Cup after a seven-year layoff.
Elmer Lach scored the series-winning goal at 1:22 of overtime in the fifth game.

1952-53 — Montreal Canadiens — Gerry McNeil, Jacques Plante, Doug Harvey, Emile Bouchard, Tom Johnson, Dollard St. Laurent, Bud MacPherson, Maurice Richard, Elmer Lach, Bert Olmstead, Bernie Geoffrion, Floyd Curry, Paul Masnick, Billy Reay, Dickie Moore, Ken Mosdell, Dick Gamble, Johnny McCormack, Lorne Davis, Calum McKay, Eddie Mazur, Frank Selke (manager), Dick Irvin (coach), Hector Dubois (trainer).
Scores: April 9, at Montreal — Canadiens 4, Boston 2; April 11, at Montreal — Boston 4, Canadiens 1; April 12, at Boston — Canadiens 3, Boston 0; April 14, at Boston — Canadiens 7, Boston 3; April 16, at Montreal — Canadiens 1, Boston 0.

1952 – DETROIT RED WINGS

Terry Sawchuk made his debut in the Finals, recording two shutouts and limiting Montreal to just two goals in the four-game series. Meanwhile, Gordie Howe contributed his first two goals in a Stanley Cup championship series.
The Red Wings set a new NHL record by winning all eight post-season games, including a four-game sweep of Toronto in the first round.

1951-52 — Detroit Red Wings — Terry Sawchuk, Bob Goldham, Ben Woit, Red Kelly, Leo Reise, Marcel Pronovost, Ted Lindsay, Tony Leswick, Gordie Howe, Metro Prystai, Marty Pavelich, Sid Abel, Glen Skov, Alex Delvecchio, John Wilson, Vic Stasiuk, Larry Zeidel, Jack Adams (manager) Tommy Ivan (coach), Carl Mattson (trainer).
Scores: April 10, at Montreal — Detroit 3, Canadiens 1; April 12 at Montreal — Detroit 2, Canadiens 1; April 13, at Detroit — Detroit 3, Canadiens 0; April 15, at Detroit — Detroit 3, Canadiens 0.

1951 – TORONTO MAPLE LEAFS

The 1951 series distinguished itself as the only Stanley Cup in which every game ended in overtime. Sid Smith, Ted Kennedy, Harry Watson and Bill Barilko notched the overtime winners for Toronto, while Maurice "Rocket" Richard, who scored goals in all five contests, netted one in Montreal's lone victory.
Richard's overtime tally was his second in a final series and the fourth of his playoff career, breaking the record of three set by Boston's Mel Hill in 1939.
For Barilko, his overtime goal would be his last, as the rugged defenseman died tragically in a plane crash during the summer.

1950-51 — Toronto Maple Leafs — Turk Broda, Al Rollins, Jim Thomson, Gus Mortson, Bill Barilko, Bill Juzda, Fern Flaman, Hugh Bolton, Ted Kennedy, Sid Smith, Tod Sloan, Cal Gardner, Howie Meeker, Harry Watson, Max Bentley, Joe Klukay, Danny Lewicki, Ray Timgren, Fleming Mackell, Johnny McCormack, Bob Hassard, Conn Smythe (manager), Joe Primeau (coach), Tim Daly (trainer).
Scores: April 11, at Toronto — Toronto 3, Canadiens 2; April 14, at Toronto — Canadiens 3, Toronto 2; April 17, at Montreal — Toronto 2, Canadiens 1; April 19, at Montreal — Toronto 3, Canadiens 2; April 21, at Toronto — Toronto 3, Canadiens 2.

1950 - DETROIT RED WINGS

Bumped from New York's Madison Square Garden by the incoming circus, the Rangers opted to play games two and three in Toronto's Maple Leaf Gardens. The initial confrontation in Toronto marked the first time since 1920, when Ottawa faced Seattle, that two teams battled for the Cup without a local club involved.

Gordie Howe failed to appear for the Wings in this series as a result of a serious head injury sustained in the first game of the semi-finals. After sliding head first into the boards, Howe required surgery to repair a fractured nose and cheekbone.

Even without Howe, Detroit managed to capture the Cup in seven games, but not without a fight. New York battled the Wings to a 3-3 tie at the end of regulation time in game seven, which the Red Wings' Pete Babando ended at the 28:31 mark of overtime. Babando's goal was the first-ever sudden-death tally in the seventh game of a Final series.

New York's Don Raleigh set a record which has never been broken when he scored two overtime goals in one Stanley Cup Final series.

1949-50 — Detroit Red Wings — Harry Lumley, Jack Stewart, Leo Reise, Clare Martin, Al Dewsbury, Lee Fogolin, Marcel Pronovost, Red Kelly, Ted Lindsay, Sid Abel, Gordie Howe, George Gee, Jimmy Peters, Marty Pavelich, Jim McFadden, Pete Babando, Max McNab, Gerry Couture, Joe Carveth, Steve Black, John Wilson, Larry Wilson, Jack Adams (manager), Tommy Ivan (coach), Carl Mattson (trainer).
Scores: April 11, at Detroit — Detroit 4, Rangers 1; April 13, at Toronto* — Rangers 3, Detroit 1; April 15, at Toronto — Detroit 4, Rangers 0; April 18, at Detroit — Rangers 4, Detroit 3; April 20, at Detroit — Rangers 2, Detroit 1; April 22, at Detroit — Detroit 5, Rangers 4; April 23, at Detroit — Detroit 4, Rangers 3. (* Ice was unavailable in Madison Square Garden and Rangers elected to play second and third games on Toronto ice.)

1949 - TORONTO MAPLE LEAFS

The Toronto Maple Leafs established two NHL records in this 1949 series. Most significantly, they captured their third straight Stanley Cup title, a feat last accomplished 44 years earlier by the Ottawa Silver Seven. They also won an unprecedented ninth straight game in Final competition, dating back to April 19, 1947.

1948-49 — Toronto Maple Leafs — Turk Broda, Jim Thomson, Gus Mortson, Bill Barilko, Garth Boesch, Bill Juzda, Ted Kennedy, Howie Meeker, Vic Lynn, Harry Watson, Bill Ezinicki, Cal Gardner, Max Bentley, Joe Klukay, Sid Smith, Don Metz, Ray Timgren, Fleming Mackell, Harry Taylor, Bob Dawes, Tod Sloan, Conn Smythe (manager), Hap Day (coach), Tim Daly (trainer).
Scores: April 8, at Detroit — Toronto 3, Detroit 2; April 10, at Detroit — Toronto 3, Detroit 1; April 13, at Toronto — Toronto 3, Detroit 1; April 16, at Toronto — Toronto 3, Detroit 1.

1948 - TORONTO MAPLE LEAFS

The series marked the beginning and end of two great Stanley Cup careers. For Detroit's Gordie Howe, it was an introduction to the rigors of championship competition. For Toronto's Syl Apps, who scored a goal in game four, it meant the conclusion of a Hall-of-Fame career.

Toronto became the fourth NHL team to repeat as Stanley Cup champions, joining the Ottawa Senators (1920-21), Montreal Canadiens (1930-31) and Detroit Red Wings (1936-37).

1947-48 — Toronto Maple Leafs — Turk Broda, Jim Thomson, Wally Stanowski, Garth Boesch, Bill Barilko. Gus Mortson, Phil Samis, Syl Apps, Bill Ezinicki, Harry Watson, Ted Kennedy, Howie Meeker, Vic Lynn, Nick Metz, Max Bentley, Joe Klukay, Les Costello, Don Metz, Sid Smith, Conn Smythe (manager), Hap Day (coach), Tim Daly (trainer).
Scores: April 7, at Toronto — Toronto 5, Detroit 3; April 10, at Toronto — Toronto 4, Detroit 2; April 11, at Detroit — Toronto 2, Detroit 0; April 14, at Detroit — Toronto 7, Detroit 2.

CUP FINALS – 1947-45

Turk Broda

1947 – TORONTO MAPLE LEAFS

In the first all-Canadian Finals in 12 years, the Maple Leafs defeated the Canadiens in six games. Toronto's Ted "Teeder" Kennedy potted three goals in the series, including the Cup-winner.

1946-47 — Toronto Maple Leafs — Turk Broda, Garth Boesch, Gus Mortson, Jim Thomson, Wally Stanowski, Bill Barilko, Harry Watson, Bud Poile, Ted Kennedy, Syl Apps, Don Metz, Nick Metz, Bill Ezinicki, Vic Lynn, Howie Meeker, Gaye Stewart, Joe Klukay, Gus Bodnar, Bob Goldham, Conn Smythe (manager), Hap Day (coach), Tim Daly (trainer).
Scores: April 8, at Montreal — Canadiens 6, Toronto 0; April 10, at Montreal — Toronto 4, Canadiens 0; April 12, at Toronto — Toronto 4, Canadiens 2; April 15, at Toronto — Toronto 2, Canadiens 1; April 17, at Montreal — Canadiens 3, Toronto 1; April 19, at Toronto — Toronto 2, Canadiens 1.

1946 – MONTREAL CANADIENS

In game one, Maurice "Rocket" Richard scored the first of his record six overtime playoff goals, and the first of his three career overtime tallies in the Finals.
Elmer Lach's playoff assist total reached 12, shattering the former assist record of 11 set by Boston's Bill Cowley in 1939 and tied by Toe Blake in 1944.

1945-46 — Montreal Canadiens — Elmer Lach, Toe Blake, Maurice Richard, Bob Fillion, Dutch Hiller, Murph Chamberlain, Ken Mosdell, Buddy O'Connor, Glen Harmon, Jim Peters, Emile Bouchard, Bill Reay, Ken Reardon, Leo Lamoureux, Frank Eddolls, Gerry Plamondon, Bill Durnan, Tommy Gorman (manager), Dick Irvin (coach), Ernie Cook (trainer).
Scores: March 30, at Montreal — Canadiens 4, Boston 3; April 2, at Montreal — Canadiens 3, Boston 2; April 4, at Boston — Canadiens 4, Boston 2; April 7, at Boston — Boston 3, Canadiens 2; April 9, at Montreal — Canadiens 6, Boston 3.

1945 – TORONTO MAPLE LEAFS

Two rookie goaltenders, Toronto's Frank McCool and Detroit's Harry Lumley, manned the opposing nets in the Cup Finals for the first time. McCool posted shutouts in each of the first three games to set a new Stanley Cup record, while Lumley rebounded with two of his own in games five and six to knot the series at three games.
McCool outworked his counterpart in game seven with help from Mel Hill and Babe Pratt, who teamed up to beat Lumley with the series-winning goal mid-way through the third period.

1944-45 — Toronto Maple Leafs — Don Metz, Frank McCool, Wally Stanowski, Reg Hamilton, Elwyn Morris, Johnny McCreedy, Tommy O'Neill, Ted Kennedy, Babe Pratt, Gus Bodnar, Art Jackson, Jack McLean, Mel Hill, Nick Metz, Bob Davidson, Dave Schriner, Lorne Carr, Conn Smythe (manager), Frank Selke (business manager), Hap Day (coach), Tim Daly (trainer).
Scores: April 6, at Detroit — Toronto 1, Detroit 0; April 8, at Detroit — Toronto 2, Detroit 0; April 12, at Toronto — Toronto 1, Detroit 0; April 14, at Toronto — Detroit 5, Toronto 3; April 19, at Detroit — Detroit 2, Toronto 0; April 21, at Toronto — Detroit 1, Toronto 0; April 22, at Detroit — Toronto 2, Detroit 1.

Elmer Lach and Toe Blake

1944 – MONTREAL CANADIENS

Making his Stanley Cup debut, Maurice "Rocket" Richard scored five goals, including the first of his three career hat-tricks in Final play. His post-season total of 12 goals in nine games set a new Stanley Cup record.

In total, the "Punch Line" of Elmer Lach, Toe Blake and Richard combined for 10 of the Canadiens' 16 goals in the series, including all five scores in the finale. Blake, who set a new playoff record with 18 points, netted the Cup-winning goal at 9:12 of overtime in game four. In that contest, Canadiens' goaltender Bill Durnan stonewalled Chicago's Virgil Johnson on the first penalty shot ever awarded in a Stanley Cup Final.

The victory gave the Canadiens their first Stanley Cup championship in 14 years, ending the longest Stanley Cup drought the club has ever faced in its 71-year NHL history.

1943-44 — Montreal Canadiens — Toe Blake, Maurice Richard, Elmer Lach, Ray Getliffe, Murph Chamberlain, Phil Watson, Emile Bouchard, Glen Harmon, Buddy O'Connor, Jerry Heffernan, Mike McMahon, Leo Lamoureux, Fernand Majeau, Bob Fillion, Bill Durnan, Tommy Gorman (manager), Dick Irvin (coach), Ernie Cook (trainer).
Scores: April 4, at Montreal — Canadiens 5, Chicago 1; April 6, at Chicago — Canadiens 3, Chicago 1; April 9, at Chicago — Canadiens 3, Chicago 2; April 13, at Montreal — Canadiens 5, Chicago 4.

1943 – DETROIT RED WINGS

After losing the Stanley Cup in 1941 and 1942, the Red Wings' third straight trip to the Finals proved successful as they swept the Bruins twice in Detroit and twice in Boston.

Goaltender Johnny Mowers blanked the Bruins at Boston Garden in the last two games.

1942-43 — Detroit Red Wings — Jack Stewart, Jimmy Orlando, Sid Abel, Alex Motter, Harry Watson, Joe Carveth, Mud Bruneteau, Eddie Wares, Johnny Mowers, Cully Simon, Don Grosso, Carl Liscombe, Connie Brown, Syd Howe, Les Douglas, Hal Jackson, Joe Fisher, Jack Adams (manager), Ebbie Goodfellow (playing-coach), Honey Walker (trainer).
Scores: April 1, at Detroit — Detroit 6, Boston 2; April 4, at Detroit — Detroit 4, Boston 3; April 7, at Boston — Detroit 4, Boston 0; April 8, at Boston — Detroit 2, Boston 0.

1942 – TORONTO MAPLE LEAFS

In one of the finest comebacks in the history of sport, Toronto rebounded from a 3-0 deficit in games to capture the Stanley Cup. The feat has never been duplicated.
 The Maple Leafs hosted the first Canadian sports crowd of over 16,000 in game seven, the first seventh game played since the expanded playoff format was adopted in 1939.
 Turk Broda was the hero for Toronto, allowing only seven goals in the final four contests.

1941-42 — Toronto Maple Leafs — Wally Stanowski, Syl Apps, Bob Goldham, Gord Drillon, Hank Goldup, Ernie Dickens, Dave Schriner, Bucko McDonald, Bob Davidson, Nick Metz, Bingo Kampman, Don Metz, Gaye Stewart, Turk Broda, Johnny McCreedy, Lorne Carr, Pete Langelle, Billy Taylor, Conn Smythe (manager), Hap Day (coach), Frank Selke (business manager), Tim Daly (trainer).
Scores: April 4, at Toronto — Detroit 3, Toronto 2; April 7, at Toronto — Detroit 4, Toronto 2; April 9, at Detroit — Detroit 5, Toronto 2; April 12, at Detroit — Toronto 4, Detroit 3; April 14, at Toronto — Toronto 9, Detroit 3; April 16, at Detroit — Toronto 3, Detroit 0; April 18, at Toronto — Toronto 3, Detroit 1.

1941 – BOSTON BRUINS

In the third-ever best-of-seven Final series, Boston set a record by winning in four straight games. Since the National Hockey League was formed in 1917, only four teams – the 1929 Boston Bruins, 1930 Montreal Canadiens, 1932 Toronto Maple Leafs and 1935 Montreal Maroons – had ever won the Cup in the fewest possible games.
 Goalie Frank Brimsek allowed only six goals in the series, while Milt Schmidt was the offensive star with three goals.

1940-41 — Boston Bruins — Bill Cowley, Des Smith, Dit Clapper, Frank Brimsek, Flash Hollett, John Crawford, Bobby Bauer, Pat McCreavy, Herb Cain, Mel Hill, Milt Schmidt, Woody Dumart, Roy Conacher, Terry Reardon, Art Jackson, Eddie Wiseman, Art Ross (manager), Cooney Weiland (coach), Win Green (trainer).
Scores: April 6, at Boston — Detroit 2, Boston 3; April 8, at Boston — Detroit 1, Boston 2; April 10, at Detroit — Boston 4, Detroit 2; April 12, at Detroit — Boston 3, Detroit 1.

1940 – NEW YORK RANGERS

With the circus heading for New York, the Rangers were forced to play the first two games on consecutive nights before vacating Madison Square Garden for the rest of the playoffs.
 Three of the Rangers' four game-winning goals were scored in overtime, including the Cup-winner by Bryan Hextall in game six. Hextall's goal marked the third time in NHL history that the last goal of the season had been tallied in overtime.
 This would be the last Stanley Cup championship for the Rangers, whose ensuing 47-year drought has become the longest by any NHL team in the history of Stanley Cup play.
 Lynn and Murray Patrick skated for the winners to become the third and fourth members of the Patrick family (joining father Lester and uncle Frank) to have their names engraved on the Stanley Cup.
 Frank Boucher, who had played on the Rangers' first two Stanley Cup winners in 1928 and 1933, became the seventh rookie coach in NHL history to win the championship.

1939-40 — New York Rangers — Dave Kerr, Art Coulter, Ott Heller, Alex Shibicky, Mac Colville, Neil Colville, Phil Watson, Lynn Patrick, Clint Smith, Muzz Patrick, Babe Pratt, Bryan Hextall, Kilby Macdonald, Dutch Hiller, Alf Pike, Sanford Smith, Lester Patrick (manager), Frank Boucher (coach), Harry Westerby (trainer).
Scores: April 2, at New York — Rangers 2, Toronto 1; April 3, at New York — Rangers 6, Toronto 2; April 6, at Toronto — Rangers 1, Toronto 2; April 9, at Toronto — Rangers 0, Toronto 3; April 11, at Toronto — Rangers 2, Toronto 1; April 13, at Toronto — Rangers 3, Toronto 2.

Manager Weston Adams and coach Art Ross

1939 – BOSTON BRUINS

During the off-season the NHL expanded the Finals to a best-of-seven format. Goaltender Frank Brimsek held the Toronto Maple Leafs to 6 goals in 5 games as the Boston Bruins took the Cup for the first time in 10 seasons.

Mel Hill of Boston, who set an NHL record with three overtime goals in the first round of the playoffs, scored twice in the series, and Bill Cowley led all playoff scorers with 11 assists and 14 points to set modern records in both categories.

Boston manager Art Ross said after the series that the Bruins were the greatest team he had seen in his 37 years of hockey.

1938-39 — **Boston Bruins** — Bobby Bauer, Mel Hill, Flash Hollett, Roy Conacher, Gord Pettinger, Milt Schmidt, Woody Dumart, Jack Crawford, Ray Getliffe, Frank Brimsek, Eddie Shore, Dit Clapper, Bill Cowley, Jack Portland, Red Hamill, Cooney Weiland, Art Ross (manager-coach), Win Green (trainer).
Scores: April 6, at Boston — Toronto 1, Boston 2; April 9, at Boston — Toronto 3, Boston 2; April 11, at Toronto — Toronto 1, Boston 3; April 13 at Toronto — Toronto 0, Boston 2; April 16, at Boston — Toronto 1, Boston 3.

1938 – CHICAGO BLACKHAWKS

The Blackhawks entered the Finals without top goaltender Mike Karakas, who had played every game during the season but broke his big toe on April 3. Chicago was forced to sign the New York Americans' Alfred Moore, who played game one and posted a win in his only Stanley Cup appearance.

Following the victory, NHL President Frank Calder ruled Moore ineligible for further play, and Chicago had to call on minor-league goalie Paul Goodman, who lost his first NHL start in game two.

For games three and four, Karakas returned with a steel-plated boot to protect his toe and won both starts. Teammate Doc Romnes wore a football helmet to guard a broken nose and scored the winning goal in game three before a record crowd of 18,497.

Eight Americans – Karakas, Romnes, Alex Levinsky, Carl Voss, Carl Dahlstrom, Roger Jenkins, Louis Trudel and Virgil Johnson – skated for the Blackhawks to set a record for U.S. players on a Cup-winning team.

Former baseball umpire Bill Stewart of Chicago became the 6th NHL rookie coach to win the Stanley Cup.

1937-38 — Chicago Black Hawks — Art Wiebe, Carl Voss, Hal Jackson, Mike Karakas, Mush March, Jack Shill, Earl Seibert, Cully Dahlstrom, Alex Levinsky, Johnny Gottselig, Lou Trudel, Pete Palangio, Bill MacKenzie, Doc Romnes, Paul Thompson, Roger Jenkins, Alf Moore, Bert Connolly, Virgil Johnson, Paul Goodman, Bill Stewart (manager-coach), Eddie Froelich (trainer).
Scores: April 5, at Toronto — Chicago 3, Toronto 1; April 7, at Toronto — Chicago 1, Toronto 5; April 10 at Chicago — Chicago 2, Toronto 1; April 12, at Chicago — Chicago 4, Toronto 1.

1937 – DETROIT RED WINGS

The Rangers, turned away again from Madison Square Garden by the incoming circus after game one, agreed to play the remainder of the series on Detroit ice.

First-year goaltender Earl Robertson, who would never play a regular-season game for the Red Wings, became the first rookie netminder to post two shutouts in the Finals, blanking the Rangers in the last two games of the series.

With their second straight Stanley Cup, Detroit became the first U.S.-based team to repeat as champions.

1936-37 — Detroit Red Wings — Normie Smith, Pete Kelly, Larry Aurie, Herbie Lewis, Hec Kilrea, Mud Bruneteau, Syd Howe, Wally Kilrea, Jimmy Franks, Bucko McDonald, Gordon Pettinger, Ebbie Goodfellow, Johnny Gallagher, Scotty Bowman, Johnny Sorrell, Marty Barry, Earl Robertson, Johnny Sherf, Howard Mackie, Jack Adams (manager-coach), Honey Walker (trainer).
Scores: April 6, at New York — Detroit 1, Rangers 5; April 8, at Detroit — Detroit 4, Rangers 2; April 11, at Detroit — Detroit 0, Rangers 1; April 13, at Detroit — Detroit 1, Rangers 0; April 15, at Detroit — Detroit 3, Rangers 0.

1936 – DETROIT RED WINGS

Under the coaching of Jack Adams, the Detroit Red Wings captured their first Stanley Cup after 10 NHL seasons.

1935-36 — Detroit Red Wings — Johnny Sorrell, Syd Howe, Marty Barry, Herbie Lewis, Mud Bruneteau, Wally Kilrea, Hec Kilrea, Gordon Pettinger, Bucko McDonald, Scotty Bowman, Pete Kelly, Doug Young, Ebbie Goodfellow, Normie Smith, Jack Adams (manager-coach), Honey Walker (trainer).
Scores: April 5, at Detroit — Detroit 3, Toronto 1; April 7, at Detroit — Detroit 9, Toronto 4; April 9, at Toronto — Detroit 3, Toronto 4; April 11, at Toronto — Detroit 3, Toronto 1.

1935 – MONTREAL MAROONS

In the first All-Canadian Final since 1926, the Maroons battled to their second Stanley Cup championship in nine seasons with a sweep of Toronto. Montreal netminder Alex Connell allowed four goals in three games.

1934-35 — Montreal Maroons — Marvin (Cy) Wentworth, Alex Connell, Toe Blake, Stew Evans, Earl Robinson, Bill Miller, Dave Trottier, Jimmy Ward, Larry Northcott, Hooley Smith, Russ Blinco, Allan Shields, Sammy McManus, Gus Marker, Bob Gracie, Herb Cain, Tommy Gorman (manager), Lionel Conacher (coach), Bill O'Brien (trainer).
Scores: April 4, at Toronto — Montreal 3, Toronto 2; April 6, at Toronto — Montreal 3, Toronto 1; April 9, at Montreal — Montreal 4, Toronto 1.

1934 – CHICAGO BLACKHAWKS

For the second year in a row, the Stanley Cup-winning goal was scored in overtime, as Chicago's Harold "Mush" March netted the winner and gave the Blackhawks their first Cup.

Chicago's Chuck Gardiner limited Detroit to two goals in his club's three victories, while Detroit's Wilf Cude led the Red Wings to their only win in game three, despite suffering a broken nose mid-way through the contest.

1933-34 — Chicago Black Hawks — Taffy Abel, Lolo Couture, Lou Trudel, Lionel Conacher, Paul Thompson, Leroy Goldsworthy, Art Coulter, Roger Jenkins, Don McFayden, Tommy Cook, Doc Romnes, Johnny Gottselig, Mush March, Johny Sheppard, Chuck Gardiner (captain), Bill Kendall, Tommy Gorman (manager-coach), Eddie Froelich (trainer).
Scores: April 3, at Detroit — Detroit 1, Chicago 2; April 5, at Detroit — Detroit 1, Chicago 4; April 8, at Chicago — Detroit 5, Chicago 2; April 10, at Chicago — Detroit 0, Chicago 1.

1933 – NEW YORK RANGERS

Again the circus forced the Rangers out of New York, with all but game one contested on Toronto ice.

In the final match, the Rangers' Bill Cook became the first of 12 players to register a Cup-winning goal in overtime when he snapped a scoreless tie at 7:33 of the fourth period. Goalie Andy Aitkenhead posted the fourth shutout by an NHL rookie in the Finals.

1932-33 — New York Rangers — Ching Johnson, Butch Keeling, Frank Boucher, Art Somers, Babe Siebert, Bun Cook, Andy Aitkenhead, Ott Heller, Ozzie Asmundson, Gord Pettinger, Doug Brennan, Cecil Dillon, Bill Cook (captain), Murray Murdock, Earl Seibert, Lester Patrick (manager-coach), Harry Westerby (trainer).
Scores: April 4, at New York — Toronto 1, Rangers 5; April 8, at Toronto — Toronto 1, Rangers 3; April 11, at Toronto — Toronto 3, Rangers 2; April 13, at Toronto — Toronto 0, Rangers 1.

The Toronto Maple Leafs, Stanley Cup Champions, 1931-'32. Front row, left to right: Charlie Conacher, Joe Primeau, King Clancy, Frank Selke, Conn Smythe, Dick Irvin, Hap Day, Ace Bailey, Busher Jackson. Top row: Harold Darragh, Tim Daley, Alex Levinsky, Red Horner, Andy Blair, Lorne Chabot, Harold Cotton, Bob Gracie, Ken Doraty. Missing: Earl Miller, Fred Robertson

1932 – TORONTO MAPLE LEAFS

After losing to Toronto in game one, the Rangers lost the home-ice advantage because the circus had once again invaded Madison Square Garden. Game two was moved to Boston.

Toronto's famed "Kid Line" – Harvey "Busher" Jackson, Charlie Conacher and Joe Primeau – made its Stanley Cup debut, combining for eight goals in three games.

The Leafs' Dick Irvin, who coached Chicago in the 1931 Finals, earned his first title as a coach.

1931-32 — Toronto Maple Leafs — Charlie Conacher, Harvey Jackson, King Clancy, Andy Blair, Red Horner, Lorne Chabot, Alex Levinsky, Joe Primeau, Hal Darragh, Hal Cotton, Frank Finnigan, Hap Day, Ace Bailey, Bob Gracie, Fred Robertson, Earl Miller, Conn Smythe (manager), Dick Irvin (coach), Tim Daly (trainer).
Scores: April 5 at New York — Toronto 6, New York Rangers 4; April 7, at Boston* — Toronto 6, New York Rangers 2; April 9, at Toronto — Toronto 6, New York Rangers 4.

* Ice was unavailable in Madison Square Garden and Rangers elected to play the second game on neutral ice.

1931 – MONTREAL CANADIENS

The Montreal Canadiens became the second NHL team to repeat as champions, duplicating the feat accomplished the Ottawa Senators in 1920-21.

Chicago's Dick Irvin made his Stanley Cup coaching debut against the team which he would later lead to three Cups.

Over 18,000 fans packed Chicago Stadium for game two to set a new record for the largest attendance in hockey history.

1930-31 — Montreal Canadiens — George Hainsworth, Wildor Larochelle, Marty Burke, Sylvio Mantha, Howie Morenz, Johnny Gagnon, Aurel Joliat, Armand Mondou, Pit Lepine, Albert Leduc, Georges Mantha, Art Lesieur, Nick Wasnie, Bert McCaffrey, Gus Rivers, Jean Pusie, Leo Dandurand (manager), Cecil Hart (coach), Ed Dufour (trainer).
Scores: April 3, at Chicago — Canadiens 2, Chicago 1; April 5, at Chicago — Canadiens 1, Chicago 2; April 9, at Montreal — Canadiens 2, Chicago 3; April 11, at Montreal — Canadiens 4, Chicago 2; April 14, at Montreal — Canadiens 2, Chicago 0.

1930 – MONTREAL CANADIENS

The defending champion Boston Bruins, who skated to the NHL's top regular-season record at 38-5-1, suffered their first back-to-back defeats all season as the Canadiens won the Stanley Cup.

1929-30 — Montreal Canadiens — George Hainsworth, Marty Burke, Sylvio Mantha, Howie Morenz, Bert McCaffrey, Aurel Joliat, Albert Leduc, Pit Lepine, Wildor Larochelle, Nick Wasnie, Gerald Carson, Armand Mondou, Georges Mantha, Gus Rivers, Leo Dandurand (manager), Cecil Hart (coach), Ed Dufour (trainer).
Scores: April 1 — Canadiens 3, Boston 0; April 3 — Canadiens 4, Boston 3.

1929 – BOSTON BRUINS

This series between the Bruins and Rangers marked the first time in Stanley Cup play that two American teams had clashed in the Finals.

Goalie Cecil "Tiny" Thompson backstopped the Bruins to consecutive wins, allowing just one goal as Boston captured its first Cup.

Dit Clapper and Harry Oliver scored the two game-winning goals.

1928-29 — Boston Bruins — Cecil (Tiny) Thompson, Eddie Shore, Lionel Hitchman, Perk Galbraith, Eric Pettinger, Frank Fredrickson, Mickey Mackay, Red Green, Dutch Gainor, Harry Oliver, Eddie Rodden, Dit Clapper, Cooney Weiland, Lloyd Klein, Cy Denneny, Bill Carson, George Owen, Myles Lane, Art Ross (manager-coach), Win Green (trainer).
Scores: March 28 — Rangers 0, Boston 2; March 29 — Rangers 1, Boston 2.

1928 – NEW YORK RANGERS

When the Rangers moved into the Finals, the circus moved into New York's Madison Square Garden and took priority over the hockey team. As a result, club management decided to play the entire series in Montreal.

After losing goalie Lorne Chabot to an eye injury mid-way through game two, 45-year-old Rangers' coach and former defenseman Lester Patrick took over between the pipes, inspiring the New Yorkers to a 2-1 overtime victory. The following day the Rangers signed New York Americans' netminder Joe Miller, who responded with two wins including the second shutout by an NHL rookie in Stanley Cup history.

In only their second NHL season, the Rangers captured their first Stanley Cup and became only the second American team in history, joining the 1917 Seattle Metropolitans of the PCHA, to possess the trophy.

1927-28 — New York Rangers — Lorne Chabot, Taffy Abel, Leon Bourgault, Ching Johnson, Bill Cook, Bun Cook, Frank Boucher, Billy Boyd, Murray Murdoch, Paul Thompson, Alex Gray, Joe Miller, Patsy Callighen, Lester Patrick (manager-coach), Harry Westerby (trainer).
Scores: April 5 — Rangers 0, Montreal 2; April 7 — Rangers 2, Montreal 1; April 10 — Rangers 0, Montreal 2; April 12 — Rangers 1, Montreal 0; April 14 — Rangers 2, Montreal 1.

1927 – OTTAWA SENATORS

The WCHL had folded the previous spring, and since no other major professional league existed, the Stanley Cup now became sole property of the NHL.

The American Division champion Boston Bruins met the Canadian champion Ottawa Senators in what became the first Stanley Cup Final of the modern era.

Cy Denneny led the Senators with four of the team's seven total goals, including the game-winners in both victories.

1926-27 — **Ottawa Senators** — Alex Connell, King Clancy, George (Buck) Boucher, Ed Gorman, Frank Finnigan, Alex Smith, Hec Kilrea, Hooley Smith, Cy Denneny, Frank Nighbor, Jack Adams, Milt Halliday, Dave Gil (manager-coach).
Scores: April 7 — Boston 0, Ottawa 0; April 9 — Boston 1, Ottawa 3; April 11 — Boston 1, Ottawa 1; April 13 — Boston 1, Ottawa 3.

The 1926 Montreal Maroons

1926 – MONTREAL MAROONS (NHL)

The Maroons had a new home for 1925-26 in the newly constructed Montreal Forum which had artificial ice, allowing the Stanley Cup Finals to start later than ever.

In his first Cup series defenseman Nels Stewart scored six of Montreal's 10 goals, and goaltender Clint Benedict recorded an unprecedented three shutouts en route to the Maroons' first Stanley Cup in the club's second NHL season.

1925-26 — **Montreal Maroons** — Clint Benedict, Reg Noble, Frank Carson, Dunc Munro, Nels Stewart, Harry Broadbent, Babe Siebert, Dinny Dinsmore, Bill Phillips, Hobart (Hobie) Kitchen, Sammy Rothschiel, Albert (Toots) Holway, Shorty Horne, Bern Brophy, Eddie Gerard (manager-coach), Bill O'Brien (trainer).
Scores: at Montreal, Maroons 3, Victoria 0; Maroons 3, Victoria 0; Victoria 3, Maroons 2; Maroons 2, Victoria 0. Total goals: Montreal 10, Victoria 3.

1925 – VICTORIA COUGARS (WCHL)

The Victoria Cougars, who joined the WCHL after the PCHA folded, became the last non-NHL team ever to win the Stanley Cup and only the third west coast club to capture the trophy, joining the 1915 Vancouver Millionaires and the 1917 Seattle Metropolitans as champions.

The Canadiens' were paced by the formidable Speedball Line of Howie Morenz, Aurel Joliat and Billy Boucher, who scored all eight Canadiens goals, but Victoria posted a more balanced attack with eight different skaters combining for 16 goals.

1924-25 — Victoria Cougars — Harry (Happy) Holmes, Clem Loughlin, Gordie Fraser, Frank Fredrickson, Jack Walker, Harold (Gizzy) Hart, Harold (Slim) Halderson, Frank Foyston, Wally Elmer, Harry Meeking, Jocko Anderson, Lester Patrick (manager-coach).
Scores: at Victoria, Victoria 5, Montreal Canadiens 2; Victoria 3, Canadiens 1; Canadiens 4, Victoria 2; Victoria 6, Canadiens 1. Total goals: Victoria 16, Canadiens 8.

1924 – MONTREAL CANADIENS (NHL)

21-year-old, 160-pound rookie forward Howie Morenz paced the Montreal attack with a hat-trick in game one and added another in game two as the Canadiens rolled past the Calgary Tigers to complete a sweep of both 1924 series.

Morenz, Aurel Joliat and Sylvio Mantha all made their first appearances on a Stanley Cup winner.

Billy Boucher scored three of the Canadiens' five goals, including both game-winning tallies, to lift Montreal over Vancouver, which lost its chance at the Stanley Cup for the third straight year.

1923-24 — Montreal Canadiens — Georges Vezina, Sprague Cleghorn, Billy Couture, Howie Morenz, Aurel Joliat, Billy Boucher, Odie Cleghorn, Sylvio Mantha, Bobby Boucher, Billy Bell, Billy Cameron, Joe Malone, Fortier, Leo Dandurand (manager-coach).
Scores: at Montreal, Canadiens 3, Vancouver 2; Canadiens 2, Vancouver 1. Total goals, Canadiens 5, Vancouver 3. Canadiens 6, Calgary 1; (the second game was transferred to Ottawa to benefit from artificial ice surface) Canadiens 3, Calgary 0. Total goals: Canadiens 9, Calgary 1. [Because of an agreement between the NHL and the two western Leagues (WCHL and PCHA) Canadiens had to play the champions of each league in the Stanley Cup series in 1924.]

1923 – OTTAWA SENATORS (NHL)

The western playoff format had been abandoned, and when Ottawa had disposed of Vancouver of the PCHA (formerly the WCHA) the WCHL champions were given the opportunity to compete for the Stanley Cup in a best-of-three series. The Eskimos gave the battle-weary Senators a difficult time, but Ottawa came through with one-goal victories in each game. Cy Denneny and Harry Broadbent scored the game-winners.

For the first time in Stanley Cup history, brothers opposed each other in the Finals. Not one but two sets of siblings – Cy and Corb Denneny and George and Frank Boucher – stood on opposite sides of the center line for the opening face-off – Cy and George with Ottawa, Corb and Frank with Vancouver. Neither of the Dennenys scored in the series, but each of the Bouchers scored twice.

Ottawa's Harry Broadbent, who posted the only goal in game one, scored five for the series to lead the Senators, whom Vancouver coach Frank Patrick called the greatest team he had ever seen.

1922-23 — Ottawa Senators — George (Buck) Boucher, Lionel Hitchman, Frank Nighbor, King Clancy, Harry Helman, Clint Benedict, Jack Darragh, Eddie Gerard, Cy Denneny, Harry Broadbent, Tommy Gorman (manager), Pete Green (coach), F. Dolan (trainer).
Scores: at Vancouver, Ottawa 1, Vancouver 0; Vancouver 4, Ottawa 1; Ottawa 3, Vancouver 2; Ottawa 5, Vancouver 1, Ottawa also met and defeated Edmonton Eskimos, Champions of the WCHL. The scores: Ottawa 2, Edmonton 1; Ottawa 1, Edmonton 0. Total goals: Ottawa 10, Vancouver 7; Ottawa 3, Edmonton 1.

1922 – TORONTO ST. PATRICKS (NHL)

With the inception of the Western Canada Hockey League (WCHL) in 1921-1922, a new playoff structure was designed to match the champions of the two west coast leagues against each other with the winner to meet the NHL champions for the Stanley Cup.

After defeating the WCHL's Regina Capitals in the preliminary series, the WCHA's Vancouver Millionaires set out for Toronto, where the NHL champion St. Pats awaited their arrival.

Cecil "Babe" Dye notched nine of his club's 16 goals, including two game-winners, and goaltender John Roach, who recorded the first Stanley Cup shutout ever by an NHL rookie, posted a 1.80 average as Toronto won its second Stanley Cup.

Jack Adams, who had been lured away from Toronto by Vancouver in 1920, returned to the eastern city and scored six goals in the series.

1921-22 — Toronto St. Pats — Ted Stackhouse, Corb Denneny, Rod Smylie, Lloyd Andrews, John Ross Roach, Harry Cameron, Bill (Red) Stuart, Cecil (Babe) Dye, Ken Randall, Reg Noble, Eddie Gerard (borrowed for one game from Ottawa), Stan Jackson, Nolan Mitchell, Charlie Querrie (manager), Eddie Powers (coach).
Scores: at Toronto, Vancouver 4, Toronto 3; Toronto 2, Vancouver 1; Vancouver 3, Toronto 0; Toronto 6, Vancouver 0; Toronto 5, Vancouver 1. Total goals: Toronto 16, Vancouver 9.

1921 – OTTAWA SENATORS (NHL)

11,000 fans, the largest crowd ever to see a hockey game at the time, jammed the Vancouver arena for the first game of this series, and an estimated 51,000 tickets were sold for the entire five-game series.

Jack Darragh was the hero for the second straight year, scoring both Ottawa goals in the finale as the Senators became the first NHL club to capture back-to-back Stanley Cups and the first team since the 1912-13 Quebec Bulldogs to repeat as champions.

1920-21 — Ottawa Senators — Jack McKell, Jack Darragh, Morley Bruce, George (Buck) Boucher, Eddie Gerard, Clint Benedict, Sprague Cleghorn, Frank Nighbor, Harry Broadbent, Cy Denneny, Leth Graham, Tommy Gorman (manager), Pete Green (coach), F. Dolan (trainer).
Scores: at Vancouver, Vancouver 2, Ottawa 1; Ottawa 4, Vancouver 3; Ottawa 3, Vancouver 2; Vancouver 3, Ottawa 2; Ottawa 2, Vancouver 1; Total goals: Ottawa 12, Vancouver 11.

1920 – OTTAWA SENATORS (NHL)

When the Mets arrived in Ottawa, it became apparent that their red, white and green barber pole uniforms were all too similar to the Senators' red, white and black pattern. Ottawa agreed to play in white jerseys.

Poor ice conditions marred the first three games, and the series was shifted to the artifical surface at Toronto's Mutual Arena. Jack Darragh, who tallied the winning marker in game one, lifted Ottawa to the championship with a hat-trick in the decisive game.

Pete Green became the second rookie coach in the NHL to win the Cup, joining Dick Carroll of the 1918 Toronto Arenas.

1919-20 — Ottawa Senators — Jack McKell, Jack Darragh, Morley Bruce, Horrace Merrill, George (Buck) Boucher, Eddie Gerard, Clint Benedict, Sprague Cleghorn, Frank Nighbor, Harry Broadbent, Cy Denneny, Price, Tommy Gorman (manager), Pete Green (coach).
Scores: at Ottawa, Ottawa 3, Seattle 2; Ottawa 3, Seattle 0; Seattle 3, Ottawa 1. Mild weather ruined natural ice surface at Ottawa rink and necessitated the transfer of two games of the series to Toronto's artificial rink. At Toronto — Seattle 5, Ottawa 2; Ottawa 6, Seattle 1. Total goals: Ottawa 15, Seattle 11.

Joe Hall

1919 – NO DECISION

Seattle's Frank Foyston and Montreal's Newsy Lalonde, two of the greatest scorers of the early 1900s, were at their best in this series. Foyston notched nine goals and Lalonde six as the clubs stood even at two wins and one tie apiece after five games.

But at that point several of the players became seriously sick with the flu, which had reached epidemic proportions throughout the country, and health officials were forced to cancel the remaining games. Canadiens' defenseman Joe Hall, hospitalized with a severe case, died on April 5, 1919, in Seattle.

Scores: at Seattle, Seattle 7, Canadiens 0; Canadiens 4, Seattle 2; Seattle 7, Canadiens 2; Seattle 0, Canadiens 0 (20 minutes overtime); Canadiens 4, Seattle 3 (15:57 overtime). Total goals: Seattle 19, Canadiens 10.

1918 – TORONTO ARENAS (NHL)

Prior to the start of the 1917-18 campaign, the NHA dissolved and the NHL took its place. The new league started with four teams – Montreal Canadiens, Montreal Wanderers, Ottawa Senators and Toronto Arenas – but the Wanderers withdrew after the Montreal Arena burned down.

After capturing the first NHL title, Toronto played host to Vancouver, with the series alternating between eastern rules in the odd-numbered games and western rules in the even-numbered games. Toronto won the series, with the advantage of playing the final game under eastern rules.

Alf Skinner led the Arenas with eight goals, while Fred "Cyclone" Taylor paced Vancouver with nine. Rookie coach Dick Carroll steered his team to the NHL's first Stanley Cup championship.

1917-18 — Toronto Arenas — Rusty Crawford, Harry Meeking, Ken Randall, Corb Denneny, Harry Cameron, Jack Adams, Alf Skinner, Harry Mummery, Harry (Happy) Holmes, Reg Noble, Sammy Hebert, Jack Marks, Jack Coughlin, Neville, Charlie Querrie (manager), Dick Carroll (coach), Frank Carroll (trainer).
Scores: at Toronto, Toronto 5, Vancouver 3; Vancouver 6, Toronto 4; Toronto 6, Vancouver 3; Vancouver 8, Toronto 1; Toronto 2, Vancouver 1. Total goals: Vancouver 21, Toronto 18.

The 1900 Montreal Shamrocks defeated teams from Winnipeg and Halifax.

The 1906 Kenora Thistles were a team of stars and future Hall of Famers including Joe Hall, top row right, Si Griffis, bottom row left and Art Ross, bottom row right.

STANLEY CUP WINNERS PRIOR TO FORMATION OF NHL IN 1917

Season	Champions	Season	Champions
1916-17	Seattle Metropolitans	1903-04	Ottawa Silver Seven
1915-16	Montreal Canadiens	1902-03	Ottawa Silver Seven
1914-15	Vancouver Millionaires	1901-02	Montreal A.A.A.
1913-14	Toronto Blueshirts	1900-01	Winnipeg Victorias
1912-13**	Quebec Bulldogs	1899-1900	Montreal Shamrocks
1911-12	Quebec Bulldogs	1898-99	Montreal Shamrocks
1910-11	Ottawa Senators	1897-98	Montreal Victorias
1909-10	Montreal Wanderers	1896-97	Montreal Victorias
1908-09	Ottawa Senators	1895-96	Montreal Victorias (December, 1896)
1907-08	Montreal Wanderers		
1906-07	Montreal Wanderers (March)	1895-96	Winnipeg Victorias (February)
1906-07	Kenora Thistles (January)	1894-95	Montreal Victorias
1905-06	Montreal Wanderers	1893-94	Montreal A.A.A.
1904-05	Ottawa Silver Seven	1892-93	Montreal A.A.A.

**Victoria defeated Quebec in challenge series.

Stanley Cup Championship Teams

1987-1893

A total of 782 players have skated for Stanley Cup championship teams since the trophy was first awarded to the Montreal Amateur Athletic Association (AAA) hockey club in 1893. Of the 782, 396 players (50.6%) have played on one Cup winner, while 386 (49.4%) have won on two or more occasions.

Stanley Cups/players

Wins	Total	1	2	3	4	5	6	7	8	9	10	11
Players	782	396	202	72	67	25	11	2	3	1	2	2
%	(100.0)	(50.6)	(25.8)	(9.2)	(8.6)	(3.2)	(1.4)					

Henri Richard holds the record for most times on a Stanley Cup winning team with 11. Richard won all of his 11 as a player with the Montreal Canadiens. Toe Blake also captured 11, three as a player, with the Montreal Maroons and Canadiens, and eight as coach of the Canadiens. During Richard's 20-year NHL career from 1955-56 to 1974-75, "The Pocket Rocket" never played more than four consecutive seasons without earning a new Stanley Cup ring.

Henri Richard

Jean Beliveau and Yvan Cournoyer of the Canadiens share second place behind Richard with 10 Cups apiece, and Montreal's Claude Provost ranks third with nine. Red Kelly, Maurice Richard and Jacques Lemaire are tied with eight, while Serge Savard and Jean-Guy Talbot have seven each.

20 players have captured six or more Stanley Cups, but Kelly is the only one who did not play for the Canadiens. Kelly played for a total of eight Cup champions, four with the Detroit Red Wings and four with the Toronto Maple Leafs.

Of the 384 players to win more than one Stanley Cup, 307 won with the same team every time. 71 players won with two teams, while five won with three and one won with four.

Jack Marshall owns the record for playing with four different teams to win the Stanley Cup. Marshall played on championship teams with the 1901 Winnipeg Vics, 1902 Montreal Maroons, 1907 and 1910 Montreal Wanderers and 1914 Toronto Blueshirts.

Five players skated for three different Stanley Cup winning franchises in their careers. Frank Foyston and Jack Walker won three Cups in their careers with three different clubs, while Larry Hillman, Harry Holmes and Gordon Pettinger won four Cups with three teams.

Of the 782 players to have played for a Stanley Cup champion, 283 won at least once as a member of a Montreal-based team, including 182 with the Montreal Canadiens.

Stanley Cup Championship Teams
Index of Players, 1987-1893

-A-

Abel, Clarence "Taffy"   NY Rangers 1928; Chicago 1934
Abel, Sid   Detroit 1943, 1950, 1952
Adams, Jack   Toronto 1918; Ottawa 1927
Aitkenhead, Andy   NY Rangers 1933
Allen, "Bones"   Ottawa 1905
Allen, Keith   Detroit 1954
Anderson, Doug   Montreal 1953
Anderson, Glenn   Edmonton 1984-85, 1987
Anderson, Jocko   Victoria 1925
Andrews, Lloyd   Toronto 1922
Apps, Syl   Toronto 1942, 1947-48
Arbour, Al   Chicago 1961; Toronto 1962, 1964
Arbour, Amos   Montreal 1916
Armitage, J.C.   Winnipeg Vics 1896
Armstrong, George   Toronto 1962-63-64, 1967
Arnold, Josh   Mtl. Wanderers 1906
Ashbee, Barry   Philadelphia 1974
Asmundson, Ossie   NY Rangers 1933
Aurie, Larry   Detroit 1936-37
Awrey, Don   Boston 1970, 1972

-B-

Babando, Pete   Detroit 1950
Backor, Peter   Toronto 1945
Backstrom, Ralph   Montreal 1959-60, 1965-66, 1968-69
Bailey, Garnet   Boston 1972
Bailey, Irvin "Ace"   Toronto 1932
Bain, Dan   Winnipeg Vics 1896, 1901
Balfour, Earl   Chicago 1961
Balfour, Murray   Chicago 1961
Balon, Dave   Montreal 1965-66
Barber, Bill   Philadelphia 1974-75
Barilko, Bill   Toronto 1947-48-49, 1951
Barlow, Billy   Mtl. AAA 1893-94
Barry, Marty   Detroit 1936-37
Bathgate, Andy   Toronto 1964
Bauer, Bobby   Boston 1939, 1941
Baun, Bob   Toronto 1962-63-64, 1967
Beaudro, Roxy   Kenora 1907
Beliveau, Jean   Montreal 1956-57-58-59-60, 1965-66, 1968-69, 1971
Bell, Billy   Montreal 1924
Bellingham, Billy   Mtl. AAA 1902
Benedict, Clint   Ottawa 1920-21, 1923; Mtl. Maroons 1926
Benoit, Joe   Montreal 1946
Bentley, Max   Toronto 1948-49, 1951
Berenson, Gordon "Red"   Montreal 1965-66
Berlinquette, Louis   Montreal 1916
Beukeboom, Jeff   Edmonton 1987
Blachford, Cecil   Mtl. Wanderers 1906-07-08, 1910
Black, Stephen   Detroit 1950
Bladon, Tom   Philadelphia 1974-75
Blair, Andy   Toronto 1932
Blake, Hector "Toe"   Mtl. Maroons 1935; Montreal 1944, 1946
Blinco, Russ   Mtl. Maroons 1935
Bodnar, Gus   Toronto 1945, 1947
Boesch, Garth   Toronto 1947-48-49
Boisvert, Serge   Montreal 1986
Bonin, Marcel   Detroit 1955; Montreal 1958-59-60
Boon, Dick   Mtl. AAA 1902
Bordeleau, Christian   Montreal 1969
Bossy, Mike   NY Islanders 1980-81-82-83
Bouchard, Emile "Butch"   Montreal 1944, 1946, 1953, 1956
Bouchard, Pierre   Montreal 1971, 1973, 1976-77-78
Boucher, Billy   Montreal 1924
Boucher, Bobby   Montreal 1924
Boucher, Frank   NY Rangers 1928, 1933
Boucher, George   Ottawa 1920-21, 1923, 1927
Bourgeault, Leo   NY Rangers 1928
Bourne, Bob   NY Islanders 1980-81-82-83
Boutilier, Paul   NY Islanders 1983
Bower, Johnny   Toronto 1962-63-64, 1967
Bowman, Ralph "Scotty"   Detroit 1936-37
Boyd, Bill   NY Rangers 1928
Brannen, Jack   Mtl. Shamrocks 1899-1900
Brennan, Doug   NY Rangers 1933
Brewer, Carl   Toronto 1962-63-64
Brimsek, Frank   Boston 1931, 1941
Broadbent, Harry   Ottawa 1920-21, 1923; Mtl. Maroons 1926
Broda, Walter "Turk"   Toronto 1942, 1947-48-49, 1951
Broden, Connie   Montreal 1957-58
Brophy, Bernie   Mtl. Maroons 1926
Brown, A.   Winnipeg Vics 1901
Brown, Adam   Detroit 1943
Brown, Pat   Detroit 1943
Bruce, Morley   Ottawa 1920-21
Bruneteau, Modere "Mud"   Detroit 1936-37, 1943
Buchberger, Kelly   Edmonton 1987
Bucyk, Johnny   Boston 1970, 1972
Burke, Marty   Montreal 1930-31

-C-

Cain, Herb   Mtl. Maroons 1935; Boston 1941
Cain, J.   Mtl. Maroons 1926
Callighen, Pat   NY Rangers 1928
Cameron, Allan   Mtl. AAA 1893-94
Cameron, Billy   Montreal 1924
Cameron, Harry   Toronto 1914, 1918, 1922
Campbell, C.J.   Winnipeg Vics 1896
Carbonneau, Guy   Montreal 1986
Carleton, Wayne   Boston 1970
Carpenter, Ed   Seattle 1917
Carr, Lorne   Toronto 1942, 1945
Carroll, Billy   NY Islanders 1981-82-83; Edmonton 1985
Carson, Bill   Boston 1929
Carson, Frank   Mtl. Maroons 1926
Carson, Gerald   Montreal 1930
Carveth, Joe   Detroit 1943, 1950
Cashman, Wayne   Boston 1970, 1972
Chabot, Lorne   NY Rangers 1928; Toronto 1932
Chamberlain, Erwin "Murph"   Montreal 1944, 1946
Chartraw, Rick   Montreal 1976-77-78-79
Cheevers, Gerry   Boston 1970, 1972
Chelios, Chris   Montreal 1986
Clancy, Frank "King"   Ottawa 1923, 1927; Toronto 1932
Clapper, Aubrey "Dit"   Boston 1929, 1939, 1941
Clarke, Bobby   Philadelphia 1974-75
Cleghorn, Odie   Montreal 1924
Cleghorn, Sprague   Ottawa 1920-21; Montreal 1924
Clement, Bill   Philadelphia 1974-75
Coffey, Paul   Edmonton 1984-85, 1987
Collins, Herb   Mtl. AAA 1894
Colville, Mac   NY Rangers 1940
Colville, Neil   NY Rangers 1940
Conacher, Brian   Toronto 1967
Conacher, Charlie   Toronto 1932
Conacher, Lionel   Chicago 1934; Mtl. Maroons 1935
Conacher, Pat   Edmonton 1984
Conacher, Roy   Boston 1939, 1941
Connell, Alex   Ottawa 1927; Mtl. Maroons 1935
Connolly, Bert   Chicago 1938
Connor, Cam   Montreal 1979
Cook, Bill   NY Rangers 1928, 1933
Cook, Fred "Bun"   NY Rangers 1928, 1933
Cook, Lloyd   Vancouver 1915

Cook, Tom   *Chicago 1934*
Corbeau, Bert   *Montreal 1916*
Corbeau, Con   *Toronto 1914*
Costello, Les   *Toronto 1948*
Cotton, Harold "Baldy"   *Toronto 1932*
Coughlin, Jack   *Toronto 1918*
Coulter, Art   *Chicago 1934; NY Rangers 1940*
Cournoyer, Yvan   *Montreal 1965-66, 1968-69, 1971, 1973, 1976-77-78-79*
Couture, Billy "Coutu"   *Montreal 1924*
Couture, Gerald "Doc"   *Detroit 1950*
Cowick, Bruce   *Philadelphia 1974*
Cowley, Bill   *Boston 1939, 1941*
Crawford, Jack   *Boston 1931, 1941*
Crawford, Russell "Rusty"   *Quebec 1913; Toronto 1918*
Creighton, Billy   *Quebec 1913*
Crisp, Terry   *Philadelphia 1974-75*
Currie, Alex   *Ottawa 1911*
Curry, Floyd   *Montreal 1953, 1956-57-58*

Floyd Curry

-D-
Dahlin, Kjell   *Montreal 1986*
Dahlstrom, Carl "Cully"   *Chicago 1938*
Dalby   *Mtl. Shamrocks 1899*
Darragh, Harold   *Toronto 1932*
Darragh, Jack   *Ottawa 1911, 1920-21, 1923*
Davidson, Bob   *Toronto 1942, 1945*
Davidson, Cam   *Mtl. Victorias 1896-97-98*
Davidson, Shirley   *Mtl. Victorias 1895-96-97*
Davis, Lorne   *Montreal 1953*
Dawes, Robert   *Toronto 1949*
Day, Clarence "Hap"   *Toronto 1932*
DeBlois, Lucien   *Montreal 1986*
Delvecchio, Alex   *Detroit 1952, 1954-55*
Denneny, Corb   *Toronto 1918, 1922*
Denneny, Cy   *Ottawa 1920-21, 1923, 1927; Boston 1929*
Dewsbury, Al   *Detroit 1950*
Dey, Edgar   *Ottawa 1909*
Dickens, Ernie   *Toronto 1942*
Dillon, Cecil   *NY Rangers 1933*
Dineen, Bill   *Detroit 1954-55*
Dinsmore, Chuck   *Mtl. Maroons 1926*
Doak, Gary   *Boston 1970*
Dornhoefer, Gary   *Philadelphia 1974-75*
Douglas, Kent   *Toronto 1963*
Douglas, Les   *Detroit 1943*
Drillon, Gordie   *Toronto 1942*
Drinkwater, Graham   *Mtl. Victorias 1895-96-97-98*

Dryden, Ken   *Montreal 1971, 1973, 1976-77-78-79*
Dube, Gilles   *Detroit 1954*
Duff, Dick   *Toronto 1962-63; Montreal 1965-66, 1968-69*
Dumart, Woody   *Boston 1931, 1941*
Dupont, Andre "Moose"   *Philadelphia 1974-75*
Durnan, Bill   *Montreal 1944, 1946*
Dye, Cecil "Babe"   *Toronto 1922*

-E-
Eddolls, Frank   *Montreal 1946*
Ehman, Gerry   *Toronto 1964*
Elliot, Roland   *Mtl. Victorias 1895; Mtl. AAA 1902*
Ellis, Ron   *Toronto 1967*
Elmer, Wally   *Victoria 1925*
Engblom, Brian   *Montreal 1977-78-79*
Erickson, Aut   *Toronto 1967*
Esposito, Phil   *Boston 1970, 1972*
Esposito, Tony   *Montreal 1969*
Evans, Jack   *Chicago 1961*
Evans, Stewart   *Mtl. Maroons 1935*
Ewing, J.   *Mtl. Victorias 1897-98*
Ezinicki, Bill   *Toronto 1947-48-49*

-F-
Farrell, Art   *Mtl. Shamrocks 1899-1900*
Fenwick, Art   *Mtl. Victorias 1895*
Ferguson, John   *Montreal 1965-66, 1968-69, 1971*
Fillion, Bob   *Montreal 1944, 1946*
Finnie, Dave   *Ottawa 1905*
Finnigan, Frank   *Ottawa 1927; Toronto 1932*
Fisher, Joe   *Detroit 1943*
Flaman, Fern   *Toronto 1951*
Fleming, Reg   *Chicago 1961*
Flett, Bill   *Philadelphia 1974*
Flett, Magnus   *Winnipeg Vics 1901*
Flett, Rod   *Winnipeg Vics 1896, 1901*
Fogolin, Lee Sr.   *Detroit 1950*
Fogolin, Lee Jr.   *Edmonton 1984-85*
Fortier, Charles   *Montreal 1924*
Fournier, Jack   *Montreal 1916*
Foyston, Frank   *Toronto 1914; Seattle 1917; Victoria 1925*
Franks, Jim   *Detroit 1937*
Fraser   *Ottawa 1903*
Fraser, Gordon   *Victoria 1925*
Fredrickson, Frank   *Victoria 1925, Boston 1929*
Fuhr, Grant   *Edmonton 1984-85, 1987*

-G-
Gagnon, John   *Montreal 1931*
Gainey, Bob   *Montreal 1976-77-78-79, 1986*
Gainor, Norman "Dutch"   *Boston 1929; Montreal 1944*
Galbraith, Percy "Perk"   *Boston 1929*
Gallagher, John   *Detroit 1937*
Gamble, Dick   *Montreal 1953, 1956*
Gardiner, Charlie   *Chicago 1934*
Gardner, Cal   *Toronto 1949, 1951*
Gardner, Jimmy   *Mtl. AAA 1902; Mtl. Wanderers 1910*
Gaul, Horace   *Ottawa 1905, 1911*
Gauthier, Jean   *Montreal 1965*
Gee, George   *Detroit 1950*
Geoffrion, Bernie "Boom Boom"   *Montreal 1953, 1956-57-58-59-60*
Gerard, Eddie   *Ottawa 1920-21, 1923; Toronto 1922*
Geroux, Eddie   *Kenora 1907*
Getliffe, Ray   *Boston 1939; Montreal 1944*
Gilbert, Greg   *NY Islanders 1982-83*
Gillelan, D.   *Mtl. Victorias 1896-97*
Gillies, Clark   *NY Islanders 1980-81-82-83*
Gilmour, Billy   *Ottawa 1903-04-05, 1909*
Gilmour, Dave   *Ottawa 1903*

Gilmour, Larry Mtl. Wanderers 1908
Gilmour, Suddy Ottawa 1903-04
Gingras, Gaston Montreal 1986
Gingras, Tony Winnipeg Vics 1901
Glass, Frank "Pud" Mtl. Wanderers 1906-07-08, 1910
Goldham, Bob Toronto 1942; Detroit 1952, 1954-55
Goldsworthy, Leroy Chicago 1934
Goldup, Hank Toronto 1942
Goodenough, Larry Philadelphia 1975
Goodfellow, Ebbie Detroit 1936-37, 1943
Goodman, Paul Chicage 1938
Goring, Butch NY Islanders 1980-81-82-83
Gorman, Ed Ottawa 1927
Gottselig, John Chicago 1934, 1938
Goyette, Phil Montreal 1957-58-59-60
Gracie, Bob Toronto 1932; Mtl. Maroons 1935
Graham, Leth Ottawa 1921
Grant, Danny Montreal 1968
Grant, Mike Mtl. Victorias 1895-96-97-98
Gray, Alex NY Rangers 1928
Green, Red Boston 1929
Green, Rick Montreal 1986
Green, Ted Boston 1972
Gregg, Randy Edmonton 1984-85, 1987
Grenier, Lucien Montreal 1969
Gretzky, Wayne Edmonton 1984-85, 1987
Griffis, Si Kenora 1907; Vancouver 1915
Grosso, Don Detroit 1943

-H-

Haidy, Gordon Detroit 1950
Hainsworth, George Montreal 1930-31
Halderson, Harold "Slim" Victoria 1925
Hall, Glenn Chicago 1961
Hall, Joe Quebec 1912-13
Halliday, Milt Ottawa 1927
Hallin, Mats NY Islanders 1983
Hamill, Robert Boston 1939
Hamilton, Reg Toronto 1942, 1945
Harmon, Glen Montreal 1944, 1946
Harper, Terry Montreal 1965-66, 1968-69, 1971
Harris, Ted Montreal 1965-66, 1968-69;
 Philadelphia 1975
Harris, Billy Toronto 1962-63-64
Harriston Toronto 1914
Hart, Harold "Gizzy" Victoria 1925
Harvey, Doug Montreal 1953, 1956-57-58-59-60
Hay, James Detroit 1955
Hay, Bill Chicago 1961
Hayes, Chris Boston 1972
Hebert, Sammy Toronto 1918
Heffernan, Gerry Montreal 1944
Heller, Ott NY Rangers 1933. 1940
Helman, Harry Ottawa 1923
Henderson, Harold Mtl. Victorias 1895-96-97
Henning, Lorne NY Islanders 1980-81
Hern, Riley Mtl. Wanderers 1907-08, 1910
Hextall, Bryan Sr. NY Rangers 1940
Hicke, Bill Montreal 1959-60
Hicks, Wayne Chicago 1961
Higginbotham Winnipeg Vics 1896
Hill, Mel Boston 1939, 1941; Toronto 1945
Hiller, Wilbur "Dutch" NY Rangers 1940;
 Montreal 1946
Hillman, Larry Detroit 1955; Toronto 1964, 1967;
 Montreal 1969
Hillman, Wayne Chicago 1961
Hitchman, Lionel Ottawa 1923; Boston 1929
Hodge, Charlie Montreal 1965
Hodge, Ken Boston 1970, 1972
Hodge, Tom Mtl. AAA 1902
Hodgson, Archie Mtl. AAA 1893-94
Hoerner Mtl. Shamrocks 1899
Hollett, Bill Boston 1939, 1941
Holmes, Harry Toronto 1914, 1918; Seattle 1917;
 Victoria 1925
Holway, Albert "Toots" Mtl. Maroons 1926
Hooper, Art Mtl. AAA 1902

Tim Horton

Hooper, Tom Kenora 1907; Mtl. Wanderers 1908
Horne, George "Shorty" Mtl. Maroons 1926
Horner, Reg Toronto 1932
Horton, Tim Toronto 1962-63-64, 1967
Houle, Rejean Montreal 1971, 1973, 1977-78-79
Howard, Howard Winnipeg Vics 1896
Howatt, Garry NY Islanders 1980-81
Howe, Gordie Detroit 1950, 1952, 1954-55
Howe, Syd Detroit 1936-37, 1943
Huddy, Charlie Edmonton 1984-85, 1987
Hughes, Pat Montreal 1979; Edmonton 1984-85
Hull, Bobby Chicago 1961
Hunter, Dave Edmonton 1984-85, 1987
Hutton, Bouse Ottawa 1903-04
Hyland, Harry Mtl. Wanderers 1910

-I-

Irving, Alex Mtl. AAA 1893-84

-J-

Jackson, Art Boston 1941; Toronto 1945
Jackson, Don Edmonton 1984-85
Jackson, Harold Chicago 1938; Detroit 1943
Jackson, Harvey "Busher" Toronto 1932
Jackson, Stan Toronto 1922
James, G. Mtl. AAA 1894
Jarvis, Doug Montreal 1976-77-78-79
Jeffrey, Larry Toronto 1967
Jenkins, Roger Chicago 1934, 1938
Johnson, Ernie Mtl. Wanderers 1906-07-08, 1910
Johnson, Ivan NY Rangers 1928, 1933
Johnson, Tom Montreal 1953, 1956-57-58-59-60
Johnson, Virgil Chicago 1938
Johnston, Ed Boston 1970, 1972
Johnstone, Charles Winnipeg Vics 1896, 1901
Johnstone, Ross Toronto 1945
Joliat, Aurel Montreal 1924, 1930-31
Jones, Robert Mtl. Victorias 1895-96
Jonsson, Tomas NY Islanders 1982-83
Juzda, Bill Toronto 1951

-K-

Kallur, Anders NY Islanders 1980-81-82-83
Kampman, Bingo Toronto 1942
Karakas, Mike Chicago 1938
Keeling, Melville "Butch" NY Rangers 1933
Kelly, Bob Philadelphia 1974-75
Kelly, Leonard "Red" Detroit 1950, 1952, 1954-55;
 Toronto 1962-63-64, 1967
Kelly, Pete Detroit 1936-37
Kendall, Bill Chicago 1934
Kennedy, Rod Mtl. Wanderers 1906-07

CUP-WINNERS ROSTER, K...Mc

Kennedy, Ted "Teeder"   Toronto 1945, 1947-48-49, 1951
Keon, Dave   Toronto 1962-63-64, 1967
Kerr, Albert "Dubbie"   Ottawa 1909, 1911
Kerr, Dave   NY Rangers 1940
Kilrea, Hec   Ottawa 1927; Detroit 1936-37
Kindrachuk, Orest   Philadelphia 1974-75
Kingan, A.   Mtl. AAA 1893-94
Kitchen, Chapman "Hobey"   Mtl. Maroons 1926
Klein, Lloyd   Boston 1929
Klukay, Joe   Toronto 1947-48-49, 1951
Kordic, John   Montreal 1986
Krushelnyski, Mike   Edmonton 1985, 1987
Kurri, Jari   Edmonton 1984-85, 1987
Kurvers, Tom   Montreal 1986

-L-

Lach, Elmer   Montreal 1944, 1946, 1953
Lafleur, Guy   Montreal 1973, 1976-77-78-79
Lake, Fred   Ottawa 1909, 1911
Lalonde, Edouard "Newsy"   Montreal 1916
Lalor, Mike   Montreal 1986
Lambert, Yvon   Montreal 1976-77-78-79
Lamoureux, Leo   Montreal 1944, 1946
Lane, Gord   NY Islanders 1980-81-82-83
Lane, Myles   Boston 1929
Langelle, Pete   Toronto 1942
Langevin, Dave   NY Islanders 1980-81-82-83
Langlois, Al   Montreal 1958-59-60
Langway, Rod   Montreal 1979
Laperriere, Jacques   Montreal 1965-66, 1968-69, 1971, 1973
Lapointe, Guy   Montreal 1971, 1973, 1976-77-78-79
Larochelle, Wildor   Montreal 1930-31
Larocque, Michel "Bunny"   Montreal 1976-77-78-79
Larose, Claude   Montreal 1965-66, 1968, 1971, 1973
Larouche, Pierre   Montreal 1979
Laviolette, Jack   Montreal 1916
Leach, Reggie   Philadelphia 1975
Leclair, Jack   Montreal 1956
LeDuc, Albert   Montreal 1930-31
Lefley, Chuck   Montreal 1971, 1973
Lehman, Hugh   Vancouver 1915
Lemaire, Jacques   Montreal 1968-69, 1971, 1973, 1976-77-78-79
Lemay, Moe   Edmonton 1987
Lemieux, Claude   Montreal 1986
Leonard   Quebec 1912
Lepine, Alfred "Pit"   Montreal 1930-31
Lesieur, Art   Montreal 1931
Lesueur, Percy   Ottawa 1909, 1911
Lesuk, Bill   Boston 1970
Leswick, Jack   Chicago 1934
Leswick, Tony   Detroit 1952, 1954-55
Levinsky, Alex   Toronto 1932; Chicago 1938
Lewicki, Dan   Toronto 1951
Lewis, Gordon   Mtl. Victorias 1896-97-98
Lewis, Herbie   Detroit 1936-37
Liffiton, Charles   Mtl. AAA 1902; Mtl. Wanderers 1908
Lindsay, Ted   Detroit 1950, 1952, 1954-55
Lindstrom, Willy   Edmonton 1984-85
Linseman, Ken   Edmonton 1984
Liscombe, Carl   Detroit 1943
Litzenberger, Eddie   Chicago 1961; Toronto 1962-63-64
Lonsberry, Ross   Philadelphia 1974-75
Lorentz, Jim   Boston 1970
Lorimer, Bob   NY Islanders 1980-81
Loughlin, Clem   Victoria 1925
Lowe, J.   Mtl. AAA 1893
Lowe, Kevin   Edmonton 1984-85, 1987
Lowery, Fred "Frock"   Mtl. Maroons 1926
Ludwig, Craig   Montreal 1986
Lumley, Dave   Edmonton 1984-85
Lumley, Harry   Detroit 1950
Lupien, Gilles   Montreal 1978-79
Lynn, Vic   Toronto 1947-48-49

-M-

MacAdam, Al   Philadelphia 1974
MacDonald, Kilby   NY Rangers 1940
MacKay, Calum "Baldy"   Montreal 1953
MacKay, Mickey   Vancouver 1915; Boston 1929
Mackie, Howie   Detroit 1937
Mackell, Fleming "Mac"   Toronto 1949, 1951
MacLeish, Rick   Philadelphia 1974-75
MacMillan, John   Toronto 1962-63
MacTavish, Craig   Edmonton 1987
MacPherson, James "Bud"   Montreal 1953
Mahovlich, Frank   Toronto 1962-63-64, 1967; Montreal 1971, 1973
Mahovlich, Peter   Montreal 1971, 1973, 1976-77
Majeau, Fern   Montreal 1944
Maki, Ronald "Chico"   Chicago 1961
Maley, Dave   Montreal 1986
Mallen, Ken   Vancouver 1915
Malone, Jeff   Quebec 1913
Malone, Joe   Quebec 1912-13; Montreal 1924
Mantha, George   Montreal 1930-31
Mantha, Sylvio   Montreal 1924, 1930-31
Marcetta, Milan   Toronto 1967
March, Harold "Mush"   Chicago 1934, 1938
Marcotte, Don   Boston 1970, 1972
Marini, Hector   NY Islanders 1981-82
Marker, Gus   Mtl. Maroons 1935
Marks, Jack   Quebec 1912-13; Toronto 1918
Marshall, Don   Montreal 1956-57-58-59-60
Marshall, Jack   Winnipeg Vics 1901; Mtl. Maroons 1902; Mtl. Wanderers 1907, 1910; Toronto 1914
Martin, Clare   Detroit 1950
Masnick, Paul   Montreal 1953
Matz, Johnny   Vancouver 1915
Mazur, Eddie   Montreal 1953
McCaffrey, Bert   Montreal 1930-31
McClelland, Kevin   Edmonton 1984-85, 1987
McCool, Frank   Toronto 1945
McCormack, John   Montreal 1953
McCreavy, Pat   Boston 1941
McCreedy, John   Toronto 1942, 1945
McDonald   Ottawa 1905
McDonald, Ab   Montreal 1958-59-60; Chicago 1961
McDonald, Jack   Quebec 1912
McDonald, Wilfred "Bucko"   Detroit 1936-37; Toronto 1942
McDougall, A.   Mtl. Victorias 1895
McDougall, Bob   Mtl. Victorias 1895-96-97-98

Ed Litzenberger

McDougall, Hartland *Mtl. Victorias 1895-96-97-98*
McEwen, Mike *NY Islanders 1981-82-83*
McFadden, Jim *Detroit 1950*
McFadyen, Don *Chicago 1934*
McGee, Frank *Ottawa 1903-04-05*
McGee, Jim *Ottawa 1904*
McGiffen, Roy "Minnie" *Toronto 1914*
McGimsie, Billy *Kenora 1907*
McKay, Doug *Detroit 1950*
McKell, Jack *Ottawa 1921*
McKendry, Alex *NY Islanders 1980*
McKenna, Joe *Mtl. Shamrocks 1899-1900*
McKenney, Don *Toronto 1964*
McKenzie, Bill *Chicago 1938*
McKenzie, John *Boston 1970, 1972*
McLea, Ernest *Mtl. Victorias 1896-97-98*
McLean, Jack *Toronto 1945*
McLellan *Mtl. Victorias 1897*
McMahon, Mike *Montreal 1944*
McManus, Sam *Mtl. Maroons 1935*
McNab, Max *Detroit 1950*
McNamara, George *Toronto 1914*
McNamara, Howard *Montreal 1916*
McNeil, Gerry *Montreal 1953*
McPhee, Mike *Montreal 1986*
McSorley, Marty *Edmonton 1987*
Meeker, Howie *Toronto 1947-48, 1951*
Meeking, Harry *Toronto 1918; Victoria 1925*
Meger, Paul *Montreal 1953*
Melanson, Roland *NY Islanders 1981-82-83*
Melnyk, Larry *Edmonton 1985*
Menard, H. *Mtl. Wanderers 1906*
Merrick, Wayne *NY Islanders 1980-81-82-83*
Merrill, Horace *Ottawa 1920*
Merritt, G.H. *Winnipeg Vics 1896*
Messier, Mark *Edmonton 1984-85*
Metz, Don *Toronto 1942, 1945, 1947-48-49*
Metz, Nick *Toronto 1942, 1945, 1947-48*
Mikita, Stan *Chicago 1961*
Miller, Bill *Mtl. Maroons 1935*
Miller, Earl *Toronto 1932*
Mitchell, Ivan *Toronto 1922*
Molson, Percy *Mtl. Victorias 1897*
Mondou, Armand *Montreal 1930-31*
Mondou, Pierre *Montreal 1977-78-79*
Moog, Andy *Edmonton 1984-85, 1987*
Moore, Alfie *Chicago 1938*
Moore, Art *Ottawa 1903-04-05*
Moore, Dickie *Montreal 1953, 1956-57-58-59-60*
Moran, Paddy *Quebec 1912-13*
Morenz, Howie *Montreal 1924, 1930-31*
Morris, Bernie *Seattle 1917*
Morris, Elwyn "Moe" *Toronto 1945*
Morrow, Ken *NY Islanders 1980-81-82-83*
Mortson, Gus *Toronto 1947-48-49, 1951*
Mosdell, Kenny *Montreal 1946, 1953, 1956, 1959*
Motter, Alex *Detroit 1943*
Mowers, Johnny *Detroit 1943*
Mummery, Harry *Quebec 1913; Toronto 1918*
Muni, Craig *Edmonton 1987*
Munro, Dunc *Mtl. Maroons 1926*
Murdoch, Bob *Montreal 1971, 1973*
Murdoch, Murray *NY Rangers 1928, 1933*
Murphy, Ron *Chicago 1961*
Mussen, Clare *Mtl. AAA 1894*

-N-

Napier, Mark *Montreal 1979; Edmonton 1985*
Naslund, Mats *Montreal 1986*
Nesterenko, Eric *Chicago 1961*
Neville, Mike *Toronto 1918*
Nevin, Bob *Toronto 1962-63*
Nicholson, Billy *Mtl. AAA 1902*
Nighbor, Frank *Vancouver 1915; Ottawa 1920-21, 1923, 1927*

Nilan, Chris *Montreal 1986*
Nilsson, Kent *Edmonton 1987*
Noble, Reg *Toronto 1918, 1922; Mtl. Maroons 1926*
Nolan, Pat *Toronto 1922*
Nolet, Simon *Philadelphia 1974*
Northcott, Lawrence "Baldy" *Mtl. Maroons 1935*
Nyrop, Bill *Montreal 1976-77-78*
Nystrom, Bob *NY Islanders 1980-81-82-83*

-O-

Oatman, Eddie *Quebec 1912*
O'Brien, E. *Mtl. AAA 1894*
O'Connor, Herbert *Montreal 1944, 1946*
Oliver, Harry *Boston 1929*
Olmstead, Bert *Montreal 1953, 1956-57-58; Toronto 1962*
O'Neill, Tom *Toronto 1945*
Orlando, Jim *Detroit 1943*
Orr, Bobby *Boston 1970, 1972*
Owen, George *Boston 1929*

-P-

Palangio, Pete *Chicago 1938*
Pappin, Jim *Toronto 1964, 1967*
Parent, Bernie *Philadelphia 1974-75*
Paton, Tom *Mtl. AAA 1893*
Patrick, Frank *Vancouver 1915*
Patrick, Lester *Mtl. Wanderers 1906-07; NY Rangers 1928*
Patrick, Lynn *NY Rangers 1940*
Patrick, Murray *NY Rangers 1940*
Pavelich, Marty *Detroit 1950, 1952, 1954-55*
Persson, Stefan *NY Islanders 1980-81-82-83*
Peters, Garry *Boston 1972*
Peters, Jim *Montreal 1946; Detroit 1950, 1954*
Pettinger, Gordon *NY Rangers 1933; Detroit 1936-37; Boston 1939*

Frank Nighbor

Lynn Patrick

Phillips, Bill   *Mtl. Maroons 1926*
Phillips, Tom   *Kenora 1907*
Picard, Noel   *Montreal 1965*
Pike, Alf   *NY Rangers 1940*
Pilote, Pierre   *Chicago 1961*
Pitre, Didier "Pit"   *Montreal 1916*
Plamondon, Gerry   *Montreal 1946*
Plante, Jacques   *Montreal 1956-57-58-59-60*
Plasse, Michel   *Montreal 1973*
Poile, Norman "Bud"   *Toronto 1947*
Polich, Mike   *Montreal 1977*
Portland, Jack   *Boston 1939*
Potvin, Denis   *NY Islanders 1980-81-82-83*
Potvin, Jean   *NY Islanders 1980*
Poulin "Skinner"   *Montreal 1916*
Pouzar, Jaroslav   *Edmonton 1984-85, 1987*
Power "Rocket"   *Quebec 1913*
Pratt, Walter "Babe"   *NY Rangers 1940; Toronto 1945*
Price   *Ottawa 1920*
Price, Noel   *Montreal 1966*
Primeau, Joe   *Toronto 1932*
Prodgers, George "Goldie"   *Quebec 1912; Montreal 1916*
Pronovost, Andre   *Montreal 1957-58-59-60*
Pronovost, Marcel   *Detroit 1950, 1952, 1954-55; Toronto 1967*
Provost, Claude   *Montreal 1956-57-58-59-60, 1965-66, 1968-69*
Prystai, Metro   *Detroit 1952, 1954*

Pulford, Bob   *Toronto 1962-63-64, 1967*
Pulford, Harvey   *Ottawa 1903-04-05*
Pullan   *Mtl. Victorias 1895*
Pusie, Jean   *Montreal 1931*

-R-

Randall, Ken   *Toronto 1918, 1922*
Rankin, N.   *Mtl. Victorias 1895*
Reardon, Ken   *Montreal 1946*
Reardon, Terry   *Boston 1941*
Reay, Billy   *Montreal 1946, 1953*
Redmond, Mickey   *Montreal 1968-69*
Reibel, Earl   *Detroit 1954-55*
Reise, Leo Jr.   *Detroit 1950, 1952*
Resch, Glenn "Chico"   *NY Islanders 1980*
Richard, Henri   *Montreal 1956-57-58-59-60, 1965-66, 1968-69, 1971, 1973*
Richard, Maurice "Rocket"   *Montreal 1944, 1946, 1953, 1956-57-58-59-60*
Richardson, Frank   *Mtl. Victorias 1898*
Richer, Stephane   *Montreal 1986*
Rickey, Roy   *Seattle 1917*
Ridpath, Bruce   *Ottawa 1911*
Riley, Jim   *Seattle 1917*
Risebrough, Doug   *Montreal 1976-77-78-79*
Rivers, Gus   *Montreal 1930-31*
Roach, John   *Toronto 1922*
Roberto, Phil   *Montreal 1971*
Roberts, Jimmy   *Montreal 1965-66, 1973, 1976-77*
Robertson, Earl   *Detroit 1937*
Robertson, Fred   *Toronto 1932*
Robinson, Earl   *Mtl. Maroons 1935*
Robinson, Larry   *Montreal 1973, 1976-77-78-79, 1986*
Rochefort, Leon   *Montreal 1966, 1971*
Rodden, Eddie   *Boston 1929*
Rollins, Al   *Toronto 1951*
Romnes, Elwyn "Doc"   *Chicago 1934, 1938*
Ronan, Skene   *Montreal 1916*
Rooney, Steve   *Montreal 1986*
Rooney, Walter   *Quebec 1912*
Ross, Art   *Kenora 1907; Mtl. Wanderers 1908*
Rothchild, Sam   *Mtl. Maroons 1926*
Roulston, William "Rolly"   *Detroit 1937*
Rousseau, Bobby   *Montreal 1965-66, 1968-69*
Routh, Harvie   *Mtl. AAA 1983-94*
Rowe, Bob   *Seattle 1917*
Roy, Patrick   *Montreal 1986*
Ruotsalainen, Reijo   *Edmonton 1987*
Russell, Ernie   *Mtl. Wanderers 1906-07-08, 1910*

-S-

St. Laurent, Dollard   *Montreal 1953, 1956-57-58; Chicago 1961*
Saleski, Don   *Philadelphia 1974-75*
Samis, Phil   *Toronto 1948*
Sanderson, Derek   *Boston 1970, 1972*
Sands, Charlie   *Boston 1939*
Savard, Serge   *Montreal 1968-69, 1973, 1976-77-78-79*
Sawchuk, Terry   *Detroit 1952, 1954-55*
Scanlon, Fred   *Mtl. Shamrocks 1899, 1900*
Schmidt, Milton   *Boston 1939, 1941*
Schriner, David   *Toronto 1942, 1945*
Schultz, Dave   *Philadelphia 1974-75*
Scott   *Ottawa 1904*
Scott, Laurie   *NY Rangers 1928*
Seaborn, Jimmy   *Vancouver 1915*
Seibert, Earl   *NY Rangers 1933; Chicago 1938*
Semenko, Dave   *Edmonton 1984-85*
Sevigny, Richard   *Montreal 1979*
Shack, Edward   *Toronto 1962-63-64, 1967*
Sheehan, Bobby   *Montreal 1971*
Sheppard, John   *Chicago 1934*
Sherf, John   *Detroit 1937*
Shewchuk, Jack   *Boston 1941*
Shibicky, Alex   *NY Rangers 1940*
Shields, Allan   *Mtl. Maroons 1935*

Shill, Jack   *Chicago 1938*
Schock, Dan   *Boston 1970*
Shore, Eddie   *Boston 1929, 1939*
Shore, Hamby   *Ottawa 1905, 1911*
Shutt, Steve   *Montreal 1973, 1976-77-78-79*
Siebert, Albert "Babe"   *Mtl. Maroons 1926; NY Rangers 1933*
Simmons, Donald   *Toronto 1962*
Simms, Percy   *Ottawa 1903*
Simon, John   *Detroit 1943*
Skinner, Alf   *Toronto 1918*
Skov, Glen   *Detroit 1952, 1954-55*
Skrudland, Brian   *Montreal 1986*
Sloan, Tod   *Toronto 1951; Chicago 1961*
Smail, Wally   *Mtl. Wanderers 1908*
Smith, Alex   *Ottawa 1927*
Smith, Alf   *Ottawa 1904-05*
Smith, Billy   *NY Islanders 1980-81-82-83*
Smith, Bobby   *Montreal 1986*
Smith, Clint   *NY Rangers 1940*
Smith, Dallas   *Boston 1970, 1972*
Smith, Des   *Boston 1941*
Smith, Norman   *Detroit 1936-37*
Smith, Reginald "Hooley"   *Ottawa 1927; Mtl. Maroons 1935*
Smith, Rick   *Boston 1970*
Smith, Sid   *Toronto 1948-49, 1951*
Smith, Stan   *NY Rangers 1940*
Smith, Steve   *Edmonton 1987*
Smylie, Rod   *Toronto 1922*
Soetaert, Doug   *Montreal 1986*
Somers, Art   *NY Rangers 1933*
Sorrell, John   *Detroit 1936-37*
Speer, Bill   *Boston 1970*
Spittal, Charles   *Ottawa 1923*
Stackhouse, Ted   *Toronto 1922*
Stanfield, Fred   *Boston 1970, 1972*
Stanley, Allan   *Toronto 1962-63-64, 1967*
Stanley, Barney   *Vancouver 1915*
Stanowski, Wally   *Toronto 1942, 1945, 1947-48*
Starr, Wilf   *Detroit 1936*
Stasiuk, Vic   *Detroit 1952, 1955*
Stemkowski, Peter   *Toronto 1967*
Stephenson, Wayne   *Philadelphia 1975*
Stewart, Gaye   *Toronto 1942, 1947*
Stewart, "Black" Jack   *Detroit 1943, 1950*
Stewart, James   *Mtl. AAA 1893-94*
Stewart, Nels   *Mtl. Maroons 1926*
Stewart, Ron   *Toronto 1962-63-64*
Strachan, Billy   *Mtl. Wanderers 1906-07*
Stuart, Bill   *Toronto 1922*
Stuart, Bruce   *Mtl. Wanderers 1908; Ottawa 1909, 1911*
Stuart, Hod   *Mtl. Wanderers 1907*
Sutter, Brent   *NY Islanders 1982-83*
Sutter, Duane   *NY Islanders 1980-81-82-83*
Svoboda, Petr   *Montreal 1986*

-T-

Talbot, Jean-Guy   *Montreal 1956-57-58-59-60, 1965-66*
Tambellini, Steve   *NY Islanders 1980*
Tansey, Frank   *Mtl. Shamrocks 1899, 1900*
Tardif, Marc   *Montreal 1971, 1973*
Taylor, Bill   *Toronto 1942*
Taylor, Bobby   *Philadelphia 1974*
Taylor, Fred "Cyclone"   *Ottawa 1909; Vancouver 1915*
Taylor, Harry   *Toronto 1949*
Thompson, Cecil "Tiny"   *Boston 1929*
Thompson, Paul   *NY Rangers 1928; Chicago 1934, 1938*
Thomson, Jimmy   *Toronto 1947-48-49, 1951*
Tikkanen, Esa   *Edmonton 1985, 1987*
Timgren, Ray   *Toronto 1949, 1951*
Tonelli, John   *NY Islanders 1980-81-82-83*
Tremblay, Gilles   *Montreal 1966, 1968*
Tremblay, J.C.   *Montreal 1965-66, 1968-69, 1971*
Tremblay, Mario   *Montreal 1976-77-78-79, 1986*
Trihey, Harry   *Mtl. Shamrocks 1899, 1900*

Bryan Trottier

Trottier, Bryan   *NY Islanders 1980-81-82-83*
Trottier, Dave   *Mtl. Maroons 1935*
Trudel, Louis   *Chicago 1934, 1938*
Turner, Bob   *Montreal 1956-57-58-59-60*

-V-

Vachon, Rogie   *Montreal 1968-69, 1971*
Vadnais, Carol   *Montreal 1968; Boston 1972*
Van Impe, Ed   *Philadelphia 1974-75*
Vasko, Elmer   *Chicago 1961*
Vezina, Georges   *Montreal 1916, 1924*
Voss, Carl   *Chicago 1938*

-W-

Walker, Jack   *Toronto 1914; Seattle 1917; Victoria 1925*
Wall, Frank   *Mtl. Shamrocks 1899, 1900*
Wallace, W.   *Mtl. Victorias 1896*
Walsh, Marty   *Ottawa 1909, 1911*
Walter, Ryan   *Montreal 1986*
Walton, Mike   *Toronto 1967; Boston 1972*
Ward, Jimmy   *Mtl. Maroons 1935*
Wares, Eddie   *Detroit 1943*
Wasnie, Nick   *Montreal 1930-31*
Watson, Harry   *Detroit 1943; Toronto 1947-48-49, 1951*
Watson, Jim   *Philadelphia 1974-75*
Watson, Joe   *Philadelphia 1974-75*
Watson, Phil   *NY Rangers 1940; Montreal 1944*
Waud, A.   *Mtl. AAA 1894*
Weiland, Ralph "Cooney"   *Boston 1929, 1939*
Wentworth, Marvin "Cy"   *Mtl. Maroons 1935*
Westfall, Ed   *Boston 1970, 1972*
Westwick, Harry   *Ottawa 1903-04-05*
Wharram, Ken   *Chicago 1961*
White, Frank   *Ottawa 1905*
Wiebe, Art   *Chicago 1938*
Willett, S.   *Mtl. Victorias 1896*
Wilson, Carol "Cully"   *Toronto 1914; Seattle 1917*
Wilson, Johnny   *Detroit 1950, 1952, 1954-55*
Wilson, Larry   *Detroit 1950*
Wilson, Murray   *Montreal 1973, 1976-77*
Wiseman, Eddie   *Boston 1941*
Woit, Benny   *Detroit 1952, 1954-55*
Wood, Burke   *Winnipeg Vics 1901*
Wood, F.   *Ottawa 1903*
Worsley, Lorne "Gump"   *Montreal 1965-66, 1968-69*

-Y-

Young, Doug   *Detroit 1936, 1937*

-Z-

Zeidel, Larry   *Detroit 1952*

Championship Trophies

PRINCE OF WALES TROPHY

Beginning with the 1981-82 season, the club which advances to the Stanley Cup Finals as the winner of the Wales Conference is presented with the Prince of Wales Trophy.

History: His Royal Highnesss, the Prince of Wales, donated the trophy to the National Hockey League in 1924. From 1927-28 through 1937-38, the award was presented to the team finishing first in the American Division of the NHL. From 1938-39, when the NHL reverted to one section, to 1966-67, it was presented to the team winning the NHL championship. With expansion in 1967-68, it again became a divisional trophy through the 1973-74 season. Beginning in 1974-75, it was awarded to the regular-season winner of the conference bearing the name of the trophy. Starting with the 1981-82 season the trophy was presented to the playoff champion in the Wales Conference.

1986-87 Winner: Philadelphia Flyers

The Philadelphia Flyers captured their eighth conference championship and second Prince of Wales Trophy with a six-game victory over the Montreal Canadiens. The Flyers split the first two contests in the series on home ice before winning games three and four in Montreal. The Canadiens came back to win game five, but a 4-3 Philadelphia win in game six clinched the series for the Flyers.

PRINCE OF WALES TROPHY WINNERS

1986-87	Philadelphia Flyers
1985-86	Montreal Canadiens
1984-85	Philadelphia Flyers
1983-84	New York Islanders
1982-83	New York Islanders
1981-82	New York Islanders
1980-81	Montreal Canadiens
1979-80	Buffalo Sabres
1978-79	Montreal Canadiens
1977-78	Montreal Canadiens
1976-77	Montreal Canadiens
1975-76	Montreal Canadiens
1974-75	Buffalo Sabres
1973-74	Boston Bruins
1972-73	Montreal Canadiens
1971-72	Boston Bruins
1970-71	Boston Bruins
1969-70	Chicago Black Hawks
1968-69	Montreal Canadiens
1967-68	Montreal Canadiens
1966-67	Chicago Black Hawks
1965-66	Montreal Canadiens
1964-65	Detroit Red Wings
1963-64	Montreal Canadiens
1962-63	Toronto Maple Leafs
1961-62	Montreal Canadiens
1960-61	Montreal Canadiens
1959-60	Montreal Canadiens
1958-59	Montreal Canadiens
1957-58	Montreal Canadiens
1956-57	Detroit Red Wings
1955-56	Montreal Canadiens
1954-55	Detroit Red Wings
1953-54	Detroit Red Wings
1952-53	Detroit Red Wings
1951-52	Detroit Red Wings
1950-51	Detroit Red Wings
1949-50	Detroit Red Wings
1948-49	Detroit Red Wings
1947-48	Toronto Maple Leafs
1946-47	Montreal Canadiens
1945-46	Montreal Canadiens
1944-45	Montreal Canadiens
1943-44	Montreal Canadiens
1942-43	Detroit Red Wings
1941-42	New York Rangers
1940-41	Boston Bruins
1939-40	Boston Bruins
1938-39	Boston Bruins
1937-38	Boston Bruins
1936-37	Detroit Red Wings
1935-36	Detroit Red Wings
1934-35	Boston Bruins
1933-34	Detroit Red Wings
1932-33	Boston Bruins
1931-32	New York Rangers
1930-31	Boston Bruins
1929-30	Boston Bruins
1928-29	Boston Bruins
1927-28	Boston Bruins
1926-27	Ottawa Senators
1925-26	Montreal Maroons
1924-25	Montreal Canadiens

Prince of Wales Trophy

CLARENCE S. CAMPBELL BOWL

Beginning with the 1981-82 season, the club which advances to the Stanley Cup Finals as the winner of the Campbell Conference championship is presented with the Clarence S. Campbell Bowl.

History: Presented by the member clubs in 1968 for perpetual competition by the National Hockey League in recognition of the services of Clarence S. Campbell, President of the NHL from 1946 to 1977. From 1967-68 through 1973-74, the trophy was awarded to the champions of the West Division. The trophy itself is a hallmark piece made of sterling silver and was crafted by a British silversmith in 1878.

1986-87 Winner: Edmonton Oilers

The Edmonton Oilers were champions of the Campbell Conference Championship for the fifth time in the past six seasons in 1986-87, defeating the Detroit Red Wings in a five-game series. The Red Wings won the first game of the series 3-1, but the Oilers won the next four matches, outscoring Detroit 16-10 over the five games.

CLARENCE S. CAMPBELL BOWL WINNERS

1986-87	Edmonton Oilers
1985-86	Calgary Flames
1984-85	Edmonton Oilers
1983-84	Edmonton Oilers
1982-83	Edmonton Oilers
1981-82	Vancouver Canucks
1980-81	New York Islanders
1979-80	Philadelphia Flyers
1978-79	New York Islanders
1977-78	New York Islanders
1976-77	Philadelphia Flyers
1975-76	Philadelphia Flyers
1974-75	Philadelphia Flyers
1973-74	Philadelphia Flyers
1972-73	Chicago Black Hawks
1971-72	Chicago Black Hawks
1970-71	Chicago Black Hawks
1969-70	St. Louis Blues
1968-69	St. Louis Blues
1967-68	Philadelphia Flyers

Clarence Campbell Bowl

Penalty Shots in Stanley Cup Playoff Games

Date	Player	Goaltender	Scored	Final Score	Series
Mar. 25/37	Lionel Conacher, Mtl. Maroons	Tiny Thompson, Boston	No	Mtl. 0 at Bos.	4 QF
Apr. 15/37	Alex Shibicky, NY Rangers	Earl Robertson, Detroit	No	NYR 0 at Det.	3 F
Apr. 13/44	Virgil Johnson, Chicago	Bill Durnan, Montreal	No	Chi. 4 at Mtl.	5* F
Apr. 9/68	Wayne Connelly, Minnesota	Terry Sawchuk, Los Angeles	Yes	L.A. 5 at Min.	7 QF
Apr. 27/68	Jim Roberts, St. Louis	Cesare Maniago, Minnesota	No	St. L. 4 at Min.	3 SF
May 16/71	Frank Mahovlich, Montreal	Tony Esposito, Chicago	No	Chi. 3 at Mtl.	4 F
May 7/75	Bill Barber, Philadelphia	Glenn Resch, NY Islanders	No	Phi. 3 at NYI	4 SF
Apr. 20/79	Mike Walton, Chicago	Glenn Resch, NY Islanders	No	NYI 4 at Chi.	0 QF
Apr. 9/81	Peter McNab, Boston	Don Beaupre, Minnesota	No	Min. 5 at Bos.	4* P
Apr. 17/81	Anders Hedberg, NY Rangers	Mike Liut, St. Louis	Yes	NYR 6 at St. L.	4 QF
Apr. 9/83	Denis Potvin, NY Islanders	Pat Riggin, Washington	No	NYI 6 at Wash.	2 DSF
Apr. 28/84	Wayne Gretzky, Edmonton	Don Beaupre, Minnesota	Yes	Edm. 8 at Min.	5 CF
May 1/84	Mats Naslund, Montreal	Bill Smith, NY Islanders	No	Mtl. 1 at NYI	3 CF
Apr. 14/85	Bob Carpenter, Washington	Bill Smith, NY Islanders	No	Wash.4 at NYI.	6 DF
May 28/85	Ron Sutter, Philadelphia	Grant Fuhr, Edmonton	No	Phi 3 at Edm.	5 F
May 30/85	Dave Poulin, Philadelphia	Grant Fuhr, Edmonton	No	Phi. 3 at Edm.	8 F

* Game was decided in overtime, but shot taken during regulation time.

Other Hockey Championships

Year	World/Olympic Champions	Memorial Cup (Canadian Jr.)	Allan Cup (Canadian Sr.)
1986-87	Swedish Nationals	Medicine Hat Tigers	Brantford Motts
1985-86	Soviet Nationals	Guelph Platers	Cornerbrook Royals
1984-85	Czech Nationals	Prince Albert Raiders	Thunder Bay Twins
1983-84	Soviet Nationals	Ottawa 67's	Thunder Bay Twins
1982-83	Soviet Nationals	Portland Winter Hawks	Cambridge Hornets
1981-82	Soviet Nationals	Kitchener Rangers	Cranbrook Royals
1980-81	Soviet Nationals	Cornwall Royals	Petrolia Squires
1979-80	U.S.A. Nationals	Cornwall Royals	Spokane Flyers
1978-79	Soviet Nationals	Peterborough Petes	Petrolia Squires
1977-78	Soviet Nationals	New Westminster Bruins	Kimberley Dynamiters
1976-77	Czech Nationals	New Westminster Bruins	Brantford Alexanders
1975-76	Czech Nationals	Hamilton Fincups	Spokane Flyers
1974-75	Soviet Nationals	Toronto Marlboros	Thunder Bay Twins
1973-74	Soviet Nationals	Regina Pats	Barrie Flyers
1972-73	Soviet Nationals	Toronto Marlboros	Orillia Terriers
1971-72	Soviet Nationals (Olympic) Czech Nationals (World)	Cornwall Royals	Spokane Jets
1970-71	Soviet Nationals	Quebec Remparts	Galt Hornets
1969-70	Soviet Nationals	Montreal Jr. Canadiens	Spokane Jets
1968-69	Soviet Nationals	Montreal Jr. Canadiens	Galt Hornets
1967-68	Soviet Nationals	Niagara Falls Flyers	Victoriaville Tigers
1966-67	Soviet Nationals	Toronto Marlboros	Drummondville Eagles
1965-66	Soviet Nationals	Edmonton Oil Kings	Drumheller Miners
1964-65	Soviet Nationals	Niagara Falls Flyers	Sherbrooke Beavers
1963-64	Soviet Nationals	Toronto Marlboros	Winnipeg Maroons
1962-63	Soviet Nationals	Edmonton Oil Kings	Windsor Bulldogs
1961-62	Swedish Nationals	Hamilton Red Wings	Trail Smoke Eaters
1960-61	Canada – Trail Smoke Eaters	Toronto St. Michael's Majors	Galt Terriers
1959-60	U.S.A. Nationals	St. Catharines Tee Pees	Chatham Maroons
1958-59	Canada – Belleville McFarlands	Winnipeg Braves	Whitby Dunlops
1957-58	Canada – Whitby Dunlops	Ottawa-Hull Canadiens	Belleville McFarlands
1956-57	Swedish Nationals	Flin Flon Bombers	Whitby Dunlops
1955-56	Soviet Nationals	Toronto Marlboros	Vernon Canadiens
1954-55	Canada – Penticton V's	Toronto Marlboros	Kitchener-Waterloo Dutchmen
1953-54	Soviet Nationals	St. Catharines Tee Pees	Penticton V's
1952-53	Swedish Nationals	Barrie Flyers	Kitchener-Waterloo Dutchmen
1951-52	Canada – Edmonton Mercurys	Guelph Biltmores	Fort Francis Canadiens
1950-51	Canada – Lethbridge Maple Leafs	Barrie Flyers	Owen Sound Mercurys
1949-50	Canada – Edmonton Mercurys	Montreal Canadiens	Toronto Marlboros
1948-49	Czech Nationals	Montreal Royals	Ottawa Senators
1947-48	Canada – RCAF Flyers	Port Arthur West End Bruins	Edmonton Flyers
1946-47	Czech Nationals	Toronto St. Michael's	Montreal Royals
1945-46	– no competition –	Winnipeg Monarchs	Calgary Stampeders
1944-45	– no competition –	Toronto St. Michael's	– no competition –
1943-44	– no competition –	Oshawa Generals	Quebec Aces
1942-43	– no competition –	Winnipeg Rangers	Ottawa Commandos
1941-42	– no competition –	Portage La Prairie	Ottawa RCAF
1940-41	– no competition –	Winnipeg Rangers	Regina Rangers
1939-40	– no competition –	Oshawa Generals	Kirkland Lake Blue Devils
1938-39	Canada – Trail Smoke Eaters	Oshawa Generals	Port Arthur
1937-38	Canada – Sudbury Wolves	St. Boniface Seals	Trail Smoke Eaters
1936-37	Canada – Kimberley Dynamiters	Winnipeg Monarchs	Sudbury Tigers
1935-36	British Nationals	West Toronto Redmen	Kimberley Dynamiters
1934-35	Canada – Winnipeg Monarchs	Winnipeg Monarchs	Halifax Wolverines
1933-34	Canada – Saskatoon Quakers	Toronto St. Michael's	Moncton Hawks
1932-33	U.S.A. – Boston Olympics	Newmarket Jr. Hockey Club	Moncton Hawks
1931-32	Canada – Winnipeg	Sudbury Wolves	Toronto Nationals
1930-31	Canada – Manitoba Grads	Winnipeg Elmwoods	Winnipeg Hockey Club
1929-30	Canada – Toronto	Regina Pats	Montreal AAA
1928-29		Toronto Marlboros	Port Arthur
1927-28	Canada – Toronto Varsity Grads	Regina Monarchs	University of Manitoba
1926-27		Owen Sound Greys	Toronto Varsity Grads
1925-26		Calgary Canadiens	Port Arthur
1924-25		Regina Pats	Port Arthur
1923-24	Canada – Toronto Granites	Owen Sound Greys	Sault Ste. Marie Greyhounds
1922-23		University of Manitoba Winnipeg	Toronto Granites
1921-22		Fort William War Veterans	Toronto Granites
1920-21		Winnipeg Falcons	University of Toronto
1919-20	Canada – Winnipeg Falcons	Toronto Canoe Club	Winnipeg Falcons
1918-19		University of Toronto Schools	Hamilton Tigers
1917-18			Kitchener Hockey Club
1916-17			Toronto Dentals
1915-16			Winnipeg 61st Battalion
1914-15			Winnipeg Monarchs
1913-14			Regina Victorias
1912-13			Winnipeg Hockey Club
1911-12			Winnipeg Victorias
1910-11			Winnipeg Victorias
1909-10			Toronto St. Michael's
1908-09			Kingston Queen's University
1907-08			Ottawa Cliffsides

193

OTHER HOCKEY CHAMPIONSHIPS

Year	Calder Cup (AHL)	Turner Cup (IHL)	NCAA Champions
1986-87	Rochester Americans	Salt Lake Golden Eagles	North Dakota Fighting Sioux
1985-86	Adirondack Red Wings	Muskegon Lumberjacks	Michigan State Spartans
1984-85	Sherbrooke Jets	Peoria Rivermen	RPI Engineers
1983-84	Maine Mariners	Flint Generals	Bowling Green Falcons
1982-83	Rochester Americans	Toledo Goaldiggers	Wisconsin Badgers
1981-82	New Brunswick Hawks	Toledo Goaldiggers	North Dakota Fighting Sioux
1980-81	Adirondack Red Wings	Saginaw Gears	Wisconsin Badgers
1979-80	Hershey Bears	Kalamazoo Wings	North Dakota Fighting Sioux
1978-79	Maine Mariners	Kalamazoo Wings	Minnesota Golden Gophers
1977-78	Maine Mariners	Toledo Goaldiggers	Boston University Terriers
1976-77	Nova Scotia Voyageurs	Saginaw Gears	Wisconsin Badgers
1975-76	Nova Scotia Voyageurs	Dayton Gems	Minnesota Golden Gophers
1974-75	Springfield Indians	Toledo Goaldiggers	Michigan Tech Huskies
1973-74	Hershey Bears	Des Moines Capitals	Minnesota Golden Gophers
1972-73	Cincinnati Swords	Fort Wayne Komets	Wisconsin Badgers
1971-72	Nova Scotia Voyageurs	Port Huron Flags	Boston University Terriers
1970-71	Springfield Kings	Port Huron Flags	Boston University Terriers
1969-70	Buffalo Bisons	Dayton Gems	Cornell Big Red
1968-69	Hershey Bears	Dayton Gems	Denver Pioneers
1967-68	Rochester Americans	Muskegon Mohawks	Denver Pioneers
1966-67	Pittsburgh Hornets	Toledo Blades	Cornell Big Red
1965-66	Rochester Americans	Port Huron Flags	Michigan State Spartans
1964-65	Rochester Americans	Fort Wayne Komets	Michigan Tech Huskies
1963-64	Cleveland Barons	Toledo Blades	Michigan Wolverines
1962-63	Buffalo Bisons	Fort Wayne Komets	North Dakota Fighting Sioux
1961-62	Springfield Indians	Muskegon Zephyrs	
1960-61	Springfield Indians	St. Paul Saints	Michigan Tech Huskies
1959-60	Springfield Indians	St. Paul Saints	Denver Pioneers
1958-59	Hershey Bears	Louisville Rebels	Denver Pioneers
1957-58	Hershey Bears	Indianapolis Chiefs	North Dakota Fighting Sioux
1956-57	Cleveland Barons	Cincinnati Mohawks	Denver Pioneers
1955-56	Providence Reds	Cincinnati Mohawks	Colorado College Tigers
1954-55	Pittsburgh Hornets	Cincinnati Mohawks	Michigan Wolverines
1953-54	Cleveland Barons	Cincinnati Mohawks	Michigan Wolverines
1952-53	Cleveland Barons	Cincinnati Mohawks	RPI Engineers
1951-52	Pittsburgh Hornets	Toledo Mercurys	Michigan Wolverines
1950-51	Cleveland Barons	Toledo Mercurys	Michigan Wolverines
1949-50	Indianapolis Caps	Chatham Maroons	Michigan Wolverines
1948-49	Providence Reds	Windsor Hettche Spitfires	Colorado College Tigers
1947-48	Cleveland Barons	Toledo Mercurys	Boston College Eagles
1946-47	Hershey Bears	Windsor Spitfires	Michigan Wolverines
1945-46	Buffalo Bisons	Detroit Auto Club	
1944-45	Cleveland Barons		
1943-44	Buffalo Bisons		
1942-43	Buffalo Bisons		
1941-42	Indianapolis Caps		
1940-41	Cleveland Barons		
1939-40	Providence Reds		
1938-39	Cleveland Barons		
1937-38	Providence Reds		
1936-37	Syracuse Stars		

Year	CIAU Champions	World Jr. Champions	Canada Cup
1986-87	Trois-Rivieres Patriotes	Finland	Team Canada
1985-86	Alberta Golden Bears	Soviet Union	
1984-85	York Yeomen	Canada	
1983-84	University of Toronto Blues	Soviet Union	Team Canada
1982-83	Saskatchewan Huskies	Soviet Union	
1981-82	Moncton Blue Eagles	Canada	
1980-81	Moncton Blue Eagles	Sweden	Soviet Nationals
1979-80	Alberta Golden Bears	Soviet Union	
1978-79	Alberta Golden Bears	Soviet Union	
1977-78	Alberta Golden Bears	Soviet Union	
1976-77	University of Toronto Blues	Soviet Union	
1975-76	University of Toronto Blues		Team Canada
1974-75	Alberta Golden Bears		
1973-74	Waterloo Warriors		
1972-73	University of Toronto Blues		
1971-72	University of Toronto Blues		
1970-71	University of Toronto Blues		
1969-70	University of Toronto Blues		
1968-69	University of Toronto Blues		
1967-68	Alberta Golden Bears		
1966-67	University of Toronto Blues		
1965-66	University of Toronto Blues		
1964-65	Manitoba Bisons		
1963-64	Alberta Golden Bears		
1962-63	McMaster Marlins		

Stanley Cup Playoff Records
1918-1987
Team Records

MOST STANLEY CUP CHAMPIONSHIPS:
- 22 — **Montreal Canadiens** 1924-30-31-44-46-53-56-57-58-59-60-65-66-68-69-71-73-76-77-78-79-86
- 13 — Toronto Maple Leafs 1918-22-32-42-45-47-48-49-51-62-63-64-67
- 7 — Detroit Red Wings 1936-37-43-50-52-54-55

MOST FINAL SERIES APPEARANCES:
- 30 — **Montreal Canadiens in 70-year history.**
- 21 — Toronto Maple Leafs in 70-year history.
- 18 — Detroit Red Wings in 61-year history.

MOST YEARS IN PLAYOFFS:
- 62 — **Montreal Canadiens in 70-year history.**
- 52 — Toronto Maple Leafs in 70-year history.
- 48 — Boston Bruins in 63-year history.

MOST CONSECUTIVE STANLEY CUP CHAMPIONSHIPS:
- 5 — **Montreal Canadiens** (1956-57-58-59-60)
- 4 — New York Islanders (1980-81-82-83)
- — Montreal Canadiens (1976-77-78-79)

MOST CONSECUTIVE FINAL SERIES APPEARANCES:
- 10 — **Montreal Canadiens** (1951-60, inclusive)

MOST CONSECUTIVE PLAYOFF APPEARANCES:
- 21 — **Montreal Canadiens** (1949-69, inclusive)
- 20 — Detroit Red Wings (1939-58, inclusive)

MOST GOALS BOTH TEAMS, ONE PLAYOFF SERIES:
- 69 — **Edmonton Oilers, Chicago Black Hawks** in 1985 Campbell Conference Final. Edmonton won best-of-seven series 4-2, outscoring Chicago 44-25.

MOST GOALS ONE TEAM, ONE PLAYOFF SERIES:
- 44 — **Edmonton Oilers** in 1985 Campbell Conference Final. Edmonton won best-of-seven series 4-2, outscoring Chicago 44-25.

LONGEST OVERTIME:
116 Minutes, 30 Seconds — **Detroit, Montreal Maroons** at Montreal, March 24-25, 1936. Detroit 1, Maroons 0. Mud Bruneteau scored, assisted by Hec Kilrea, at 16:30 of sixth overtime period, or after 176 minutes, 30 seconds from start of game, which ended at 2:25 a.m. Detroit won best-of-five semi-final 3-0.

SHORTEST OVERTIME:
9 Seconds — **Montreal Canadiens, Calgary Flames,** at Calgary, May 18, 1986. Montreal won game 3-2 on Brian Skrudland's goal and captured the best-of-seven Final series 4-1.

MOST OVERTIME GAMES, ONE PLAYOFF YEAR:
- 16 — **1982.** Of 71 games played, 16 went into overtime: one in Division Semi-Final won by Quebec 3-2 against Montreal; two in Division Semi-Final won by NY Islanders 3-2 against Pittsburgh; one in Division Semi-Final won by Chicago 3-1 against Minnesota; two in Division Semi-Final won by Los Angeles 3-2 against Edmonton; one in Division Semi-Final won by Vancouver 3-0 against Calgary; two in Division Final won by Quebec 4-3 against Boston; one in Division Final won by NY Islanders 4-2 against NY Rangers; one in Division Final won by Chicago 4-2 against St. Louis; two in Division Final won by Vancouver 4-1 against Los Angeles; one in Conference Championship won by NY Islanders 4-0 against Quebec; one in Conference Championship won by Vancouver 4-1 against Chicago; one in Stanley Cup Championship won by NY Islanders 4-0 against Vancouver.

FEWEST OVERTIME GAMES, ONE PLAYOFF YEAR:
- 0 — **1963.** None of the 16 games went into overtime, the only year since 1926 that no overtime was required in any playoff series.

MOST OVERTIME-GAME VICTORIES, ONE TEAM, ONE PLAYOFF YEAR:
- 6 — **New York Islanders,** 1980. One against Los Angeles in the Preliminary Round; two against Boston in the Quarter-Final; one against Buffalo in the Semi-Final; and two against Philadelphia in the Final. Islanders played 21 games.

MOST OVERTIME GAMES, FINAL SERIES:
- 5 — **Toronto, Montreal Canadiens** in 1951. Toronto defeated Canadiens 4-1 in best-of-seven series

MOST GAMES PLAYED BY ALL TEAMS, ONE PLAYOFF YEAR:
- 87 — **1987.** There were 44 Division Semi-Final, 25 Division Final, 11 Conference Championships and 7 Stanley Cup games.

MOST GAMES PLAYED, ONE TEAM, ONE PLAYOFF YEAR:
26 — **Philadelphia Flyers,** 1987. Won Patrick DSF 4-2 against NY Rangers, Patrick DF 4-3 against NY Islanders, Wales CC 4-2 against Montreal, and lost Stanley Cup Final 4-3 against Edmonton.

MOST CONSECUTIVE PLAYOFF GAME VICTORIES:
12 — **Edmonton Oilers.** Streak began May 15, 1984 at Edmonton with a 7-2 win over New York Islanders in third game of Final series, and ended May 9, 1985 when Chicago Black Hawks defeated Edmonton 5-2 at Chicago. Included in the streak were three wins over the Islanders, in 1984, three over the Los Angeles Kings, four over the Winnipeg Jets and two over the Black Hawks, all in 1985.

MOST POWER-PLAY GOALS, ONE TEAM, ONE PLAYOFF YEAR:
31 — **New York Islanders,** 1981. 6 against Toronto in Preliminary Round, won by Islanders 3-0; 13 against Edmonton in Quarter-Final, won by Islanders 4-2; 7 against NY Rangers in Semi-Final, won by Islanders 4-0; and 5 in Final against Minnesota, won by Islanders 4-1.

MOST POWER-PLAY GOALS, BOTH TEAMS, ONE SERIES:
21 — **New York Islanders, Philadelphia Flyers** in 1980 Final Series, won by Islanders 4-2. Islanders had 15 and Flyers 6.
— **New York Islanders, Edmonton Oilers** in 1981 Quarter-Final, won by Islanders 4-2. Islanders had 13 and Oilers 8.

MOST POWER-PLAY GOALS, ONE TEAM, ONE SERIES:
15 — **New York Islanders** in 1980 Final Series against Philadelphia. Islanders won series 4-2.

MOST POWER-PLAY GOALS, BOTH TEAMS, ONE GAME:
7 — **Minnesota North Stars, Edmonton Oilers,** April 28, 1984 at Minnesota. Minnesota had 4, Edmonton 3. Edmonton won game 8-5.
— **Philadelphia Flyers, New York Rangers,** April 13, 1985 at New York. Philadelphia had 4, New York 3. Philadelphia won game 6-5.
— **Edmonton Oilers, Chicago Black Hawks,** May 14, 1985 at Edmonton. Chicago had 5, Edmonton 2. Edmonton won game 10-5.

MOST POWER-PLAY GOALS, ONE TEAM, ONE GAME:
6 — **Boston Bruins,** April 2, 1969, at Boston against Toronto Maple Leafs. Boston won game 10-0.

MOST POWER-PLAY GOALS, BOTH TEAMS, ONE PERIOD:
5 — **Minnesota North Stars, Edmonton Oilers,** April 28, 1984, second period, at Minnesota. North Stars had four and Oilers one. Edmonton won game 8-5.

MOST POWER-PLAY GOALS, ONE TEAM, ONE PERIOD:
4 — **Toronto Maple Leafs,** March 26, 1936, second period against Boston at Toronto. Toronto won game 8-3.
— **Minnesota North Stars,** April 28, 1984, second period against Edmonton. Oilers won game 8-5.

MOST SHORTHAND GOALS BY ALL TEAMS, ONE PLAYOFF YEAR:
27 — **1986,** during 72 games.
26 — **1981,** during 68 games.

MOST SHORTHAND GOALS, ONE TEAM, ONE PLAYOFF YEAR:
10 — **Edmonton Oilers 1983, in 16 games.**

MOST SHORT-HAND GOALS, BOTH TEAMS, ONE SERIES:
7 — **Boston Bruins (4), New York Rangers (3),** in 1958 semi-final, won by Boston 4-2.
— **Edmonton Oilers (5), Calgary Flames (2),** in 1983 Smythe Division Final won by Edmonton 4-1.

MOST SHORT-HAND GOALS, ONE TEAM, ONE SERIES:
5 — **Edmonton Oilers** in 1983 best-of-seven Smythe Division Final won by Edmonton 4-1.
— **New York Rangers** in 1979 against Philadelphia Flyers in best-of-seven Quarter-Final, won by Rangers 4-1.

MOST SHORTHAND GOALS, BOTH TEAMS, ONE GAME:
4 — **New York Islanders, New York Rangers,** April 17, 1983 at NY Rangers. The Islanders scored 3 shorthand goals, Rangers 1. The Rangers won 7-6.
— **Boston Bruins, Minnesota North Stars,** April 11, 1981, at Minnesota. Boston had 3 shorthand goals, Minnesota 1. Minnesota won 6-3.

MOST SHORTHAND GOALS, ONE TEAM, ONE GAME:
3 — **Boston Bruins,** April 11, 1981, at Minnesota. Minnesota won 6-3.

MOST SHORT-HAND GOALS, BOTH TEAMS, ONE PERIOD:
3 — **Toronto Maple Leafs, Detroit Red Wings,** April 5, 1947, at Toronto, first period. Toronto scored two short-hand goals; Detroit one. Toronto won game 6-1.

MOST SHORT-HAND GOALS ONE TEAM, ONE PERIOD:
2 — **By several teams.**

Individual Records
Career

MOST YEARS IN PLAYOFFS:
20 — **Gordie Howe, Detroit, Hartford** (1947-58 incl.; 60-61; 63-66 incl.; 70 and 80)
19 — Red Kelly, Detroit, Toronto
18 — Stan Mikita, Chicago Black Hawks

Brad Park *Jean Beliveau*

MOST CONSECUTIVE YEARS IN PLAYOFFS:
17 — **Brad Park, New York Rangers, Boston, Detroit** (1969-1985 inclusive).
16 — Jean Beliveau, Montreal Canadiens (1954-69, inclusive).

MOST PLAYOFF GAMES:
180 — Henri Richard, Montreal Canadiens

MOST POINTS IN PLAYOFFS (CAREER):
209 — **Wayne Gretzky, Edmonton Oilers**, 64 goals, 111 assists.
176 — Jean Beliveau, Montreal Canadiens, 79 goals, 97 assists.
169 — Bryan Trottier, New York Islanders

MOST GOALS IN PLAYOFFS (CAREER):
85 — **Mike Bossy, New York Islanders**
82 — Maurice Richard, Montreal Canadiens
79 — Jean Beliveau, Montreal Canadiens

MOST GAME-WINNING GOALS IN PLAYOFFS (CAREER):
18 — **Maurice Richard, Montreal Canadiens**

MOST OVERTIME GOALS IN PLAYOFFS (CAREER):
6 — **Maurice Richard, Montreal Canadiens.** (1 in 1946; 3 in 1951; 1 in 1957; 1 in 1958.)

MOST POWER-PLAY GOALS IN PLAYOFFS (CAREER):
35 — **Mike Bossy, New York Islanders**

MOST SHORTHAND GOALS IN PLAYOFFS (CAREER):
9 — **Mark Messier, Edmonton Oilers**

MOST THREE-OR-MORE-GOAL GAMES IN PLAYOFFS (CAREER):
7 — **Maurice Richard, Montreal Canadiens.** Four three-goal games; two four-goal games; one five-goal game.
— **Wayne Gretzky, Edmonton Oilers.** Two four-goal games; five three-goal games.

MOST ASSISTS IN PLAYOFFS (CAREER):
140 — **Wayne Gretzky, Edmonton Oilers**
106 — Bryan Trottier, New York Islanders
104 — Denis Potvin, New York Islanders

MOST SHUTOUTS IN PLAYOFFS (CAREER):
14 — **Jacques Plante, Montreal Canadiens, St. Louis Blues** in 16 playoff years.
13 — Turk Broda, Toronto Maple Leafs
12 — Terry Sawchuk, Detroit, Toronto, Los Angeles

MOST PLAYOFF GAMES APPEARED IN BY A GOALTENDER (CAREER):
132 — **Bill Smith, NY Islanders**

Single Playoff Year

MOST POINTS, ONE PLAYOFF YEAR:
47 — **Wayne Gretzky, Edmonton Oilers,** in 1985. 17 goals, 30 assists in 18 games.

MOST POINTS BY A DEFENSEMAN, ONE PLAYOFF YEAR:
37 — **Paul Coffey, Edmonton Oilers,** in 1985. 12 goals, 25 assists in 18 games against Los Angeles, Winnipeg, Chicago and Philadelphia.

MOST POINTS BY A ROOKIE, ONE PLAYOFF YEAR:
21 — **Dino Ciccarelli, Minnesota North Stars,** in 1981. 14 goals, 7 assists in 19 games against Boston, Buffalo, Calgary and NY Islanders.

MOST GOALS, ONE PLAYOFF YEAR:
19 — **Reggie Leach, Philadelphia Flyers,** 1976. 16 games.
— **Jari Kurri, Edmonton Oilers,** 1985. 18 games.

MOST GOALS BY A DEFENSEMAN, ONE PLAYOFF YEAR:
12 — **Paul Coffey, Edmonton Oilers,** 1985. 18 games.

MOST GOALS BY A ROOKIE, ONE PLAYOFF YEAR:
14 — **Dino Ciccarelli, Minnesota North Stars,** 1981. 19 games.

MOST GAME-WINNING GOALS, ONE PLAYOFF YEAR:
5 — **Mike Bossy, New York Islanders,** 1983. 19 games.
— **Jari Kurri, Edmonton Oilers,** 1987. 21 games.

MOST OVERTIME GOALS, ONE PLAYOFF YEAR:
3 — **Mel Hill, Boston Bruins,** 1939. All against New York Rangers in best-of-seven Semi-Final, won by Boston 4-3.
— **Maurice Richard, Montreal Canadiens,** 1951. 2 against Detroit Red Wings in best-of-seven Semi-Final, won by Montreal 4-2; 1 against Toronto Maple Leafs in best-of-seven Final, won by Toronto 4-1.

MOST POWER-PLAY GOALS, ONE PLAYOFF YEAR:
9 — **Mike Bossy, New York Islanders,** 1981. 18 games against Toronto, Edmonton, NY Rangers and Minnesota.

MOST SHORTHAND GOALS, ONE PLAYOFF YEAR:
3 — **Derek Sanderson, Boston Bruins,** 1969.
— **Bill Barber, Philadelphia Flyers,** 1980.
— **Lorne Henning, New York Islanders,** 1980.
— **Wayne Gretzky, Edmonton Oilers,** 1983.

MOST THREE-OR-MORE GOAL GAMES, ONE PLAYOFF YEAR:
4 — **Jari Kurri, Edmonton Oilers,** 1985. 1 four-goal game, 3 three-goal games.

LONGEST CONSECUTIVE GOAL-SCORING STREAK, ONE PLAYOFF YEAR:
9 Games — **Reggie Leach, Philadelphia Flyers,** 1976. Streak started April 17 at Toronto and ended May 9 at Montreal. He scored one goal in each of seven games; two in one game; and five in another; a total 14 goals.

MOST ASSISTS, ONE PLAYOFF YEAR:
30 — **Wayne Gretzky, Edmonton Oilers,** 1985. 18 games.

MOST ASSISTS BY A DEFENSEMAN, ONE PLAYOFF YEAR:
25 — **Paul Coffey, Edmonton Oilers,** 1985. 18 games.

MOST WINS BY A GOALTENDER, ONE PLAYOFF YEAR:
15 — **Bill Smith, New York Islanders,** 1980. 20 games.
— **Bill Smith, New York Islanders,** 1982. 18 games.
— **Grant Fuhr, Edmonton, Oilers,** 1985. 18 games.
— **Patrick Roy, Montreal Canadiens,** 1986. 20 games.
— **Ron Hextall, Philadelphia Flyers,** 1987. 26 games.

MOST CONSECUTIVE WINS BY A GOALTENDER, ONE PLAYOFF YEAR:
10 — **Gerry Cheevers, Boston Bruins,** 1970. 2 wins against NY Rangers in Quarter-Final, won by Boston 4-2; 4 wins against Chicago in Semi-Final, won by Boston 4-0; and 4 wins against St. Louis in Final, won by Boston 4-0.

PLAYOFF RECORDS

Ken Dryden

MOST SHUTOUTS, ONE PLAYOFF YEAR:
4 — **Clint Benedict, Montreal Maroons,** 1928. 9 games.
— **Dave Kerr, New York Rangers,** 1937. 9 games.
— **Frank McCool, Toronto Maple Leafs,** 1945. 13 games.
— **Terry Sawchuk, Detroit Red Wings,** 1952. 8 games.
— **Bernie Parent, Philadelphia Flyers,** 1975. 17 games.
— **Ken Dryden, Montreal Canadiens,** 1977. 14 games.

MOST CONSECUTIVE SHUTOUTS:
3 — **Frank McCool, Toronto Maple Leafs,** 1945. McCool shut out Detroit Red Wings 1-0, April 6; 2-0, April 8; 1-0, April 12. Toronto won the best-of-seven Final 4-3.

One-Series Records

MOST POINTS IN FINAL SERIES:
12 — **Gordie Howe, Detroit Red Wings,** in 1955, during 7 games against Montreal. 5 goals, 7 assists.
— **Yvan Cournoyer, Montreal Canadiens,** in 1973, during 6 games against Chicago. 6 goals, 6 assists.
— **Jacques Lemaire, Montreal Canadiens,** in 1973, during 6 games against Chicago. 3 goals, 9 assists.

MOST GOALS IN FINAL SERIES:
7 — **Jean Beliveau, Montreal Canadiens,** in 1956, during 5 games against Detroit.
— **Mike Bossy, New York Islanders,** in 1982, during 4 games against Vancouver.
— **Wayne Gretzky, Edmonton Oilers,** in 1985, during 5 games against Philadelphia.

MOST ASSISTS IN FINAL SERIES:
9 — **Jacques Lemaire, Montreal Canadiens,** in 1973, during 6 games against Chicago.
— **Wayne Gretzky, Edmonton Oilers,** in 1987, during 7 games against Philadelphia.

MOST POINTS IN ONE SERIES (OTHER THAN FINAL):
19 — **Rick Middleton, Boston Bruins,** in 1983, during 7 games against Buffalo. 5 goals, 14 assists.

MOST GOALS IN ONE SERIES (OTHER THAN FINAL):
12 — **Jari Kurri, Edmonton Oilers,** in 1985, during 6 games against Chicago.

MOST ASSISTS IN ONE SERIES (OTHER THAN FINAL):
14 — **Rick Middleton, Boston Bruins,** in 1983, during 7 games against Buffalo.
— **Wayne Gretzky, Edmonton Oilers,** in 1985, during 6 games against Chicago.

MOST OVERTIME GOALS, ONE PLAYOFF SERIES:
3 — **Mel Hill, Boston Bruins,** 1939, in Semi-Final series against New York Rangers, won by Boston 4-3. Hill scored at 59:25 overtime March 21 for a 2-1 win; at 8:24, March 23 for a 3-2 win; and at 48:00 April 2 for a 2-1 win.

MOST POWER-PLAY GOALS, ONE PLAYOFF SERIES:
5 — **Andy Bathgate, Detroit Red Wings,** 1966, Semi-Final against Chicago, won by Detroit 4-2.
— **Denis Potvin, New York Islanders,** 1981, Quarter-Final against Edmonton, won by Islanders 4-2.
— **Ken Houston, Calgary Flames,** 1981, Quarter-Final against Philadelphia, won by Calgary 4-3.

MOST SHORTHAND GOALS, ONE PLAYOFF SERIES:
3 — **Bill Barber, Philadelphia Flyers,** 1980, Semi-Final against Minnesota, won by Philadelphia 4-1.

MOST THREE-OR-MORE-GOAL GAMES, ONE PLAYOFF SERIES:
3 — **Jari Kurri, Edmonton Oilers,** 1985, Campbell Conference Championship against Chicago. Kurri scored three goals May 7 in 7-3 win at Edmonton; three goals May 14 in 10-5 win at Edmonton; and four goals May 16 in 8-2 win at Chicago.

Single-Game Records

MOST POINTS, ONE GAME:
7 — **Wayne Gretzky, Edmonton Oilers,** April 17, 1983 at Calgary during 10-2 win. Gretzky had 4 goals, 3 assists.
— **Wayne Gretzky, Edmonton Oilers,** April 25,1985 at Winnipeg during 8-3 win. Gretzky had 3 goals, 4 assists.
— **Wayne Gretzky, Edmonton Oilers,** April 9, 1987, at Edmonton during 13-3 win over Los Angeles. Gretzky had one goal, six assists.

MOST POINTS BY A DEFENSEMAN, ONE GAME:
6 — **Paul Coffey, Edmonton Oilers,** May 14, 1985 at Edmonton. 1 goal, 5 assists. Edmonton won 10-5.

MOST GOALS, ONE GAME:
5 — **Maurice Richard, Montreal Canadiens,** March 23, 1944, at Montreal. Final score: Canadiens 5, Toronto 1.
— **Darryl Sittler, Toronto Maple Leafs,** April 22, 1976, at Toronto. Final score: Toronto 8, Philadelphia 5.
— **Reggie Leach, Philadelphia Flyers,** May 6, 1976, at Philadelphia. Final score: Philadelphia 6, Boston 3.

MOST GOALS BY A DEFENSEMAN, ONE GAME:
3 — **Bobby Orr, Boston Bruins,** April 11, 1971 at Montreal. Final score: Boston 5, Montreal 2.
— **Dick Redmond, Chicago Black Hawks,** April 4, 1973 at Chicago. Final score: Chicago 7, St. Louis 1.
— **Denis Potvin, NY Islanders,** April 17, 1981 at Long Island. Final score: NY Islanders 6, Edmonton 3.
— **Paul Reinhart, Calgary Flames,** April 14, 1983 at Edmonton. Final score: Edmonton 6, Calgary 3.
— **Paul Reinhart, Calgary,** April 8, 1984 at Vancouver. Final score: Calgary 5, Vancouver 1.
— **Doug Halward, Vancouver Canucks,** April 7, 1984 at Vancouver. Final score: Vancouver 7, Calgary 0.

MOST POWER-PLAY GOALS, ONE GAME:
3 — **Syd Howe, Detroit Red Wings,** March 23, 1939, at Detroit against Montreal Canadiens. Detroit won 7-3.
— **Sid Smith, Toronto Maple Leafs,** April 10, 1949, at Toronto against Detroit Red Wings. Toronto won 3-1.
— **Phil Esposito, Boston Bruins,** April 2, 1969, at Boston against Toronto Maple Leafs. Boston won 10-0.
— **John Bucyk, Boston Bruins,** April 21, 1974, at Boston against Chicago Black Hawks. Boston won 8-6.
— **Denis Potvin, New York Islanders,** April 17, 1981, at New York against Edmonton Oilers. Islanders won 6-3.
— **Tim Kerr, Philadelphia Flyers,** April 13, 1985, at New York against Rangers. Philadelphia won 6-5.
— **Jari Kurri, Edmonton Oilers,** April 9, 1987, at Edmonton against Los Angeles Kings. Edmonton won 13-3.

Dave Keon

MOST SHORTHAND GOALS, ONE GAME:
2 — **Dave Keon, Toronto Maple Leafs,** April 18, 1963, at Toronto, in 3-1 win against Detroit.
— **Bryan Trottier, New York Islanders,** April 8, 1980 at Long Island, in 8-1 win against Los Angeles.
— **Bobby Lalonde, Boston Bruins,** April 11, 1981 at Minnesota. Final score: Minnesota 6, Boston 3.
— **Wayne Gretzky, Edmonton Oilers,** April 6, 1983 at Edmonton, in 6-3 win against Winnipeg.
— **Jari Kurri, Edmonton Oilers,** April 24, 1983 at Edmonton. Final score: Edmonton 8, Chicago 4.

MOST ASSISTS, ONE GAME:
6 — **Mikko Leinonen, New York Rangers,** April 8, 1982, at New York. Final score: NY Rangers 7, Philadelphia 3.
— **Wayne Gretzky, Edmonton Oilers,** April 9, 1987, at Edmonton. Final score: Edmonton 13, Los Angeles 3.

Tim Kerr

One-Period Records

MOST POINTS, ONE PERIOD:
4 — **Maurice Richard, Montreal Canadiens,** March 29, 1945, at Montreal against Toronto. Third period, three goals, one assist. Final score: Montreal 10, Toronto 3.
 — **Dickie Moore, Montreal Canadiens,** March 25, 1954, at Montreal against Boston. First period, two goals, two assists. Final score: Montreal 8, Boston 1.
 — **Barry Pederson, Boston Bruins,** April 8, 1982, at Boston against Buffalo. Second period, three goals, one assist. Final score: Boston 7, Buffalo 3.
 — **Peter McNab, Boston Bruins,** April 11, 1982, at Buffalo. Second period, one goal, three assists. Final score: Boston 5, Buffalo 2.
 — **Tim Kerr, Philadelphia Flyers,** April 13, 1985 at New York. Second period, four goals. Final score: Philadelphia 6, Rangers 5.
 — **Ken Linseman, Boston Bruins,** April 14, 1985 at Boston against Montreal. Second period, two goals, two assists. Final score: Boston 7, Montreal 6.
 — **Wayne Gretzky, Edmonton Oilers,** April 12, 1987, at Edmonton against Los Angeles. Third period, one goal, three assists. Final score: Edmonton 6, Los Angeles 3.

MOST GOALS, ONE PERIOD:
4 — **Tim Kerr, Philadelphia Flyers,** April 13, 1985, at New York against Rangers, second period. Final score: Philadelphia 6, Rangers 5.

MOST POWER PLAY GOALS, ONE PERIOD:
3 — **Tim Kerr, Philadelphia Flyers,** April 13, 1985 at New York, second period in 6-5 win against Rangers.

MOST SHORTHAND GOALS, ONE PERIOD:
2 — **Bryan Trottier, New York Islanders,** April 8, 1980, second period at New York in 8-1 win against Los Angeles Kings.
 — **Bobby Lalonde, Boston Bruins,** April 11, 1981, third period at Minnesota in 6-3 win by North Stars.
 — **Jari Kurri, Edmonton Oilers,** April 24, 1983, third period at Edmonton in 8-4 win against Chicago Black Hawks.

MOST ASSISTS, ONE PERIOD:
3 — **By several players.**

The Longest Game in Stanley Cup History

At the Forum, March 24-25, 1936, between Detroit Red Wings and Montreal Maroons. Mud Bruneteau scored, assisted by Hec Kilrea, after 116 minutes, 30 seconds of overtime to give Detroit a 1-0 victory. Total playing time for the game was 176 minutes, 30 seconds. The game started at 8:34 p.m., March 24, and ended five hours, 51 minutes later at 2:25 a.m., March 25. It was the first game of a best-of-five Semi-Final, won by Detroit 3-0.

SUMMARY
First Period
No scoring.
Penalties: McDonald (minor) 12:07, Trottier (minor) 15:48, Shields (minor) 17:30.
Second Period
No scoring.
Penalties: H. Kilrea (minor) 5:05, Barry, Ward (minors) 10:24, McDonald (minor) 12:07.
Third Period
No scoring.
Penalty: W. Kilrea (minor) 9:08
First Overtime Period
No scoring.
Penalties: none.
Second Overtime Period
No scoring.
Penalties: none.
Third Overtime Period
No scoring. Penalties: none.
Fourth Overtime Period
No scoring.
Penalty: H. Smith (minor) 0:09.
Fifth Overtime Period
No scoring. Penalties: none.
Sixth Overtime Period
1. — Detroit, Bruneteau (H. Kilrea) 16:30.
Penalties: none.

LINEUP
DETROIT:
Goal — Norm Smith. Defense — Doug Young, Bucko McDonald, Ebbie Goodfellow, Scotty Bowman. Forwards — Herbie Lewis, Larry Aurie, Marty Barry, Syd Howe, Wally Kilrea, Johnny Sorrell, Gordie Pettinger, Hec Kilrea, Pete Kelly, Mud Bruneteau.
MONTREAL MAROONS:
Goal — Lorne Chabot. Defence — Cy Wentworth, Lionel Conacher, Stew Evans, Alan Shields. Forwards — Jimmy Ward, Baldy Northcott, Hooley Smith, Dave Trottier, Gus Marker, Herb Cain, Bob Gracie, Russ Blinco, Earle Robinson, Joe Lamb.

OFFICIALS
Referees — A.G. Smith, Bill Stewart. Penalty recorders — Bill Graham of Toronto, H. Hayter of Montreal. Umpires (goal judges) — Bill Campbell, Wirey Hagen of Toronto. Timekeeper — Bill Christie of Toronto. Scorer — Elmer Ferguson of Montreal.

Mud Bruneteau

OVERTIME

Pat LaFontaine's goal in the fourth overtime period eliminated the Washington Capitals in game seven of the 1987 Patrick Division Semi-Final.

Ten Longest Overtime Games

Mar. 24/36	Mtl.	SF	Det. 1	Mtl. M. 0	Mud Bruneteau	116:30	Det.
Apr. 3/33	Tor.	SF	Tor. 1	Bos. 0	Ken Doraty	104:46	Tor.
Mar. 23/43	Det.	SF	Tor. 3	Det. 2	Jack McLean	70:18	Det.
Mar. 28/30	Mtl.	SF	Mtl. 2	NYR 1	Gus Rivers	68:52	Mtl.
Apr. 18/87	Wsh.	DSF	NYI 3	Wsh. 2	Pat LaFontaine	68:47	NYI
Mar. 27/51	Det.	SF	Mtl. 3	Det. 2	Maurice Richard	61:09	Mtl.
Mar. 26/32	Mtl.	SF	NYR 4	Mtl. 3	Fred Cook	59:32	NYR
Mar. 21/39	NY	SF	Bos. 2	NYR 1	Mel Hill	59:25	Bos.
Apr. 9/31	Mtl.	F	Chi. 3	Mtl. 2	Cy Wentworth	53:50	Mtl.
Mar. 26/61	Chi.	SF	Chi. 2	Mtl. 1	Murray Balfour	52:12	Chi.

Overtime Record of Current Teams
(Listed by number of OT games played)

	Overall				Home				Road					
Team	GP	W	L	T	GP	W	L	T	Last OT Game	GP	W	L	T	Last OT Game
Montreal	90	46	42	2	41	25	15	1	Apr. 9/87	49	21	27	1	May 4/86
Boston	74	30	41	3	34	17	16	1	Apr. 24/83	40	13	25	2	Apr. 9/87
Toronto	73	35	37	1	47	22	24	1	Apr. 27/87	26	13	13	0	Apr. 9/87
NY Rangers	46	23	23	0	19	9	10	0	May 5/86	27	14	13	0	Apr. 17/86
Detroit	44	20	24	0	26	10	16	0	Apr. 18/84	18	10	8	0	Apr. 27/87
Chicago	40	21	17	2	21	12	8	1	Apr. 28/85	19	9	9	1	Apr. 30/85
NY Islanders	29	22	7	0	12	10	2	0	Apr. 13/84	17	12	5	0	Apr. 18/87
Philadelphia	29	16	13	0	10	7	3	0	May 4/80	19	9	10	0	May 20/87
St. Louis	23	12	11	0	10	8	2	0	May 12/86	13	4	9	0	Apr. 9/87
Minnesota	21	10	11	0	12	5	7	0	Apr. 30/85	9	5	4	0	Apr. 28/85
Buffalo	15	9	6	0	10	7	3	0	Apr. 16/81	5	2	3	0	Apr. 24/83
Quebec	15	9	6	0	9	5	4	0	Apr. 26/87	6	4	2	0	Apr. 8/87
Los Angeles	14	6	8	0	7	3	4	0	Apr. 13/85	7	3	4	0	Apr. 10/85
*Calgary	14	7	7	0	4	2	2	0	May 18/86	10	5	5	0	Apr. 11/87
Edmonton	13	7	6	0	9	6	3	0	May 20/87	4	1	3	0	Apr. 13/85
Vancouver	9	3	6	0	3	1	2	0	Apr. 10/83	6	2	4	0	Apr. 6/83
Pittsburgh	6	3	3	0	2	1	1	0	Apr. 10/82	4	2	2	0	Apr. 13/82
Washington	6	2	4	0	4	2	2	0	Apr. 18/87	2	0	2	0	Apr. 23/86
Hartford	6	3	3	0	3	2	1	0	Apr. 9/87	3	1	2	0	Apr. 16/87
Winnipeg	5	2	3	0	3	1	2	0	Apr. 11/87	2	1	1	0	Apr. 21/87
**New Jersey	1	0	1	0	0	0	0	0		1	0	1	0	Apr. 11/78

* Totals include those of Atlanta 1974-80.
** Totals include those of Kansas City and Colorado 1975-82.

Stanley Cup Coaching Records

Coaches listed in order of total games coached in playoffs. Minimum: 65 games.

Coach	Team	Years	Series	Series W	L	G	Games W	L	T	Cups	%
Irvin, Dick	Chicago	1	3	2	1	9	5	3	1	0	.611
	Toronto	9	20	12	8	66	33	32	1	1	.508
	Montreal	14	22	11	11	115	62	53	0	3	.539
	TOTALS	24	45	25	20	190	100	88	2	4	.532
Bowman, Scott	St. Louis	4	10	6	4	52	26	26	0	0	.500
	Montreal	8	19	16	3	98	70	28	0	5	.714
	Buffalo	5	8	3	5	36	18	18	0	0	.500
	TOTALS	17	37	25	12	186	114	72	0	5	.612
Arbour, Al	St. Louis	1	2	1	1	11	4	7	0	0	.364
	NY Islanders	12	35	27	8	171	109	62	0	4	.637
	TOTALS	13	37	28	9	182	113	69	0	4	.621
Blake, Toe	Montreal	13	23	18	5	119	82	37	0	8	.689
Reay, Billy	Chicago	12	22	10	12	117	57	60	0	0	.487
Shero, Fred	Philadelphia	6	16	12	4	83	48	35	0	2	.578
	NY Rangers	2	5	3	2	25	13	12	0	0	.520
	TOTALS	8	21	15	6	108	61	47	0	2	.565
Adams, Jack	Detroit	15	27	15	12	105	52	52	1	3	.500
Francis, Emile	NY Rangers	9	14	5	9	75	34	41	0	0	.453
	St. Louis	3	4	1	3	18	6	12	0	0	.333
	TOTALS	12	18	6	12	93	40	53	0	0	.430
Imlach, Punch	Toronto	11	17	10	7	92	44	48	0	4	.478
Sather, Glen	Edmonton	7	18	13	5	80	54	26	0	2	.675
Day, Hap	Toronto	9	14	10	4	80	49	31	0	5	.613
Abel, Sid	Chicago	1	1	0	1	7	3	4	0	0	.429
	Detroit	8	12	4	8	69	29	40	0	0	.420
	TOTALS	9	13	4	9	76	32	44	0	0	.421
Ross, Art	Boston	12	19	9	10	70	32	33	5	2	.493
Ivan, Tommy	Detroit	7	12	8	4	67	36	31	0	3	.537
Pulford, Bob	Los Angeles	4	6	2	4	26	11	15	0	0	.423
	Chicago	5	9	4	5	41	17	24	0	0	.415
	TOTALS	9	15	6	9	67	28	39	0	0	.418
Patrick, Lester	NY Rangers	12	24	14	10	65	31	26	8	2	.538

Professional Hockey Index 1988

AHL	American Hockey League
AJHL	Alberta Junior Hockey League
AUAA	Atlantic Universities Athletic Association
BCJHL	British Columbia Junior Hockey League
CCHA	Central Collegiate Hockey Association
COJHL	Central Ontario Junior Hockey League
CWUAA	Canada West Universities Athletic Association
ECAC	Eastern Collegiate Athletic Association
H.E.	Hockey East
IHL	International Hockey League
MJHL	Manitoba Junior Hockey League
NHL	**National Hockey League**
OHL	Ontario Hockey League
OPJHL	Ontario Provincial Junior Hockey League
OUAA	Ontario Universities Athletic Association
QMJHL	Quebec Major Junior Hockey League
SJHL	Saskatchewan Junior Hockey League
WCHA	Western Collegiate Hockey Association
WHL	Western Hockey League

Abbreviations: A – assists; G – goals; GP – games played; PIM – penalties in minutes; TP – total points; * – league-leading total.

SECTION 1: FORWARDS AND DEFENSEMEN

The Professional Hockey Index lists the 1986-87 statistical record and NHL totals of more than 1,600 forwards and defensemen who played in the NHL, minor professional, junior, college or European leagues last season. Included are skaters who played in the NHL in 1986-87, draft choices from the first and second rounds of the 1986 and 1987 NHL Entry Drafts and players on the reserve lists of NHL clubs.

PLAYER	CLUB	LEAGUE	GP	G	A	TP	PIM	GP	G	A	TP	PIM
Acton, Keith	**Minnesota**	**NHL**	78	16	29	45	56	....	....	....	....	....
	NHL Totals		525	157	247	404	535	39	8	18	26	46
Adams, Greg	**New Jersey**	**NHL**	72	20	27	47	19	....	....	....	....	....
	NHL Totals		186	67	78	145	63	....	....	....	....	....
Adams, Gregory	**Washington**	**NHL**	67	14	30	44	184	7	1	3	4	38
	NHL Totals		371	57	114	171	870	22	2	6	8	74
Agnew, Jim	**Vancouver**	**NHL**	4	0	0	0	0	....	....	....	....	....
	Fredericton	AHL	67	0	5	5	261	....	....	....	....	....
	NHL Totals		4	0	0	0	0	....	....	....	....	....
Aitken, Brad	S.S. Marie	OHL	52	27	38	65	86	4	1	2	3	5
Akervik, Andrew	U. of Wisconsin	WCHA	18	3	3	6	4	....	....	....	....	....
Albelin, Tommy	Djurgardens	Swe.	33	7	5	12	49	....	....	....	....	....
Albrecht, Cliff	Newmarket	AHL	63	2	5	7	20	....	....	....	....	....
Alexander, Bob	Minn.-Duluth	WCHA	37	12	6	18	40	....	....	....	....	....
Allison, David	Muskegon	IHL	67	11	35	46	337	15	4	3	7	20
	NHL Totals		3	0	0	0	12	....	....	....	....	....
Allison, Mike	**Toronto**	**NHL**	71	7	16	23	66	13	3	5	8	15
	NHL Totals		337	70	118	188	363	66	7	17	24	107
Allison, Ray	**Philadelphia**	**NHL**	2	0	0	0	0	....	....	....	....	....
	Hershey	AHL	78	29	55	84	57	5	3	1	4	12
	NHL Totals		238	64	93	157	223	12	2	3	5	20

| | | | \multicolumn{4}{c}{Regular Season} | | \multicolumn{5}{c}{Playoffs} |
PLAYER	CLUB	LEAGUE	GP	G	A	TP	PIM	GP	G	A	TP	PIM
Ames, Paul	U. of Lowell	H.E.	34	7	16	23	43	....	....	....	....	....
Anderson, David	Maine	AHL	59	9	9	18	80	....	....	....	....	....
Anderson, Glenn	Edmonton	NHL	80	35	38	73	65	21	14	13	27	59
	NHL Totals		522	301	316	617	454	98	55	65	120	196
Anderson, John	Hartford	NHL	76	31	44	75	19	6	1	2	3	0
	NHL Totals		689	249	293	542	215	33	9	17	26	0
Anderson, John	Oshawa	OHL	45	11	13	24	24	....	....	....	....	....
Anderson, Mark	Ohio State	CCHA	43	21	26	47	74	....	....	....	....	....
Anderson, Perry	New Jersey	NHL	57	10	9	19	107	....	....	....	....	....
	Maine	AHL	9	5	4	9	42	....	....	....	....	....
	NHL Totals		252	39	39	78	553	22	2	0	2	38
Anderson, Shawn	Buffalo	NHL	41	2	11	13	23	....	....	....	....	....
	Rochester	AHL	15	2	5	7	11	....	....	....	....	....
	NHL Totals		41	2	11	13	23	....	....	....	....	....
Anderson, Will	Victoria	WHL	69	17	43	60	96	5	1	3	4	6
Andersson, Mikael	Buffalo	NHL	16	0	3	3	0	....	....	....	....	....
	Rochester	AHL	42	6	20	26	14	9	1	2	3	2
	NHL Totals		48	1	12	13	4	....	....	....	....	....
Andonoff, Jim	Flint	IHL	34	7	11	18	24	1	0	1	1	2
Andreychuk, Dave	Buffalo	NHL	77	25	48	73	46	....	....	....	....	....
	NHL Totals		342	144	194	338	219	11	5	3	8	10
Arabski, Rob	Guelph	OHL	64	29	60	89	36	....	....	....	....	....
Archibald, Dave	Portland	WHL	65	50	57	107	40	20	10	18	28	11
Archibald, James	Minnesota	NHL	1	0	0	0	2	....	....	....	....	....
	Springfield	AHL	66	10	17	27	303	....	....	....	....	....
	NHL Totals		16	1	2	3	45	....	....	....	....	....
Armstrong, Harry	Ill.-Chicago	CCHA	15	1	3	4	32	....	....	....	....	....
Armstrong, Ian	Hershey	AHL	68	0	7	7	148	3	0	0	0	2
Armstrong, Tim	Newmarket	AHL	5	3	0	3	2	....	....	....	....	....
	Toronto	OHL	66	29	55	84	61	....	....	....	....	....
Arndt, Troy	Brandon	WHL	38	1	8	9	154	....	....	....	....	....
Arniel, Scott	Buffalo	NHL	63	11	14	25	59	....	....	....	....	....
	NHL Totals		394	86	109	195	308	18	1	2	3	26
Arthur, Chad	Bowling Green	CCHA	20	6	4	10	41	....	....	....	....	....
Ashton, Brent	Quebec	NHL	46	25	19	44	17	....	....	....	....	....
	Detroit	NHL	35	15	16	31	22	16	4	9	13	6
	NHL Totals		584	165	188	353	351	56	14	16	30	56
Aubertin, Eric	Laval	QMJHL	59	33	51	84	70	15	2	5	7	20
Aubry, Pierre	Adirondack	AHL	17	3	7	10	23	9	1	3	4	32
	NHL Totals		202	24	26	50	133	20	1	1	2	32
Babcock, Bobby	S.S. Marie	OHL	62	7	8	15	243	4	0	0	0	11
Babe, Warren	Swift Current	WHL	16	8	12	20	19	....	....	....	....	....
	Kamloops	WHL	52	28	45	73	109	11	4	6	10	8
Babych, Dave	Hartford	NHL	66	8	33	41	44	6	1	1	2	14
	NHL Totals		518	91	324	415	472	32	6	14	20	63
Babych, Wayne	Hartford	NHL	4	0	0	0	4	....	....	....	....	....
	Binghamton	AHL	6	2	5	7	6	....	....	....	....	....
	NHL Totals		519	192	246	438	498	41	7	9	16	24
Badeau, Rene	Saginaw	IHL	69	4	13	17	39	10	0	0	0	4
Baillargeon, Joel	Winnipeg	NHL	11	0	1	1	15	....	....	....	....	....
	Sherbrooke	AHL	44	9	18	27	137	6	2	2	4	27
	Fort Wayne	IHL	4	1	1	2	37	....	....	....	....	....
	NHL Totals		11	0	1	1	15	....	....	....	....	....
Baker, Sean	U. of Michigan	CCHA	31	3	3	6	24	....	....	....	....	....
Bakovic, Peter	Moncton	AHL	77	17	34	51	280	6	3	3	6	54
Baldris, Miguel	St. Jean	QMJHL	67	7	34	41	72	8	0	0	0	9
Ballantyne, Jeff	Ottawa	OHL	65	2	13	15	75	5	0	0	0	9
Bar, Mark	Peterborough	OHL	36	2	12	14	38	12	1	1	2	25
Barbe, Mario	Granby	QMJHL	65	7	25	32	356	7	1	5	6	38
Barber, Don	Bowling Green	CCHA	43	29	34	63	107	....	....	....	....	....
Baron, Murray	North Dakota	WCHA	41	4	10	14	62	....	....	....	....	....
Barr, Dave	St. Louis	NHL	2	0	0	0	0	....	....	....	....	....
	Hartford	NHL	30	2	4	6	19	....	....	....	....	....
	Detroit	NHL	37	13	13	26	49	....	....	....	....	....
	NHL Totals		235	45	74	119	179	28	2	1	3	18

PLAYER	CLUB	LEAGUE	GP	Regular Season G	A	TP	PIM	GP	Playoffs G	A	TP	PIM
Barraket, Tim	Harvard	ECAC	34	25	29	54	12	....	....	....	....	....
Barrett, John	Washington	NHL	55	2	2	4	43	....	....	....	....	....
	NHL Totals		487	20	76	96	642	16	2	2	4	50
Bartel, Robin	Vancouver	NHL	40	0	1	1	14	....	....	....	....	....
	Fredericton	AHL	10	0	2	2	15	....	....	....	....	....
	NHL Totals		41	0	1	1	14	6	0	0	0	16
Bassegio, David	Yale	ECAC	29	8	17	25	52	....	....	....	....	....
Bassen, Bob	NY Islanders	NHL	77	7	10	17	89	14	1	2	3	21
	NHL Totals		88	9	11	20	95	17	1	3	4	21
Bateman, Robinson	Vermont	ECAC	32	2	3	5	78	....	....	....	....	....
Baumgartner, Ken	New Haven	AHL	13	0	3	3	99	6	0	0	0	60
Bawa, Robin	Kamloops	WHL	62	57	56	113	91	13	6	7	13	22
Baxter, Paul	Calgary	NHL	18	0	2	2	66	2	0	0	0	10
	NHL Totals		472	48	121	169	1564	40	0	5	5	162
Bean, Tim	North Bay	OHL	65	24	39	63	134	21	4	12	16	65
Beaudette, Dan	Miami-Ohio	CCHA	31	5	9	14	26	....	....	....	....	....
Beaudoin, Yves	Washington	NHL	6	0	0	0	5	....	....	....	....	....
	Binghamton	AHL	63	11	25	36	35	11	0	1	1	6
	NHL Totals		10	0	0	0	5	••••	••••	••••	••••	••••
Beaulieu, Nicolas	Drummondville	QMJHL	69	19	34	53	198	....	....	....	....	....
Beck, Barry	DID NOT PLAY											
	NHL Totals		563	103	244	347	963	51	10	23	33	77
Beck, Brad	Saginaw	IHL	82	10	24	34	114	10	0	2	2	24
Becker, Russ	Michigan Tech	WCHA	27	0	1	1	46	....	....	....	....	....
Beers, Bob	U. Maine	H.E.	38	0	13	13	45	....	....	....	....	....
Beers, Eddie	DID NOT PLAY											
	NHL Totals		250	94	116	210	256	41	7	10	17	47
Belanger, Roger	Baltimore	AHL	32	9	11	20	14	....	....	....	....	....
	Muskegon	IHL	5	1	2	3	0	....	....	....	....	....
	NHL Totals		44	3	5	8	32	••••	••••	••••	••••	••••
Bell, Bruce	St. Louis	NHL	45	3	13	16	18	4	1	1	2	7
	NHL Totals		195	11	62	73	105	34	3	5	8	41
Belland, Brad	Cornwall	OHL	50	28	25	53	31	5	1	3	4	8
Belland, Neil	Pittsburgh	NHL	3	0	1	1	0	....	....	....	....	....
	Baltimore	AHL	61	6	18	24	12	....	....	....	....	....
	NHL Totals		109	13	32	45	54	21	2	9	11	23
Bellefeuille, Brian	Ill-Chicago	CCHA	2	0	0	0	2	....	....	....	....	....
Bellows, Brian	Minnesota	NHL	65	26	27	53	34	....	....	....	....	....
	NHL Totals		376	159	183	342	251	39	14	20	34	49
Benic, Geoff	Windsor	OHL	63	9	7	16	169	14	2	1	3	22
Bennett, Ric	Providence	H.E.	32	15	12	27	34	....	....	....	....	....
Benning, Brian	St. Louis	NHL	78	13	36	49	110	6	0	4	4	9
	NHL Totals		82	13	38	51	110	12	1	6	7	22
Benning, Jim	Toronto	NHL	5	0	0	0	4	....	....	....	....	....
	Newmarket	AHL	10	1	5	6	0	....	....	....	....	....
	Vancouver	NHL	54	2	11	13	40	....	....	....	....	....
	NHL Totals		418	39	147	186	329	4	1	1	2	2
Benoit, Guy	New Haven	AHL	41	14	15	29	10	6	2	2	4	16
	Cdn. Olympic	....	15	5	2	7	0	....	....	....	....	....
Beraldo, Paul	S.S. Marie	OHL	63	39	51	90	117	4	3	2	5	6
Berezan, Perry	Calgary	NHL	24	5	3	8	24	2	0	2	2	7
	NHL Totals		88	20	26	46	67	12	2	3	5	17
Berg, Bill	Springfield	AHL	4	1	1	2	4	....	....	....	....	....
	Toronto	OHL	57	3	15	18	138	....	....	....	....	....
Bergen, Todd	Springfield	AHL	27	12	11	23	14	....	....	....	....	....
	NHL Totals		14	11	5	16	4	17	4	9	13	8
Berger, Mike	Indianapolis	IHL	4	0	3	3	4	6	0	1	1	13
	Spokane	WHL	65	26	49	75	80	2	0	0	0	2
Bergevin, Marc	Chicago	NHL	66	4	10	14	66	3	1	0	1	2
	NHL Totals		197	11	23	34	180	12	1	3	4	4
Bergland, Tim	U. of Minnesota	WCHA	49	18	17	35	48	....	....	....	....	....
Bernard, Larry	Seattle	WHL	70	40	46	86	159	....	....	....	....	....
Berry, Brad	Winnipeg	NHL	52	2	8	10	60	7	0	1	1	14
	NHL Totals		65	3	8	11	70	10	0	1	1	14

Players: BERTUZZI...BOUTILIER

PLAYER	CLUB	LEAGUE	Regular Season GP	G	A	TP	PIM	Playoffs GP	G	A	TP	PIM
Bertuzzi, Brian	Fredericton	AHL	55	7	8	15	50	....	....	....	....	....
Berube, Craig	Philadelphia	NHL	7	0	0	0	57	5	0	0	0	17
	Hershey	AHL	63	7	17	24	325	....	....	....	....	....
	NHL Totals		7	0	0	0	57	5	0	0	0	17
Beukeboom, Jeff	Edmonton	NHL	44	3	8	11	124	....	....	....	....	....
	Nova Scotia	AHL	14	1	7	8	35	....	....	....	....	....
	NHL Totals		44	3	8	11	124	1	0	0	0	4
Beukeboom, John	Kalamazoo	IHL	80	8	24	32	270	5	1	1	2	16
Biggs, Don	Nova Scotia	AHL	80	22	25	47	165	5	1	2	3	4
	NHL Totals		1	0	0	0	0	....	....	....	....	....
Biotti, Chris	Harvard	ECAC	30	1	6	7	23	....	....	....	....	....
Bishop, Michael	Colgate	ECAC	30	7	17	24	68	....	....	....	....	....
Bissett, Tom	Michigan Tech	WCHA	40	16	19	35	12	....	....	....	....	....
Bisson, Steve	S.S. Marie	OHL	52	5	15	20	38	4	1	1	2	4
Bjorkman, John	U. of Michigan	CCHA	25	4	0	4	6	....	....	....	....	....
Bjugstad, Scott	Minnesota	NHL	39	4	9	13	43	....	....	....	....	....
	Springfield	AHL	11	6	4	10	7	....	....	....	....	....
	NHL Totals		196	58	46	104	101	5	0	1	1	0
Bjuhr, Thomas	Portland	WHL	39	28	26	54	23	....	....	....	....	....
Blaisdell, Mike	Pittsburgh	NHL	10	1	1	2	2	....	....	....	....	....
	Baltimore	AHL	43	12	12	24	47	....	....	....	....	....
	NHL Totals		316	66	82	148	160	....	....	....	....	....
Bloemberg, Jeff	North Bay	OHL	60	5	13	18	91	21	1	6	7	13
Blomqvist, Timo	New Jersey	NHL	20	0	2	2	29	....	....	....	....	....
	NHL Totals		243	4	53	57	293	13	0	0	0	24
Blomsten, Arto	Djurgardens	Swe.	29	2	4	6	28	....	....	....	....	....
Bloom, Scott	U. Minnesota	WCHA	44	6	11	17	28	....	....	....	....	....
Blum, John	Washington	NHL	66	2	8	10	133	6	0	1	1	4
	NHL Totals		223	7	33	40	532	17	0	1	1	27
Bobyck, Brent	North Dakota	WCHA	46	8	11	19	16	....	....	....	....	....
Bodak, Robert Peter	Moncton	AHL	48	11	20	31	75	6	1	1	2	18
Bodger, Doug	Pittsburgh	NHL	76	11	38	49	52	....	....	....	....	....
	NHL Totals		220	20	97	117	182	....	....	....	....	....
Boettger, Dwayne	Fredericton	AHL	22	0	2	2	11	....	....	....	....	....
	Flint	IHL	41	0	6	6	44	....	....	....	....	....
Boh, Rick	Colorado	WCHA	38	22	42	64	37	....	....	....	....	....
Bois, Jean	Shawinigan	QMJHL	69	35	59	94	112	13	4	6	10	46
Boisvert, Serge	Montreal	NHL	1	0	0	0	0	....	....	....	....	....
	Sherbrooke	AHL	78	27	54	81	29	15	8	10	18	15
	NHL Totals		41	4	6	10	6	20	3	6	9	2
Boland, Sean	Toronto	OHL	17	0	4	4	23	....	....	....	....	....
Bonar, Graeme	Sherbrooke	AHL	21	6	6	12	7	....	....	....	....	....
Borrell, John	U. of Lowell	H.E.	34	5	10	15	43	....	....	....	....	....
Borsato, Luciano	Clarkson	ECAC	31	16	41	57	55	....	....	....	....	....
Boschman, Laurie	Winnipeg	NHL	80	17	24	41	152	10	2	3	5	32
	NHL Totals		570	156	246	402	1469	36	5	9	14	105
Bossy, Mike	NY Islanders	NHL	63	38	37	75	33	6	2	3	5	0
	NHL Totals		752	573	553	1126	210	129	85	75	160	38
Bothwell, Tim	Hartford	NHL	4	1	0	1	0	....	....	....	....	....
	St. Louis	NHL	72	5	16	21	46	6	0	0	0	6
	NHL Totals		402	22	80	102	292	39	0	2	2	38
Boudreau, Bruce	Nova Scotia	AHL	78	35	47	82	40	5	3	3	6	4
	NHL Totals		141	28	42	70	46	9	2	0	2	0
Bourbeau, Allen	Harvard	ECAC	33	23	34	57	46	....	....	....	....	....
Bourgeois, Charlie	St. Louis	NHL	66	2	12	14	164	6	0	0	0	27
	NHL Totals		259	16	53	69	710	40	2	3	5	194
Bourne, Bob	Los Angeles	NHL	78	13	9	22	35	5	2	1	3	0
	NHL Totals		892	251	313	564	577	134	40	55	95	108
Bourque, Phil	Pittsburgh	NHL	22	2	3	5	32	....	....	....	....	....
	Baltimore	AHL	49	15	16	31	183	....	....	....	....	....
	NHL Totals		31	2	4	6	46	....	....	....	....	....
Bourque, Raymond	Boston	NHL	78	23	72	95	36	4	1	2	3	0
	NHL Totals		580	176	437	613	454	54	12	37	49	59
Boutilier, Paul	Boston	NHL	52	5	9	14	84	....	....	....	....	....
	Minnesota	NHL	10	2	4	6	8	....	....	....	....	....
	NHL Totals		275	27	82	109	342	36	1	9	10	30

Players: BOYD...BUCHBERGER

PLAYER	CLUB	LEAGUE	Regular Season GP	G	A	TP	PIM	Playoffs GP	G	A	TP	PIM
Boyd, Randy	NY Islanders	NHL	30	7	17	24	37	4	0	1	1	6
	Springfield	AHL	48	9	30	39	96	....	....	....	....	....
	NHL Totals		195	13	50	63	264	13	0	2	2	26
Bozek, Steve	Calgary	NHL	71	17	18	35	22	4	1	0	1	2
	NHL Totals		359	107	108	215	150	41	11	8	19	59
Bozon, Philippe	Peoria	IHL	28	4	11	15	17	....	....	....	....	....
	St. Jean	QMJHL	25	20	21	41	75	8	5	5	10	30
Braccia, Rick	Boston College	H.E.	30	4	5	9	52	....	....	....	....	....
Bradley, Brian	Calgary	NHL	40	10	18	28	16	....	....	....	....	....
	Moncton	AHL	20	12	16	28	8	....	....	....	....	....
	NHL Totals		45	10	19	29	16	1	0	0	0	0
Brady, Neil	Medicine Hat	WHL	57	19	64	83	126	18	1	4	5	25
Brant, Chris	Salt Lake	IHL	67	27	38	65	107	17	11	10	21	23
Brennan, Stephen	Clarkson	ECAC	29	3	3	6	17	....	....	....	....	....
Brickley, Andy	New Jersey	NHL	51	11	12	23	8	....	....	....	....	....
	NHL Totals		149	37	48	85	27	....	....	....	....	....
Bridgman, Mel	New Jersey	NHL	51	8	31	39	80	....	....	....	....	....
	Detroit	NHL	13	2	2	4	19	16	5	2	7	28
	NHL Totals		905	242	435	677	1573	102	23	36	59	276
Britz, Greg	Hartford	NHL	1	0	0	0	0	....	....	....	....	....
	Binghamton	AHL	74	25	16	41	66	13	3	3	6	6
	NHL Totals		8	0	0	0	4	....	....	....	....	....
Brochu, Stephane	St. Jean	QMJHL	DID NOT PLAY					8	0	2	2	11
Brodeur, Lee	W. Michigan	CCHA	25	3	3	6	8	....	....	....	....	....
Brooke, Bob	NY Rangers	NHL	15	3	5	8	20	....	....	....	....	....
	Minnesota	NHL	65	10	18	28	78	....	....	....	....	....
	NHL Totals		240	45	54	99	292	24	6	9	15	43
Broten, Aaron	New Jersey	NHL	80	26	53	79	36	....	....	....	....	....
	NHL Totals		439	110	199	309	170	....	....	....	....	....
Broten, Neal	Minnesota	NHL	46	18	35	53	33	....	....	....	....	....
	NHL Totals		437	166	314	480	259	62	12	27	39	35
Broten, Paul	U. of Minnesota	WCHA	48	17	22	39	52	....	....	....	....	....
Brown, Allister	N. Hampshire	H.E.	33	0	10	10	38	....	....	....	....	....
Brown, Cal	Colorado	WCHA	41	7	17	24	80	....	....	....	....	....
Brown, David	Philadelphia	NHL	62	7	3	10	274	26	1	2	3	59
	NHL Totals		216	21	21	42	819	44	1	2	3	146
Brown, Doug	New Jersey	NHL	4	0	1	1	0	....	....	....	....	....
	Maine	AHL	73	24	34	58	15	....	....	....	....	....
	NHL Totals		4	0	1	1	0	....	....	....	....	....
Brown, Greg	Boston College	H.E.	37	10	27	37	22	....	....	....	....	....
Brown, Jeff	Quebec	NHL	44	7	22	29	16	13	3	3	6	2
	Fredericton	AHL	26	2	14	16	16	....	....	....	....	....
	NHL Totals		52	10	24	34	22	14	3	3	6	2
Brown, Keith	Chicago	NHL	73	4	23	27	86	4	0	1	1	6
	NHL Totals		512	45	198	243	475	43	2	14	16	78
Brown, Rob	Kamloops	WHL	63	76	136	212	101	5	6	5	11	6
Brownschidle, Jack	Rochester	AHL	74	8	22	30	13	12	1	3	4	0
	NHL Totals		494	39	162	201	151	....	....	....	....	....
Brubaker, Jeff	Nova Scotia	AHL	47	10	16	26	80	....	....	....	....	....
	Hershey	AHL	12	1	2	3	30	3	2	0	2	10
	NHL Totals		146	14	9	23	434	....	....	....	....	....
Bruce, David	Vancouver	NHL	50	9	7	16	109	....	....	....	....	....
	Fredericton	AHL	17	7	6	13	73	....	....	....	....	....
	NHL Totals		62	9	8	17	123	1	0	0	0	0
Brumwell, Murray	New Jersey	NHL	1	0	0	0	2	....	....	....	....	....
	Maine	AHL	69	10	38	48	30	....	....	....	....	....
	NHL Totals		125	12	30	42	68	2	0	0	0	2
Brunet, Benoit	Hull	QMJHL	60	43	67	110	105	6	7	5	12	8
Bryden, Rob	W. Michigan	CCHA	43	46	32	78	82	....	....	....	....	....
Brydges, Paul	Buffalo	NHL	15	2	2	4	6	....	....	....	....	....
	Rochester	AHL	54	13	17	30	54	1	0	0	0	0
	NHL Totals		15	2	2	4	6	....	....	....	....	....
Buchberger, Kelly	Edmonton	NHL	....	....	....	....	....	3	0	1	1	5
	Nova Scotia	AHL	70	12	20	32	257	5	0	1	1	23
	NHL Totals		....	....	....	....	....	3	0	1	1	5

Players: BUCKLEY...CARNELLEY

PLAYER	CLUB	LEAGUE	GP	Regular Season G	A	TP	PIM	GP	Playoffs G	A	TP	PIM
Buckley, David	Boston College	H.E.	34	3	5	8	9	....	....	....	....	....
Bucyk, Randy	Sherbrooke	AHL	70	24	39	63	28	17	3	11	14	2
	NHL Totals		17	4	2	6	8	2	0	0	0	0
Buda, David	Northeastern	H.E.	37	15	15	30	32	....	....	....	....	....
Bullard, Mike	Pittsburgh	NHL	14	2	10	12	17	....	....	....	....	....
	Calgary	NHL	57	28	26	54	34	5	4	2	6	2
	NHL Totals		439	213	201	414	422	5	4	2	6	2
Bureau, Marc	Longueuil	QMJHL	66	54	58	112	68	20	17	20	37	12
Burnie, Stuart	Springfield	AHL	76	21	30	51	62	....	....	....	....	....
Burr, Shawn	Detroit	NHL	80	22	25	47	107	16	7	2	9	20
	NHL Totals		94	23	25	48	113	16	7	2	9	20
Burridge, Randy	Boston	NHL	23	1	4	5	16	2	1	0	1	2
	Moncton	AHL	47	26	41	67	139	3	1	2	3	30
	NHL Totals		75	18	29	47	33	5	1	4	5	14
Burt, Adam	North Bay	OHL	57	4	27	31	138	24	1	6	7	68
Buskas, Rod	Pittsburgh	NHL	68	3	15	18	123	....	....	....	....	....
	NHL Totals		297	11	35	46	635	....	....	....	....	....
Butcher, Garth	Vancouver	NHL	70	5	15	20	207	....	....	....	....	....
	NHL Totals		303	15	44	59	695	7	1	0	1	0
Butler, Bill	Vermont	ECAC	32	0	7	7	14	....	....	....	....	....
Byce, John	U. Wisconsin	WCHA	40	1	4	5	12	....	....	....	....	....
Byers, Lyndon	Boston	NHL	18	2	3	5	53	1	0	0	0	0
	Moncton	AHL	27	5	5	10	63	....	....	....	....	....
	NHL Totals		66	7	17	24	135	1	0	0	0	0
Byram, Shawn	Prince Albert	WHL	67	19	21	40	147	7	1	1	2	10
Byrnes, Brian	Milwaukee	IHL	82	2	26	28	70	....	....	....	....	....
Bzdel, Gerald	Seattle	WHL	48	4	12	16	137	....	....	....	....	....
Cain, Kelly	London	OHL	5	4	3	7	18	....	....	....	....	....
	Kitchener	OHL	28	18	19	37	48	....	....	....	....	....
	Kingston	OHL	12	3	5	8	15	....	....	....	....	....
Callaghan, Gary	Kitchener	OHL	56	30	30	60	23	4	2	3	5	0
Callander, Jock	Muskegon	IHL	82	54	82	136	110	15	13	7	20	23
Camazzola, James	Chicago	NHL	2	0	0	0	0	....	....	....	....	....
	Nova Scotia	AHL	48	13	18	31	31	3	0	0	0	0
	NHL Totals		3	0	0	0	0	....	....	....	....	....
Camazzola, Tony	Fort Wayne	IHL	74	21	16	37	137	11	4	1	5	44
	NHL Totals		1	0	0	0	0	....	....	....	....	....
Campbell, Wade	Boston	NHL	14	0	3	3	24	4	0	0	0	11
	Moncton	AHL	64	12	23	35	34	....	....	....	....	....
	NHL Totals		207	9	26	35	284	10	0	0	0	20
Campbell, William	Sherbrooke	AHL	60	1	13	14	21	9	1	3	4	4
Campedelli, Dom	Sherbrooke	AHL	7	3	2	5	2	....	....	....	....	....
	Hershey	AHL	45	7	15	22	70	....	....	....	....	....
	Nova Scotia	AHL	12	0	4	4	7	5	0	0	0	17
	NHL Totals		2	0	0	0	0	....	....	....	....	....
Capello, Jeff	U. Vermont	ECAC	32	17	26	43	56	....	....	....	....	....
Capuano, Dave	Maine	H.E.	38	18	41	59	14	....	....	....	....	....
Capuano, Jack	Maine	H.E.	42	10	34	44	20	....	....	....	....	....
Carbonneau, Guy	Montreal	NHL	79	18	27	45	68	17	3	8	11	20
	NHL Totals		395	103	157	260	311	67	18	19	37	77
Carkner, Terry	NY Rangers	NHL	52	2	13	15	118	1	0	0	0	0
	New Haven	AHL	12	2	6	8	56	3	1	0	1	0
	NHL Totals		52	2	13	15	118	1	0	0	0	0
Carlile, Todd	Indianapolis	IHL	50	11	29	40	102	....	....	....	....	....
Carlson, Kent	DID NOT PLAY -	INJURED										
	NHL Totals		111	6	11	17	148	5	0	0	0	11
Carlson, Steve	Baltimore	AHL	67	12	13	25	32	....	....	....	....	....
	NHL Totals		52	9	12	21	23	4	1	1	2	7
Carlsson, Anders	New Jersey	NHL	48	2	18	20	14	....	....	....	....	....
	Maine	AHL	6	0	6	6	2	....	....	....	....	....
	NHL Totals		48	2	18	20	14	....	....	....	....	....
Carlyle, Randy	Winnipeg	NHL	71	16	26	42	93	10	1	5	6	18
	NHL Totals		706	113	373	486	950	59	8	22	30	104
Carnelley, Todd	Muskegon	IHL	71	4	29	33	75	2	0	0	0	0

PLAYER	CLUB	LEAGUE	GP	Regular Season G	A	TP	PIM	GP	Playoffs G	A	TP	PIM
Carpenter, Bob	Washington	NHL	22	5	7	12	21	....	....	....	....	....
	NY Rangers	NHL	28	2	8	10	20	....	....	....	....	....
	Los Angeles	NHL	10	2	3	5	6	5	1	2	3	2
	NHL Totals		460	181	201	382	423	31	10	11	21	49
Carroll, Billy	Detroit	NHL	31	1	2	3	6	....	....	....	....	....
	NHL Totals		322	30	54	84	113	71	6	12	18	18
Carson, Jimmy	Los Angeles	NHL	80	37	42	79	22	5	1	2	3	6
	NHL Totals		80	37	42	79	22	5	1	2	3	6
Carson, Lindsay	Philadelphia	NHL	71	11	15	26	141	24	3	5	8	22
	NHL Totals		310	59	69	128	457	44	3	8	11	56
Carter, John	Boston	NHL	8	0	1	1	0	....	....	....	....	....
	Moncton	AHL	58	25	30	55	60	6	2	3	5	5
	NHL Totals		11	0	1	1	0	••••	••••	••••	••••	••••
Cassels, Andrew	Ottawa	OHL	66	26	66	92	28	11	5	9	14	7
Cassidy, Bruce	Chicago	NHL	2	0	0	0	0	....	....	....	....	....
	Nova Scotia	AHL	19	2	8	10	4	....	....	....	....	....
	Cdn. Olympic	....	12	3	6	9	4	....	....	....	....	....
	Saginaw	IHL	10	2	13	15	6	2	1	1	2	0
	NHL Totals		4	0	0	0	0	••••	••••	••••	••••	••••
Caufield, Jay	NY Rangers	NHL	13	2	1	3	45	3	0	0	0	12
	Flint	IHL	12	4	3	7	59	....	....	....	....	....
	New Haven	AHL	13	0	0	0	43	....	....	....	....	....
	NHL Totals		13	2	1	3	45	3	0	0	0	12
Cavallini, Gino	St. Louis	NHL	80	18	26	44	54	6	3	1	4	2
	NHL Totals		164	37	48	85	130	26	7	6	13	16
Cavallini, Paul	Washington	NHL	6	0	2	2	8	....	....	....	....	....
	Binghamton	AHL	66	12	24	36	188	13	2	7	9	35
	NHL Totals		6	0	2	2	8	••••	••••	••••	••••	••••
Chabot, John	Pittsburgh	NHL	72	14	22	36	8	....	....	....	....	....
	NHL Totals		282	55	129	184	41	11	1	4	5	0
Chambers, Shawn	Alaska-Fair.	G.N.	28	8	29	37	84					
Channell, Craig	Fort Wayne	IHL	81	12	42	54	90	11	2	1	3	29
Channell, Todd	Binghamton	AHL	12	1	4	5	4	....	....	....	....	....
	Salt Lake	IHL	59	22	19	41	28	17	8	10	18	8
Chapdelaine, Rene	Lake Superior	CCHA	28	1	5	6	51	....	....	....	....	....
Charbonneau, Jose	Sherbrooke	AHL	72	14	27	41	94	16	5	12	17	17
Charlesworth, Todd	Pittsburgh	NHL	1	0	0	0	0	....	....	....	....	....
	Baltimore	AHL	75	5	21	26	64	....	....	....	....	....
	NHL Totals		80	1	9	10	39	••••	••••	••••	••••	••••
Chaulk, Landis	Moncton	AHL	14	1	0	1	13	....	....	....	....	....
Chelios, Chris	Montreal	NHL	71	11	33	44	124	17	4	9	13	38
	NHL Totals		198	28	116	144	290	61	9	35	44	121
Chernomaz, Rich	New Jersey	NHL	25	6	4	10	8	....	....	....	....	....
	Maine	AHL	58	35	27	62	65	....	....	....	....	....
	NHL Totals		37	8	7	15	12	••••	••••	••••	••••	••••
Chiasson, Steve	Detroit	NHL	45	1	4	5	73	2	0	0	0	19
	NHL Totals		45	1	4	5	73	2	0	0	0	19
Chisholm, Colin	Minnesota	NHL	1	0	0	0	0	....	....	....	....	....
	Springfield	AHL	75	1	11	12	141	....	....	....	....	....
	NHL Totals		1	0	0	0	0	••••	••••	••••	••••	••••
Choma, Peter	Belleville	OHL	64	18	17	35	34	6	1	3	4	7
Chorske, Tom	U. of Minnesota	WCHA	47	20	22	42	20	....	....	....	....	....
Chrest, Blaine	Portland	WHL	5	1	4	5	0	....	....	....	....	....
	Saskatoon	WHL	62	27	44	71	17	11	3	7	10	0
Christensen, Matt	DID NOT PLAY											
Christian, Dave	Washington	NHL	76	23	27	50	8	7	1	3	4	6
	NHL Totals		546	198	294	492	140	36	11	13	24	13
Churla, Shane	Hartford	NHL	20	0	1	1	78	2	0	0	0	42
	Binghamton	AHL	24	1	5	6	249	....	....	....	....	....
	NHL Totals		20	0	1	1	78	2	0	0	0	42
Chychrun, Jeff	Philadelphia	NHL	1	0	0	0	4	....	....	....	....	....
	Hershey	AHL	74	1	17	18	239	4	0	0	0	10
	NHL Totals		1	0	0	0	4	••••	••••	••••	••••	••••
Chynoweth, Dean	Medicine Hat	WHL	67	3	18	21	285	13	4	2	6	28

PLAYER	CLUB	LEAGUE	GP	Regular Season G	A	TP	PIM	GP	Playoffs G	A	TP	PIM
Chyzowski, Barry	Minn.-Duluth	WCHA	39	5	11	16	16	....	....	....	....	....
Ciccarelli, Dino	Minnesota	NHL	80	52	51	103	88	....	....	....	....	....
	NHL Totals		470	259	247	506	499	62	28	23	51	79
Cichocki, Chris	Detroit	NHL	2	0	0	0	2	....	....	....	....	....
	Adirondack	AHL	55	31	34	65	27	....	....	....	....	....
	Maine	AHL	7	2	2	4	0	.....	....	....	....	....
	NHL Totals		61	10	11	21	23	....	....	....	....	....
Cirella, Joe	New Jersey	NHL	65	9	22	31	111	....	....	....	....	....
	NHL Totals		343	39	109	148	594	....	....	....	....	....
Clark, Kerry	Saskatoon	WHL	54	12	10	22	229	8	0	1	1	23
Clark, Wendel	Toronto	NHL	80	37	23	60	271	13	6	5	11	38
	NHL Totals		146	71	34	105	498	23	11	6	17	85
Clarke, Doug	Colorado	WCHA	37	11	37	48	73	....	....	....	....	....
Claviter, Bill	North Dakota	WCHA	20	2	2	4	10	....	....	....	....	....
Clemens, Kevin	Seattle	WHL	26	5	4	9	21	....	....	....	....	....
	Brandon	WHL	43	11	16	27	29	....	....	....	....	....
Clement, Sean	Michigan State	CCHA	41	3	11	14	70	....	....	....	....	....
Clements, Scott	Newmarket	AHL	70	1	14	15	77	....	....	....	....	....
Clouston, Sean	Portland	WHL	70	6	25	31	93	19	0	5	5	45
Cloutier, Rejean	Sherbrooke	AHL	76	7	37	44	182	17	3	9	12	59
	NHL Totals		5	0	2	2	2	....	....	....	....	....
Cochrane, Glen	Vancouver	NHL	14	0	0	0	52	....	....	....	....	....
	NHL Totals		320	16	64	80	1287	13	1	1	2	29
Coffey, Paul	Edmonton	NHL	59	17	50	67	49	17	3	8	11	30
	NHL Totals		532	209	460	669	693	94	36	67	103	167
Cole, Danton	Michigan State	CCHA	44	9	15	24	16	....	....	....	....	....
Conacher, Pat	Maine	AHL	56	12	14	26	47	....	....	....	....	....
	NHL Totals		69	2	16	18	41	6	1	1	2	4
Copeland, Todd	U. of Michigan	CCHA	34	2	11	13	59	....	....	....	....	....
Corkum, Bob	Maine	H.E.	35	18	11	29	24	....	....	....	....	....
Cornelius, Jeff	Baltimore	AHL	7	0	2	2	25	....	....	....	....	....
Corriveau, Yvon	Washington	NHL	17	1	1	2	24	....	....	....	....	....
	Binghamton	AHL	7	0	0	0	2	8	0	1	1	2
	Toronto	OHL	23	14	19	33	23	....	....	....	....	....
	NHL Totals		19	1	1	2	24	4	0	3	3	2
Corson, Shayne	Montreal	NHL	55	12	11	23	144	17	6	5	11	30
	NHL Totals		58	12	11	23	146	17	6	5	11	30
Costello, Rich	Newmarket	AHL	48	6	11	17	53	....	....	....	....	....
	NHL Totals		12	2	2	4	2	....	....	....	....	....
Cote, Alain	Quebec	NHL	80	12	24	36	38	13	2	3	5	2
	NHL Totals		565	97	164	261	343	67	9	15	24	44
Cote, Alain G.	Boston	NHL	3	0	0	0	0	....	....	....	....	....
	Granby	QMJHL	43	7	24	31	185	4	0	3	3	3
	NHL Totals		35	0	6	6	5	....	....	....	....	....
Cote, Matt	Lake Superior	CCHA	36	1	8	9	30	....	....	....	....	....
Cote, Ray	Adirondack	AHL	0	0	0	0	0	9	2	6	8	6
	Cdn. Olympic	....	68	20	30	50	34	....	....	....	....	....
	NHL Totals		15	0	0	0	4	14	3	2	5	0
Cote, Sylvain	Hartford	NHL	67	2	8	10	20	2	0	2	2	2
	Binghamton	AHL	12	2	4	6	0	....	....	....	....	....
	NHL Totals		136	5	17	22	37	2	0	2	2	2
Coulis, Tim	Springfield	AHL	38	12	19	31	212	....	....	....	....	....
	NHL Totals		47	4	5	9	138	3	1	0	1	2
Coulter, Neal	NY Islanders	NHL	9	2	1	3	7	....	....	....	....	....
	Springfield	AHL	47	12	13	25	63	....	....	....	....	....
	NHL Totals		25	5	5	10	11	1	0	0	0	0
Courteau, Yves	Hartford	NHL	4	0	0	0	0	....	....	....	....	....
	Binghamton	AHL	57	15	28	43	8	7	1	4	5	12
	NHL Totals		22	2	5	7	4	1	0	0	0	0
Courtnall, Geoff	Boston	NHL	65	13	23	36	117	1	0	0	0	0
	NHL Totals		197	46	55	101	260	9	0	2	2	9
Courtnall, Russ	Toronto	NHL	79	29	44	73	90	13	3	4	7	11
	NHL Totals		235	66	101	167	192	23	6	10	16	19
Cousins, Steve	U. Alberta	CWUAA	45	4	15	19	105	....	....	....	....	....

PLAYER	CLUB	LEAGUE	GP	Regular Season G	A	TP	PIM	GP	Playoffs G	A	TP	PIM
Cowan, David	Minn.-Duluth	WCHA	31	2	9	11	24	....	....	....	....	....
Coxe, Craig	Vancouver	NHL	15	1	0	1	31	....	....	....	....	....
	Fredericton	AHL	46	1	12	13	168	....	....	....	....	....
	NHL Totals		81	4	5	9	256	3	0	0	0	2
Cramarossa, Vito	Toronto	OHL	59	24	50	74	130	....	....	....	....	....
Craven, Murray	Philadelphia	NHL	77	19	30	49	38	12	3	1	4	9
	NHL Totals		281	70	109	179	114	36	7	10	17	24
Crawford, Louis	Nova Scotia	AHL	35	3	4	7	48	....	....	....	....	....
Crawford, Marc	Vancouver	NHL	21	0	3	3	67	....	....	....	....	....
	Fredericton	AHL	25	8	11	19	21	....	....	....	....	....
	NHL Totals		176	19	31	50	229	20	1	2	3	44
Crawford, Bob	NY Rangers	NHL	3	0	0	0	2	....	....	....	....	....
	New Haven	AHL	4	3	0	3	7	....	....	....	....	....
	Washington	NHL	12	0	0	0	0	....	....	....	....	....
	Binghamton	AHL	5	0	2	2	0	....	....	....	....	....
	Salt Lake	IHL	2	0	1	1	0	....	....	....	....	....
	NHL Totals		246	71	71	142	72	11	0	1	1	8
Crawford, Wayne	Adirondack	AHL	2	1	1	2	0	....	....	....	....	....
	Kalamazoo	IHL	52	27	21	48	38	....	....	....	....	....
	Milwaukee	IHL	15	5	8	13	23	6	0	3	3	0
Creighton, Adam	Buffalo	NHL	56	18	22	40	26	....	....	....	....	....
	NHL Totals		112	23	33	56	65	....	....	....	....	....
Cristofoli, Ed	Denver	WCHA	40	14	15	29	52	....	....	....	....	....
Cronin, Shawn	Salt Lake	IHL	53	8	16	24	118	....	....	....	....	....
	Binghamton	AHL	12	0	1	1	60	10	0	0	0	41
Crossman, Doug	Philadelphia	NHL	78	9	31	40	29	26	4	14	18	31
	NHL Totals		475	51	199	250	284	77	11	31	42	73
Crossman, Jeff	New Haven	AHL	61	2	3	5	133	2	0	0	0	20
Crowder, Keith	Boston	NHL	58	22	30	52	106	4	0	1	1	4
	NHL Totals		470	187	214	401	929	45	10	11	21	128
Crowder, Troy	North Bay	OHL	56	11	16	27	142	23	3	9	12	99
Cruickshank, Gord	Providence	H.E.	31	27	18	45	38	....	....	....	....	....
Culhane, Jim	W. Michigan	CCHA	43	9	24	33	163	....	....	....	....	....
Cullen, John	Boston U.	H.E.	36	23	29	52	35	....	....	....	....	....
Cunneyworth, Randy	Pittsburgh	NHL	79	26	27	53	142	....	....	....	....	....
	NHL Totals		175	43	61	104	265	....	....	....	....	....
Cupolo, Mark	Peoria	IHL	37	4	7	11	22	....	....	....	....	....
Curran, Brian	NY Islanders	NHL	68	0	10	10	356	8	0	0	0	51
	NHL Totals		183	3	17	20	763	13	0	0	0	62
Currie, Dan	S.S. Marie	OHL	66	31	52	83	53	4	2	1	3	2
Curtale, Tony	Peoria	IHL	72	8	21	29	126	....	....	....	....	....
	NHL Totals		2	0	0	0	0	....	....	....	....	....
Cusack, Mike	U. of Michigan	CCHA	17	1	1	2	43	....	....	....	....	....
Cyr, Denis	Peoria	IHL	81	29	41	70	10	....	....	....	....	....
	NHL Totals		193	41	43	84	36	4	0	0	0	0
Cyr, Paul	Buffalo	NHL	73	11	16	27	122	....	....	....	....	....
	NHL Totals		322	84	110	194	416	18	3	6	9	79
Dagenais, Mike	Peterborough	OHL	56	1	17	18	66	12	4	1	5	20
Dahlen, Ulf	Ostersund	Swe.	31	9	12	21	20	....	....	....	....	....
Dahlin, Kjell	Montreal	NHL	41	12	8	20	0	8	2	4	6	0
	NHL Totals		118	44	47	91	4	24	4	7	11	4
Dahlquist, Chris	Pittsburgh	NHL	19	0	1	1	20	....	....	....	....	....
	Baltimore	AHL	51	1	16	17	50	....	....	....	....	....
	NHL Totals		24	1	3	4	22	....	....	....	....	....
Daigneault, J.-J.	Philadelphia	NHL	77	6	16	22	56	9	1	0	1	0
	NHL Totals		208	15	62	77	170	12	1	2	3	0
Dalgarno, Brad	Hamilton	OHL	60	27	32	59	100	9	4	6	10	11
	NHL Totals		2	1	0	1	0	....	....	....	....	....
Dallman, Marty	Newmarket	AHL	42	24	24	48	44	....	....	....	....	....
	Baltimore	AHL	6	0	1	1	0	....	....	....	....	....
Dallman, Rod	Prince Albert	WHL	47	13	21	34	240	5	0	1	1	32
Damphousse, Vincent	Toronto	NHL	80	21	25	46	26	12	1	5	6	8
	NHL Totals		80	21	25	46	26	12	1	5	6	8
Daneyko, Ken	New Jersey	NHL	79	2	12	14	183	....	....	....	....	....
	NHL Totals		135	3	26	29	310	....	....	....	....	....

Players: DANIELS...DONATELLI

PLAYER	CLUB	LEAGUE	Regular Season GP	G	A	TP	PIM	Playoffs GP	G	A	TP	PIM
Daniels, Jeff	Oshawa	OHL	54	14	9	23	22	15	3	2	5	5
Daoust, Dan	Toronto	NHL	33	4	3	7	35	13	5	2	7	42
	Newmarket	AHL	1	0	0	0	4	....	....	....	....	....
	NHL Totals		322	64	143	207	344	23	7	4	11	61
Dark, Michael	St. Louis	NHL	13	2	0	2	2	....	....	....	....	....
	Peoria	IHL	42	4	11	15	93	....	....	....	....	....
	NHL Totals		13	2	0	2	2	....	....	....	....	....
Davey, Neil	Maine	AHL	6	0	0	0	2	....	....	....	....	....
	Indianapolis	IHL	44	2	11	13	34	3	0	1	1	2
Davidson, Lee	North Dakota	WCHA	41	16	12	28	65	....	....	....	....	....
Davidson, Sean	Toronto	OHL	66	30	32	62	24	....	....	....	....	....
Deasley, Bryan	U. Michigan	CCHA	38	13	11	24	74	....	....	....	....	....
DeBlois, Lucien	NY Rangers	NHL	40	3	8	11	27	2	0	0	0	2
	NHL Totals		659	201	196	397	475	43	6	6	12	32
DeCarle, Mike	Lake Superior	CCHA	38	34	18	52	122	....	....	....	....	....
Deegan, Shannon	Vermont	ECAC	29	19	21	40	44	....	....	....	....	....
Defazio, Dean	Newmarket	AHL	76	7	13	20	116	....	....	....	....	....
	NHL Totals		22	0	2	2	28	....	....	....	....	....
DeGaetano, Phil	Adirondack	AHL	78	7	23	30	75	10	0	1	1	51
Degray, Dale	Calgary	NHL	27	6	7	13	29	....	....	....	....	....
	Moncton	AHL	45	10	22	32	57	5	2	1	3	19
	NHL Totals		28	6	7	13	29	....	....	....	....	....
Degrio, Gary	Salt Lake	IHL	54	12	19	31	10	17	5	5	10	2
Delcol, John	Baltimore	AHL	54	4	5	9	100	....	....	....	....	....
Delcourt, Grant	Spokane	WHL	57	34	44	78	75	5	1	1	2	4
Delorme, Gilbert	Quebec	NHL	19	2	0	2	14	....	....	....	....	....
	Detroit	NHL	24	2	3	5	33	16	0	2	2	14
	NHL Totals		390	25	74	99	344	35	1	5	6	32
Demers, Eric	Drummondville	QMJHL	29	3	11	14	93	....	....	....	....	....
DePalma, Larry	Minnesota	NHL	56	9	6	15	219	....	....	....	....	....
	Springfield	AHL	9	2	2	4	82	....	....	....	....	....
	NHL Totals		57	9	6	15	219	....	....	....	....	....
Derlago, Bill	Winnipeg	NHL	30	3	6	9	12	....	....	....	....	....
	Quebec	NHL	18	3	5	8	6	....	....	....	....	....
	Fredericton	AHL	16	7	8	15	2	....	....	....	....	....
	NHL Totals		555	189	227	416	247	13	5	0	5	8
Desjardins, Eric	Granby	QMJHL	66	14	24	38	178	8	3	2	5	10
Desjardins, Martin	Longueuil	QMJHL	68	39	61	100	89	19	8	10	18	18
Desmond, Ned	Dartmouth	ECAC	24	4	9	13	28	....	....	....	....	....
Devereaux, John	Boston College	H.E.	39	14	20	34	16	....	....	....	....	....
Diduck, Gerald	NY Islanders	NHL	30	2	3	5	67	14	0	1	1	35
	Springfield	AHL	45	6	8	14	120	....	....	....	....	....
	NHL Totals		105	5	13	18	149	14	0	1	1	35
DiFiore, Ralph	Saginaw	IHL	36	1	5	6	49	....	....	....	....	....
DiMuzio, Frank	Ottawa	OHL	61	59	30	89	57	7	5	1	6	21
Dineen, Gord	NY Islanders	NHL	71	4	10	14	110	7	0	4	4	4
	NHL Totals		221	7	41	48	316	29	1	5	6	60
Dineen, Kevin	Hartford	NHL	78	40	39	79	110	6	2	1	3	31
	NHL Totals		192	98	90	188	354	16	8	8	16	49
Dineen, Peter	Los Angeles	NHL	11	0	2	2	8	....	....	....	....	....
	New Haven	AHL	59	2	17	19	140	7	0	1	1	27
	NHL Totals		11	0	2	2	8	....	....	....	....	....
Dion, Grant	Nova Scotia	AHL	14	1	4	5	2	....	....	....	....	....
	Muskegon	IHL	40	7	15	22	46	13	1	6	7	6
Dionne, Marcel	Los Angeles	NHL	67	24	50	74	54	....	....	....	....	....
	NY Rangers	NHL	14	4	6	10	6	6	1	1	2	2
	NHL Totals		1244	693	990	1683	526	49	21	24	45	17
Dirk, Robert	Peoria	IHL	76	5	17	22	155	....	....	....	....	....
Djoos, Per	Brynas	Swe.	23	1	2	3	16	....	....	....	....	....
Dobbin, Brian	Philadelphia	NHL	12	2	1	3	14	....	....	....	....	....
	Hershey	AHL	52	26	35	61	66	5	4	2	6	15
	NHL Totals		12	2	1	3	14	....	....	....	....	....
Dollas, Bobby	Sherbrooke	AHL	75	6	18	24	87	16	2	4	6	13
	NHL Totals		56	0	5	5	66	3	0	0	0	2
Donahue, Andy	Dartmouth	ECAC	18	0	7	7	10	....	....	....	....	....
Donatelli, Clark	Boston U.	H.E.	37	15	23	38	46	....	....	....	....	....

PLAYER	CLUB	LEAGUE	GP	G	A	TP	PIM	GP	G	A	TP	PIM
Donnelly, Dave	Chicago	NHL	71	6	12	18	81	1	0	0	0	0
	NHL Totals		133	15	24	39	146	5	0	0	0	0
Donnelly, Gord	Quebec	NHL	38	0	2	2	143	13	0	0	0	53
	NHL Totals		134	2	9	11	321	14	0	0	0	53
Donnelly, Mike	NY Rangers	NHL	5	1	1	2	0	....	....	....	....	....
	New Haven	AHL	58	27	34	61	52	7	2	0	2	9
	NHL Totals		5	1	1	2	0	....	....	....	....	....
Dorion, Dan	Maine	AHL	70	16	22	38	47	....	....	....	....	....
	NHL Totals		3	1	1	2	1	....	....	....	....	....
Dornbach, Greg	Miami-Ohio	CCHA	39	11	28	39	42	....	....	....	....	....
Doucet, Benoit	Cdn. Olympic	....	63	27	31	58	86	....	....	....	....	....
	Moncton	AHL	....	....	....	....	....	5	0	3	3	18
Douris, Peter	Winnipeg	NHL	6	0	0	0	0	....	....	....	....	....
	Sherbrooke	AHL	62	14	28	42	24	17	7	15	22	16
	NHL Totals		17	0	0	0	0	....	....	....	....	....
Doyle, Rob	Colorado	WCHA	42	17	37	54	72	....	....	....	....	....
Doyle, Shane	Oshawa	OHL	46	9	13	22	168	23	4	4	8	115
Doyon, Mario	Drummondville	QMJHL	65	18	47	65	150	8	1	3	4	30
Driver, Bruce	New Jersey	NHL	74	6	28	34	36	....	....	....	....	....
	NHL Totals		185	18	68	86	104	....	....	....	....	....
Druce, John	Binghamton	AHL	77	13	9	22	131	12	0	3	3	28
Drulia, Stan	Hamilton	OHL	55	27	51	78	26	....	....	....	....	....
Duchesne, Gaetan	Washington	NHL	74	17	35	52	53	7	3	0	3	14
	NHL Totals		451	87	138	225	244	33	10	6	16	39
Duchesne, Steve	Los Angeles	NHL	75	13	25	38	74	5	2	2	4	4
	NHL Totals		75	13	25	38	74	5	2	2	4	4
Ducolon, Toby	U. of Vermont	ECAC	32	9	11	20	42	....	....	....	....	....
Dufresne, Donald	Longueuil	QMJHL	67	5	29	34	97	20	1	8	9	38
Duggan, Ken	Flint	IHL	66	2	23	25	51	....	....	....	....	....
Duguay, Ron	Pittsburgh	NHL	40	5	13	18	30	....	....	....	....	....
	NY Rangers	NHL	34	9	12	21	9	6	2	0	2	4
	NHL Totals		731	261	319	580	494	76	31	22	53	112
Dumas, Claude	Granby	QMJHL	67	50	82	132	59	8	6	6	12	2
	Fort Wayne	IHL	3	1	3	4	4	7	4	0	4	0
Dumont, Marc	Laval	QMJHL	67	29	47	76	53	15	10	8	18	6
Dunbar, Dale	Peoria	IHL	46	2	8	10	32	....	....	....	....	....
	NHL Totals		1	0	0	0	2	....	....	....	....	....
Duncan, Iain	Winnipeg	NHL	6	1	2	3	0	7	0	2	2	6
	Bowling Green	CCHA	39	28	40	68	141	....	....	....	....	....
	NHL Totals		6	1	2	3	0	7	0	2	2	6
Duncanson, Craig	Los Angeles	NHL	2	0	0	0	24	....	....	....	....	....
	Cornwall	OHL	52	22	45	67	88	5	4	3	7	20
	NHL Totals		4	0	1	1	24	....	....	....	....	....
Dundas, Rocky	Spokane	WHL	19	13	17	30	69	....	....	....	....	....
	Medicine Hat	WHL	29	22	24	46	63	20	4	8	12	44
Dunn, Richie	Buffalo	NHL	2	0	1	1	2	....	....	....	....	....
	Rochester	AHL	64	6	26	32	47	18	1	6	7	6
	NHL Totals		467	34	139	173	304	36	3	15	18	24
Dupont, Jerome	Toronto	NHL	13	0	0	0	23	....	....	....	....	....
	Newmarket	AHL	29	1	8	9	47	....	....	....	....	....
	NHL Totals		214	7	29	36	468	20	0	2	2	56
Duvall, Harold	Colgate	ECAC	32	9	17	26	65	....	....	....	....	....
Dykstra, Steven	Buffalo	NHL	37	0	1	1	179	....	....	....	....	....
	Rochester	AHL	18	0	0	0	77	....	....	....	....	....
	NHL Totals		101	4	22	26	287	....	....	....	....	....
Dzikowski, John	Hershey	AHL	61	13	13	26	90	....	....	....	....	....
	Kalamazoo	IHL	21	2	4	6	72	5	1	0	1	2
Eagles, Mike	Quebec	NHL	73	13	19	32	55	4	1	0	1	10
	NHL Totals		148	24	31	55	106	7	1	0	1	12
Eakin, Bruce	Springfield	AHL	11	0	5	5	6	....	....	....	....	....
	NHL Totals		13	2	2	4	4	....	....	....	....	....
Eakins, Dallas	Peterborough	OHL	54	3	11	14	145	12	1	4	5	37
Eaves, Murray	Nova Scotia	AHL	76	26	38	64	46	4	1	1	2	2
	NHL Totals		49	4	12	16	7	4	0	1	1	2

PLAYER	CLUB	LEAGUE	Regular Season GP	G	A	TP	PIM	Playoffs GP	G	A	TP	PIM
Edlund, Par	Bjorkleven	Swe.	4	0	0	0	0	....	....	....	....	....
Eklund, Per-Erik	Philadelphia	NHL	72	14	41	55	2	26	7	20	27	2
	NHL Totals		142	29	92	121	14	31	7	22	29	2
Ekroth, Peter	Sodertalje	Swe.	33	6	13	19	70	....	....	....	....	....
Ellett, David	Winnipeg	NHL	78	13	31	44	53	10	0	8	8	2
	NHL Totals		238	39	89	128	234	21	1	14	15	6
Elynuik, Pat	Prince Albert	WHL	64	51	62	113	40	8	5	5	10	12
Emerson, Nelson	Bowling Green	CCHA	45	26	35	61	28	....	....	....	....	....
Emery, Robert	Fredericton	AHL	42	2	0	2	63	....	....	....	....	....
Endean, Craig	Winnipeg	NHL	2	0	1	1	0	....	....	....	....	....
	Regina	WHL	76	69	77	146	34	3	5	0	5	4
	NHL Totals		2	0	1	1	0	....	....	....	....	....
Engblom, Brian	Calgary	NHL	32	0	4	4	28	....	....	....	....	....
	NHL Totals		659	29	177	206	599	48	3	9	12	43
Engevik, Glen	U. Denver	WCHA	40	10	8	18	32	....	....	....	....	....
English, John	New Haven	AHL	3	0	0	0	6	....	....	....	....	....
	Flint	IHL	18	1	2	3	83	6	1	2	3	12
Ennis, Jim	Boston U.	H.E.	26	3	4	7	27	....	....	....	....	....
Erickson, Bryan	Los Angeles	NHL	68	20	30	50	26	3	1	1	2	0
	NHL Totals		225	67	83	150	101	11	3	4	7	7
Eriksson, Patrick	Brynas	Swe.	25	10	5	15	8	....	....	....	....	....
Erixon, Jan	NY Rangers	NHL	68	8	18	26	24	6	1	0	1	0
	NHL Totals		240	22	82	104	77	25	3	1	4	10
Ernst, Gordon	Brown	ECAC	15	5	6	11	10	....	....	....	....	....
Errey, Bob	Pittsburgh	NHL	72	16	18	34	46	....	....	....	....	....
	NHL Totals		190	36	39	75	90	....	....	....	....	....
Espe, David	U. of Minnesota	WCHA	45	4	8	12	28	....	....	....	....	....
Evans, Daryl	Newmarket	AHL	74	27	46	73	17	....	....	....	....	....
	Toronto	NHL	2	1	0	1	0	1	0	0	0	0
	NHL Totals		113	22	30	52	25	11	5	8	13	12
Evans, Doug	St. Louis	NHL	53	3	13	16	91	5	0	0	0	10
	Peoria	IHL	18	10	15	25	39	....	....	....	....	....
	NHL Totals		66	4	13	17	93	5	0	0	0	10
Evans, Shawn	Nova Scotia	AHL	55	7	28	35	29	5	0	4	4	6
Evason, Dean	Hartford	NHL	80	22	37	59	67	5	3	2	5	35
	NHL Totals		154	45	69	114	136	15	4	6	10	45
Evtushevski, Greg	Maine	AHL	17	1	1	2	55	....	....	....	....	....
	Kalamazoo	IHL	47	23	26	49	114	....	....	....	....	....
	Indianapolis	IHL	8	1	6	7	4	....	....	....	....	....
Ewen, Dean	Spokane	WHL	66	8	14	22	236	....	....	....	....	....
Ewen, Todd	St. Louis	NHL	23	2	0	2	84	4	0	0	0	23
	Peoria	IHL	16	3	3	6	110	....	....	....	....	....
	NHL Totals		23	2	0	2	84	4	0	0	0	23
Fauss, Ted	Toronto	NHL	15	0	1	1	11	....	....	....	....	....
	Newmarket	AHL	59	0	5	5	81	....	....	....	....	....
	NHL Totals		15	0	1	1	11	....	....	....	....	....
Featherstone, Glen	Windsor	OHL	47	6	11	17	154	14	2	6	8	19
Federko, Bernie	St. Louis	NHL	64	20	52	72	32	6	3	3	6	18
	NHL Totals		782	310	607	917	357	71	29	52	81	63
Fedyk, Brent	Regina	WHL	12	9	6	15	9	....	....	....	....	....
	Seattle	WHL	13	5	11	16	9	....	....	....	....	....
	Portland	WHL	11	5	4	9	6	14	5	6	11	0
Felix, Chris	Cdn. Olympic	....	78	14	38	52	36	....	....	....	....	....
Fenton, Paul	NY Rangers	NHL	8	0	0	0	2	....	....	....	....	....
	New Haven	AHL	70	37	38	75	45	7	6	4	10	6
	NHL Totals		42	7	5	12	12	....	....	....	....	....
Fenyves, David	Buffalo	NHL	7	1	0	1	0	....	....	....	....	....
	Rochester	AHL	71	6	16	22	57	18	3	12	15	10
	NHL Totals		148	2	27	29	87	11	0	0	0	9
Fergus, Tom	Toronto	NHL	57	21	28	49	57	2	0	1	1	2
	Newmarket	AHL	1	0	1	1	0	....	....	....	....	....
	NHL Totals		424	150	208	358	258	41	12	10	22	36
Ferguson, John	Providence	H.E.	23	0	0	0	6	....	....	....	....	....
Ferner, Mark	Buffalo	NHL	13	0	3	3	9	....	....	....	....	....
	Rochester	AHL	54	0	12	12	157	....	....	....	....	....
	NHL Totals		13	0	3	3	9	....	....	....	....	....

PLAYER	CLUB	LEAGUE	GP	G	A	TP	PIM	GP	G	A	TP	PIM
Ferraro, Ray	Hartford	NHL	80	27	32	59	42	6	1	1	2	8
	NHL Totals		200	68	96	164	139	16	4	7	11	12
Ferreira, Brian	RPI	ECAC	30	17	15	32	22	....	....	....	....	....
Finley, Jeff	Portland	WHL	72	13	53	66	113	20	1	21	22	27
Finn, Steven	Quebec	NHL	36	2	5	7	40	13	0	2	2	29
	Fredericton	AHL	38	7	19	26	73	....	....	....	....	....
	NHL Totals		53	2	6	8	68	13	0	2	2	29
Fishback, Bruce	Minn.-Duluth	WCHA	18	1	3	4	6	....	....	....	....	....
Fitzgerald, Tom	Providence	H.E.	27	8	14	22	22	....	....	....	....	....
Fitzpatrick, Ross	Hershey	AHL	66	45	40	85	34	5	1	4	5	10
	NHL Totals		20	5	2	7	0	....	....	....	....	....
Flaherty, Jeff	Lowell	H.E.	28	4	5	9	37	....	....	....	....	....
Flanagan, Mike	Providence	H.E.	25	1	2	3	18	....	....	....	....	....
Flanagan, Tim	Calgary	WHL	45	13	14	27	83	....	....	....	....	....
Flatley, Pat	NY Islanders	NHL	63	16	35	51	81	11	3	2	5	6
	NHL Totals		230	56	107	163	259	39	13	8	21	47
Fletcher, Steven	Sherbrooke	AHL	70	15	11	26	261	17	5	5	10	82
Flichel, Todd	Bowling Green	CCHA	42	4	15	19	77	....	....	....	....	....
Flockhart, Ron	St. Louis	NHL	60	16	19	35	12	....	....	....	....	....
	NHL Totals		428	140	179	319	204	19	4	6	10	14
Florio, Perry	Providence	H.E.	23	1	6	7	58	....	....	....	....	....
Floyd, Larry	Maine	AHL	77	30	44	74	50	....	....	....	....	....
	NHL Totals		12	2	3	5	9	....	....	....	....	....
Fogarty, Bryan	Kingston	OHL	56	20	50	70	70	12	2	3	5	5
Fogolin, Lee	Edmonton	NHL	35	1	3	4	17	....	....	....	....	....
	Buffalo	NHL	9	0	2	2	8	....	....	....	....	....
	NHL Totals		924	44	195	239	1318	108	5	19	24	173
Foligno, Mike	Buffalo	NHL	75	30	29	59	176	....	....	....	....	....
	NHL Totals		609	249	267	516	1280	22	7	7	14	79
Forst, Rick	North Dakota	WCHA	1	0	0	0	0	....	....	....	....	....
Fortier, Marc	Chicoutimi	QMJHL	65	66	135	201	39	19	11	40	51	20
Foster, Dwight	Boston	NHL	47	4	12	16	37	3	0	0	0	0
	NHL Totals		541	111	163	274	420	35	5	12	17	4
Fotiu, Nick	Calgary	NHL	42	5	3	8	145	....	....	....	....	....
	NHL Totals		622	60	77	137	1322	38	0	4	4	67
Fowler, Rob	Merrimack	ECAC	35	2	25	27	49	....	....	....	....	....
Fox, Jimmy	Los Angeles	NHL	76	19	42	61	48	5	3	2	5	0
	NHL Totals		499	169	257	426	125	21	4	8	12	0
Franceschetti, Lou	Washington	NHL	75	12	9	21	127	7	0	0	0	23
	NHL Totals		205	25	40	65	326	23	1	1	2	61
Francis, Bobby	Salt Lake	IHL	82	29	69	98	86	17	9	8	17	13
Francis, Ron	Hartford	NHL	75	30	63	93	45	6	2	2	4	6
	NHL Totals		418	157	335	492	291	16	3	4	7	10
Fraser, Curt	Chicago	NHL	75	25	25	50	182	2	1	1	2	10
	NHL Totals		624	182	228	410	1131	65	15	18	33	198
Fraser, Jay	Rochester	AHL	36	8	12	20	159	6	0	1	1	17
Frawley, Dan	Pittsburgh	NHL	78	14	14	28	218	....	....	....	....	....
	NHL Totals		180	28	28	56	456	1	0	0	0	0
Freer, Mark	Philadelphia	NHL	1	0	1	1	0	....	....	....	....	....
	Peterborough	OHL	65	39	43	82	44	12	2	6	8	5
	NHL Totals		1	0	1	1	0	....	....	....	....	....
Frycer, Miroslav	Toronto	NHL	29	7	8	15	28	....	....	....	....	....
	NHL Totals		339	122	150	272	380	14	3	8	11	10
Gage, Jody	Rochester	AHL	70	26	39	65	60	17	14	5	19	24
	NHL Totals		57	14	14	28	24	....	....	....	....	....
Gagne, Simon	Laval	QMJHL	66	19	35	54	90	15	9	11	20	12
Gagne, Wayne	W. Michigan	CCHA	43	13	76	89	38	....	....	....	....	....
Gagner, Dave	NY Rangers	NHL	10	1	4	5	12	....	....	....	....	....
	New Haven	AHL	56	22	41	63	50	7	1	5	6	18
	NHL Totals		80	11	16	27	47	....	....	....	....	....
Gainey, Bob	Montreal	NHL	47	8	8	16	19	17	1	3	4	6
	NHL Totals		1033	218	244	462	537	160	24	43	67	137
Gallant, Bernie	Saginaw	IHL	66	24	38	62	77	....	....	....	....	....

PLAYER	CLUB	LEAGUE	Regular Season GP	G	A	TP	PIM	Playoffs GP	G	A	TP	PIM
Gallant, Gerard	Detroit	NHL	80	38	34	72	216	16	8	6	14	43
	NHL Totals		164	64	65	129	388	19	8	6	14	54
Galley, Garry	Los Angeles	NHL	30	5	11	16	57	....	....	....	....	....
	Washington	NHL	18	1	10	11	10	2	0	0	0	0
	NHL Totals		175	23	64	87	195	5	1	0	1	2
Ganchar, Perry	Sherbrooke	AHL	68	22	29	51	64	17	9	8	17	37
	NHL Totals		8	0	2	2	0	7	3	1	4	0
Gans, David	New Haven	AHL	29	10	11	21	20	....	....	....	....	....
	Hershey	AHL	20	7	8	15	28	....	....	....	....	....
	NHL Totals		6	0	0	0	2	....	....	....	....	....
Gardner, Bill	Hartford	NHL	8	0	1	1	0	....	....	....	....	....
	Binghamton	AHL	50	17	44	61	18	13	4	8	12	14
	NHL Totals		372	71	114	~185	66	45	3	8	11	17
Gardner, Joel	Colgate	ECAC	31	10	20	30	20	....	....	....	....	....
Gare, Danny	Edmonton	NHL	18	1	3	4	6	....	....	....	....	....
	NHL Totals		827	354	331	685	1285	64	25	21	46	195
Garpenlov, Johan	Djurgardens	Swe.	29	5	8	13	20	....	....	....	....	....
Gartner, Mike	Washington	NHL	78	41	32	73	61	7	4	3	7	14
	NHL Totals		622	323	330	653	626	33	13	23	36	47
Gasseau, James	Rochester	AHL	7	0	2	2	6	....	....	....	....	....
Gatzos, Steve	DID NOT PLAY -	INJURED										
	NHL Totals		89	15	20	35	83	1	0	0	0	0
Gaulin, Jean-Marc	Fredericton	AHL	17	1	1	2	15	....	....	....	....	....
	Muskegon	IHL	5	1	3	4	6	....	....	....	....	....
	NHL Totals		26	4	3	7	8	1	0	0	0	0
Gaume, Dallas	Binghamton	AHL	77	18	39	57	31	12	1	1	2	7
Gavin, Stewart	Hartford	NHL	79	20	21	41	28	6	2	4	6	10
	NHL Totals		423	80	98	178	293	20	6	5	11	23
Geist, Rich	Yale	ECAC	28	9	14	23	41	....	....	....	....	....
Gerlitz, Paul	Fredericton	AHL	8	0	1	1	0	....	....	....	....	....
	Muskegon	IHL	54	10	10	20	26	1	0	0	0	2
Germain, Eric	Fredericton	AHL	44	2	8	10	28	....	....	....	....	....
Gibson, Don	Michigan St.	CCHA	43	3	3	6	74	....	....	....	....	....
Giffen, Lee	Pittsburgh	NHL	8	1	1	2	0	....	....	....	....	....
	Oshawa	OHL	48	31	69	100	46	23	17	19	36	14
	NHL Totals		8	1	1	2	0	....	....	....	....	....
Giguere, Stephane	St. Jean	QMJHL	69	45	45	90	129	8	3	5	8	11
Gilbert, Greg	NY Islanders	NHL	51	6	7	13	26	10	2	2	4	6
	NHL Totals		294	68	97	165	233	47	9	10	19	70
Gilchrist, Brent	Spokane	WHL	46	45	55	100	71	5	2	7	9	6
	Sherbrooke	AHL	....	....	....	....	....	10	2	7	9	2
Giles, Curt	Minnesota	NHL	11	0	3	3	4	....	....	....	....	....
	NY Rangers	NHL	61	2	17	19	50	5	0	0	0	6
	NHL Totals		542	31	150	181	436	75	4	14	18	90
Gilhen, Randy	Winnipeg	NHL	2	0	0	0	0	....	....	....	....	....
	Sherbrooke	AHL	75	36	29	65	44	17	7	13	20	10
	NHL Totals		4	0	1	1	0	....	....	....	....	....
Gill, Todd	Toronto	NHL	61	4	27	31	92	13	2	2	4	42
	Newmarket	AHL	11	1	8	9	33	....	....	....	....	....
	NHL Totals		86	6	29	35	133	14	2	2	4	42
Gillies, Clark	Buffalo	NHL	61	10	17	27	81	....	....	....	....	....
	NHL Totals		933	314	276	590	972	159	47	46	93	262
Gillis, Jere	Philadelphia	NHL	1	0	0	0	0	....	....	....	....	....
	Hershey	AHL	47	13	22	35	32	5	0	0	0	9
	NHL Totals		386	78	95	173	230	19	4	7	11	9
Gillis, Paul	Quebec	NHL	76	13	26	39	267	13	2	4	6	65
	NHL Totals		297	54	89	143	699	35	3	13	16	154
Gilmour, Doug	St. Louis	NHL	80		154							
Gilmour, Doug	St. Louis	NHL	80	42	63	105	58	6	2	2	4	16
	NHL Totals		312	113	155	268	205	39	14	24	38	53
Gingras, Gaston	Montreal	NHL	66	11	34	45	21	5	0	2	2	0
	NHL Totals		354	51	141	192	135	35	5	14	19	14
Ginnell, Erin	Swift Current	WHL	73	33	21	54	35	4	1	0	1	0

PLAYER	CLUB	LEAGUE	Regular Season GP	G	A	TP	PIM	Playoffs GP	G	A	TP	PIM
Glasgow, Robert	U. Alberta	CWUAA	24	5	4	9	8	....	....	....	....	....
Glynn, Brian	Saskatoon	WHL	44	2	26	28	163	11	1	3	4	19
Goertz, Dave	Baltimore	AHL	16	0	3	3	8	....	....	....	....	....
	Muskegon	IHL	44	3	17	20	44	15	0	4	4	14
Golden, Mike	Maine	H.E.	36	19	23	42	37	....	....	....	....	....
Gosselin, Guy	Minn.-Duluth	WCHA	33	7	8	15	66	....	....	....	....	....
Gotaas, Steve	Prince Albert	WHL	68	53	55	108	94	8	5	6	11	16
Gould, Bobby	**Washington**	**NHL**	78	23	27	50	74	7	0	3	3	8
	NHL Totals		473	120	115	235	359	41	12	10	22	33
Goulet, Michel	**Quebec**	**NHL**	75	49	47	96	61	13	9	5	14	35
	NHL Totals		607	366	364	730	448	66	34	30	64	98
Gourlie, David	U. Denver	WCHA	37	3	9	12	34	....	....	....	....	....
Gradin, Thomas	**Boston**	**NHL**	64	12	31	43	18	4	0	4	4	0
	NHL Totals		677	209	384	593	298	42	17	25	42	20
Graham, Dirk	**Minnesota**	**NHL**	76	25	29	54	142	....	....	....	....	....
	NHL Totals		198	60	74	134	252	15	3	5	8	11
Graham, Robb	Guelph	OHL	45	13	14	27	37	....	....	....	....	....
Granato, Tony	U. of Wisconsin	WCHA	42	28	45	73	64	....	....	....	....	....
Grannis, David	U. of Minnesota	WCHA	46	10	12	22	32	....	....	....	....	....
Grant, Kevin	Kitchener	OHL	52	5	18	23	125	4	0	1	1	16
Gratton, Dan	New Haven	AHL	49	6	10	16	45	2	0	0	0	0
Graves, Adam	Windsor	OHL	66	45	55	100	70	14	9	8	17	32
	Adirondack	AHL	....	....	....	....	....	5	0	1	1	0
Graves, Steve	**Edmonton**	**NHL**	12	2	0	2	0	....	....	....	....	....
	Nova Scotia	AHL	59	18	10	28	22	5	1	1	2	2
	NHL Totals		14	2	0	2	0	....	....	....	....	....
Green, Rick	**Montreal**	**NHL**	72	1	9	10	10	17	0	4	4	8
	NHL Totals		645	38	181	219	506	65	2	13	15	65
Greenlaw, Jeff	**Washington**	**NHL**	22	0	3	3	44	....	....	....	....	....
	Binghamton	AHL	4	0	2	2	0	....	....	....	....	....
	NHL Totals		22	0	3	3	44	....	....	....	....	....
Greenough, Glenn	Saginaw	IHL	70	38	43	81	6	10	1	2	3	8
Gregg, Randy	**Edmonton**	**NHL**	52	8	16	24	42	18	3	6	9	17
	NHL Totals		333	32	111	143	231	84	9	23	32	75
Gregoire, Bill	Victoria	WHL	15	6	3	9	41	....	....	....	....	....
	Calgary	WHL	34	7	14	21	132	....	....	....	....	....
	Moncton	AHL	7	0	0	0	29	6	0	2	2	48
Greschner, Ron	**NY Rangers**	**NHL**	61	6	34	40	62	6	0	5	5	0
	NHL Totals		818	176	407	583	997	70	17	31	48	84
Gretzky, Keith	Hamilton	OHL	64	35	66	101	18	9	5	9	14	4
Gretzky, Wayne	**Edmonton**	**NHL**	79	62	121	183	28	21	5	29	34	6
	NHL Totals		632	543	977	1520	299	101	69	140	209	40
Gronstrand, Jari	**Minnesota**	**NHL**	47	1	6	7	27	....	....	....	....	....
	NHL Totals		47	1	6	7	27	....	....	....	....	....
Groulx, Wayne	Fredericton	AHL	30	11	7	18	8	....	....	....	....	....
	Muskegon	IHL	38	18	22	40	49	....	....	....	....	....
	NHL Totals		1	0	0	0	0	....	....	....	....	....
Gruhl, Scott	Muskegon	IHL	67	34	39	73	157	15	5	7	12	54
	NHL Totals		14	2	3	5	6	....	....	....	....	....
Guay, Francois	Laval	QMJHL	63	52	77	129	67	14	5	13	18	18
Guay, Paul	**Los Angeles**	**NHL**	35	2	5	7	16	2	0	0	0	0
	New Haven	AHL	6	1	3	4	11	....	....	....	....	....
	NHL Totals		74	7	15	22	48	5	0	0	0	4
Guden, Dave	Providence	H.E.	33	4	2	6	22	....	....	....	....	....
Guerard, Stephane	Shawinigan	QMJHL	31	5	16	21	57	12	2	9	11	36
Guidotti, Vincent	Maine	H.E.	24	2	2	4	10	....	....	....	....	....
Gustafsson, Bengt	Swe. National	Swe.	10	3	8	11	....	....	....	....	....	....
	NHL Totals		479	160	272	432	149	14	3	7	10	4
Guy, Kevan	**Calgary**	**NHL**	24	0	4	4	19	4	0	1	1	23
	Moncton	AHL	46	2	10	12	38	....	....	....	....	....
	NHL Totals		24	0	4	4	19	4	0	1	1	23
Haanpaa, Ari	**NY Islanders**	**NHL**	41	6	4	10	17	6	0	0	0	10
	NHL Totals		59	6	11	17	37	6	0	0	0	10
Haarmann, Mark	S.S. Marie	OHL	60	6	30	36	25	....	....	....	....	....

PLAYER	CLUB	LEAGUE	Regular Season GP	G	A	TP	PIM	Playoffs GP	G	A	TP	PIM
Haas, David	London	OHL	5	1	0	1	5	....	....	....	....	....
	Kitchener	OHL	4	0	1	1	4	....	....	....	....	....
	Belleville	OHL	55	10	13	23	86	6	3	0	3	13
Habscheid, Marc	Minnesota	NHL	15	2	0	2	2	....	....	....	....	....
	Cdn. Olympic	....	51	29	32	61	70	....	....	....	....	....
	NHL Totals		95	14	19	33	28	2	0	0	0	0
Hachborn, Len	Hershey	AHL	17	4	10	14	2	5	0	2	2	2
	NHL Totals		102	20	39	59	29	7	0	3	3	7
Hajdu, Richard	Buffalo	NHL	2	0	0	0	0	....	....	....	....	....
	Rochester	AHL	58	7	15	22	90	11	1	1	2	9
	NHL Totals		5	0	0	0	4	....	....	....	....	....
Hajt, Bill	Buffalo	NHL	23	0	2	2	4	....	....	....	....	....
	NHL Totals		854	42	202	244	433	80	2	16	18	70
Halkidis, Bob	Buffalo	NHL	6	1	1	2	19	....	....	....	....	....
	Rochester	AHL	59	1	8	9	144	8	0	0	0	43
	NHL Totals		43	2	10	12	134	4	0	0	0	19
Hall, Taylor	Vancouver	NHL	4	0	0	0	0	....	....	....	....	....
	Fredericton	AHL	36	21	20	41	23	....	....	....	....	....
	NHL Totals		34	7	9	16	25	....	....	....	....	....
Hallin, Mats	Minnesota	NHL	6	0	0	0	4	....	....	....	....	....
	NHL Totals		152	17	14	31	193	15	1	0	1	13
Halward, Doug	Vancouver	NHL	10	0	3	3	34	....	....	....	....	....
	Detroit	NHL	11	0	3	3	19	....	....	....	....	....
	NHL Totals		541	64	195	259	583	37	6	6	12	95
Hamel, Gilles	Winnipeg	NHL	79	27	21	48	24	8	2	0	2	2
	NHL Totals		444	119	135	254	239	26	4	5	9	10
Hamilton, Brad	Michigan State	CCHA	45	3	29	32	54	....	....	....	....	....
Hammond, Ken	Los Angeles	NHL	10	0	2	2	11	....	....	....	....	....
	New Haven	AHL	66	1	15	16	76	6	0	1	1	21
	NHL Totals		16	1	3	4	13	3	0	0	0	4
Hamway, Mark	NY Islanders	NHL	2	0	1	1	0	....	....	....	....	....
	Springfield	AHL	59	25	31	56	8	....	....	....	....	....
	NHL Totals		53	5	13	18	9	1	0	0	0	0
Handy, Ron	Indianapolis	IHL	82	55	80	135	57	6	4	3	7	2
	NHL Totals		10	0	2	2	0	....	....	....	....	....
Hanley, Tim	New Hampshire	H.E.	37	11	23	34	34	....	....	....	....	....
Hannan, Dave	Pittsburgh	NHL	58	10	15	25	56	....	....	....	....	....
	NHL Totals		262	46	65	111	350	....	....	....	....	....
Hanson, Dave	Denver	WCHA	36	7	17	24	64	....	....	....	....	....
Harding, Jeff	St. Michael's	Jr. B	22	22	8	30	97	....	....	....	....	....
Hardy, Mark	Los Angeles	NHL	73	3	27	30	120	5	1	2	3	10
	NHL Totals		528	47	222	269	728	26	4	8	12	34
Harlow, Scott	Sherbrooke	AHL	66	22	26	48	6	15	5	6	11	6
Harper, Warren	Rochester	AHL	61	13	27	40	50	11	1	4	5	18
Hartman, Mike	Buffalo	NHL	17	3	3	6	69	....	....	....	....	....
	North Bay	OHL	32	15	24	39	144	19	7	8	15	88
	NHL Totals		17	3	3	6	69	....	....	....	....	....
Hartsburg, Craig	Minnesota	NHL	73	11	50	61	93	....	....	....	....	....
	NHL Totals		513	91	285	376	742	61	15	27	42	70
Hatcher, Kevin	Washington	NHL	78	8	16	24	144	7	1	0	1	20
	NHL Totals		159	18	26	44	263	17	2	1	3	39
Hawerchuk, Dale	Winnipeg	NHL	80	47	53	100	52	10	5	8	13	4
	NHL Totals		479	268	363	631	321	26	10	24	34	21
Hawgood, Greg	Kamloops	WHL	61	30	83	123	139	....	....	....	....	....
Hawkins, Todd	Belleville	OHL	60	47	40	87	187	6	3	5	8	16
Hawley, Kent	Ottawa	OHL	64	29	53	82	86	11	0	5	5	43
Haworth, Alan	Washington	NHL	50	25	16	41	43	6	0	3	3	7
	NHL Totals		422	166	177	343	313	42	12	16	28	28
Hawryliw, Neil	Kalamazoo	IHL	56	9	23	32	84	5	0	1	1	4
	NHL Totals		1	0	0	0	0	....	....	....	....	....
Hayton, Brian	Guelph	OHL	63	6	19	25	113	5	2	1	3	0
Headon, Peter	Boston U.	H.E.	4	0	0	0	0	....	....	....	....	....
Heffernan, Kevin	Northeastern	H.E.	36	14	22	36	30	....	....	....	....	....
Hejna, Tony	RPI	ECAC	31	12	18	30	18	....	....	....	....	....

PLAYER	CLUB	LEAGUE	Regular Season GP	G	A	TP	PIM	Playoffs GP	G	A	TP	PIM
Helmer, Tim	Indianapolis	IHL	74	17	17	34	21	3	0	0	0	0
Helminen, Raimo	NY Rangers	NHL	21	2	4	6	2	....	....	....	....	....
	New Haven	AHL	6	0	2	2	0	....	....	....	....	....
	Minnesota	NHL	6	0	1	1	0	....	....	....	....	....
	NHL Totals		93	12	35	47	12	2	0	0	0	0
Henderson, Archie	Maine	AHL	67	4	6	10	246	....	....	....	....	....
	NHL Totals		23	3	1	4	92	....	....	....	....	....
Henry, Dale	NY Islanders	NHL	19	3	3	6	46	8	0	0	0	2
	Springfield	AHL	23	9	14	23	49	....	....	....	....	....
	NHL Totals		42	6	7	13	80	8	0	0	0	2
Hepple, Alan	Maine	AHL	74	6	19	25	137	....	....	....	....	....
	NHL Totals		3	0	0	0	7	....	....	....	....	....
Herbert, Rick	Spokane	WHL	2	0	1	1	0	....	....	....	....	....
	Brandon	WHL	65	3	34	37	129	....	....	....	....	....
	Saginaw	IHL	3	0	0	0	0	8	0	2	2	9
Herniman, Steve	Cornwall	OHL	64	2	8	10	121	3	0	0	0	0
Herom, Kevin	Moose Jaw	WHL	72	34	33	67	111	9	3	2	5	24
Heroux, Yves	Quebec	NHL	1	0	0	0	0	....	....	....	....	....
	Fredericton	AHL	37	8	6	14	13	....	....	....	....	....
	Muskegon	IHL	25	6	8	14	31	2	0	0	0	0
	NHL Totals		1	0	0	0	0	....	....	....	....	....
Herring, Graham	Saginaw	IHL	4	0	1	1	0	....	....	....	....	....
Hie, Danny	Ottawa	OHL	4	3	6	9	16	....	....	....	....	....
	Hamilton	OHL	15	2	14	16	25	....	....	....	....	....
	Sudbury	OHL	19	1	5	6	47	....	....	....	....	....
Hiemer, Ullie	New Jersey	NHL	40	6	14	20	45	....	....	....	....	....
	Maine	AHL	26	4	3	7	51	....	....	....	....	....
	NHL Totals		143	19	54	73	176	....	....	....	....	....
Higgins, Tim	Detroit	NHL	77	12	14	26	124	12	0	1	1	16
	NHL Totals		602	137	176	313	563	51	4	8	12	51
Hill, Alan	Philadelphia	NHL	7	0	2	2	4	9	2	1	3	0
	Hershey	AHL	76	13	35	48	124	5	0	1	1	2
	NHL Totals		209	39	55	94	217	50	8	10	18	39
Hill, Bruce	Denver	WCHA	38	14	16	30	28	....	....	....	....	....
Hillier, Randy	Pittsburgh	NHL	55	4	8	12	97	....	....	....	....	....
	NHL Totals		292	9	60	69	459	11	0	1	1	20
Hiltner, Mike	Alaska-Anch.	G.N.	30	19	20	39	76	....	....	....	....	....
Hjalm, Michael	Bjorkloven	Swe.	34	9	13	22	16	....	....	....	....	....
Hoard, Brian	Hamilton	OHL	1	0	1	1	0	....	....	....	....	....
	Belleville	OHL	9	0	0	0	31	....	....	....	....	....
	S.S. Marie	OHL	44	4	8	12	137	4	0	0	0	2
Hobson, Doug	Prince Albert	WHL	69	3	20	23	83	8	2	3	5	12
Hodge, Ken	Boston College	H.E.	37	29	33	62	30	....	....	....	....	....
Hodgson, Dan	Vancouver	NHL	43	9	13	22	25	....	....	....	....	....
	Newmarket	AHL	20	7	12	19	16	....	....	....	....	....
	NHL Totals		83	22	25	47	37	....	....	....	....	....
Hoffman, Mike	Binghamton	AHL	74	9	32	41	120	13	2	2	4	23
	NHL Totals		9	1	3	4	2	....	....	....	....	....
Hofford, James	Buffalo	NHL	12	0	0	0	40	....	....	....	....	....
	Rochester	AHL	54	1	8	9	204	13	1	0	1	57
	NHL Totals		17	0	0	0	45	....	....	....	....	....
Hogue, Benoit	Rochester	AHL	52	14	20	34	52	12	5	4	9	8
Holland, Dennis	Portland	WHL	51	43	62	105	40	20	7	14	21	20
Hollett, Steve	S.S. Marie	OHL	65	35	41	76	63	4	0	1	1	7
Holmes, Daril	Kitchener	OHL	64	17	24	41	84	3	0	0	0	7
Hooey, Todd	Salt Lake	IHL	82	47	48	95	60	17	14	8	22	21
Hoover, Ron	W. Michigan	CCHA	34	7	10	17	22	....	....	....	....	....
Hoover, Tim	Flint	IHL	75	3	23	26	26	5	0	4	4	0
Hopkins, Dean	Nova Scotia	AHL	59	20	25	45	84	1	0	0	0	5
	NHL Totals		218	23	49	72	302	18	1	5	6	29
Horacek, Tony	Hershey	AHL	1	0	0	0	0	1	0	0	0	0
	Spokane	WHL	64	23	37	60	177	5	1	3	4	18
Horachek, Peter	Saginaw	IHL	77	30	34	64	26	10	2	3	5	0
Horner, Steve	New Hampshire	H.E.	33	19	17	36	14	....	....	....	....	....
Hospodar, Ed	Philadelphia	NHL	45	2	2	4	136	5	0	0	0	2
	NHL Totals		408	17	50	67	1216	44	4	1	5	206

PLAYER	CLUB	LEAGUE	GP	Regular Season G	A	TP	PIM	GP	Playoffs G	A	TP	PIM
Hostak, Martin	Sparta Praha	Czech	34	6	2	8	0	....	....	....	....	....
Hotham, Greg	Newmarket	AHL	51	4	9	13	60	....	....	....	....	....
	NHL Totals		230	15	74	89	139	5	0	3	3	6
Houck, Paul	Minnesota	NHL	12	0	2	2	2	....	....	....	....	....
	Springfield	AHL	64	29	18	47	58	....	....	....	....	....
	NHL Totals		15	1	2	3	2	....	....	....	....	....
Houda, Doug	Adirondack	AHL	77	6	23	29	142	11	1	8	9	50
	NHL Totals		3	1	0	1	0	....	....	....	....	....
Hough, Mike	Quebec	NHL	56	6	8	14	79	9	0	3	3	26
	Fredericton	AHL	10	1	3	4	20	....	....	....	....	....
	NHL Totals		56	6	8	14	79	9	0	3	3	26
Houlder, Bill	North Bay	OHL	62	17	51	68	68	22	4	19	23	20
Houle, Kevin	Sherbrooke	AHL	4	0	3	3	0	....	....	....	....	....
	Saginaw	IHL	39	6	12	18	27	5	1	1	2	0
Housley, Phil	Buffalo	NHL	78	21	46	67	57	....	....	....	....	....
	NHL Totals		382	102	239	341	211	18	6	6	12	10
Howard, Tarek	North Dakota	WCHA	32	1	9	10	38	....	....	....	....	....
Howe, Mark	Philadelphia	NHL	69	15	43	58	37	26	2	10	12	4
	NHL Totals		579	147	368	515	258	59	6	26	32	18
Hrdina, Jiri	Sparta Praha	Czech	31	18	18	36	24	....	....	....	....	....
Hrkac, Tony	St. Louis	NHL	....	....	....	....	....	3	0	0	0	0
	North Dakota	WCHA	48	46	79	125	48	....	....	....	....	....
	NHL Totals		....	....	....	....	....	3	0	0	0	0
Hrynewich, Tim	Milwaukee	IHL	82	39	37	76	78	6	2	3	5	2
Huber, Willy	NY Rangers	NHL	66	8	22	30	68	6	0	2	2	6
	NHL Totals		599	95	195	290	880	28	5	5	10	33
Huddy, Charlie	Edmonton	NHL	58	4	15	19	35	21	1	7	8	21
	NHL Totals		418	51	181	232	289	78	7	43	50	70
Hudson, Mike	Sudbury	OHL	63	40	57	97	18	....	....	....	....	....
Huffman, Kerry	Philadelphia	NHL	9	0	0	0	2	....	....	....	....	....
	Hershey	AHL	3	0	1	1	0	4	0	0	0	0
	Guelph	OHL	44	4	31	35	20	5	0	2	2	8
	NHL Totals		9	0	0	0	2	....	....	....	....	....
Hughes, Pat	St. Louis	NHL	43	1	5	6	26	....	....	....	....	....
	Hartford	NHL	2	0	0	0	2	3	0	0	0	0
	NHL Totals		573	130	128	258	653	71	8	25	33	77
Hull, Brett	Calgary	NHL	5	1	0	1	0	4	2	1	3	0
	Moncton	AHL	67	50	42	92	16	3	2	2	4	2
	NHL Totals		5	1	0	1	0	6	2	1	3	0
Hull, Jody	Peterborough	OHL	49	18	34	52	22	12	4	9	13	14
Hulst, Kent	Windsor	OHL	37	18	20	38	49	....	....	....	....	....
	Belleville	OHL	27	13	10	23	17	6	1	1	2	0
Hunt, Curtis	Prince Albert	WHL	47	6	31	37	101	8	1	3	4	4
Hunter, Dale	Quebec	NHL	46	10	29	39	135	13	1	7	8	56
	NHL Totals		523	140	318	458	1545	67	16	26	42	319
Hunter, Dave	Edmonton	NHL	77	6	9	15	79	21	3	3	6	20
	NHL Totals		600	113	163	276	752	99	16	24	40	211
Hunter, Mark	St. Louis	NHL	74	36	33	69	167	5	0	3	3	10
	NHL Totals		348	133	98	231	719	54	9	14	23	160
Hunter, Tim	Calgary	NHL	73	6	15	21	361	6	0	0	0	51
	NHL Totals		271	30	37	67	1104	45	1	3	4	274
Huscroft, Jamie	Seattle	WHL	21	1	18	19	99	....	....	....	....	....
	Medicine Hat	WHL	35	4	21	25	170	20	0	3	3	125
Husgen, Jamie	Ill.-Chicago	CCHA	31	2	8	10	59	....	....	....	....	....
	Sherbrooke	AHL	2	0	0	0	0	....	....	....	....	....
Hussey, Tom												
Hutton, Dwaine	Flint	IHL	48	13	24	37	71	....	....	....	....	....
	Milwaukee	IHL	5	2	3	5	0	4	3	0	3	0
Hynes, Gord	Moncton	AHL	69	2	19	21	21	4	0	0	0	2
Iafrate, Al	Toronto	NHL	80	9	21	30	55	13	1	3	4	11
	NHL Totals		213	22	62	84	146	23	1	6	7	15
Ihnacak, Miroslav	Toronto	NHL	34	6	5	11	12	1	0	0	0	0
	Newmarket	AHL	32	11	17	28	6	....	....	....	....	....
	NHL Totals		55	8	9	17	39	1	0	0	0	0

PLAYER	CLUB	LEAGUE	Regular Season GP	G	A	TP	PIM	Playoffs GP	G	A	TP	PIM
Ihnacak, Peter	Toronto	NHL	58	12	27	39	16	13	2	4	6	9
	Newmarket	AHL	8	2	6	8	0	....	....	....	....	....
	NHL Totals		318	90	127	217	124	23	4	7	11	21
Illikainen, Darin	Minn.-Duluth	WCHA	32	5	4	9	20	....	....	....	....	....
Ingman, Jan	Farjestad	Swe.	29	10	11	21	14	....	....	....	....	....
Issel, Kim	Prince Albert	WHL	70	31	44	75	55	6	1	2	3	17
Jackson, Don	NY Rangers	NHL	22	1	0	1	91	....	....	....	....	....
	NHL Totals		311	16	52	68	640	53	4	5	9	147
Jablonski, Jeff	Lake Superior	CCHA	40	17	10	27	42	....	....	....	....	....
Jackson, James	Rochester	AHL	71	19	38	57	48	16	5	4	9	6
	NHL Totals		107	15	30	45	20	14	3	2	5	6
Jackson, Jeff	Toronto	NHL	55	8	7	15	64	....	....	....	....	....
	Newmarket	AHL	7	3	6	9	13	....	....	....	....	....
	NY Rangers	NHL	9	5	1	6	15	6	1	1	2	16
	NHL Totals		86	14	11	25	105	6	1	1	2	16
James, Val	Toronto	NHL	4	0	0	0	14	....	....	....	....	....
	Newmarket	AHL	74	4	3	7	71	....	....	....	....	....
	NHL Totals		11	0	0	0	30	....	....	....	....	....
Janney, Craig	Boston College	H.E.	37	26	55	81	6	....	....	....	....	....
Janostin, Pat	Minn.-Duluth	WCHA	22	0	1	1	8	....	....	....	....	....
Janssens, Mark	Regina	WHL	68	24	38	62	209	3	0	1	1	14
Jarvenpaa, Hannu	Winnipeg	NHL	20	1	8	9	8	....	....	....	....	....
	NHL Totals		20	1	8	9	8	....	....	....	....	....
Jarvis, Doug	Hartford	NHL	80	9	13	22	20	6	0	0	0	4
	NHL Totals		962	139	264	403	261	105	14	27	41	42
Jarvis, Wes	Toronto	NHL	....	....	....	....	....	2	0	0	0	2
	Newmarket	AHL	70	28	50	78	32	....	....	....	....	....
	NHL Totals		236	31	55	86	98	2	0	0	0	2
Jennings, Grant	Fort Wayne	IHL	3	0	0	0	0	....	....	....	....	....
	Binghamton	AHL	47	1	5	6	125	13	0	2	2	17
Jensen, Chris	NY Rangers	NHL	37	6	7	13	21	....	....	....	....	....
	New Haven	AHL	14	4	9	13	41	....	....	....	....	....
	NHL Totals		46	7	10	17	21	....	....	....	....	....
Jensen, David A.	Washington	NHL	46	8	8	16	12	7	0	0	0	2
	Binghamton	AHL	6	2	5	7	0	....	....	....	....	....
	NHL Totals		64	9	12	21	18	11	0	0	0	2
Jerrard, Paul	Lake Superior	CCHA	35	10	19	29	56	....	....	....	....	....
Johannesen, Glen	Springfield	AHL	54	10	6	16	156	....	....	....	....	....
	NHL Totals		2	0	0	0	0	....	....	....	....	....
Johnson, Jim	Pittsburgh	NHL	80	5	25	30	116	....	....	....	....	....
	NHL Totals		160	8	51	59	231	....	....	....	....	....
Johnson, Mark	New Jersey	NHL	68	25	26	51	22	....	....	....	....	....
	NHL Totals		512	160	232	392	210	17	6	4	10	6
Johnson, Scott	Baltimore	AHL	63	8	7	15	27	....	....	....	....	....
Johnson, Steve	North Dakota	WCHA	48	26	44	70	38	....	....	....	....	....
Johnson, Terry	Toronto	NHL	48	0	1	1	104	2	0	0	0	0
	Newmarket	AHL	24	0	1	1	37	....	....	....	....	....
	NHL Totals		285	3	24	27	580	35	0	4	4	108
Johnston, Greg	Boston	NHL	76	12	15	27	79	4	0	0	0	0
	NHL Totals		117	14	18	32	81	4	0	0	0	0
Johnston, Jay	Fort Wayne	IHL	31	0	8	8	92	....	....	....	....	....
	NHL Totals		8	0	0	0	13	....	....	....	....	....
Johnstone, Eddie	Detroit	NHL	6	0	0	0	0	....	....	....	....	....
	Adirondack	AHL	61	30	22	52	83	5	1	0	1	2
	NHL Totals		426	122	136	258	375	55	13	10	23	83
Jones, Brad	Winnipeg	NHL	4	1	0	1	0	....	....	....	....	....
	U. of Michigan	CCHA	40	32	46	78	64	....	....	....	....	....
	NHL Totals		4	1	0	1	0	....	....	....	....	....
Jonsson, Tomas	NY Islanders	NHL	47	6	25	31	36	10	1	4	5	6
	NHL Totals		407	69	185	254	311	71	7	24	31	81
Joseph, Chris	Seattle	WHL	67	13	45	58	155	....	....	....	....	....
Joseph, Fabian	Cdn. Olympic	....	74	15	30	45	26	....	....	....	....	....
Joyce, Bobby	North Dakota	WCHA	48	52	37	89	42	....	....	....	....	....

PLAYER	CLUB	LEAGUE	Regular Season GP	G	A	TP	PIM	Playoffs GP	G	A	TP	PIM
Julien, Claude	Fredericton	AHL	17	1	6	7	22	....	....	...	....	....
	NHL Totals		14	0	1	1	25	....	....	...	....	....
Kaese, Trent	Calgary	WHL	68	30	24	54	117	....	....	...	....	....
	Swift Current	WHL	2	1	0	1	4	....	....	...	....	....
	Flint	IHL	1	0	0	0	0	6	4	1	5	9
Kaminski, Kevin	Saskatoon	WHL	67	26	44	70	35	11	5	6	11	45
Karalis, Tom	Fredericton	AHL	37	0	3	3	64	....	....	...	....	....
	Muskegon	IHL	28	3	9	12	94	15	2	12	14	28
Kasper, Steve	Boston	NHL	79	20	30	50	51	3	0	2	2	0
	NHL Totals		436	99	160	259	366	40	7	10	17	52
Kastelic, Ed	Washington	NHL	23	1	1	2	83	5	1	0	1	13
	Binghamton	AHL	48	17	11	28	124	....	....	...	....	....
	NHL Totals		38	1	1	2	156	5	1	0	1	13
Keane, Mike	Moose Jaw	WHL	53	25	45	70	107	9	3	9	12	11
	Sherbrooke	AHL	....	....	....	....	....	9	2	2	4	16
Keczmer, Dan	Lake Superior	CCHA	38	3	5	8	26	....	....	...	....	....
Kelfer, Mike	Boston U.	H.E.	33	21	19	40	20	....	....	...	....	....
Kellin, Tony	Binghamton	AHL	66	8	27	35	65	5	1	1	2	2
Kelly, Paul	Guelph	OHL	61	27	48	75	67	5	2	4	6	0
Kennedy, Dean	Los Angeles	NHL	66	6	14	20	91	5	0	2	2	10
	NHL Totals		236	9	41	50	370	5	0	2	2	10
Kerr, Alan	NY Islanders	NHL	72	7	10	17	175	14	1	4	5	25
	NHL Totals		98	10	12	22	215	19	2	4	6	29
Kerr, Kevin	Windsor	OHL	63	27	41	68	264	14	3	8	11	45
Kerr, Tim	Philadelphia	NHL	75	58	37	95	57	12	8	5	13	2
	NHL Totals		457	278	207	485	450	48	24	17	41	27
Ketola, Marty	Colorado	WCHA	41	4	4	8	55	....	....	...	....	....
King, Derek	NY Islanders	NHL	2	0	0	0	0	....	....	...	....	....
	Oshawa	OHL	57	53	53	106	74	17	14	10	24	40
	NHL Totals		2	0	0	0	0	....	....	...	....	....
King, Kris	Binghamton	AHL	7	0	0	0	18	....	....	...	....	....
	Peterborough	OHL	46	23	33	56	160	12	5	8	13	41
Kirton, Doug	Colorado	WCHA	38	10	10	20	42	....	....	...	....	....
Kirton, Mark	Fredericton	AHL	80	27	37	64	20	....	....	...	....	....
	NLH Totals		266	57	56	113	121	4	1	2	3	7
Kisio, Kelly	NY Rangers	NHL	70	24	40	64	73	4	0	1	1	2
	NHL Totals		306	92	169	261	248	11	1	3	4	8
Kivell, Rob	Moncton	AHL	3	0	0	0	2	....	....	...	....	....
Kleinendorst, Scot	Hartford	NHL	66	3	9	12	130	4	1	3	4	20
	NHL Totals		195	8	35	43	304	20	1	6	7	40
Klima, Petr	Detroit	NHL	77	30	23	53	42	13	2	1	3	4
	NHL Totals		151	62	47	109	58	13	2	1	3	4
Kluzak, Gord	DID NOT PLAY											
	NHL Totals		220	19	64	83	395	23	2	5	7	70
Kocur, Joey	Detroit	NHL	77	9	9	18	276	16	2	3	5	71
	NHL Totals		153	19	15	34	717	19	3	3	6	76
Kolstad, Dean	Prince Albert	WHL	72	17	37	54	112	8	1	5	6	8
Konroyd, Steve	NY Islanders	NHL	72	5	16	21	70	14	1	4	5	10
	NHL Totals		435	23	104	127	472	41	5	11	16	56
Kontos, Chris	Pittsburgh	NHL	31	8	9	17	6	....	....	...	....	....
	New Haven	AHL	36	14	17	31	29	....	....	...	....	....
	NHL Totals		109	20	25	45	71	....	....	...	....	....
Kopechy, Bill	RPI	ECAC	30	13	8	21	27	....	....	...	....	....
Korchinsky, Jeff	Clarkson	ECAC	30	5	8	13	40	....	....	...	....	....
Kordic, John	Montreal	NHL	44	5	3	8	151	11	2	0	2	19
	Sherbrooke	AHL	10	4	4	8	49	....	....	...	....	....
	NHL Totals		49	5	4	9	163	29	2	0	2	72
Korn, Jim	Buffalo	NHL	52	4	10	14	158	....	....	...	....	....
	NHL Totals		434	41	88	129	1273	3	0	0	0	26
Korol, David	Adirondack	AHL	48	1	4	5	67	11	2	2	4	21
Kortko, Roger	Springfield	AHL	75	16	30	46	54	....	....	...	....	....
	NHL Totals		79	7	17	24	28	10	0	3	3	17
Kostynski, Doug	Moncton	AHL	74	21	45	66	22	6	2	1	3	0
	NHL Totals		15	3	1	4	4	....	....	...	....	....

			Regular Season					Playoffs				
PLAYER	CLUB	LEAGUE	GP	G	A	TP	PIM	GP	G	A	TP	PIM
Kotsopoulous, Chris	Toronto	NHL	43	2	10	12	75	7	0	0	0	14
	NHL Totals		399	41	93	134	754	31	1	3	4	91
Koudys, Jim	Peoria	IHL	9	3	2	5	4	....	....	...	....	....
Krakiwsky, Sean	Spokane	WHL	57	19	42	61	57	5	2	4	6	4
Krayer, Ed	Harvard	ECAC	14	2	9	11	4	....	....	...	....	....
Krentz, Dale	Detroit	NHL	8	0	0	0	0	....	....	...	....	....
	Adirondack	AHL	71	32	39	71	68	11	3	4	7	10
	NHL Totals		8	0	0	0	0	....	....	...	....	....
Kromm, Rich	NY Islanders	NHL	70	12	17	29	20	14	1	3	4	4
	NHL Totals		273	62	85	147	114	31	2	6	8	17
Krupp, Uwe	Buffalo	NHL	26	1	4	5	23	....	....	...	....	....
	Rochester	AHL	42	3	19	22	50	17	1	11	12	16
	NHL Totals		26	1	4	5	23	....	....	...	....	....
Kruppke, Gord	Prince Albert	WHL	49	2	10	12	129	8	0	0	0	9
Krushelnyski, Mike	Edmonton	NHL	80	16	35	51	67	21	3	4	7	18
	NHL Totals		376	126	169	295	249	69	20	23	43	70
Kudelski, Bob	Yale	ECAC	30	25	22	47	34	....	....	...	....	....
Kulak, Stu	Vancouver	NHL	28	1	1	2	37	....	....	...	....	....
	Edmonton	NHL	23	3	1	4	41	....	....	...	....	....
	NY Rangers	NHL	3	0	0	0	0	....	....	...	....	....
	NHL Totals		58	5	3	8	78	....	....	...	....	....
Kumpel, Mark	Quebec	NHL	40	1	8	9	16	....	....	...	....	....
	Detroit	NHL	5	0	1	1	0	8	0	0	0	4
	Adirondack	AHL	7	2	3	5	0	1	1	0	1	0
	NHL Totals		134	19	28	47	59	28	4	4	8	8
Kurri, Jari	Edmonton	NHL	79	54	54	108	41	21	15	10	25	20
	NHL Totals		520	354	398	752	201	98	65	73	138	65
Kurvers, Tom	Montreal	NHL	1	0	0	0	0	....	....	...	....	....
	Buffalo	NHL	55	6	17	23	22	....	....	...	....	....
	NHL Totals		193	23	75	98	88	12	0	6	6	6
Kurzawski, Mark	Windsor	OHL	65	5	23	28	98	14	3	4	7	38
Kushner, Dale	Medicine Hat	WHL	65	34	34	68	250	25	0	5	5	14
Kypreos, Nick	Hershey	AHL	10	0	1	1	4	....	....	...	....	....
	North Bay	OHL	46	49	41	90	54	24	11	5	16	78
Kyte, Jim	Winnipeg	NHL	72	5	5	10	162	10	0	4	4	36
	NHL Totals		274	7	13	20	454	24	0	4	4	73
Lackten, Kurt	Swift Current	WHL	65	20	20	40	97	3	0	1	1	4
Lacombe, Normand	Buffalo	NHL	39	4	7	11	8	....	....	...	....	....
	Rochester	AHL	13	6	5	11	4	....	....	...	....	....
	Edmonton	NHL	1	0	0	0	2	....	....	...	....	....
	Nova Scotia	AHL	10	3	5	8	4	5	1	1	2	6
	NHL Totals		95	12	18	30	48	....	....	...	....	....
Lacroix, Daniel	Granby	QMJHL	54	9	16	25	311	8	1	2	3	22
Ladouceur, Randy	Detroit	NHL	34	3	6	9	70	....	....	...	....	....
	Hartford	NHL	36	2	3	5	51	6	0	2	2	12
	NHL Totals		326	16	70	86	499	13	2	2	4	18
LaFontaine, Pat	NY Islanders	NHL	80	38	32	70	70	14	5	7	12	10
	NHL Totals		227	100	96	196	151	42	10	15	25	22
Laforge, Marc	Binghamton	AHL	....	....	....	....	....	4	0	0	0	7
	Kingston	OHL	53	2	10	12	224	12	1	0	1	79
Lafreniere, Jason	Quebec	NHL	56	13	15	28	8	12	1	5	6	2
	Fredericton	AHL	11	3	11	14	0	....	....	...	....	....
	NHL Totals		56	13	15	28	8	12	1	5	6	2
Laidlaw, Tom	NY Rangers	NHL	63	1	10	11	65	....	....	...	....	....
	Los Angeles	NHL	11	0	3	3	4	5	0	0	0	2
	NHL Totals		521	20	102	122	565	43	2	9	11	54
Lakso, Bob	Indianapolis	IHL	79	39	55	94	6	6	2	2	4	0
Lalonde, Todd	Sudbury	OHL	29	5	11	16	71	....	....	...	....	....
Lalor, Mike	Montreal	NHL	57	0	10	10	47	13	2	1	3	29
	NHL Totals		119	3	15	18	103	30	3	2	5	58
Lamb, Jeff	U. Denver	WCHA	40	10	24	34	58	....	....	...	....	....
Lamb, Mark	Detroit	NHL	22	2	1	3	8	11	0	0	0	11
	Adirondack	AHL	49	14	36	50	45	....	....	...	....	....
	NHL Totals		23	2	1	3	8	11	0	0	0	11

			Regular Season					Playoffs				
PLAYER	CLUB	LEAGUE	GP	G	A	TP	PIM	GP	G	A	TP	PIM
Lambert, Lane	NY Rangers	NHL	18	2	2	4	33	....	....	...	....	....
	New Haven	AHL	11	3	3	6	19	....	....	...	....	....
	Quebec	NHL	15	5	5	10	18	13	2	4	6	30
	NHL Totals		209	43	36	79	400	17	2	4	6	40
Lambert, Richard	N. Hampshire	H.E.	34	1	5	6	63	....	....	...	....	....
Lammens, Hank	St. Lawrence	ECAC	35	6	13	19	92	....	....	...	....	....
LaMoine, Mike	North Dakota	WCHA	47	2	17	19	36	....	....	...	....	....
Lamoureux, Mitch	Hershey	AHL	78	43	46	89	122	5	1	2	3	8
Langevin, Dave	Los Angeles	NHL	11	0	4	4	7	....	....	...	....	....
	New Haven	AHL	10	1	1	2	7	....	....	...	....	....
	NHL Totals		513	12	107	119	530	87	2	15	17	106
Langway, Rod	Washington	NHL	78	2	25	27	53	7	0	1	1	2
	NHL Totals		656	45	218	263	651	59	4	15	19	62
Laniel, Marc	Oshawa	OHL	63	14	31	45	42	26	3	13	16	20
Lanigan, Mark	N. Michigan	WCHA	34	2	9	11	46	....	....	...	....	....
Lanthier, Jean-Marc	Fredericton	AHL	78	15	38	53	24	....	....	...	....	....
	NHL Totals		100	15	15	30	27	....	....	...	....	....
Lanz, Rick	Vancouver	NHL	17	1	6	7	10	....	....	...	....	....
	Toronto	NHL	44	2	19	21	32	13	1	3	4	27
	NHL Totals		461	58	190	248	363	27	3	8	11	33
Lanza, Matt	RPI	ECAC	16	0	1	1	31	....	....	...	....	....
Laplante, Richard	Vermont	ECAC	3	2	4	6	6	....	....	...	....	....
Lappin, Peter	St. Lawrence	ECAC	35	34	24	58	32	....	....	...	....	....
Larmer, Steve	Chicago	NHL	80	28	56	84	22	4	0	0	0	2
	NHL Totals		407	183	229	412	147	38	16	25	41	35
Larocque, Denis	Guelph	OHL	45	4	10	14	82	5	0	2	2	9
Larose, Guy	Ottawa	OHL	66	28	49	77	77	11	6	2	8	10	27
Larouche, Pierre	NY Rangers	NHL	73	28	35	63	12	6	3	2	5	4
	NHL Totals		802	392	418	810	224	64	20	34	54	16
Larson, Reed	Boston	NHL	66	12	24	36	95	4	0	2	2	2
	NHL Totals		787	203	410	613	1230	21	4	6	10	53
Latreille, Martin	Laval	QMJHL	59	1	16	17	118	15	0	2	2	6
Latta, David	Kitchener	OHL	50	32	46	78	46	4	0	3	3	2
	NHL Totals		1	0	0	0	0	....	....	...	....	....
Lauer, Brad	NY Islanders	NHL	61	7	14	21	65	6	2	0	2	4
	NHL Totals		61	7	14	21	65	6	2	0	2	4
Laughlin, Craig	Washington	NHL	80	22	30	52	67	1	0	0	0	0
	NHL Totals		424	117	179	296	291	30	6	5	11	18
LaVallee, Kevin	Pittsburgh	NHL	33	8	20	28	4	....	....	...	....	....
	NHL Totals		366	110	125	235	85	32	5	8	13	24
Lavarre, Mark	Chicago	NHL	58	8	15	23	33	....	....	...	....	....
	Nova Scotia	AHL	17	12	8	20	8	....	....	...	....	....
	NHL Totals		60	8	15	23	33	....	....	...	....	....
Laviolette, Peter	Indianapolis	IHL	72	10	20	30	146	5	0	1	1	12
Lavoie, Dominic	ST. Jean	QMJHL	64	12	42	54	97	8	2	7	9	2
Lawless, Paul	Hartford	NHL	60	22	32	54	14	2	0	2	2	2
	NHL Totals		177	45	65	110	38	3	0	2	2	2
Lawrence, Brett	Colgate	ECAC	33	8	7	15	22	....	....	...	....	....
Lawton, Brian	Minnesota	NHL	66	21	23	44	86	....	....	...	....	....
	NHL Totals		229	54	67	121	179	8	0	1	1	12
Laxdal, Derek	Toronto	NHL	2	0	0	0	7	....	....	...	....	....
	Newmarket	AHL	78	24	20	44	69	....	....	...	....	....
	NHL Totals		5	0	0	0	13	....	....	...	....	....
Leach, Jamie	Hamilton	OHL	64	12	19	31	67	....	....	...	....	....
Leach, Steve	Washington	NHL	15	1	0	1	6	....	....	...	....	....
	Binghamton	AHL	54	18	21	39	39	13	3	1	4	6
	NHL Totals		26	2	1	3	8	6	0	1	1	0
Leavins, Jim	NY Rangers	NHL	4	0	1	1	4	....	....	...	....	....
	New Haven	AHL	54	7	21	28	16	7	0	4	4	2
	NHL Totals		41	2	12	14	30	....	....	...	....	....
LeBeau, Stephane	Shawinigan	QMJHL	65	77	90	167	60	14	9	20	29	20
Leblanc, Jean	Vancouver	NHL	2	1	0	1	0	....	....	...	....	....
	Fredericton	AHL	75	40	30	70	27	....	....	...	....	....
	NHL Totals		2	1	0	1	0	....	....	...	....	....

PLAYER	CLUB	LEAGUE	Regular Season GP	G	A	TP	PIM	Playoffs GP	G	A	TP	PIM
LeClair, John	Bellows	HS	27	44	40	84	30	....	....	....	....	....
Ledyard, Grant	Los Angeles	NHL	67	14	23	37	93	5	0	0	0	10
	NHL Totals		188	31	62	93	244	8	0	2	2	14
Leeman, Gary	Toronto	NHL	80	21	31	52	66	5	0	1	1	14
	NHL Totals		238	39	88	127	189	17	2	11	13	16
Leetch, Brian	Boston College	H.E.	37	9	38	47	10	....	....	....	....	....
Lefebvre, Sylvain	Laval	QMJHL	70	10	36	46	44	15	1	6	7	12
Lehman, Tom	AIK	Swe.	32	25	26	51	12	....	....	....	....	....
Leiter, Ken	NY Islanders	NHL	74	9	20	29	30	11	0	5	5	6
	NHL Totals		88	10	23	33	38	11	0	5	5	6
Lemay, Moe	Vancouver	NHL	52	9	17	26	128	....	....	....	....	....
	Edmonton	NHL	10	1	2	3	36	9	2	1	3	11
	NHL Totals		289	71	94	165	403	13	2	1	3	23
Lemieux, Alain	Pittsburgh	NHL	1	0	0	0	0	....	....	....	....	....
	Baltimore	AHL	72	41	56	97	62	....	....	....	....	....
	NHL Totals		119	28	44	72	38	19	4	6	10	0
Lemieux, Claude	Montreal	NHL	76	27	26	53	156	17	4	9	13	41
	NHL Totals		95	29	30	59	197	37	14	15	29	109
Lemieux, Jocelyn	St. Louis	NHL	53	10	8	18	94	5	0	1	1	6
	NHL Totals		53	10	8	18	94	5	0	1	1	6
Lemieux, Mario	Pittsburgh	NHL	63	54	53	107	57	....	....	....	....	....
	NHL Totals		215	145	203	348	154	....	....	....	....	....
Lenardon, Tim	New Jersey	NHL	7	1	1	2	0	....	....	....	....	....
	Maine	AHL	61	28	35	63	30	....	....	....	....	....
	NHL Totals		7	1	1	2	0	....	....	....	....	....
Leonard, John	Bowdoin	ECAC	28	15	17	32	34	....	....	....	....	....
Lessard, Rick	Ottawa	OHL	66	5	36	41	188	11	1	7	8	30
Lever, Don	Buffalo	NHL	10	3	2	5	4	....	....	....	....	....
	Rochester	AHL	57	29	25	54	69	18	4	3	7	14
	NHL Totals		1020	313	367	680	593	30	7	10	17	26
Levie, Craig	Vancouver	NHL	9	0	1	1	13	....	....	....	....	....
	NHL Totals		183	22	53	75	177	16	2	3	5	32
Levasseur, Chris	Alaska-Anch.	G.N.	28	15	17	32	34	....	....	....	....	....
Lewis, Dave	Detroit	NHL	58	2	5	7	66	14	0	4	4	10
	NHL Totals		1002	36	187	223	935	91	1	20	21	143
Lidster, Doug	Vancouver	NHL	80	12	51	63	40	....	....	....	....	....
	NHL Totals		244	30	91	121	155	5	0	2	2	2
Lindstrom, Willy	Pittsburgh	NHL	60	10	13	23	6	....	....	....	....	....
	NHL Totals		582	161	162	323	200	57	14	18	32	24
Linseman, Ken	Boston	NHL	64	15	34	49	126	4	1	1	2	22
	NHL Totals		586	182	407	589	1204	88	32	62	94	269
Loach, Lonnie	Guelph	OHL	56	31	24	55	42	5	2	1	3	2
Lockwood, Joe	U. Michigan	CCHA	39	13	5	18	62	....	....	....	....	....
Lofthouse, Mark	New Haven	AHL	47	18	27	45	34	4	0	1	1	2
	NHL Totals		181	42	38	80	73	....	....	....	....	....
Logan, Robert	Buffalo	NHL	22	7	3	10	0	....	....	....	....	....
	Rochester	AHL	56	30	14	44	27	18	5	10	15	4
	NHL Totals		22	7	3	10	0	....	....	....	....	....
Loiselle, Claude	New Jersey	NHL	75	16	24	40	137	....	....	....	....	....
	NHL Totals		203	38	46	84	373	3	0	2	2	0
Lomow, Byron	Indianapolis	IHL	81	28	43	71	225	6	3	5	8	21
Loney, Troy	Pittsburgh	NHL	23	8	7	15	22	....	....	....	....	....
	Baltimore	AHL	40	13	14	27	134	....	....	....	....	....
	NHL Totals		129	21	24	45	185	....	....	....	....	....
Loob, Hakan	Calgary	NHL	68	18	26	44	26	5	1	2	3	0
	NHL Totals		291	116	122	238	98	42	10	18	28	8
Lorden, Gary	U. of Michigan	CCHA	1	0	1	1	2	....	....	....	....	....
Lorenz, Tom	Minn.-Duluth	WCHA	22	4	1	5	14	....	....	....	....	....
Loven, Tim	Milwaukee	IHL	7	0	0	0	0	....	....	....	....	....
Lovesin, Ken	U. Saskatchewan	CWUAA	28	5	15	20	22	....	....	....	....	....
Lowe, Kevin	Edmonton	NHL	77	8	29	37	94	21	2	4	6	22
	NHL Totals		614	45	216	261	617	99	7	33	40	72
Lowes, Glen	Toronto	OHL	49	10	14	24	118	....	....	....	....	....

PLAYER	CLUB	LEAGUE	Regular Season GP	G	A	TP	PIM	Playoffs GP	G	A	TP	PIM
Lowney, Ed	Boston U.	H.E.	37	22	22	44	6	....	....	....	....	....
Lowry, Dave	Vancouver	NHL	70	8	10	18	176	....	....	....	....	....
	NHL Totals		143	18	18	36	319	3	0	0	0	0
Ludvig, Jan	New Jersey	NHL	47	7	9	16	98	....	....	....	....	....
	Maine	AHL	14	6	4	10	46	....	....	....	....	....
	NHL Totals		288	53	79	132	314	....	....	...	....	....
Ludwig, Craig	Montreal	NHL	75	4	12	16	105	17	2	3	5	30
	NHL Totals		376	18	73	91	369	67	2	8	10	109
Ludzik, Steve	Chicago	NHL	52	5	12	17	34	4	0	0	0	0
	NHL Totals		334	39	77	116	279	39	4	7	11	57
Lukowich, Morris	Los Angeles	NHL	60	14	21	35	64	3	0	0	0	8
	NHL Totals		582	199	219	418	584	11	0	2	2	24
Lumley, Dave	Edmonton	NHL	1	0	0	0	0	....	....	....	....	....
	NHL Totals		437	98	160	258	680	61	6	8	14	131
Lumme, Jyrkki	Ilves	Fin.	43	12	12	24	52	....	....	....	....	....
Luongo, Chris	Michigan St.	CCHA	27	4	16	20	38	....	....	....	....	....
Lyons, Marc	Kingston	OHL	47	5	11	16	32	12	0	1	1	44
MacDermid, Paul	Hartford	NHL	72	7	11	18	202	6	2	1	3	34
	NHL Totals		190	25	29	54	395	16	4	2	6	54
Macdonald, Brett	Fredericton	AHL	49	0	9	9	29	....	....	....	....	....
MacDonald, Bruce	Loomis Chaffee	HS	25	30	33	63	54	....	....	....	....	....
MacDonald, Lane	Harvard	ECAC	34	37	30	67	26	....	....	....	....	....
MacEachern, Shane	Hull	QMJHL	69	43	67	110	105	8	6	7	13	8
MacInnis, Allan	Calgary	NHL	79	20	56	76	97	4	1	0	1	0
	NHL Totals		290	57	202	259	299	40	8	29	37	51
MacInnis, Joseph	Northeastern	H.E.	29	7	8	15	33	....	....	....	....	....
MacIntyre, Duncan	Fredericton	AHL	37	6	15	21	30	....	....	....	....	....
MacIver, Norm	NY Rangers	NHL	3	0	1	1	0	....	....	....	....	....
	New Haven	AHL	71	6	30	36	73	7	0	0	0	9
	NHL Totals		3	0	1	1	0	....	....	...	....	....
Mack, Craig	U. of Minnesota	WCHA	20	1	4	5	24	....	....	....	....	....
MacKenzie, Jean-Marc	London	OHL	63	49	56	105	20	....	....	....	....	....
Mackey, David	Saginaw	IHL	81	26	49	75	173	10	5	6	11	22
MacLean, John	New Jersey	NHL	80	31	36	67	120	....	....	....	....	....
	NHL Totals		238	66	92	158	186	....	....	...	....	....
MacLean, Paul	Winnipeg	NHL	72	32	42	74	75	10	5	2	7	16
	NHL Totals		451	208	231	439	650	30	14	10	24	53
MacLean, Terry	Trois-Rivieres	QMJHL	69	41	76	117	20	....	....	....	....	....
MacLellan, Brian	Minnesota	NHL	76	32	31	63	69	....	....	....	....	....
	NHL Totals		314	104	146	250	240	19	2	5	7	15
Macoun, Jamie	Calgary	NHL	79	7	33	40	111	3	0	1	1	8
	NHL Totals		320	37	111	148	381	49	3	9	12	43
MacPherson, Duncan	Springfield	AHL	26	1	0	1	86	....	....	....	....	....
MacSwain, Steve	U. Minnesota	WCHA	48	31	29	60	24	....	....	....	....	....
MacTavish, Craig	Edmonton	NHL	79	20	19	39	55	21	1	9	10	16
	NHL Totals		370	87	109	196	199	59	10	17	27	52
MacTavish, Scott	Verdun	QMJHL	11	1	2	3	30	....	....	....	....	....
MacVicar, Andrew	Peterborough	OHL	64	6	13	19	33	11	2	1	3	7
MacWilliam, Mike	Medicine Hat	WHL	44	7	17	24	134	19	1	0	1	35
Madill, Jeff	Ohio State	CCHA	43	38	32	70	139	....	....	....	....	....
Magnan, Marc	Indianapolis	IHL	77	11	21	32	353	6	0	0	0	22
	NHL Totals		4	0	1	1	5	....	....	...	....	....
Maguire, Kevin	Toronto	NHL	17	0	0	0	74	1	0	0	0	0
	Newmarket	AHL	51	4	2	6	131	....	....	....	....	....
	NHL Totals		17	0	0	0	74	1	0	0	0	0
Mahoney, Scott	Oshawa	OHL	54	13	9	22	161	22	4	1	5	117
Major, Bruce	Maine	H.E.	37	14	10	24	12	....	....	....	....	....
Makela, Mikko	NY Islanders	NHL	80	24	33	57	24	11	2	4	6	8
	NHL Totals		138	40	53	93	52	11	2	4	6	8
Maki, Jyrki	U. of Lowell	H.E.	25	2	2	4	8	....	....	....	....	....
Maley, David	Montreal	NHL	48	6	12	18	55	....	....	....	....	....
	Sherbrooke	AHL	11	1	5	6	25	12	7	7	14	10
	NHL Totals		51	6	12	18	55	7	1	3	4	2
Malone, Greg	Quebec	NHL	6	0	1	1	0	1	0	0	0	0
	Fredericton	AHL	49	13	22	35	50	....	....	....	....	....
	NHL Totals		704	191	310	501	661	20	3	5	8	32

PLAYER	CLUB	LEAGUE	Regular Season GP	G	A	TP	PIM	Playoffs GP	G	A	TP	PIM
Maloney, Don	NY Rangers	NHL	72	19	38	57	117	6	2	1	3	6
	NHL Totals		556	179	277	456	663	85	22	35	57	91
Maltais, Steve	Cornwall	OHL	65	32	12	44	29	5	0	0	0	2
Mann, Jimmy	DID NOT PLAY		....	....	....	....	....	....	....	....	....	....
	NHL Totals		284	10	20	30	842	22	0	0	0	89
Mann, Russ	St. Lawrence	ECAC	34	2	14	16	30	....	....	....	....	....
Mansi, Maurice	RPI	ECAC	22	3	7	10	19	....	....	....	....	....
Manson, Dave	Chicago	NHL	63	1	8	9	146	3	0	0	0	10
	NHL Totals		63	1	8	9	146	3	0	0	0	10
Mantha, Moe	Pittsburgh	NHL	62	9	31	40	44	....	....	....	....	....
	NHL Totals		387	55	203	258	336	9	4	5	9	16
Marchment, Bryan	Belleville	OHL	52	6	38	44	238	6	0	4	4	17
Marcov, Peter	Cornell	ECAC	27	10	6	16	6	....	....	....	....	....
Marcinyshyn, David	Kamloops	WHA	68	5	27	32	106	13	0	3	3	35
Mark, Gordon	New Jersey	NHL	36	3	5	8	82	....	....	....	....	....
	Maine	AHL	29	4	10	14	66	....	....	....	....	....
	NHL Totals		36	3	5	8	82	....	....	....	....	....
Markwart, Nevin	Boston	NHL	64	10	9	19	225	4	0	0	0	9
	Moncton	AHL	3	3	3	6	11	....	....	....	....	....
	NHL Totals		225	31	44	75	589	5	0	0	0	9
Marois, Daniel	Chicoutimi	QMJHL	40	22	26	48	143	16	7	14	21	25
Marois, Mario	Winnipeg	NHL	79	4	40	44	106	10	1	3	4	23
	NHL Totals		645	60	268	328	1260	86	4	30	34	139
Marsh, Brad	Philadelphia	NHL	77	2	9	11	124	26	3	4	7	16
	NHL Totals		701	14	128	142	896	81	4	18	22	114
Marshall, Paul	Boston College	H.E.	36	4	10	14	30	....	....	....	....	....
Marston, Stuart	Laval	QMJHL	16	0	8	8	24	....	....	....	....	....
Martin, Brian	Flint	IHL	11	1	0	1	15	....	....	....	....	....
	Milwaukee	IHL	5	0	1	1	0	....	....	....	....	....
Martin, Grant	Washington	NHL	9	0	0	0	4	1	1	0	1	2
	Binghamton	AHL	63	30	23	53	86	12	3	1	4	16
	NHL Totals		44	0	4	4	55	1	1	0	1	2
Martin, Terry	Newmarket	AHL	72	8	7	15	8	....	....	....	....	....
	NHL Totals		479	104	101	205	202	21	4	2	6	26
Martin, Tom	Winnipeg	NHL	11	1	0	1	49	....	....	....	....	....
	Adirondack	AHL	18	5	6	11	57	....	....	....	....	....
	NHL Totals		24	2	0	2	91	3	0	0	0	2
Martinson, Steven	Hershey	AHL	17	0	3	3	85	....	....	....	....	....
	Adirondack	AHL	14	1	1	2	78	11	2	0	2	108
Maruk, Dennis	Minnesota	NHL	67	16	30	46	52	....	....	....	....	....
	NHL Totals		860	349	517	866	744	34	14	22	36	26
Massey, Peter	Northeastern	H.E.	16	0	1	1	6	....	....	....	....	....
Mathias, Scott	U. Denver	WCHA	40	11	13	24	22	....	....	....	....	....
Mathiasen, Dwight	Pittsburgh	NHL	6	0	1	1	2	....	....	....	....	....
	Baltimore	AHL	61	23	22	45	49	....	....	....	....	....
	NHL Totals		10	1	1	2	4	....	....	....	....	....
Matikainen, Petri	Oshawa	OHL	50	8	34	42	53	21	2	12	14	36
Matteau, Stephane	Hull	QMJHL	69	27	48	75	113	8	3	7	10	8
Matulik, Ivan	Bratislava	Czech.	25	1	3	4	....	....	....	....	....	....
Maurice, Mike	Kingston	OHL	60	48	44	92	69	12	11	2	13	21
Maurice, Paul	Windsor	OHL	63	4	15	19	87	14	2	1	3	18
Maxwell, Brad	Vancouver	NHL	30	1	7	8	28	....	....	....	....	....
	NY Rangers	NHL	9	0	4	4	6	....	....	....	....	....
	Minnesota	NHL	17	2	7	9	9	....	....	....	....	....
	NHL Totals		612	98	270	368	1270	79	12	49	61	178
Maxwell, Kevin	Hershey	AHL	56	12	20	32	139	3	1	0	1	30
May, Andy	Northeastern	H.E.	26	5	5	10	17	....	....	....	....	....
Mayer, Derek	Denver	WCHA	38	5	17	22	87	....	....	....	....	....
Mayer, Patrick	Muskegon	IHL	71	4	14	18	387	13	0	1	1	53
McBain, Andrew	Winnipeg	NHL	71	11	21	32	106	9	0	2	2	10
	NHL Totals		254	32	58	90	205	19	3	2	5	10
McBean, Wayne	Medicine Hat	WHL	71	12	41	53	163	20	2	8	10	40
McCarthy, Kevin	Philadelphia	NHL	2	0	0	0	0	....	....	....	....	....
	Hershey	AHL	74	6	44	50	86	5	0	4	4	4
	NHL Totals		537	67	191	258	527	21	2	3	5	20

PLAYER	CLUB	LEAGUE	GP	Regular Season G	A	TP	PIM	GP	Playoffs G	A	TP	PIM
McCarthy, Tom	Boston	NHL	68	30	29	59	31	4	1	1	2	4
	Moncton	AHL	2	1	0	1	0	....	....	...	....	....
	NHL Totals		453	176	216	392	324	55	9	22	31	49
McCaughey, Brad	U. of Michigan	CCHA	30	26	23	49	53	....	....	...	....	....
McClelland, Kevin	Edmonton	NHL	72	12	13	25	238	21	2	3	5	43
	NHL Totals		337	47	85	132	975	72	9	13	22	197
McColgan, Gary	Indianapolis	IHL	75	30	25	55	15	6	0	2	2	0
McCormack, Scott	Harvard	ECAC	10	1	1	2	0	....	....	...	....	....
McCrady, Scott	Medicine Hat	WHL	70	10	66	76	157	20	2	21	23	30
McCreary, Bill	Milwaukee	IHL	74	30	35	65	64	6	2	2	4	10
	NHL Totals		12	1	0	1	4	....	....	...	....	....
McCrimmon, Brad	Philadelphia	NHL	71	10	29	39	52	26	3	5	8	30
	NHL Totals		595	52	189	241	680	61	8	8	16	87
McCrory, Scott	Oshawa	OHL	66	51	99	150	35	24	15	22	37	20
McCutcheon, Darwin	Moncton	AHL	69	1	10	11	187	4	0	1	1	51
McDonald, Lanny	Calgary	NHL	58	14	12	26	54	5	0	0	0	2
	NHL Totals		1000	479	486	965	816	94	40	36	76	85
McEwen, Mike	Hartford	NHL	48	8	8	16	32	1	1	1	2	0
	NHL Totals		707	108	293	401	450	76	12	34	46	46
McGeough, Jim	Pittsburgh	NHL	11	1	4	5	8	....	....	...	....	....
	Baltimore	AHL	45	18	19	37	37	....	....	...	....	....
	Muskegon	IHL	18	13	15	28	6	15	14	8	22	10
	NHL Totals		57	7	10	17	32	....	....	...	....	....
McGeough, Peter	St. Lawrence	ECAC	30	7	14	21	90	....	....	...	....	....
McGill, Bob	Toronto	NHL	56	1	4	5	103	3	0	0	0	0
	NHL Totals		298	3	25	28	954	12	0	0	0	35
McGill, Ryan	Swift Current	WHL	72	12	36	48	226	4	1	0	1	9
McIntyre, John	Guelph	OHL	47	8	22	30	95	....	....	...	....	....
McKay, Darren	Indianapolis	IHL	58	9	29	38	64	6	0	4	4	13
McKay, Randy	Michigan Tech	WCHA	39	5	11	16	46	....	....	...	....	....
McKechney, Garnet	Peoria	IHL	70	16	11	27	32	....	....	...	....	....
McKee, Brian	Bowling Green	CCHA	40	18	31	49	93	....	....	...	....	....
	Indianapolis	IHL	4	0	2	2	4	....	....	...	....	....
McKegney, Tony	Minnesota	NHL	11	2	3	5	16	....	....	...	....	....
	NY Rangers	NHL	64	29	17	46	56	6	0	0	0	12
	NHL Totals		640	220	235	455	276	65	21	16	37	44
McKenna, Sean	Los Angeles	NHL	69	14	19	33	10	5	0	1	1	0
	NHL Totals		336	74	72	146	137	13	1	2	3	2
McKinley, Jamie	Guelph	OHL	57	23	50	73	109	5	2	3	5	0
McKinnon, Brian	Hershey	AHL	7	3	2	5	2	....	....	...	....	....
	Flint	IHL	50	16	23	39	40	3	1	1	2	0
McLay, David	Hershey	AHL	7	1	2	3	15	....	....	...	....	....
	Portland	WHL	57	35	42	77	151	18	9	15	24	51
McLellan, Todd	Saskatoon	WHL	60	34	39	73	66	6	1	1	2	2
McLlwain, Dave	North Bay	OHL	60	46	73	119	35	24	7	18	25	40
McMillan, Bill	Peterborough	OHL	38	14	14	28	32	8	4	4	8	5
McMurchy, Tom	Nova Scotia	AHL	67	21	35	56	99	4	3	2	5	4
	NHL Totals		46	4	3	7	57	....	....	...	....	....
McNab, Peter	New Jersey	NHL	46	8	12	20	8	....	....	...	....	....
	NHL Totals		954	363	450	813	179	107	40	42	82	20
McPhee, George	NY Rangers	NHL	21	4	4	8	34	6	1	0	1	28
	NHL Totals		109	21	24	45	247	29	5	3	8	69
McPhee, Mike	Montreal	NHL	79	18	21	39	58	17	7	2	9	13
	NHL Totals		233	59	66	125	288	64	15	7	22	123
McRae, Basil	Detroit	NHL	36	2	2	4	193	....	....	...	....	....
	Quebec	NHL	33	9	5	14	149	13	3	1	4	99
	NHL Totals		119	16	11	27	496	22	4	1	5	133
McRae, Chris	Newmarket	AHL	51	3	6	9	193	....	....	...	....	....
McRae, Ken	Hamilton	OHL	41	19	27	46	65	7	1	1	2	12
McReynolds, Brian	Michigan St.	CCHA	45	16	24	40	68	....	....	...	....	....
McSorley, Chris	New Haven	AHL	22	2	2	4	116	....	....	...	....	....
	Muskegon	IHL	47	18	17	35	293	15	1	3	4	87
McSorley, Marty	Edmonton	NHL	41	2	4	6	159	21	4	3	7	65
	Nova Scotia	AHL	7	2	2	4	48	....	....	...	....	....
	NHL Totals		187	15	23	38	663	29	4	5	9	115

| | | | Regular Season | | | | | Playoffs | | | | |
PLAYER	CLUB	LEAGUE	GP	G	A	TP	PIM	GP	G	A	TP	PIM
McSween, Don	Michigan St.	CCHA	45	7	23	30	34	....	....	....	....	....
Meagher, Rick	St. Louis	NHL	80	18	21	39	54	6	0	0	0	11
	NHL Totals		437	100	117	217	201	25	4	4	8	23
Measures, Allan	Fredericton	AHL	29	3	8	11	12	....	....	....	....	....
Megannety, Neil	Tyringe	Swe.	40	30	20	50	32	....	....	....	....	....
	Adirondack	AHL	22	7	3	10	7	11	3	4	7	5
	Kalamazoo	IHL	37	11	15	26	26	5	1	1	2	0
Meitner, Charles	Peoria	IHL	38	12	10	22	12	....	....	....	....	....
Mellanby, Scott	Philadelphia	NHL	71	11	21	32	94	24	5	5	10	46
	NHL Totals		73	11	21	32	94	24	5	5	10	46
Melnyk, Larry	NY Rangers	NHL	73	3	12	15	182	6	0	0	0	4
	NHL Totals		228	6	46	52	406	62	2	9	11	125
Melrose, Barry	Adirondack	AHL	55	4	9	13	170	11	1	2	3	107
	NHL Totals		300	10	23	33	728	7	0	2	2	38
Melrose, Kevan	Cdn. Olympic	....	8	1	0	1	4	....	....	....	....	....
Mercier, Don	Moncton	AHL	74	5	11	16	107	4	0	0	0	15
Merkosky, Glenn	Adirondack	AHL	77	54	31	85	66	11	6	8	14	7
	NHL Totals		63	5	12	17	22	....	....	....	....	....
Messier, Mark	Edmonton	NHL	77	37	70	107	73	21	12	16	28	16
	NHL Totals		570	265	371	636	776	100	55	68	123	102
Messier, Mitch	Michigan State	CCHA	45	44	48	92	89	....	....	....	....	....
Mersh, Mike	Salt Lake	IHL	43	3	12	15	101	17	0	10	10	14
Metcalfe, Scott	Windsor	OHL	57	25	57	82	156	13	5	5	10	27
Meyer, Jayson	Flint	IHL	73	17	51	68	77	....	....	....	....	....
	Rochester	AHL	3	0	2	2	12	18	2	8	10	14
Michayluk, David	Muskegon	IHL	82	47	53	100	29	15	2	14	16	8
	NHL Totals		14	2	6	8	8	....	....	....	....	....
Micheletti, Pat	Springfield	AHL	67	17	26	43	39	....	....	....	....	....
Middendorf, Max	Quebec	NHL	6	1	4	5	4	....	....	....	....	....
	Kitchener	OHL	48	38	44	82	13	4	2	5	7	5
	NHL Totals		6	1	4	5	4	....	....	....	....	....
Middleton, Rick	Boston	NHL	76	31	37	68	6	4	2	2	4	0
	NHL Totals		946	435	521	956	146	95	40	50	90	15
Miehm, Kevin	Oshawa	OHL	61	12	27	39	19	26	1	8	9	12
Milani, Mario	Verdun	QMJHL	60	15	27	42	83	....	....	....	....	....
Milbury, Mike	Boston	NHL	68	6	16	22	96	4	0	0	0	4
	NHL Totals		754	49	189	238	1552	86	4	24	28	219
Millar, Mike	Hartford	NHL	10	2	2	4	0	....	....	....	....	....
	Binghamton	AHL	61	45	32	77	38	13	7	4	11	27
	NHL Totals		10	2	2	4	0	....	....	....	....	....
Millen, Corey	U. of Minnesota	WCHA	42	36	29	65	62	....	....	....	....	....
Miller, Brad	Regina	WHA	67	10	38	48	154	3	0	0	0	6
Miller, Jay	Boston	NHL	55	1	4	5	208	....	....	....	....	....
	NHL Totals		101	4	4	8	386	2	0	0	0	17
Miller, Keith	Guelph	OHL	66	50	31	81	44	5	6	2	8	0
Miller, Kelly	NY Rangers	NHL	38	6	14	20	22	....	....	....	....	....
	Washington	NHL	39	10	12	22	26	7	2	2	4	0
	NHL Totals		156	29	48	77	102	26	5	6	11	6
Miller, Kevin	Michigan State	CCHA	42	25	56	81	63	....	....	....	....	....
Millier, Pierre	Chicoutimi	QMJHL	68	37	57	94	92	15	5	2	7	42
Mills, Chris	Clarkson	ECAC	30	3	14	17	32	....	....	....	....	....
Miner, John	Nova Scotia	AHL	45	5	28	33	38	5	0	3	3	4
Minor, Gerry	Indianapolis	IHL	68	17	22	39	93	15	3	9	12	32
	NHL Totals		140	11	21	32	173	12	1	3	4	25
Mokosak, Carl	Pittsburgh	NHL	3	0	0	0	4	....	....	....	....	....
	Baltimore	AHL	67	23	27	50	228	....	....	....	....	....
	NHL Totals		76	11	15	26	139	....	....	....	....	....
Mokosak, John	Binghamton	AHL	72	2	15	17	187	9	0	2	2	42
Mollard, Jim	Nova Scotia	AHL	2	0	1	1	0	....	....	....	....	....
	Muskegon	IHL	67	25	38	63	78	14	4	5	9	20
Moller, Mike	Edmonton	NHL	6	2	1	3	0	....	....	....	....	....
	Nova Scotia	AHL	70	14	33	47	28	1	0	0	0	0
	NHL Totals		134	15	28	43	41	3	0	1	1	0

PLAYER	CLUB	LEAGUE	GP	G	A	TP	PIM	GP	G	A	TP	PIM
Moller, Randy	**Quebec**	**NHL**	**71**	**5**	**9**	**14**	**144**	**13**	**1**	**4**	**5**	**23**
	NHL Totals		368	23	75	98	697	48	5	6	11	138
Momesso, Sergio	**Montreal**	**NHL**	**59**	**14**	**17**	**31**	**96**	**11**	**1**	**3**	**4**	**31**
	Sherbrooke	AHL	6	1	6	7	10	....	....	....	....	....
	NHL Totals		84	22	24	46	142	11	1	3	4	31
Moore, Steve	RPI	ECAC	30	2	15	17	43	....	....	....	....	....
More, Jayson	New Westminster	WHL	64	8	29	37	217	....	....	....	....	....
Moria, Steve	New Haven	AHL	31	5	8	13	8	....	....	....	....	....
Morris, Jon	U. of Lowell	H.E.	35	28	33	61	48	....	....	....	....	....
Morrison, Doug	Salt Lake	IHL	73	48	39	87	24	17	9	8	17	26
	NHL Totals		23	7	3	10	15	....	....	....	....	....
Morrow, Ken	**NY Islanders**	**NHL**	**64**	**3**	**8**	**11**	**32**	**13**	**1**	**3**	**4**	**2**
	NHL Totals		403	15	81	96	237	121	11	22	33	89
Morton, Dean	Oshawa	OHL	62	1	11	12	165	23	3	6	9	112
Moylan, Dave	Kitchener	OHL	51	6	13	19	98	3	2	0	2	11
Mullen, Brian	**Winnipeg**	**NHL**	**69**	**19**	**32**	**51**	**20**	**9**	**4**	**2**	**6**	**0**
	NHL Totals		372	124	172	296	132	26	7	9	16	16
Mullen, Joe	**Calgary**	**NHL**	**79**	**47**	**40**	**87**	**14**	**6**	**2**	**1**	**3**	**0**
	NHL Totals		409	214	246	460	70	47	23	19	42	8
Muller, Kirk	**New Jersey**	**NHL**	**79**	**26**	**50**	**76**	**75**	....	....	....	....	....
	NHL Totals		236	68	128	196	189	....	....	....	....	....
Mullins, Dwight	Calgary	WHL	31	12	8	20	71	....	....	....	....	....
Mullowney, Michael	Boston College	H.E.	30	0	2	2	22	....	....	....	....	....
Muni, Craig	**Edmonton**	**NHL**	**79**	**7**	**22**	**29**	**85**	**14**	**0**	**2**	**2**	**17**
	NHL Totals		98	7	24	31	91	14	0	2	2	17
Murano, Eric	U. Denver	WCHA	31	5	7	12	12	....	....	....	....	....
Murphy, Gary	Lowell	H.E.	21	3	4	7	13	....	....	....	....	....
Murphy, Gordon	Oshawa	OHL	56	7	30	37	95	24	6	16	22	22
Murphy, Joe	**Detroit**	**NHL**	**5**	**0**	**1**	**1**	**2**	....	....	....	....	....
	Adirondack	AHL	71	21	38	59	61	10	2	1	3	33
	NHL Totals		5	0	1	1	2	....	....	....	....	....
Murphy, Kelly	Michigan Tech	WCHA	14	0	1	1	14	....	....	....	....	....
Murphy, Larry	**Washington**	**NHL**	**80**	**23**	**58**	**81**	**39**	**7**	**2**	**2**	**4**	**6**
	NHL Totals		551	122	332	454	445	43	10	21	31	32
Murphy, Rob	Laval	QMJHL	70	35	54	89	86	14	3	4	7	15
Murray, Mike	Hershey	AHL	70	8	16	24	10	2	0	0	0	0
Murray, Rob	Peterborough	OHL	62	17	37	54	204	3	1	4	5	8
Murray, Robert	**Chicago**	**NHL**	**79**	**6**	**38**	**44**	**80**	**4**	**1**	**0**	**1**	**4**
	NHL Totals		882	119	339	458	757	75	14	27	41	74
Murray, Troy	**Chicago**	**NHL**	**77**	**28**	**43**	**71**	**59**	**4**	**0**	**0**	**0**	**5**
	NHL Totals		353	122	160	282	307	35	7	14	21	43
Murzyn, Dana	**Hartford**	**NHL**	**74**	**9**	**19**	**28**	**95**	**6**	**2**	**1**	**3**	**29**
	NHL Totals		152	12	42	54	220	10	2	1	3	39
Musil, Frantisek	**Minnesota**	**NHL**	**72**	**2**	**9**	**11**	**148**	....	....	....	....	....
	NHL Totals		72	2	9	11	148	....	....	....	....	....
Nachbaur, Don	Philadelphia	NHL	23	0	2	2	87	7	1	1	2	15
	Hershey	AHL	57	18	17	35	274	5	0	3	3	47
	NHL Totals		186	22	41	63	367	9	1	1	2	22
Nanne, Marty	U. Minnesota	WCHA	31	3	4	7	41	....	....	....	....	....
Napier, Mark	**Edmonton**	**NHL**	**62**	**8**	**13**	**21**	**2**	....	....	....	....	....
	Buffalo	NHL	15	5	5	10	0	....	....	....	....	....
	NHL Totals		654	214	281	495	116	73	17	21	38	11
Naslund, Mats	**Montreal**	**NHL**	**79**	**25**	**55**	**80**	**16**	**17**	**7**	**15**	**22**	**11**
	NHL Totals		390	165	239	404	60	67	29	38	67	25
Nattress, Ric	**St. Louis**	**NHL**	**73**	**6**	**22**	**28**	**24**	**6**	**0**	**0**	**0**	**2**
	NHL Totals		230	11	58	69	112	29	1	4	5	38
Natyshak, Mike	Bowling Green	CCHA	45	5	10	15	101	....	....	....	....	....
Nault, Jean-Francois	Granby	QMJHL	53	36	49	85	68	8	1	6	7	4
Neely, Cam	**Boston**	**NHL**	**75**	**36**	**36**	**72**	**143**	**4**	**5**	**1**	**6**	**8**
	NHL Totals		276	87	89	176	463	11	7	1	8	16
Neill, Mike	Springfield	AHL	32	3	4	7	67	....	....	....	....	....
	Indianapolis	IHL	43	2	10	12	83	....	....	....	....	....
Nelson, Brian	Minn.-Duluth	WCHA	1	0	0	0	0	....	....	....	....	....
Nemeth, Steve	Kamloops	WHL	10	10	4	14	0	13	11	9	20	12
	Cdn. Olympic	....	43	14	7	21	12	....	....	....	....	....

			Regular Season					Playoffs			
PLAYER	CLUB	LEAGUE	GP	G	A	TP	PIM	GP	G	A	TP	PIM
Nesich, Jim	Verdun	QMJHL	62	20	50	70	133	....	....	....	....	....
Neufeld, Ray	Winnipeg	NHL	80	18	18	36	105	8	1	1	2	30
	NHL Totals		471	133	177	310	567	13	4	1	5	40
Newberry, John	Karpat	Fin.	39	16	14	30	63	....	....	....	....	....
	NHL Totals		22	0	4	4	6	2	0	0	0	0
Newhouse, Jim	U. of Lowell	H.E.	31	12	24	36	17	....	....	....	....	....
Nicholls, Bernie	Los Angeles	NHL	80	33	48	81	101	5	2	5	7	6
	NHL Totals		411	198	257	455	489	18	7	6	13	38
Nichols, Jamie	Portland	WHL	59	28	37	65	42	20	6	4	10	17
Nicoletti, Martin	UQTR	QUAA	18	7	20	27	45	....	....	....	....	....
Nison, Len	Sherbrooke	AHL	3	1	0	1	0	5	1	1	2	0
	Regina	WHL	72	36	100	136	32	3	0	4	4	0
Nienhuis, Kraig	Boston	NHL	16	4	2	6	2	....	....	....	....	....
	Moncton	AHL	54	10	17	27	44	....	....	....	....	....
	NHL Totals		86	20	16	36	39	2	0	0	0	14
Nieuwendyk, Joe	Calgary	NHL	9	5	1	6	0	6	2	2	4	0
	Cornell	ECHA	23	26	26	52	26	....	....	....	....	....
	NHL Totals		9	5	1	6	0	6	2	2	4	0
Nilan, Chris	Montreal	NHL	44	4	16	20	266	17	3	0	3	75
	NHL Totals		456	80	79	159	1965	77	8	4	12	407
Nill, Jim	Winnipeg	NHL	36	3	4	7	52	3	0	0	0	7
	NHL Totals		378	47	66	113	654	37	4	4	8	116
Nilsson, Kent	Minnesota	NHL	44	13	33	46	12	....	....	....	....	....
	Edmonton	NHL	17	5	12	17	4	21	6	13	19	6
	NHL Totals		547	263	422	685	116	59	11	41	52	14
Nilsson, Stefan	Lulea	Swe.	23	3	9	12	14	....	....	....	....	....
Noble, Jeff	Kitchener	OHL	66	29	57	86	55	4	2	0	2	20
Noonan, Brian	Nova Scotia	AHL	70	25	26	51	30	5	3	1	4	4
Nordmark, Robert	Lulea	Swe.	32	7	8	15	52	....	....	....	....	....
Norton, Chris	Cornell	ECAC	24	10	21	31	79	....	....	....	....	....
Norton, Jeff	U. of Michigan	CCHA	39	12	36	48	92	....	....	....	....	....
Norwood, Lee	Detroit	NHL	57	6	21	27	163	16	1	6	7	31
	Adirondack	AHL	3	0	3	3	0	....	....	....	....	....
	NHL Totals		175	19	57	76	447	38	3	13	16	97
Novak, Richard	Michigan Tech.	WCHA	7	0	0	0	4	....	....	....	....	....
Numminen, Teppo	Tappara	Fin.	44	9	9	18	16	....	....	....	....	....
Nylund, Gary	Chicago	NHL	80	7	20	27	190	4	0	2	2	11
	NHL Totals		298	14	70	84	588	14	0	4	4	36
Oates, Adam	Detroit	NHL	76	15	32	47	21	16	4	7	11	6
	NHL Totals		114	24	43	67	31	16	4	7	11	6
O'Brien, David	Northeastern	H.E.	35	16	24	40	12	....	....	....	....	....
O'Callahan, Jack	Chicago	NHL	48	1	13	14	59	2	0	0	0	2
	NHL Totals		303	15	64	79	393	27	3	8	11	35
O'Connell, Mike	Detroit	NHL	77	5	26	31	70	16	1	4	5	14
	NHL Totals		680	94	292	386	504	66	8	20	28	52
O'Conner, Myles	U. of Michigan	CCHA	39	15	39	54	111	....	....	....	....	....
Octeau, Jay	Boston U.	H.E.	37	5	23	28	40	....	....	....	....	....
Odelein, Lyle	Moose Jaw	WHL	59	9	50	59	70	9	2	5	7	26
Odelein, Selmar	Nova Scotia	AHL	2	0	1	1	2	....	....	....	....	....
	NHL Totals		4	0	0	0	0	....	....	....	....	....
O'Dwyer, Bill	New Haven	AHL	65	22	42	64	74	3	0	0	0	14
	NHL Totals		18	1	0	1	15	....	....	....	....	....
Ogrodnick, John	Detroit	NHL	39	12	28	40	6	....	....	....	....	....
	Quebec	NHL	32	11	16	27	4	13	9	4	13	6
	NHL Totals		571	270	291	561	152	20	10	5	15	6
Ojanen, Janne	Tappara	Fin.	40	18	13	31	21	....	....	....	....	....
Okerlund, Todd	U. of Minnesota	WCHA	4	0	7	7	0	....	....	....	....	....
Olausson, Fredrik	Winnipeg	NHL	72	7	29	36	24	10	2	3	5	4
	NHL Totals		72	7	29	36	24	10	2	3	5	4
Olczyk, Ed	Chicago	NHL	79	16	35	51	119	4	1	1	2	4
	NHL Totals		228	65	115	180	233	22	7	6	13	15
Oliverio, Michael	S.S. Marie	OHL	66	35	58	93	34	4	0	3	3	0
Olivier, Martin	Granby	QMJHL	51	5	17	22	132	8	0	1	1	2
Olsen, Darryl	N. Michigan	WCHA	37	5	20	25	46	....	....	....	....	....

PLAYER	CLUB	LEAGUE	GP	G	A	TP	PIM	GP	G	A	TP	PIM
Olsen, Mark	Colorado	WCHA	42	2	4	6	38	....	....	....	....	....
O'Regan, Tom	Adirondack	AHL	58	20	42	....	78	11	3	9	12	10
	NHL Totals		60	5	12	17	10	....	....	....	....	....
Orlando, Gates	Buffalo	NHL	27	2	8	10	16	....	....	....	....	....
	Rochester	AHL	44	22	42	64	42	18	9	13	22	14
	NHL Totals		98	18	26	44	51	5	0	4	4	14
Orn, Mike	Miami-Ohio	CCHA	36	22	23	45	70	....	....	....	....	....
Orth, Steve	U. of Minnesota	WCHA	37	8	7	15	18	....	....	....	....	....
Osborne, Keith	North Bay	OHL	61	34	55	89	31	24	11	11	22	25
Osborne, Mark	NY Rangers	NHL	58	17	15	32	101	....	....	....	....	....
	Toronto	NHL	16	5	10	15	12	9	1	3	4	6
	NHL Totals		392	110	146	256	458	32	3	7	10	43
Oswald, Randy	Michigan Tech.	WCHA	39	3	17	20	67	....	....	....	....	....
O'Toole, Mike	Mich. State	CCHA	43	2	13	15	74	....	....	....	....	....
Otto, Joel	Calgary	NHL	68	19	31	50	185	2	0	2	2	6
	NHL Totals		164	48	73	121	403	27	7	13	20	96
Paddock, Gordon	Springfield	AHL	78	6	11	17	127	....	....	....	....	....
Paek, Jim	Oshawa	OHL	57	5	17	22	75	26	1	14	15	43
Paiement, Wilf	Buffalo	NHL	56	20	17	37	108	....	....	....	....	....
	NHL Totals		923	354	452	806	1718	69	18	17	35	185
Paluch, Scott	Bowling Green	CCHA	45	13	38	51	88	....	....	....	....	....
Pardoski, Ryan	U. Michigan	CCHA	39	4	9	13	26	....	....	....	....	....
Parent, Russel	North Dakota	WCHA	47	2	17	19	50	....	....	....	....	....
Parker, Jeff	Buffalo	NHL	15	3	3	6	7	....	....	....	....	....
	Rochester	AHL	54	14	8	22	75	14	1	3	4	19
	NHL Totals		15	3	3	6	7	....	....	....	....	....
Parker, John	U. Wisconsin	WCHA	8	0	1	1	4	....	....	....	....	....
Parks, Malcolm	North Dakota	WCHA	48	18	21	39	50	....	....	....	....	....
Pasin, Dave	Moncton	AHL	66	27	25	52	47	6	1	1	2	14
	NHL Totals		71	18	19	37	50	3	0	1	1	0
Paslawski, Greg	St. Louis	NHL	76	29	35	64	27	6	1	3	4	2
	NHL Totals		264	82	76	158	87	35	12	8	20	21
Paterson, Joe	Los Angeles	NHL	45	2	1	3	158	2	0	0	0	0
	NHL Totals		218	17	30	47	569	22	3	4	7	77
Paterson, Mark	Moncton	AHL	70	6	21	27	112	3	0	0	0	0
	NHL Totals		29	3	3	6	33	....	....	....	....	....
Paterson, Rick	Chicago	NHL	22	1	2	3	6	....	....	....	....	....
	Nova Scotia	AHL	31	5	7	12	2	5	0	1	1	10
	NHL Totals		430	50	43	93	136	61	7	10	17	51
Patrick, James	NY Rangers	NHL	78	10	45	55	62	6	1	2	3	2
	NHL Totals		240	33	109	142	223	30	2	10	12	42
Patterson, Colin	Calgary	NHL	68	13	14	27	41	6	0	2	2	2
	NHL Totals		242	62	62	124	83	40	7	6	13	23
Pavelich, Mark	Minnesota	NHL	12	4	6	10	10	....	....	....	....	....
	NHL Totals		353	137	191	328	336	23	7	17	24	14
Pavese, Jim	St. Louis	NHL	69	2	9	11	127	2	0	0	0	2
	NHL Totals		259	10	33	43	477	29	0	5	5	66
Pawlowski, Jerry	Harvard	ECAC	18	1	5	6	26	....	....	....	....	....
Payne, Steve	Minnesota	NHL	48	4	6	....	19	....	....	....	....	....
	NHL Totals		604	227	235	462	423	71	35	35	70	60
Paynter, Kent	Nova Scotia	AHL	66	2	6	8	57	2	0	0	0	0
Pearson, Ted	Salt Lake	IHL	17	6	8	14	10	17	3	12	15	10
Pederson, Allan	Boston	NHL	79	1	11	12	71	4	0	0	0	4
	NHL Totals		79	1	11	12	71	4	0	0	0	4
Pederson, Barry	Vancouver	NHL	79	24	52	76	50	....	....	....	....	....
	NHL Totals		426	187	297	484	290	34	22	30	52	25
Pederson, Mark	Medicine Hat	WHL	69	56	46	102	58	20	19	7	26	14
Peer, Brit	Peoria	IHL	20	3	3	6	5	....	....	....	....	....
	Muskegon	IHL	11	1	0	1	9	....	....	....	....	....
Peerless, Blaine	Milwaukee	IHL	74	5	31	36	71	6	0	1	1	4
Peluso, Mike	Alaska-Anch.	G.N.	30	5	21	26	68	....	....	....	....	....
Peplinski, Jim	Calgary	NHL	80	18	32	50	181	6	1	0	1	24
	NHL Totals		545	127	206	333	977	70	14	20	34	262

			Regular Season					Playoffs			
PLAYER	CLUB	LEAGUE	GP	G	A	TP	PIM	GP	G	A	TP	PIM
Perkins, Terry	Fredericton	AHL	44	10	11	21	35	....	....	....	....	....
	Muskegon	IHL	12	4	8	12	31	....	....	....	....	....
Perreault, Gilbert	**Buffalo**	**NHL**	20	9	7	16	6	....	....	....	....	....
	NHL Totals		1191	512	814	1326	500	90	33	70	103	44
Persson, Joakim	Brynas	Swe.	34	9	8	17	10	....	....	....	....	....
Persson, Lars	Ostersund	Swe.	31	10	11	21	2	....	....	....	....	....
Pesetti, Ron	Fort Wayne	IHL	79	12	39	51	62	5	0	2	2	5
Pesklewis, Matt	Boston U.	H.E.	24	0	2	2	28	....	....	....	....	....
Peterson, Brent	**Vancouver**	**NHL**	69	7	15	22	77	....	....	....	....	....
	NHL Totals		502	66	121	187	383	25	4	3	7	59
Petit, Michel	**Vancouver**	**NHL**	69	12	13	25	131	....	....	....	....	....
	NHL Totals		216	24	54	78	338	1	0	0	0	0
Phair, Lyle	**Los Angeles**	**NHL**	5	2	0	2	2	....	....	....	....	....
	New Haven	AHL	65	19	27	46	77	7	0	3	3	13
	NHL Totals		20	2	1	3	4	....	....	....	....	....
Picard, Robert	**Quebec**	**NHL**	78	8	20	28	71	13	2	10	12	10
	NHL Totals		716	94	284	378	813	36	5	15	20	39
Pichette, Dave	Maine	AHL	61	6	16	22	69	....	....	....	....	....
	NHL Totals		316	40	137	177	344	28	3	7	10	54
Pickell, Doug	Kamloops	WHL	70	34	24	58	182	13	0	4	4	15
Pilon, Neil	Moose Jaw	WHL	72	2	23	25	119	9	0	5	5	22
Pilon, Richard	Prince Albert	WHL	68	4	21	25	192	7	1	6	7	17
Pitlick, Lance	U. Minnesota	WCHA	45	0	9	9	88	....	....	....	....	....
Pivonka, Michal	**Washington**	**NHL**	73	18	25	43	41	7	1	1	2	2
	NHL Totals		73	18	25	43	41	7	1	1	2	2
Plante, Cam	Newmarket	AHL	19	3	4	7	14	....	....	....	....	....
	Milwaukee	IHL	56	7	47	54	44	5	2	2	4	4
	NHL Totals		2	0	0	0	0	....	....	....	....	....
Playfair, Jim	Nova Scotia	AHL	60	1	21	22	82	....	....	....	....	....
	NHL Totals		2	1	1	2	2	....	....	....	....	....
Playfair, Larry	**Los Angeles**	**NHL**	37	2	7	9	181	....	....	....	....	....
	NHL Totals		582	26	80	106	1487	39	0	6	6	97
Plett, Willi	**Minnesota**	**NHL**	67	6	5	11	263	....	....	....	....	....
	NHL Totals		769	220	212	432	2402	66	22	18	40	392
Poddubny, Walt	**NY Rangers**	**NHL**	75	40	47	87	49	6	0	0	0	8
	NHL Totals		265	99	133	232	227	19	7	2	9	12
Podloski, Ray	Moncton	AHL	70	23	27	50	12	3	0	0	0	15
Poeschek, Rudy	Kamloops	WHL	54	13	18	31	153	13	1	4	5	39
Polonich, Denis	Muskegon	IHL	22	2	9	11	24	....	....	....	....	....
	NHL Totals		390	59	82	141	1242	7	1	0	1	19
Poner, Jiri	Landshut	W. Ger.	34	17	22	39	115	....	....	....	....	....
Pooley, Paul	Fort Wayne	IHL	77	28	44	72	47	2	1	2	3	2
	NHL Totals		15	0	3	3	0	....	....	....	....	....
Pooley, Perry	Fort Wayne	IHL	82	30	31	61	31	11	5	3	8	4
Porter, Don	Michigan Tech	WCHA	36	7	3	10	42	....	....	....	....	....
Posa, Victor	Nova Scotia	AHL	2	1	0	1	2	....	....	....	....	....
	Saginaw	IHL	61	13	27	40	203	7	1	0	1	34
Posavad, Mike	**St. Louis**	**NHL**	2	0	0	0	0	....	....	....	....	....
	Peoria	IHL	77	2	15	17	77	....	....	....	....	....
	NHL Totals		8	0	0	0	0	....	....	....	....	....
Posma, Mike	W. Michigan	CCHA	35	12	31	43	42	....	....	....	....	....
Potvin, Denis	**NY Islanders**	**NHL**	58	12	30	42	70	10	2	2	4	21
	NHL Totals		988	291	710	1001	1244	180	55	104	159	247
Potvin, Marc	Bowling Green	CCHA	43	5	15	20	74	....	....	....	....	....
Poudrier, Daniel	**Quebec**	**NHL**	6	0	0	0	0	....	....	....	....	....
	Fredericton	AHL	69	8	18	26	11	....	....	....	....	....
	NHL Totals		19	1	5	6	10	....	....	....	....	....
Poulin, David	**Philadelphia**	**NHL**	75	25	45	70	53	15	3	3	6	14
	NHL Totals		302	115	176	291	210	37	9	11	20	33
Pound, Ian	Toronto	OHL	65	2	13	15	126	....	....	....	....	....
Powers, Bill	U. of Michigan	CCHA	36	13	16	29	18	....	....	....	....	....
Prajsler, Petr	Pardubice	Czech.	32	2	3	5	....	....	....	....	....	....
Pratt, Tom	Bowling Green	CCHA	41	1	7	8	46	....	....	....	....	....
Premak, Garth	Kamloops	WHL	70	8	28	36	8	13	1	3	4	14
Presley, Wayne	**Chicago**	**NHL**	80	32	29	61	114	4	1	0	1	9
	NHL Totals		121	39	38	77	152	7	1	0	1	9

PLAYER	CLUB	LEAGUE	Regular Season GP	G	A	TP	PIM	Playoffs GP	G	A	TP	PIM
Preston, Rich	Chicago	NHL	73	8	9	17	19	4	0	2	2	4
	NHL Totals		580	127	164	291	348	47	4	18	22	56
Price, Pat	Quebec	NHL	47	0	6	6	81	....	....	....	....	....
	Fredericton	AHL	7	0	0	0	14	....	....	....	....	....
	NY Rangers	NHL	13	0	2	2	49	6	0	1	1	27
	NHL Totals		712	43	216	259	1436	74	2	10	12	195
Priestlay, Ken	Buffalo	NHL	34	11	6	17	8	....	....	....	....	....
	Victoria	WHL	33	43	39	82	37	....	....	....	....	....
	Rochester	AHL	....	....	....	....	....	8	3	2	5	4
	NHL Totals		34	11	6	17	8	....	....	....	....	....
Probert, Bob	Detroit	NHL	63	13	11	24	221	16	3	4	7	63
	Adirondack	AHL	8199									
Propp, Brian	Philadelphia	NHL	53	31	36	67	45	26	12	16	28	10
	NHL Totals		599	297	369	666	525	91	34	49	83	99
Pryor, Chris	Minnesota	NHL	50	1	3	4	49	....	....	....	....	....
	Springfield	AHL	5	0	2	2	17	....	....	....	....	....
	NHL Totals		61	1	4	5	65	....	....	....	....	....
Pulis, Paul	Ill.-Chicago	CCHA	24	10	9	19	32	....	....	....	....	....
Purves, John	Hamilton	OHL	28	12	11	23	37	9	2	0	2	12
Quenneville, Joel	Hartford	NHL	37	3	7	10	24	6	0	0	0	0
	NHL Totals		604	47	117	164	595	22	0	3	3	6
Quinn, Dan	Calgary	NHL	16	3	6	9	14	....	....	....	....	....
	Pittsburgh	NHL	64	28	43	71	40	....	....	....	....	....
	NHL Totals		286	100	162	262	140	29	11	12	23	14
Quinn, David	Boston U.	H.E.	27	1	11	12	34	....	....	....	....	....
Quinn, Joe	Bowling Green	CCHA	39	4	13	17	22	....	....	....	....	....
Quinney, Ken	Quebec	NHL	25	2	7	9	16	....	....	....	....	....
	Fredericton	AHL	48	14	27	41	20	....	....	....	....	....
	NHL Totals		25	2	7	9	16	....	....	....	....	....
Quintal, Stephane	Granby	QMJHL	67	13	41	54	178	8	0	9	9	10
Racine, Yves	Longueuil	QMJHL	70	7	43	50	50	30	3	11	14	14
Raglan, Herb	St. Louis	NHL	62	6	10	16	159	4	0	0	0	2
	NHL Totals		69	6	10	16	164	14	1	1	2	26
Ramage, Rob	St. Louis	NHL	59	11	28	39	108	6	2	2	4	21
	NHL Totals		608	100	286	386	1300	43	5	26	31	147
Ramsey, Mike	Buffalo	NHL	80	8	31	39	109	....	....	....	....	....
	NHL Totals		549	51	169	220	583	43	6	12	18	90
Randall, Dave	Cdn. Olympic	....	17	1	4	5	6	....	....	....	....	....
Ranger, Joe	DID NOT PLAY -	INJURED										
Ranheim, Paul	U. of Wisconsin	WCHA	42	24	35	59	54	....	....	....	....	....
Raus, Marty	Northeastern	H.E.	26	0	7	7	24	....	....	....	....	....
Ray, Derek	Fort Wayne	IHL	75	16	23	39	156	11	2	1	3	10
Redmond, Craig	Los Angeles	NHL	16	1	7	8	8	....	....	....	....	....
	New Haven	AHL	5	2	2	4	6	....	....	....	....	....
	NHL Totals		168	13	58	71	122	3	1	0	1	2
Reeds, Mark	St. Louis	NHL	68	9	16	25	16	6	0	1	1	2
	NHL Totals		320	45	105	150	98	53	8	9	17	23
Reekie, Joe	Buffalo	NHL	56	1	8	9	82	....	....	....	....	....
	Rochester	AHL	22	0	6	6	52	....	....	....	....	....
	NHL Totals		59	1	8	9	96	....	....	....	....	....
Regan, Brent	Bowling Green	CCHA	43	12	17	29	22	....	....	....	....	....
Reid, David	Boston	NHL	12	3	3	6	0	2	0	0	0	0
	Moncton	AHL	40	12	22	34	23	5	0	1	1	0
	NHL Totals		92	28	26	54	39	7	1	0	1	0
Reierson, Dave	Moncton	AHL	....	....	....	....	....	6	0	1	1	12
	Cdn. Olympic	....	61	1	17	18	36					
Reinhart, Paul	Calgary	NHL	76	15	54	69	22	4	0	1	1	6
	NHL Totals		503	109	333	442	193	68	19	44	63	32
Rendall, Bruce	Michigan State	CCHA	44	11	14	25	113	....	....	....	....	....
Reynolds, Bobby	Michigan State	CCHA	40	20	13	33	40	....	....	....	....	....
Rezansoff, Grant	Peoria	IHL	82	25	44	69	33	....	....	....	....	....
Ribble, Pat	Salt Lake	IHL	80	4	19	28	55	17	1	5	6	2
	NHL Totals		349	19	60	79	365	8	0	1	1	12
Richard, Jean-Marc	Chicoutimi	QMJHL	67	21	81	102	105	16	6	25	31	28
Richards, Todd	U. of Minnesota	WCHA	49	8	43	51	70	....	....	....	....	....

PLAYER	CLUB	LEAGUE	GP	G	A	TP	PIM	GP	G	A	TP	PIM
Richardson, Luke	Peterborough	OHL	59	13	32	45	70	12	0	5	5	24
Richer, Stephane	Montreal	NHL	57	20	19	39	80	5	3	2	5	0
	Sherbrooke	AHL	12	10	4	14	11	....	....	....	....	....
	NHL Totals		123	41	35	76	130	21	7	3	10	23
Richmond, Steve	New Jersey	NHL	44	1	7	8	143	....	....	....	....	....
	NHL Totals		150	4	21	25	488	4	0	0	0	12
Richter, Dave	Vancouver	NHL	78	2	15	17	172	....	....	....	....	....
	NHL Totals		248	6	31	37	707	22	1	0	1	80
Ridley, Mike	NY Rangers	NHL	38	16	20	36	20	....	....	....	....	....
	Washington	NHL	40	15	19	34	20	7	2	1	3	6
	NHL Totals		158	53	82	135	109	23	8	9	17	32
Risebrough, Doug	Calgary	NHL	22	2	3	5	66	4	0	1	1	2
	NHL Totals		740	185	286	471	1542	124	21	37	58	238
Ristau, Andrew	Rochester	AHL	23	1	1	2	113	5	0	0	0	31
	Flint	IHL	31	5	7	12	267	....	....	....	....	....
Rivington, Dale	Moncton	AHL	15	0	0	0	4	....	....	....	....	....
	Salt Lake	IHL	37	0	9	9	18	4	0	0	0	9
Roberts, Gary	Calgary	NHL	32	5	9	14	85	2	0	0	0	4
	Moncton	AHL	38	20	18	38	72	....	....	....	....	....
	NHL Totals		32	5	9	14	85	2	0	0	0	4
Roberts, Gordie	Minnesota	NHL	67	3	10	13	68	....	....	....	....	....
	NHL Totals		614	42	253	295	899	64	7	31	38	97
Robertson, Geordie	Adirondack	AHL	63	28	41	69	94	....	....	....	....	....
	NHL Totals		5	1	2	3	7	....	....	....	....	....
Robertson, Torrie	Hartford	NHL	20	1	0	1	98	....	....	....	....	....
	NHL Totals		298	42	80	122	1199	10	1	0	1	67
Robidoux, Florent	Milwaukee	IHL	15	2	7	9	16	6	3	3	6	13
	NHL Totals		52	7	4	11	75	....	....	....	....	....
Robinson, Larry	Montreal	NHL	70	13	37	50	44	17	3	17	20	6
	NHL Totals		1075	187	626	813	654	171	22	97	119	170
Robitaille, Luc	Los Angeles	NHL	79	45	39	84	28	5	1	4	5	2
	NHL Totals		79	45	39	84	28	5	1	4	5	2
Rochefort, Normand	Quebec	NHL	70	6	9	15	46	13	2	1	3	26
	NHL Totals		434	29	94	123	403	59	5	4	9	56
Rohlicek, Jeff	Fredericton	AHL	70	19	37	56	22	....	....	....	....	....
Rohlik, Steve	U. of Wisconsin	WCHA	31	3	0	3	34	....	....	....	....	....
Ronning, Cliff	St. Louis	NHL	42	11	14	25	6	4	0	1	1	0
	NHL Totals		42	11	14	25	6	9	1	2	3	2
Rooney, Larry	Thayer	HS	26	15	26	41	....	....	....	....	....	....
Rooney, Steve	Montreal	NHL	2	0	0	0	22	....	....	....	....	....
	Sherbrooke	AHL	22	4	11	15	66	....	....	....	....	....
	Winnipeg	NHL	30	2	3	5	57	8	0	0	0	34
	NHL Totals		73	5	6	11	200	20	2	2	4	53
Root, Bill	Toronto	NHL	34	3	3	6	37	13	1	0	1	12
	Newmarket	AHL	32	4	11	15	23	....	....	....	....	....
	NHL Totals		214	10	21	31	158	20	1	2	3	25
Rose, Jay	Clarkson	ECAC	29	2	10	12	74	....	....	....	....	....
Roth, Mike	N. Hampshire	H.E.	22	1	2	3	11	....	....	....	....	....
Rouleau, Guy	Sherbrooke	AHL	10	4	3	7	2	2	0	0	0	0
Roupe, Magnus	Farjestad	Swe.	31	11	6	17	58	....	....	....	....	....
Rouse, Bob	Minnesota	NHL	72	2	10	12	179	....	....	....	....	....
	NHL Totals		211	5	33	38	443	3	0	0	0	2
Routhier, Jean-Marc	Hull	QMJHL	59	17	18	35	98	....	....	....	....	....
Rowe, Mike	Pittsburgh	NHL	2	0	0	0	0	....	....	....	....	....
	Baltimore	AHL	79	1	18	19	64	....	....	....	....	....
	NHL Totals		11	0	0	0	11	....	....	....	....	....
Roy, Darcy	Kalamazoo	IHL	72	24	27	51	85	5	0	1	1	4
Roy, Stephane	Granby	QMJHL	45	23	44	67	54	7	2	3	5	50
	Cdn. Olympic	....	9	1	2	3	4	....	....	....	....	....
Rucinski, Mike	Moncton	AHL	42	5	9	14	14	....	....	....	....	....
	Salt Lake	IHL	29	16	25	41	19	17	9	18	27	18
Rude, Blaine	U. of Minnesota	WCHA	6	1	1	2	2	....	....	....	....	....
Ruff, Lindy	Buffalo	NHL	50	6	14	20	74	....	....	....	....	....
	NHL Totals		468	94	149	243	861	36	11	8	19	141

| | | | | Regular Season | | | | | Playoffs | | | |
PLAYER	CLUB	LEAGUE	GP	G	A	TP	PIM	GP	G	A	TP	PIM
Rumble, Darren	Kitchener	OHL	64	11	32	43	44	4	0	1	1	9
Ruotsalinen, Reijo	Edmonton	NHL	16	5	8	13	6	21	2	5	7	10
	NHL Totals		405	104	225	329	160	64	13	21	34	32
Ruskowski, Terry	Pittsburgh	NHL	70	14	37	51	145	....	....	....	....	....
	NHL Totals		580	107	300	407	1276	21	1	6	7	86
Russell, Cam	Hull	QMJHL	66	3	16	19	119	8	0	1	1	16
Russell, Phil	Buffalo	NHL	6	0	2	2	12	....	....	....	....	....
	NHL Totals		1016	99	325	424	2038	73	4	22	26	202
Ruuttu, Christian	Buffalo	NHL	76	22	43	65	62	....	....	....	....	....
	NHL Totals		76	22	43	65	62	....	....	....	....	....
Ryan, Tom	Boston U.	H.E.	37	1	7	8	20	....	....	....	....	....
Rychel, Warren	Kitchener	OHL	49	16	12	28	96	4	0	0	0	9
Saatzer, Ron	Miami-Ohio	CCHA	31	5	8	13	44	....	....	....	....	....
Sabol, Shawn	U. of Wisconsin	WCHA	40	7	16	23	98	....	....	....	....	....
Sabourin, Ken	Moncton	AHL	75	1	10	11	166	6	0	1	1	27
Sagissor, Tom	U. of Wisconsin	WCHA	41	1	4	5	32	....	....	....	....	....
Sakic, Joe	Swift Current	WHL	72	60	73	133	31	4	0	1	1	0
Salming, Borje	Toronto	NHL	56	4	16	20	42	13	0	3	3	14
	NHL Totals		970	143	579	722	1124	75	11	34	45	83
Sampson, Gary	Washington	NHL	25	1	2	3	4	....	....	....	....	....
	Binghamton	AHL	37	12	16	28	10	11	4	2	6	0
	NHL Totals		105	13	22	35	25	12	1	0	1	0
Samuelsson, Kjell	NY Rangers	NHL	30	2	6	8	50	....	....	....	....	....
	Philadelphia	NHL	46	1	6	7	86	26	0	4	4	25
	NHL Totals		85	3	12	15	146	35	0	5	5	33
Samuelsson, Ulf	Hartford	NHL	78	2	31	33	162	5	0	1	1	
	NHL Totals		199	9	56	65	419	15	1	3	4	79
Sandelin, Scott	Montreal	NHL	1	0	0	0	0	....	....	....	....	....
	Sherbrooke	AHL	74	7	22	29	35	16	2	4	6	2
	NHL Totals		1	0	0	0	0	....	....	....	....	....
Sandlak, Jim	Vancouver	NHL	78	15	21	36	66	....	....	....	....	....
	NHL Totals		101	16	24	40	76	3	0	1	1	0
Sandstrom, Tomas	NY Rangers	NHL	64	40	34	74	60	6	1	2	3	20
	NHL Totals		211	94	92	186	220	25	5	10	15	40
Sanipass, Everett	Chicago	NHL	7	1	3	4	2	....	....	....	....	....
	Granby	QMJHL	35	34	48	82	220	8	6	4	10	48
	NHL Totals		7	1	3	4	2	....	....	....	....	....
Sapergia, Brent	Kalpa	Fin.	33	25	13	38	117	....	....	....	....	....
	New Haven	AHL	2	0	1	1	0	....	....	....	....	....
Sasso, Tom	Babson	ECAC	29	22	31	53	8	....	....	....	....	....
Saunders, David	St. Lawrence	ECAC	34	18	34	52	44	....	....	....	....	....
Sauve, Jean	Quebec	NHL	14	2	3	5	4	....	....	....	....	....
	NHL Totals		290	65	138	203	117	36	9	12	21	10
Savard, Denis	Chicago	NHL	70	40	50	90	108	4	1	0	1	12
	NHL Totals		538	257	463	720	574	58	34	40	74	121
Sawkins, Peter	New Haven	AHL	23	1	1	2	8	....	....	....	....	....
	Flint	IHL	29	1	5	6	15	....	....	....	....	....
Scanlon, Pat	Minn-Duluth	WCHA	22	2	2	4	14	....	....	....	....	....
Sceviour, Darin	Chicago	NHL	1	0	0	0	0	....	....	....	....	....
	Cdn. Olympic	....	5	2	0	2	17	....	....	....	....	....
	Saginaw	IHL	37	13	18	31	4	10	10	2	12	0
	NHL Totals		1	0	0	0	0	....	....	....	....	....
Schafhauser, Bill	Kalamazoo	IHL	82	6	49	55	52	5	1	0	1	2
Schamehorn, Kevin	Milwaukee	IHL	82	35	35	70	102	6	3	3	6	6
	NHL Totals		10	0	0	0	17	....	....	....	....	....
Scheifele, Steve	Boston Coll.	H.E.	38	13	13	26	28	....	....	....	....	....
Schenna, Rob	RPI	ECAC	30	1	9	10	32	....	....	....	....	....
Schmalzbauer, Tony	St. Cloud	NCAA	33	4	4	8	27	....	....	....	....	....
Schmidt, Norm	Pittsburgh	NHL	20	1	5	6	4	....	....	....	....	....
	Baltimore	AHL	36	4	7	11	25	....	....	....	....	....
	NHL Totals		120	22	31	53	73	....	....	....	....	....
Schneider, Mathieu	Cornwall	OHL	63	7	29	36	75	5	0	0	0	22
Schneider, Scott	Colorado	WCHA	42	21	22	43	36	....	....	....	....	....
Schofield, Dwight	Pittsburgh	NHL	25	1	6	7	59	....	....	....	....	....
	Baltimore	AHL	20	1	5	6	58	....	....	....	....	....
	NHL Totals		193	8	22	30	598	9	0	0	0	55

			Regular Season					Playoffs			
PLAYER	CLUB	LEAGUE	GP	G	A	TP	PIM	GP	G	A	TP	PIM
Schrader, Kevin	N. Hampshire	H.E.	27	1	4	5	16	....	....	....	....	....
Schreiber, Wally	Cdn. Olympic	....	70	40	37	77	27	....	....	....	....	....
Seabrooke, Glen	Philadelphia	NHL	10	1	4	5	2	....	....	....	....	....
	Peterborough	OHL	48	30	39	69	29	4	3	3	6	6
	NHL Totals		10	1	4	5	2	....	....	....	....	....
Secord, Al	Chicago	NHL	77	29	29	58	196	4	0	0	0	21
	NHL Totals		589	238	178	416	1632	70	22	30	52	327
Seftel, Steve	Kingston	OHL	54	21	43	64	55	12	1	4	5	9
Seiling, Ric	Detroit	NHL	74	3	8	11	49	7	0	0	0	5
	NHL Totals		738	179	208	387	573	62	14	14	28	36
Semenko, Dave	Edmonton	NHL	5	0	0	0	0	....	....	....	....	....
	Hartford	NHL	51	4	8	12	87	4	0	0	0	15
	NHL Totals		505	63	85	148	1068	73	6	6	12	208
Seppo, Jukka	Tappara	Fin.	39	11	16	27	50	....	....	....	....	....
Servinis, George	Indianapolis	IHL	70	41	54	95	54	....	....	....	....	....
Sexsmith, Dean	Seattle	WHL	65	14	24	38	46	....	....	....	....	....
Shanahan, Brendan	London	OHL	56	39	53	92	92	....	....	....	....	....
Shannon, Darryl	Windsor	OHL	64	23	27	50	83	14	4	8	12	18
Sharples, Jeff	Detroit	NHL	3	0	1	1	2	2	0	0	0	2
	Portland	WHL	44	25	35	60	92	20	7	15	22	23
	NHL Totals		3	0	1	1	2	2	0	0	0	2
Shaunessy, Scott	Quebec	NHL	3	0	0	0	7	....	....	....	....	....
	Boston U.	H.E.	32	2	13	15	71	....	....	....	....	....
	NHL Totals		3	0	0	0	7	....	....	....	....	....
Shaw, Brad	Hartford	NHL	2	0	0	0	0	....	....	....	....	....
	Binghamton	AHL	77	9	30	39	43	12	1	8	9	2
	NHL Totals		10	0	2	2	4	....	....	....	....	....
Shaw, Brian	Peoria	IHL	38	9	12	21	77	....	....	....	....	....
Shaw, David	Quebec	NHL	75	0	19	19	69	....	....	....	....	....
	NHL Totals		165	7	38	45	158	....	....	....	....	....
Shaw, Larry	Peterborough	OHL	61	4	13	17	145	12	1	2	3	35
Shea, Dan	Boston College	H.E.	38	21	45	66	56	....	....	....	....	....
Shedden, Doug	Detroit	NHL	33	6	12	18	6	....	....	....	....	....
	Adirondack	AHL	5	2	2	4	4	....	....	....	....	....
	Quebec	NHL	16	0	2	2	8	....	....	....	....	....
	Fredericton	AHL	15	12	6	18	0	....	....	....	....	....
	NHL Totals		392	131	176	307	164	....	....	....	....	....
Sheehy, Neil	Calgary	NHL	54	4	6	10	151	6	0	0	0	21
	NHL Totals		151	10	26	36	533	28	0	2	2	100
Sheppard, Ray	Rochester	AHL	55	18	13	31	11	15	12	3	15	2
Sherven, Gord	Hartford	NHL	7	0	0	0	0	....	....	....	....	....
	Cdn. Olympic	....	56	14	22	36	30	....	....	....	....	....
	NHL Totals		96	13	22	35	33	3	0	0	0	0
Shibicky, Bill	Michigan State	CCHA	42	43	36	79	100	....	....	....	....	....
	Adirondack	AHL	2	0	0	0	0	3	0	0	0	0
Shoebottom, Bruce	Fort Wayne	IHL	75	2	10	12	309	10	0	0	0	31
Shold, Terry	Minn-Duluth	WCHA	11	1	1	2	2	....	....	....	....	....
Shudra, Ron	Kamloops	WHL	71	49	70	119	68	11	7	3	10	10
Siltala, Michael	NY Rangers	NHL	1	0	0	0	0	....	....	....	....	....
	New Haven	AHL	17	13	6	19	20	....	....	....	....	....
	NHL Totals		4	1	0	1	2	....	....	....	....	....
Siltanen, Risto	Quebec	NHL	66	10	29	39	32	13	1	9	10	8
	Fredericton	AHL	6	2	4	6	6	....	....	....	....	....
	NHL Totals		562	90	265	355	266	32	6	12	18	30
Simard, Martin	Granby	QMJHL	41	30	47	77	105	8	3	7	10	21
Simmer, Charlie	Boston	NHL	80	29	40	69	59	1	0	0	0	2
	NHL Totals		662	331	352	683	520	24	9	9	18	32
Simonetti, Frank	Boston	NHL	25	1	0	1	17	4	0	0	0	6
	Moncton	AHL	7	0	1	1	6	....	....	....	....	....
	NHL Totals		85	3	5	8	57	12	0	1	1	8
Simpson, Craig	Pittsburgh	NHL	72	26	25	51	57	....	....	....	....	....
	NHL Totals		148	37	42	79	106	....	....	....	....	....
Simpson, Robert	Salt Lake	IHL	9	2	3	5	12	....	....	....	....	....
	Peoria	IHL	58	14	29	43	32	....	....	....	....	....
	NHL Totals		175	35	29	64	98	6	0	1	1	2

PLAYER	CLUB	LEAGUE	Regular Season GP	G	A	TP	PIM	Playoffs GP	G	A	TP	PIM
Sinisalo, Ilkka	Philadelphia	NHL	42	10	21	31	8	18	5	1	6	4
	NHL Totals		386	150	163	313	122	51	16	7	23	6
Siren, Ville	Pittsburgh	NHL	69	5	17	22	50	....	....	....	....	....
	NHL Totals		129	9	25	34	82	....	....	....	....	....
Skarda, Randy	U. Minnesota	WCHA	43	3	10	13	77	....	....	....	....	....
Skriko, Petri	Vancouver	NHL	76	33	41	74	44	....	....	....	....	....
	NHL Totals		228	92	95	187	88	3	0	0	0	0
Skrudland, Brian	Montreal	NHL	79	11	17	28	107	14	1	5	6	29
	NHL Totals		144	20	30	50	164	34	3	9	12	105
Smail, Doug	Winnipeg	NHL	78	25	18	43	36	10	4	0	4	10
	NHL Totals		479	134	151	285	307	31	7	2	9	27
Smith, Brad	Toronto	NHL	47	5	7	12	172	11	1	1	2	24
	NHL Totals		222	28	34	62	591	20	3	3	6	49
Smith, Dennis	Adirondack	AHL	64	4	24	28	120	6	0	0	0	8
Smith, Derrick	Philadelphia	NHL	71	11	21	32	34	26	6	4	10	26
	NHL Totals		217	34	49	83	122	49	8	9	17	52
Smith, Doug	Buffalo	NHL	62	16	24	40	106	....	....	....	....	....
	Rochester	AHL	15	5	6	11	35	....	....	....	....	....
	NHL Totals		396	98	109	207	397	13	4	2	6	15
Smith, Geoff	St. Albert	AJHL	57	7	28	35	101	....	....	....	....	....
Smith, Greg	Washington	NHL	45	0	9	9	31	7	0	0	0	11
	NHL Totals		775	55	226	281	1043	54	4	7	11	83
Smith, J. Steven	Edmonton	NHL	62	7	15	22	165	15	1	3	4	45
	NHL Totals		119	11	35	46	333	21	1	4	5	59
Smith, Jim	Adirondack	AHL	77	8	27	35	43	....	....	....	....	....
Smith, Nathan	Princeton	ECAC	25	0	3	3	10	....	....	....	....	....
Smith, Randy	Minnesota	NHL	2	0	0	0	0	....	....	....	....	....
	Springfield	AHL	75	20	44	64	24	....	....	....	....	....
	NHL Totals		3	0	0	0	0	....	....	....	....	....
Smith, Robert	Montreal	NHL	80	28	47	75	72	17	9	9	18	19
	NHL Totals		680	257	473	730	556	111	40	68	108	123
Smith, Sandy	Minn-Duluth	WCHA	35	3	3	6	26	....	....	....	....	....
Smith, Scott	New Haven	AHL	39	0	8	8	63	3	0	0	0	12
Smith, Steve	Philadelphia	NHL	2	0	0	0	6	....	....	....	....	....
	Hershey	AHL	66	11	26	37	191	5	0	2	2	8
	NHL Totals		14	0	1	1	15	....	....	....	....	....
Smith, Vern	Springfield	AHL	41	1	10	11	58	....	....	....	....	....
	NHL Totals		1	0	0	0	0	....	....	....	....	....
Smyl, Stan	Vancouver	NHL	66	20	23	43	84	....	....	....	....	....
	NHL Totals		672	240	341	581	1186	34	16	17	33	55
Smyth, Greg	Philadelphia	NHL	1	0	0	0	0	1	0	0	0	2
	Hershey	AHL	35	0	2	2	158	2	0	0	0	19
	NHL Totals		1	0	0	0	0	1	0	0	0	2
Snepsts, Harold	Detroit	NHL	54	1	13	14	129	11	0	2	2	18
	NHL Totals		843	35	175	210	1787	57	1	10	11	135
Snuggerud, Dave	U. Minnesota	WCHA	39	30	29	59	38	....	....	....	....	....
Soberlak, Peter	Swift Current	WHL	68	33	42	75	45	....	....	....	....	....
Sommer, Roy	Muskegon	IHL	65	14	13	27	219	15	3	3	6	44
	NHL Totals		3	1	0	1	7	....	....	....	....	....
Spangler, Ken	Calgary	WHL	49	12	24	36	185	....	....	....	....	....
Speers, Ted	Adirondack	AHL	80	24	37	61	39	11	2	0	2	4
	NHL Totals		4	1	1	2	0	....	....	....	....	....
Sprenger, Jim	Minn.-Duluth	WCHA	39	5	14	19	30	....	....	....	....	....
Sprott, Jim	London	OHL	66	8	30	38	153	....	....	....	....	....
Stafford, Gord	Milwaukee	IHL	71	28	34	62	42	6	3	2	5	2
Stanley, Darryl	Philadelphia	NHL	33	1	2	3	76	13	0	0	0	9
	NHL Totals		89	2	8	10	216	17	0	0	0	30
Stanton, Paul	U. of Wisconsin	WCHA	41	5	17	22	70	....	....	....	....	....
Stapleton, Mike	Chicago	NHL	39	3	6	9	6	4	0	0	0	2
	Cdn. Olympic	....	21	2	4	6	4	....	....	....	....	....
	NHL Totals		39	3	6	9	6	4	0	0	0	2
Stark, Jay	Portland	WHL	70	2	14	16	321	20	0	6	6	58
Stastny, Anton	Quebec	NHL	77	27	35	62	8	13	3	8	11	6
	NHL Totals		526	218	309	527	124	66	20	32	52	31

PLAYER	CLUB	LEAGUE	Regular Season GP	G	A	TP	PIM	Playoffs GP	G	A	TP	PIM
Stastny, Peter	Quebec	NHL	64	24	53	77	43	13	6	9	15	12
	NHL Totals		527	275	515	790	477	64	24	57	81	96
Steen, Thomas	Winnipeg	NHL	75	17	33	50	59	10	3	4	7	8
	NHL Totals		458	125	241	366	386	31	6	15	21	40
Stefanski, Ed	Maine	AHL	29	9	12	21	34	....	....	....	....	....
	NHL Totals		1	0	0	0	0	....	....	....	....	....
Steinberg, Trevor	Quebec	NHL	6	1	0	1	12	....	....	....	....	....
	Fredericton	AHL	48	14	12	26	123	....	....	....	....	....
	NHL Totals		8	2	0	2	12	1	0	0	0	0
Stepan, Brad	Windsor	OHL	54	18	21	39	58	13	2	5	7	14
Stevens, John	Philadelphia	NHL	6	0	2	2	14	....	....	....	....	....
	Hershey	AHL	63	1	15	16	131	3	0	0	0	7
	NHL Totals		6	0	2	2	14	....	....	....	....	....
Stevens, Kevin	Boston College	H.E.	39	35	35	70	54	....	....	....	....	....
Stevens, Mike	Fredericton	AHL	71	7	18	25	258	....	....	....	....	....
	NHL Totals		6	0	3	3	6	....	....	....	....	....
Stevens, Scott	Washington	NHL	77	10	51	61	283	7	0	5	5	19
	NHL Totals		385	68	181	249	1065	33	5	22	27	98
Stewart, Allan	New Jersey	NHL	7	1	0	1	26	....	....	....	....	....
	Maine	AHL	74	14	24	38	143	....	....	....	....	....
	NHL Totals		11	1	0	1	47	....	....	....	....	....
Stewart, Ryan	Brandon	WHL	15	7	9	16	15	....	....	....	....	....
	Portland	WHL	7	5	2	7	12	17	7	11	18	34
	NHL Totals		3	1	0	1	0	....	....	....	....	....
Stiles, Tony	Cdn. Olympic	....	70	4	18	22	58	....	....	....	....	....
	NHL Totals		30	2	7	9	20	....	....	....	....	....
Stothers, Mike	Philadelphia	NHL	2	0	0	0	4	2	0	0	0	7
	Hershey	AHL	75	5	11	16	283	5	0	0	0	10
	NHL Totals		9	0	1	1	10	5	0	0	0	11
Stromback, Doug	Belleville	OHL	65	32	46	78	23	6	2	2	4	10
Strong, Ken	Adirondack	AHL	31	7	13	20	18	11	6	7	13	12
	NHL Totals		15	2	2	4	6	....	....	....	....	....
Strueby, Todd	Muskegon	IHL	82	28	41	69	208	13	4	6	10	53
	NHL Totals		5	0	1	1	2	....	....	....	....	....
Sulliman, Doug	New Jersey	NHL	78	27	26	53	14	....	....	....	....	....
	NHL Totals		492	135	144	279	145	3	1	0	1	0
Summanen, Raimo	Edmonton	NHL	48	10	7	17	15	....	....	....	....	....
	Vancouver	NHL	10	4	4	8	0	....	....	....	....	....
	NHL Totals		142	34	37	71	33	10	2	5	7	0
Sundstrom, Patrik	Vancouver	NHL	72	29	42	71	40	....	....	....	....	....
	NHL Totals		374	133	209	342	181	11	1	1	2	9
Sundstrom, Peter	Bjorkloven	Swe.	36	16	32	38	44	....	....	....	....	....
	NHL Totals		206	48	62	110	70	9	1	3	4	2
Suter, Gary	Calgary	NHL	68	9	40	49	70	6	0	3	3	10
	NHL Totals		148	27	90	117	211	16	2	11	13	12
Sutter, Brent	NY Islanders	NHL	69	27	36	63	73	5	1	0	1	4
	NHL Totals		397	171	185	356	509	77	20	31	51	100
Sutter, Brian	St. Louis	NHL	14	3	3	6	18	....	....	....	....	....
	NHL Totals		703	288	311	599	1639	55	21	18	39	200
Sutter, Darryl	Chicago	NHL	44	8	6	14	16	2	0	0	0	0
	NHL Totals		406	161	118	279	288	51	24	19	43	26
Sutter, Duane	NY Islanders	NHL	80	14	17	31	169	14	1	0	1	26
	NHL Totals		547	121	171	292	894	120	22	30	52	321
Sutter, Rich	Vancouver	NHL	74	20	22	42	113	....	....	....	....	....
	NHL Totals		287	56	69	125	494	19	5	0	5	44
Sutter, Ron	Philadelphia	NHL	39	10	17	27	69	16	1	7	8	12
	NHL Totals		276	64	121	185	432	43	5	17	22	72
Sutton, Boyd	Miami-Ohio	CCHA	39	19	18	37	44	....	....	....	....	....
Svanberg, Bo	Farjestad	Swe.	29	4	3	7	8	....	....	....	....	....
Sveen, Jeff	Boston U.	H.E.	34	8	6	14	32	....	....	....	....	....
Svoboda, Petr	Montreal	NHL	70	5	17	22	63	14	0	5	5	10
	NHL Totals		216	10	62	72	221	29	1	6	7	43

PLAYER	CLUB	LEAGUE	Regular Season GP	G	A	TP	PIM	Playoffs GP	G	A	TP	PIM
Sweeney, Bob	Boston	NHL	14	2	4	6	21	3	0	0	0	0
	Moncton	AHL	58	29	26	55	81	4	0	2	2	13
	NHL Totals		14	2	4	6	21	3	0	0	0	0
Sweeney, Don	Harvard	ECAC	34	7	4	11	22	....	....	....	....	....
Sweeney, Tim	Boston College	H.E.	38	31	18	49	28	....	....	....	....	....
Sykes, Phil	Los Angeles	NHL	58	6	15	21	133	5	0	1	1	8
	NHL Totals		223	45	54	99	272	8	0	2	2	12
Taglianetti, Peter	Winnipeg	NHL	3	0	0	0	12	....	....	....	....	....
	Sherbrooke	AHL	54	5	14	19	104	10	2	5	7	25
	NHL Totals		22	0	0	0	60	4	0	0	0	2
Tait, Terry	Springfield	AHL	73	26	39	65	48	6	5	2	7	7
Talakoski, Ron	NY Rangers	NHL	3	0	0	0	21	....	....	....	....	....
	New Haven	AHL	26	2	2	4	58	1	0	0	0	0
	NHL Totals		3	0	0	0	21	....	....	....	....	....
Tambellini, Steve	Vancouver	NHL	72	16	20	36	14	....	....	....	....	....
	NHL Totals		512	149	140	289	97	2	0	1	1	0
Tanner, David	Yale	ECAC	30	10	11	21	20	....	....	....	....	....
Tanti, Tony	Vancouver	NHL	77	41	38	79	84	....	....	....	....	....
	NHL Totals		343	173	140	313	280	11	1	4	5	11
Tarasuk, Allen	Indianapolis	IHL	46	8	12	20	173	6	1	2	3	10
Taylor, Darren	Seattle	WHL	60	13	13	26	112	....	....	....	....	....
Taylor, Dave	Los Angeles	NHL	67	18	44	62	84	5	2	3	5	6
	NHL Totals		684	321	473	794	996	30	12	14	26	55
Taylor, Mark	Binghamton	AHL	67	16	37	53	40	13	2	6	8	9
	NHL Totals		209	42	68	110	73	6	0	0	0	0
Taylor, Randy	Harvard	ECAC	34	3	35	38	30	....	....	....	....	....
Taylor, Scott	Kitchener	OHL	53	6	16	22	123	4	0	0	0	9
Tebbutt, Greg	Saginaw	IHL	81	27	59	86	215	8	6	5	11	34
	NHL Totals		26	0	3	3	35	....	....	....	....	....
Teevens, Mark	Baltimore	AHL	71	15	16	31	34	....	....	....	....	....
Terrion, Greg	Toronto	NHL	67	7	8	15	6	13	0	2	2	14
	NHL Totals		497	89	134	223	274	30	2	7	9	37
Terwilliger, Tom	Miami-Ohio	CCHA	26	2	1	3	24	....	....	....	....	....
Thacker, Rod	Hamilton	OHL	6	0	0	0	0	....	....	....	....	....
	Ottawa	OHL	31	1	3	4	36	....	....	....	....	....
	S.S. Marie	OHL	26	0	6	6	28	4	0	1	1	8
Thayer, Chris	Kent	HS	22	15	22	37	0	....	....	....	....	....
Thelin, Mats	Boston	NHL	59	1	3	4	69	....	....	....	....	....
	NHL Totals		163	8	19	27	107	5	0	0	0	6
Thelven, Michael	Boston	NHL	34	5	15	20	18	....	....	....	....	....
	NHL Totals		94	11	35	46	66	3	0	0	0	0
Thibodeau, Gilles	Montreal	NHL	9	1	3	4	2	....	....	....	....	....
	Sherbrooke	AHL	62	27	40	67	26	....	....	....	....	....
	NHL Totals		9	1	3	4	2	....	....	....	....	....
Thomas, Steve	Toronto	NHL	78	35	27	62	114	13	2	3	5	13
	NHL Totals		161	56	65	121	152	23	8	11	19	22
Thomlinson, Dave	Brandon	WHL	2	0	1	1	9	....	....	....	....	....
	Moose Jaw	WHL	70	44	36	80	117	9	7	3	10	19
Thomson, Jim	Washington	NHL	10	0	0	0	35	....	....	....	....	....
	Binghamton	AHL	57	13	10	23	360	10	0	1	1	40
	NHL Totals		10	0	0	0	35	....	....	....	....	....
Tiano, John	RPI	ECAC	....	....	....	....	....	....	....	....	....	....
Tikkanen, Esa	Edmonton	NHL	76	34	44	78	120	21	7	2	9	22
	NHL Totals		111	41	50	91	148	32	10	4	14	31
Tilley, Tom	Michigan State	CCHA	42	7	14	21	48	....	....	....	....	....
Tinordi, Mark	Calgary	WHL	61	29	37	66	148	....	....	....	....	....
	New Haven	AHL	2	0	0	0	2	2	0	0	0	0
Tippet, Dave	Hartford	NHL	80	9	22	31	42	6	0	2	2	4
	NHL Totals		257	34	56	90	74	16	2	4	6	8
Tirkkonen, Pekka	Sapko	Fin.	40	14	22	36	8	....	....	....	....	....
Tocchet, Rick	Philadelphia	NHL	69	21	26	47	288	26	11	10	21	72
	NHL Totals		213	49	72	121	753	50	15	16	31	170
Todd, Kevin	Prince Albert	WHL	71	39	46	85	92	8	2	5	7	17
Toivola, Tero	Tappara	Fin.	11	0	0	0	0	....	....	....	....	....

PLAYER	CLUB	LEAGUE	Regular Season GP	G	A	TP	PIM	Playoffs GP	G	A	TP	PIM
Tomlinson, Kirk	Hamilton	OHL	65	33	37	70	169	9	4	6	10	28
Tonelli, John	Calgary	NHL	78	20	31	51	72	3	0	0	0	4
	NHL Totals		681	229	373	602	555	138	35	64	99	166
Tookey, Tim	Philadelphia	NHL	2	0	0	0	0	10	1	3	4	2
	Hershey	AHL	80	51	73	124	45	5	5	4	9	0
	NHL Totals		79	19	29	48	59	10	1	3	4	2
Toomey, Sean	Minnesota	NHL	1	0	0	0	0	....	....	....	....	....
	Minn.-Duluth	WCHA	39	26	17	43	34	....	....	....	....	....
	Indianapolis	IHL	13	3	3	6	0	5	2	2	4	2
	NHL Totals		1	0	0	0	0	....	....	....	....	....
Torkki, Jiri	Lukko	Fin.	44	27	8	35	42	....	....	....	....	....
Tory, Paul	Ill.-Chicago	CCHA	34	17	21	38	73	....	....	....	....	....
Tracy, Joe	Ohio State	CCHA	37	8	13	21	49	....	....	....	....	....
Trader, Larry	St. Louis	NHL	5	0	0	0	8	....	....	....	....	....
	Cdn. Olympic	....	48	4	16	20	56	....	....	....	....	....
	NHL Totals		60	3	9	12	53	3	0	0	0	0
Trapp, Doug	Buffalo	NHL	2	0	0	0	0	....	....	....	....	....
	Rochester	AHL	68	27	35	62	80	16	0	9	9	5
	NHL Totals		2	0	0	0	0	....	....	....	....	....
Trottier, Bryan	NY Islanders	NHL	80	23	64	87	50	14	8	5	13	12
	NHL Totals		914	440	762	1202	677	165	63	106	169	206
Trottier, Rocky	Maine	AHL	77	9	14	23	41	....	....	....	....	....
	NHL Totals		38	6	4	10	2	....	....	....	....	....
Tsujiura, Steve	Maine	AHL	80	24	41	65	73	....	....	....	....	....
Tucker, John	Buffalo	NHL	54	17	34	51	21	....	....	....	....	....
	NHL Totals		214	82	99	181	85	8	2	5	7	0
Tuer, Al	New Haven	AHL	69	1	14	15	273	5	0	1	1	48
	NHL Totals		45	0	1	1	150	....	....	....	....	....
Tuite, Steve	Milwaukee	IHL	33	4	10	14	22	1	0	0	0	2
	Muskegon	IHL	39	0	4	4	28	....	....	....	....	....
Turcotte, Alfie	Nova Scotia	AHL	70	27	41	68	37	5	2	4	6	2
	NHL Totals		85	15	23	38	47	5	0	0	0	0
Turcotte, Darren	North Bay	OHL	55	30	48	78	20	18	12	8	20	6
Turgeon, Pierre	Granby	QMJHL	58	69	85	154	8	7	9	6	15	15
Turgeon, Sylvain	Hartford	NHL	41	23	13	36	45	6	1	2	3	4
	NHL Totals		257	139	110	249	255	15	3	5	8	8
Turnbull, Perry	Winnipeg	NHL	26	1	5	6	44	1	0	0	0	10
	NHL Totals		557	178	154	332	1163	33	6	7	13	84
Turnbull, Randy	Salt Lake	IHL	60	2	6	8	212	10	0	0	0	56
	NHL Totals		1	0	0	0	2	....	....	....	....	....
Turner, Brad	Michigan	CCHA	40	3	10	13	40	....	....	....	....	....
Tutt, Brian	Maine	AHL	41	6	15	21	19	....	....	....	....	....
	Kalamazoo	IHL	19	2	7	9	10	....	....	....	....	....
Tuttle, Steve	U. of Wisconsin	WCHA	42	31	21	52	14	....	....	....	....	....
Tyers, Shawn	Kitchener	OHL	....	....	....	....	....	....	....	....	....	....
Urban, Jeff	U. of Michigan	CCHA	28	3	4	7	18	....	....	....	....	....
Vaive, Rick	Toronto	NHL	73	32	34	66	61	13	4	2	6	23
	NHL Totals		581	312	246	558	1051	32	14	9	23	53
Valimont, Carl	U. of Lowell	H.E.	36	8	9	17	36	....	....	....	....	....
Vandermast, Howie	Potsdam State	ECAC	28	21	18	39	32	....	....	....	....	....
Van Dorp, Wayne	Edmonton	NHL	3	0	0	0	25	3	0	0	0	2
	Rochester	AHL	47	7	3	10	192	....	....	....	....	....
	Nova Scotia	AHL	11	2	3	5	37	5	0	0	0	56
	NHL Totals		3	0	0	0	36	3	0	0	0	2
Vani, Carmine	Newmarket	AHL	27	1	1	2	31	....	....	....	....	....
	Milwaukee	IHL	2	0	1	1	0	....	....	....	....	....
	Saginaw	IHL	19	5	10	15	52	....	....	....	....	....
	Flint	IHL	14	4	6	10	53	....	....	....	....	....
	Fort Wayne	IHL	6	1	1	2	2	....	....	....	....	....
Vargas, Ernie	Sherbrooke	AHL	69	22	32	54	52	16	6	3	9	13
Vaske, Dennis	U. of Minnesota	WCHA	33	0	2	2	40	....	....	....	....	....
Veilleux, Steve	Trois Rivieres	QMJHL	62	6	22	28	227	....	....	....	....	....
Veitch, Darren	Detroit	NHL	77	13	45	58	52	12	3	4	7	8
	NHL Totals		409	38	168	206	235	22	3	6	9	27
Velischek, Randy	New Jersey	NHL	64	2	16	18	52	....	....	....	....	....
	NHL Totals		199	10	34	44	129	19	2	3	5	8

| | | | \multicolumn{4}{c}{Regular Season} | | | \multicolumn{4}{c}{Playoffs} |
PLAYER	CLUB	LEAGUE	GP	G	A	TP	PIM	GP	G	A	TP	PIM
Vellucci, Mike	Salt Lake	IHL	60	5	30	35	94	....	....	....	....	....
Verbeek, Brian	Salt Lake	IHL	52	22	15	37	119	....	....	....	....	....
Verbeek, Pat	**New Jersey**	**NHL**	74	35	24	59	120	....	....	....	....	....
	NHL Totals		313	98	99	197	527	....	....	....	....	....
Vermette, Mark	Lake Superior	CCHA	38	19	17	36	59	....	....	....	....	....
Verret, Claude	Rochester	AHL	36	13	12	25	2	8	3	3	6	0
	NHL Totals		14	2	5	7	2	....	....	....	....	....
Verstraete, Leigh	Newmarket	AHL	57	9	7	16	179	....	....	....	....	....
	NHL Totals		5	0	0	0	5	....	....	....	....	....
Vesey, Jim	Merrimack	ECAC	35	22	36	58	57	....	....	....	....	....
Vey, Greg	Peterborough	OHL	57	8	22	30	105	12	1	5	6	7
Vichorek, Mark	Binghamton	AHL	64	1	12	13	63	....	....	....	....	....
	Salt Lake	IHL	16	1	0	1	32	17	0	8	8	23
Vilgrain, Claude	Cdn. Olympic	....	78	28	42	70	38	....	....	....	....	....
Villeneuve, Andre	Hershey	AHL	7	0	2	2	2	....	....	....	....	....
	Sherbrooke	AHL	49	3	16	19	69	15	1	2	3	38
Vincelette, Daniel	Drummondville	QMJHL	50	34	35	69	288	8	6	5	11	17
Virta, Hannu	T.P.S.	Fin.	41	13	30	43	20	....	....	....	....	....
	NHL Totals		245	25	101	126	66	17	1	3	4	6
Vitale, Luke	Providence	H.E.	32	4	7	11	14	....	....	....	....	....
Viveiros, Emanuel	**Minnesota**	**NHL**	1	0	1	1	0	....	....	....	....	....
	Springfield	AHL	76	7	35	42	38	....	....	....	....	....
	NHL Totals		5	0	2	2	0	....	....	....	....	....
Volcan, Mickey	Baltimore	AHL	72	8	36	44	118	....	....	....	....	....
	NHL Totals		162	8	33	41	146	....	....	....	....	....
Volhoffer, Troy	Baltimore	AHL	67	11	25	36	90	....	....	....	....	....
Vos, Ralph	N. Michigan	WCHA	18	4	12	16	18	....	....	....	....	....
Wahlsten, Sami	TPS	Fin.	40	15	13	28	22	....	....	....	....	....
Walker, Gord	**NY Rangers**	**NHL**	1	1	0	1	4	....	....	....	....	....
	New Haven	AHL	59	24	20	44	58	7	3	2	5	0
	NHL Totals		1	1	0	1	4	....	....	....	....	....
Walter, Bret	Alberta	GPAC	....	....	....	....	....	....	....	....	....	....
	Cdn. Olympic	....	2	0	0	0	0	....	....	....	....	....
Walter, Ryan	**Montreal**	**NHL**	76	23	23	46	34	17	7	12	19	10
	NHL Totals		677	220	314	534	729	52	11	21	32	40
Ware, Michael	Cornwall	OHL	50	5	19	24	173	5	0	1	1	10
Warus, Mike	Lake Superior	CCHA	38	6	15	21	113	....	....	....	....	....
Waslen, Gerard	Newmarket	AHL	79	22	30	52	64	....	....	....	....	....
Watson, Bill	**Chicago**	**NHL**	51	13	19	32	6	4	0	1	1	0
	NHL Totals		103	21	35	56	8	6	0	2	2	0
Watters, Tim	**Winnipeg**	**NHL**	63	3	13	16	119	10	0	0	0	21
	NHL Totals		402	21	101	122	654	28	1	2	3	49
Weinrich, Eric	U. of Maine	H.E.	41	12	32	44	59	....	....	....	....	....
Weiss, Tom	Springfield	AHL	46	6	10	16	47	....	....	....	....	....
Wells, Jay	**Los Angeles**	**NHL**	77	7	29	36	155	5	1	2	3	10
	NHL Totals		546	32	120	152	1287	26	2	6	8	89
Wenaas, Jeff	Medicine Hat	WHL	70	42	29	71	68	17	9	9	18	28
Werenka, Brad	N. Michigan	WCHA	30	4	4	8	35	....	....	....	....	....
Wesley, Blake	Newmarket	AHL	79	1	12	13	170	....	....	....	....	....
	NHL Totals		298	18	46	64	486	19	2	2	4	30
Wesley, Glen	Portland	WHL	63	16	46	62	72	20	8	18	26	27
Wheeldon, Simon	Salt Lake	IHL	41	17	53	70	20	....	....	....	....	....
	New Haven	AHL	38	11	28	39	39	5	0	0	0	6
Whelan, Shane	London	OHL	52	13	19	32	68	....	....	....	....	....
Whistle, Rob	New Haven	AHL	55	4	12	16	30	7	1	1	2	7
	NHL Totals		32	4	2	6	10	3	0	0	0	2
Whitaker, Gord	Colorado	WCHA	34	21	17	38	69	....	....	....	....	....
White, George	Milwaukee	IHL	60	15	27	42	50	6	3	3	6	7
White, Scott	Michigan Tech	WCHA	36	4	15	19	58	....	....	....	....	....
Whitham, Shawn	Providence	H.E.	31	9	11	20	57	....	....	....	....	....
Whyte, David	Boston College	H.E.	28	2	2	4	26	....	....	....	....	....
Wickenheiser, Doug	**St. Louis**	**NHL**	80	13	15	28	37	6	0	0	0	2
	NHL Totals		432	100	133	233	226	36	4	7	11	16
Wiemer, Jim	New Haven	AHL	6	0	7	7	6	....	....	....	....	....
	Nova Scotia	AHL	59	9	25	34	72	5	0	4	4	2
	NHL Totals		103	15	20	35	84	10	1	0	1	6
Wiest, Rich	Kamloops	WHL	44	13	22	35	69	10	1	4	5	16
	Swift Current	WHL	24	6	5	11	60	....	....	....	....	....

PLAYER	CLUB	LEAGUE	GP	G	A	TP	PIM	GP	G	A	TP	PIM
Wiitala, Marty	U.S. Olympic	.....	5	1	1	2	2	....	....	....	....	....
Wilkie, Bob	Swift Current	WHL	65	12	38	50	50	4	1	3	4	2
Wilks, Brian	**Los Angeles**	**NHL**	1	0	0	0	0	....	....	....	....	....
	New Haven	AHL	43	16	20	36	23	7	1	3	4	7
	NHL Totals		46	4	8	12	25	....	....	....	....	....
Williams, Brian	Sherbrooke	AHL	9	0	0	0	6	....	....	....	....	....
	Saginaw	IHL	6	1	5	6	8	....	....	....	....	....
Williams, Dave	Los Angeles	NHL	76	16	18	34	358	5	3	2	5	30
	NHL Totals		934	235	272	507	3873	83	12	23	35	455
Williams, Rod	Brandon	WHL	33	6	10	16	98	....	....	....	....	....
	Regina	WHL	18	2	4	6	59	....	....	....	....	....
	Medicine Hat	WHL	16	3	3	6	59	13	0	0	0	12
Williams, Sean	Oshawa	OHL	62	21	23	44	32	25	7	5	12	19
Wilson, Behn	DID NOT PLAY -	INJURED										
	NHL Totals		543	92	237	329	1314	64	12	29	41	184
Wilson, Carey	**Calgary**	**NHL**	80	20	36	56	42	6	1	1	2	6
	NHL Totals		245	75	118	193	95	25	4	4	8	10
Wilson, Doug	**Chicago**	**NHL**	69	16	32	48	36	4	0	0	0	0
	NHL Totals		724	168	404	572	595	66	13	46	59	68
Wilson, Mitch	Pittsburgh	NHL	17	2	1	3	83	....	....	....	....	....
	Baltimore	AHL	58	8	9	17	353	....	....	....	....	....
	NHL Totals		26	2	3	5	104	....	....	....	....	....
Wilson, Rik	Nova Scotia	AHL	45	8	13	21	109	5	1	3	4	20
	NHL Totals		237	21	60	81	214	22	0	4	4	23
Wilson, Rob	Sudbury	OHL	58	1	27	28	135	....	....	....	....	....
Wilson, Ron	**Minnesota**	**NHL**	65	12	29	41	36	....	....	....	....	....
	NHL Totals		140	20	47	67	50	8	0	5	5	6
Wilson, Ronald	**Winnipeg**	**NHL**	80	3	13	16	13	10	1	2	3	0
	NHL Totals		467	70	126	196	208	22	7	6	13	2
Wilson, Ross	Peterborough	OHL	66	28	11	39	91	12	3	5	8	16
Wolak, Michael	Kitchener	OHL	9	3	6	9	6	....	....	....	....	....
	Belleville	OHL	25	20	16	36	18	....	....	....	....	....
	Windsor	OHL	26	7	14	21	26	14	2	7	9	2
Wolanin, Craig	**New Jersey**	**NHL**	68	4	6	10	109	....	....	....	....	....
	NHL Totals		112	6	22	28	183	....	....	....	....	....
Wood, Randy	NY Islanders	NHL	6	1	0	1	4	13	1	3	4	14
	Springfield	AHL	75	23	24	47	57	....	....	....	....	....
	NHL Totals		6	1	0	1	4	13	1	3	4	14
Woodley, Dan	Portland	WHL	47	30	50	80	81	19	19	17	36	52
Wright, Kory	N. Michigan	WCHA	36	11	14	25	22	....	....	....	....	....
Yake, Terry	Brandon	WHL	71	44	58	102	64	....	....	....	....	....
Yaremchuk, Gary	Jokerit	Fin.	20	7	21	28	116	....	....	....	....	....
	NHL Totals		34	1	4	5	28	....	....	....	....	....
Yaremchuk, Ken	**Toronto**	**NHL**	20	3	8	11	16	6	0	0	0	0
	Newmarket	AHL	14	2	4	6	21	....	....	....	....	....
	NHL Totals		208	33	51	84	94	25	6	6	12	39
Yawney, Trent	Cdn. Olympic	....	51	4	15	19	37	....	....	....	....	....
Young, Scott	Boston U.	H.E.	33	15	21	36	24	....	....	....	....	....
Young, Warren	**Pittsburgh**	**NHL**	50	8	13	21	103	....	....	....	....	....
	Baltimore	AHL	22	8	7	15	95	....	....	....	....	....
	NHL Totals		229	72	77	149	457	....	....	....	....	....
Ysabaert, Paul	Bowling Green	CCHA	45	27	58	85	44	....	....	....	....	....
	Cdn. Olympic	....	5	1	0	1	4	....	....	....	....	....
Yzerman, Steve	**Detroit**	**NHL**	80	31	59	90	43	16	5	13	18	8
	NHL Totals		291	114	194	308	150	23	10	17	27	10
Zalapski, Zarley	Cdn. Olympic	....	74	11	29	40	28	....	....	....	....	....
Zemlack, Richard	**Quebec**	**NHL**	20	0	2	2	47	....	....	....	....	....
	Fredericton	AHL	29	9	6	15	201	....	....	....	....	....
	NHL Totals		20	0	2	2	47	....	....	....	....	....
Zettler, Rob	S.S. Marie	OHL	64	13	22	35	89	4	0	0	0	0
Zezel, Peter	**Philadelphia**	**NHL**	71	33	39	72	71	25	3	10	13	10
	NHL Totals		215	65	122	187	173	49	7	19	26	42
Zombo, Rick	**Detroit**	**NHL**	44	1	4	5	59	7	0	1	1	9
	Adirondack	AHL	25	0	6	6	22	....	....	....	....	....
	NHL Totals		59	1	5	6	75	7	0	1	1	9

Professional Hockey Index 1988

Abbreviations:

Avg – goals against per game average;
GA – goals against;
GP – games played; **L** – losses;
SO – shutouts; **T** – ties; **W** – wins.

To calculate a goaltender's goals-against-per-game average **(Avg)**, divide goals against **(GA)** by minutes played **(Mins)** and multiply this result by **60**.

SECTION 2: GOALTENDERS

The Professional Hockey Index lists the 1986-87 statistical record and NHL totals of more than 150 goaltenders who played in the NHL, minor professional, junior, college or European leagues last season. Included are goaltenders who played in the NHL in 1986-87, draft choices from the first and second rounds of the 1986 and 1987 NHL Entry Drafts and players on the reserve lists of NHL clubs.

					Regular Season								Playoffs			
GOALTENDER	CLUB	LEAGUE	GP	W	L	T	Mins	GA	SO	Avg	GP	W	L	Mins	GA	SO	Avg
Bannerman, Murray	Chicago	NHL	39	9	18	8	2059	142	0	4.14	....	....	....	....	....	....	....
	NHL Totals		289	116	125	33	16470	1051	8	3.83	40	20	18	2322	165	0	4.26
Barrasso, Tom	Buffalo	NHL	46	17	23	2	2501	152	2	3.65	....	....	....	....	....	....	....
	NHL Totals		202	97	77	20	11785	627	11	3.19	8	2	5	439	30	0	4.10
Beals, Darren	Kitchener	OHL	49	20	16	3	2582	190	1	4.42	2	0	2	120	9	0	4.50
Beaupre, Don	Minnesota	NHL	47	17	20	6	2622	174	1	3.98	....	....	....	....	....	....	....
	NHL Totals		272	116	102	42	15486	947	3	3.67	34	15	16	1931	119	1	3.70
Beedon, Roger	Ohio State	CCHA	24	8	13	1	1322	114	1	5.17	....	....	....	....	....	....	....
Behrend, Marc	Sherbrooke	AHL	19	8	5	0	1124	62	0	3.31	1	0	1	59	3	0	3.05
	NHL Totals		38	12	19	0	1946	160	1	4.93	7	1	3	312	19	0	3.65
Bernhardt, Tim	Toronto	NHL	1	0	0	0	20	3	0	9.00	....	....	....	....	....	....	....
	Newmarket	AHL	31	6	17	0	1705	117	1	4.12	....	....	....	....	....	....	....
	NHL Totals		67	17	36	7	3748	267	0	4.27	....	....	....	....	....	....	....
Berthiaume, Daniel	Winnipeg	NHL	31	18	7	3	1758	93	1	3.17	8	4	4	439	21	0	2.87
	Sherbrooke	AHL	7	4	3	0	420	23	0	3.29	....	....	....	....	....	....	....
	NHL Totals		31	18	7	3	1758	93	1	3.17	9	4	5	507	25	0	2.96
Bester, Allan	Toronto	NHL	36	10	14	3	1808	110	2	3.65	1	0	0	39	1	0	1.54
	Newmarket	AHL	3	1	0	0	190	6	0	1.89	....	....	....	....	....	....	....
	NHL Totals		84	24	39	8	4443	300	3	4.05	1	0	0	39	1	0	1.54

Goaltenders: BILLINGTON...GILLES

GOALTENDER	CLUB	LEAGUE	GP	W	L	T	Mins	GA	SO	Avg	GP	W	L	Mins	GA	SO	Avg
Billington, Craig	New Jersey	NHL	22	4	13	2	1114	89	0	4.79	....	....	....	....	....	....	....
	Maine	AHL	20	9	7	0	1151	70	0	3.65	....	....	....	....	....	....	....
	NHL Totals		40	8	22	3	2016	166	0	4.94	....	....	....	....	....	....	....
Blair, Grant	Salt Lake	IHL	25	7	15	1	1431	108	0	4.53	1	0	1	60	6	0	6.00
Blue, John	U. Minnesota	WCHA	33	21	9	1	1889	99	3	3.14							
Bohemier, Eric	Granby	QMJHL	35	27	7	0	1846	133	1	4.32	3	0	3	129	13	0	6.05
Brodeur, Richard	Vancouver	NHL	53	20	25	5	2972	178	1	3.59	....	....	....	....	....	....	....
	NHL Totals		368	124	168	60	20958	1346	6	3.85	29	12	17	1809	99	1	3.28
Brower, Scott	North Dakota	WCHA	15	11	4	0	803	44	0	3.29							
Brunetta, Mario	Laval	QMJHL	59	27	25	4	3469	261	1	4.51	14	8	6	820	63	0	4.61
Burke, Sean	Can. Olympic	....	42	27	13	2	2550	130	0	3.05							
Caprice, Frank	Vancouver	NHL	25	8	11	2	1390	89	0	3.84							
	Fredericton	AHL	12	5	5	0	686	47	0	4.11							
	NHL Totals		80	24	30	9	4339	304	1	4.20	....	....	....	....	....	....	....
Casey, Jon	Springfield	AHL	13	1	8	0	770	56	0	4.36							
	Indianapolis	IHL	31	14	15	0	1794	133	0	4.45							
	NHL Totals		28	12	11	1	1486	97	0	3.92	....	....	....	....	....	....	....
Chabot, Frederic	Drummondville	QMJHL	62	31	29	0	3508	293	1	5.01	8	2	6	481	40	0	4.99
Chevrier, Alan	New Jersey	NHL	58	24	26	2	3153	227	0	4.32							
	NHL Totals		95	35	44	4	5015	370	0	4.43	....	....	....	....	....	....	....
Clifford, Chris	Kingston	OHL	44	18	25	0	2596	191	1	4.41	12	6	6	730	42	0	3.45
Cloutier, Jacques	Buffalo	NHL	40	11	19	5	2167	137	0	3.79							
	NHL Totals		88	31	36	13	4805	284	1	3.55	....	....	....	....	....	....	....
Cooper, Jeff	Muskegon	IHL	45	23	21	1	2673	147	2	3.30	1	0	1	8	1	0	7.50
Craig, Mike	Rochester	AHL	23	6	10	0	1192	82	0	4.13							
	Flint	IHL	2	2	0	0	120	5	0	2.50							
Dadswell, Doug	Calgary	NHL	2	0	1	1	125	10	0	4.80							
	Moncton	AHL	42	23	12	0	2276	138	1	3.64	6	2	4	326	23	0	4.23
	NHL Totals		2	0	1	1	125	10	0	4.80	....	....	....	....	....	....	....
D'Amour, Marc	Binghamton	AHL	8	5	3	0	461	30	0	3.90							
	Salt Lake	IHL	10	3	6	0	523	37	0	4.24							
	Can. Olympic	....	1	0	0	0	30	4	0	8.00							
	NHL Totals		15	2	4	2	560	32	0	3.43	....	....	....	....	....	....	....
Daskalakis, Cleon	Boston	NHL	2	2	0	0	97	7	0	4.33							
	Moncton	AHL	27	8	14	0	1452	118	0	4.88	1	0	0	36	2	0	3.33
	NHL Totals		12	3	4	1	506	41	0	4.86	....	....	....	....	....	....	....
Dowie, Bruce	Newmarket	AHL	4	0	2	0	155	13	0	5.03							
	NHL Totals		2	0	1	0	72	4	0	3.33	....	....	....	....	....	....	....
Draper, Tom	U. Vermont	ECAC	29	16	13	0	1662	96	2	3.47							
Dufor, Michel	Muskegon	IHL	3	1	2	0	179	11	0	3.69							
	Fort Wayne	IHL	40	24	14	0	2247	126	1	3.36	6	3	3	346	17	0	2.95
Edmands, Jim	Cornell	ECAC	18	7	7	0	953	60	1	3.78							
Eliot, Darren	Los Angeles	NHL	24	8	13	2	1404	103	1	4.40	1	0	0	40	7	0	10.50
	New Haven	AHL	4	2	2	0	239	15	0	3.77							
	NHL Totals		84	25	41	11	4767	361	1	4.54	1	0	0	40	7	0	10.50
Essensa, Bob	Michigan State	CCHA	25	19	3	1	1383	64	2	2.78							
Evoy, Sean	Oshawa	OHL	31	23	3	1	1702	89	2	3.14	14	8	3	720	31	2	2.58
Exelby, Randy	Lake Superior	CCHA	28	12	9	1	1357	91	0	4.02							
Fitzpatrick, Mark	Medicine Hat	WHL	50	31	11	4	2844	159	4	3.35	20	12	8	1224	71	1	3.48
Ford, Brian	Baltimore	AHL	32	10	11	0	1541	99	0	3.85							
	NHL Totals		11	3	7	0	580	61	0	6.31	....	....	....	....	....	....	....
Foster, Norm	Michigan State	CCHA	24	14	7	1	1383	90	1	3.90							
Franzosa, John	Flint	IHL	5	1	2	0	192	18	0	5.63							
Friesen, Karl	New Jersey	NHL	4	0	2	1	130	16	0	7.38							
	NHL Totals		4	0	2	1	130	16	0	7.38	....	....	....	....	....	....	....
Froese, Bob	Philadelphia	NHL	3	3	0	0	180	8	0	2.67							
	NY Rangers	NHL	28	14	11	0	1474	92	0	3.74	4	1	1	165	10	0	3.64
	NHL Totals		172	106	40	12	9575	462	12	2.90	16	3	7	758	47	0	3.72
Fuhr, Grant	Edmonton	NHL	44	22	13	3	2388	137	0	3.44	19	14	5	1148	47	0	2.46
	NHL Totals		255	148	56	33	14406	902	2	3.76	68	47	19	3956	200	1	3.03
Furlan, Frank	Mich. Tech	WCHA	11	1	10	0	623	66	0	6.36							
Gamble, Troy	Vancouver	NHL	1	0	1	0	60	4	0	4.00							
	Spokane	WHL	38	17	17	0	2155	163	0	4.54	5	0	5	298	35	0	7.05
	Medicine Hat	WHL	11	7	3	0	646	46	0	4.27							
	NHL Totals		1	0	1	0	60	4	0	4.00	....	....	....	....	....	....	....
Gilles, Bruce	Fort Wayne	IHL	5	1	4	0	289	17	0	3.53							

Goaltenders: GILMOUR...MASON

GOALTENDER	CLUB	LEAGUE	GP	W	Regular Season L	T	Mins	GA	SO	Avg	GP	W	Playoffs L	Mins	GA	SO	Avg
Gilmour, Darryl	Moose Jaw	WHL	31	14	13	2	1776	123	2	4.16	....	....	....	....	....	....	....
	Portland	WHL	24	15	7	1	1460	111	0	4.56	19	12	7	1167	83	1	4.27
Gordon, Scott	Fredericton	AHL	32	9	12	2	1616	120	0	4.46	....	....	....	....	....	....	....
Gosselin, Mario	**Quebec**	**NHL**	30	13	11	1	1625	86	0	3.18	11	7	4	654	37	0	3.39
	NHL Totals		**100**	**48**	**36**	**5**	**5519**	**311**	**4**	**3.38**	**29**	**16**	**13**	**1753**	**96**	**0**	**3.29**
Gowans, Mark	Oshawa	OHL	10	7	2	0	571	21	0	2.21							
	Hamilton	OHL	20	8	10	0	1106	82	0	4.45	3	0	2	157	14	0	5.35
Gravel, Francois	Shawinigan	QMJHL	40	18	17	5	2415	194	0	4.82	11	8	3	678	47	0	4.16
Greenlay, Mike	Lake Superior	CCHA	17	7	5	0	744	44	0	3.54	....	....	....	....	....	....	....
Guenette, Steve	**Pittsburgh**	**NHL**	2	0	2	0	113	8	0	4.25	....	....	....	....	....	....	....
	Baltimore	AHL	54	21	23	0	3035	157	5	3.10							
	NHL Totals		**2**	**0**	**2**	**0**	**113**	**8**	**0**	**4.25**							
Gunn, Royden	Springfield	AHL	29	10	13	4	1599	107	0	4.02	....	....	....	....	....	....	....
Hackett, Jeff	Oshawa	OHL	31	18	9	2	1672	85	2	3.05	15	8	7	895	40	0	2.68
Hanlon, Glen	**Detroit**	**NHL**	36	11	16	5	1963	104	1	3.18	8	5	2	467	13	2	1.67
	NHL Totals		**327**	**113**	**147**	**40**	**18170**	**1096**	**7**	**3.62**	**25**	**7**	**10**	**1247**	**63**	**3**	**3.03**
Hansch, Randy	Kalamazoo	IHL	16	8	7	0	926	60	0	3.89	....	....	....	....	....	....	....
	Adirondack	AHL	10	5	4	0	544	36	0	3.97	10	5	4	579	34	0	3.52
Harris, Peter	Lowell	H.E.	6	1	2	1	279	22	0	4.73	....	....	....	....	....	....	....
Hayward, Brian	**Montreal**	**NHL**	37	19	13	4	2178	102	1	2.81	13	6	5	708	32	0	2.71
	NHL Totals		**202**	**82**	**88**	**21**	**11350**	**756**	**2**	**4.00**	**24**	**8**	**13**	**1245**	**75**	**0**	**3.61**
Healy, Glen	New Haven	AHL	47	21	15	0	2828	173	1	3.67	7	3	4	427	19	0	2.67
	NHL Totals		**1**	**0**	**0**	**0**	**51**	**6**	**0**	**6.00**							
Heinz, Rick	Salt Lake	IHL	51	29	20	0	3026	201	1	3.99	16	12	4	912	57	0	3.75
	NHL Totals		**49**	**14**	**19**	**5**	**2356**	**159**	**2**	**4.05**							
Helmuth, Andy	Guelph	OHL	48	17	26	1	2637	188	3	4.28	5	1	4	300	21	0	4.20
Hextall, Ron	**Philadelphia**	**NHL**	66	37	21	6	3799	190	1	3.00	26	15	11	1540	71	2	2.77
	NHL Totals		**66**	**37**	**21**	**6**	**3799**	**190**	**1**	**3.00**	**26**	**15**	**11**	**1540**	**71**	**2**	**2.77**
Horn, Bill	W. Michigan	CCHA	36	19	16	0	2065	136	2	3.95							
Hrudey, Kelly	**NY Islanders**	**NHL**	46	21	15	7	2634	145	0	3.30	14	7	7	842	38	0	2.71
	NHL Totals		**144**	**66**	**49**	**18**	**8067**	**451**	**3**	**3.35**	**21**	**8**	**12**	**1243**	**52**	**0**	**2.51**
Hyduke, John	Minn.-Duluth	WCHA	23	7	15	0	1359	99	0	4.37	....	....	....	....	....	....	....
Jablonski, Pat	Windsor	OHL	41	22	14	2	2328	128	3	3.30	12	8	4	710	38	0	3.21
Janecyk, Bob	**Los Angeles**	**NHL**	7	4	3	0	420	34	0	4.86	....	....	....	....	....	....	....
	NHL Totals		**104**	**42**	**43**	**13**	**5917**	**407**	**2**	**4.13**	**3**	**0**	**3**	**184**	**10**	**0**	**3.26**
Jeffrey, Mike	N. Michigan	WCHA	28	13	12	1	1601	102	0	3.82							
Jensen, Al	**Washington**	**NHL**	6	1	3	1	328	27	0	4.94	....	....	....	....	....	....	....
	Binghamton	AHL	13	5	6	0	684	42	0	3.68							
	Los Angeles	NHL	5	1	4	0	300	27	0	5.40	....	....	....	....	....	....	....
	NHL Totals		**179**	**95**	**53**	**18**	**9974**	**557**	**8**	**3.35**	**12**	**5**	**5**	**598**	**32**	**0**	**3.21**
Jensen, Darren	Hershey	AHL	60	26	26	0	3429	215	0	3.76	4	1	2	203	15	0	4.43
	NHL Totals		**30**	**15**	**10**	**1**	**1496**	**95**	**2**	**3.81**	....	....	....	....	....	....	....
Keans, Doug	**Boston**	**NHL**	36	18	8	4	1942	108	0	3.34	2	0	2	120	11	0	5.50
	NHL Totals		**180**	**80**	**53**	**26**	**9728**	**576**	**3**	**3.55**	**9**	**2**	**6**	**432**	**34**	**0**	**4.72**
Kemp, John	Hershey	AHL	30	13	9	0	1349	80	1	3.56	2	0	2	96	9	0	5.63
Kilroy, Shawn	Kalamazoo	IHL	25	8	17	0	1476	107	0	4.35	....	....	....	....	....	....	....
King, Scott	U. Maine	H.E.	21	11	6	1	1111	58	0	3.13							
Kleisinger, Terry	New Haven	AHL	1	0	1	0	40	4	0	6.00	....	....	....	....	....	....	....
	Flint	IHL	2	0	0	0	53	5	0	5.66							
	Indianapolis	IHL	4	0	4	0	240	25	0	6.25	....	....	....	....	....	....	....
	NHL Totals		**4**	**0**	**2**	**0**	**191**	**14**	**0**	**4.40**	....	....	....	....	....	....	....
Knickle, Rick	Saginaw	IHL	26	9	13	0	1413	113	0	4.80	5	1	4	329	21	0	3.83
Kosti, Rick	Cdn. Olympic	....	30	20	8	2	1736	85	2	2.94	....	....	....	....	....	....	....
Kruzich, Gary	Bowling Green	WCHA	38	27	7	2	2229	123	1	3.31	....	....	....	....	....	....	....
Laforest, Mark	**Detroit**	**NHL**	5	2	1	0	219	12	0	3.29	....	....	....	....	....	....	....
	Adirondack	AHL	37	23	8	0	2229	105	3	2.83	....	....	....	....	....	....	....
	NHL Totals		**33**	**6**	**22**	**0**	**1602**	**126**	**1**	**4.72**	....	....	....	....	....	....	....
Lemelin, Reggie	**Calgary**	**NHL**	34	16	9	1	1735	94	3	3.25	2	0	1	101	6	0	3.56
	NHL Totals		**324**	**144**	**90**	**46**	**17698**	**1082**	**6**	**3.67**	**31**	**11**	**15**	**1619**	**109**	**1**	**4.04**
Liut, Mike	**Hartford**	**NHL**	59	31	22	5	3476	187	4	3.23	6	2	4	332	25	0	4.52
	NHL Totals		**476**	**214**	**185**	**62**	**27559**	**1617**	**17**	**3.52**	**53**	**24**	**26**	**3099**	**172**	**2**	**3.33**
MacKenzie, Shawn	Maine	AHL	6	3	2	0	321	19	1	3.55	....	....	....	....	....	....	....
	NHL Totals		**4**	**0**	**1**	**0**	**130**	**15**	**0**	**6.91**	....	....	....	....	....	....	....
Malarchuk, Clint	**Quebec**	**NHL**	54	18	26	9	3092	175	1	3.40	3	0	2	140	8	0	3.43
	NHL Totals		**140**	**62**	**53**	**18**	**7984**	**482**	**5**	**3.62**	**7**	**0**	**4**	**283**	**19**	**0**	**4.03**
Mason, Bob	**Washington**	**NHL**	45	20	18	5	2536	137	0	3.24	4	2	2	309	9	1	1.75
	NHL Totals		**60**	**31**	**20**	**8**	**3333**	**171**	**1**	**3.08**	**4**	**2**	**2**	**309**	**9**	**1**	**1.75**

Goaltenders: MAY...ROMANO 249

GOALTENDER	CLUB	LEAGUE	GP	W	L	T	Mins	GA	SO	Avg	GP	W	L	Mins	GA	SO	Avg
May, Darrell	Peoria	IHL	58	26	31	1	3420	214	2	3.75	....	....	....	....	....	....	....
	NHL Totals		3	1	2	0	184	13	0	4.23	....	....	....	....	....	....	....
McLean, Kirk	New Jersey	NHL	4	1	1	0	160	10	0	3.75	....	....	....	....	....	....	....
	Maine	AHL	45	15	23	4	2606	140	1	3.22	....	....	....	....	....	....	....
	NHL Totals		6	2	2	0	271	21	0	4.65	....	....	....	....	....	....	....
Melanson, Roland	Los Angeles	NHL	46	18	21	6	2734	168	1	3.69	5	1	4	260	24	0	5.54
	NHL Totals		230	106	82	26	13086	757	2	3.47	22	4	8	741	50	0	4.05
Meloche, Gilles	Pittsburgh	NHL	43	13	19	7	2343	134	0	3.43	....	....	....	....	....	....	....
	NHL Totals		761	262	342	126	44007	2661	20	3.63	45	21	19	2464	143	2	3.48
Merten, Matt	Providence	H.E.	24	6	14	2	1455	104	0	4.29	....	....	....	....	....	....	....
Meszaros, Dave	Saginaw	IHL	7	2	4	1	427	28	0	3.93	....	....	....	....	....	....	....
	Flint	IHL	9	3	4	0	442	34	0	4.62	....	....	....	....	....	....	....
Micalef, Corrado	Adirondack	AHL	1	0	1	0	59	5	0	5.08	....	....	....	....	....	....	....
	NHL Totals		113	26	59	15	5794	409	2	4.24	....	....	....	....	....	....	....
Millen, Greg	St.Louis	NHL	42	15	18	9	2482	146	0	3.53	4	1	3	250	10	0	2.40
	NHL Totals		442	150	217	67	26059	1730	9	3.98	25	11	13	1521	81	0	3.20
Moog, Andy	Edmonton	NHL	46	28	11	3	2461	144	0	3.51	2	2	0	120	8	0	4.00
	NHL Totals		235	118	52	15	12901	777	4	3.61	37	23	9	1938	101	0	3.13
Olsen, Chris	U. Denver	WCHA	24	10	11	1	1327	92	1	4.16	....	....	....	....	....	....	....
Pang, Darren	Nova Scotia	AHL	7	4	2	0	389	21	0	3.24	3	1	2	200	11	0	3.30
	Saginaw	IHL	44	25	16	0	2500	151	0	3.62	....	....	....	....	....	....	....
	NHL Totals		1	0	0	0	60	4	0	3.90	....	....	....	....	....	....	....
Parro, Dave	Indianapolis	IHL	32	16	14	0	1780	124	0	4.18	....	....	....	....	....	....	....
	NHL Totals		77	21	36	10	4015	274	2	4.09	....	....	....	....	....	....	....
Peeters, Pete	Washington	NHL	37	17	11	4	2002	107	0	3.21	3	1	2	180	9	0	3.00
	Binghamton	AHL	4	3	0	0	245	4	1	0.98	....	....	....	....	....	....	....
	NHL Totals		371	202	116	37	21539	1115	13	3.11	53	26	26	3187	174	2	3.28
Penney, Steve	Winnipeg	NHL	7	1	4	1	327	25	0	4.59	....	....	....	....	....	....	....
	Sherbrooke	AHL	4	1	2	0	199	12	0	3.62	....	....	....	....	....	....	....
	NHL Totals		83	33	34	11	4809	283	1	3.53	27	15	12	1604	72	4	2.69
Perreault, Jocelyn	Sherbrooke	AHL	13	8	4	0	722	40	0	3.32	6	3	0	258	9	0	2.09
Perry, Alan	Peoria	IHL	6	0	5	0	312	36	0	6.92	....	....	....	....	....	....	....
	Belleville	OHL	15	7	7	1	843	64	0	4.56	6	2	4	367	18	1	2.94
Pietrangelo, Frank	Muskegon	IHL	35	23	11	0	2090	119	2	3.42	15	10	4	923	46	0	2.99
Puppa, Darren	Buffalo	NHL	3	0	2	1	185	13	0	4.22	....	....	....	....	....	....	....
	Rochester	AHL	57	33	14	0	3129	146	1	2.80	16	10	6	944	48	1	3.05
	NHL Totals		10	3	6	1	586	34	1	3.48	....	....	....	....	....	....	....
Pusey, Chris	Adirondack	AHL	11	4	5	0	617	40	0	3.89	....	....	....	....	....	....	....
	Indianapolis	IHL	6	1	4	0	330	36	0	6.55	....	....	....	....	....	....	....
	NHL Totals		1	0	0	0	40	3	0	4.50	....	....	....	....	....	....	....
Quigley, Dave	U. Moncton	AUAA	19	...	...	...	985	45	0	2.74	....	....	....	....	....	....	....
Racine, Bruce	Northeastern	H.E.	33	12	18	3	1966	133	0	4.06	....	....	....	....	....	....	....
Ralph, Jim	Milwaukee	IHL	2	0	2	0	120	9	0	4.50	....	....	....	....	....	....	....
Ranford, Bill	Boston	NHL	41	16	20	2	2234	124	3	3.33	2	0	2	123	8	0	3.90
	Moncton	AHL	3	3	0	0	180	6	0	2.00	....	....	....	....	....	....	....
	NHL Totals		45	19	21	2	2474	134	3	3.25	4	0	4	243	15	0	3.70
Raymond, Alain	Fort Wayne	IHL	45	23	16	0	2433	134	1	3.30	6	2	3	320	23	0	4.31
Reaugh, Daryl	Nova Scotia	AHL	46	19	22	0	2637	163	1	3.71	2	0	2	120	13	0	6.50
	NHL Totals		1	0	1	0	60	5	0	5.00	....	....	....	....	....	....	....
Reddick, Eldon	Winnipeg	NHL	48	21	21	4	2762	149	0	3.24	3	0	2	166	10	0	3.61
	NHL Totals		48	21	21	4	2762	149	0	3.24	3	0	2	166	10	0	3.61
Reese, Jeff	Newmarket	AHL	50	11	29	0	2822	193	1	4.10	....	....	....	....	....	....	....
Reid, John	North Bay	OHL	47	33	12	1	2737	142	1	3.11	24	14	10	1496	92	0	3.69
Rein, Kenton	Prince Albert	WHL	51	29	18	3	2996	159	0	3.18	8	3	5	443	31	0	4.20
Resch, Chico	Philadelphia	NHL	17	6	5	2	867	42	0	2.91	2	0	0	36	1	0	1.67
	NHL Totals		571	231	224	82	32279	1761	26	3.27	41	17	17	2044	85	2	2.50
Richter, Mike	U. of Wisconsin	WCHA	36	19	16	1	2136	126	0	3.54	....	....	....	....	....	....	....
Riendeau, Vincent	Sherbrooke	AHL	41	25	14	0	2363	114	2	2.89	13	8	5	742	47	0	3.80
Riggin, Pat	Boston	NHL	10	3	5	1	513	29	0	3.39	....	....	....	....	....	....	....
	Moncton	AHL	14	6	5	0	798	34	1	2.56	....	....	....	....	....	....	....
	Pittsburgh	NHL	17	8	6	3	988	55	0	3.34	....	....	....	....	....	....	....
	NHL Totals		328	146	112	48	18703	1059	11	3.40	25	8	13	1336	72	0	3.23
Roach, Dave	Michigan Tech	WCHA	30	10	18	1	1811	151	0	5.00	....	....	....	....	....	....	....
Romano, Roberto	Pittsburgh	NHL	25	9	11	2	1438	87	0	3.63	....	....	....	....	....	....	....
	Baltimore	AHL	5	0	3	0	274	18	0	3.94	....	....	....	....	....	....	....
	Boston	NHL	1	0	1	0	60	6	0	6.00	....	....	....	....	....	....	....
	Moncton	AHL	1	0	0	0	65	3	0	2.77	....	....	....	....	....	....	....
	NHL Totals		125	45	64	7	7046	474	4	4.04	....	....	....	....	....	....	....

GOALTENDER	CLUB	LEAGUE	GP	W	L	T	Mins	GA	SO	Avg	GP	W	L	Mins	GA	SO	Avg
Roy, Patrick	Montreal	NHL	46	22	16	6	2686	131	1	2.93	6	4	2	330	22	0	4.00
	NHL Totals		93	45	35	9	5337	281	2	3.16	26	19	7	1548	61	1	2.36
St. Laurent, Sam	Detroit	NHL	6	1	2	2	342	16	0	2.81	....	....	....	....	....	....	....
	Adirondack	AHL	25	7	13	0	1397	98	1	4.21	3	0	2	105	10	0	5.71
	NHL Totals		10	3	3	2	530	29	1	3.28	....	....	....	....	....	....	....
Sands, Mike	Minnesota	NHL	3	0	2	0	163	12	0	4.42	....	....	....	....	....	....	....
	Springfield	AHL	19	4	10	0	1048	77	0	4.41	....	....	....	....	....	....	....
	NHL Totals		6	0	5	0	302	26	0	5.17	....	....	....	....	....	....	....
Sauve, Bob	Chicago	NHL	46	19	19	5	2660	159	1	3.59	4	0	4	245	15	0	3.67
	NHL Totals		371	168	133	54	21187	1214	8	3.44	29	13	15	1612	82	4	3.05
Scott, Ron	NY Rangers	NHL	1	0	0	1	65	5	0	4.62	....	....	....	....	....	....	....
	New Haven	AHL	29	16	7	0	1744	107	2	3.68	....	....	....	....	....	....	....
	NHL Totals		14	2	6	4	706	45	0	3.82	....	....	....	....	....	....	....
Sevigny, Richard	Quebec	NHL	4	0	2	0	144	11	0	4.58	....	....	....	....	....	....	....
	Fredericton	AHL	14	4	10	0	884	62	0	4.21	....	....	....	....	....	....	....
	NHL Totals		176	90	44	20	9485	507	5	3.21	6	0	3	208	13	0	3.75
Sharples, Warren	U. Michigan	CCHA	32	12	16	1	1720	148	1	5.14	....	....	....	....	....	....	....
Sidorkiewicz, Peter	Binghamton	AHL	57	23	16	0	3304	161	4	2.92	13	6	7	794	36	0	2.72
Simpson, Shawn	S.S. Marie	OHL	46	20	22	2	2673	184	0	4.13	4	0	4	243	17	0	4.20
Skorodenski, Warren	Chicago	NHL	3	1	0	1	155	7	0	2.71	....	....	....	....	....	....	....
	Nova Scotia	AHL	32	10	15	0	1813	121	2	4.00	....	....	....	....	....	....	....
	Saginaw	IHL	6	4	1	0	319	21	0	3.95	6	2	2	304	24	0	4.74
	NHL Totals		32	12	11	4	1671	93	2	3.34	2	0	0	33	6	0	10.91
Smith, Bill	NY Islanders	NHL	40	14	18	5	2252	132	1	3.52	2	0	0	67	1	0	0.90
	NHL Totals		625	281	191	95	35594	1864	20	3.14	132	88	36	7645	348	5	2.73
Soetaert, Doug	NY Rangers	NHL	13	2	7	2	675	58	0	5.16	....	....	....	....	....	....	....
	NHL Totals		284	110	103	44	15583	1030	6	3.97	5	1	2	180	14	0	4.67
Stefan, Greg	Detroit	NHL	43	20	17	3	2351	135	1	3.45	9	4	5	508	24	0	2.83
	NHL Totals		213	76	96	22	11621	781	4	4.03	15	5	10	856	49	0	3.43
Strauber, Rob	U. Minnesota	WCHA	20	13	5	0	1072	63	0	3.53	....	....	....	....	....	....	....
Strome, Greg	North Dakota	WCHA	1	0	0	0	40	3	0	4.50	....	....	....	....	....	....	....
Tabaracci, Richard	Cornwall	OHL	59	23	32	3	3347	290	1	5.20	5	1	4	303	26	0	3.17
Taillefer, Terry	Boston U.	H.E.	22	10	10	1	1260	82	0	3.90	....	....	....	....	....	....	....
Takko, Kari	Minnesota	NHL	38	13	18	4	2075	119	0	3.44	....	....	....	....	....	....	....
	Springfield	AHL	5	3	2	0	300	16	1	3.20	....	....	....	....	....	....	....
	NHL Totals		39	13	19	4	2135	122	0	3.43	....	....	....	....	....	....	....
Terreri, Chris	New Jersey	NHL	7	0	3	1	286	21	0	4.41	....	....	....	....	....	....	....
	Maine	AHL	14	4	8	0	765	57	0	4.47	....	....	....	....	....	....	....
	NHL Totals		7	0	3	1	286	21	0	4.41	....	....	....	....	....	....	....
Tessier, Brian	Toronto	OHL	3	0	3	0	147	26	0	10.61	....	....	....	....	....	....	....
	Belleville	OHL	17	5	9	0	854	68	0	4.78	....	....	....	....	....	....	....
	Kingston	OHL	8	4	3	1	506	39	0	4.62	....	....	....	....	....	....	....
Titus, Steve	London	OHL	47	15	22	1	2476	195	1	4.73	....	....	....	....	....	....	....
Tugnutt, Ron	Peterborough	OHL	31	21	7	2	1891	88	2	2.79	6	3	3	374	21	1	3.37
Vanbiesbrouck, John	NY Rangers	NHL	50	18	20	5	2656	161	0	3.64	4	1	3	195	11	1	3.38
	NHL Totals		157	64	66	13	8580	522	4	3.65	22	9	11	1115	60	2	3.23
Vernon, Mike	Calgary	NHL	54	30	21	1	2957	178	1	3.61	5	2	3	263	16	0	3.65
	NHL Totals		75	39	27	4	3989	245	2	3.69	26	14	12	1492	76	0	3.06
Volpe, Mike	Toronto	OHL	10	1	6	0	473	26	0	3.30	....	....	....	....	....	....	....
Waite, Jimmy	Chicoutimi	QMJHL	50	23	17	3	2569	209	2	4.48	11	4	6	576	54	1	5.63
Wakaluk, Darcy	Rochester	AHL	11	2	2	0	545	26	0	2.86	5	2	0	141	11	0	4.68
Wakelyn, Marty	Springfield	AHL	21	7	7	0	1144	75	0	3.93	....	....	....	....	....	....	....
Wamsley, Rick	St. Louis	NHL	41	17	15	6	2410	142	0	3.54	2	1	1	120	5	0	2.50
	NHL Totals		254	134	82	30	14621	816	6	3.35	23	7	16	1293	59	0	2.74
Weeks, Steve	Hartford	NHL	25	12	8	2	1367	78	1	3.42	1	0	0	36	1	0	1.67
	NHL Totals		169	76	66	18	9621	607	5	3.79	9	2	4	346	19	0	3.29
Whitmore, Kay	Peterborough	OHL	36	14	17	5	2159	118	1	3.28	7	3	3	366	17	1	2.79
Wregget, Ken	Toronto	NHL	56	22	28	3	3026	200	0	3.97	13	7	6	761	29	1	2.29
	NHL Totals		112	34	57	11	6035	430	0	4.28	23	13	10	1368	61	2	2.68
Young, Wendell	Vancouver	NHL	8	1	6	1	420	35	0	5.00	....	....	....	....	....	....	....
	Fredericton	AHL	30	11	16	0	1676	118	0	4.22	....	....	....	....	....	....	....
	NHL Totals		30	5	15	4	1443	96	0	3.99	1	0	1	60	5	0	5.00
Zanier, Mike	Indianapolis	IHL	14	6	8	0	807	60	0	4.46	6	2	4	359	21	0	3.51
	NHL Totals		3	1	1	1	185	12	0	3.89	....	....	....	....	....	....	....

NHL Schedule 1987-88

Visitor	Home
Thur. Oct. 8	
WSH	BOS
QUE	HFD
MIN	BUF
MTL	PHI
NYI	L.A.
PIT	NYR
TOR	CHI
DET	CGY
ST.L.	VAN
Fri. Oct. 9	
PIT	N.J.
DET	EDM
Sat. Oct. 10	
BOS	QUE
NYR	HFD
BUF	MTL
NYI	VAN
N.J.	TOR
PHI	MIN
CHI	WSH
ST.L.	L.A.
WPG	CGY
Sun. Oct. 11	
HFD	BOS
WSH	BUF
PHI	CHI
EDM	L.A.
Mon. Oct. 12	
QUE	MTL
MIN	NYR
DET	VAN
CGY	WPG
Tues. Oct. 13	
BUF	PIT
Wed. Oct. 14	
HFD	N.J.
TOR	MIN
ST.L.	CHI
CGY	EDM
Thur. Oct. 15	
BOS	L.A.
NYI	PHI
NYR	PIT

Visitor	Home
Fri. Oct. 16	
HFD	WSH
QUE	BUF
MTL	N.J.
TOR	DET
EDM	CGY
Sat. Oct. 17	
BOS	EDM
N.J.	HFD
BUF	QUE
PIT	MTL
PHI	NYI
NYR	WSH
DET	TOR
CHI	ST.L.
WPG	MIN
Sun. Oct. 18	
BOS	CGY
PIT	PHI
WPG	CHI
VAN	L.A.
Mon. Oct. 19	
MIN	MTL
WSH	NYR
Tues. Oct. 20	
CGY	NYI
WPG	ST.L.
Wed. Oct. 21	
BOS	VAN
HFD	BUF
MTL	TOR
CGY	NYR
N.J.	PIT
CHI	DET
L.A.	EDM
Thur. Oct. 22	
MIN	QUE
WSH	PHI
Fri. Oct. 23	
MTL	BUF
NYI	N.J.
CHI	NYR
PIT	DET
L.A.	WPG
EDM	VAN

Visitor	Home
Sat. Oct. 24	
BOS	ST.L.
CHI	HFD
BUF	PIT
MTL	WSH
CGY	QUE
N.J.	NYI
NYR	PHI
MIN	TOR
VAN	EDM
Sun. Oct. 25	
*L.A.	WPG
Mon. Oct. 26	
CGY	MTL
PHI	NYR
Tues. Oct. 27	
EDM	QUE
CHI	NYI
PHI	N.J.
L.A.	PIT
WSH	VAN
MIN	ST.L.
Wed. Oct. 28	
BUF	HFD
EDM	MTL
NYI	TOR
L.A.	NYR
DET	WPG
Thur. Oct. 29	
QUE	BOS
TOR	PIT
ST.L.	MIN
Fri. Oct. 30	
L.A.	BUF
MTL	DET
WSH	WPG
CGY	VAN

Visitor	Home
Sat. Oct. 31	
BOS	MTL
PHI	HFD
PIT	QUE
NYR	NYI
EDM	N.J.
WSH	MIN
CHI	TOR
DET	ST.L.
Sun. Nov. 1	
NYI	BOS
HFD	QUE
CHI	BUF
EDM	NYR
L.A.	PHI
VAN	WPG
Mon. Nov. 2	
ST.L.	MTL
Tues. Nov. 3	
ST.L.	QUE
N.J.	NYI
NYR	CGY
PHI	PIT
VAN	WSH
MIN	DET
Wed. Nov. 4	
BOS	HFD
BUF	L.A.
MTL	CHI
NYR	EDM
WPG	TOR
DET	MIN
Thur. Nov. 5	
TOR	BOS
PIT	NYI
ST.L.	N.J.
VAN	PHI
EDM	CGY
Fri. Nov. 6	
HFD	DET
QUE	WSH
CHI	WPG

continued

* AFTERNOON GAME

251

1987-88 NHL Schedule *continued*

Visitor	Home
Sat. Nov. 7	
PIT	BOS
QUE	HFD
BUF	EDM
PHI	MTL
DET	NYI
NYR	L.A.
WSH	N.J.
ST.L.	TOR
VAN	MIN
Sun. Nov. 8	
BUF	CGY
N.J.	PHI
MIN	CHI
VAN	WPG
Mon. Nov. 9	
BOS	QUE
TOR	MTL
Tues. Nov. 10	
WSH	NYI
N.J.	NYR
PHI	ST.L.
CGY	WPG
EDM	L.A.
Wed. Nov. 11	
BOS	TOR
MTL	HFD
BUF	VAN
WSH	PIT
DET	CHI
CGY	MIN
Thur. Nov. 12	
MTL	BOS
NYI	ST.L.
WPG	N.J.
PIT	PHI
Fri. Nov. 13	
MIN	BUF
QUE	VAN
L.A.	CGY
Sat. Nov. 14	
HFD	BOS
CHI	MTL
QUE	L.A.
WPG	NYI
NYR	PIT
*DET	N.J.
*TOR	PHI
MIN	WSH
EDM	ST.L.
Sun. Nov. 15	
TOR	BUF
WPG	NYR
EDM	CHI
VAN	CGY
Mon. Nov. 16	
HFD	MTL

Visitor	Home
Tues. Nov. 17	
BOS	CGY
L.A.	NYI
PIT	VAN
DET	WSH
Wed. Nov. 18	
BOS	WPG
BUF	HFD
NYI	MTL
QUE	EDM
PHI	N.J.
ST.L.	TOR
MIN	CHI
Thur. Nov. 19	
QUE	CGY
NYR	MIN
L.A.	PHI
TOR	ST.L.
VAN	DET
Fri. Nov. 20	
WSH	BUF
NYR	WIN
CHI	N.J.
PIT	EDM
Sat. Nov. 21	
BOS	MIN
WSH	HFD
N.J.	MTL
NYI	PHI
PIT	CGY
L.A.	TOR
VAN	ST.L.
Sun. Nov. 22	
BOS	DET
L.A.	BUF
VAN	CHI
EDM	WPG
Mon. Nov. 23	
MTL	QUE
N.J.	CGY
Tues. Nov. 24	
TOR	NYI
Wed. Nov. 25	
BOS	WSH
MTL	HFD
BUF	PHI
QUE	PIT
TOR	NYR
N.J.	EDM
WPG	DET
CHI	L.A.
ST.L.	MIN
CGY	VAN
Thur. Nov. 26	
WPG	BOS

Visitor	Home
Fri. Nov. 27	
HFD	BUF
MTL	MIN
N.J.	VAN
PIT	WSH
ST.L.	DET
CHI	EDM
Sat. Nov. 28	
DET	BOS
HFD	TOR
MTL	WPG
PHI	QUE
NYR	NYI
WSH	PIT
MIN	ST.L.
CGY	L.A.
Sun. Nov. 29	
EDM	BUF
NYI	NYR
N.J.	L.A.
Mon. Nov. 30	
BOS	MTL
CHI	CGY
Tues. Dec. 1	
VAN	QUE
EDM	WSH
TOR	MIN
WIN	L.A.
Wed. Dec. 2	
BOS	HFD
VAN	MTL
NYI	PIT
EDM	DET
CHI	ST.L.
Thur. Dec. 3	
NYR	BOS
HFD	PHI
QUE	BUF
ST.L.	N.J.
TOR	CGY
WPG	L.A.
Fri. Dec. 4	
NYI	WSH
CHI	DET
Sat. Dec. 5	
CHI	BOS
BUF	HFD
L.A.	MTL
N.J.	QUE
NYR	ST.L.
VAN	PIT
TOR	EDM
MIN	CGY
Sun. Dec. 6	
VAN	BUF
N.J.	PHI
L.A.	WSH
MIN	EDM

Visitor	Home
Mon. Dec. 7	
DET	TOR
Tues. Dec. 8	
BOS	PHI
HFD	QUE
MTL	NYI
CGY	WSH
MIN	VAN
Wed. Dec. 9	
WSH	HFD
BUF	CHI
MTL	NYR
L.A.	N.J.
CGY	PIT
ST.L.	DET
WIN	EDM
Thur. Dec. 10	
L.A.	BOS
NYR	PHI
ST.L.	MIN
Fri. Dec. 11	
QUE	WPG
NYI	PIT
CGY	N.J.
PHI	DET
VAN	EDM
Sat. Dec. 12	
*BUF	BOS
L.A.	HFD
DET	MTL
QUE	MIN
N.J.	NYI
NYR	TOR
PIT	ST.L.
CHI	WSH
EDM	VAN
Sun. Dec. 13	
CGY	BUF
PHI	WPG
TOR	CHI
Mon. Dec. 14	
DET	NYR
Tues. Dec. 15	
VAN	HFD
ST.L.	NYI
PHI	PIT
WSH	TOR
Wed. Dec. 16	
QUE	MTL
N.J.	NYR
WSH	DET
CHI	MIN
WPG	CGY
EDM	L.A.

1987-88 NHL SCHEDULE

*AFTERNOON GAME

Visitor	Home
Thur. Dec. 17	
VAN	BOS
ST.L.	HFD
NYI	PHI
PIT	N.J.
Fri. Dec. 18	
MTL	BUF
TOR	WSH
MIN	DET
WPG	EDM
Sat. Dec. 19	
*ST.L.	BOS
HFD	EDM
BUF	MTL
PHI	NYI
NYR	PIT
N.J.	MIN
CHI	TOR
CGY	L.A.
Sun. Dec. 20	
BOS	CHI
HFD	VAN
*DET	QUE
PIT	NYR
N.J.	WPG
*ST.L.	WSH
L.A.	CGY
Mon. Dec. 21	
MIN	TOR
Tues. Dec. 22	
BUF	BOS
HFD	CGY
WSH	QUE
NYI	WPG
PHI	NYR
L.A.	EDM
Wed. Dec. 23	
BUF	DET
WSH	MTL
NYI	CHI
N.J.	PIT
MIN	PHI
TOR	ST.L.
L.A.	VAN
Sat. Dec. 26	
BOS	NYI
QUE	HFD
MTL	TOR
*NYR	N.J.
PHI	WSH
DET	PIT
ST.L.	CHI
MIN	WPG
EDM	CGY
VAN	L.A.

Visitor	Home
Sun. Dec. 27	
BOS	NYR
*HFD	QUE
PIT	BUF
DET	MIN
CHI	ST.L.
Mon. Dec. 28	
MTL	CGY
NYI	N.J.
WSH	TOR
WPG	L.A.
VAN	EDM
Tues. Dec. 29	
BOS	PIT
BUF	QUE
MTL	VAN
NYR	NYI

Visitor	Home
Wed. Dec. 30	
TOR	HFD
WSH	N.J.
PHI	EDM
DET	ST.L.
MIN	CHI
WPG	L.A.
Thur. Dec. 31	
BOS	BUF
QUE	NYR
PHI	CGY
ST.L.	DET
CHI	MIN
WPG	VAN
Fri. Jan. 1	
*PIT	WSH

Visitor	Home
Sat. Jan. 2	
*QUE	BOS
N.J.	HFD
BUF	TOR
MTL	L.A.
PIT	NYI
NYR	MIN
PHI	VAN
*EDM	WSH
CGY	ST.L.
Sun. Jan. 3	
QUE	BUF
DET	WPG
CGY	CHI
Mon. Jan. 4	
EDM	BOS
ST.L.	NYR
L.A.	N.J.
VAN	TOR

continued

Jari Kurri

1987-88 NHL Schedule *continued*

Visitor	Home	Visitor	Home	Visitor	Home	Visitor	Home
Tues. Jan. 5		**Thur. Jan. 14**		**Sat. Jan. 23**		**Mon. Feb. 1**	
MIN	NYI	MTL	BOS	*PHI	BOS	BOS	CHI
WSH	PHI	HFD	ST.L.	MIN	HFD	HFD	MTL
L.A.	PIT	BUF	PHI	BUF	WSH	N.J.	CGY
Wed. Jan. 6		QUE	NYI	PIT	MTL	ST.L.	TOR
EDM	HFD	**Fri. Jan. 15**		ST.L.	QUE	**Tues. Feb. 2**	
BUF	MTL	TOR	N.J.	EDM	NYI	BUF	QUE
QUE	CHI	PHI	PIT	CHI	TOR	NYR	NYI
VAN	NYR	MIN	DET	*CGY	DET	WSH	PIT
MIN	TOR	WPG	EDM	**Sun. Jan. 24**		L.A.	VAN
ST.L.	DET	CGY	VAN	DET	HFD	**Wed. Feb. 3**	
WPG	CGY	**Sat. Jan. 16**		MTL	QUE	MTL	HFD
Thur. Jan. 7		*BUF	BOS	MIN	PHI	N.J.	EDM
BOS	PIT	HFD	L.A.	VAN	CHI	DET	CHI
VAN	N.J.	NYR	MTL	*L.A.	WPG	ST.L.	MIN
ST.L.	PHI	CHI	QUE	**Mon. Jan. 25**		CGY	WPG
Fri. Jan. 8		N.J.	NYI	BUF	N.J.	VAN	L.A.
HFD	BUF	PIT	TOR	EDM	PIT	**Thur. Feb. 4**	
NYI	CGY	WSH	ST.L.	CGY	TOR	MTL	BOS
NYR	WSH	DET	MIN	**Tues. Jan. 26**		NYR	QUE
TOR	CHI	**Sun. Jan. 17**		L.A.	QUE	TOR	PHI
L.A.	DET	NYI	BUF	WPG	WSH	MIN	PIT
EDM	WPG	PHI	NYR	CHI	DET	**Fri. Feb. 5**	
Sat. Jan. 9		WSH	CHI	VAN	ST.L.	TOR	BUF
BOS	ST.L.	VAN	WPG	**Wed. Jan. 27**		NYI	WSH
PIT	HFD	**Mon. Jan. 18**		HFD	CGY	N.J.	VAN
PHI	MTL	EDM	MTL	MTL	BUF	CGY	DET
VAN	QUE	TOR	DET	NYI	MIN	CHI	WPG
NYI	EDM	**Tues. Jan. 19**		WPG	PIT	**Sat. Feb. 6**	
N.J.	MIN	HFD	MIN	L.A.	TOR	*BOS	QUE
Sun. Jan. 10		EDM	QUE	**Thur. Jan. 28**		HFD	PIT
NYR	BUF	PIT	NYI	QUE	BOS	BUF	NYI
N.J.	PHI	NYR	L.A.	NYR	PHI	DET	MTL
PIT	DET	N.J.	WSH	PIT	N.J.	NYR	WSH
WSH	CGY	ST.L.	WPG	MIN	ST.L.	PHI	ST.L.
TOR	WPG	VAN	CGY	**Fri. Jan. 29**		WPG	MIN
L.A.	CHI	**Wed. Jan. 20**		HFD	VAN	EDM	L.A.
Mon. Jan. 11		BOS	BUF	NYI	BUF	**Sun. Feb. 7**	
HFD	BOS	PIT	CHI	MTL	WSH	*N.J.	BOS
CHI	NYR	**Thur. Jan. 21**		CHI	N.J.	TOR	HFD
WSH	EDM	MIN	BOS	TOR	DET	*CHI	QUE
L.A.	MIN	NYI	HFD	CGY	EDM	*PIT	NYR
Tues. Jan. 12		ST.L.	MTL	**Sat. Jan. 30**		CGY	L.A.
BUF	ST.L.	QUE	TOR	*NYR	BOS	**Tues. Feb. 9**	
NYI	PIT	DET	N.J.	HFD	EDM	All-Star Game
WPG	VAN	EDM	PHI	MTL	NYI	ST. LOUIS
Wed. Jan. 13		L.A.	CGY	QUE	ST.L.	**Thur. Feb. 11**	
BOS	MTL	**Fri. Jan. 22**		*WPG	PHI	MTL	N.J.
HFD	CHI	N.J.	BUF	CHI	PIT	QUE	L.A.
QUE	N.J.	NYR	VAN	DET	TOR	NYI	TOR
DET	NYR	L.A.	WPG	MIN	L.A.	WSH	NYR
WSH	L.A.			VAN	CGY	EDM	VAN
TOR	MIN			**Sun. Jan. 31**			
WPG	VAN			*WPG	BUF		
CGY	EDM			*PHI	WSH		

1987-88 NHL SCHEDULE

*AFTERNOON GAME

Visitor	Home
Fri. Feb. 12	
BOS	EDM
BUF	WPG
NYI	WSH
N.J.	DET
CGY	PHI
ST.L.	CHI
Sat. Feb. 13	
BOS	VAN
HFD	MTL
QUE	MIN
PHI	TOR
PIT	L.A.
DET	ST.L.
Sun. Feb. 14	
*BUF	CHI
QUE	WPG
*NYI	NYR
N.J.	TOR
*CGY	WSH
VAN	EDM
Mon. Feb. 15	
*HFD	PHI
*MTL	NYR
*DET	L.A.
Tues. Feb. 16	
BUF	ST.L.
WPG	QUE
CGY	NYI
Wed. Feb. 17	
BOS	MTL
WPG	HFD
CGY	NYR
WSH	N.J.
PIT	VAN
TOR	EDM
DET	CHI
L.A.	MIN
Thur. Feb. 18	
NYI	PHI
L.A.	ST.L.
Fri. Feb. 19	
PHI	BUF
NYR	N.J.
PIT	EDM
WSH	WPG
TOR	VAN
Sat. Feb. 20	
HFD	NYI
QUE	MTL
WSH	MIN
TOR	L.A.
*CHI	DET
CGY	ST.L.

Visitor	Home
Sun. Feb. 21	
*BOS	N.J.
NYI	HFD
QUE	BUF
VAN	NYR
*DET	PHI
ST.L.	PIT
CGY	CHI
*EDM	WPG
Mon. Feb. 22	
TOR	MIN
Tues. Feb. 23	
BOS	HFD
MTL	QUE
VAN	NYI
PHI	DET
WPG	PIT
EDM	ST.L.
Wed. Feb. 24	
VAN	MTL
WPG	N.J.
WSH	L.A.
MIN	TOR
EDM	CHI
Thur. Feb. 25	
HFD	BOS
ST.L.	BUF
CHI	NYI
PIT	NYR
Fri. Feb. 26	
QUE	DET
NYR	N.J.
CGY	VAN

Visitor	Home
Sat. Feb. 27	
*MIN	BOS
BUF	HFD
WPG	MTL
DET	QUE
WSH	NYI
PHI	L.A.
ST.L.	TOR
Sun. Feb. 28	
WPG	BUF
*MIN	N.J.
*PIT	CHI
CGY	EDM
L.A.	VAN
Mon. Feb. 29	
MTL	QUE
ST.L.	NYR
Tues. Mar. 1	
HFD	WPG
BUF	DET
ST.L.	NYI
N.J.	WSH
PHI	VAN
MIN	PIT
L.A.	EDM
Wed. Mar. 2	
HFD	CHI
QUE	TOR
NYI	NYR
WSH	N.J.

Visitor	Home
Thur. Mar. 3	
TOR	BOS
MTL	ST.L.
PHI	CGY
MIN	DET
VAN	WPG
Fri. Mar. 4	
NYR	BUF
QUE	WSH
PHI	EDM
Sat. Mar. 5	
*N.J.	BOS
NYR	HFD
MTL	L.A.
*NYI	PIT
WPG	TOR
DET	ST.L.
CHI	MIN
EDM	CGY
Sun. Mar. 6	
BOS	BUF
*NYI	QUE
*PHI	N.J.
*VAN	WSH
DET	CHI
Mon. Mar. 7	
PIT	CGY
EDM	WPG

continued

Troy Murray

1987-88 NHL Schedule *continued*

*AFTERNOON GAME

Visitor	Home
Tues. Mar. 8	
BOS	DET
HFD	QUE
VAN	NYI
N.J.	NYR
TOR	ST.L.
Wed. Mar. 9	
L.A.	HFD
BUF	MIN
MTL	EDM
TOR	CHI
CGY	WPG
Thur. Mar. 10	
L.A.	BOS
QUE	NYI
WSH	PHI
PIT	ST.L.
VAN	DET
WPG	CGY
Sat. Mar. 12	
BOS	QUE
HFD	MTL
BUF	CGY
DET	NYI
NYR	WSH
*N.J.	PHI
*PIT	MIN
CHI	TOR
EDM	VAN
Sun. Mar. 13	
WSH	BOS
QUE	HFD
BUF	VAN
NYI	DET
PHI	CHI
*PIT	WPG
ST.L.	L.A.
Mon. Mar. 14	
MTL	MIN
Tues. Mar. 15	
CGY	HFD
BUF	EDM
TOR	QUE
PHI	NYR
CHI	ST.L.
Wed. Mar. 16	
MTL	WPG
WSH	NYR
TOR	PIT
DET	MIN
VAN	L.A.

Visitor	Home
Thur. Mar. 17	
CGY	BOS
QUE	N.J.
CHI	PHI
MIN	ST.L.
Fri. Mar. 18	
NYI	WSH
WPG	EDM
L.A.	VAN
Sat. Mar. 19	
*BUF	BOS
HFD	ST.L.
CHI	MTL
CGY	QUE
NYR	TOR
PHI	PIT
DET	L.A.
Sun. Mar. 20	
*BOS	BUF
HFD	NYR
*NYI	WPG
*N.J.	WSH
PIT	PHI
ST.L.	CHI
EDM	MIN
Mon. Mar. 21	
CGY	MTL
NYI	MIN
Tues. Mar. 22	
BOS	PHI
WPG	HFD
BUF	NYR
ST.L.	WSH
TOR	VAN
EDM	DET
Wed. Mar. 23	
QUE	MTL
NYI	L.A.
WSH	PIT
MIN	CHI
Thur. Mar. 24	
WPG	BOS
HFD	DET
EDM	NYR
N.J.	ST.L.
TOR	CGY
Fri. Mar. 25	
N.J.	BUF
MTL	PIT
PHI	WSH
CHI	VAN

Visitor	Home
Sat. Mar. 26	
*QUE	BOS
MIN	HFD
EDM	NYI
*NYR	DET
WPG	PHI
TOR	ST.L.
CHI	L.A.
VAN	CGY
Sun. Mar. 27	
MTL	HFD
DET	BUF
*PIT	QUE
*NYR	N.J.
Mon. Mar. 28	
EDM	TOR
CHI	MIN
ST.L.	CGY
Tues. Mar. 29	
BUF	QUE
PHI	NYI
PIT	N.J.
DET	WSH
WPG	VAN
Wed. Mar. 30	
NYR	CHI
MIN	EDM
CGY	L.A.

Visitor	Home
Thur. Mar. 31	
MTL	BOS
HFD	BUF
QUE	PHI
WSH	NYI
N.J.	PIT
Fri. Apr. 1	
NYR	WPG
TOR	DET
ST.L.	EDM
MIN	VAN
L.A.	CGY
Sat. Apr. 2	
BOS	HFD
BUF	MTL
PHI	QUE
*NYI	N.J.
PIT	WSH
DET	TOR
Sun. Apr. 3	
NYI	BOS
HFD	PIT
MTL	BUF
QUE	NYR
N.J.	CHI
WSH	PHI
*ST.L.	WPG
*MIN	CGY
L.A.	EDM

Craig Laughlin

Copyright © 1987 by the National Hockey League. All rights reserved. Reproduction in whole or in part without permission of the National Hockey League is strictly prohibited. Publication of this schedule is permitted for the sole purpose of informing members of the public who wish to attend or view on television National Hockey League games. Any other publication or use of any portion of this schedule, including for the purpose of lottery or other form of gambling, whether such gambling is legal or illegal, is strictly prohibited.